JEAN-JACQUES ROUSSEAU

CONFESSIONS

Rousseau's ideas have influenced almost every major political development of the last two hundred years, and are crucial to an understanding of phenomena as diverse as the French Revolution, modern educational theory, and the contemporary environmental movement. This is reason enough to draw attention to his startlingly alive autobiography. But the CONFESSIONS is also among the greatest self-portraits in world literature – which suggests, even more than the impact of Rousseau's thought, the extent to which the very high opinion he had of himself was ultimately justified.

EVERYMAN,
I WILL GO WITH THEE,
AND BE THY GUIDE,
IN THY MOST NEED
TO GO BY THY SIDE

JEAN-JACQUES ROUSSEAU

CONFESSIONS

EDITED AND INTRODUCED
BY P. N. FURBANK

EVERYMAN'S LIBRARY
Alfred A. Knopf New York London Toronto
84

THIS IS A BORZOI BOOK
PUBLISHED BY ALFRED A. KNOPF

First included in Everyman's Library, 1931
Introduction, Bibliography, Chronology and editorial matter
Copyright © 1992 by Everyman's Library
Typography by Peter B. Willberg
Fourth printing (US)

US website: www.randomhouse.com/everymans

ISBN: 978-0-679-40998-4 (US)
978-1-85715-084-1 (UK)

A CIP catalogue reference for this book is available from the
British Library

Library of Congress Cataloging-in-Publication Data
Rousseau, Jean-Jacques, 1712–1778.
[Confessions.   English]
Confessions / Jean-Jacques Rousseau.
p.   cm.—(Everyman's library)
Translation of: Les confessions.
ISBN 978-0-679-40998-4
1. Rousseau, Jean-Jacques, 1712–1778—Biography.   2. Authors,
French—18th century—Biography.   1. Title.   II. Series.
PQ2036.A5   1992   91-53194
848'.509—dc20   CIP
[B]

Book design by Barbara de Wilde and Carol Devine Carson

Printed and bound in Germany by GGP Media GmbH, Pössneck

C O N T E N T S

INTRODUCTION

Rousseau's public career as a writer was as brief as it was dazzling. He was already thirty-seven when, in 1750, he published his first substantial work, the *Discourse on the Arts and Sciences*; and the last important work that he would publish, his *Letters Written from the Mountain*, came out only some fourteen years later.

The story of how he became a writer is a famous and very stirring one. The year was 1749. His great friend, the atheist philosopher and Encyclopaedist Denis Diderot, was imprisoned in the royal dungeon of Vincennes, and on a sweltering day in late summer Rousseau set out on foot to visit him. To relieve the tedium of the journey, he read as he walked, and in the pages of the *Mercure de France* he happened to read the announcement of the annual essay competition of the Academy of Dijon. The essay topic for the coming year was 'Whether the progress of the arts and sciences has contributed to the purifying of morals'*, and from the moment of reading these words, so Rousseau would later write, he 'beheld another world and became another man'. He entered the competition, with an essay arguing that progress had emphatically *not* helped to purify morals, and won the prize; and when his essay was published, his diatribe against advanced civilization and his plea for 'ignorance, innocence and poverty' made him famous overnight.

Then in 1752 he achieved a further and quite different form of celebrity. A pastoral opera by him, *Le Devin du village* (*The Village Soothsayer*), was performed before the King at Fontainebleau, to great applause, and was soon staged with equal success at the Paris Opéra. (It would remain in the repertory for half a century or more.) It tells us a good deal about Rousseau that, very soon afterwards, this successful author of a French opera published a savage *Letter on French Music*,

---

*The word *moeurs* in the French combines the meanings of 'morals' and 'manners'.

scornfully attacking French operas and French orchestras and asserting that France had never had, and what is more never could have, a music of her own.

At this early period of his writing career Rousseau was closely involved with the circle of rationalists and freethinkers known as *philosophes* (the term has a more specialized and radical flavour than its English equivalent, 'philosophers'). It was under their influence, and especially his friend Diderot's, that he composed a second 'Discourse', *On the Origins of Inequality*, in which he extended his analysis of civilization and gave a conjectural account of the origins of society. Within a few years, however, he became disgusted with Paris *salon* talk and with the whole (as he considered it) over-rationalistic outlook of the *philosophes*, and he deserted Paris for a cottage, 'The Hermitage', in the woods of Montmorency – lent to him by a wealthy friend, Louise de Lalive d'Epinay. It was a symbolic move, and in his friends' eyes a dangerous one for him. They may have been right; for in the year 1757 he was involved in a shattering quarrel, known nowadays as the 'Hermitage affair', which severed him from some of his closest friends. It was, nevertheless, in the semi-solitude of Montmorency (first in The Hermitage, and then in nearby Montlouis) that three of his best-known works were composed: his novel *Julie, ou la Nouvelle Héloïse*, his educational treatise *Émile* and his political testament, *Le Contrat social*. They were books (at all events the latter two) which represented for him the working out of the original 'illumination' received on the road to Vincennes.

The Hermitage affair had been much publicized, and public interest in Rousseau continued to be intense. From time to time, accordingly, his publisher Marc-Michel Rey (the Swissborn director of a firm in Amsterdam specializing in 'dangerous' publications) would urge him to write his memoirs. He came back to this theme insistently in 1761, and Rousseau, who found the notion attractive, began to assemble letters and other materials against the day when he might undertake such a work. He decided that, if he ever embarked on it, he would make it a work of 'unexampled veracity', so that once at least in the world's history people might 'see a man as he was within'.

The year 1761, however, proved to be a deeply disturbing one for Rousseau. In February *La Nouvelle Héloïse* was issued in Paris, achieving instant and quite overwhelming success. Letters poured in to him from all quarters, and strangers wrote to tell him how he had changed their life or begging him to become their spiritual director. He was, for the moment, a more famous writer even perhaps than Voltaire, and he basked in the praise, believing it to be his due. But at this high point in his fortunes he fell seriously ill. His chronic ailment, a retention of urine, had flared up, and so violently that he believed he might be dying. He became alarmed, among other things, about the fate of his unpublished writings – especially *Émile*, which he thought of as his masterpiece – and he wrote to a friend of his named Moultou, asking him to oversee the publishing of a general edition. He was also inspired to write a 'dying' letter to his friend the Maréchale de Luxembourg, revealing to her the painful and long-kept secret that he had had five children by his mistress Thérèse Levasseur and that they had all been taken to the Foundlings' Hospital.

Soon he recovered, and he was able to make arrangements on his own account for the printing of *Émile* and *The Social Contract*. *Émile* was to be seen through the press by no less a person than the King's own appointed Director of the Publishing Trade, Lamoignon de Malesherbes, a most enlightened man and a friend and protector to Rousseau and to all the *philosophes*. However, by autumn, for reasons Rousseau could not understand, all work on *Émile* seemed to have stopped. He had moreover fallen ill again, with a further attack of his bladder disease, and a catheter had broken off in his urethra. Once again it seemed to him he might be dying, and in these extremities he began to have nightmarish fears about *Émile*, convincing himself that it had been seized by his enemies the Jesuits and that they were waiting for him to die so that they could publish it in distorted and mangled form. Eventually the kindly Malesherbes, alarmed by his letters, came to visit him and managed to quieten his fears; and with a return to sanity Rousseau felt ashamed to have troubled him. 'I do not know,' he told him, 'what blindness or attack of melancholia, brought on by solitude and a dreadful malady, made me invent this tissue of horrors.' He felt the need to justify himself in Malesherbes' eyes; and in the course of the succeeding January (1762) he composed a sequence of four letters to him, giving a portrait of himself, or, as he said, 'exposing the true motives of my conduct and faithfully describing my tastes, my inclinations, my character and everything that has taken place in my heart'. It was, as one might say, a preliminary sketch for the *Confessions*.

Rousseau had always expected that *Émile*, and especially the challenging and freethinking 'Confession of a Savoyard Vicar' that featured in it, would cause trouble, and trouble was not long in coming. In June the Paris Parlement had the book seized and a copy of it burnt by the public executioner, and it issued a warrant for Rousseau's arrest. Friends gave him warning just in time, and he fled to Yverdon in Switzerland; when expelled from this temporary refuge, he moved on to Môtiers-Travers, in the principality of Neuchâtel. Thérèse came to join him there, and it was to be their home for the next three years.

In Môtiers Rousseau was under the protection of Frederick the Great of Prussia; and from this relative security he became engaged in furious polemics over the government of his birthplace Geneva. The Procureur-General of Geneva, Jean-Robert Tronchin, attacked him for impiety and sedition in some *Letters Written from the Country*, and he replied in his *Letters Written from the Mountain*. Meanwhile the idea of a 'General Edition' of his writings, perhaps to include a volume of memoirs, began to take more definite shape. There was even talk of installing a printing press in Neuchâtel for the purpose. Rousseau spoke about the proposed memoirs to various friends, in vague terms, and he seems at this time to have begun to sketch some fragmentary reminiscences. He was feeling the need of some decisive act of self-justification, for various damaging rumours about him were circulating in Geneva, including whispered reports of his abandonment of his children. Also, he wanted to record his own account of the 'Hermitage affair' and to air a growing suspicion that his friends had conspired against him. For the moment, though, since he would have to be discussing living people, he did not envisage publishing the work (should he ever complete it) in his own lifetime.

Then, on the very last day of 1764, he suffered an appalling blow. He received in the post an anonymous pamphlet – written, though he did not realize the fact, by Voltaire – claiming to voice the 'Sentiment of the Citizens' about himself, this disturber of the Genevan peace, and openly accusing him of being pox-ridden, of having killed Thérèse's mother by his unkindness, of being a systematic sower of sedition and – most wounding of all, because half true – of having exposed his children on the steps of the Foundlings' Hospital. This public revelation of his secret, a staggering blow to a writer who had so much taken his stand on 'Virtue', overwhelmed him and shook his hold on life. For some days he could not think what to do. Then he adopted a strange course and sent the pamphlet on to his publisher in Paris, instructing him to reprint it with a Preface and some notes by Rousseau himself. In these notes he dealt with the leading accusation in thoroughly Jesuitical fashion, denying – as of course he was technically entitled to do – that he had ever *exposed* children on the Foundlings' Hospital steps.

As Rousseau almost instantly saw, his way was now plain: he must at all costs write those long-projected memoirs and, by confessing his own faults and crimes, earn the right to expose those of his enemies. High on the list of these latter he placed his one-time friend and protectress Madame d'Epinay, who had been at the centre of the 'Hermitage affair'; and on 13 January, for the moment filled with vengeful thoughts, he drafted a significant letter to his friend, the Academician Charles Duclos.

They are doing their best to make it easy for me to write my Life, as you have been reminding me to do. An appalling libel has just appeared in Geneva, for which the d'Epinay woman has supplied information of the kind she specializes in, so putting me thoroughly at my ease as regards her and circle. God preserve me, all the same, from imitating her in the way I defend myself! But without revealing secrets she herself has confided in me, I know enough that did not come from her to be able to make her known for what she is in all that concerns myself. She does not realize how well-informed I am;

but, since she forces me to it, she will learn one day how discreet I have been. I confess, though, I still find it hard to overcome my repugnance, and I shall at least take steps to see that nothing appears in my lifetime. But I have much to say, and I shall say it all; I shall not omit one of my faults, or even one of my evil thoughts. I shall paint myself as I am: evil will almost always offset good; yet, despite that, I find it hard to believe that any of my readers will dare to say to himself, 'I was better than that man'.

In this letter, which may well never have been sent, the *Confessions* have taken definite shape, and certain of its most famous words have already been framed.

Through much of 1765, with the aid of a mass of documents, Rousseau worked at a first sketch of his early history. It was a year full of storms for him. He was commanded, but refused, to appear before the Môtiers Consistory to defend his religious beliefs. In September, his house was stoned. Seeking sanctuary in the Ile Saint-Pierre, in Bernese territory, he was expelled; became for a month or two an outlaw and wanderer; returned, risking arrest, to Paris, where his presence, in his recently adopted Armenian costume, created a great stir; and in January 1766, under the protection of the philosopher David Hume, he eventually took refuge in England. For a few weeks he lived in London, and then, accompanied by Thérèse, he took up residence in Wootton in Staffordshire.

He had some time before appointed a new literary executor, named du Peyrou, and du Peyrou forwarded his papers and MSS. to him, enabling him to continue work on his auto-biography. Before long, however, Rousseau had begun to nurse all sorts of suspicions against his benefactor Hume; and in the July of 1766 he wrote the bewildered philosopher a terrifying letter, accusing him of conspiring against him. It is fair to say that Rousseau, a sick man, living in a strange country whose language he did not speak and ceaselessly revolving in his mind the extraordinary vicissitudes of his last few years, had for the moment, and in some part of his mind, gone mad. It thus proves the true extraordinariness of this man that, at this very time, he was composing the wonderful – strange and touching and miraculously fresh and living – earlier chapters of his *Confessions*.

INTRODUCTION

In the autumn of 1766 Hume published, in Paris, a *Succinct Account* of his troubles with Rousseau. It made Rousseau more and more convinced of some mysterious plot against himself. He began to picture his papers, if not his life itself, as being in danger, and by the following spring he had more or less stopped writing and had parcelled up all his manuscripts and documents, to be put in safe keeping with a friend of du Peyrou's in Lincolnshire. Returning to France in May, he found shelter with the Prince de Conti at the Château de Trye, adopting the pseudonym of 'Renou'. Here he was able to complete the First Part of the *Confessions*, and for the moment he decided to write no more.

It was meanwhile a question, as always, where he should live. For a moment he contemplated quitting France for Italy or elsewhere. By now his papers had been returned, and in preparation for departure he was beginning to prune them so as to lighten his baggage, when he noticed what seemed to be a mysterious gap in the sequence. It pertained to the year 1757, the year of the 'Hermitage affair', and, in a flash, the 'truth' dawned on him: the baffling conspiracy surrounding him must date back to that by now far-off time. Hume no doubt had become party to it, but its real architects were the circle of *philosophes* to which Rousseau himself had once belonged: Madame d'Epinay, her lover Melchior Grimm, d'Alembert, d'Holbach and – the most-loved of all his friends at that time – Denis Diderot. Seventeen-fifty-seven was also the year of Damiens' attempt to assassinate Louis XV. Was it not very likely, Rousseau said to himself, that they had planned to associate him with the crime and had stolen the papers to deprive him of evidence in his own defence? Spurred by this new 'revelation', he gave up all thoughts of emigrating and decided to return to Paris, to confront his enemies.

His presence in Paris created great excitement. On several occasions, when he appeared at the café de la Régence, a great crowd gathered, and he received a warning from the police to be more discreet. He had resumed his old humble profession of music-copier, and meanwhile he was continuing his *Confessions*. It was well known by now that he was writing them, and he had been forced to give a pledge to the authorities that he would not publish them. As a next best, therefore, he decided to give public readings from them, in various aristocratic households. One of these readings went on from nine a.m. till three o'clock the next morning, and – according to a participant – when he came to the passage in Book VII, describing how he abandoned his children, his listeners, who were at first embarrassed, were reduced to tears by his visible grief. His own account of a reading at the Comtesse d'Egmont's is more chilly. 'Thus I concluded the reading of my Confessions, and everyone was silent. Madame d'Egmont was the only person who appeared to be affected; she trembled visibly, but she quickly recovered herself and remained silent, like the rest of the company. Such were the results of this reading and my declaration.' These form the last words of the *Confessions* and register his sense that the whole enterprise had ended in disappointment. He had projected a third book, carrying the story on from the year 1766 and his departure for England, but it never came to be written.

*

'I am commencing an undertaking, hitherto without precedent, and which will never find an imitator.' So runs the first sentence of Jean-Jacques Rousseau's *Confessions*. These claims of Rousseau's are vast ones, but on reflection one is forced to admit that they both of them are, in fact, justified. As for the actual title of his book, it is plain that he took it from the famous *Confessions* of Saint Augustine. (It is worth reminding oneself that, both for Augustine and for Rousseau, the term 'confessions' means not only 'admission of sin' but also 'profession of faith'.) The title has led some to argue that Augustine was his model and that his work belongs to the tradition of 'spiritual autobiography': that is to say that we should think of it as a quasi-religious narrative of 'testing' and conversion, on the lines of Augustine's, or of Bunyan's *Grace Abounding*. Many such narratives were in fact produced by French Jansenists in the seventeenth century, and Rousseau knew them, as he tells us himself in Book VI of the *Confessions*. All, the same, it is not a very convincing theory; and the reasons why not lead us right away to a point of great significance.

For it was fundamental with Rousseau to reject the Augustinian doctrine, revived with such force by Pascal and La Rochefoucauld in the seventeenth century, that love of self and self-approval were the root of all evil. This idea was entirely alien to him. His position is plain: one simply *has* to think well of oneself. 'What can one be pleased with in life,' he once wrote grimly to a friend, 'if one is not pleased with the only man one can never be separated from?' The theory led him to draw a basic distinction between two attitudes towards the self. There was love-of-self, an innocent, and indeed inescapable, emotion; and then there was *amour propre* (or as one might render it, 'self-conceit') which was a vice and a form of corruption. Love-of-self was limited to the individual; *amour propre*, by contrast, was a matter of wanting the good opinion of others, and it was an endless and never-to-be-satisfied quest since (so Rousseau argued) 'it requires that others should prefer us to themselves, which is an impossibility'.

With this defence of love-of-self went the theory that only we ourselves can judge ourselves, for we alone know what takes place in our heart. 'I can see by the way in which those who think they know me interpret my actions and my conduct that they know nothing,' he once wrote. 'No one in the world knows me except myself.' Rousseau's theory of the Self was a strange and thoroughly original one – it is hard to think of anyone else who has held it in quite that form – and it has important bearings on the *Confessions*.

Another model sometimes suggested for the *Confessions* is Montaigne's *Essays*, and certainly Rousseau knew Montaigne's work very well and once spoke of him as 'the master of us all'. All the same, his judgement of Montaigne is clear. It is the one we read in Book X of the *Confessions*: 'I had always ridiculed the false ingenuousness of Montaigne, who, while pretending to confess his defects, is most careful to attribute to himself only such as are amiable; whereas I, who have always believed, and still believe, myself to be, all things considered, the best of men, felt that there is no human heart, however pure it may be, which does not conceal some odious vice.' That Rousseau found it possible to admit to not just 'amiable', but hateful, vices, is a fact that everyone knows about his *Confessions*. One is struck, therefore, by those words 'believe myself to be, all things considered, the best of men'. One needs to remember them when reading that very striking passage at the very beginning of the *Confessions*: 'Eternal Being, gather round me the countless host of my fellow-men; let them hear my confessions, lament for my unworthiness, and blush for my imperfections. Then let each of them in turn reveal, with the same frankness, the secrets of his heart at the foot of the Throne, and say, if he dare, "*I was better than that man!*".' One tends to read this as paraphrasing Christ's 'He that is without sin among you, let him first cast a stone' – that is to say, as affirming that Rousseau was no worse, if no better, than any other human. Probably, indeed, this is the right reading; but there were moods in which Rousseau was inclined to claim much more and to represent himself as, literally, 'the best of men'. The theory of love-of-self allowed for humility but not for modesty or the making light of one's own virtues. One can scarcely think of an occasion, in the *Confessions* or elsewhere, when Rousseau practises the common social virtue of modesty.

I said that we might grant Rousseau his two great opening claims. There are other assertions, too, in those opening pages, which we must allow: for instance 'I know the feelings of my heart, and I know men. I am not made like any of those I have seen; I venture to believe that I am not made like any of those who are in existence. If I am not better, at least I am different.' Few, having read the *Confessions*, would disagree. It would be an incompetent reader of this book who finished it regarding Rousseau as a mere 'example' of something or other, heroic or otherwise, or as some kind of 'case'. Further, one can grant to Rousseau that he 'knew men'. He was often a prey to delusions and mad conspiracy-theories; nevertheless he was endowed by nature with a good deal of shrewdness about human beings. He was, above all, quick to sense their weak spots, and the *Confessions* are dotted here and there with devastating little satirical portraits.

Paul de Man once wrote of Rousseau as one of a group of writers who tend to be misread almost on principle. 'It is as if the conspiracy that Rousseau's paranoia imagined during his lifetime came into being after his death, uniting friend and

foe alike in a concerted effort to misrepresent his thought.'
Moreover, says de Man, the misreading is almost always
accompanied by 'an overtone of intellectual and moral superiority', as if the critic 'knows exactly what ails Rousseau and
can therefore observe, judge, and assist him from a position of
unchallenged authority, like an ethnocentric anthropologist
observing a native or a doctor advising a patient'.

There is a lot of truth in this. One of the most impressive of
more recent studies of Rousseau is Jean Starobinski's *Jean-
Jacques Rousseau: la Transparence et l'obstacle*. It is Starobinski who
pointed out the all-importance for Rousseau of the notion
of 'transparency'. It is, for him, a doctrine about the heart.
('Throughout the course of my life, as has been seen,' he writes
in the *Confessions*, 'my heart, transparent as crystal, has never
been able to conceal, even for a moment, any feelings at all
lively which may have taken refuge in it.') But equally, as
Starobinski shows, it helps to explain his political theories –
the conception of the 'General Will', so important in *Le Contrat
social*, presupposing the transparency of one citizen's consciousness to another's.

Nevertheless, as de Man rightly says, for all the closeness of
Starobinski's reading of Rousseau's texts, the ultimate effect of
his book is to explain them away: to represent Rousseau's
'splendid phrases' as a mere substitute for pre-verbal emotional
states, into which he himself had no insight.

The temptation to put Rousseau right is really very hard to
resist, and especially perhaps with the *Confessions*; for the reader
cannot but help observe there what an appalling mess Rousseau makes of his personal life, how much wanton havoc he
creates for himself and for others. Nevertheless the *Confessions*
is a very great book. Thus it is a matter of looking for its
greatness in the right place.

What I think may help in this is to notice, what is not always
stressed by critics, that the reader of the *Confessions* finds two
large and separate subjects presented with equal vividness:
namely, the self that was given to Rousseau by Nature, and
the self or selves that he created for himself. One looks for
light on such complexities where one can, and we may find
help in Yeats's theory that happiness and active virtue depend

upon the power to create an anti-self – to assume a face that is not our own. ('Active virtue, as distinguished from the passive acceptance of a code, is therefore theatrical, consciously dramatic, the wearing of a mask.') It is a fruitful hypothesis and seems to say something, though certainly not everything, about Rousseau.

What Rousseau himself tells us is that, by nature, he was lazy and a liver-in-the-moment, was impatient of dictation and referred everything to the 'heart', despised money (finding it incomprehensible) but prized solid goods; was incapable of planning evil but was prone to succumb to momentary temptation: the vice most natural to him was theft. When, however, at that epoch-making moment on the road to Vincennes, he discovered he was to be a writer – an event that he liked to describe as the beginning of all his misfortunes – he recognized at once that all must be different. He was now, or must become – these are his words – 'another man'. That man we may call 'Jean-Jacques', and he was a most impressive creation, incarnating austerity, stern moral effort and an enthusiasm for truth, liberty and virtue. By his own calculation, he was this exalted figure – with a fervour few have paralleled – for 'more than four or five years'. Thus in some sense this must have been the Jean-Jacques who wrote the famous books. In some sense only; since – still going by what he tells us himself – we have to cope with an important rider. For he claims that during those first few years of authorship, and under the influence of his friend Diderot, he adopted a 'hard' manner of writing which was not really natural to him. He only found his right 'tone' after he had shaken the dust of Paris from his feet. These two accounts of self-transformation do not so much contradict each other as provide an example of repetition-with-a-difference – a phenomenon that we often meet with in the *Confessions*.

At all events it is with perfect consistency that he tells us in Book XII of the *Confessions*, that when he felt his career as an author was at an end, and he had found what he thought might be his last refuge, on the island of Saint-Pierre, he happily reverted to his old aimless, cheerfully idle natural self. His picture of his few weeks in this tiny island paradise –

rowing, day-dreaming, learning, forgetting and learning again the names of wild flowers – is enchanting and almost completely persuasive. If this too was some kind of fiction, it was a work of genius and no banal piece of self-deception.

Rousseau's concern with his two selves, a natural and a created one, was thus no passing fantasy but an organizing principle in the story he chose to tell. Indeed it helps to shape the whole two-part structure of the *Confessions*. I have described how, soon after his return to France in 1767, he gave up work on his memoirs, not returning to them for the space of two years. When he resumed, beginning what is now regarded as the Second Part, it was with a prefatory declaration, explaining the pattern of his life as the tragedy of a man forced against his will and inclinations into 'greatness' and the virtues which went with it.

After two years of silence and patience, in spite of my resolutions, I again take up my pen. Reader, suspend your judgment upon the reasons which force me to do so; you cannot judge of them until you have read the story of my life.

You have seen my peaceful youth pass away in a tolerably uniform and agreeable manner, without great disappointments or remarkable prosperity. This absence of extremes was in great part the result of my passionate but weak disposition, which, more easily discouraged than prompt to undertake, only quitted its state of repose when rudely shocked, but fell back into it again from weariness and natural inclination; and which, while keeping me away from great virtues, and still further from great vices, led me back steadily to the indolent and peaceful life for which I felt Nature intended me, and never permitted me to attain to greatness in anything, either good or bad. What a different picture I shall soon have to draw! Destiny, which for thirty years favoured my inclinations, during a second thirty thwarted them, and this continued opposition between my position and inclinations will be seen to have produced monstrous errors, unheard-of misfortunes, and all the virtues that can render adversity honourable, with the exception of strength of character.

It is a memorable passage and a most remarkable 'plot' to have given the story of a life. How the mind lingers over that 'all the virtues that can render adversity honourable, with the exception of strength of character'. Rousseau was a myth-maker of genius, and we shall only understand the greatness of

the *Confessions* if we take this myth with the utmost seriousness –
indeed, perhaps, see it, as he wants us to, as the organizing
theme of the whole work.

In what I have been saying about the two selves presented
in the *Confessions*, I did not mention the word 'hypocrisy', for
it was not at issue there. All the same, it is a subject we need
to think about. For it seems plain that Rousseau had a very
pronounced inborn tendency to falsity. He admitted it himself,
though not in so many words, in the famous anecdote of the
stolen ribbon: the pitiful story of how, as a young lackey in
Turin, he stole a ribbon from his employers and, when charged
with the theft, blamed it on a fellow-servant named Marion,
saying she had stolen it to give it to him, and persisted bare-
facedly in the accusation even when they confronted him with
the poor girl herself – with the result that she was dismissed in
disgrace and perhaps driven to her ruin. Rousseau was
intensely remorseful over this example of falsity, and to tell it
to the world seems to have been one of his motives for undertaking the *Confessions*. All the same, we cannot write it off as
just an isolated episode. As we saw, when he was publicly
accused of abandoning his children, he responded altogether
Jesuitically and disingenuously; and during his love affair with
Sophie d'Houdetot, related in Book IX of the *Confessions*, he
behaved once or twice – indeed one is tempted to say, throughout – with quite outrageous hypocrisy. At one point of this
affair he and Sophie grew alarmed that Sophie's lover Saint-
Lambert might have discovered their relationship, and his
solution was to write to Saint-Lambert, in a tone of pained
innocence, asking him to explain why Sophie had recently
been so strangely cold in her manner towards him!

I am not suggesting that hypocrisy was Rousseau's ruling
passion and the key to unlock his whole character – if for no
other reason because, on his own showing, he had other vices
and weaknesses as well, of equal importance – as very likely
many of his readers do. It is that 'on his own showing' which
counts. For the fact that, by nature, he had a marked bent
towards falsity gives the true measure of his greatness, the
scale of the obstacle he overcame, in achieving veracity – a
truthfulness of a kind never attempted before and hardly since.

There is no doubt that it was an ethical novelty: this disciplining of his writing self to depict things that were personally shameful with perfect freedom, describing them exactly and detachedly, without embarrassment or bravado or any of the normal tactics of defensiveness. There is a heroic purity of purpose, a writerly honour, in such passages which continues to astonish. Who else could have handled the Mademoiselle Lambercier episode – his discovery of the pleasures of masochism – with such unabashed curiosity and delicate relish of the absurd? Who else would have related so sympathetically the grotesque scene of his exposing his bare bottom to the young women at the well? The episode is told with such detachment and even a certain tender amusement: how he is arrested by a tall man with moustachios, leading a posse of old women armed with broom-handles; how he improvises an improbable romantic explanation of his behaviour and, against all odds, is half believed; and how, a few days later, he runs into his captor again in the street and is received with the mocking words 'I am a prince, I am a prince, and I am a coward. Don't let his highness come back again!' – The tone is neither defiant, nor clinical, nor Rabelaisian; it is altogether strange and without precedent.

Who else, again – we might ask – would have ventured on that infinitely humiliating, infinitely touching confession concerning Claude Anet's coat? The grave and admirable Anet, Madame de Warens' ex-servant and lover, a sort of father-figure to Rousseau, unexpectedly dies of pleurisy. Rousseau's text continues:

The next day, I was speaking of him to mamma with the most lively and sincere affliction; when suddenly, in the midst of our conversation, the vile and unworthy thought came across my mind, that I should inherit his wardrobe, particularly a nice black coat, which had caught my fancy. I thought of this, and consequently gave utterance to my thought; for when I was with her, to think and speak was the same thing for me. Nothing made her feel more keenly the loss which she had sustained than this contemptible and hateful remark, disinterestedness and nobility of soul being qualities for which the deceased had been pre-eminently distinguished. The poor woman, without answering a word, turned away from me and began to cry.

Or let us take just one more example of Rousseau's heroic veracity, recalling that he was a vain man and that, as he says himself, petty indignities take more courage to confess to than great crimes. I have in mind the anecdote of the after-dinner reading at Saint-Lambert's. To Rousseau's alarm, in the middle of his entanglement with Sophie d'Houdetot, Saint-Lambert returned unexpectedly to France: more, he called on him with Sophie to invite him to dinner. However earnestly he managed to reassure himself about his recent doings with Sophie, Rousseau felt sheepish in Saint-Lambert's presence; and he noticed that, at the dinner party, Saint-Lambert – it was his sole revenge – was inclined to take advantage of the fact to humiliate him. After dinner, no doubt in response to polite request, Rousseau read to the company his letter to Voltaire on Providence and the Lisbon earthquake, a piece he thought very well of. Saint-Lambert, however, fell asleep. Despite this, says Rousseau wryly:

I, formerly so proud, now so foolish, did not venture to discontinue reading, and read on while he snored. Thus did I humble myself; thus did he avenge himself; but his generosity never permitted him to do so except when we three were alone.

It could have been no small challenge to depict this comedy of humiliation, but Rousseau's writing self carries it off with perfect composure. It will be seen that I regard his 'writing self' as a 'created' self, and the most valuable of all his selves or anti-selves.

In his capacity as myth-maker, Rousseau's greatest achievement of all in the *Confessions* is the 'idyll' of Les Charmettes, the story of his brief period of perfect intimacy with Madame de Warens. 'Here begins the brief happiness of my life,' he writes on the opening page of Book VI. 'Here approach the peaceful, but rapid moments which have given me the right to say, "I have lived."' He had stumbled on the long-sought secret of happiness.

I got up at sunrise, and was happy; I walked, and was happy; I saw mamma, and was happy; I left her, and was happy; I roamed the forests and hills, I wandered in the valleys, I read, I did nothing, I worked in the garden, I picked the fruit, I helped in the work of the house, and happiness followed me everywhere – happiness, which could not be referred to any definite object, but dwelt entirely within myself, and which never left me for a single instant.

The myth, as Rousseau creates it here, is all in extremes and uniquenesses. His relationship with Madame de Warens at Les Charmettes is a mutual possession 'perhaps unique of its kind among human beings', just as the earlier *ménage à trois* with Claude Anet had been 'a society without any other example perhaps on earth'. It is also, as it were, artistically planned by destiny. In his days with Madame de Warens at Annecy, years earlier, he had once had a prophetic dream, seeing himself 'transported ... in ecstasy, into that happy time and place, wherein my heart, possessing all the happiness it could desire, tasted it with inexpressible rapture, without even a thought of sensual pleasure'. Now one day (it is 'Mamma's' name-day) at Les Charmettes, when the two are out on a country expedition, the thought occurs to him that his dream has at last been fulfilled in every particular. He kisses Madame de Warens passionately, exclaiming that the day has been promised for very long, and he can see nothing beyond it.

This episode of Les Charmettes, as Rousseau recreates it in the *Confessions*, becomes for him the central point or pivot of his emotional career: before it, his imagination had always looked forward, after it, it would always look back. As we sense, he is describing not so much what actually happened as what it would entail – how things would have had to have been – if he were ever to be happy. He implies as much himself in the double-edged words that he speaks to Madame de Warens on their arrival at Les Charmettes: 'This is the abode of happiness and innocence. If we do not find both here, it will be useless to look for them anywhere else.' It is this that gives the whole episode its force and requires us to call it a myth.

For it is a point very important to remember, and Rousseau makes it abundantly plain: this inspiring idyll was for him also the moment of an acute nervous collapse. The country air at Les Charmettes fails to restore his health. He tries the then fashionable 'water-cure', wildly overdoes it as one might have expected, and one day suffers an alarming psychosomatic crisis, experiencing a sort of 'storm' in his body, an extraordinary convulsion of the arteries, and a humming, tinkling and whistling in his ears which leaves him permanently deafened. The crisis makes him believe he has not long to live and induces in him a state of 'calm, even sensual' tranquillity and resignation. The quasi-incestuous relationship of the motherless Rousseau to his 'Mamma' has become the acme of passivity: 'I became altogether her work, altogether her child, and more so than if she had been my real mother.' This episode of Les Charmettes, so infinitely charming seen from one angle, appears from another angle, on evidence faithfully supplied by Rousseau himself, as morbidly relaxed and deathly.

Such a languid and perfervid state, following upon one equally enervating, when he was 'burning with passion without an object', is plainly not designed to last. The truth becomes obvious as soon as he gets away from Les Charmettes – before even he has got to Montpellier, where the doctors are to cure him of his imaginary 'polypus of the heart' – for on the way there, he has a cheerful affair with the accommodating Madame de Larnage, and at once 'good-bye to fever, hysteria, and polypus.' (It is another 'uniqueness', the only time in his life that he makes love with untroubled enjoyment.)

The affair with Madame de Larnage, not very important in itself, has a further function in the book, for in the account of it we are given a subtle foretaste of the metamorphosis to come: the transformation of the hedonistic Jean-Jacques into the austere author of *Émile*. (Such overlappings of themes are important to the book's structure.) Having parted from Madame de Larnage, but intending to rejoin her very soon, Rousseau pays a visit to the great Roman aqueduct, the Pont du Gard, and it inspires him with ancient-Roman thoughts and hankerings after greatness – the very kind that will soon dominate him as a writer.

The echo of my footsteps under these immense vaults made me imagine that I hear the sturdy voices of those who had built them. I felt myself lost like an insect in this immensity. I felt, in spite of my sense of littleness, as if my soul was somehow or other elevated, and I said to myself with a sigh, 'Why was I not born a Roman?'

He remains there day-dreaming for several hours and, he writes with delicious irony, 'this dreaminess was not favourable to Madame de Larnage. She had been careful to warn me against the girls of Montpellier, but not against the Pont du Gard. One never thinks of everything!'

The conception of happiness that Rousseau presents in his marvellous pages on the idyll of Les Charmettes is of something that must inevitably be lost. He is inventing a lost Eden, and the light-hearted affair with Madame de Larnage stands in very conveniently for the Fall. Thus, fittingly, and with admirable artistry, the de Warens story is brought to a close with expulsion from Eden. Jean-Jacques finds that, in his absence from Madame de Warens, he has been supplanted by the intruder Vintzenried.

I asked her whether she had received my letter. She answered 'Yes'. 'I should not have thought so,' I said, and the explanation ended there. A young man was with her. I remembered having seen him in the house before I left, but now he seemed established there, as in fact he was. In a word, I found my place filled.

*

A lot of research has been done on Rousseau's 'idyll' and a great deal written about it, from which it emerges that, in certain very significant ways, his account is not actually true to historical fact. It seems plain that, before he returned to Madame de Warens from Montpellier, he already knew that he had lost her favour, for he wrote her an agonized (and petulant) letter, to be allowed to come back to her on any terms: 'Ah, my dear *maman*,' he apostrophizes her, 'are you then no longer my dear *maman*?' The scene of his return, as related in the *Confessions*, and his sudden recognition that his 'place was taken', are thus a dramatic fiction. More importantly, whatever the correctness of his explanation of the rift with Madame de Warens, he is not telling the literal truth in writing that, since his situation had become 'unendurable', he soon decided to leave and make a new life for himself, as a tutor in Lyons. In fact, it seems, for as long as two aimless and humiliating years he continued to depend on Madame de Warens' bounty. He was living – for most of the time in solitude – in the house as Les Charmettes, communicating with Madame de Warens by letter, and was pursuing vague money-making schemes – making efforts to obtain a pension from the Sardinian Treasury or to lay hands on his brother's unclaimed inheritance.

These are facts it is certainly fascinating to know. But the trouble is, most of the best scholarship about the *Confessions* has been very largely about such questions, matters connected with the literal truthfulness or otherwise of what Rousseau has written, or alternatively with the enticing subject of his psychology. It has had rather little to say about Rousseau's prodigious creative force, his artistic motives in remodelling historic fact. It seems an oddly one-sided approach to a great work of art.

But then, it cannot help striking one that the *Confessions* have enjoyed a strange fate. It is one of the most famous of books and, I would suggest, much the greatest of Rousseau's writings, a work that can vitally concern us even now; yet all along even Rousseau's admirers have been half reluctant to consider it as a work of art. They have been keener to interest themselves in its subject, the erring, sinning and deluded 'citizen of Geneva', than in its masterly creator. (I should add that, when I speak of the literary greatness of the *Confessions*, I am thinking pre-dominantly of the First Part. For the Second Part, with all its amazing interest, is by no means so successful – a fact Rousseau knew very well himself and lamented – indeed it is sometimes so obsessional as to make painful reading.)

*

Few books have been awaited with such excitement as Rous-seau's *Confessions*, and when the First Part was published in 1782 the disappointment was intense, both among his admirers and his detractors. They had expected all sorts of revelations, hoped to be told the secret history of his quarrels and persecu-tions and be treated to lurid disclosures about the famous and the great; and here, instead, was this rambling and pettifogging tale of an obscure private life, full of the most puerile details, and some of them (though the editors had bowdlerized the text) very sordid into the bargain. The book was altogether too much for his sometime friend, the aristocratic-minded Comtesse de Boufflers. 'It seems to me,' she wrote (1 May 1782) to the future King of Sweden, 'that they [the *Confessions*] could be those of some miserable lackey, perhaps even worse – in all points lunatic and disgustingly vicious. The passages where extravagance and vice are least in evidence are of intolerable heaviness and tediousness; but his mad avowal of all his own basenesses seems to me an effect of Providence, which has compelled this unworthy man to strip the mask of hypocrisy off with his own hand. I cannot forgive myself for the cult I once made of him – for that is what it was.' The great naturalist Buffon, who had been another admirer, felt much the same. 'I used to have some love for him, but when I saw his *Confessions* I ceased to esteem him. His soul revolts me.' The *Année littéraire* found the book 'an unbelievable tissue of puerilities, stupidities and extravagances'. How utterly indecent of Rousseau, was the verdict of other readers, to expose the frailties of a woman he had loved (Madame de Warens) to the public gaze. Rousseau's admirers made the best of what they, too, evidently felt to be a bad business, saying that he must be loved in spite of it. 'I know the judgements that people have passed on the *Confessions*,' wrote the future Girondin leader Brissot. 'I know that people have painted him as a scoundrel, a calumniator, a hypocrite and a criminal. The most moderate have called him a madman. I have the misfortune to love, to adore this madman, and I share the misfortune with a crowd of other sensitive and virtuous souls.' When, in 1788, on the eve of the appearance of the Second Part of the *Confessions*, that ardent Rousseauist Madame de Staël published her *Letters on the Works and Character of Jean-Jacques Rousseau*, she admitted in it that there were details in the book which 'revolted noble souls'. All the same, she held, one should believe Rousseau when he laid claim to being a good man. Intentions sometimes counted more than actions in life; and his stoopings were somehow accidental, not truly a part of the man himself: 'He is not, if one may so put it, the tree which bears these fruits.' The villain of the story, she held, was that 'unnatural mother', Thérèse Levasseur; it was she who had been the real cause of Rousseau's abandoning his children, and if, as was rumoured, he had committed suicide, it was her misconduct which had driven him to it.

A year or two after this, another great admirer, Louis-Sebastien Mercier, offered his own peculiar explanation of the *Confessions*, in his *Jean-Jacques Rousseau: Considered as one of the First Authors of the Revolution*. The book was, he argued, a fiction or allegory. Rousseau had never in fact abandoned his children. He merely meant to evoke an 'ideal picture' of how indigence and misfortune might drag down a man of superior parts. Unwisely perhaps, Rousseau had indulged himself in the sport of 'mystifying posterity'.

*

The shock caused by the *Confessions* was considerable, but it had little or no effect on the growth of the Rousseau cult. At his death, his grave on the Isle of Poplars at Ermenonville had become a place of pilgrimage. (Even Marie-Antoinette came to pay a visit to it.) Plays were performed about him, and academies set up competitions for a eulogy on him. His face looked out from plates and snuff boxes, clocks and playing cards, and Moreau le Jeune's print 'The Arrival of Jean-Jacques Rousseau in the Elysian Fields' sold in thousands. With the coming of the Revolution, the cult intensified and grew to amazing proportions. At a Festival of Triumph, on the first anniversary of the fall of the Bastille, a bust of Rousseau, carved from one of the stones from the fortress, was borne in procession before six hundred white-gowned young women, escorted by troops of guardsmen, their muskets garlanded with flowers. Four years later, in October, there was an even more fantastic pageant, when his coffin, borne on a car adorned with poplar branches, was transported from Ermenonville to the Panthéon in Paris, amid vast weeping crowds. (The much-abused Thérèse, who had hoped to take part in the ceremony, was refused permission and had to watch from an inn window.)

Equally spectacular was the reversal of the Rousseau cult at the Restoration. In May 1814 his remains, together with those of Voltaire, were secretly removed from their tomb in the Panthéon and would only find their way back there in 1830; and during the century that ensued he continued, more perhaps than any other individual, even including Napoleon, to be a bone of contention among the French. Under Louis-

Philippe he was a hero to the Romantics and to the Saint-Simonians and Fourierists and anathema to all conservative elements. There was an outburst of Rousseau-phobia in the 1870s, at the time of the debate on popular sovereignty, and another very violent one during the Dreyfus affair; and the bicentenary celebrations in 1912 were nearly broken up by Action Française, Charles Maurras being particularly rancorous at the time about this 'disgusting hog', this 'vomit of the desert', this 'inventor of the *stupid* style' and 'enemy of France'.

In all this, as regards the *Confessions*, a clear pattern emerges. Rousseau's idolaters and ideological partisans would never feel quite comfortable about the book and would be inclined to draw attention away from it; and on the other hand, to anti-Rousseauists, it offered the most deliciously tempting ways of barbing their epigrams or insults. Edgar Quinet would write in 1865, in his book on the French Revolution, that the Revolution resembled Rousseau, being as touchy and suspicious as he was and as prone to believe itself betrayed by a universal conspiracy. In the 1920s the novelist François Mauriac, in an Introduction to the *Confessions*, would write that 'Rousseau treats his crimes as he treated his children; he does not recognize them', and the neo-Thomist Jacques Maritain would vilify Rousseau as a 'lackey of genius', a man to whom we owed 'this corpse of the Christian idea whose immense putrefaction today poisons the universe'.

As for England, from the first, the *Confessions* were a gift to Rousseau's enemies and enemies of the Revolution, and Edmund Burke would exploit them with ferocious relish. 'Everybody knows,' he wrote in a *Letter to a Member of the* [French] *National Assembly*, 'that there is a great dispute amongst their leaders, which of them is the best resemblance of Rousseau.'

In truth they all resemble him. His blood they transfuse into their minds and into their manners ... Rousseau is their canon of holy writ; in his life he is their canon of *Polycletus*; he is their standard figure of perfection. To this man and this writer, as a pattern to authors and to Frenchmen, the foundries of Paris are now running for statues, with the kettles of their poor and the bells of their churches.

And why should this be, asks Burke? It is because the French have found a substitute for old-fashioned duty and humility in a new social principle, that of *vanity*; and Rousseau is the supreme exemplar of vanity. When Rousseau came to England, he left no doubt in Burke's mind that vanity possessed him almost to the point of madness; and 'It is from the same deranged, eccentric vanity, that this, the insane *Socrates* of the National Assembly, was impelled to publish a mad confession of his mad faults, and to attempt a new sort of glory from bringing hardily to light the obscure and vulgar vices, which we know may sometimes be blended with eminent talents.' It was the same omnivorous vanity, writes Burke, that led Rousseau to 'exhaust the stores of his powerful rhetoric in the expression of universal benevolence; whilst his heart was incapable of harbouring one spark of common affection'.

He melts with tenderness for those only who touch him by the remotest relation, and then, without one natural pang, casts away, as a sort of offal and excrement, the spawn of his disgustful amours, and sends his children to the hospital of foundlings.

That the *Confessions* were useful to Rousseau's detractors is thus beyond dispute. Usefulness, however, is not the same as influence. To what degree did Rousseau's book have 'influence'? It is not, actually, a question very easy to answer. One feels that it should have done so to an enormous degree; and Marcel Raymond, the editor of the Pléiade edition of the *Confessions*, evidently holds that it did. He claims that Rousseau enriched the tradition of autobiographical writing in all its three main forms (Memoirs, 'Souvenirs' or 'Reveries', and the autobiographical novel) and, by implication, was an influence upon a whole string of famous authors: Restif de la Bretonne, Chateaubriand, Stendhal, Senancour, Constant, Nerval, Musset, the young Flaubert and Gide. One wonders if this is right, and if so, in what sense. Actually, I find it is hard to think of a single major author of whom one could say that, without question, he or she was a true disciple of the *Confessions*. Chateaubriand's bombastic *Mémoires d'outre-tombe* scarcely for a moment recall the *Confessions*, a work which anyway he thought 'vulgar, cynical and in bad taste'; nor does one ever get the feeling that Alfred de Musset had fathomed their secret. For Stendhal, certainly, Rousseau's book was a constant presence; indeed his *Vie de Henry Brulard* is actually referred to as a '*Confessions*'. Nevertheless he always preserved an ironic distance from Rousseau's book. He once said of it that Jean-Jacques suffered so many misfortunes 'through lack of two or three principles of *Beylism*'. For the young and callow Julien Sorel, in Stendhal's *Le Rouge et le Noir*, the *Confessions*, together with the *Memoirs of St Helena*, are his bible and his sole guide on all worldly problems; but it is not long before he has learned to despise them.

For influence, of the profound kind that Rousseau's book deserved, one seems to have to look elsewhere. Occasionally, in reading Dostoevsky or Proust, one receives a powerful feeling that the page one is reading could never have been written if the *Confessions* had not existed. It is a matter, in each of their cases – though in quite different ways – of their attitude towards shame, a concern so fundamental to Rousseau. Dostoevsky, so fascinated by shame, seems to imagine shame as overcome by driving it to its extreme; Proust writes like a man 'dead' to shame. But if there is a connection with Rousseau here, there is no proving it, and neither of those writers paid any public homage to Rousseau's book.

In a way, one might say, Rousseau did his work too well. The fascinating nature of his subject – the appealing, half-crazed, 'impossible' and all-too-human Jean-Jacques – continues to deflect attention from the extraordinary thing he has done with this subject, the revolutionary work of art he has derived from it. There are secrets in this masterpiece that still await their expositor.

P. N. Furbank

NOTE ON THE TEXT

The text of the present edition is, with some changes and emendations, that of the anonymous translation (the first un-expurgated version in English) first published in 1904. The present editor has also combined some of the notes from the 1904 edition with his own. Rousseau's own notes have been distinguished by the symbol '(R)'.

SELECT BIBLIOGRAPHY

———

CRANSTON, MAURICE, *Jean-Jacques: the Early Life and Works of Jean-Jacques Rousseau 1712–1754*, Allen Lane, 1983.

——*The Noble Savage: Jean-Jacques Rousseau 1754–1762*, Allen Lane, 1991. The first two volumes of an excellent scholarly biography, drawing on much recent work not available to Guéhenno (*q.v.*). A further volume is still to come.

DE SAUSSURE, H., *Rousseau et les Mss. des 'Confessions'*, 1958.

GAGNEBIN, B., 'L'Etrange accueil fait aux *Confessions* de Rousseau au dix-huitième siècle', *Annales de la Société Jean-Jacques Rousseau*, vol. 38, 1974, pp. 105–26.

GREEN, F. C., *Jean-Jacques Rousseau: a Critical Study of his Life and Writings*, Cambridge University Press, 1955. A helpful general study of Rousseau.

GRIMSLEY, R., *Jean-Jacques Rousseau: a Study in Self-Awareness*, University of Wales Press, 1961. A valuable psychological study, drawing extensively on the *Confessions*.

GUÉHENNO, J., *Jean-Jacques Rousseau*, trans. J. & D. Weightman, 2 vols, Routledge, 1966. An admirably vivid and humane biography.

SCHINZ, A., 'L'Idylle des Charmettes', *Revue de France*, 1934.

WILLIAMS, H., *Rousseau and Romantic Autobiography*, Oxford University Press, 1983. A wide-ranging examination of Rousseau's contribution to the autobiographical genre.

CHRONOLOGY

DATE	AUTHOR'S LIFE	LITERARY CONTEXT
1712	Born (28 June), in Geneva, the son of Isaac Rousseau, watchmaker. His mother dies in childbirth.	
1721		Montesquieu: *Persian Letters*.
1722–4	Boards with Pastor Lambercier at Bossey.	Defoe: *Moll Flanders* (1722). Marivaux founds the *Spectateur français* (1722).
1725	Is apprenticed as an engraver.	
1726		Swift: *Gulliver's Travels*.
1728	Absconds from Geneva and finds welcome with Madame de Warens at Annecy. Attends hospice for catechumens in Turin and adopts Catholic faith. Works as a lackey.	Gay: *The Beggar's Opera*.
1730–31	Lives by music teaching in Lausanne and Neuchâtel.	
1731	Goes to live with Madame de Warens at Chambéry.	Prévost: *Manon Lescaut*. Marivaux: *La Vie de Marianne* (to 1748).
1733–5		Voltaire: *Philosophical Letters* (1734).
1736	His 'idyll' at Les Charmettes.	
1737	Goes to Montpellier for his health.	Marivaux: *Les Fausses Confidences*.
1738/9	Lives, largely alone, at Les Charmettes.	
1740	Becomes tutor in the de Mably household in Lyons.	
1741 (or early 1742)	Arrives in Paris, having invented new system of musical notation. Gets to know Diderot.	
1742		Prévost's translation of Richardson's *Pamela*.
1743	Goes to Venice as Secretary to Ambassador.	Voltaire: *Merope*.
1744	Returns to Paris.	

HISTORICAL EVENTS

Peace of Utrecht (1713–15) ends War of Spanish Succession. Bull Unigenitus (1713): papal condemnation of Jansenism. Accession of George I (first Hanoverian monarch) in England (1714). Death of Louis XIV (1715). Regency of Philippe of Orleans (to 1723).

Marriage of Louis XV to Marie Leszczynska of Poland. Fleury chief minister in France.

Walpole engineers treaty of Vienna with Emperor Charles VI (1731). End of close alliance between England and France inaugurated by Stanhope in 1716.

War of Polish Succession.

Outbreak of war between England and Spain (1739).

Frederick the Great King of Prussia (to 1786). Death of Charles VI.

Franco-Prussian alliance. France enters War of Austrian Succession (to 1748).

Death of Walpole (chief minister in England since 1721).

Death of Fleury.

Illness of Louis XV at Metz. Strike of silk workers at Lyons.

DATE	AUTHOR'S LIFE	LITERARY CONTEXT
1745	Begins relationship with Thérèse Levasseur.	Crébillon *fils*: *The Sofa*.
1746/7	His first child by Thérèse Levasseur is born and taken to Foundlings' Hospital, as will be his succeeding children.	Diderot: *Philosophical Thoughts* (1746). Condillac: *Essay on the Origins of Human Knowledge* (1746). Voltaire: *Zadig* (1747).
1748		Montesquieu: *The Spirit of Laws*. Diderot: *Indiscreet Jewels*. Toussaint: *Treatise on Morals*. La Mettrie: *Man the Machine*.
1749	Receives 'revelation' on the road to Vincennes, where Diderot is imprisoned.	Diderot: *Letter on the Blind*. First three volumes of Buffon's *Natural History*. Fielding: *Tom Jones*.
1750	His *Discourse on the Arts and Sciences* wins essay award from the Academy of Dijon and is published. He composes articles on music and economics for the *Encyclopaedia* (ed. Diderot and d'Alembert).	
1751		First volume of the *Encyclopaedia*, with a *Preliminary Discourse* by d'Alembert. Prévost's translation of Richardson's *Clarissa*.
1752	His opera *The Village Soothsayer* is performed before Louis XV at Fontainebleau. His one-act play *Narcissus* is performed by the Théâtre Français.	Hume: *Political Discourses*. Voltaire: *Micromegas*.
1753	Publishes controversial *Letter on French Music*.	
1754	Visits Geneva and returns to the Protestant communion.	Condillac: *Treatise on the Senses*.
1755	Publishes *Discourse on the Origins of Inequality*. Article on *Political Economy* appears in volume V of the *Encyclopaedia*.	Death of Montesquieu.
1756	Goes to live at 'The Hermitage', near Montmorency. Begins *Julie, or the New Héloïse*.	Voltaire: 'Poem on the Disaster at Lisbon'.
1757	Falls in love with his friend Saint-Lambert's mistress,	Burke: *A Philosophical Enquiry into the Sublime and the Beautiful*.

CHRONOLOGY

Jacobite Rebellion in England and Scotland. Marshal de Saxe wins battle of Fontenoy, last glorious victory of the *ancien régime*. Madame de Pompadour becomes titular mistress of Louis XV.
Death of Philip V of Spain. Accession of Ferdinand VI (1746).

Treaty of Aix-la-Chapelle (effectively no more than an armistice for the protagonists, France and England. From henceforward main theatre of war shifts from Europe to colonies.)

Machault's tax of the *vingtième*; within two years his financial reforms have failed. In England Pelham introduces measures which successfully reduce interest on the National Debt.

Dupleix appointed Governor General of India (to 1754) where French and British interests increasingly conflict.

'War' between the supporters of French and of Italian music – 'Guerre des Bouffons' (to 1753).

Dispute over *billets de confession*; exile (May) and recall (October) of the Paris Parlement.

Lisbon earthquake. English attacks on French ships off Newfoundland.

Treaty of Versailles between France and Austria. Agreement of Westminster between England and Prussia. Beginning of Seven Years' War. English war effort masterminded by the elder Pitt.
Damiens attempts to assassinate Louis XV. D'Alembert's inflammatory article 'Geneva' is published. Clive victorious at battle of Plassey.

DATE	AUTHOR'S LIFE	LITERARY CONTEXT
1757 *cont*	Sophie d'Houdetot. Quarrels with Madame d'Epinay, Grimm and Diderot. Quits 'The Hermitage'.	Hume: *Four Dissertations.* Diderot: *The Natural Son.*
1758	Publishes *Letter to d'Alembert on Stage Spectacles*, in the Preface to which he announces his break with Diderot.	Helvétius: *On Human Intelligence.*
1759	Is befriended by the Luxembourg family. Writes much of *Émile*.	Voltaire: *Candide.* Sterne: *Tristram Shandy* (to 1767). Johnson: *Rasselas.*
1760	Rousseau and Diderot are satirized (May) in Palissot's comedy *The Philosophers*.	Diderot begins *The Nun.*
1761	*The New Héloïse* goes on sale (February) in Paris.	Death of Richardson.
1762	Writes four autobiographical letters to Malesherbes (April). His *Social Contract* is published in Amsterdam; its entry into France is banned. His *Émile* is issued (May) in Paris. *Émile* is condemned (June) by Parlement, and Rousseau, threatened with arrest, takes refuge in Switzerland.	Birth of Cobbett. Diderot begins to write *Rameau's Nephew.* Wilkes founds political periodical *The North Briton.*
1763		
1764	James Boswell visits Rousseau at Môtiers. *Letters Written from the Mountain.* Rousseau's abandonment of his children is revealed (December) in an anonymous pamphlet by Voltaire, 'The Sentiment of the Citizens'.	Voltaire: *Philosophical Dictionary.* Walpole: *The Castle of Otranto.*
1765	Begins his *Confessions*. Is stoned (September) at Môtiers. Short period of happiness on the island of Saint-Pierre in the lake of Bienne. Returns to Paris, braving arrest.	Sedaine: *A Philosopher Without Knowing It.*
1766	Leaves for England (January) with David Hume. Moves (March) with Thérèse to Wootton in	Marmontel: *Belisarius.* Goldsmith: *The Vicar of Wakefield.*

HISTORICAL EVENTS

Choiseul Secretary of Foreign Affairs.

The *Encyclopaedia* is suppressed (March) but is continued secretly. British Museum opens. French lose Quebec, Guadaloupe and Martinique. Etienne de Silhouette, Controller-General (March–November), fails to reform finances.
George III succeeds George II as King of England.

Family Compact between France and Spain.

Execution of Calas, and later of La Barre (1765) fuels anti-clerical campaign. Catherine the Great becomes Empress of Russia.

Peace of Paris establishes England as major colonial power at the expense of France. Issue 45 of *The North Briton* denounces the King's Speech; Wilkes is arrested, and in a series of cases triumphs against the Crown and is popularly regarded as a symbol of 'Liberty'.
Secularization of Church lands in Russia. The Jesuit Order in France is suppressed. Death of Madame de Pompadour.

Death of the Dauphin. Grenville's Stamp Act antagonizes both American colonists and radical opposition in England.

Lorraine incorporated in France. Provincial parlements, led by Brittany, challenge royal authority; Louis XV repudiates their claims in a *lit de justice*. Catherine the Great's 'Instruction', inspired by philosophy of the French

DATE	AUTHOR'S LIFE	LITERARY CONTEXT
1766 *cont*	Staffordshire, where he works on his *Confessions*. Writes letter (July) to Hume accusing him of treachery. Hume publishes in Paris (October) a *Succinct Account* of his troubles with Rousseau.	Smollett: *Travels through France and Italy.*
1767	Returns (May) with Thérèse to France and is given shelter by the Prince de Conti at Trye-le-Château.	Voltaire: *The Ingenu.* Ferguson: *Essay on the History of Civil Society.*
1768	Goes through a marriage ceremony with Thérèse.	
1770	Writes to Saint-Germain announcing his discovery of a 'conspiracy' against him by his so-called friends. Returns to Paris and begins readings from his *Confessions*.	d'Holbach: *System of Nature.* Birth of Wordsworth.
1771	His readings are prohibited by the police.	Smollett: *Humphry Clinker.* Mackenzie: *The Man of Feeling.*
1772–6	He is writing *Rousseau Judge of Jean-Jacques* and *Reveries of a Solitary Walker*. On Christmas Eve 1776 he attempts to place the MS. of *Rousseau Judge of Jean-Jacques* on the high altar of Notre-Dame.	Diderot begins *Jacques the Fatalist* (c. 1773). Goethe: *The Sorrows of Young Werther* (1774). Beaumarchais: *The Barber of Seville* (1775).
1776	Suffers street accident near Ménilmontant.	First volume of Gibbon's *Decline and Fall of the Roman Empire.* Smith: *The Wealth of Nations.*
1778	He and Thérèse move (May) to cottage at Ermenonville, on the estate of the Marquis de Girardin. Diderot makes veiled but bitter reference to him in his *Life of Seneca*. He dies (2 July). Is buried on the Isle of Poplars at Ermenonville, soon to become a place of pilgrimage.	Death of Voltaire (30 May).
1781		Schiller: *The Robbers.*
1782	The First Part of the *Confessions* is published in Geneva.	Laclos: *Dangerous Liaisons.*
1787		
1789	The Second Part of the *Confessions* is published in Geneva.	Madame de Staël: *Letters on the Works and Character of Jean-Jacques Rousseau.* Blake: *Songs of Innocence.*

CHRONOLOGY

Enlightenment, proposes new liberal and rational methods of government – some of which are later put into practice.

French purchase Corsica from Genoa. Riots in London – British Government again humiliated over Wilkes affair.
Marriage of the future Louis XVI to Marie-Antoinette. Fall of Choiseul. Succeeded by Maupeou and Terray (to 1774).

Exile of parlements.

The Boston Tea Party (1773). American War of Independence with Washington as commander-in-chief (1775–83). Peasant rebellion in Russia led by Pugachev. Death of Louis XV; accession of Louis XVI. Maurepas chief influence in government. Recall of parlements (1774).

Turgot (Controller-General since 1774) is dismissed and Necker replaces him.

France enters American War of Independence. In England the Roman Catholic Relief Bill passes, repealing the most repressive anti-Catholic laws.

Necker's *Compte rendu*; dismissal of Necker.

Edict of toleration of Protestants.
Summoning of the French States-General (1788) which becomes the National Assembly (1789). The French Revolution with the storming of the Bastille (14 July 1789). Feudal privileges abolished. Secularization of Church lands. Louis XVI put in prison.

xliii

CONFESSIONS

THE CONFESSIONS OF JEAN-JACQUES ROUSSEAU

PART THE FIRST

BOOK I [1712–1719]

Intus, et in cute[1]

I AM commencing an undertaking, hitherto without precedent, and which will never find an imitator. I desire to set before my fellows the likeness of a man in all the truth of nature, and that man myself.

Myself alone! I know the feelings of my heart, and I know men. I am not made like any of those I have seen; I venture to believe that I am not made like any of those who are in existence. If I am not better, at least I am different. Whether Nature has acted rightly or wrongly in destroying the mould in which she cast me, can only be decided after I have been read.

Let the trumpet of the Day of Judgment sound when it will, I will present myself before the Sovereign Judge with this book in my hand. I will say boldly: "This is what I have done, what I have thought, what I was. I have told the good and the bad with equal frankness. I have neither omitted anything bad, nor interpolated anything good. If I have occasionally made use of some immaterial embellishments, this has only been in order to fill a gap caused by lack of memory. I may have assumed the truth of that which I knew might have been true, never of that which I knew to be false. I have shown myself as I was: mean and contemptible, good, high-minded and sublime, according as I was one or the other. I have unveiled my inmost self even as Thou hast seen it, O Eternal Being. Gather round me the countless host of my fellow-men; let them hear my confessions, lament for my unworthiness, and blush for my imperfections. Then let each of them in turn reveal, with the same frankness, the secrets of his heart at the foot of the Throne, and say, if he dare, *'I was better than that man!'* "

---

[1] *Intus, et in cute.* An allusion to Persius, *Satire* III, line 30: *Ego te intus et in cute novi* ("I know you from within and under the skin").

I was born at Geneva, in the year 1712,[1] and was the son of Isaac Rousseau[2] and of Susanne Bernard, citizen.[3] The distribution of a very moderate inheritance amongst fifteen children had reduced my father's portion almost to nothing; and his only means of livelihood was his trade of watchmaker, in which he was really very clever. My mother, a daughter of the Protestant minister Bernard, was better off. She was clever and beautiful, and my father had found difficulty in obtaining her hand. Their affection for each other had commenced almost as soon as they were born. When only eight years old, they walked every evening upon the Treille;[4] at ten, they were inseparable. Sympathy and union of soul strengthened in them the feeling produced by intimacy. Both, naturally full of tender sensibility, only waited for the moment when they should find the same disposition in another – or, rather, this moment waited for them, and each abandoned their heart to the first which opened to receive it. Destiny, which appeared to oppose their passion, only encouraged it. The young lover, unable to obtain possession of his mistress, was consumed by grief. She advised him to travel, and endeavour to forget her. He travelled, but without result, and returned more in love than ever. He found her whom he loved still faithful and true. After this trial of affection, nothing was left for them but to love each other all their lives. This they swore to do, and Heaven blessed their oath.

Gabriel Bernard, my mother's brother, fell in love with one of my father's sisters, who only consented to accept the hand of the brother, on condition that her own brother married the sister. Love arranged everything, and the two marriages took place on

---

[1] He was born 28 June 1712, in the rue de la Boulangerie, now no. 40 Grand'Rue.

[2] [Rousseau, Isaac] See *Biographies*, p. 713.

[3] There were four different legal statuses in Geneva. *Citoyen*, for which one had to be the child of a *bourgeois* and born in the city. (Only *citoyens* could become magistrates.) *Bourgeois, i.e.*, child of a *citoyen* or *bourgeois* but born outside the city, or having received the rights of *bourgeoisie* from the magistracy. (A *bourgeois* could belong to the General Council and the Council of 200.) *Habitant*: foreigner permitted to live in Geneva. *Natif*: child of a *habitant*, with certain privileges but excluded from government.

[4] A fashionable promenade in Geneva.

the same day. Thus my uncle became the husband of my aunt, and their children were doubly my first cousins. At the end of a year, a child was born to both, after which they were again obliged to separate.

My uncle Bernard was an engineer. He took service in the Empire and in Hungary, under Prince Eugène. He distinguished himself at the siege and battle of Belgrade. My father, after the birth of my only brother, set out for Constantinople, whither he was summoned to undertake the post of watchmaker to the Sultan. During his absence, my mother's beauty, intellect and talents gained for her the devotion of numerous admirers.* M. de la Closure, the French Resident, was one of the most eager to offer his. His passion must have been great, for, thirty years later, I saw him greatly affected when speaking to me of her. To enable her to resist such advances, my mother had more than her virtue: she loved her husband tenderly. She pressed him to return; he left all, and returned. I was the unhappy fruit of this return. Ten months later I was born, a weak and ailing child; I cost my mother her life, and my birth was the first of my misfortunes.

I have never heard how my father bore this loss, but I know that he was inconsolable. He believed that he saw his wife again in me, without being able to forget that it was I who had robbed him of her; he never embraced me without my perceiving, by his sighs and the convulsive manner in which he clasped me to his breast, that a bitter regret was mingled with his caresses, which were on that account only the more tender. When he said to me,

---

* Her talents were too brilliant for her position, since her father, the minister, who worshipped her, had educated her with great care. She drew, sang, accompanied herself on the téorbe; † she read much, and wrote tolerable verses. During the absence of her husband and her brother, while walking with her sister-in-law and their two children, she delivered the following impromptu, when someone happened to mention them:

> Ces deux messieurs, qui sont absents,
> Nous sont chers de bien des manières:
> Ce sont nos amis, nos amants:
> Ce sont nos maris et nos frères,
> Et les pères de ces enfants. (R)
> † A stringed instrument, resembling a lute.

"Jean Jacques, let us talk of your mother," I used to answer, "Well, then, my father, we will weep!" – and this word alone was sufficient to move him to tears. "Ah!" said he, with a sigh, "give her back to me, console me for her loss, fill the void which she has left in my soul. Should I love you as I do, if you were only my son?" Forty years after he had lost her, he died in the arms of a second wife, but the name of the first was on his lips and her image at the bottom of his heart.

Such were the authors of my existence. Of all the gifts which Heaven had bestowed upon them, a sensitive heart is the only one they bequeathed to me; it had been the source of their happiness, but for me it proved the source of all the misfortunes of my life.

I was brought into the world in an almost dying condition; little hope was entertained of saving my life. I carried within me the germs of a complaint which the course of time has strengthened, and which at times allows me a respite only to make me suffer more cruelly in another manner. One of my father's sisters, an amiable and virtuous young woman, took such care of me that she saved my life. At this moment, while I am writing, she is still alive, at the age of eighty, nursing a husband younger than herself, but exhausted by excessive drinking. Dear aunt, I forgive you for having preserved my life; and I deeply regret that, at the end of your days, I am unable to repay the tender care which you lavished upon me at the beginning of my own.[1] My dear old nurse Jacqueline is also still alive, healthy and robust. The hands which opened my eyes at my birth will be able to close them for me at my death.

I felt before I thought: this is the common lot of humanity. I experienced it more than others. I do not know what I did until I was five or six years old. I do not know how I learned to read; I only remember my earliest reading, and the effect it had upon me; from that time I date my uninterrupted self-consciousness. My mother had left some romances behind her, which my father and I began to read after supper. At first it was only a question of

[1] The name of this aunt was Madame Gonceru. In March, 1767, Rousseau settled upon her an income of one hundred livres, and, even in the time of his greatest distress, always paid it with scrupulous exactitude.

practising me in reading by the aid of amusing books; but soon the interest became so lively, that we used to read in turns without stopping, and spent whole nights in this occupation. We were unable to leave off until the volume was finished. Sometimes, my father, hearing the swallows begin to twitter in the early morning, would say, quite ashamed, "Let us go to bed; I am more of a child than yourself."

In a short time I acquired, by this dangerous method, not only extreme facility in reading and understanding what I read, but a knowledge of the passions that was unique in a child of my age. I had no idea of things in themselves, although all the feelings of actual life were already known to me. I had conceived nothing, but felt everything. These confused emotions which I felt one after the other, certainly did not warp the reasoning powers which I did not as yet possess; but they shaped them in me of a peculiar stamp, and gave me odd and romantic notions of human life, of which experience and reflection have never been able wholly to cure me.

[1719–1723.] – The romances came to an end in the summer of 1719. The following winter brought us something different. My mother's library being exhausted, we had recourse to the share of her father's which had fallen to us. Luckily, there were some good books in it; in fact, it could hardly have been otherwise, for the library had been collected by a minister, who was even a learned man according to the fashion of the day, and was at the same time a man of taste and intellect. The "History of the Empire and the Church," by Le Sueur; Bossuet's "Treatise upon Universal History"; Plutarch's "Lives of Famous Men"; Nani's "History of Venice"; Ovid's "Metamorphoses"; "La Bruyère"; Fontenelle's "Worlds"; his "Dialogues of the Dead"; and some volumes of Molière – all these were brought over into my father's room, and I read to him out of them while he worked. I conceived a taste for them that was rare and perhaps unique at my age. Plutarch, especially, became my favourite author. The pleasure I took in reading him over and over again cured me a little of my taste for romance, and I soon preferred Agesilaus, Brutus and Aristides to Orondates, Artamenes, and Juba. This interesting reading, and the conversations between my father and myself to which it gave rise, formed in me the free and republican spirit, the proud and indomitable character unable to endure slavery or servitude, which has tormented me throughout my life in situations the least fitted to afford it scope. Unceasingly occupied with thoughts of Rome and Athens, living as it were amongst their great men, myself by birth the citizen of a republic and the son of a father whose patriotism was his strongest passion, I was fired by his example; I believed myself a Greek or a Roman; I lost my identity in that of the individual whose life I was reading; the recitals of the qualities of endurance and intrepidity which arrested my attention made my eyes glisten and strengthened my voice. One day, while I was relating the history of Scaevola at table, those present were alarmed to see me come forward and hold my hand over a chafing-dish, to illustrate his action.

I had a brother seven years older than myself, who was learning my father's trade. The excessive affection which was lavished upon myself caused him to be somewhat neglected, which treatment I cannot approve of. His education felt the consequences of this neglect. He took to evil courses before he was old enough to be a regular profligate. He was put with another master, from whom he was continually running away, as he had done from home. I hardly ever saw him; I can scarcely say that I knew him; but I never ceased to love him tenderly, and he loved me as much as a vagabond can love anything. I remember that, on one occasion, when my father was chastising him harshly and in anger, I threw myself impetuously between them and embraced him closely. In this manner I covered his body with mine, and received the blows which were aimed at him; I so obstinately maintained my position that at last my father was obliged to leave off, being either disarmed by my cries and tears, or afraid of hurting me more than him. At last, my brother turned out so badly that he ran away and disappeared altogether. Some time afterwards we heard that he was in Germany. He never once wrote to us. From that time nothing more has been heard of him, and thus I have remained an only son.

If this poor boy was carelessly brought up, this was not the case with his brother; the children of kings could not be more carefully looked after than I was during my early years – worshipped by all around me, and, which is far less common, treated as a beloved, never as a spoiled child. Till I left my father's house, I was never once allowed to run about the streets by myself with the other children; in my case no one ever had to satisfy or check any of those fantastic whims which are attributed to Nature, but are all in reality the result of education. I had the faults of my age: I was a chatterbox, a glutton, and, sometimes, a liar. I would have stolen fruits, bonbons, or eatables; but I have never found pleasure in doing harm or damage, in accusing others, or in tormenting poor dumb animals. I remember, however, that I once made water in a saucepan belonging to one of our neighbours, Madame Clot, while she was at church. I declare that, even now, the recollection of this makes me laugh, because Madame Clot, a good woman in other respects, was the most confirmed old grumbler I have ever known. Such is the brief and true story of all my childish offences.

How could I become wicked, when I had nothing but examples of gentleness before my eyes, and none around me but the best people in the world? My father, my aunt, my nurse, my relations, our friends, our neighbours, all who surrounded me, did not, it is true, obey me, but they loved me; and I loved them in return. My wishes were so little excited and so little opposed, that it did not occur to me to have any. I can swear that, until I served under a master, I never knew what a fancy was. Except during the time I spent in reading or writing in my father's company, or when my nurse took me for a walk, I was always with my aunt, sitting or standing by her side, watching her at her embroidery or listening to her singing; and I was content. Her cheerfulness, her gentleness and her pleasant face have stamped so deep and lively an impression on my mind that I can still see her manner, look, and attitude; I remember her affectionate language: I could describe what clothes she wore and how her head was dressed, not forgetting the two little curls of black hair on her temples, which she wore in accordance with the fashion of the time.

I am convinced that it is to her I owe the taste, or rather passion, for music, which only became fully developed in me a long time afterwards. She knew a prodigious number of tunes and songs which she used to sing in a very thin, gentle voice. This excellent woman's cheerfulness of soul banished dreaminess and melancholy from herself and all around her. The attraction which her singing possessed for me was so great, that not only have several of her songs always remained in my memory, but even now, when I have lost her, and as I grew older, many of them, totally forgotten since the days of my childhood, return to my mind with inexpressible charm. Would anyone believe that I, an old dotard, eaten up by cares and troubles, sometime find myself weeping like a child, when I mumble one of those little airs in a voice already broken and trembling? One of them, especially, has come back to me completely, as far as the tune is concerned; the second half of the words, however, has obstinately resisted all my efforts to recall it, although I have an indistinct recollection of the rhymes. Here is the beginning, and all that I can remember of the rest:

> Tircis, je n'ose
> Écouter ton chalumeau
> Sous l'ormeau:
> Car on en cause
> Déjà dans notre hameau.
> . . . .
> . . . . un berger
> . . . . s'engager
> . . . . sans danger
> Et toujours l'épine est sous la rose.[1]

I ask, where is the affecting charm which my heart finds in this song? it is a whim, which I am quite unable to understand; but,

---

[1] This song, well-known in Paris, is still sung by the working classes. The sixth and following lines run:
> "Un cœur s'expose
> À trop s'engager
> Avec un berger,
> Et toujours l'épine est sous la rose."

[Tircis, I dare not listen to your pipe under the elm; people are beginning to talk about it in the village. It is dangerous for a heart to have too much to do with a shepherd; there is no rose without its thorn.]

be that as it may, it is absolutely impossible for me to sing it through without being interrupted by my tears. I have intended, times without number, to write to Paris to make inquiries concerning the remainder of the words, in case anyone should happen to know them; but I am almost certain that the pleasure which I feel in recalling the air would partly disappear, if it should be proved that others besides my poor aunt Suson have sung it.

Such were my earliest emotions on my entry into life; thus began to form or display itself in me that heart at once so proud and tender, that character so effeminate but yet indomitable, which, ever wavering between timidity and courage, weakness and self-control, has throughout my life made me inconsistent, and has caused abstinence and enjoyment, pleasure and prudence equally to elude my grasp.

This course of education was interrupted by an accident, the consequences of which have exercised an influence upon the remainder of my life. My father had a quarrel with a captain in the French army, named Gautier, who was connected with some of the members of the Common Council. This Gautier, a cowardly and insolent fellow (whose nose happened to bleed during the affray), in order to avenge himself, accused my father of having drawn his sword within the city walls. My father, whom they wanted to send to prison, persisted that, in accordance with the law, the accuser ought to be imprisoned as well as himself. Being unable to have his way in this, he preferred to quit Geneva and expatriate himself for the rest of his life, than to give way on a point in which honour and liberty appeared to him to be compromised.

I remained under the care of my uncle Bernard, who was at the time employed upon the fortifications of Geneva. His eldest daughter was dead, but he had a son of the same age as myself. We were sent together to Bossey, to board with the Protestant minister Lambercier, in order to learn, together with Latin, all the sorry trash which is included under the name of education.

Two years spent in the village in some degree softened my Roman roughness and made me a child again. At Geneva, where no tasks were imposed upon me, I loved reading and study,

which were almost my only amusements; at Bossey, my tasks
made me love the games which formed a break in them. The
country was so new to me, that my enjoyment of it never palled.
I conceived so lively an affection for it, that it has never since
died out. The remembrance of the happy days I have spent there
filled me with regretful longing for its pleasures, at all periods
of my life, until the day which has brought me back to it.
M. Lambercier was a very intelligent person, who, without
neglecting our education, never imposed excessive tasks upon
us. The fact that, in spite of my dislike to restraint, I have never
recalled my hours of study with any feeling of disgust – and also
that, even if I did not learn much from him, I learnt without
difficulty what I did learn and never forgot it – is sufficient proof
that his system of instruction was a good one.

The simplicity of this country life was of inestimable value to
me, in that it opened my heart to friendship. Up to that time
I had only known lofty but imaginary sentiments. The habit of
living peacefully together with my cousin Bernard drew us
together in tender bonds of union. In a short time, my feelings
towards him became more affectionate than those with which I
had regarded my brother, and they have never been effaced. He
was a tall, lanky, weakly boy, as gentle in disposition as he was
feeble in body, who never abused the preference which was
shown to him in the house as the son of my guardian. Our tasks,
our amusements, our tastes were the same: we were alone, we
were of the same age, each of us needed a companion: separation was to us, in a manner, annihilation. Although we had few
opportunities of proving our mutual attachment, it was very
great; not only were we unable to live an instant apart, but we did
not imagine it possible that we could ever be separated. Being,
both of us, ready to yield to tenderness, and docile, provided
compulsion was not used, we always agreed in everything. If, in
the presence of those who looked after us, he had some advantage over me in consequence of the favour with which they
regarded him, when we were alone I had an advantage over him
which restored the equilibrium. When we were saying our
lessons, I prompted him if he hesitated; when I had finished
my exercise, I helped him with his; and in our amusements, my

more active mind always led the way. In short, our two characters harmonised so well, and the friendship which united us was so sincere, that, in the five years and more, during which, whether at Bossey or Geneva, we were almost inseparable, although I confess that we often fought, it was never necessary to separate us, none of our quarrels ever lasted longer than a quarter of an hour, and neither of us ever made any accusation against the other. These observations are, if you will, childish, but they furnish an example which, since the time that there have been children, is perhaps unique.

The life which I led at Bossey suited me so well that, had it only lasted longer, it would have completely decided my character. Tender, affectionate and gentle feelings formed its foundation. I believe that no individual of our species was naturally more free from vanity than myself. I raised myself by fits and starts to lofty flights, but immediately fell down again into my natural languor. My liveliest desire was to be loved by all who came near me. I was of a gentle disposition; my cousin and our guardians were the same. During two whole years I was neither the witness nor the victim of any violent feeling. Everything nourished in my heart those tendencies which it received from Nature. I knew no higher happiness than to see all the world satisfied with me and with everything. I shall never forget how, if I happened to hesitate when saying my catechism in church, nothing troubled me more than to observe signs of restlessness and dissatisfaction on Mademoiselle Lambercier's face. That alone troubled me more than the disgrace of failing in public, which, nevertheless, affected me greatly: for, although little susceptible to praise, I felt shame keenly; and I may say here that the thought of Mademoiselle's reproaches caused me less uneasiness than the fear of offending her.

When it was necessary, however, neither she nor her brother were wanting in severity; but, since this severity was nearly always just, and never passionate, it pained me without making me insubordinate. Failure to please grieved me more than punishment, and signs of dissatisfaction hurt me more than corporal chastisement. It is somewhat embarrassing to explain myself more clearly, but, nevertheless, I must do so. How differently would one deal with youth, if one could more clearly see the remote effects of the usual method of treatment, which is employed always without discrimination, frequently without discretion! The important lesson which may be drawn from an example as common as it is fatal makes me decide to mention it.

As Mademoiselle Lambercier had the affection of a mother for us, she also exercised the authority of one, and sometimes carried it so far as to inflict upon us the punishment of children when we had deserved it. For some time she was content with threats, and this threat of a punishment that was quite new to me appeared very terrible; but, after it had been carried out, I found the reality less terrible than the expectation; and, what was still more strange, this chastisement made me still more devoted to her who had inflicted it. It needed all the strength of this devotion and all my natural docility to keep myself from doing something which would have deservedly brought upon me a repetition of it; for I had found in the pain, even in the disgrace, a mixture of sensuality which had left me less afraid than desirous of experiencing it again from the same hand. No doubt some precocious sexual instinct was mingled with this feeling, for the same chastisement inflicted by her brother would not have seemed to me at all pleasant. But, considering his disposition, there was little cause to fear the substitution; and if I kept myself from deserving punishment, it was solely for fear of displeasing Mademoiselle Lambercier; for, so great is the power exercised over me by kindness, even by that which is due to the senses, that it has always controlled the latter in my heart.

The repetition of the offence, which I avoided without being afraid of it, occurred without any fault of mine, that is to say, of my will, and I may say that I profited by it without any qualm of conscience. But this second time was also the last; for Mademoiselle Lambercier, who had no doubt noticed something which convinced her that the punishment did not have the desired effect, declared that it tired her too much, and that she would abandon it. Until then we had slept in her room, sometimes even in her bed during the winter. Two days afterwards we were put to sleep in another room, and from that time I had the

honour, which I would gladly have dispensed with, of being
treated by her as a big boy.

Who would believe that this childish punishment, inflicted
upon me when only eight years old by a young woman of thirty,
disposed of my tastes, my desires, my passions, and my own self
for the remainder of my life, and that in a manner exactly
contrary to that which should have been the natural result?
When my feelings were once inflamed, my desires so went astray
that, limited to what I had already felt, they did not trouble
themselves to look for anything else. In spite of my hot blood,
which has been inflamed with sensuality almost from my birth, I
kept myself free from every taint until the age when the coldest
and most sluggish temperaments begin to develop. In torments
for a long time, without knowing why, I devoured with burning
glances all the pretty women I met; my imagination unceasingly
recalled them to me, only to make use of them in my own
fashion, and to make of them so many Mlles. Lambercier.

Even after I had reached years of maturity, this curious taste,
always abiding with me and carried to depravity and even frenzy,
preserved my morality, which it might naturally have been
expected to destroy. If ever a bringing-up was chaste and modest, assuredly mine was. My three aunts were not only models of
propriety, but reserved to a degree which has long since been
unknown amongst women. My father, a man of pleasure, but a
gallant of the old school, never said a word, even in the presence
of women whom he loved more than others, which would have
brought a blush to a maiden's cheek; and the respect due to
children has never been so much insisted upon as in my family
and in my presence. In this respect I found M. Lambercier
equally careful; and an excellent servant was dismissed for having used a somewhat too free expression in our presence. Until I
was a young man, I not only had no distinct idea of the union of
the sexes, but the confused notion which I had regarding it never
presented itself to me except in a hateful and disgusting form.
For common prostitutes I felt a loathing which has never been
effaced: the sight of a profligate always filled me with contempt,
even with affright. My horror of debauchery became thus pronounced ever since the day when, walking to Little Sacconex by

a hollow way, I saw on both sides holes in the ground, where I was told that these creatures carried on their intercourse. The thought of the one always brought back to my mind the copulation of dogs, and the bare recollection was sufficient to disgust me.

This tendency of my bringing-up, in itself adapted to delay the first outbreaks of an inflammable temperament, was assisted, as I have already said, by the direction which the first indications of sensuality took in my case. Only busying my imagination with what I had actually felt, in spite of most uncomfortable effervescence of blood, I only knew how to turn my desires in the direction of that kind of pleasure with which I was acquainted, without ever going as far as that which had been made hateful to me, and which, without my having the least suspicion of it, was so closely related to the other. In my foolish fancies, in my erotic frenzies, in the extravagant acts to which they sometimes led me, I had recourse in my imagination to the assistance of the other sex, without ever thinking that it was serviceable for any purpose than that for which I was burning to make use of it.

In this manner, then, in spite of an ardent, lascivious and precocious temperament, I passed the age of puberty without desiring, even without knowing of any other sensual pleasures than those of which Mademoiselle Lambercier had most innocently given me the idea; and when, in course of time, I became a man, that which should have destroyed me again preserved me. My old childish taste, instead of disappearing, became so associated with the other, that I could never banish it from the desires kindled by my senses; and this madness, joined to my natural shyness, has always made me very unenterprising with women, for want of courage to say all or power to do all. The kind of enjoyment, of which the other was only for me the final consummation, could neither be appropriated by him who longed for it, nor guessed by her who was able to bestow it. Thus I have spent my life in idle longing, without saying a word, in the presence of those whom I loved most. Too bashful to declare my taste, I at least satisfied it in situations which had reference to it and kept up the idea of it. To lie at the feet of an imperious mistress, to obey her commands, to ask her forgive-ness – this was for me a sweet enjoyment; and, the more my lively imagination heated my blood, the more I presented the appearance of a bashful lover. It may be easily imagined that this manner of making love does not lead to very speedy results, and is not very dangerous to the virtue of those who are its object. For this reason I have rarely possessed, but have none the less enjoyed myself in my own way – that is to say, in imagination. Thus it has happened that my senses, in harmony with my timid disposition and my romantic spirit, have kept my sentiments pure and my morals blameless, owing to the very tastes which, combined with a little more impudence, might have plunged me into the most brutal sensuality.

I have taken the first and most difficult step in the dark and dirty labyrinth of my confessions. It is easier to admit that which is criminal than that which is ridiculous and makes a man feel ashamed. Henceforth I am sure of myself; after having ventured to say so much, I can shrink from nothing. One may judge what such confessions have cost me, from the fact that, during the whole course of my life, I have never dared to declare my folly to those whom I loved with the frenzy of a passion which deprived me of sight and hearing, which robbed me of my senses and caused me to tremble all over with a convulsive movement. I have never brought myself, even when on most intimate terms, to ask women to grant me the only favour of all which was wanting. This never happened to me but once – in my child-hood, with a girl of my own age; even then, it was she who first proposed it.

While thus going back to the first traces of my inner life, I find elements which sometimes appear incompatible, and yet have united in order to produce with vigour a simple and uniform effect; and I find others which, although apparently the same, have formed combinations so different, owing to the co-opera-tion of certain circumstances, that one would never imagine that these elements were in any way connected. Who, for instance, would believe that one of the most powerful movements of my soul was tempered in the same spring from which a stream of sensuality and effeminacy has entered my blood? Without

leaving the subject of which I have just spoken, I shall produce
by means of it a very different impression.

One day I was learning my lesson by myself in the room next
to the kitchen. The servant had put Mademoiselle Lambercier's
combs in front of the fire-place to dry. When she came back to
fetch them, she found one with a whole row of teeth broken.
Who was to blame for the damage? No one except myself had
entered the room. On being questioned, I denied that I had
touched the comb. M. and Mademoiselle Lambercier both
began to admonish, to press, and to threaten me; I obstinately
persisted in my denial; but the evidence was too strong, and
outweighed all my protestations, although it was the first time
that I had been found to lie so boldly. The matter was regarded
as serious, as in fact it deserved to be. The mischievousness, the
falsehood, the obstinacy appeared equally deserving of punishment; but this time it was not by Mademoiselle Lambercier that
chastisement was inflicted. My uncle Bernard was written to,
and he came. My poor cousin was accused of another equally
grave offence; we were involved in the same punishment. It was
terrible. Had they wished to look for the remedy in the evil itself
and to deaden for ever my depraved senses, they could not have
set to work better, and for a long time my senses left me
undisturbed.

They could not draw from me the desired confession.
Although I was several times brought up before them and
reduced to a pitiable condition, I remained unshaken. I would
have endured death, and made up my mind to do so. Force was
obliged to yield to the diabolical obstinacy of a child – as they
called my firmness. At last I emerged from this cruel trial, utterly
broken, but triumphant.

It is now nearly fifty years since this incident took place, and I
have no fear of being punished again for the same thing. Well,
then, I declare in the sight of heaven that I was innocent of the
offence, that I neither broke nor touched the comb, that I never
went near the fire-place, and had never even thought of doing
so. It would be useless to ask me how the damage was done: I do
not know, and I cannot understand; all that I know for certain is,
that I had nothing to do with it.

Imagine a child, shy and obedient in ordinary life, but fiery, proud, and unruly in his passions: a child who had always been led by the voice of reason and always treated with gentleness, justice, and consideration, who had not even a notion of injustice, and who for the first time becomes acquainted with so terrible an example of it on the part of the very people whom he most loves and respects! What an upset of ideas! what a disturbance of feelings! what revolution in his heart, in his brain, in the whole of his little intellectual and moral being! Imagine all this, I say, if possible. As for myself, I feel incapable of disentangling and following up the least trace of what then took place within me.

I had not yet sense enough to feel how much appearances were against me, and to put myself in the place of the others. I kept to my own place, and all that I felt was the harshness of a frightful punishment for an offence which I had not committed. The bodily pain, although severe, I felt but little: all I felt was indignation, rage, despair. My cousin, whose case was almost the same, and who had been punished for an involuntary mistake as if it had been a premeditated act, following my example, flew into a rage, and worked himself up to the same pitch of excitement as myself. Both in the same bed, we embraced each other with convulsive transports: we felt suffocated; and when at length our young hearts, somewhat relieved, were able to vent their wrath, we sat upright in bed and began to shout, times without number, with all our might: *Carnifex! carnifex! carnifex!*[1]

While I write these words, I feel that my pulse beats faster; those moments will always be present to me though I should live a hundred thousand years. That first feeling of violence and injustice has remained so deeply graven on my soul, that all the ideas connected with it bring back to me my first emotion; and this feeling, which, in its origin, had reference only to myself, has become so strong in itself and so completely detached from all personal interest, that, when I see or hear of any act of injustice – whoever is the victim of it, and wherever it is committed – my heart kindles with rage, as if the effect of it recoiled upon

[1] Executioner, torturer.

myself. When I read of the cruelties of a ferocious tyrant, the crafty atrocities of a rascally priest, I would gladly set out to plunge a dagger into the heart of such wretches, although I had to die for it a hundred times. I have often put myself in a perspiration, pursuing or stoning a cock, a cow, a dog, or any animal which I saw tormenting another merely because it felt itself the stronger. This impulse may be natural to me, and I believe that it is; but the profound impression left upon me by the first injustice I suffered was too long and too strongly connected with it, not to have greatly strengthened it.

With the above incident the tranquillity of my childish life was over. From that moment I ceased to enjoy a pure happiness, and even at the present day I feel that the recollection of the charms of my childhood ceases there. We remained a few months longer at Bossey. We were there, as the first man is represented to us – still in the earthly paradise, but we no longer enjoyed it; in appearance our condition was the same, in reality it was quite a different manner of existence. Attachment, respect, intimacy, and confidence no longer united pupils and guides: we no longer regarded them as gods, who were able to read in our hearts; we became less ashamed of doing wrong and more afraid of being accused; we began to dissemble, to be insubordinate, to lie. All the vices of our age corrupted our innocence and threw a veil of ugliness over our amusements. Even the country lost in our eyes that charm of gentleness and simplicity which goes to the heart. It appeared to us lonely and sombre: it seemed as it were covered with a veil which concealed its beauties from our eyes. We ceased to cultivate our little gardens, our plants, our flowers. We no longer scratched up the ground gently, or cried with joy when we saw the seed which we had sown beginning to sprout. We were disgusted with the life, and others were disgusted with us; my uncle took us away, and we separated from M. and Mademoiselle Lambercier, having had enough of each other, and feeling but little regret at the separation.

Nearly thirty years have passed since I left Bossey, without my recalling to mind my stay there with any connected and pleasurable recollections; but, now that I have passed the prime of life and am approaching old age, I feel these same recollections springing up again while others disappear; they stamp themselves upon my memory with features, the charm and strength of which increase daily, as if, feeling life already slipping away, I were endeavouring to grasp it again by its commencement. The most trifling incidents of that time please me, simply because they belong to that period. I remember all the details of place, persons, and time. I see the maid or the manservant busy in the room, a swallow darting through the window, a fly settling on my hand while I was saying my lesson: I see the whole arrangement of the room in which we used to live; M. Lambercier's study on the right, a copperplate engraving of all the Popes, a barometer, a large almanack hanging on the wall, the raspberry bushes which, growing in a garden situated on very high ground facing the back of the house, shaded the window and sometimes forced their way through it. I am quite aware that the reader does not want to know all this; but I am bound to tell him. Why have I not the courage to relate to him in like manner all the trifling anecdotes of that happy time, which still make me tremble with joy when I recall them? Five or six in particular – but let us make a bargain. I will let you off five, but I wish to tell you one, only one, provided that you will permit me to tell it in as much detail as possible, in order to prolong my enjoyment.

If I only had your pleasure in view, I might choose the story of Mademoiselle Lambercier's backside, which, owing to an unfortunate somersault at the bottom of the meadow, was exhibited in full view to the King of Sardinia,[1] who happened to be passing by; but that of the walnut-tree on the terrace is more amusing for me who took an active part in it, whereas I was merely a spectator of the somersault; besides, I declare that I found absolutely nothing to laugh at in an accident which, although comic in itself, alarmed me for the safety of a person whom I loved as a mother and, perhaps, even more.

Now, O curious readers of the important history of the walnut-tree on the terrace, listen to the horrible tragedy, and keep from shuddering if you can!

[1] [Victor Amadeus II] See *Biographies*, p. 714.

Outside the gate of the court, on the left of the entrance, there was a terrace, where we often went to sit in the afternoon. As it was entirely unprotected from the sun, M. Lambercier had a walnut-tree planted there. The process of planting was carried out with the greatest solemnity. The two boarders were its godfathers; and, while the hole was being filled up, we each of us held the tree with one hand and sang songs of triumph. In order to water it, a kind of basin was made round the foot. Every day, eager spectators of this watering, my cousin and I became more strongly convinced, as was natural, that it was a finer thing to plant a tree on a terrace than a flag upon a breach, and we resolved to win this glory for ourselves without sharing it with anyone.

With this object, we proceeded to cut a slip from a young willow, and planted it on the terrace, at a distance of about eight or ten feet from the august walnut-tree. We did not forget to dig a similar trench round our tree; the difficulty was how to fill it, for the water came from some distance, and we were not allowed to run and fetch it. However, it was absolutely necessary to have some for our willow. For a few days, we had recourse to all kinds of devices to get some, and we succeeded so well that we saw it bud and put forth little leaves, the growth of which we measured every hour, convinced that, although not yet a foot high, it would soon afford us a shade.

As our tree so completely claimed our attention that we were quite incapable of attending to or learning anything else, and were in a sort of delirium: as our guardians, not knowing what was the matter with us, kept a tighter hand upon us, we saw the fatal moment approaching when we should be without water, and were inconsolable at the thought of seeing our tree perish from drought. At length necessity, the mother of invention, suggested to us how to save ourselves from grief and the tree from certain death; this was, to make a channel underground, which should secretly conduct part of the water intended for the walnut-tree to our willow. This undertaking was at first unsuccessful, in spite of the eagerness with which it was carried out. We had made the incline so clumsily that the water did not run at all. The earth fell in and stopped up the channel; the entrance was filled with mud; everything went wrong. But nothing disheartened us: *Labor omnia vincit improbus*.[1] We dug our basin deeper, in order to allow the water to run; we cut some bottoms of boxes into small narrow planks, some of which were laid flat, one after the other, and others set up on both sides of these at an angle, thus forming a triangular canal for our conduit. At the entrance we stuck small pieces of wood, some little distance apart, which, forming a kind of grating or lattice-work, kept back the mud and stones, without stopping the passage of the water. We carefully covered our work with well-trodden earth; and when all was ready, we awaited, in the greatest excitement of hope and fear, the time of watering. After centuries of waiting, the hour at length arrived; M. Lambercier came as usual to assist at the operation, during which we both kept behind him, in order to conceal our tree, to which very luckily he turned his back.

No sooner had the first pail of water been poured out, than we saw some of it running into our basin. At this sight, our prudence deserted us: we began to utter cries of joy which made M. Lambercier turn round; this was a pity, for he took great delight in seeing how good the soil of the walnut-tree was, and how greedily it absorbed the water. Astonished at seeing it distribute itself into two basins, he cried out in his turn, looked, perceived the trick, ordered a pickaxe to be brought, and, with one blow, broke off two or three pieces from our planks; then, crying loudly, "An aqueduct, an aqueduct!" he dealt merciless blows in every direction, each of which went straight to our hearts. In a moment planks, conduit, basin, willow, everything was destroyed and uprooted, without his having uttered a single word, during this terrible work of destruction, except the exclamation which he incessantly repeated. "An aqueduct!" he cried, while demolishing everything, "an aqueduct, an aqueduct!"

It will naturally be imagined that the adventure turned out badly for the little architects: that would be a mistake: it was all over. M. Lambercier never uttered a single word of reproach, or looked upon us with displeasure, and said nothing more about it;

[1] Persistent effort overcomes all difficulties.

shortly afterwards, we even heard him laughing loudly with his sister, for his laughter could be heard a long way off; and what was still more astonishing, when the first fright was over, we ourselves were not much troubled about the matter. We planted another tree somewhere else, and often reminded ourselves of the disaster that overtook the first, by repeating with emphasis, "An aqueduct, an aqueduct!" Hitherto I had had intermittent attacks of pride, when I was Aristides or Brutus; then it was that I felt the first well-defined promptings of vanity. To have been able to construct an aqueduct with our own hands, to have put a cutting in competition with a large tree, appeared to me the height of glory. At ten years of age I was a better judge on this point than Caesar at thirty.

The thought of this walnut-tree and the little history connected with it has remained so vivid in my memory, or returned to it, that one of the plans which gave me the greatest pleasure, on my journey to Geneva, in 1754, was to go to Bossey and revisit the memorials of my boyish amusements, above all, the dear walnut-tree, which by that time must have been a third of a century old; but I was so continually occupied, so little my own master, that I could never find the moment to afford myself this satisfaction. There is little prospect of the opportunity ever occurring again; yet the wish has not disappeared with the hope; and I am almost certain that, if ever I should return to those beloved spots and find my dear walnut-tree still alive, I should water it with my tears.

After my return to Geneva, I lived for two or three years with my uncle, waiting until my friends had decided what was to be done with me. As he intended his own son to be an engineer, he made him learn a little drawing and taught him the elements of Euclid. I learned these subjects together with him, and acquired a taste for them, especially for drawing. In the meantime, it was debated whether I should be a watchmaker, an attorney, or a minister. My own preference was for the last, for preaching seemed to me to be a very fine thing; but the small income from my mother's property, which had to be divided between my brother and myself, was not sufficient to allow me to prosecute my studies. As, considering my age at that time, there was no immediate need to decide, I remained for the present with my uncle, making little use of my time and, in addition, as was only fair, paying a tolerably large sum for my board. My uncle, a man of pleasure like my father, was unable, like him, to tie himself down to his duties, and troubled himself little enough about us. My aunt was somewhat of a pietist, and preferred to sing psalms rather than attend to our education. We were allowed almost absolute freedom, which we never abused. Always inseparable, we were quite contented with our own society; and, having no temptation to make companions of the street boys of our own age, we learned none of the dissolute habits into which idleness might have led us. I am even wrong in saying that we were idle, for we were never less so in our lives; and the most fortunate thing was, that all the ways of amusing ourselves, with which we successively became infatuated, kept us together busy in the house, without our being even tempted to go out into the street. We made cages, flutes, shuttlecocks, drums, houses, squirts,[1] and cross-bows. We spoilt my good old grandfather's tools in trying to make watches as he did. We had a special taste for wasting paper, drawing, painting in water-colours, illuminating, and spoiling colours. An Italian showman, named Gamba-Corta, came to Geneva; we went to see him once and never wanted to go again. But he had a marionette-show, and we proceeded to make marionettes; his marionettes played comedies and we composed comedies for ours. For want of a squeaker, we imitated Punch's voice in our throat, in order to play the charming comedies, which our poor and kind relations had the patience to sit and listen to. But, my uncle Bernard having one day read aloud in the family circle a very fine sermon which he had composed himself, we abandoned comedy and began to write sermons. These details are not very interesting, I confess, but they show how exceedingly well-conducted our early education must have been, seeing that we, almost masters of our time and ourselves at so tender an age, were so little tempted to abuse our opportunities. We had so little need of making companions, that we even neglected the chances of doing so. When we went for a walk, we looked at their

[1] Genevan term for a form of pop-gun.

amusements as we passed by without the slightest desire, or even
the idea of taking part in them. Our friendship so completely
filled our hearts, that it was enough for us to be together to make
the simplest amusements a delight.

Being thus inseparable, we began to attract attention: the
more so as, my cousin being very tall while I was very short,
we made an oddly-assorted couple. His long, slim figure, his
little face like a boiled apple, his gentle manner, and his slovenly
walk excited the children's ridicule. In the *patois* of the district he
was nicknamed Barna Bredanna, and, directly we went out, we
heard nothing but "Barna Bredanna!"[1] all round us. He endured
it more quietly than I did: I lost my temper and wanted to fight.
This was just what the little rascals desired. I fought and was
beaten. My poor cousin helped me as well as he could; but he
was weak, and a single blow of the fist knocked him down. Then
I became furious. However, although I received blows in abundance, I was not the real object of attack, but Barna Bredanna;
but my obstinate anger made matters so much worse, that, in
future, we only ventured to go out during school-hours, for fear
of being hooted and followed.

Behold me already a redresser of wrongs! In order to be a
regular Paladin I only wanted a lady; I had two. From time to
time I went to see my father at Nyon, a little town in the Vaud
country, where he had settled. He was very much liked, and his
son felt the effects of his popularity. During the short time
I stayed with him, friends vied with each other in making me
welcome. A certain Madame de Vulson, especially, bestowed a
thousand caresses upon me, and, to crown all, her daughter took
me for her lover. It is easy to understand the meaning of a lover
eleven years old for a girl of twenty-two. But all these roguish
young women are so ready to put little puppets in front in order
to hide larger ones, or to tempt them with the idea of an
amusement which they know how to render attractive! As for
myself, I saw no incongruity between us and took the matter
seriously; I abandoned myself with all my heart, or rather with all

---

[1] A play of words (in the Savoy *patois*) on "Bernard", the name of the man
on a donkey in the *Roman de Renart*.

my head – for it was only in that part of me that I was in love, although madly – and my transports, excitement and frenzy produced scenes enough to make anyone split his sides with laughing.

I am acquainted with two very distinct and very real kinds of love, which have scarcely anything in common, although both are very fervent, and which both differ from tender friendship. The whole course of my life has been divided between these two kinds of love, essentially so different, and I have even felt them both at the same time; for instance, at the time of which I am speaking, while I took possession of Mademoiselle de Vulson so openly and so tyrannically that I could not endure that any man should approach her, I had several meetings, brief but lively, with a certain little Mademoiselle Goton, in which she deigned to play the schoolmistress, and that was all; but this all, which was really all for me, seemed to me the height of happiness; and, already feeling the value of the mystery, although I only knew how to make use of it as a child, I paid Mademoiselle de Vulson, who had scarcely any suspicion of it, in the same coin, for the assiduity with which she made use of me to conceal other amours. But, to my great regret, my secret was discovered, or not so well kept on the part of my little schoolmistress as on my own; we were soon separated; and, some time afterwards, on my return to Geneva, while passing through Coutance, I heard some little girls cry, in an undertone, "Goton tic-tac Rousseau!"

This little Mademoiselle Goton was really a singular person. Without being pretty, she had a face which was not easy to forget, and which I still recall to mind, often too tenderly for an old fool. Neither her form, nor her manner, nor, above all, her eyes were in keeping with her age. She had a proud and commanding air, which suited her part admirably, and which in fact had suggested the first idea of it to us. But the oddest thing about her was a mixture of impudence and reserve which it was difficult to comprehend. She took the greatest liberties with me, but never allowed me to take any with her. She treated me just like a child, which makes me believe, either that she was no longer one herself, or that, on the contrary, she was still childish enough to see nothing but an amusement in the danger to which she exposed herself.

I belonged entirely, so to say, to each of these two persons, and so completely, that, when I was with one, I never thought of the other. In other respects, there was not the slightest similarity between the feelings with which they inspired me. I could have spent all my life with Mademoiselle de Vulson, without ever thinking of leaving her; but, when I approached her, my joy was tranquil and free from emotion. I loved her above all in fashionable society; the witty sallies, railleries, and even the petty jealousies attracted and interested me; I felt a pride and glory in the marks of preference she bestowed upon me in the presence of grown-up rivals whom she appeared to treat with disdain. I was tormented, but I loved the torment. The applause, encouragement, and laughter warmed and inspirited me. I had fits of passion and broke out into audacious sallies. In society, I was transported with love; in a *tête-à-tête* I should have been constrained, cold, perhaps wearied. However, I felt a real tenderness for her; I suffered when she was ill; I would have given my own health to restore her own, and, observe! I knew very well from experience the meaning of illness and health. When absent from her, I thought of her and missed her; when I was by her side, her caresses reached my heart – not my senses. I was intimate with her with impunity; my imagination demanded no more than she granted; yet I could not have endured to see her do even as much for others. I loved her as a brother, but I was as jealous of her as a lover.

I should have been as jealous of Mademoiselle Goton as a Turk, a madman, or a tiger, if I had once imagined that she could accord the same treatment to another as to myself; for even that was a favour which I had to ask on my knees. I approached Mademoiselle de Vulson with lively pleasure, but without emotion; whereas, if I only saw Mademoiselle Goton, I saw nothing else, all my senses were bewildered. With the former I was familiar without familiarity; while on the contrary, in the presence of the latter, I was as bashful as I was excited, even in the midst of our greatest familiarities. I believe that, if I had remained with her long, I should have died; the throbbings of my heart would have suffocated me. I was equally afraid of displeasing either; but I was more attentive to the one and more obedient to the other. Nothing in the world would have made me annoy Mademoiselle de Vulson; but if Mademoiselle Goton had ordered me to throw myself into the flames, I believe I should have obeyed her immediately.

My amour, or rather my meetings, with the latter, continued only for a short time – happily for both of us. Although my relations with Mademoiselle de Vulson had not the same danger, they were not without their catastrophe, after they had lasted a little longer. The end of all such connections should always be somewhat romantic, and furnish occasion for exclamations of sorrow. Although my connection with Mademoiselle de Vulson was less lively, it was perhaps closer. We never separated without tears, and it is remarkable into what an overwhelming void I felt myself plunged as soon as I had left her. I could speak and think of nothing but her; my regret was genuine and lively; but I believe that, at bottom, this heroic regret was not felt altogether for her, and that, without my perceiving it, the amusements, of which she was the centre, played their part in it. To moderate the pangs of absence, we wrote letters to each other, pathetic enough to melt the heart of a stone. At last I triumphed; she could endure it no longer, and came to Geneva to see me. This time my head was completely turned; I was drunk and mad during the two days she remained. When she left I wanted to throw myself in the water after her, and the air resounded with my screams. Eight days afterwards she sent me some bonbons and gloves, which I should have considered a great compliment, if I had not learnt at the same time that she was married, and that the visit with which she had been pleased to honour me was really made in order to buy her wedding-dress. I will not attempt to describe my fury; it may be imagined. In my noble rage I swore that I would never see the faithless one again, being unable to imagine a more terrible punishment for her. She did not, however, die of it; for, twenty years afterwards, when on a visit to my father, while rowing with him on the lake, I asked who the ladies were whom I saw in a boat not far from ours. "What!" said my father with a smile, "does not your heart tell you? it is your old love, Mademoiselle de Vulson that was, now Madame Cristin." I started at the almost forgotten name, but I told the boatmen to change their course. Although I had a fine opportunity of avenging myself at that moment, I did not think it worth while to perjure myself and to renew a quarrel, twenty years old, with a woman of forty.

[1723–1728.] – Thus the most valuable time of my boyhood was wasted in follies, before my future career had been decided upon. After long deliberation as to the bent of my natural inclination, a profession was determined upon for which I had the least taste; I was put with M. Masseron, the town clerk, in order to learn, under his tuition, the useful trade of a *fee-grabber*.[1] This nickname was extremely distasteful to me; the hope of gaining a number of crowns in a somewhat sordid business by no means flattered my pride; the occupation itself appeared to me wearisome and unendurable; the constant application, the feeling of servitude completed my dislike, and I never entered the office without a feeling of horror, which daily increased in intensity. M. Masseron, on his part, was ill-satisfied with me, and treated me with contempt; he continually reproached me with my dulness and stupidity, dinning into my ears every day that my uncle had told him that I knew something, whereas, in reality, I knew nothing; that he had promised him a sharp lad, and had given him a jackass. At last I was dismissed from the office in disgrace as being utterly incapable, and M. Masseron's clerks declared that I was good for nothing except to handle a file.

My calling being thus settled, I was apprenticed, not, however, to a watchmaker, but to an engraver. The contempt with which I had been treated by M. Masseron had made me very humble, and I obeyed without a murmur. My new master, M. Ducommun, was a rough and violent young man, who in a short time succeeded in tarnishing all the brightness of my childhood, stupefying my loving and lively nature, and reducing me, in mind as well as in position, to a real state of apprenticeship. My Latin, my antiquities, my history, were all for a long time forgotten; I did not even remember that there had ever

---

[1] *Grapignan*: a slang term for a lawyer.

been any Romans in the world. My father, when I went to see him, no longer found in me his idol; for the ladies I was no longer the gallant Jean Jacques; and I felt so certain myself that the Lamberciers would not have recognised their pupil in me, that I was ashamed to pay them a visit, and have never seen them since. The vilest tastes, the lowest street-blackguardism took the place of my simple amusements and effaced even the remembrance of them. I must, in spite of a most upright training, have had a great propensity to degenerate; for the change took place with great rapidity, without the least trouble, and never did so precocious a Caesar so rapidly become a Laridon.[1]

The trade in itself was not disagreeable to me; I had a decided taste for drawing; the handling of a graving-tool amused me; and as the claims upon the skill of a watchmaker's engraver were limited, I hoped to attain perfection. I should, perhaps, have done so, had not my master's brutality and excessive restraint disgusted me with my work. I stole some of my working hours to devote to similar occupations, but which had for me the charm of freedom. I engraved medals for an order of knighthood for myself and my companions. My master surprised me at this contraband occupation, and gave me a sound thrashing, declaring that I was training for a coiner, because our medals bore the arms of the Republic. I can swear that I had no idea at all of bad, and only a very faint one of good, money. I knew better how the Roman *As* was made than our three-sou pieces.

My master's tyranny at length made the work, of which I should have been very fond, altogether unbearable, and filled me with vices which I should otherwise have hated, such as lying, idleness and thieving. The recollection of the alteration produced in me by that period of my life has taught me, better than anything else, the difference between filial dependence and abject servitude. Naturally shy and timid, no fault was more foreign to my disposition than impudence; but I had enjoyed an honourable liberty, which hitherto had only been gradually restrained, and at length disappeared altogether. I was

---

[1] A degenerate dog in La Fontaine's fable *L'Education*, the last line of which runs: "Oh how many Caesars become Laridons!"

bold with my father, unrestrained with M. Lambercier, and modest with my uncle; I became timid with my master, and from that moment I was a lost child. Accustomed to perfect equality in my intercourse with my superiors, knowing no pleasure which was not within my reach, seeing no dish of which I could not have a share, having no desire which I could not have openly expressed, and carrying my heart upon my lips – it is easy to judge what I was bound to become, in a house in which I did not venture to open my mouth, where I was obliged to leave the table before the meal was half over, and the room as soon as I had nothing more to do there; where, incessantly fettered to my work, I saw only objects of enjoyment for others and of privation for myself; where the sight of the liberty enjoyed by my master and companions increased the weight of my servitude; where, in disputes about matters as to which I was best informed, I did not venture to open my mouth; where, in short, everything that I saw became for my heart an object of longing, simply because I was deprived of all. From that time my ease of manner, my gaiety, the happy expressions which, in former times, when I had done something wrong, had gained me immunity from punishment – all were gone. I cannot help laughing when I remember how, one evening, at my father's house, having been sent to bed without any supper for some piece of roguery, I passed through the kitchen with my melancholy piece of bread, and, seeing the joint turning on the spit, sniffed at it. All the household was standing round the hearth, and, in passing, I was obliged to say good-night to everybody. When I had gone the round, I winked at the joint, which looked so nice and smelt so good, and could not help bowing to it as well, and saying in a mournful voice, "Good-night, roast beef!" This naïve sally amused them so much that they made me stop to supper. Perhaps it might have had the same effect with my master, but I am sure that it would never have occurred to me, and that I should not have had the courage, to say it in his presence.

In this manner I learnt to covet in silence, to dissemble, to lie, and, lastly, to steal – an idea which, up to that time, had never even entered my mind, and of which since then I have never been able to cure myself completely. Covetousness and weakness always lead in that direction. This explains why all servants are rogues, and why all apprentices ought to be; but the latter, in a peaceful state of equality, where all that they see is within their reach, lose, as they grow up, this disgraceful propensity. Not having had the same advantages, I have not been able to reap the same benefits.

It is nearly always good, but badly-directed, principles, that make a child take the first step towards evil. In spite of continual privations and temptations, I had been more than a year with my master without being able to make up my mind to take anything, even eatables. My first theft was a matter of obliging some one else, but it opened the door to others, the motive of which was not so praiseworthy.

My master had a journeyman, named M. Verrat, whose house was in the neighbourhood, and had a garden some way off which produced very fine asparagus. M. Verrat, who was not too well supplied with money, conceived the idea of stealing some of his mother's young asparagus and selling it in order to provide himself with two or three good breakfasts. As he was unwilling to run the risk himself, and was not very active, he selected me for the expedition. After some preliminary cajoleries, which the more easily succeeded with me as I did not see their aim, he proposed it to me as an idea that had struck him on the spur of the moment. I strongly opposed it; he persisted. I have never been able to resist flattery: I gave in. I went every morning to gather a crop of the finest asparagus, and carried it to the Molard, where some good woman, who saw that I had just stolen it, told me so to my face in order to get it cheaper. In my fright I took whatever she chose to offer me, and took it to Verrat. The amount was immediately converted into a breakfast, of which I was the purveyor, and which he shared with another companion; I myself was quite satisfied with a few scraps, and never even touched their wine.

This little arrangement continued several days, without its even occurring to me to rob the robber, and to levy my tithe of the proceeds of M. Verrat's asparagus. I performed my part in the transaction with the greatest loyalty; my only motive was to please him who prompted me to carry it out. And yet, if I had been caught, what blows, abuse, and cruel treatment should I have had to endure, while the wretch, who would have been sure to give me the lie, would have been believed on his word, and I should have suffered double punishment for having had the impudence to accuse him, seeing that he was a journeyman, while I was only an apprentice! So true it is that, in every condition of life, the strong man who is guilty saves himself at the expense of the innocent who is weak.

In this manner I learned that stealing was not so terrible a thing as I had imagined, and I soon knew how to make such good use of my discovery, that nothing I desired, if it was within my reach, was safe from me. I was not absolutely ill-fed, and abstinence was only rendered difficult to me from seeing that my master observed it so ill himself. The custom of sending young people from the table when the most appetising dishes are brought on appears to me admirably adapted to make them gluttons as well as thieves. In a short time I became both the one and the other; and, as a rule, I came off very well; occasionally, when I was caught, very badly.

I shudder, and at the same time laugh, when I remember an apple-hunt which cost me dear. These apples were at the bottom of a store-room, which was lighted from the kitchen by means of a high grating. One day, when I was alone in the house, I climbed upon the kneading-trough, in order to look at the precious fruit in the garden of the Hesperides, which was out of my reach. I went to fetch the spit to see if I could touch the apples; it was too short. To make it longer, I tied on to it another little spit which was used for small game, for my master was very fond of sport. I thrust several times without success; at last, to my great delight, I felt that I had secured an apple. I pulled very gently; the apple was close to the grating; I was ready to catch hold of it. But who can describe my grief, when I found that it was too large to pass through the bars? How many expedients I tried, to get it through! I had to find supports to keep the spit in its place, a knife long enough to divide the apple, a lath to hold it up. At last I managed to divide it, and hoped to be able to pull the pieces towards me one after the other; but no sooner were they separated than they both fell into the store-room. Compassionate reader, share my affliction!

I by no means lost courage; but I had lost considerable time. I was afraid of being surprised. I put off a more lucky attempt till the following day, and returned to my work as quietly as if I had done nothing, without thinking of the two tell-tale witnesses in the store-room.

The next day, finding the opportunity favourable, I made a fresh attempt. I climbed upon my stool, lengthened the spit, adjusted it, and was ready to make a lunge .... but, unfortunately, the dragon was not asleep; all at once the door of the store-room opened, my master came out, folded his arms, looked at me, and said, "Courage!"... the pen falls from my hand.

In consequence of continuous ill-treatment I soon became less sensitive to it, and regarded it as a kind of compensation for theft, which gave me the right to continue the latter. Instead of looking back and considering the punishment, I looked forward and thought of revenge. I considered that, if I were beaten as a rogue, I was entitled to behave like one. I found that stealing and a flogging went together, and constituted a sort of bargain, and that, if I performed my part, I could safely leave my master to carry out his own. With this idea, I began to steal more quietly than before. I said to myself: "What will be the result? I shall be flogged. Never mind; I am made to be flogged."

I am fond of eating, but am not greedy; I am sensual, but not a gourmand; too many other tastes prevent that. I have never troubled myself about my food except when my heart has been unoccupied: and that has so seldom been the case during my life that I have scarcely had time to think about dainties. For this reason I did not long confine my thievish propensities to eatables, but soon extended them to everything which tempted me; and, if I did not become a regular thief, it was because I have never been much tempted by money. Leading out of the common workshop was a private room belonging to my master, the door of which I found means to open and shut without being noticed. There I laid under contribution his best tools, drawings, proofs – in fact, everything which attracted me and which he purposely kept out of my reach. At bottom, these thefts were quite innocent, being only committed to serve him; but I was transported with joy at having these trifles in my power; I thought that I was robbing him of his talent together with its productions. Besides, I found boxes containing gold and silver filings, little trinkets, valuables and coins. When I had four or five sous in my pocket, I thought I was rich; and yet, far from touching anything of what I found there, I do not even remember that I ever cast longing eyes upon it. I looked upon it with more affright than pleasure. I believe that this horror of stealing money and valuables was in great part the result of my bringing-up. With it were combined secret thoughts of disgrace, prison, punishment and the gallows, which would have made me shudder if I had been tempted; whereas my tricks only appeared to me in the light of pieces of mischief, and in fact were nothing else. They could lead to nothing but a sound flogging from my master, and I prepared myself for that beforehand.

But, I repeat, I never felt sufficient longing to need to control myself; I had nothing to contend with. A single sheet of fine drawing-paper tempted me more than money enough to buy a ream of it. This singularity is connected with one of the peculiarities of my character; it has exercised such great influence upon my conduct that it is worth while to explain it.

I am a man of very strong passions, and, while I am stirred by them, nothing can equal my impetuosity; I forget all discretion, all feelings of respect, fear and decency; I am cynical, impudent, violent and fearless; no feeling of shame keeps me back, no danger frightens me; with the exception of the single object which occupies my thoughts, the universe is nothing to me. But all this lasts only for a moment, and the following moment plunges me into complete annihilation. In my calmer moments I am indolence and timidity itself; everything frightens and discourages me; a fly, buzzing past, alarms me; a word which I have to say, a gesture which I have to make, terrifies my idleness; fear and shame overpower me to such an extent that I would gladly hide myself from the sight of my fellow-creatures. If I have to act, I do not know what to do; if I have to speak, I do not know what to say; if anyone looks at me, I am put out of countenance. When I am strongly moved I sometimes know how to find the right words, but in ordinary conversation I can find absolutely nothing, and my condition is unbearable for the simple reason that I am obliged to speak.

Add to this, that none of my prevailing tastes centre in things that can be bought. I want nothing but unadulterated pleasures, and money poisons all. For instance, I am fond of the pleasures of the table; but, as I cannot endure either the constraint of good society or the drunkenness of the tavern, I can only enjoy them with a friend; alone, I cannot do so, for my imagination then occupies itself with other things, and eating affords me no pleasure. If my heated blood longs for women, my excited heart longs still more for affection. Women who could be bought for money would lose for me all their charms; I even doubt whether it would be in me to make use of them. I find it the same with all pleasures within my reach; unless they cost me nothing, I find them insipid. I only love those enjoyments which belong to no one but the first man who knows how to enjoy them.

Money has never appeared to me as valuable as it is generally considered. More than that, it has never even appeared to me particularly convenient. It is good for nothing in itself; it has to be changed before it can be enjoyed; one is obliged to buy, to bargain, to be often cheated, to pay dearly, to be badly served. I should like something which is good in quality; with my money I am sure to get it bad. If I pay a high price for a fresh egg, it is stale; for a nice piece of fruit, it is unripe; for a girl, she is spoilt. I am fond of good wine, but where am I to get it? At a wine merchant's? Whatever I do, he is sure to poison me. If I really wish to be well served, what trouble and embarrassment it entails! I must have friends, correspondents, give commissions, write, go backwards and forwards, wait, and in the end be often deceived! What trouble with my money! my fear of it is greater than my fondness for good wine.

Times without number, during my apprenticeship and afterwards, I have gone out with the intention of buying some delicacy. Coming to a pastrycook's shop, I notice some women at the counter; I think I can already see them laughing amongst themselves at the little glutton. I go on to a fruiterer's; I eye the fine pears; their smell tempts me. Two or three young people close by me look at me; a man who knows me is standing in front of his shop; I see a girl approaching in the distance: is it the housemaid? My short-sightedness causes all kinds of illusions. I take all the passers-by for acquaintances; everywhere I am intimidated, restrained by some obstacle; my desire increases with my shame, and at last I return home like a fool, consumed with longing, having in my pocket the means of satisfying it, and yet not having had the courage to buy anything.

I should enter into the most insipid details if, in relating how my money was spent by myself or others, I were to describe the embarrassment, the shame, the repugnance, the inconvenience, the annoyances of all kinds which I have always experienced. In proportion as the reader, following the course of my life, becomes acquainted with my real temperament, he will understand all this, without my taking the trouble to tell him.

This being understood, it will be easy to comprehend one of my apparent inconsistencies – the union of an almost sordid avarice with the greatest contempt for money. It is a piece of furniture in which I find so little convenience, that it never enters my mind to long for it when I have not got it, and that, when I have got it, I keep it for a long time without spending it, for want of knowing how to make use of it in a way to please myself; but if a convenient and agreeable opportunity presents itself, I make such good use of it that my purse is empty before I know it. Besides this, one need not expect to find in me that curious characteristic of misers – that of spending for the sake of ostentation; on the contrary, I spend in secret for the sake of enjoyment; far from glorying in my expenditure, I conceal it. I feel so strongly that money is of no use to me, that I am almost ashamed to have any, still more to make use of it. If I had ever had an income sufficient to live comfortably upon, I am certain that I should never have been tempted to be a miser. I should have spent it all, without attempting to increase it; but my precarious circumstances make me careful. I worship freedom; I abhor restraint, trouble, dependence. As long as the money in my purse lasts, it assures my independence; it relieves me of the trouble of finding expedients to replenish it, a necessity which always inspired me with dread; but the fear of seeing it exhausted makes me hoard it carefully. The money which a man possesses is the instrument of freedom; that which we eagerly pursue is the instrument of slavery. Therefore I hold fast to that which I have, and desire nothing.

My disinterestedness is, therefore, nothing but idleness; the pleasure of possession is not worth the trouble of acquisition. In like manner, my extravagance is nothing but idleness; when the opportunity of spending agreeably presents itself, it cannot be too profitably employed. Money tempts me less than things, because between money and the possession of the desired object there is always an intermediary, whereas between the thing itself and the enjoyment of it there is none. If I see the thing, it tempts me; if I only see the means of gaining possession of it, it does not. For this reason I have committed thefts, and even now I sometimes pilfer trifles which tempt me, and which I prefer to take rather than to ask for; but neither when a child nor a grown-up man do I ever remember to have robbed anyone of a farthing, except on one occasion, fifteen years ago, when I stole seven *livres* ten *sous*. The incident is worth recording, for it contains a most extraordinary mixture of folly and impudence, which I should have found difficulty in believing if it concerned anyone but myself.

It took place at Paris. I was walking with M. de Franceuil in the Palais-Royal about five o'clock. He pulled out his watch, looked at it, and said: "Let us go to the Opera." I agreed; we went. He took two tickets for the amphitheatre, gave me one, and went on in front with the other. I followed him; he went in. Entering after him, I found the door blocked. I looked, and seeing everybody standing up, thought it would be easy to lose myself in the crowd, or at any rate to make M. de Franceuil believe that I had lost myself. I went out, took back my check, then my money, and went off, without thinking that as soon as I had reached the door everybody had taken their seats, and that M. de Franceuil clearly saw that I was no longer there.[1]

---

[1] According to George Sand, in her "Histoire de ma Vie," M. de Francueil, who was her grandfather, has always absolutely denied the truth of this story.

As nothing was ever more foreign to my disposition than such behaviour, I mention it in order to show that there are moments of semi-delirium during which men must not be judged by their actions. I did not exactly want to steal the money, I wanted to steal the employment of it; the less of a theft it was, the greater its disgracefulness.

I should never finish these details if I were to follow all the paths along which, during my apprenticeship, I descended from the sublimity of heroism to the depths of worthlessness. And yet, although I adopted the vices of my position, I could not altogether acquire a taste for them. I wearied of the amusements of my companions; and when excessive restraint had rendered work unendurable to me, I grew tired of everything. This renewed my taste for reading, which I had for some time lost. This reading, for which I stole time from my work, became a new offence which brought new punishment upon me. The taste for it, provoked by constraint, became a passion, and soon a regular madness. La Tribu, a well-known lender of books, provided me with all kinds of literature. Good or bad, all were alike to me; I had no choice, and read everything with equal avidity. I read at the work-table, I read on my errands, I read in the wardrobe, and forgot myself for hours together; my head became giddy with reading; I could do nothing else. My master watched me, surprised me, beat me, took away my books. How many volumes were torn, burnt, and thrown out of the window! how many works were left in odd volumes in La Tribu's stock! When I had no more money to pay her, I gave her my shirts, neckties and clothes; my three sous of pocket-money were regularly taken to her every Sunday.

Well, then, I shall be told, money had become necessary to me. That is true; but it was not until my passion for reading had deprived me of all activity. Completely devoted to my new hobby, I did nothing but read, and no longer stole. Here again is one of my characteristic peculiarities. In the midst of a certain attachment to any manner of life, a mere trifle distracts me, alters me, rivets my attention, and finally becomes a passion. Then everything is forgotten; I no longer think of anything except the new object which engrosses my attention. My heart beat with impatience to turn over the leaves of the new book which I had in my pocket; I pulled it out as soon as I was alone, and thought no more of rummaging my master's work-room. I can hardly believe that I should have stolen even if I had had more expensive tastes. Limited to the present, it was not in my way to make preparations in this manner for the future. La Tribu gave me credit, the payments on account were small, and, as soon as I had my book in my pocket, I forgot everything else. The money which came to me honestly passed in the same manner into the hands of this woman; and, when she pressed me, nothing was easier to dispose of than my own property. It required too much foresight to steal in advance, and I was not even tempted to steal in order to pay.

In consequence of quarrels, blows, and secret and ill-chosen reading, my disposition became savage and taciturn; my mind became altogether perverted, and I lived like a misanthrope. However, if my good taste did not keep me from silly and insipid books, my good fortune preserved me from such as were filthy and licentious; not that La Tribu, a woman in all respects most accommodating, would have made any scruple about lending them to me; but, in order to increase their importance, she always mentioned them to me with an air of mystery which had just the effect of making me refuse them, as much from disgust as from shame; and chance aided my modest disposition so well, that I was more than thirty years old before I set eyes upon any of those dangerous books which a fine lady finds inconvenient because they can only be read with one hand.

In less than a year I exhausted La Tribu's little stock, and want of occupation, during my spare time, became painful to me. I had been cured of my childish and knavish propensities by my passion for reading, and even by the books I read, which, although ill-chosen and frequently bad, filled my heart with nobler sentiments than those with which my sphere of life had inspired me. Disgusted with everything that was within my reach, and feeling that everything which might have tempted me was too far removed from me, I saw nothing possible which might have flattered my heart. My excited senses had long clamoured for an enjoyment, the object of which I could not even imagine. I was as far removed from actual enjoyment as if I had been sexless; and, already fully developed and sensitive, I sometimes thought of my crazes, but saw nothing beyond them. In this strange situation, my restless imagination entered upon an occupation which saved me from myself and calmed my growing sensuality. This consisted in feeding myself upon the situations which had interested me in the course of my reading, in recalling them, in varying them, in combining them, in making them so truly my own that I became one of the persons who filled my imagination, and always saw myself in the situations most agreeable to my taste; and that, finally, the fictitious state in which I succeeded in putting myself made me forget my actual state with which I was so dissatisfied. This love of imaginary objects, and the readiness with which I occupied myself with them, ended by disgusting me with everything around me, and decided that liking for solitude which has never left me. In the sequel we shall see more than once the curious effects of this disposition, apparently so gloomy and misanthropic, but which is really due to a too affectionate, too loving and too tender heart, which, being unable to find any in existence resembling it, is obliged to nourish itself with fancies. For the present, it is sufficient for me to have defined the origin and first cause of a propensity which has modified all my passions, and which, restraining them by means of themselves, has always made me slow to act, owing to my excessive impetuosity in desire.

In this manner I reached my sixteenth year, restless, dissatisfied with myself and everything, without any of the tastes of my condition of life, without any of the pleasures of my age, consumed by desires of the object of which I was ignorant, weeping without any cause for tears, sighing without knowing why – in short, tenderly caressing my chimeras, since I saw nothing around me which counterbalanced them. On Sundays, my fellow-apprentices came to fetch me after service to go and amuse myself with them. I would gladly have escaped from them if I had been able; but, once engaged in their amusements, I became more excited and went further than any of them; it was as difficult to set me going as to stop me. Such was always my disposition. During our walks outside the city I always went further than any of them without thinking about my return, unless others thought of it for me. Twice I was caught: the gates were shut before I could get back. The next day I was treated as may be imagined; the second time I was promised such a reception if it ever happened again, that I resolved not to run the risk of it; yet this third time, so dreaded, came to pass. My watchfulness was rendered useless by a confounded Captain Minutoli, who always shut the gate at which he was on guard half-an-hour before the others. I was returning with two companions. About half a league from the city I heard the retreat sounded: I doubled my pace: I heard the tattoo beat, and ran with all my might. I arrived out of breath and bathed in perspiration; my heart beat; from a distance I saw the soldiers at their posts; I rushed up and cried out with a voice half-choked. It was too late! Twenty paces from the outposts, I saw the first bridge raised. I shuddered when I saw those terrible horns rising in the air – a sinister and fatal omen of the destiny which that moment was opening for me.

In the first violence of my grief I threw myself on the *glacis* and bit the ground. My companions, laughing at their misfortune, immediately made up their minds what to do. I did the same, but my resolution was different from theirs. On the spot I swore never to return to my master; and the next morning, when they entered the city after the gates were opened, I said good-bye to them for ever,[1] only begging them secretly to inform my cousin Bernard of the resolution I had taken, and of the place where he might be able to see me once more.

After I had entered upon my apprenticeship I saw less of him. For some time we used to meet on Sunday, but gradually each of us adopted other habits, and we saw one another less frequently. I am convinced that his mother had much to do with this change. He was a child of the upper city;[2] I, a poor apprentice, was only a child of Saint-Gervais. In spite of our relationship, there was no longer any equality between us; it was derogatory to

[1] Rousseau decided to quit Geneva on Sunday, 14 March 1728.
[2] *Enfant du haut – i.e.*, of the upper, more fashionable part of the city; while Saint-Gervais, on the right bank of the Rhône, was the quarter inhabited by the poorer population.

him to associate with me. However, relations were not entirely
broken off between us, and, as he was a good-natured lad, he
sometimes followed the dictates of his heart instead of his
mother's instructions. When he was informed of my resolution,
he hastened to me, not to try and dissuade me from it or to share
it, but to lessen the inconveniences of my flight by some small
presents, since my own resources could not take me very far.
Amongst other things he gave me a small sword, which had
taken my fancy exceedingly, and which I carried as far as Turin,
where necessity obliged me to dispose of it, and where, as the
saying is, I passed it through my body. The more I have since
reflected upon the manner in which he behaved towards me at
this critical moment, the more I have felt convinced that he
followed the instructions of his mother, and perhaps of his
father; for it is inconceivable that, left to himself, he would not
have made some effort to keep me back, or would not have been
tempted to follow; but, no! he rather encouraged me in my plan
than tried to dissuade me; and, when he saw me quite determined, he left me without shedding many tears. We have never
corresponded or seen each other since. It is a pity: his character
was essentially good; we were made to love each other.

Before I abandon myself to the fatality of my lot, allow me to
turn my eyes for a moment upon the destiny which, in the nature
of things, would have awaited me if I had fallen into the hands of
a better master. Nothing was more suitable to my disposition or
better adapted to make me happy than the quiet and obscure lot
of a respectable artisan, especially of a certain class such as that
of the engravers of Geneva. Such a position, sufficiently lucrative to afford a comfortable livelihood, but not sufficiently so to
lead to fortune, would have limited my ambition for the rest of
my days, and, leaving me an honourable leisure to cultivate
modest tastes, would have confined me within my own sphere,
without offering me the means of getting out of it. My imaginat-
ive powers were rich enough to beautify all callings with their
chimeras, and strong enough to transport me, so to speak, at will
from one to another; so it would have been immaterial to me in
what position I actually found myself. It could not have been so
far from the place where I was to my first castle in the air, that I

could not have taken up my abode there without any difficulty. From this alone it followed that the simplest vocation, that which involved the least trouble and anxiety, that which allowed the greatest mental freedom, was the one which suited me best: and that was exactly my own. I should have passed a peaceful and quiet life, such as my disposition required, in the bosom of my religion, my country, my family and my friends, in the monotony of a profession that suited my taste, and in a society after my own heart. I should have been a good Christian, a good citizen, a good father of a family, a good friend, a good workman, a good man in every relation of life. I should have loved my position in life, perhaps honoured it; and, having spent a life – simple, indeed, and obscure, but calm and serene – I should have died peacefully in the bosom of my family. Though, doubtless, soon forgotten, I should at least have been regretted as long as anyone remembered me.

Instead of that – what picture am I going to draw? Let us not anticipate the sorrows of my life; I shall occupy my readers more than enough with this melancholy subject.

BOOK II

H<small>OWEVER</small> mournful the moment, when terror suggested to me the idea of flight, had appeared – the moment when I carried it into execution appeared equally delightful. While still a child, to leave my country, my parents, my means of support, my resources; to give up an apprenticeship half-served, without a sufficient knowledge of my trade to earn my livelihood; to abandon myself to the horrors of want, without any means of saving myself from it; to expose myself, at the age of innocence and weakness, to all the temptations of vice and despair; to seek, in the distance, suffering, error, snares, servitude, and death, beneath a yoke far more unbending than that which I had been unable to endure – this was what I was going to do, this was the prospect which I ought to have considered. How different was that which my fancy painted! The independence which I believed I had gained was the only feeling which moved me. Free, and my own master, I believed I could do everything, attain to everything; I had only to launch myself forth, to mount and fly through the air. I entered the vast world with a feeling of security; it was to be filled with the fame of my achievements; at every step I was to find festivities, treasures, adventures, friends ready to serve me, mistresses eager to please me; I had only to show myself, to engage the attention of the whole world – and yet not the whole world; to a certain extent I could dispense with it, and did not want so much. Charming society was enough for me, without troubling myself about the rest. In my modesty I limited myself to a narrow, but delightfully select circle, in which my sovereignty was assured. A single castle was the limit of my ambition. As the favourite of the lord and the lady, as the lover of the daughter, as the friend of the son and protector of the neighbours, I was content – I wanted no more.

In the expectation of this modest future, I wandered for some days round the city, lodging with some peasants whom I knew, who all received me with greater kindness than any of the inhabitants of the city would have done. They took me in, lodged me, and fed me with too much kindness to make a merit of it. It could not be called charity; they did not bestow it with a sufficient air of superiority.

Travelling and roaming about in this manner, I reached Confignon, in the district of Savoy, two leagues from Geneva. The name of the *curé* was M. de Pontverre. This name, famous in the history of the Republic, arrested my attention. I was curious to see what the descendants of the Knights of the Spoon[1] looked like.

I called upon M. de Pontverre. He received me kindly, talked about the heresy of Geneva, the authority of the Holy Mother Church, and invited me to dinner. I found little to reply to arguments which ended in this manner, and I formed the opinion that *curés* who dined so well were at least as good as our ministers. I was certainly more learned than M. de Pontverre, in spite of his birth; but I was too good a guest to be as good a theologian, and his Frangi wine, which appeared to me excellent, argued so triumphantly in his favour that I should have been ashamed to stop the mouth of so admirable a host. I therefore gave in, or at least offered no open resistance. To see the carefulness I exhibited, one would have believed me false; but that would have been a mistake. I only behaved with common courtesy, that is certain. Flattery, or rather condescension, is not always a vice; it is more often a virtue, especially in young people. The kindness with which a person treats us endears him to us; we give in to him, not in order to abuse his kindness, but to avoid annoying him, or returning him evil for good. What interest had M. de Pontverre in receiving me, treating me kindly, or trying to convince me? No other than my own; my young heart told me that. I was moved with gratitude and respect for the good priest. I felt my superiority; I did not wish to overwhelm him with it as the reward of his hospitality. In this attitude there was nothing hypocritical; I

---

[1] These Catholic knights, subjects of the Duke of Savoy, formed a league against the Genevese in the time of the Reformation, and were so called because they boasted of having "eaten their enemies with a spoon," and carried a spoon hung round their necks. They were headed by a De Pontverre.

never thought of changing my religion; and, far from familiaris-
ing myself so rapidly with this idea, I only regarded it with a
feeling of horror which was destined to keep it away from me for
a long time; my only wish was to avoid annoying those who
treated me kindly with the object of converting me; I wished to
cultivate their goodwill, and to leave them the hope of success,
by appearing less completely armed than I really was. My fault in
that respect resembled the coquetry of respectable women, who
sometimes, in order to attain their object, without allowing or
promising anything, know how to excite greater hopes than they
mean to fulfil.

Reason, pity, and regard for discipline required that, far from
assisting my folly, people should have saved me from the ruin
which I ran to meet and sent me back to my family. That is what
every truly virtuous man would have done or attempted to do.
But, although M. de Pontverre was a good man, he was certainly
not a virtuous man; on the contrary, he was an enthusiast who
knew no other virtue except worshipping images and telling his
beads – a kind of missionary who could think of nothing better
for the good of the faith than writing libels against the ministers
of Geneva. Far from thinking of sending me back to my home,
he took advantage of the desire I felt to get away from it, to make
it impossible for me to return even though I should wish to do
so. It was any odds that he was sending me to perish in misery or
to become a worthless scamp. But that was not what he looked
at; he only saw a soul saved from heresy and restored to the
Church. Honest man or scamp – what did it matter, provided I
went to mass? One must not, however, believe that this way of
thinking is peculiar to Catholics; it is common to all dogmatic
religions in which faith, not works, is considered the principal
thing.

"God calls you," said M. de Pontverre; "go to Annecy; there
you will find a good and charitable lady, whom the King's
kindness has placed in a position to rescue other souls from
the error from which she herself has been delivered." The lady in
question was Madame de Warens,[1] a new convert, who in reality

---

[1] [Warens] See *Biographies*, p. 716.

had been forced by the priests to share, with the rabble which came to sell its faith, a pension of two thousand francs which she received from the King of Sardinia. I felt very humiliated at requiring the assistance of a good and charitable lady. I was very desirous of having my wants supplied, but not of receiving alms, and a devotee did not sound very attractive to me. However, urged by M. de Pontverre, and hard pressed by hunger and pleased at the idea of making a journey with a definite object, I made up my mind, although with some difficulty, and set out for Annecy. I could easily have reached the place in one day; but, as I did not hurry, it took three. I never saw a *château* on the right or left without going in search of the adventure which I felt sure awaited me there. I did not dare to enter the *château* or knock at the door, being naturally very shy; but I sang under the window which looked most promising from outside, and, after having tired out my lungs by continued efforts, was surprised that I beheld neither ladies nor maidens attracted by the beauty of my voice or the spirit of my songs, seeing that I knew some admirable compositions which my companions had taught me and which I sang in a manner equally admirable.

At last I arrived: I saw Madame de Warens. That epoch of my life decided my character; I cannot bring myself to pass lightly over it. I was in the middle of my sixteenth year. Without being what is called a handsome lad, I was well set up, I had a pretty foot, a fine leg, an easy manner, lively features, a pretty little mouth, black hair and eyebrows, small and even sunken eyes, which, however, vigorously darted forth the fire with which my blood was kindled. Unhappily, I knew nothing of that, and it has never occurred to me during my life to think about my personal appearance except when it was too late to profit by it. With the timidity of my age was united that of a very loving disposition, always troubled by the fear of displeasing. Besides, although my mind was tolerably well formed, I had never seen the world, and was entirely wanting in manners, and my knowledge, far from supplementing this defect, only served to intimidate me still more by making me feel how sadly I needed them.

Fearing, therefore, that my first appearance would not pre-judice Madame de Warens in my favour, I had recourse to other expedients. I composed a beautiful letter in oratorical style, in which, intermingling phrases out of books with the language of an apprentice, I displayed all my eloquence in order to gain her goodwill. I enclosed M. de Pontverre's letter in my own, and set out for the dreaded interview. Madame de Warens was not at home. I was told that she had just gone to church. It was Palm-Sunday in 1728. I ran after her. I saw her; I overtook her; I addressed her. I ought to remember the spot. Since then I have often wetted it with my tears and covered it with my kisses. I should like to surround this happy spot with a railing of gold. I should like to draw upon it the homage of the world. Whoever loves to honour the monuments of the salvation of men should only approach them on his knees.

It was in a passage behind her house, leading between a brook on the right, which separated the house from the garden, and the court-wall on the left, through a back-gate to the Franciscan[1] church. Just as she was going to enter, Madame de Warens, hearing my voice, turned round. How did the sight of her strike me! I had pictured to myself an old, grim, religious enthusiast; in my opinion, M. de Pontverre's pious lady could be nothing else. Instead, I beheld a face full of charm, beautiful blue eyes – full of gentleness – a dazzling complexion, the outlines of an enchanting throat. Nothing escaped the rapid glance of the young proselyte – for at that moment I became hers, feeling convinced that a religion preached by such apostles must inevitably lead to paradise. With a smile, she took the letter which I presented to her with a trembling hand, opened it, glanced at that of M. de Pontverre, returned to mine, read it through, and would have read it again, had not her servant reminded her that it was time to go in. "Well, my child," she said to me in a tone which made me tremble, "so you are wandering about the country at your age; that is indeed a pity." Then, without waiting for me to answer, she added, "Go and wait for me; tell them to give you some breakfast. After mass I will come and talk to you."

[1] *Les Cordeliers*: a religious order, founded by St. Francis of Assisi in 1223. The name was afterwards also given to a club founded in 1790 by Danton, Marat, and Desmoulins, which held its meetings in the old Franciscan convent at Paris.

Louise Éléonore de Warens was a young lady who belonged to the house of La Tour de Pil, an ancient and noble family of Vévai, a town in the canton of Vaud. When very young she had married M. de Warens, of the house of Loys, the eldest son of M. de Villardin, of Lausanne. This marriage, which proved childless, was not a happy one, and Madame de Warens, driven by some domestic grief, seized the opportunity of the presence of King Victor Amadeus at Évian to cross the lake and throw herself at the feet of this prince, thus abandoning her husband, her family and her country through a piece of folly which much resembled mine, and which she, like myself, has had ample time to lament. The King, who was fond of posing as a zealous Catholic, took her under his protection, and settled on her an annuity of 1,500 Piedmontese livres,[1] a tolerably large sum for a prince who, as a rule, was little inclined to be generous. Afterwards, finding that he was reported to be in love with her in consequence of the manner in which he had received her, he sent her to Annecy under the escort of a detachment of his guards, where, under the spiritual guidance of Michel-Gabriel de Bernex, titular Bishop of Geneva, she renounced the Protestant faith in the Convent of the Visitation.

She had been six years in Annecy when I arrived there, and was twenty-eight years of age, having been born with the century. Her beauty was of the kind which lasts, consisting rather in the expression than the features; besides, hers was still in its first brilliancy. She had a caressing and tender air, a gentle look, an angelic smile, a mouth like my own, ashen-grey hair of rare beauty, which she wore in a careless fashion, which gave her a very piquant appearance. She was small of stature, even short — somewhat dumpy, although not disagreeably so; but a more beautiful head and bosom, more beautiful hands and arms, could not have been seen.

Her education had been very peculiar. Like myself, she had lost her mother at her birth, and, receiving instruction indiscriminately, just as it happened to offer itself, she had learnt a little

[1] 1,500 Piedmontese *livres* were the equivalent of about 1,750 French *livres* (or francs).

from her governess, a little from her father, a little from her masters, and a great deal from her lovers, especially from one M. de Tavel, who, being a man of taste and learning, adorned the object of his affections with his own excellences. But so many different kinds of instruction impeded each other, and, as she pursued her studies without any regular system, her naturally sound understanding was by no means improved. Thus, although she knew something about the principles of philosophy and physics, she still preserved her father's taste for empirical medicine and alchemy; she prepared elixirs, tinctures, balsams, and magisteries.[1] She claimed to possess secret remedies. Quacks, profiting by her weakness, got hold of her, pestered her, ruined her, and, in the midst of crucibles and drugs, squandered her intellect, her talents, and her charms, with which she might have graced the highest society.

But, although vile rascals abused her ill-directed education, in order to obscure the light of her reason, her excellent heart stood the test and always remained the same; her loving and gentle character, her sympathy with the unfortunate, her inexhaustible goodness, her cheerful, frank, and open disposition never changed; and, even when old age came upon her, surrounded by want, suffering, and calamities of all kinds, the calmness of her beautiful soul preserved for her to the end of her life all the gaiety of her happiest days.

Her errors were due to an inexhaustible fund of activity which needed incessant occupation. She wanted no intrigues like other women, but enterprises to direct and carry out. She was born to take part in important affairs. In her place, Madame de Longueville would have been a mere intriguer; in the place of Madame de Longueville, she would have governed the State. Her talents were misplaced, and that which would have brought fame to her in a more exalted position proved her ruin in that in which she lived. In everything which was within the reach of her mental capacity, she always enlarged her plan in her head and saw its object magnified, the result of this being that she employed means better proportioned to her views than her

---

[1] Magisteries were secret alchemical preparations.

strength; she failed through the fault of others; and, when her project failed to succeed, she was ruined, where others would scarcely have lost anything. This eagerness for business, which did her so much harm, was at least of great service to her, in her monastic retreat, in that it prevented her from settling there for the rest of her life as she had intended. The regular and simple life of the nuns, the idle gossip of the parlour, could not possibly be agreeable to a mind which was continually in movement, and which, inventing new systems every day, required freedom in order to devote itself to them. The good Bishop of Bernex, though not so clever as François de Sales,[1] resembled him in many points and Madame de Warens, whom he called his daughter, and who resembled Madame de Chantal[2] in many other points, might have resembled her even in her retirement, had not the idle life of a convent been distasteful to her. It was not from want of zeal that this amiable woman did not devote herself to the trifling exercises of devotion, which appeared suitable to a new convert living under the guidance of a prelate. Whatever may have been the motive that induced her to change her religion, she was certainly sincere in that which she had embraced. She may have repented of having taken the step; certainly she never wished to retrace it. She not only died a good Catholic; she proved herself one during her lifetime; and I, who believe that I have read her inmost soul, dare to affirm that it was solely owing to a horror of affectation that she never played the devotee in public; her piety was too genuine for her to make a show of devotion. But this is not the place to discuss her principles; I shall have other opportunities of speaking of them.

Those who deny the sympathy of souls may explain, if they can, how, from the first interview, from the first word, from the first look, Madame de Warens inspired me, not only with the liveliest feelings of attachment, but with a perfect confidence which has never belied itself. Granted that my sentiments for her were really love, which will at least appear doubtful to those who follow the history of our relations, how came it that this

[1]   Bishop of Geneva (1567–1622).
[2]   A lady, distinguished for her great piety, the foundress of the Order of the Visitation; she was canonised by Clement XIII.

passion was from the outset accompanied by the feelings which it least inspires – peace of heart, calm, cheerfulness, confidence, trust? How was it that, when for the first time I approached an amiable, refined, and dazzlingly beautiful woman, a lady of higher position than my own, the like of whom I had never addressed, upon whom my destiny in a manner depended, according as she interested herself more or less on my behalf – how came it, I repeat, that, in spite of all this, I immediately felt as free and completely at my ease as if I had been perfectly certain of pleasing her? How was it that I did not for a single moment experience a feeling of embarrassment, timidity, or awkwardness? Naturally bashful and easily put out of countenance, knowing nothing of the world, how was it that from the first day, from the first moment, I was able to assume with her the easy manners, the tender language, the familiar tone which prevailed between us ten years later, when our close intimacy had made it natural? Is it possible to love, I do not say without desires, for those I had, but without jealousy? Does not one at least wish to learn from the object of one's affection whether one is loved in return? It has no more occurred to me in the course of my life ever to ask her this question than to ask myself whether I loved her; and she has never shown greater curiosity in regard to myself. There was certainly something singular in my feelings for this charming woman, and, in the course of the narrative, the reader will find unexpected singularities.

It was a question what was to become of me; and, in order to discuss my future more at leisure, she kept me to dinner. It was the first meal in my life at which my appetite failed me; and her maid, who waited upon us, said that I was the first traveller of my age and class that she had ever seen in such a condition. This remark, which did me no harm in the eyes of her mistress, struck home to a great lout who was dining with us, and who devoured by himself quite a respectable dinner for six. As for myself, I was in a state of rapture which did not allow me to eat. My heart fed upon an entirely new feeling, with which my whole being was filled, and which left me no inclination for doing anything else.

Madame de Warens wanted to know the details of my little history; and in relating them I recovered all the fire and vivacity which I had lost during my apprenticeship. The more I interested this excellent soul in my favour, the more she lamented the lot to which I intended to expose myself. She did not venture to advise me to return to Geneva; in her position that would have been an act of treason to the Catholic faith; and she knew only too well how she was watched and how her words were weighed. But she spoke to me so touchingly of my father's affliction, that it was easy to see that she would have approved of my going to console him. She did not know how strongly, without knowing it, she was pleading against herself. I think I have already said that my mind was made up; the more eloquent and persuasive her words, the more they went to my heart, the less I was able to make up my mind to separate from her. I felt that to return to Geneva would be to put an almost insurmountable barrier between herself and me, unless I again took the step which I had already taken, and by which it was better to abide once and for all. I accordingly remained firm. Madame de Warens, seeing that her efforts were unavailing, did not persist in them, to avoid compromising herself, but she said to me, with a look of compassion, "Poor little one, you must go where God calls you; but when you are grown up, you will think of me." I believe she herself had no idea how cruelly this prediction was to be fulfilled.

The difficulty was great. How was I, young as I was, to find a livelihood so far from home? Having served scarcely half my apprenticeship, I was very far from knowing my trade. Even if I had known it, I should have been unable to earn a living by it in Savoy, for the country was too poor to support the arts. The lout who was eating our dinners for us, being obliged to stop to give his jaws a rest, made a proposal which he declared was inspired by heaven, but which, to judge from its results, was rather inspired by the opposite place. This proposal was that I should go to Turin, where I should find spiritual and bodily support in a hospice established for the instruction of catechumens, until, after I had been received into the bosom of the Church, I should find suitable employment by the kindness of the charitable. "As to the expenses of his journey," continued my friend, "his lordship the bishop will no doubt be kind enough to provide for them, if Madame suggests this holy work to him, and, doubtless, Madame la Baronne," he added, bending over his plate, "who is so charitable, will also be eager to contribute towards them." I found the idea of so much charity very distasteful; I was sick at heart, and said nothing. Madame de Warens, without embracing the suggestion as eagerly as it was offered, contented herself with replying that everyone ought to do good to the best of his power, and that she would speak to the bishop about it; but my confounded friend, who had a little interest of his own in the matter, and was afraid that she might not speak of it exactly as he wished, hastened to warn the almoners, and worked upon the good priests so cleverly that, when Madame de Warens, who feared the journey for me, wished to speak about it to the bishop, she found that everything had been arranged, and he immediately handed her over the money destined for my humble travelling expenses. She did not venture to insist upon my remaining, for I was approaching an age when a woman of her own years could not with propriety express a desire to keep a young man with her.

My journey being thus arranged by those who took charge of me, I was obliged to submit, and I even did so without much reluctance. Although Turin was further than Geneva, I judged that, being the capital, it was more closely connected with Annecy than a town of different faith and in a foreign land; and, besides, as I was setting out in obedience to Madame de Warens, I considered myself as remaining under her guidance and that was more than living in her neighbourhood. Lastly, the idea of a long journey flattered my fondness for roaming, which was already beginning to declare itself. It appeared to me a fine thing to cross mountains at my age, and to elevate myself above my comrades by the whole height of the Alps. There is a charm in seeing different countries which a Genevese can scarcely ever resist; I, therefore, gave my consent. My lout intended to set out in two days with his wife, and I was intrusted to their care. My funds, which Madame de Warens had augmented, were handed over to them. She also gave me privately a little pocket-money, and much good advice; and, on the Wednesday in Passion week, we set out on our journey.

On the day after I left Annecy my father arrived, having followed on my track with his friend, M. Rival, a watchmaker like himself, a talented and even a witty man, who wrote better verses than La Motte, and was almost as good a speaker; in addition, he was a thoroughly good fellow; but his misplaced taste for literature led to no other result than sending one of his sons on the stage.

These gentlemen saw Madame de Warens, and contented themselves with lamenting my lot, instead of following and overtaking me, as they could easily have done, since they were on horseback while I was on foot. My uncle Bernard had done the same; he had gone as far as Confignon, whence he returned to Geneva, after he heard that I was at Annecy. It seemed as if my relations were in league with my unlucky star to hand me over to the destiny which awaited me. My brother had been lost through similar negligence, and so completely, that it has never been known what became of him.

My father was not only a man of honour, he was a man of proved uprightness, and he had one of those strong souls which are capable of great virtues; in addition to which, he was a good father, especially towards myself. He loved me very tenderly, but he also loved his pleasures, and, since I had lived apart from him, other tastes had rendered his paternal affection somewhat luke-warm. He had married again at Nyon; and although his wife was no longer of an age to present me with brothers, she had relations. This created another family, other aims, a new estab-lishment, which no longer so frequently recalled the memory of myself. My father was growing old, and had nothing to live upon; but my brother and myself had a small property from our mother, the interest of which could be claimed by my father during our absence. This idea did not present itself to him directly, and by no means prevented him from doing his duty; but it exercised a secret influence without his being aware of it, and sometimes moderated his zeal, which he would have pushed further had it not been for that. That, I believe, was the reason why, having originally gone to Annecy to find me out, he did not follow me as far as Chambéri, where he would have been morally certain to find me. That again was the reason why, when I went to pay him a visit, as I frequently did after my flight, he always received me with the caresses of a father, but without making any serious efforts to keep me with him.

This behaviour on the part of a father, whose tenderness and uprightness I knew so well, led me to reflections upon myself, which have in no small degree contributed to keep my heart in a healthy condition. From these I have drawn the great moral lesson, perhaps the only one of any practical value, to avoid those situations of life which bring our duties into conflict with our interests, and which show us our own advantage in the misfortunes of others; for it is certain that, in such situations, however sincere our love of virtue, we must, sooner or later, inevitably grow weak without perceiving it, and become unjust and wicked in act, without having ceased to be just and good in our hearts.

This principle, deeply imprinted on the bottom of my heart, which, although somewhat late, in practice guided my whole conduct, is one of those which have caused me to appear a very strange and foolish creature in the eyes of the world, and, above all, amongst my acquaintances. I have been reproached with wanting to pose as an original, and different from others. In reality, I have never troubled about acting like other people or differently from them. I sincerely desired to do what was right. I withdrew, as far as it lay in my power, from situations which opposed my interests to those of others, and might, consequently, inspire me with a secret, though involuntary, desire of injuring them.

Two years ago my Lord Marshal[1] wanted to put my name in his will; I strongly opposed this. I told him that I would not for the world know that my name was down in anyone's will, least of all in his. He gave in; but insisted upon bestowing upon me a pension for life, to which I offered no opposition. It will be said that I gain by this alteration; that may be so, but I know, oh! father and benefactor, that, if I unhappily survive you, in losing you I have everything to lose and nothing to gain.

[1] Marshal Keith; see *Biographies*, p. 712.

That, in my opinion, is the true philosophy, the only philo-sophy which is really suited for the human heart. I am more impressed every day by its profound solidity, and in all my recent writings I have presented it under various aspects; but the public is superficial, and has not known how to recognise it. If, after I have finished my present task, I live long enough to undertake another, I propose to give, in the sequel to "Émile,"[1] so attrac-tive and striking an example of this maxim, that the reader will be compelled to notice it. But enough reflections for a traveller; it is time to continue my journey!

I found it more agreeable than I had expected, and my lout was not so sulky as he looked. He was a man of middle age, who wore his black hair, which was beginning to grow grey, in a *queue*; he looked like a grenadier, had a strong voice, was pretty cheer-ful, could walk well and eat better, and practised all sorts of trades, for want of knowing any. I believe he had proposed to establish some kind of manufactory at Annecy, and Madame de Warens had not failed to approve of the idea. It was in order to make the attempt to gain the minister's approval also, that, well furnished with money, he was making the journey to Turin. Our friend possessed a talent for intrigue, always making himself agreeable to the priests; and, while showing great eagerness to serve them, he had caught from their school a certain pious jargon of which he made incessant use, and boasted of being a great preacher. He even knew one passage of the Bible in Latin; and, as he repeated it a thousand times a day, it was as if he had known a thousand. He was seldom short of money, when he knew that others had any in their purse. He was rather clever than a rogue, and, when he recited his *capucinades*[2] in the tone of a recruiting officer, he resembled Peter the Hermit preaching the Crusade sword in hand.

As for his wife, Madame Sabran, she was a good woman enough, who was quieter during the day than at night. As I always slept in their room, her noisy sleeplessness often woke

---

[1] The sequel, never completed, was entitled *Emile et Sophie, ou les solitaires*. Some fragments were published after Rousseau's death, in 1780.

[2] Insipid discourses upon religious matters, like those of the Capucin friars.

me, and would have kept me awake still more, if I had known the reason of it; but I had not the least suspicion; and my stupidity on this point left the duty of instructing me to nature alone.

I proceeded gaily on my way with my pious guide and his lively companion. No mishap disturbed my journey; I was happier, in body and mind, than I have ever been in my life. Young, vigorous, in perfect health, without a care, full of confidence in myself and others, I was enjoying that short but precious moment of life when its expansive fulness, so to speak, enlarges our being in all our sensations, and beautifies in our eyes the whole aspect of nature by the charm of our existence. My pleasant restlessness had an object which restrained it and steadied my imagination. I looked upon myself as the work, the pupil, the friend, almost as the lover of Madame de Warens. The polite things she had said to me, the little caresses which she had bestowed upon me, the tender interest which she had seemed to take in me, her friendly looks, which appeared to me full of love, since they inspired me with that feeling – all this occupied my thoughts during the journey, and plunged me in delicious reveries undisturbed by any fear or doubt concerning my future. I considered that, in sending me to Turin, they had undertaken to support me there, and to find me a suitable situation. I felt that I need not trouble further about myself; others had undertaken the charge. So I went on my way with light step, freed from this burden; youthful desires, enchanting hopes, brilliant plans filled my soul. Everything that I saw appeared to assure my early happiness. In the houses I pictured to myself rustic festivities; in the meadows, playful romps; on the banks of the rivers, baths, walks, fishing; on the trees, delicious fruit; under their shade, loving *tête-à-têtes*; on the mountains, pails full of milk and cream, a charming idleness, peace, simplicity, and the pleasure of going I knew not where. In short, nothing met my eyes without conveying to my heart some attraction of enjoyment. The grandeur, the variety, the real beauty of the sight around me rendered this attraction worthy of reason; even vanity claimed its share. It appeared to me an honour beyond my years to visit Italy while still so young, to have already seen so much of the world, to follow Hannibal across the mountains. Besides this, we frequently halted at good inns; I had a good appetite and plenty to satisfy it; for it was really not worth while to deny myself anything, since my own meals were nothing in comparison with those of M. Sabran.

During the whole course of my life, I never remember a time when I have been so completely free from care and trouble as during the seven or eight days of our journey; for Madame Sabran's rate of travelling, by which we were obliged to regulate our own, made it nothing but a long walk. This recollection has left me the liveliest taste for everything connected with it, especially for mountains and walks. I have never journeyed on foot except in my younger days, and then always with the greatest pleasure. Duties, business, luggage, soon obliged me to play the gentleman and take a carriage; gnawing cares, perplexities, and discomfort got in with me, and from that moment, instead of feeling, as before, nothing but the pleasure of travelling, my only anxiety was to reach the end of my journey. For a long time I endeavoured to find in Paris two companions of the same tastes as myself willing to spend fifty *louis* of their money and a year of their time upon a walking tour through Italy with me, with only a single lad to carry our travelling-bags. Many appeared enchanted with the idea, but in reality considered it as nothing but a castle in the air, only fit to talk about without any idea of putting it into execution. I remember that Diderot and Grimm, with whom I once discussed the idea with enthusiasm, at last became enamoured of it. Once I thought the matter settled, but it all ended in their wanting to make a journey on paper, in which Grimm found nothing so delightful as making Diderot commit a number of impieties and handing me over to the inquisition in his stead.

My regret at arriving so soon at Turin was lessened by the pleasure of seeing a large city, and by the hope of soon playing a part worthy of myself; for already the fumes of ambition were mounting to my brain; already I regarded myself as infinitely raised above my former condition of apprentice, and I was far from suspecting that, in a short time, I was destined to fall far below it.

Before I continue, I must excuse or justify myself to the reader for the trivial details into which I have already entered, or into which I shall enter in the course of my narrative, and which in his eyes can have no interest. The task which I have undertaken, of showing myself completely without reserve to the public, requires that nothing that concerns myself shall remain obscure or hidden; that I shall keep myself continually before its eyes; that it shall accompany me in all the errors of my heart, into all the secret corners of my life; that it shall not lose sight of me for a single instant, for fear that, if it finds in my narrative the least gap, the least blank, it may ask, What was he doing during that time? and accuse me of unwillingness to tell all. My writings expose me sufficiently to the spite of mankind, without my exposing myself to it still more by my silence.

My little pocket-money was gone. I had chattered, and my guides were not slow to take advantage of my indiscretion. Madame Sabran managed to get everything from me, even a small piece of ribbon covered with silver, which Madame de Warens had given me for my little sword, and which I regretted more than anything else. The sword itself would have remained in their hands if I had resisted less firmly. They had faithfully defrayed my expenses during the journey, but they had left me nothing. I reached Turin without clothes, without money, without linen, and was obliged to leave entirely to my merits the honour of the fortune I was going to make.

I had some letters. I presented them, and was immediately conducted to the hospice for catechumens, to be instructed in the religion with which I was to purchase my livelihood.[1] On my arrival, I beheld a large gate with iron bars, which was double-locked behind me as soon as I had passed through it. This introduction struck me as more imposing than agreeable, and was beginning to afford me food for reflection, when I was conducted into a tolerably large room. All its furniture consisted of a wooden altar, surmounted by a large crucifix, at the end of the room, in front of which stood four or five chairs, also made of wood, which looked as if they had been polished, but in reality had become shiny merely from constant use and rubbing. In this

---

[1] According to the register of the Hospice, Rousseau entered on 12 April 1728 and was baptised eleven days later.

assembly-room were four or five frightful villains – my fellow-students – who seemed to be rather the devil's constables than aspirants to the honour of sons of God. Two of these rascals were Slavonians, who called themselves Jews or Moors, and, as they confessed to me, spent their life in wandering through Spain and Italy, embracing Christianity and submitting to be baptised where they found it worth their while. Another iron door was then thrown open, which divided into two a large balcony running along the courtyard. Through this door our sisters entered, catechumens who, like myself, were to be born again, not by means of baptism, but by a solemn abjuration of their faith. They were certainly the greatest sluts and the most disgusting vagabonds who ever contaminated the sheepfold of the Lord. Only one appeared to me pretty and attractive; she was about my own age, perhaps two or three years older. She had roguish eyes, which sometimes met mine. This inspired me with a desire to make her acquaintance; but, during nearly two months, which she spent in the house after my arrival – she had already been there three months – I found it absolutely impossible to speak to her, so strictly had she been recommended to the care of our old jaileress, and so carefully was she watched by the holy missionary, who laboured with more zeal than diligence to convert her. She must have been extremely dull, although she did not appear so, for never did tuition require so long a time. The holy man always found her unfit for the act of abjuration; but she grew weary of her confinement, and declared that she wanted to leave – Christian or no Christian. They were obliged to take her at her word, while she still showed herself ready to become one, for fear she might become refractory and refuse.

The little community was assembled in honour of the new-comer. A short address was delivered to us, in which I was exhorted to consent to respond to the favour which God extended to me, while the others were invited to pray for me and edify me by their example. After this, our virgins returned to their seclusion, and I had time to meditate with astonishment upon my own situation to my heart's content.

Next morning we were again assembled to receive instruction; and then, for the first time, I began to reflect upon the step

I was going to take, and upon the circumstances which had led me to do so.

I have said – I repeat it, and shall, perhaps, repeat it again, as I am daily more convinced of its truth – that, if ever a child received a sensible and sound education, it was myself. I belonged to a family which was distinguished by its manners from the common people; from all my relations I had learnt nothing but lessons of wisdom, and had had honourable examples before my eyes. My father, although fond of pleasure, was not only a man of strict integrity but of considerable religious feeling. A man of gallantry in the world and a Christian at heart, he had early instilled into me the sentiments which he felt. Of my three aunts, who were all prudent and virtuous, the two eldest were pious; the youngest, a girl full of grace, talent and good sense, was perhaps even more pious, although she made less show of it. From the bosom of this estimable family I went to M. Lambercier, who, though a churchman and preacher, was at heart a believer, and nearly always practised what he preached. He and his sister, by gentle and judicious training, cultivated the principles of piety which they found in my heart. These worthy people, with this object, employed means so sincere, so prudent and so sensible that, far from being wearied by their preaching, I always felt deeply affected by it and formed the best resolutions, which I rarely forgot to carry out when I thought of them. In the case of my aunt Bernard, her piety was somewhat more distasteful to me, because she made a trade of it. While serving my apprenticeship I scarcely thought of it, without, however, changing my views. I never came into contact with any young people who might have corrupted me; I became vagabond, but not dissipated.

I consequently knew as much about religion as was possible for a child of my age. I even knew more, for why should I conceal my thoughts? My childhood was not that of a child; I always felt and thought as a man. It was only when I grew up that I re-entered the class of ordinary individuals; as a child I did not belong to it. The reader will laugh to find me modestly representing myself as a prodigy. So be it; but when he has laughed sufficiently, let him find a child who, in his sixth year, is so attracted, interested and carried away by romances as to shed hot tears over them; then I shall feel that my vanity is ridiculous, and will confess that I am wrong.

If I have said that we ought not to speak about religion to children, if we wish them to possess any, and, further, that they are incapable of knowing God, even according to our ideas, I have drawn this conviction from my observations, not from my own experience, for I knew that no conclusion could be drawn from it in regard to others. Find me Jean Jacques Rousseaus of six years old, and speak to *them* of God when they are seven; I will guarantee that you run no risk.

I think it will be admitted that, in the case of a child, and even of a man, to have religion means to follow that in which he is born. This faith is sometimes lessened, rarely enlarged; dogmatic belief is one of the fruits of education. Besides this general principle which attached me to the religious creed of my fathers, I had the aversion for Catholicism peculiar to our village, which represented it as a frightful idolatry, and painted its priests in the blackest colours. This feeling was so strong in me, that at first I never looked into the inside of a church, never met a priest in a surplice, never heard the processional bell, without a shudder of terror and alarm, which soon left me in the towns, but has often come upon me again in country parishes, more like those where I had first felt it. It is true that this impression contrasted singularly with the recollections of the caresses which the priests of the environs of Geneva were fond of bestowing upon the children of the city. While the bell announcing supreme unction alarmed me, the bell for mass and vespers reminded me of breakfast, collation, fresh butter, fruit, and milk-food. M. de Pontverre's good dinner still produced a great effect. Thus I had easily driven all such thoughts out of my mind. Seeing papism only in its connection with amusement and good living, I had readily accustomed myself to the idea of living in its midst; but the idea of solemnly going over to the Church of Rome had only presented itself to me for a moment, as possible in a distant future. At the present moment it was no longer possible to deceive myself; I saw with horror the kind of consent which I had given, and its inevitable consequences. The future neophytes around me were not calculated to sustain my courage by their example, and I could not conceal from myself that the holy work, which I intended to carry out, was in the main the action of a bandit; for, young as I was, I felt that, whatever religion might be the true one, I was going to sell my own, and that, even though I made a good choice, in the bottom of my heart I should lie to the Holy Spirit and deserve the contempt of men. The more I thought of it, the more indignant I became with myself; and I sighed over the destiny which had brought me to this pass, as if this destiny had not been my own work. There were moments when these reflections became so strong, that, if I had found the door open for a moment, I should certainly have run away; but this was impossible, and my resolution was not strong enough. Too many secret desires combated it not to overcome it. Besides, my fixed determination not to return to Geneva, shame, the difficulty of crossing the mountains again, the embarrassment of finding myself far from my country, without friends and without resources – all these feelings combined to make me regard my prickings of conscience as a too tardy repentance; I pretended to reproach myself for what I had done, in order to excuse what I was going to do. While aggravating the errors of the past, I regarded the future as their necessary result. Instead of saying to myself, "Nothing is done yet, and you can be innocent if you wish," I said, "Sigh for the crime of which you have made yourself guilty, and which you have made it necessary for yourself to carry out."

In fact, what uncommon strength of mind would have been necessary, at my age, in order to recall everything that I had hitherto promised or given hopes of, to break the bonds which I had placed upon myself, to declare boldly that I desired at all risks to continue in the religion of my fathers! Such vigour was not natural to one of my age, and it is not very probable that it would have succeeded. Things had gone too far for them not to feel ashamed if they did not succeed; and, the greater my resistance, the more they would have felt themselves bound, by some means or other, to overcome it.

The sophism which ruined me, is that common to most men who complain of want of strength when it is already too late to make use of it. Virtue only becomes difficult by our own fault; if we could always be prudent, we should rarely need to be virtuous. But inclinations, easily surmountable, hurry us along without resistance; we yield to trifling temptations, the danger of which we despise. Imperceptibly we fall into perilous situations, from which we could easily have protected ourselves, but from which we can no longer extricate ourselves without heroic efforts which appal us; and at last we fall into the abyss, reproaching God, "Why hast Thou made me so weak?" But, in spite of ourselves, He replies to our consciences, "I have made you too weak to save yourself from the abyss, because I made you strong enough not to fall into it."

I did not exactly resolve to become a Catholic; but, seeing the time still far off, I profited by the occasion to accustom myself gradually to the idea, and in the meantime I hoped for some unforeseen circumstance which would get me out of the difficulty. In order to gain time, I resolved to make the best defence of which I was capable. But soon my vanity relieved me from thinking of my resolution; and, as soon as I observed that I sometimes embarrassed those who desired to instruct me, that was sufficient to make me endeavour to floor them altogether. I even exhibited ridiculous eagerness in this undertaking; for, while they were working upon me, I wanted to work upon them. I honestly believed that I had only to convince them, to make them turn Protestants.

Consequently, they did not find in me nearly as much tractability as they had expected, either in regard to my knowledge or good will. Protestants are generally better instructed than Catholics. This is only natural; the doctrine of the one requires discussion, that of the other submission. The Catholic is obliged to embrace the decision that is put before him; the Protestant must learn to decide for himself. This was well known; but no great difficulties were expected for persons of experience from one of my age and position. Besides, I had not yet received my first Communion, nor received the instructions connected with it; that, too, was known. But what they did not know was that, to make up for this, I had been well taught at M. Lambercier's, and that, in addition, I had by me a little storehouse, very inconvenient for these gentlemen, in the history of the Church and the Empire, which, while living with my father, I had learnt almost by heart, and since then almost forgotten, but which came back to me in proportion as the dispute grew warmer.

A little, old, but somewhat venerable priest held the first meeting of all of us together. For my companions this meeting was rather a catechism than a discussion, and he had more to do with instructing them than with removing their objections. In my own case it was different. When my turn came, I stopped him at every point, and spared him no single difficulty which I was able to throw in his way. This protracted the meeting, and made it very tedious for those who were present. My old priest spoke much, grew excited, wandered from his subject, and got himself out of the difficulty by declaring that he did not know French well. The next day, for fear that my indiscreet objections might give offence to my companions, I was put into another room with another priest, who was younger and a good speaker – that is to say, a coiner of fine phrases – and satisfied with himself, if ever a teacher was. I did not, however, allow myself to be too much cowed by his imposing manner; and feeling that, after all, I was able to hold my own, I proceeded to answer him with tolerable confidence, and to press him on all sides to the best of my ability. He thought to overwhelm me with St. Augustine, St. Gregory, and the other fathers, but found, to his incredible surprise, that I handled all the fathers nearly as readily as he did; not that I had ever read them, as neither perhaps had he, but I remembered several passages out of my "Le Sueur"; and, as soon as he quoted one, without stopping to dispute it, I answered it by another from the same Father, which frequently caused him considerable embarrassment. However, in the end he gained the victory, for two reasons. In the first place, he was the stronger, and, feeling that I was, so to speak, at his mercy, I correctly judged, young as I was, that it would not do to press him – to drive him to extremities; for I saw clearly enough that the little old priest had conceived no great affection for myself or my learning. In the second place, the young priest was an educated man, while I was not. This caused him to employ in his manner of argument a method which I was unable to follow, and, as soon as he felt himself pushed by some unforeseen objection, he put it off until the next day, declaring that I was wandering from the point. Sometimes he even refused to accept my quotations, declaring that they were false; and, offering to go and fetch the book for me, defied me to find them. He felt that he did not risk much, and that, with all my borrowed learning, I was not sufficiently experienced in handling books, and did not know enough Latin to find a passage in a large volume, even though I might be certain that it was there. I even suspected him of making use of the same dishonesty of which he accused our ministers, and of sometimes inventing passages, in order to extricate himself from a difficulty which embarrassed him.

While these petty disputes about trifles lasted, and the time was spent in arguing, mumbling prayers, and doing nothing, a disgusting little adventure happened to me, which very nearly turned out very badly for me.

There is no soul so vile, no heart so barbarous, that it is not susceptible of some kind of attachment. One of the two vagabonds who called themselves Moors conceived an affection for me. He was fond of accosting me, talked to me in his jargon, rendered me slight services, sometimes gave me part of his food, and frequently kissed me with an ardour which was very annoying to me. In spite of the natural alarm which I felt at his gingerbread face decorated with a long scar, and his inflamed countenance which appeared more furious than tender, I endured his kisses, saying to myself: "The poor fellow has conceived a lively friendship for me. I should be wrong to repulse him." He gradually began to take greater liberties, and sometimes made such curious proposals to me, that I thought he was mad. One night, he wanted to sleep with me. I refused, saying that my bed was too small. He pressed me to go to his, but I again refused, for the wretch was so dirty and stunk so strongly of chewed tobacco, that he made me quite sick.

Early on the following morning, we were both alone in the assembly-room. He recommenced his caresses, but with such violent movements, that it became quite alarming. At last, he wanted to take the most disgusting liberties with me, and, taking hold of my hand, tried to make me take the same with him. I uttered a loud cry, and, jumping back, freed myself from him; and, without exhibiting anger or indignation, for I had not the least idea what it was all about, I expressed my surprise and disgust so energetically, that he left me where I was; but, while he was finishing his efforts, I saw something white, like glue, shoot towards the fireplace and fall upon the ground, which turned my stomach. I rushed upon the balcony, more moved, more troubled, more frightened than I had ever been in my life, and prepared to find myself ill.

I could not understand what had been the matter with the wretch. I believed that he was attacked by epilepsy, or some other madness even more terrible; and in truth, I know nothing more hideous for any cool-blooded person to see than such filthy and dirty behaviour, and a frightful countenance inflamed by brutal lust. I have never seen another man in a similar condition; but if we are like it when we are with women, their looks must certainly be bewitched, for them not to feel disgusted at us.

I was in a great hurry to go and tell everyone what had just happened to me. Our old intendant bade me hold my tongue; but I saw that my story had greatly affected her, and I heard her mutter: *Can maledet! brutta bestia!*[1]

Not understanding why I ought to hold my tongue, I went my own way in spite of her prohibition, and I talked so much that, the next day, one of the governors came at an early hour to administer a sharp reproof to me, accusing me of compromising the honour of a holy house, and of making a great fuss about a trifle.

He spun out his lecture by explaining to me many things of which I was ignorant, but which he did not believe he was teaching me, for he was convinced that I had defended myself because I was unwilling to consent, not because I did not know what the Moor wanted from me. He told me gravely that it was an action forbidden as highly immoral, the desire of which, however, was not an affront to the person who was the object of it, and that there was no need to be so annoyed at having

---

[1] Cursed dog! brute beast!

been considered worthy of affection. He told me plainly that he himself, during his youth, had had the same honour paid to him, and that, having been surprised when he was not in a condition to offer any resistance, he had not found it particularly painful. He was so shameless as to make use of plain language; and, imagining that the reason of my resistance was the fear of pain, he assured me that I need have no fear, and that I ought not to be alarmed where there was no reason for it.

I listened to this wretch with an astonishment which was increased by the fact that he did not speak for himself, but only appeared to be instructing me for my good. The subject appeared to him so simple, that he did not even attempt to ensure privacy; and our conversation was heard by a third party in the person of an ecclesiastic who seemed no more frightened by it than himself. This air of naturalness so imposed upon me, that I was convinced that it was no doubt a custom recognised in the world, as to which I had not had the opportunity of being instructed sooner. This made me listen without anger, but not without disgust. The image of what had happened to me, but above all of what I had seen, remained so deeply impressed upon my memory that, when I thought of it, I still felt disgusted. Without knowing any more about it, my aversion for the thing itself extended to its apologist; and I could not restrain myself sufficiently to prevent him seeing the bad effect of his lessons. He cast a glance at me that was by no means affectionate and from that time spared no efforts to make my stay in the hospice disagreeable. He succeeded so well that, seeing that there was only one way of getting away, I hastened to take it with as much eagerness as I had up till then exhibited in order to keep away from it.

This adventure assured me for the future against the attempts of the "Knights of the Cuff";[1] and the sight of people who were supposed to belong to their order, by recalling to my mind the appearance and gestures of my frightful Moor, always inspired me with such horror, that I had difficulty in concealing it. On the

---

[1] *Chevaliers de la manchette*: pederasts.

other hand, women, to my mind, gained much by comparison; it appeared to me that I owed them tender feelings and personal homage by way of reparation for the insults of my sex; and the ugliest strumpet became in my eyes an object of adoration, when I remembered the false African.

As for him, I do not know what may have been said to him; it did not appear to me that anybody, with the exception of mistress Lorenza, looked upon him less favourably than before. However, he neither accosted nor spoke to me again. Eight days afterwards, he was baptised with great solemnity, dressed in white from head to foot, in token of the purity of his regenerated soul. The next day he left the hospice, and I have never seen him since.

My turn came a month later; for it required all that time to procure for the directors of my conscience the honour of a difficult conversion, and I was obliged to examine and go through all the dogmas, in order that my new docility might be triumphantly paraded.

At last, sufficiently instructed and sufficiently prepared to satisfy my masters, I was conducted in solemn procession to the metropolitan church of St. John, to make a public abjuration of faith, and to receive the accessories of baptism, although I was not really rebaptised; but, as the ceremonies are almost the same, it serves to delude the people with the idea that Protestants are not Christians. I was clothed in a grey coat adorned with white frogs, which was used on such occasions. Two men, before and behind me, carried copper basins, which they beat with a key, and into which each threw his alms in proportion to his piety or the interest which he took in the new convert. Briefly, nothing of the pomp of the Catholic Church was omitted, in order to render the ceremony at once more edifying to the people, and more humiliating for myself. Only the white robe was wanting, which would have been very useful to me, and which was not given to me as to the Moor, seeing that I had not the honour to be a Jew.

This was not all. I was next obliged to go to the Inquisition to receive absolution from the crime of heresy, and to re-enter the bosom of the Church with the ceremony to which Henry IV was subjected in the person of his ambassador.[1] The behaviour and look of the reverend father inquisitor were not calculated to remove the secret terror which had seized upon me when I entered the house. After several questions about my belief, my position, and my family, he abruptly asked me whether my mother was damned. Fright caused me to repress the first movement of my indignation. I contented myself with answering that I ventured to hope that she was not, and that God might have enlightened her at her last hour. The monk was silent, but made a grimace which by no means appeared to me a sign of approval.

When all was over, at the moment when I expected to be provided for in accordance with my hopes, I was put out of doors with a little more than twenty francs in small money – the result of the collection made for me. I was recommended to live as a good Christian, to remain true to grace; they wished me good luck, shut the door upon me, and I saw no more of them.

Thus, in an instant, all my great expectations disappeared, and the only result of the self-seeking step that I had just taken, was the consciousness of having been an apostate and a dupe at the same time. It may be easily imagined what a sudden revolution took place in my ideas, when I saw myself dashed down from my brilliant dreams of fortune into utter misery, and when, after having deliberated in the morning upon the choice of the palace I should inhabit, I found myself in the evening obliged to go to bed in the street. It will be imagined that I began by abandoning myself to a feeling of despair, the more cruel in proportion as regret for my errors was aggravated by the reproach that all my misfortune was my own work. Nothing of the kind. For the first time in my life, I had just been shut up for more than two months. My first sensation was one of joy at the recovery of my liberty. After a long period of slavery, again master of myself and my actions, I beheld myself in the midst of a large city, abounding in resources, full of persons of distinction, by whom

---

[1] Cardinals Du Perron and Ossat did public penance before Pope Clement VIII in 1595 to obtain absolution for Henri IV from the bull of excommunication of Sixtus V.

I could not fail to be welcomed in consequence of my good qualities and my talents as soon as I became known. Besides, I had plenty of time to wait, and the twenty francs, which I had in my pocket, appeared to me an inexhaustible treasure. I could spend them as I pleased, without being accountable to anybody. It was the first time that I had ever been so well off. Far from becoming disheartened or shedding tears, I only changed my hopes, and my *amour-propre* lost nothing by the exchange. I had never felt so confident and secure; I believed my fortune already made, and I considered it a fine thing to have no one but myself to thank for it.

The first thing I did was to satisfy my curiosity by going round the city, if only to enjoy the sweets of liberty. I went to see the soldiers mount guard; the military music pleased me exceedingly. I followed processions; I delighted in the church-music of the priests. I went to see the King's palace; I approached it with awe; but, seeing others go in, I did the same without being stopped. Perhaps I owed this favour to the little parcel which I carried under my arm. Anyhow, I began to entertain a high opinion of myself when I found myself in this palace; I already began to consider myself a resident in it. At last, I grew tired of going backwards and forwards; I was hungry; it was hot; I went into a milk-shop; I bought some *giunca*[1] and sour milk; and with two slices of the excellent Piedmontese bread, which I prefer to any other, for my five or six *sous* I had one of the best meals I have ever had in my life.

I was obliged to look for a lodging. As I already knew enough Piedmontese to make myself understood it was easy to find one, and I was prudent enough to make my choice more in accordance with my means than my taste. I was told of a soldier's wife in the Rue du Pô who took in servants out of employment for a *sou* a night. She had a bed empty, and I took it. She was young and recently married, although she already had five or six children. We all slept in the same room, mother, children, and lodgers, and continued to do so as long as I remained with her. In other respects she was a good woman, who swore like

[1]   Fresh cheese and cream brought to market on rushes.

a carter, whose breast was always exposed and her hair untidy, but kind-hearted and obliging; she took a liking to me, and was even useful to me.

I spent several days in abandoning myself solely to the delights of independence and curiosity. I wandered about inside and outside the city, prying everywhere, looking at everything which appeared to me new or curious; and this was the case with everything to a young man who had just left his shell, and had never seen a capital. I was above all very regular in going to court, and was particular in my attendance every morning at the royal mass. I thought it a fine thing to be in the same chapel as the prince and his suite; but my passion for music, which was beginning to make itself felt, had more to do with my regular appearance than the pomp of the court, which, soon seen and always the same, soon loses the charm of novelty. The King of Sardinia at that time had the best choir in Europe. Somis, Desjardins, the Bezuzzi, were successively its brilliant ornaments. This was more than sufficient to attract a young man whom the sound of the most wretched instrument, if only correctly played, was enough to enchant. Besides, the admiration I felt for the magnificence which dazzled my eyes was senseless and aroused no envy. The only thing which interested me in all the brilliancy of the court was to see whether there was not some young princess, worthy of my homage, with whom I might carry on a romance.

I was nearly commencing one in a less brilliant circle, but one in which, if I had carried it out, I should have found pleasures a thousand times more delicious.

Although I lived most economically, my purse was gradually becoming exhausted. Besides, my economy was not so much the effect of prudence as of a simplicity of taste which, even at the present day, familiarity with the tables of the great has not changed. I did not know, and do not know even now, better cheer than a country meal. Anyone may feel sure of entertaining me handsomely with milk-food, eggs, vegetables, cheese, black bread, and tolerable wine; my excellent appetite will do the rest; while a *maître-d'hôtel* and footmen about me with their troublesome officiousness can never satisfy me. At that time I made far better meals at a cost of six or seven *sous*, than I have made since for six or seven francs. I was temperate, because I had no temptation to be otherwise; and yet I am wrong to say I was temperate, for I had at the same time all possible sensual enjoyments. My pears, my *giunca*, my cheese, my slices of bread, and a few glasses of a full-bodied Montferrat wine, which could have been cut into slices, made me the happiest of gourmands. And yet, in spite of all that, the end of my twenty francs was visible. This I became more sensibly aware of every day; and, in spite of the thoughtlessness of my years, my uneasiness regarding the future soon became real alarm. Of all my castles in the air nothing remained to me but the necessity of finding a means of livelihood, which was by no means easy to procure. I thought of my old trade, but I did not know enough of it to work for a master, and, besides, there were not many masters in Turin. While waiting for something better, I took to going from shop to shop to offer my services for engraving figures or coats-of-arms on silver, hoping to tempt customers by my cheapness, since I left the amount of payment to them. This plan did not prove very successful. I was generally shown the door; and the work I got was so little, that I scarcely earned enough to pay for two or three meals. One day, however, as I was walking at an early hour through the *Contrada nova*, I saw through a shop window a young woman of so kindly and attractive an appearance, that, in spite of my shyness with women, I entered without hesitation and placed my humble talents at her disposal. She did not repulse me, but made me sit down and tell her my little history, pitied me, bade me cheer up, since assuredly good Christians would not desert me, and, having sent to a neighbouring goldsmith for the tools which I told her I wanted, she went into the kitchen and fetched me some breakfast with her own hands. This beginning appeared to me to promise well; the result did not give the lie to it. She appeared satisfied with my bit of work, and still more with my humble chatter, when I was a little more at my ease; for she was brilliant and handsomely dressed, and, in spite of her gracious manner, her appearance had inspired me with awe. But her kindly reception, her compassionate voice, her gentle and caressing manners, soon put me at my ease. I saw that I was successful, and this increased my success. But, although she was an Italian and too pretty not to be somewhat of a coquette, she was at the same time so modest, and I was so shy, that it was difficult for it to lead to anything further. We were not allowed time to finish the adventure. I remember with the greater rapture the brief moments which I spent by her side, and I can declare that in their first beginnings I tasted the sweetest and purest joys of love.

She was an extremely piquant brunette, whose liveliness was rendered somewhat touching by the expression of good nature on her pretty face. Her name was Madame Basile. Her husband, who was older than herself and somewhat jealous, left her, while he was travelling, under the care of a clerk, who appeared too disagreeable to be seductive, and yet was not without pretensions of his own, which he only showed by his bad temper. This he visited upon me, although I was very fond of hearing him play the flute, on which he was a tolerably good performer. This new Aegisthus grumbled whenever he saw me enter the place, and treated me with a contempt which his mistress returned in full. It even seemed as if it delighted her to caress me in his presence, in order to plague him; and this kind of revenge, although very much to my taste, would have been still more agreeable in a *tête-à-tête*. But she never pushed matters to that extent, or, at least, not in the same manner. Whether it was that she found me too young, or did not know how to make advances, or really intended to be discreet, she exhibited at that time a kind of reserve, which, while not repellent, intimidated me without my knowing the reason why. Although I did not feel for her the real and tender respect that I felt for Madame de Warens, I was more timid and less familiar with her. I was embarrassed and confused; I did not venture to look at her or to breathe by her side; and yet I dreaded to leave her worse than death. I devoured with a greedy eye everything I could look at without being observed: the flowers in her dress, the tips of her pretty feet, the glimpse of a firm white arm which I caught between her glove and her cuff, and of her bosom, which was sometimes visible between her tucker and her neckerchief. Each object strengthened the impression made by the rest. From looking at what I could see, and even further than that, my eyes became troubled, my breast felt oppressed; my respiration became every moment more choked, I could scarcely breathe, and all I could do was to heave a succession of noiseless sighs, which were very embarrassing in the complete stillness in which we often found ourselves. Luckily Madame Basile, busy with her work, did not notice it, as far as I could see. However, I sometimes saw the bosom of her dress heave as if in sympathy. This dangerous sight made me lose my head completely; but, when I was ready to give way to my transports, she quietly said something to me which immediately brought me to my senses again.

I saw her several times alone in this manner, without a word, or gesture, or even a too expressive look indicating the least understanding between us. This state of things, very tormenting for myself, was nevertheless extremely delightful, and in the simplicity of my heart I could scarcely understand why I felt so tormented. It appeared that these little *tête-à-têtes* were not unpleasant to her either; at any rate, she provided opportunity for them pretty frequently – certainly a very harmless endeavour on her part, for all the use which she made of them herself, or allowed me to make.

One day, tired of the clerk's silly conversation, she had gone upstairs to her room. I hastily finished my little task in the room behind the shop, and followed her. The door of her room was half open. I entered without being seen. She was working at her embroidery near a window, with her back turned towards the door. She could neither see me nor hear me come in, owing to the noise of the carriages in the street. She was always well dressed; on that day her toilet was almost coquettish. Her attitude was graceful; her head, slightly bent, allowed the whiteness of her neck to be seen; her hair, elegantly fastened up, was ornamented with flowers. Over her whole form was spread a charm, which I had time to consider, and which made me beside myself. I threw myself on my knees on the threshold, stretching out my arms towards her with passionate movements, feeling certain that she could not hear me, and not thinking it possible that she could see me; but over the mantelpiece was a looking-glass, which betrayed me. I do not know what effect my attack of madness produced upon her; she neither looked at me, nor said a word; but, half-turning her head, with a simple movement of her finger she pointed to the mat at her feet. To tremble, to utter a cry, to fling myself down on the spot she had indicated, was for me the work of a moment; but it will scarcely be believed that, in this position, I did not venture to attempt anything further, to say a single word, to lift my eyes to her, or even to touch her, in my uncomfortable attitude, to support myself for an instant upon her knees. Although unable to speak or move, I was certainly not tranquil; everything about me betrayed my agitation, my joy, my gratitude, my ardent desires, which, without definite aim or object, were restrained by the fear of displeasing, in regard to which my youthful heart could not make itself easy.

She appeared no less moved and no less shy than myself. Disturbed at seeing me there, disconcerted at having drawn me thither, and beginning to feel the full consequences of a sign which she had no doubt made without due reflection, she neither drew me towards her nor repulsed me. She did not take her eyes from her work; she tried to behave as if she had not seen me at her feet; but all my stupidity could not prevent me from concluding that she shared my embarrassment, perhaps even my desires, and that she was restrained by the same feeling of shame as myself, although this did not assist me to overcome it. Being five or six years older than myself, she ought, as I considered, to have had all the boldness on her side; and I said to myself that, as she did nothing to awaken mine, she could not wish me to show any. Even now I think I was right, and certainly she was too clever not to see that a novice, such as I was, needed to be not only encouraged, but also instructed.

I do not know what would have been the end of this lively dumb show, nor how long I should have remained without moving in my ridiculous and yet delicious situation, if we had not been interrupted. At the moment of my most violent excitement, I heard the door of the kitchen, which was close to the room where we were, open, and Madame Basile, in lively alarm which showed itself in her words and gestures, said, "Get up! here comes Rosina." Hastily rising, I seized the hand which she held out to me, and imprinted two burning kisses upon it, at the second of which I felt this charming hand pressed lightly against my lips. Never in my life had I enjoyed so sweet a moment; but the opportunity which I had lost never came again, and our youthful loves stopped at that point.

This is, perhaps, the very reason why the image of that amiable woman has remained imprinted on the bottom of my heart in such charming outlines. It has even grown in beauty in proportion as my knowledge of the world and women has been enlarged. If she had only had a little experience, she would have behaved differently in order to encourage a lad; but, if her heart was weak, it was upright; she yielded involuntarily to the inclination which carried her away; it was, according to all appearance, her first infidelity, and I should, perhaps, have found more difficulty in overcoming her shyness than my own. Without having gone so far, I found in her presence indescribable happiness. None of the feelings caused by the possession of women have ever equalled the two minutes which I spent at her feet without even venturing to touch her dress. No; there is no enjoyment equal to that which a virtuous woman, whom one loves, can afford. Everything is a favour with her. A sign with the finger, a hand pressed lightly against my mouth – these are the only favours that I ever received from Madame Basile, and the recollection of these trifling tokens of regard still enchants me when I think of them.

For the two next days it was in vain that I looked out for the chance of another *tête-à-tête*; it was impossible for me to find the opportunity, and I did not observe any anxiety on her part to bring it about. Her manner, although not colder, was more reserved than usual; and I believe that she avoided my looks, for fear of being unable to control her own sufficiently. Her confounded clerk was more unbearable than ever; he even joked and bantered me, saying that I should get on with the ladies. I trembled at the thought of having been guilty of some indiscretion; and, already considering that there was an understanding between Madame Basile and myself, I wished to keep secret an inclination which, until then, had not greatly needed it. This made me more careful in seizing opportunities to satisfy it; and, as I wished them to be safe, I no longer found any at all.

This is another romantic folly of which I have never been able to cure myself, and which, combined with my natural shyness, has strikingly falsified the clerk's predictions. I loved too sincerely, too completely, I venture to say, to be able to be happy easily. Never have passions been at once more lively and purer than mine; never has love been tenderer, truer, more disinterested. I would have sacrificed my happiness a thousand times for that of the person whom I loved; her reputation was dearer to me than my life, and I would never have wished to endanger her repose for a single moment for all the pleasures of enjoyment. This feeling has made me employ such carefulness, such secrecy, and such precaution in my undertakings, that none of them have ever been successful. My want of success with women has always been caused by my excessive love for them.

To return to the flute player Aegisthus: the curious thing was that the traitor, as he became more unendurable, appeared to become more affable. From the first day that his mistress had taken a liking to me, she had thought of making me useful in the shop. I was a fairly good arithmetician. She had proposed to him to teach me to keep the books; but the boorish fellow received the proposal with a very ill grace, perhaps because he was afraid of being supplanted. Thus all my work, besides that with my graving tool, consisted in copying a few accounts and memoranda, correcting a few books, and translating a few business letters from Italian into French. Suddenly it occurred to my friend to return to the proposal which had been made and rejected. He offered to teach me double entry, and said that he wished to make me competent to offer my services to M. Basile on his return. In his voice, in his manner, there was something false, spiteful, and ironical, which did not inspire me with confidence. Madame Basile, without waiting for me to answer, said to him coldly, that I was obliged to him for his offer; that she hoped that fortune would in the end reward my good qualities, and that it would be a great pity if, with my talents, I became nothing more than a clerk.

She had on several occasions told me that she desired to introduce me to someone who might be of assistance to me. She was prudent enough to feel that it was time for us to separate. Our mute declarations had been made on a Thursday. On the following Sunday she gave a dinner, at which I was present, and amongst the guests was a monk of the Jacobin order, a man of good appearance, to whom she introduced me. He treated me very cordially, congratulated me on my conversion, and spoke to me about my history in a manner which proved to me that she had given him a full account of it; then, giving me a friendly slap on the cheek with the back of his hand, he told me to behave myself properly, to be of good courage, and to go and see him, that we might talk more at leisure. I judged, by the respect which everyone showed him, that he was a person of some importance; and, from the paternal tone which he adopted towards Madame Basile, that he was her confessor. I also remember that his respectful familiarity was united with marks of esteem and even respect for his penitent, which impressed me less at the time than they do now. If I had been more intelligent, I should have been affected at the thought of having been able to touch the feelings of a young woman so respected by her confessor. The table was not large enough for all of us; another small one was called into requisition, at which I had the pleasure of sitting opposite the clerk. As far as attention and good cheer were concerned, I lost nothing by the arrangement; several plates were sent to the little table, which were certainly not meant for him. Up to this time all was going well; the ladies were very gay, the men very attentive; Madame Basile did the honours with charming grace. In the middle of dinner, a carriage stopped at the door; someone came upstairs. It was M. Basile. I see him now, just as when he came in, dressed in a scarlet coat with gilt buttons, a colour which, since that day, I have always regarded with aversion. He was a tall, handsome man of good appearance. He entered noisily with the air of a man surprising his guests, although all who were present were friends of his. His wife flung her arms round his neck, pressed his hands, and lavished caresses upon him, which he accepted without returning. He saluted the company, and sat down to eat. The guests had scarcely begun to speak of his journey, when, turning his eyes towards the little table, he asked, in a severe tone, who the little boy was whom he saw there. Madame Basile told him everything quite simply. He asked whether I lived in the house, and being told no, he said coarsely, "Why not? since he is here in the daytime, he might as well stop during the night." The monk took up the conversation; and, after speaking of Madame Basile in terms of praise that were earnest and true, said a few words in my favour, adding that, far from blaming his wife's pious work of charity, he ought to be eager to take part in it himself, since nothing in it overstepped the bounds of discretion. M. Basile replied in a tone of annoyance, which he half concealed, out of respect for the monk's presence, but which was enough to make me feel that he had been informed about me, and that the clerk had done me an ill turn.

No sooner was the meal over, than the latter, sent by his master, came in triumph to tell me, by his orders, to leave the house at once and never set foot in it again. He seasoned his message with everything that could make it cruel and insulting. I went without saying a word, but with a heart deeply afflicted, not so much at the thought of leaving this amiable woman, as of abandoning her to her husband's brutality. He was no doubt right in wishing her not to be untrue to him; but, although intelligent and well brought up, she was an Italian, that is to say, of a sensitive and revengeful disposition; and it appears to me that he was wrong in treating her in the manner most calculated to bring upon himself the misfortune which he dreaded.

Such was the result of my first love adventure. I did not omit to pass two or three times through the street, in the hope of at least seeing again her whom my heart unceasingly regretted; but, instead of her, I only saw the husband and the watchful clerk, who, as soon as he saw me, made a movement towards me with the yard measure, which was more expressive than alluring. Seeing that I was so well watched, I lost heart and did not pass the shop again. I wished, at least, to see the patron whom Madame Basile had found for me. Unfortunately I did not know his name. I wandered several times round the convent in the hope of meeting him, but without success. At last other events banished the delightful recollections of Madame Basile, and in a short time I forgot her so completely that, simple and as great a novice as before, I did not even feel attracted by pretty women.

However, her generosity had somewhat refurnished my wardrobe, although very modestly, and with the foresight of a prudent woman who thought more of neatness than of adornment, and whose wish was to keep me from discomfort, not to deck me out. The clothes which I had brought from Geneva were still good enough to wear; she only added a hat and some linen. I had no cuffs; she would not give me any, although I was very anxious to have some. She was satisfied with putting me in a position to keep myself neat and clean, and that was a thing which there was no need to recommend me to be careful about, as long as I was in her presence.

A few days after my misfortune, my landlady who, as I have said, had taken a liking to me, told me that she had, perhaps, found me a place, and that a lady of position wanted to see me. At these words, I believed myself already in the midst of fashionable adventures; for my mind was always running upon that. This one, however, did not prove as brilliant as I had pictured to myself. I went to see the lady with the servant who had spoken of me to her. She questioned and examined me; I did not displease her, and immediately entered her service, not exactly as a favourite, but as a lackey. I was dressed in her livery; the only difference was that, while they wore shoulder knots, I had none; as there was no lace on her livery, it looked like an ordinary dress. Such was the unexpected end of all my grand hopes!

The Comtesse de Vercellis, whose service I then entered, was a widow without children; her husband was a Piedmontese. I always took her to be a Savoyard, since I could not believe that a Piedmontese could speak French so well and with so pure an accent. She was middle-aged, of distinguished appearance, possessed a cultivated mind, and was fond of French literature, of which she had an extensive knowledge. She wrote much, and always in French. Her letters had the character and almost the grace of those of Madame de Sévigné, and some of them might have been mistaken for hers. My chief employment, one that I did not dislike, was to write them from her dictation; since a cancer in the stomach, from which she suffered greatly, made it impossible for her to write them herself.

Madame de Vercellis was not only a woman of great talent, but possessed a strong and lofty soul. I was with her during her last illness. I saw her suffer and die without showing signs of weakness, even for a moment, without making the least effort to control herself, without doing anything unwomanly, without suspecting that her conduct was an example of philosophy, a word which was not as yet fashionable, and with which she was not even acquainted in the sense which it bears to-day.[1] This force of character sometimes even became coldness. She always appeared to me as little without feeling for others as for herself; and, when she did a kindness to anyone who was unfortunate, she did it rather from a desire to do what was good in itself, than from genuine feelings of pity. During the three months which I spent with her, I experienced to some extent this want of feeling. It would have been natural that she should conceive a regard for a young man of some promise, whom she had continually in her sight, and that, feeling that her end was near, she should reflect that he would afterwards stand in need of assistance and support; however, whether it was that she did not consider me worthy of special attention, or that those who besieged her did not allow her to think of anyone but themselves – she did nothing for me.

I remember very well, however, that she displayed some curiosity to know my story. She sometimes asked me questions; she liked me to show her the letters I wrote to Madame de Warens, and to give her an account of my feelings; but she certainly did not go the right way to become acquainted with them, as she never disclosed her own to me. My heart loved to unbosom itself, provided it felt that it was doing so to another heart. Cold and dry questions, without any sign of approval or blame at my answers, gave me no confidence. When there was nothing to show me whether my chatter pleased or displeased, I was always in a state of alarm, and I endeavoured, not so much

---

[1] The term *philosophie* acquired a special sense in the mid-eighteenth century in France, as signifying the outlook of the freethinking critics of church and state, such as Diderot, d'Alembert and d'Holbach.

to show what I thought as to say nothing which might do me harm. I have since observed that this dry manner of questioning people in order to find out their character, is a frequent trick with women who wish to be thought clever. They imagine that, by concealing their own feelings, they will be more likely to succeed in finding out your own; but they fail to see that, in so doing, they are depriving you of the courage to exhibit them. A man who is questioned, for that reason alone begins to put himself on his guard, and, if he believes that his questioner, without feeling any genuine interest in him, merely wants to make him talk, he either lies, holds his tongue, or redoubles his watchfulness, preferring to be thought a fool than to be the dupe of curiosity. In short, when a man desires to read the hearts of others, it is always a bad plan to make a show of concealing his own.

Madame de Vercellis never said a word to me expressive of affection, pity, or goodwill. She asked me questions with coldness; I replied with reserve. My answers were so timid that she must have found them commonplace and tedious. At length she gave up questioning me, and never spoke to me except to give me an order. She judged me less according to what I was than according to what she had made me; and, as she never saw anything in me but a lackey, she prevented me from appearing anything else.

I believe that from that time I suffered from the malicious sport of secret intrigue which has ever since thwarted me, and which has inspired me with a very natural aversion for the apparent order of things which produces it. The heir of Madame de Vercellis, who was childless, was her nephew, the Comte de la Roque, who assiduously paid court to her. Besides, her chief servants, who saw that her end was near, did not neglect their own interests; and there were so many devoted attendants round her, that it would have been difficult for her to give a thought to myself. At the head of the establishment was a certain M. Lorenzi, a clever man, whose still more clever wife had so insinuated herself into her mistress's good graces, that she stood rather on the footing of a friend than of a paid servant. She had bestowed the post of lady's-maid upon her own niece,

Mademoiselle Pontal, a sly creature, who gave herself the airs of a maid of honour, and so successfully helped her aunt to get round her mistress, that she only saw through their eyes and only acted through their hands. I had not the good fortune to please these three persons; I obeyed them, but I did not serve them; I did not consider that, besides serving our common mistress, I was obliged to be a servant to her servants. Besides, I was the kind of person who caused them uneasiness. They saw clearly that I was not in my place; they were afraid that Madame saw it as well, and that what she might do to put me in my proper position, might diminish their share of her money; for people of this class, too greedy to be just, look upon every legacy left to others as stolen from their own property. They accordingly conspired to remove me from her sight. She was fond of writing letters; it was an amusement for her in her state of health; they inspired her with disgust for it, and dissuaded her from continuing it by the advice of her physician, while persuading her that it was too tiring for her. On the pretence that I did not understand my duty, two loutish sedan-chair carriers were employed in my place; in short, they managed so cleverly that, when she made her will, I was not allowed to enter her room for eight days. It is true that I subsequently went in as before, and I showed her even more attention than anyone else; for the sufferings the poor woman endured tore my heart; the firmness with which she bore them inspired me with extreme reverence and affection for her, and I often shed tears of genuine sorrow in my room, unperceived by her or anyone else.

At length we lost her. I saw her die. Her life had been the life of a woman of talent and intelligence; her death was that of a philosopher. I can say that she inspired me with a feeling of esteem for the Catholic religion, by the cheerfulness of soul with which she fulfilled its instructions, without carelessness and without affectation. She was naturally of a serious disposition. Towards the end of her illness, she assumed a sort of gaiety, which was too regular to be unreal, and which was only a counterpoise to her melancholy condition and was the gift of reason. She only kept her bed the two last days, and continued to converse quietly with everybody to the end. At last, speaking no more, and already in the agonies of death, she broke wind loudly. "Good!" she said, turning round, "a woman who can fart is not dead!" These were the last words she uttered.

She left a year's wages to her underservants. I received nothing, not having been entered on the list of her establishment. However, the Comte de la Roque ordered thirty *livres* to be given me, and left me the new suit which I was wearing, and which M. Lorenzi wanted to take from me. He even promised to try and find a place for me, and gave me leave to go and see him. I went there two or three times without being able to speak to him. Being easily rebuffed, I did not go again. It will soon be seen that I was wrong. Would that I had finished all that I had to say about my stay at Madame de Vercellis's! But, although my condition apparently remained the same, I did not leave the house as I entered it. I carried away from it lasting recollections of crime and the insupportable weight of remorse, which, after forty years, still lies heavy on my conscience; while the bitterness of it, far from growing weaker, makes itself more strongly felt with my advancing years. Who would believe that a childish fault could have such cruel consequences? For these more than probable consequences my heart is inconsolable. I have, perhaps, caused the ruin of an amiable, honest, and estimable girl, who certainly was far more worthy than myself, and doomed her to disgrace and misery.

It is almost unavoidable that the break up of an establishment should cause some confusion in the house, and that several things should get lost; however, the servants were so honest, and the Lorenzis so watchful, that nothing was missing when the inventory was taken. Only Mademoiselle Pontal had lost a piece of old red and silver-coloured ribbon. Many other things of greater value were at my disposal; this ribbon alone tempted me; I stole it, and, as I took no trouble to conceal it, it was soon found. They wanted to know how it had come into my possession. I became confused, stammered, blushed, and at last said that Marion had given it to me. Marion was a young girl from Maurienne, whom Madame de Vercellis had taken for her cook, when she left off giving dinners and discharged her own, as she had more need of good soup than of fine stews. Marion was not only pretty but had a fresh colour, only found on the mountains, and, above all, there was something about her so gentle and modest, that it was impossible for anyone to see her without loving her; in addition to that, she was a good and virtuous girl, and of unquestionable honesty. All were surprised when I mentioned her name. We were both equally trusted and it was considered important to find out which of us two was really the thief. She was sent for; a number of people were assembled, amongst them the Comte de la Roque. When she came, the ribbon was shown to her. I boldly accused her; she was astounded, and unable to utter a word; looked at me in a manner that would have disarmed the Devil himself, but against which my barbarous heart was proof. At last, she denied the theft firmly, but without anger, addressed herself to me, exhorted me to reflect, and not to disgrace an innocent girl who had never done me any harm; but I, with infernal impudence, persisted in my story, and declared to her face that she had given me the ribbon. The poor girl began to cry, and only said to me: "Ah! Rousseau, I thought you were a good man. You make me very unhappy, but I should not like to be in your place." That was all. She proceeded to defend herself with equal simplicity and firmness, but without allowing herself to utter the slightest reproach against me. This moderation, contrasted with my decided tone, did her harm. It did not seem natural to suppose, on the one side, such devilish impudence, and, on the other, such angelic mildness. Although the matter did not appear to be absolutely settled, they were prepossessed in my favour. In the confusion which prevailed, they did not give themselves time to get to the bottom of the affair; and the Comte de la Roque, in dismissing us both, contented himself with saying that the conscience of the guilty one would amply avenge the innocent. His prediction has been fulfilled; it fulfils itself everyday.

I do not know what became of the victim of my false accusation; but it is not likely that she afterwards found it easy to get a good situation. She carried away with her an imputation upon her honesty which was in every way cruel. The theft was only a trifling one, but still it was a theft, and, what is worse, made use of to lead a young man astray; lastly, lying and obstinacy left

nothing to be hoped from one in whom so many vices were
united. I do not even consider misery and desertion as the
greatest danger to which I exposed her. At her age, who
knows to what extremes discouragement and the feeling of ill-
used innocence may have carried her? Oh, if my remorse at
having, perhaps, made her unhappy is unendurable, one may
judge what I feel at the thought of having, perhaps, made her
worse than myself!

This cruel remembrance at times so sorely troubles and
upsets me, that in my sleepless hours I seem to see the poor
girl coming to reproach me for my crime, as if it had been
committed only yesterday. As long as I have lived quietly, it
has tormented me less; but in the midst of a stormy life it robs
me of the sweet consolation of persecuted innocence, it makes
me feel what I think I have said in one of my books, that
"Remorse goes to sleep when our fortunes are prosperous,
and makes itself felt more keenly in adversity." However, I
have never been able to bring myself to unburden my heart of
this confession to a friend. The closest intimacy has never led me
so far with anyone, not even with Madame de Warens. All that I
have been able to do has been to confess that I had to reproach
myself with an atrocious act, but I have never stated wherein it
consisted. This burden has remained to this day upon my conscience without alleviation; and I can affirm that the desire of
freeing myself from it in some degree, has greatly contributed to
the resolution I have taken of writing my Confessions.

I have behaved straightforwardly in the confession which I
have just made, and it will assuredly be found that I have not
attempted to palliate the blackness of my offence. But I should
not fulfil the object of this book, if I did not at the same time set
forth my inner feelings, and hesitated to excuse myself by what is
strictly true. Wicked intent was never further from me than at
that cruel moment; and when I accused the unhappy girl, it is
singular, but it is true, that my friendship for her was the cause of
it. She was present to my thoughts; I threw the blame on the first
object which presented itself. I accused her of having done what
I meant to do, and of having given me the ribbon, because my
intention was to give it to her. When I afterwards saw her

appear, my heart was torn; but the presence of so many people was stronger than repentance. I was not afraid of punishment, I was only afraid of disgrace; and that I feared more than death, more than crime, more than anything else in the world. I should have rejoiced if the earth had suddenly opened, swallowed me up and suffocated me; the unconquerable fear of shame overcame everything, and alone made me impudent. The greater my crime, the more the dread of confessing it made me fearless. I saw nothing but the horror of being recognised and publicly declared, in my own presence, a thief, liar, and slanderer. Complete embarrassment deprived me of every other feeling. If I had been allowed to recover myself I should have assuredly confessed everything. If M. de la Roque had taken me aside and said to me: "Do not ruin this poor girl; if you are guilty, confess it to me," I should have immediately thrown myself at his feet, of that I am perfectly certain. But, when I needed encouragement, they only intimidated me. And yet it is only fair to consider my age. I was little more than a child, or rather, I still was one. In youth real crimes are even more criminal than in riper years; but that which is only weakness is less so, and my offence was at bottom scarcely anything else. Thus the recollection of it afflicts me not so much by reason of the evil in itself as on account of its evil consequences. It has even done me the good of securing me for the rest of my life against every act tending to crime, by the terrible impression which I have retained of the only offence that I have ever committed; and I believe that my horror of a lie is due in great measure to my regret at having been capable myself of telling one so shameful. If it is a crime that can be expiated, as I venture to believe, it must be expiated by all the unhappiness which has overwhelmed the last years of my life, by forty years of honourable and upright conduct in difficult circumstances; and poor Marion finds so many avengers in this world, that, however great my offence against her may have been, I have little fear of dying without absolution. This is what I have to say on this matter: permit me never to speak of it again.

BOOK III

HAVING left Madame de Vercellis's house in almost the same state as I had entered it, I went back to my old landlady, with whom I remained for five or six weeks, during which health, youth, and idleness again rendered my temperament troublesome. I was restless, absent-minded, a dreamer. I wept, I sighed, I longed for a happiness of which I had no idea, and of which I nevertheless felt the want. This state cannot be described; only few men can even imagine it, because most of them have anticipated this fulness of life, at once so tormenting and so delicious, which, in the intoxication of desire, gives a foretaste of enjoyment. My heated blood incessantly filled my brain with girls and women; but, ignorant of the relations of sex, I made use of them in my imagination in accordance with my distorted notions, without knowing what else to do with them; and these notions kept my feelings in a state of most uncomfortable activity, from which, fortunately, they did not teach me how to deliver myself. I would have given my life to have found another Mademoiselle Goton for a quarter of an hour. But it was no longer the time when childish amusements took this direction as if naturally. Shame, the companion of a bad conscience, had made its appearance with advancing years; it had increased my natural shyness to such an extent that it made it unconquerable; and never, neither then nor later, have I been able to bring myself to make an indecent proposal, unless she, to whom I made it, in some measure forced me to it by her advances, even though I knew that she was by no means scrupulous, and felt almost certain of being taken at my word.

My agitation became so strong that, being unable to satisfy my desires, I excited them by the most extravagant behaviour. I haunted dark alleys and hidden retreats, where I might be able to expose myself to women in the condition in which I should have liked to have been in their company. What they saw was not an obscene object, I never even thought of such a thing; it was a ridiculous object. The foolish pleasure I took in displaying it before their eyes cannot be described. There was only one step further necessary for me to take, in order to gain actual experience of the treatment I desired, and I have no doubt that someone would have been bold enough to afford me the amusement, while passing by, if I had had the boldness to wait. This folly of mine led to a disaster almost as comical, but less agreeable for myself.

One day, I took up my position at the bottom of a court where there was a well, from which the girls of the house were in the habit of fetching water. At this spot there was a slight descent which led to some cellars by several entrances. In the dark I examined these underground passages, and finding them long and dark, I concluded that there was no outlet, and that, if I happened to be seen and surprised, I should find a safe hiding-place in them. Thus emboldened, I exhibited to the girls who came to the well a sight more laughable than seductive. The more modest pretended to see nothing; others began to laugh; others felt insulted and made a noise. I ran into my retreat; someone followed me. I heard a man's voice, which I had not expected, and which alarmed me. I plunged underground at the risk of losing myself; the noise, the voices, the man's voice, still followed me. I had always reckoned upon the darkness; I saw a light. I shuddered, and plunged further into the darkness. A wall stopped me, and, being unable to go any further, I was obliged to await my fate. In a moment I was seized by a tall man with a big moustache, a big hat, and a big sword, who was escorted by four or five old women, each armed with a broom-handle, amongst whom I perceived the little wretch who had discovered me, and who, no doubt, wanted to see me face to face.

The man with the sword, seizing me by the arm, asked me roughly what I was doing there. It may be imagined that I had no answer ready. However, I recovered myself; and, in desperation, at this critical moment I invented a romantic excuse which proved successful. I begged him in a suppliant voice to have pity upon my age and condition; I said that I was a young stranger of good birth, whose brain was affected; that I had run away from home, because they wanted to shut me up; that I was lost if he betrayed me; but that, if he would let me go, I might some day be able to reward him for his kindness. Contrary to all expectation, my words and demeanour took effect; the terrible man was touched by them, and, after administering a short reproof, he let me go quietly without questioning me further. From the demeanour of the girl and the old women, when they saw me go, I judged that the man whom I feared so much had been of great service to me, and that I should not have got off so easily with them alone. I heard them murmur something or other to which I hardly paid attention; for, provided that the man and his sword did not interfere, I felt confident, active and vigorous as I was, of escaping from them and their cudgels.

A few days afterwards, while walking down a street with a young Abbé, my neighbour, I nearly ran into the man with the sword. He recognised me, and, imitating me mockingly, said: "I am a prince, I am a prince, and I am a coward; but don't let his highness come back again!" He said no more, and I sneaked away, not venturing to look up, and thanking him in my heart for his discretion. I judged that the confounded old women had made him ashamed of his credulity. Anyhow, Piedmontese as he was, he was a good man, and I never think of him without a feeling of gratitude; for the story was so funny that, merely from the desire of creating a laugh, anyone else in his place would have shamed me. This adventure, without having the consequences which I dreaded, nevertheless made me careful for a long time.

My stay with Madame de Vercellis had gained me some acquaintances, whom I cultivated in the hope that they might prove useful to me. Amongst others, I sometimes went to visit a Savoyard Abbé, named M. Gaime,[1] tutor to the children of the Comte de Mellarède. He was still young and went little into society, but was full of good sense, honour and intelligence, and one of the most honourable men that I have known. He was not the least use to me for the object which took me to him; he had not sufficient interest to get me a situation; but I gained from him still more precious advantages, which have been of use to me all my life, lessons of healthy morality and principles of

[1] [Gaime] See *Biographies*, p. 711.

sound reason. In my alternating tastes and ideas, I had always been too high or too low – Achilles or Thersites: now a hero, now a good-for-nothing. M. Gaime undertook to put me in my place, and to show me to myself in my true colours, without sparing or discouraging me. He spoke to me with due recognition of my natural talents, but added that he saw obstacles arising from them which would prevent me from making the best use of them; so that, in his opinion, they would be less useful to me as steps to fortune than as a means to enable me to do without it. He put before me a true picture of human life, of which I had only false ideas; he showed me how, in the midst of contrary fortune, the wise man can always strive after happiness and sail against the wind in order to reach it; that there is no true happiness without prudence, and that prudence belongs to all conditions of life. He damped my admiration for external grandeur, by proving that those who ruled others were neither happier nor wiser than the ruled. He told me one thing, which I have often remembered since then – that, if every man could read the hearts of all other men, there would be found more people willing to descend than to rise in life. This reflection, the truth of which is striking, and in which there is no exaggeration, has been of great service to me during the course of my life, by helping to make me quietly content with my position. He gave me the first true ideas of what was honourable, which my inflated genius had only grasped in its exaggerated forms. He made me feel that the enthusiasm of lofty virtues was rarely shown in society; that, in trying to climb too high, one was in danger of falling; that a continued round of trifling duties, always well performed, required no less effort than heroic actions; that from them a man gained more in the matter of honour and happiness; and that it was infinitely better to enjoy the esteem of one's fellow men at all times, than their admiration occasionally.

In order to define the duties of man, it was necessary to go back to their principles. Besides, the step which I had just taken, and of which my present condition was the result, led us to speak of religion. It will be already imagined that the honourable M. Gaime is, in great part at least, the original of the "Savoyard Vicar." Only, as prudence constrained him to speak with more reserve, he expressed himself less openly upon certain points; but, for the rest, his maxims, his sentiments, his opinions were the same, and, his advice to return home not excepted, everything was just as I have since publicly represented it. Therefore, without enlarging further upon the conversations, the substance of which is accessible to everyone, I will only say that his lessons, the wisdom of which was at first without effect, became in my heart a germ of virtue and religion which was never choked, and which only needed the care of a dearer hand in order to bear fruit.

Although, at the time, my conversion was by no means thorough, I nevertheless felt moved. Far from feeling tired of his conversations, I was attracted to them by their clearness and simplicity, and, above all, by a certain warmth of heart, by which I felt they were pervaded. I have a loving disposition, and have always attached myself to people less in proportion to the good they have done me than the good they have wished to do me; and in regard to the latter, my judgment rarely deceives me. I was also genuinely attached to M. Gaime; I was, so to speak, his second pupil, and for the moment this had for me the inestimable advantage of turning me aside from the inclination to vice, towards which my want of occupation drew me.

One day, when I least expected it, I was sent for by the Comte de la Roque. The frequent visits I had made without being able to speak to him had tired me, and I gave up going to his house; I thought that he had forgotten me, or that he had retained a bad impression of me. I was mistaken. He had more than once witnessed the pleasure with which I fulfilled my duties to his aunt. He had even spoken of it to her, and spoke of it again to me, when I had forgotten it myself. He received me kindly, told me that, instead of putting me off with idle promises, he had tried to find a place for me; that he had been successful; that he was going to put me in the way of becoming something, that it was for me to do the rest; that the house to which he had procured me admission was influential and respected; that I needed no other patrons to help me on; and that, although treated at first as a simple servant, as I had lately been, I might rest assured that they would be quite ready not to leave me in that position if my disposition and behaviour gave them reason to think that I was fit for something better. The end of the conversation cruelly belied the brilliant hopes with which the commencement had inspired me. "What! always a lackey!" I said to myself, with a feeling of bitter annoyance which confidence soon effaced. I felt too little adapted for such a position to fear that I should be left in it.

He took me to the Comte de Gouvon,[1] chief equerry to the Queen, and head of the illustrious house of Solar. The dignified air of this venerable old man made the kindness of his reception more touching. He questioned me with interest, and I answered him with sincerity. He told the Comte de la Roque that I had pleasant features, which gave promise of intelligence; that it appeared to him that in fact I was not wanting in it, but that that was not everything, and that it was necessary to see what I was in other respects. Then, turning to me, he said: "My child, in almost everything the beginning is difficult; in your case, however, it will not be so to any great extent. Be prudent, and endeavour to please everyone here; for the present, that is all you have to do; for the rest, be of good courage; you will be taken care of." Immediately afterwards, he went over to the Marquise de Breil, his step-daughter, to whom he presented me, and then to the Abbé de Gouvon, his son. This beginning seemed to promise well. I was already experienced enough to know that lackeys were not received with so much ceremony. In fact, I was not treated like one. I took my meals at the steward's table, and wore no livery; and when the Comte de Favria, an empty-headed young fool, wanted me to get up behind his carriage, his grandfather forbade my riding behind anyone's carriage, or attending upon anyone outside the house. However, I waited at table, and, in the house, performed almost the duties of a lackey; but I performed them to a certain extent voluntarily, without being especially attached to anyone. With the exception of writing a few letters from dictation, and cutting out a few

---

[1] Gouvon (or Govone), Ottavio Francesco Solaro, Comte de (1648–) minister and ambassador at the court of Sardinia.

figures for the Comte de Favria, I was master of my time for almost the whole of the day. This test, which I did not perceive, was in truth very dangerous; it was not even very kind, for this long idleness might have led me to vices which I should not otherwise have contracted.

But, happily, this did not occur. M. Gaime's lessons had made an impression upon my heart, and I conceived such a liking for them that I sometimes stole out to go and listen to them again. I believe that those who saw me leave the house secretly had not the least suspicion where I was going. Nothing could have been more sensible than the advice which he gave me concerning my behaviour. I commenced admirably; I displayed assiduity, attention, and eagerness which charmed everybody. The Abbé prudently advised me to moderate my youthful zeal, for fear that it might gradually relax and that this might be noticed. "As you begin," said he, "so will you be expected to behave as a rule; try to manage to do even more as time goes on, but beware of ever doing less."

As no one had taken much trouble to find out my poor talents, and as I was only credited with those which Nature had bestowed upon me, it did not appear to me, in spite of what M. Gouvon had told me, that anyone thought of making any use of me. Other things came in the way, and I was almost forgotten. The Marquis de Breil, the Comte de Gouvon's son, was at the time ambassador at Vienna. Events happened at court which made themselves felt in the family, and for some weeks everyone was in a state of excitement which left little time to think of me. However, up to that time I had relaxed little of my zeal. One thing did me both good and harm; good, by keeping me away from any outside distractions; harm, by making me a little less attentive to my duties.

Mademoiselle de Breil was a young lady of nearly my own age, well formed, tolerably good-looking, fresh-complexioned, with very dark hair, and, although a brunette, she had that expression of gentleness which is peculiar to fair women, and which my heart has never been able to resist. Her court dress, so becoming to young people, showed her beautiful figure to advantage, left her breast and shoulders free, and made her complexion still more dazzling by reason of the mourning[1] which was worn at the time. It will be said that a servant has no business to notice such things; I was wrong, no doubt; but I noticed them all the same, and I was not the only one who did so. The *maître d'hôtel* and the *valets de chambre* sometimes spoke of them at table with a coarseness which made me suffer cruelly. My head was not, however, so turned that I fell in love without more ado. I did not forget myself; I kept myself in my place, and even my desires were not allowed too much freedom. I liked to see Mademoiselle de Breil, to hear her say a few words which showed her intelligence, good sense and modesty; my ambition, limited to the pleasure of serving her, never went beyond my rights. At table I was always on the look out to assert them. If her footman left her chair for a moment, I was behind it immediately; otherwise I stood opposite to her; I looked in her eyes to see what she was going to ask for, and watched for the moment to change her plate. What would I not have done if she would only have deigned to give me some order, to look at me, to address a single word to me! but no! I had the mortification of being nothing to her; she did not even notice that I was there. However, on one occasion, when her brother, who sometimes spoke to me at table, addressed a somewhat uncivil remark to me, I gave him an answer, so neat and so well expressed, that she noticed it and turned her eyes upon me. This glance, rapid as it was, nevertheless enchanted me. The next day, the opportunity of winning a second glance presented itself, and I took advantage of it. A big dinner was given on that occasion, at which for the first time I saw the *maître d'hôtel*, to my great astonishment, waiting with his hat on his head and a sword at his side. By chance the conversation turned upon the motto of the house of Solar, which was embroidered under the coat-of-arms, *Tel fiert qui ne tue pas*. As the Piedmontese are not, as a rule, masters of the French language, someone detected in this motto a mistake in spelling, and declared that there should be no *t* in the word *fiert*.

---

[1] The court was in mourning for the Queen of Sardinia, Anne d'Orléans, niece of Louis XIV. The "events" were perhaps concerned with the King's intention to re-marry.

The old Comte de Gouvon was just going to answer, but, happening to look at me, saw that I was smiling without venturing to say anything, and ordered me to speak. I thereupon said that I did not believe that the *t* was unnecessary; that *fiert* was an old French word, not derived from *ferus*, proud, threatening, but from *ferit*, he strikes, he wounds; so that the meaning of the motto appeared to me to be, not, Many a man threatens, but, Many a man strikes and does not kill.

All the company looked first at me and then at themselves without saying a word. I had never seen such astonishment in my life. But what flattered me more was to see from Mademoiselle de Breil's face that she was evidently much pleased. This disdainful young lady condescended to cast a second glance at me, which, at least, was equal to the first; then, turning her eyes towards her grandfather, she appeared to be waiting with a sort of impatience for the compliment which was my due, and which he, in fact, paid me so fully and completely, and with the appearance of such satisfaction, that the whole table hastened to join in the chorus. The moment was brief, but in every respect delicious. It was one of those moments, only too rare, which replace things in their natural order, and avenge depreciated merit for the insults of fortune. A few minutes afterwards, Mademoiselle de Breil, lifting her eyes to me again, asked me, in a timid and affable voice, to give her something to drink. I need not say that I did not keep her waiting; but, as I came near to her, I trembled so violently that, having filled the glass too full, I spilt some of the water over her plate, and even over herself. Her brother asked me thoughtlessly why I was trembling so? This question did not serve to reassure me, and Mademoiselle de Breil blushed up to the whites of her eyes.

Here ended the romance, in which it will be observed, as in the case of Madame Basile and during all the rest of my life, that I am not happy in the conclusion of my amours. In vain I paid special attention to Madame de Breil's ante-room; I did not obtain another mark of attention from her daughter. She went in and out without looking at me, and, as for myself, I hardly ventured to cast eyes upon her. I was even so stupid and awkward that, one day, when she dropped her glove while passing, instead of darting upon this glove which I should have liked to cover with kisses, I did not dare to leave my place; and I allowed it to be picked up by a great lout of a valet, whom I would gladly have throttled. To complete my nervousness, I perceived that I had not the good fortune to please Madame de Breil. She not only gave me no orders, but never accepted my services; and on two occasions, finding me in her ante-room, she asked me coldly if I had not something to do. I was obliged to renounce this dear ante-room; at first I regretted it, but distractions intervened, and soon I thought no more of it.

The kindness of her step-father, who at last perceived that I was there, consoled me for the coldness of Madame de Breil. During the evening after the dinner of which I have spoken, he held a conversation with me for half-an-hour, with which he appeared satisfied, and I was delighted. This good old man, although less gifted than Madame de Vercellis, had more heart, and I got on better with him. He told me to attach myself to the Abbé de Gouvon, who had conceived a regard for me; that this regard, if I made good use of it, might be useful to me, and assist me in acquiring what I still lacked, in order to promote what they had in view for me. Next morning, I hastened to the Abbé. He did not receive me as a servant, but made me sit down by the side of the fire, and, questioning me with the greatest gentleness, soon discovered that my education, which had been commenced in so many things, was complete in none. Finding, especially, that I knew very little Latin, he undertook to teach me more. It was arranged that I should go to him every morning, and I commenced the following day. Thus, by one of those curious coincidences, which will often be found in the course of my life, I was at once above and below my station – I was pupil and valet in the same house; and, while still a servant, I had a tutor of such noble birth that he ought to have been the tutor of none but kings' sons.

The Abbé de Gouvon was a younger son, destined by his family for a bishopric; and for this reason his studies had been pushed on more than is usual in the case of children of rank. He had been sent to the University of Sienna, where he remained several years, and from which he had brought back a tolerably strong dose of *cruscantism*,[1] so that he was almost the same at Turin as the Abbé de Dangeau[2] had formerly been at Paris. Distaste for theology had driven him to *belles-lettres* – a very common thing in Italy in the case of those who are training for the rank of a prelate. He had read the poets attentively, and wrote tolerable Latin and Italian verses. In a word, he had sufficient taste to form my own, and to introduce some order into the confused mass with which my head was stuffed. But, whether it was that my chatter had given him a false idea of my knowledge, or that he could not endure the tedium of the elements of Latin, he put me far too high to begin with; and, no sooner had he made me translate a few fables of Phaedrus, than he plunged me into Virgil, of which I scarcely understood anything. It was my fate, as will be afterwards seen, often to begin Latin afresh and never to learn it. However, I worked zealously enough, and the Abbé lavished his attention upon me with a kindness of which I cannot think, even now, without emotion. I spent a good part of the morning with him, both for my own instruction and for his service – not personal service, for that he never allowed me to perform, but to write from his dictation and to do copying; and my duties as secretary were more useful to me than my studies as pupil. In this manner I not only learnt Italian in its purity, but I imbibed a taste for literature, and acquired some knowledge of good books which had been impossible at La Tribu's, and which proved very serviceable to me afterwards when I began to work by myself.

This was the period of my life when, without romantic projects, I might most reasonably have hoped for success. The Abbé, who was well satisfied with me, told everybody; and his father had conceived so special a regard for me that the Comte de Favria told me that he had spoken of me to the King. Even

---

[1] *Cruscantism* is here synonymous with *purism*. The word *cruscante*, in Italian, denotes a man who affects to use only words authorised by the *Accademia della Crusca* of Florence.

[2] The Abbé de Dangeau was a member of the *Académie française* in the middle of the previous century, and was the author of grammatical treatises on the French language.

Madame de Breil had laid aside her contemptuous demeanour towards me. In short, I became a sort of favourite in the house, to the great jealousy of the other servants, who, seeing me honoured by receiving instruction from their master's son, well understood that I was not long intended to remain one of themselves.

As far as I was able to judge of the views entertained for me from a few words hastily dropped, upon which I only reflected later, it seems to me that the house of Solar, eager for ambassadorial, and possibly, in the future, ministerial offices, would have been very glad to educate in advance a trustworthy and talented person, who being entirely dependent upon it, might have been received into its confidence and have served it faithfully. This project of the Comte de Gouvon was noble, judicious, generous, and truly worthy of a great nobleman, beneficent and far-seeing; but, not to mention that, at the time, I did not see its entire range, it was too sensible for me to understand, and required too long a period of submission. My foolish ambition only looked for good fortune in the midst of adventures; and, as no woman had anything to do with it, this means of succeeding seemed to me slow, wearisome, and dull; whereas I ought to have considered it safer and more honourable, for the very reason that no women were mixed up in it, seeing that the kind of merit which they take under their protection was assuredly not so honourable as that which I was supposed to possess.

Everything was going on admirably. I had gained, almost taken by storm, the respect of all; the time of probation was over, and in the house I was looked upon generally as a young man of great promise who was not in his proper place, but whom everyone expected to see promoted to it. But my place was not that which was generally assigned to me, and I was destined to reach it by a very different road. I now come to one of those characteristic traits which are peculiar to me, and which I need only put before the reader without further discussion.

Although there were several new converts like myself at Turin, I was not fond of them and had never wished to see any of them. But I had made the acquaintance of some Genevese who did not belong to them, amongst others, a

M. Mussard, surnamed *Tordgueule*, a miniature-painter and a sort
of connection of mine. He found out that I was staying with the
Comte de Gouvon and came to see me with another Genevese,
named Bâcle, whose companion I had been during my apprenticeship. This Bâcle was a very amusing fellow, very lively, and
full of witty sallies which his age rendered agreeable. Behold me,
then, suddenly infatuated with M. Bâcle to such a degree that
I was unable to leave him! He intended soon to set out on his
return to Geneva. What a loss for me! I realised its full extent. In
order, at least, to make the best use of the time that remained to
me, I never left his side, or rather, he never left me, for I did not
at first lose my head so entirely as to spend the day with him
outside the hotel without leave; but soon, seeing that he occupied my time entirely, they forbade him the house, and I became
so enraged that, forgetting everything except my friend Bâcle, I
never went near the Abbé or the Count, and was never seen in
the house. I paid no heed to reprimands. I was threatened with
dismissal, and this proved my ruin; it showed me that it was
possible not to let Bâcle go unaccompanied. From this moment
I saw no other pleasure, no other destiny, no other happiness,
than that of making a similar journey, and I saw nothing but the
unspeakable bliss of the journey, at the end of which, as a further
happiness, I perceived Madame de Warens, but in the remote
distance; for I never had the least idea of returning to Geneva.
Mountains, meadows, woods, brooks, villages, passed in never-
ending succession before me with fresh charms; this happy
journey appeared to absorb my whole life. I recalled with delight
how charming this same journey had seemed to me on my way
to Turin. What would it be like when, in addition to all the charm
of independence, I should enjoy the further delight of the
companionship of a friend of my own age and tastes, and of
cheerful temper, without restraint, without duties, without
check, without being obliged to go or remain anywhere unless
it pleased us! I thought that a man must be a fool to sacrifice
such good fortune to ambitious plans, slow, difficult, and uncertain of fulfilment, which, even supposing them to be some day
realised, in spite of all their brilliancy, were not worth a quarter
of an hour of real pleasure and youthful freedom.

Full of this wise idea, I behaved in such a manner that I succeeded in getting myself dismissed, although, in truth, not without considerable difficulty. One evening, on my return to the house, the *maître d'hôtel* gave me my dismissal from the Count. This was exactly what I wanted; for, well aware, in spite of myself, of the extravagance of my conduct, in order to excuse myself, I added to it injustice and ingratitude, thinking that, in this manner, I should be able to lay the blame upon others, and justify myself, as if I had been obliged to take measures for which I had been solely responsible. The Comte de Favria sent a message that I was to go and speak to him before I left on the following morning; and, as they saw that I had completely lost my head and was quite capable of doing nothing of the kind, the *maître d'hôtel* informed me that, after I had done so, he would give me a sum of money which was intended for me, and which I certainly did not deserve; for, as it had not been intended that I should remain in the position of a valet, no wages had been fixed for me.

The Comte de Favria, young and thoughtless as he was, on this occasion spoke to me most sensibly – I might almost say, most tenderly – so earnestly and in such a flattering and touching manner did he put before me his uncle's sympathy and his grandfather's intentions in regard to me. At last, after having represented to me, as strongly as he was able, all the advantages I was sacrificing in order to rush to my own destruction, he offered to make peace for me, on the sole condition that I would give up the little wretch who had led me astray. It was so evident that he did not say all this on his own responsibility, that, in spite of my foolish blindness, I was sensible of all the kindness of my old master and felt touched by it; but my beloved journey was too deeply impressed upon my imagination for anything to be able to outweigh its attractions. I was quite out of my mind; I grew callous and hardened, stood on my dignity and answered haughtily that, as I had received my dismissal, I had accepted it; that there was no time now to recall it; and that, whatever might happen to me during my life, I was determined not to allow myself to be dismissed twice from the same house. Then the young man, justly irritated, called me the names I deserved, took me by the shoulders and put me out of his room, and shut the door behind me. I went out in triumph, as if I had just gained a brilliant victory; and, for fear of being obliged to endure a second struggle, I was base enough to depart without thanking the Abbé for his kindness.

To form an idea of the lengths to which my madness carried me at this moment, one ought to know to what a degree my heart is liable to become heated about the smallest trifles, and how violently it plunges into the idea of the object which attracts it, however idle and worthless this object may be. The oddest, the most childish, the most foolish plans flatter and support my favourite idea, in order to convince me of the reasonableness of devoting myself to it. Would it be believed that anyone, almost nineteen years of age, could place his hopes of support for the rest of his life on an empty bottle? Then listen.

The Abbé de Gouvon, some weeks before, had made me a present of a pretty little heron-fountain,[1] with which I was delighted. As we were constantly playing with this artificial fountain, while talking about our journey, the wise Bâcle and myself thought that the one might prove very serviceable in lengthening the other. What could there be more curious in the world than a heron-fountain? This axiom was the foundation upon which we built the edifice of our future fortune. We need only assemble the peasants of each village round our fountain, and food and all kinds of good cheer would be showered upon us in so much greater abundance, as we were both convinced that provisions cost nothing to those who procure them, and that, if they do not stuff passers-by with them, it is pure ill-will on their part. Everywhere we expected weddings and festivities, reckoning that, without further expenditure than the breath of our lungs and the water of our fountain, it would pay our way through Piedmont, Savoy, France – in fact, all over the world. We made endless plans for our journey, and first took our way

[1] The "fountain" was invented by the Greek mathematician Heron of Alexandria (B.C. 285–222). It consisted of two sealed chambers connected by a tube. The upper chamber was filled with wine, and when water was poured into the lower one, air-pressure caused wine to spurt out, giving the impression that water was being turned into wine.

northwards, more for the pleasure of crossing the Alps than with the idea that we should be obliged to stop anywhere at last.

[1731–1732.] – Such was the plan with which I set out, abandoning without regret my protector, my tutor, my studies, my hopes and the expectation of a fortune almost assured, to begin the life of a regular vagabond. I said good-bye to the capital, to the court, to ambition, vanity, love, pretty women, and all the exciting adventures, the hope of which had brought me there the year before. I set out with my fountain and my friend Bâcle, with a light purse but a heart filled with joy, thinking of nothing but the enjoyment of this roving happiness to which I had suddenly limited my brilliant projects.

I made this extravagant journey quite as agreeably as I had expected, but not exactly in the same way; for, although our fountain amused the landladies and their servants for a few moments at the inns, we had to pay just the same when we went out. But this troubled us little, and we only thought of seriously utilising this resource when our money failed us. An accident spared us the trouble; the fountain broke when we were near Bramant; and, indeed, it was time, for we felt, without venturing to admit it, that we were beginning to get tired of it. This misfortune made us more cheerful than before, and we laughed greatly at our folly in forgetting that our clothes and boots would wear out, and in believing that we should be able to get new ones by making our fountain play. We continued our journey as cheerfully as we had commenced it, but making our way a little more directly towards the goal which the gradual exhaustion of our resources made it necessary for us to reach.

At Chambéri I became thoughtful, not on account of the folly which I had just committed – no man ever knew how to console himself so rapidly or so completely in regard to the past – but in regard to the reception which awaited me from Madame de Warens; for I looked upon her house quite as my own home. I had written to inform her of my entry into the Comte de Gouvon's house; she knew on what footing I stood there, and, while congratulating me, she had given me some excellent advice as to the manner in which I ought to requite the kindness shown to me. She looked upon my fortune as assured, unless

I destroyed it by my own fault. What would she say when she saw me arrive? The possibility of her shutting the door upon me never occurred to me; but I was afraid of the sorrow which I was about to cause her; I was afraid of her reproaches, harder for me to bear than the greatest misery. I resolved to endure all in silence, and to do all I could to calm her. In the world I saw no one but her; to live in disgrace with her was an impossibility! What troubled me most was my travelling companion, with whom I had no desire to burden her, and whom I was afraid I should find it no easy matter to get rid of. I prepared him for the separation by treating him somewhat coldly on the last day. The rascal understood me; he was more a madman than a fool. I thought he would take my fickleness to heart; I was wrong; my friend Bâcle took nothing to heart. Hardly had we set foot in Annecy, when he said to me: "Here you are at home," embraced me, said good-bye, turned round on his heel, and disappeared. I have never heard of him since. Our acquaintance and friendship lasted about six months in all; their consequences will remain as long as I live.

How my heart beat as I drew near to her house! My legs trembled beneath me; my eyes seemed covered with a veil; I saw nothing, I heard nothing, I should not have recognised anybody; I was obliged to stop several times to recover my breath and compose myself. Was it the fear of not obtaining the assistance I needed that troubled me so? does the fear of starvation cause such alarm to a person of my age? No! that I can declare with as much truth as pride; never, at any moment of my life, has self-interest or want been able to open or shut my heart. In the course of a life, uneven and memorable for its vicissitudes, often without shelter and bread, I have always looked with the same eye upon wealth and poverty. In time of need I could have begged or stolen like anybody else, but never distressed myself in consequence of being reduced to do so. Few men have sighed so much as I, few have shed so many tears in their life; but never has poverty or the fear of being reduced to it made me utter a sigh or shed a tear. My soul, proof against fortune, has never known true blessings or misfortunes other than those which do not depend upon her; and, when I am in want of nothing that is needful, that is just the time when I feel myself the unhappiest of mortals.

No sooner had I shown myself to Madame de Warens, than her manner reassured me. I trembled at the first sound of her voice. I threw myself at her feet, and, in transports of liveliest joy, I fastened my lips upon her hand. I do not know whether she had heard any news of me, but her face showed little surprise and no displeasure. "Poor little one," she said, in a caressing voice, "here you are again then? I knew you were too young for the journey. I am glad, at any rate, that it has not turned out so badly as I had feared." Then she made me tell my story, which was not a long one, and which I faithfully related, suppressing a few details, but otherwise neither sparing nor excusing myself.

It was a question where I was to sleep. She consulted her maid. I hardly ventured to breathe during the discussion; but when I heard that I was to sleep in the house I could scarcely contain myself, and I saw my little bundle carried into the room appointed for me with much the same feelings as St. Preux saw his chaise taken into Madame de Wolmar's[1] coach-house. To increase my delight, I learned that this favour was not to be a passing one, and, at the moment when I was believed to be thinking of something quite different, I heard her say: "Let them say what they like; since Providence sends him back to me, I am resolved not to abandon him."

Thus I was at last settled in her house. This settlement, however, was not as yet that from which I date the happy days of my life, but it served to pave the way for it. Although this sensibility of the heart, which makes us truly enjoy ourselves, is the work of Nature, and, perhaps, a product of the organisation, it requires certain situations to develop it. Without such developing causes, a man born with powerful susceptibilities would feel nothing, and would, perhaps, die without ever having known his real self. Up to that time, it had been so, or nearly so, with me: and I should, perhaps, have always remained such, if I had never known Madame de Warens, or if, having known

---

[1] Allusion to Saint-Preux's return to Switzerland after his voyage round the world, in Rousseau's *La Nouvelle Héloïse* (Part IV, Letter 6).

her, I had not lived with her long enough to contract the sweet
habit of affectionate feelings with which she inspired me. I
venture to say that he who only feels love does not feel what is
sweetest in life. I know another feeling, less impetuous, perhaps,
but a thousand times more delightful, which is sometimes
combined with love, but is frequently separated from it. This
feeling is not simple friendship either; it is more voluptuous,
more tender. I do not believe that it can be felt for a person of
the same sex; at any rate, I was a friend, if ever a man was, and I
never felt it in the presence of any of my friends. This is somewhat obscure, but it will become clear in the sequel; feelings can
only be satisfactorily described by their effects.

Madame de Warens lived in an old house, large enough to
contain a pretty spare room, which she made her drawing-room;
in this I was lodged. It led into the passage of which I have
already spoken, where our first interview took place; on the
other side of the brook and the gardens the country could be
seen. This view was not a matter of indifference to the youthful
occupant. Since I had lived at Bossey, it was the first time that
I had seen anything green before my windows. Always surrounded by walls, I had nothing before my eyes except the
roofs of houses or the dull grey of the streets. How vividly I
felt the charm of novelty, which strengthened my inclination to
tender emotions! I looked upon this enchanting landscape as
another of my dear patroness's kindnesses; it seemed to me that
she had put everything there on purpose for me; I placed myself
in it by her side full of peaceful contentment; I saw her everywhere, in the midst of the flowers and verdure: her charms and
those of spring melted together insensibly before my eyes. My
heart, until then restricted, expanded in this unconfined space,
and my sighs found freer vent amongst the fruit-gardens.

I did not find with Madame de Warens the magnificence
which I had seen at Turin, but I found cleanliness, neatness,
and a patriarchal abundance, with which pomp and pride are
never combined. She had little plate, no porcelain, no game in
the larder, no foreign wines in the cellar; but both kitchen and
cellar were sufficiently well furnished for anybody, and in Delft-
ware cups she provided excellent coffee. All who came to visit

her were invited to dine with her or in her house; no workman, messenger, or passer-by left without eating or drinking. Her servants consisted of a rather pretty maid from Fribourg, named Merceret; a valet from her own country, named Claude Anet, of whom more will be said later; a cook, and two hired sedan-chair carriers for the rare occasions when she went to pay a visit. That was a great deal for a yearly pension of two thousand *livres*; nevertheless, her little income, well managed, might have been sufficient in a country where the soil is very good and money very scarce. Unfortunately, economy was never her favourite virtue; she got into debt and paid what she could; the money went in all directions, and things went on as best they could.

The manner in which her establishment was arranged was just such as I should have chosen myself; it may be imagined that I was only too pleased to take advantage of it. What was less pleasant to me was to be obliged to remain a long time at table. She could scarcely endure the first smell of the soup and other dishes; the smell almost made her faint, and this feeling of aversion lasted some time. By degrees she recovered herself, talked, and ate nothing. It was at least half-an-hour before she tried to eat a morsel. I could have eaten three dinners in the time, and I had always finished my meal long before she had begun. For the sake of keeping her company, I used to begin again; in this manner I ate for two, and never felt any the worse for it. In a word, I abandoned myself the more freely to the sweet sensation of comfort, which I felt when with her, as this comfort which I enjoyed was free from all uneasiness as to the means of preserving it. Not being yet admitted with complete confidence into the state of her affairs, I imagined that the present state of things would always continue. I found the same comfort again in her house in after times; but, being better informed as to her real position, and seeing that she drew upon her income in advance, I never enjoyed it with the same content. Looking ahead always spoils my enjoyment. It is not the least use to me to foresee the future; I have never known how to avoid it.

From the first day, the most complete intimacy was established between us, which has continued during the rest of her

life. "Little one" was my name; "Mamma" was hers; and we
always remained "Little one" and "Mamma," even when advancing years had almost obliterated the difference between us. I
find that these two names give a wonderfully good idea of the
tone of our intercourse, of the simplicity of our manners, and,
above all, of the mutual relation of our hearts. For me she was
the tenderest of mothers, who never sought her own pleasure,
but always what was best for me; and if sensuality entered at all
into her attachment for me, it did not alter its character, but only
rendered it more enchanting, and intoxicated me with the
delight of having a young and pretty mamma whom it was
delightful to me to caress – I say caress in the strictest sense of
the word, for it never occurred to her to be sparing of kisses and
the tenderest caresses of a mother, and it certainly never entered
my mind to abuse them. It will be objected that, in the end, we
had relations of a different character; I admit it, but I must wait a
little – I cannot say all at once.

   The moment of our first meeting was the only really passionate moment which she has ever made me feel; yet this moment
was the work of surprise. My looks never ventured to peep
indiscreetly beneath her neckerchief, although an ill-concealed
embonpoint might very well have attracted them. I felt no transports or desires in her presence. I was in a state of charming
repose and enjoyment, without knowing in what the enjoyment
consisted. I could have spent all my life in this manner, and
eternity as well, without a moment's weariness. She is the only
person with whom I have never felt that dearth of conversation
which makes the obligation of keeping it up a martyrdom. Our
tête-à-têtes were not so much conversations as an inexhaustible
gossip, which never came to an end unless it was interrupted.
There was no need to invite me to talk; it was far more necessary
to impose silence upon me. From constantly thinking over her
plans, she often fell into a reverie. Well, then I let her alone; I
held my tongue, I looked at her, and was the happiest of men. I
had still a singular fancy. Without claiming the favour of a *tête-à-
tête*, I incessantly sought one; and enjoyed it with a passion which
degenerated into madness when troublesome visitors disturbed
it. As soon as anyone came – whether man or woman, it did not

matter which — I left the room grumbling, being unable to remain with her in the presence of a third party. I counted the minutes in her ante-room, cursing these eternal visitors a thousand times, and unable to imagine how it was that they had so much, because I myself had still more, to say.

I only felt the full strength of my attachment when I no longer saw her. When I saw her, I was only content; but, during her absence, my restlessness became painful. The need of living with her caused me outbreaks of tenderness which often ended in tears. I shall never forget how, on the day of a great festival, while she was at vespers, I went for a walk outside the town, my heart full of her image and a burning desire to spend my life with her. I had sense enough to see that at present this was impossible, and that the happiness which I enjoyed so deeply could only be short. This gave to my reflections a tinge of melancholy, about which, however, there was nothing gloomy, and which was tempered by flattering hopes. The sound of the bells, which always singularly affects me, the song of the birds, the beauty of the daylight, the enchanting landscape, the scattered country dwellings in which my fancy placed our common home — all these produced upon me an impression so vivid, tender, melancholy and touching, that I saw myself transported, as it were, in ecstasy, into that happy time and place, wherein my heart, possessing all the happiness it could desire, tasted it with inexpressible rapture, without even a thought of sensual pleasure. I never remember to have plunged into the future with greater force and illusion than on that occasion; and what has struck me most in the recollection of this dream after it had been realised, is that I have found things again exactly as I had imagined them. If ever the dream of a man awake resembled a prophetic vision, it was assuredly that dream of mine. I was only deceived in the imaginary duration; for the days, the years, and our whole life were spent in serene and undisturbed tranquillity, whereas in reality it lasted only for a moment. Alas! my most lasting happiness belongs to a dream, the fulfilment of which was almost immediately followed by the awakening.

I should never have done, if I were to enter into the details of all the follies which the remembrance of this dear mamma caused me to commit when I was no longer in her presence. How often have I kissed my bed, since she had slept in it; my curtains, all the furniture of my room, since they belonged to her, and her beautiful hand had touched them; even the floor, on which I prostrated myself, since she had walked upon it! Sometimes, even in her presence, I was guilty of extravagances, which only the most violent love seemed capable of inspiring. At table one day, just when she had put a piece of food into her mouth, I exclaimed that I saw a hair in it; she put back the morsel on her plate, and I eagerly seized and swallowed it. In a word, between myself and the most passionate lover there was only one, but that an essential, point of distinction, which makes my condition almost unintelligible and inconceivable.

I had returned from Italy not quite the same as I had entered it, but as, perhaps, no one of my age had ever returned from it. I had brought back, not my mental and moral, but my bodily virginity. I had felt the progress of years; my restless temperament had at last made itself felt, and its first outbreak, quite involuntary, had caused me alarm about my health in a manner which shows better than anything else the innocence in which I had lived up to that time. Soon reassured, I learned that dangerous means of assisting it, which cheats Nature and saves up for young men of my temperament many forms of excess at the expense of their health, strength, and, sometimes, of their life. This vice, which shame and timidity find so convenient, possesses, besides a great attraction for lively imaginations – that of being able to dispose of the whole sex as they desire, and to make the beauty which tempts them minister to their pleasures, without being obliged to obtain its consent. Seduced by this fatal advantage, I did my best to destroy the good constitution which Nature had restored to me, and which I had allowed time to strengthen itself. Add to this habit the circumstances of my position, living as I was with a beautiful woman, caressing her image in the bottom of my heart, seeing her continually throughout the day, surrounded in the evening by objects which reminded me of her, sleeping in the bed in which I knew she had slept! What causes for excitement! Many a reader, who reflects upon them, no doubt already considers me as half-dead!

Quite the contrary; that which ought to have destroyed me was just the thing that saved me, at least for a time. Intoxicated with the charm of living with her, with the ardent desire of spending my life with her, I always saw in her, whether she were absent or present, a tender mother, a beloved sister, a delightful friend, and nothing more. I saw her always thus, always the same, and I never saw anyone but her. Her image, ever present to my heart, left room for no other; she was for me the only woman in the world; and the extreme sweetness of the feelings with which she inspired me did not allow my senses time to awake for others, and protected me against her and all her sex. In a word, I was chaste, because I loved her. Considering these results, which I can only imperfectly describe, let him who can say what was the nature of my attachment for her. For myself, all that I can say about it is that, if it already seems to be very extraordinary, in the sequel it will appear far more so.

I spent my time in the pleasantest manner possible, although occupied with things which were least attractive to me. There were plans to draw up, fair copies of accounts to make, recipes to transcribe, herbs to pick out, drugs to pound, stills to work. In the midst of all this, chance travellers, beggars, and visitors of all classes kept coming in crowds; we were obliged to entertain at one and the same time a soldier, an apothecary, a canon, a fine lady, and a lay brother. I cursed, I grumbled, I swore, I wished the whole accursed gang at the devil. Madame de Warens, who took it all good-humouredly, laughed at my rage till she cried; and what made her laugh still more was to see me the more furious, as I was unable to prevent even myself from laughing. These brief interruptions, during which I had the pleasure of grumbling, were delightful, and, if another unwelcome visitor arrived during the dispute, she knew how to extract amusement from it by maliciously prolonging his visit, casting glances at me for which I should have liked to beat her. She could hardly keep from bursting out laughing, when she saw me, restrained and kept in check by politeness, glaring at her like one possessed, while in the bottom of my heart, and even in spite of myself, I found it all very amusing.

All this, without being pleasant in itself, nevertheless amused me, because it formed part of a kind of existence which was delightful to me. Of all that was going on around me, of all that I was obliged to do, nothing suited my taste, but everything suited my heart. I believe that I should have come to like medicine, had not my natural distaste for it caused those comical scenes which delighted us so much; this is, perhaps, the first time that this art has produced a similar effect. I pretended to be able to recognise a medical work by its smell, and the amusing thing is that I was rarely mistaken. She made me taste the most horrible drugs. It was no use to run away or try to defend myself; in spite of my resistance and wry faces, in spite of myself and my teeth, when I saw her pretty fingers, all besmeared, near my mouth, I was obliged at last to open it and suck them. When all her little household was assembled in the same room, to hear us running about and shrieking with laughter, anyone would have thought we were performing some farce, instead of compounding opiates and elixirs.

My time, however, was not entirely occupied with these fooleries. In the room which I occupied I had found a few books: the "Spectator," "Puffendorf,"[1] "St. Évremond," the "Henriade." Although I no longer had my old mania for reading, I read a little when I had nothing else to do. The "Spectator," especially, pleased me and proved beneficial to me. The Abbé de Gouvon had taught me to read less greedily and with more reflection; and, accordingly, my reading did me more good. I accustomed myself to think about the language and style, and the elegance of the constructions; I practised myself in distinguishing pure French from my provincial idioms. For instance, I learned to correct an orthographical error, of which I, in common with all us Genevese, was guilty, by the two following lines of the "Henriade":

"Soit qu'un ancien respect pour le sang de leurs maîtres
Parlât encore pour lui dans le cœur de ces traîtres."

[1] Samuel von Pufendorf (1632–94), German "natural law" theorist, author of *De jure naturae et gentium* (1672). St. Evremond (1613–1703), wit and essayist. *Henriade*: epic poem about Henry of Navarre (later Henri IV) by Voltaire, published in 1723.

I was struck by this word *parlât*, which taught me that the third person subjunctive must end in *t*, whereas formerly I wrote and pronounced *parla*, as if it had been the perfect indicative.

Sometimes I talked with mamma about my reading, sometimes I read to her, which afforded me great pleasure. I tried to read well, and this, also, was useful to me. I have mentioned that she had a cultivated mind, and just at that time it was in its prime. Several men of letters had shown themselves eager to win her favour and had taught her to distinguish the productions of genius. Her taste, if I may say so, smacked of Protestantism; she talked only of Bayle, and thought highly of St. Évremond, who had died some time ago in France. But this did not hinder her from an acquaintance with good literature, and she discussed it intelligently. She had been brought up in select society and had come to Savoy while still young; in the charming society of the nobility of this country she had lost the affected manners of the Vaud country, where women consider attempts at wit to be good style, and can only speak in epigrams.

Although she had only a passing acquaintance with the Court, she had cast a rapid glance at it, which had been sufficient to give her a knowledge of it. She always retained her friends there, and, in spite of secret jealousies, in spite of the disapproval excited by her conduct and her debts, she never lost her pension. She possessed knowledge of the world and that capacity of reflection which makes this knowledge useful. Worldly matters formed the chief topic of her conversations, and, considering my romantic ideas, this was exactly the kind of instruction of which I stood most in need. We read La Bruyère[1] together; he pleased her better than La Rochefoucauld, a gloomy and comfortless author, especially for the young, who do not care to see men as they are. When she moralised, she sometimes lost herself in lengthy discourses; but, by kissing her mouth or hands from time to time, I managed to endure it, and her prolixity ceased to weary me.

[1] Jean de la Bruyère (1645–96) was author of a famous series of observations on character and conduct entitled *Caractères* (1688). François, duc de La Rochefoucauld (1613–80) published his pessimistic and cynical *Maxims* in 1665.

This life was too delightful to be able to last. I felt this, and my distress at the thought of seeing it come to an end was the only thing that disturbed my enjoyment of it. In the midst of her playfulness, mamma studied, observed, and questioned me, and sketched out a number of plans for my advancement, which I could well have dispensed with. Happily, it was not enough to know my inclinations, my tastes, my abilities; it was necessary to find or to create opportunities for employing them profitably, and this was not the work of a day. The prejudices which the poor woman had conceived in favour of my talents, served to defer the moment of putting them to the proof, by making her more particular in regard to the choice of means. In short, everything went on in accordance with my wishes, thanks to her good opinion of me; but, sooner or later, this life was bound to come to an end, and, from that moment, good-bye to all hope of tranquillity. One of her relations, a M. d'Aubonne, came to pay her a visit. He was a man of considerable endowments, an intriguer, and a born schemer like herself, but too clever to allow his plans to ruin him – a sort of adventurer. He had just proposed to the Cardinal de Fleury a very intricate plan of a lottery, which had not met with approval. He was now going to lay it before the Court of Turin, where it was adopted and carried out. He remained some time at Annecy where he fell in love with the wife of the Intendant, a very amiable person much to my taste, and the only one whom I cared to see at mamma's house. M. d'Aubonne saw me; his relative spoke of me to him; he undertook to examine me, to see what I was fit for, and, if he found anything in me, to endeavour to get me a place.

Madame de Warens sent me to him on two or three successive mornings, on the pretence of executing some commission for her, and without giving me any intimation of the truth. He succeeded admirably in making me talk, became quite intimate with me, put me at my ease as far as possible, spoke to me about matters of no importance and all kinds of subjects – all without appearing to watch me, without the least formality, as if he found pleasure in my society and desired to converse with me without restraint. I was enchanted with him. The result of his observations was that, in spite of my attractive appearance and

animated features, I was, if not quite silly, a lad of little intelligence, without any ideas, almost without knowledge – in a word,
of very limited capacities in every respect; and that the highest
position to which I had any right to aspire was that of some day
becoming a village *curé*. Such was the account of me which he
gave to Madame de Warens. This was the second or the third
time that I was thus judged; it was not the last, and M. Masseron's
opinion has often been confirmed.

The reason of the judgments passed upon me is too closely
connected with my character not to require some explanation;
for to speak honestly, it will be readily understood that I cannot
subscribe to them unreservedly, and that, with all possible
impartiality, in spite of all that MM. Masseron, d'Aubonne,
and many others may have said, I cannot take them at their
word.

Two things, almost incompatible, are united in me in a
manner which I am unable to understand: a very ardent temperament, lively and tumultuous passions, and, at the same time,
slowly developed and confused ideas, which never present
themselves until it is too late. One might say that my heart and
my mind do not belong to the same person. Feeling takes
possession of my soul more rapidly than a flash of lightning;
but, instead of illuminating, inflames and dazzles me. I feel
everything and see nothing. I am carried away by my passions,
but stupid; in order to think, I must be cool. The astonishing
thing is that, notwithstanding, I exhibit tolerably sound judgment, penetration, even finesse, if I am not hurried; with
sufficient leisure I can compose excellent impromptus; but I
have never said or done anything worthy of notice on the spur of
the moment. I could carry on a very clever conversation through
the post, as the Spaniards are said to carry on a game of chess.
When I read of that Duke of Savoy, who turned round on his
journey, in order to cry, "At your throat, Parisian huckster,"
I said, "There you have myself!"

This sluggishness of thought, combined with such liveliness
of feeling, not only enters into my conversation, but I feel it even
when alone and at work. My ideas arrange themselves in my
head with almost incredible difficulty; they circulate in it with

uncertain sound, and ferment till they excite and heat me, and make my heart beat fast; and, in the midst of this excitement, I see nothing clearly and am unable to write a single word – I am obliged to wait. Imperceptibly this great agitation subsides, the confusion clears up, everything takes its proper place, but slowly, and only after a period of long and confused agitation. Have you ever been to the opera in Italy? During the changes of scene, there prevails upon the stage of those vast theatres an unpleasant disorder which continues for some time: all the decorations are mixed up, things are pulled about in different directions in a manner most painful to see, which produces the impression that everything must be upset. Gradually, however, complete order is restored, nothing is wanting, and one is quite astounded to see an enchanting spectacle succeed this long continued disorder. This mode of procedure is almost the same as that which takes place in my brain when I attempt to write. If I had known how to wait first and then to restore in all their beauty the things represented therein, few writers would have surpassed me.

Hence comes the extreme difficulty which I find in writing. My manuscripts, scratched, smeared, muddled and almost illegible, bear witness to the trouble they have cost me. There is not one of them which I have not been obliged to copy four or five times before I could give it to the printer. I have never been able to produce anything, pen in hand, in front of my table and paper; it is during a walk, in the midst of rocks and forests, at night in my bed while lying awake, that I write in my brain; one may judge how slowly, especially in the case of a man utterly without verbal memory and who has never been able to learn six lines by heart in his life. Many of my periods have been turned and turned again five or six nights in my head before they were fit to be set down on paper. This, also, is the reason why I succeed better in works which require labour than in those which require to be written with a certain lightness of style, such as letters – a style of which I have never been able to properly catch the tone, so that such occupation is a perfect torture to me. I cannot write a letter on the most trifling subject, which does not cost me hours of fatigue; or, if I try to write down immediately what occurs to me,

I know neither how to begin nor how to end; my letter is a long and confused mass of verbosity, and, when it is read, my meaning is difficult to make out.

Not only is it painful for me to put my ideas into shape: I also find a difficulty in grasping them. I have studied mankind, and believe that I am a fairly shrewd observer; nevertheless, I cannot see clearly anything of all that I perceive; I only see clearly what I remember, and only show intelligence in my recollections. Of all that is said, of all that is done, of all that goes on in my presence, I feel nothing, I see through nothing. The outward sign is the only thing that strikes me. But, later, all comes back to me: I recall place, time, manner, look, gesture, and circumstance: nothing escapes me. Then, from what people have said or done, I discover what they have thought; and I am rarely mistaken.

If, when alone with myself, I am so little master of my intellectual capacity, it may be imagined what I must be in conversation, when, in order to speak to the purpose, it is necessary to think of a thousand things at the same time and at once. The mere idea of all the usages of society – which it is so necessary to observe, and of which I am certain to forget one or other – is enough to frighten me. I do not even understand how anyone can dare to speak at all in society, where, at every word, it is essential to pass in review all those who are present; it is essential to be acquainted with all their characters and histories, in order to make sure of saying nothing which can give offence. In this respect, those who live in the world have a great advantage; since they know better than others what ought not to be spoken about, they are more confident of what they say; and yet, even they frequently let fall awkward and ill-timed remarks. How must it fare with one who drops into their midst as it were from the clouds! It is almost impossible for him to speak for a minute with impunity. In a *tête-à-tête*, there is another inconvenience which I find even worse: the necessity of talking perpetually. When one is spoken to, one is obliged to answer, and, when silence ensues, to take up the conversation again. This unbearable constraint would alone have disgusted me with society. I find no compulsion more terrible than the obligation of speaking continuously and on the spur of the moment. I do not know whether this has anything to do with my mortal aversion to constraint of any kind; but to be absolutely obliged to speak is enough to make me infallibly talk nonsense.

A still more fatal defect of mine is that, instead of being able to hold my tongue when I have nothing to say, that is just the time when, in order to discharge my debt sooner, I am mad to speak. I hasten to stammer out a few words destitute of ideas, and am only too happy when they have no meaning at all. When attempting to overcome or conceal my stupidity, I rarely fail to show it. Out of numerous instances that I could cite, I will select one which does not belong to my youthful days, but to a period of my life when, having lived several years in society, I should have caught its easy tone, if the thing had been possible. One evening, I was sitting between two great ladies and a gentleman, whose name I may mention – it was the Duc de Gontaut. There was no one else in the room, and I was doing my utmost to supply a few words – heaven knows what! – during a conversation between four persons, three of whom certainly had no need of my supplementary efforts. The mistress of the house ordered an opiate to be brought to her, which she took twice a day to ease her stomach. The other lady, seeing the wry face she made, said, laughingly: "Is it M. Tronchin's opiate?" "I don't think so," the first replied in the same tone. "I expect it is just as bad," politely added the witty Rousseau. Everyone was amazed; not a word was uttered, not a smile was seen, and immediately afterwards the conversation took a different turn.[1] In the presence of anyone else this awkward remark might have been only amusing, but, addressed to a woman who was too amiable not to have made herself somewhat talked about, and whom I most certainly had no desire to offend, it was terrible; and I believe that the two who heard it, both the lady and the gentleman, could scarcely refrain from bursting out into a laugh. Such are the flashes of genius which escape me when I attempt to speak without having anything to say. I shall not easily forget that particular instance,

[1] Tronchin used to prescribe his "opiate" for venereal infections. Thus Rousseau's remark could have been interpreted as meaning that the remedy she was using, though it was not Tronchin's, was for the same sort of disreputable complaint.

for not only is it in itself worthy of record, but I cannot help thinking that it has produced results which recall it to my mind only too often.

I think this is enough to make it intelligible how, although not a fool, I have often been taken for one, even by people who were in a position to judge correctly; what aggravates my misfortune is the fact that my eyes and features give promise of something better, and the failure of this hope makes my stupidity more startling to others. This detailed explanation, to which a special circumstance has led me, is not without its use in reference to what follows. It contains the solution of many extraordinary things which I have done, and which are attributed to an unsociable disposition which I by no means possess. I should be as fond of society as anyone else, if I was not sure of appearing in it, not only to my own disadvantage, but quite a different person from what I really am. My resolution to write and live in seclusion, is exactly that which suits me. If I had been present, my powers would never have been known, or even suspected; this actually happened in the case of Madame Dupin, although she was a woman of intelligence, and although I lived for several years in her house. Since that time, she has often told me so herself. However, this rule is liable to certain exceptions, to which I will subsequently return.

The extent of my capacities having thus been settled, and the position for which I was adapted marked out for the second time, the only question remaining was how to fit me for fulfilling my vocation. The difficulty was that I had not studied sufficiently, and did not even know enough Latin to be a priest. Madame de Warens thought of having me taught for some time at the seminary. She spoke of it to the Superior, a Lazarist,[1] named M. Gros, a good little man, lean and grey-haired, who had almost lost the sight of one eye, and who was the most intelligent and the least pedantic Lazarist that I have ever known – although, to tell the truth, that is not saying much.

He came sometimes to see mamma, who welcomed him, petted him, teased him, and sometimes made him lace her

---

[1] A monk of the order of St. Lazare.

stays, a service which he was only too glad to perform. While he was thus engaged, she ran from one side of the room to the other, doing first one thing and then another. Dragged along by her staylace, the Superior followed, grumbling and crying out every minute: "Madame, do please keep still!" It was an extremely attractive picture!

M. Gros entered heartily into mamma's plan. He was satisfied with a very modest fee for my board, and undertook to teach me. Nothing else was required except the consent of the bishop, who not alone granted it, but offered to pay the fee. He also gave me permission to wear my lay dress until the degree of success which might be hoped for could be estimated by a trial.

What a change! I was obliged to submit. I went to the seminary as I should have gone to execution. A seminary is a melancholy abode, especially for one who has just left the house of an amiable woman. I took with me only a single book, which I had begged mamma to lend me, and which was a great consolation to me. No one would guess what kind of book it was; it was a book of music. Amongst the accomplishments which she had cultivated, music had not been forgotten. She had a good voice, sang fairly well, and played the piano a little; she had been good enough to give me some lessons in singing, in which she was obliged to begin at the very beginning, for I hardly knew the music of our psalms. Eight or ten lessons, constantly interrupted, and given me by a woman, were not enough to teach me a quarter of the notes, much less to enable me to sing the scales. However, I had such a passion for the art that I determined to try to practise by myself. The volume which I took with me was not even one of the easiest; it was the cantatas of Clérambault. The doggedness of my application may be imagined, when I mention that, without any knowledge of transposition or quantity, I succeeded in deciphering and singing without a mistake the first air and recitative of the cantata *Alpheus and Arethusa*; although, certainly, this air is so correctly set, that it is only necessary to recite the verses in proper time in order to catch the air.

At the seminary there was a confounded Lazarist, who took charge of me, and disgusted me with the Latin which he wanted to teach me. He had sleek, greasy, black hair, a gingerbread face, a voice like a buffalo, the look of a night-owl and a beard like boar's bristles; his smile was sardonic, his limbs moved like those of a jointed doll. I have forgotten his hateful name, but his frightful and mawkish face has remained in my memory, and I can scarcely think of it without a shudder. I fancy I still meet him in the corridors, politely holding out his dirty square cap, as an invitation to enter his room, which was more dreadful to me than a prison cell. Imagine the impression such a teacher produced by contrast upon the pupil of a court Abbé.

If I had remained two months at the mercy of this monster, I am convinced that I should have lost my reason. But good M. Gros, who perceived that I was depressed, that I ate nothing and grew thin, guessed the reason of my grief; it was not hard to do so! He rescued me from the claws of my wild beast, and, by a still more marked contrast, handed me over to the gentlest of men, a young Abbé from Le Faucigny,[1] named Gâtier, who was going through his college course, and who, from a desire to oblige M. Gros, and also, I believe, from feelings of humanity, was so good as to rob his own studies of the time he devoted to the direction of mine. I have never seen a more touching expression than M. Gâtier's. He was fair, and his beard inclined to be red; he had the ordinary appearance of those who came from his province, who all conceal considerable intelligence under a heavy exterior; but what truly distinguished him was a tender, affectionate and loving heart. There was in his large blue eyes a mixture of gentleness, tenderness and sadness, which made it impossible for anyone to see him without being attracted by him. From the looks and manner of this poor young man, one would have said that he foresaw his destiny, and that he felt he was born to be unhappy.

His character did not belie his looks; full of patience, and ever ready to oblige, he seemed rather to study with than to teach me. That alone was more than enough to make me love him; his predecessor had made that exceedingly easy. However, in spite of all the time that he devoted to me, in spite of the hearty

---

[1] A small province of the Duchy of Savoy.

goodwill with which we both devoted ourselves to our studies, and although he went quite the right way to work, I made little progress, although I worked hard. It is singular that, although endowed with considerable powers of apprehension, I have never been able to learn anything with tutors, with the exception of my father and M. Lambercier. The little additional knowledge I possess I owe to my own unaided efforts, as will be presently seen. My spirit, impatient of any kind of constraint, cannot submit to the laws of the moment; even the fear of not learning prevents my attention; for fear of making those who are talking to me impatient, I pretend to understand them; they accordingly go on, and I understand nothing. My mind must fix its own time for work; it cannot submit to that which is fixed by another.

The time of ordination came, and M. Gâtier returned to his province in deacon's orders. He took with him my regrets, my attachment, my gratitude. I offered prayers on his behalf, which were no more granted than those which I offered for myself. Some years afterwards, I learned that, while *vicaire* of a parish, he seduced a girl, the only one whom, in spite of a very tender heart, he had ever loved. The girl had a child by him, which caused a terrible scandal in a parish which was very strictly managed. The priests, being under good regulations, are not allowed to have children – except by married women. For his offence against this rule of propriety, he was imprisoned, disgraced, and deprived of his benefice. I do not know whether he afterwards regained his position, but the thought of his misfortune, deeply graven on my heart, returned to me when I wrote "Émile"; and, uniting M. Gâtier with M. Gaime, I made of these two worthy priests the original of the "Savoyard Vicar." I flatter myself that the imitation has not disgraced its originals.

While I was at the seminary, M. d'Aubonne was obliged to leave Annecy. The Intendant took it into his head to be displeased that he made love to his wife. This was playing the part of the dog in the manger; for, although Madame Corvezi was extremely amiable, he lived on very bad terms with her; ultramontane tendencies[1] rendered her useless to him, and he treated

[1] By "ultramontane tendencies" Rousseau means homosexuality.

her so brutally that a separation was talked of. M. Corvezi was an ugly-looking fellow, black as a mole, knavish as an owl, and who, by continued abuse of his office, ended in getting dismissed himself. It is said that the natives of Provence revenge themselves upon their enemies by songs; M. d'Aubonne revenged himself upon his by a comedy; he sent the piece to Madame de Warens, who showed it to me. It pleased me, and put into my head the idea of writing one myself, in order to see whether I was really such a fool as the author had declared me to be; but I did not carry out this idea until I went to Chambéri, where I wrote *L'Amant de lui-même*.[1] Consequently, when I state in the preface to this piece that I wrote it when I was eighteen years old, I have deviated from the truth in the matter a few years.

It was nearly about this time that an event occurred, of little importance in itself, but which affected me, and made a stir in the world when I had already forgotten it. One day in every week I had permission to go out; it is not necessary to say what use I made of it. One Sunday when I was with mamma, a fire broke out in a building belonging to the Grey Friars, which adjoined the house she occupied. This building, in which was their oven, was crammed full of dry faggots. In a very short time the whole was in flames. The house was in great danger, already enveloped by the flames which the wind drove in that direction. Everyone made ready to remove the furniture as quickly as possible, and to carry it into the garden, which was opposite the windows of my old room, beyond the brook of which I have already spoken. I was so confused, that I threw out of the window promiscuously everything that came into my hands, even a large stone mortar, which at any other time I should scarcely have been able to lift; in like manner I should have thrown out a large looking-glass, had not someone stopped me. The good bishop, who had come to pay mamma a visit, did not remain idle. He took her into the garden, where he began to pray with her, and all those who were there, so that, when I came up some time later, I found all on their knees and followed their example. During the holy man's

[1] Rousseau explains in Book VII (p. 303) how his comedy *Narcisse, ou L'Amant de lui-même* (*Narcissus, or The Man in Love with Himself*) was "improved" by Marivaux and eventually staged in December 1752.

prayer, the wind changed, but so suddenly and just at the right moment, that the flames, which enveloped the house and were already making their way through the windows, were blown to the other side of the court, and the house suffered no damage. Two years later, after the death of M. de Bernex, his former brethren, the Antonines,[1] began to collect evidence which might serve towards his beatification. At the earnest request of Father Boudet, I added to this evidence an attestation of the fact which I have just related, in which I was right; but, in giving out the fact for a miracle, I was wrong. I had seen the bishop at prayers, and during his prayers I had seen the wind change, and just at the critical moment; this I was able to state and certify; but that one of these two things was the cause of the other, this I ought not to have certified, because I could not possibly know. However, as far as I can recollect my ideas, I was at that time a sincere Catholic, and therefore a good believer. The love of the marvellous, so natural to the human heart, my veneration for this virtuous prelate, the feeling of secret pride at having, perhaps, contributed to the miracle myself, helped to lead me astray; and it is quite certain that, if this miracle had been the result of fervent prayer, I might with good reason have claimed a share in it. More than thirty years afterwards, when I published my "Lettres de la Montagne," M. Fréron[2] somehow or other unearthed this testimony and made use of it in his papers. I must confess that it was a fortunate discovery, and it seemed to me very amusing that it was made at so opportune a moment.

I was destined to be the rejected of all professions. Although M. Gâtier had given the least unfavourable account of my progress that he possibly could, it was easily seen that it was out of proportion to my efforts, and that was no encouragement to make me study further. Accordingly, the bishop and the Superior refused to have any more to do with me, and gave me back to Madame de Warens as a person not even good enough for a priest; in other respects, a good enough lad, they

[1] A begging order founded in 1070.
[2] Elie-Catherine Fréron (1719–76), editor of the *Année littéraire*, was for many years a thorn in the side of the *philosophes*.

said, and free from vice: which was the reason why, in spite of so many discouraging prejudices against me, she did not desert me.

I brought back to her in triumph her volume of music, of which I had made such good use. My air of *Alpheus and Arethusa* was nearly all that I had learnt at the seminary. My marked taste for this art gave her the idea of making me a musician; the opportunity was favourable; she had music at her house at least once a week, and the choir-master of the cathedral, who directed these little concerts, was a frequent visitor. He was a Parisian, named Le Maître, a good composer, very lively, very gay, still young, tolerably good-looking, not very intelligent, but, on the whole, a good fellow. Mamma introduced me to him. I took a fancy to him, and he was not displeased with me; the fee was discussed and settled. In short, I went to his house, where I passed the winter the more agreeably, as it was only twenty yards distant from mamma's; we were with her in a moment, and very often supped there together.

It will be readily imagined that life in the choir-master's house, where singing and gaiety prevailed, together with musicians and choir-boys, pleased me far better than life in the seminary with the fathers of St. Lazare. However, this life, although more unrestrained, was not less orderly and regular. I was born to love independence, without abusing it. For six whole months, I never went out once, except to visit mamma or to attend church, nor did I ever feel tempted to do so. This period is one of those during which I have enjoyed the greatest calm, and which I recall with the greatest pleasure. Of the various situations in which I have found myself, some have been distinguished by such a feeling of comfort, that, in recalling them, I am as affected by them as if I were still similarly situated. I not only recall times, places, persons, but all the surrounding objects, the temperature of the air, its smell, its colour, a certain local impression only felt there, the lively remembrance of which stirs my old transports anew. For instance, all that was repeated in the choir-master's house, all that was sung in the choir, everything that took place there, the beautiful and majestic dress of the canons, the chasubles of the priests, the mitres of the chanters, the faces of the musicians, an old lame carpenter, who played the counterbass, a fair little Abbé who played the violin, the ragged cassock which, after laying down his sword, M. le Maître put on over his lay-coat, and the beautiful fine surplice with which he covered its rags when he went to the choir; the pride with which, holding my little flageolet, I took my place in the orchestra in the gallery, to assist in the end of a recitative which M. le Maître had composed on purpose for me; the good dinner waiting for us afterwards, the good appetite we took to it – all these objects together, recurring most vividly a hundred times to my memory, have enchanted me as much or even more than the reality had ever done. I have always preserved a tender affection for a certain air of the *Conditor alme siderum* which goes in iambics, because, one Advent Sunday, I heard from my bed this hymn being sung before daybreak on the steps of the cathedral, according to a custom of that church. Mademoiselle de Merceret, mamma's chambermaid, knew a little music. I shall never forget a little motet, called *Afferte*, which M. le Maître made me sing with her, and which her mistress listened to with great pleasure. In short, everything, down to the good servant Perrine, who was so good a girl, and whom the choir-boys teased to madness, frequently comes back to me from those innocent and happy times, to enchant and sadden me.

I lived at Annecy for nearly a year without the least reproach; everybody was satisfied with me. Since my departure from Turin I had committed no follies, nor was I guilty of any as long as I was under mamma's eyes. She guided me, and always guided me well; my attachment to her had become my only passion, and, a proof that it was not a foolish passion, my heart formed my reason. It is true that a single sentiment, absorbing, so to speak, all my faculties, put it out of my power to learn anything, even music, although I did my utmost. But it was not my fault; the most perfect goodwill was there, and steady application. But I was distracted, a dreamer; I sighed. What could I do? Nothing that depended upon me was wanting to ensure my progress; but, in order for me to commit fresh follies, I only needed a subject to put them into my head. This subject presented itself; chance arranged matters, and, as will be seen in the sequel, my stupid head knew how to profit by it.

One evening during the month of February, in very cold weather, while we were all seated round the fire, we heard a knock at the street door. Perrine took her lantern, went down and opened it; and returned with a young man, who came upstairs, introduced himself with an easy air, paid M. le Maître a short and well-turned compliment, and told us that he was a French musician, obliged by the low state of his finances to offer his services to churches, in order to pay his way. When he heard the words "French musician," Le Maître's good heart leaped for joy; he was passionately fond of his country and his profession. He received the young wayfarer, offered him a night's lodging, of which he seemed sorely in want, and which he accepted without much ceremony. I examined him while he was warming himself and chattering, while waiting for supper. He was short of stature, but broad-shouldered. There was something misshapen about his figure, without any special deformity; he was, so to speak, a hunchback with straight shoulders, and I fancy that he limped a little. His black coat was worn out by constant use rather than old, and was falling to pieces; his shirt, made of very fine linen, was very dirty; he wore beautiful fringed ruffles and gaiters, in either of which he could have put both his legs; and, by way of protection against the snow, he had a little hat only fit to carry under his arm. In this whimsical attire, however, there was something noble, to which his general demeanour did not give the lie. His expression was pleasant and intelligent: he spoke readily and well, although his language was rather too free. Everything about him showed him to be a young libertine of good education, who did not go begging like a beggar, but like a madcap. He told us that his name was Venture de Villeneuve, that he came from Paris, that he had lost his way, and, forgetting for the moment his *rôle* of musician, he added that he was going to Grenoble to see one of his relations who was a member of the parliament.

During supper the conversation turned upon music, and he spoke well upon the subject. He was acquainted with all the great virtuosi, all the famous works, all the actors and actresses, pretty women, and great noblemen. He appeared familiar with everything that was alluded to; but, directly a subject was broached, he upset the discussion with some broad joke, which made us laugh and forget what had been said. It was Saturday; on the following day there was music in the cathedral. M. le Maître proposed to him to take part in the singing; "With pleasure," he replied. Being asked what part he took, he answered, "Alto," and went on to speak of something else. Before church, his part was given him to look through; but he never even glanced at it. This piece of swagger surprised Le Maître. "You will see," he whispered to me, "that he doesn't know a note." "I am very much afraid so," I replied. I followed them full of uneasiness. When the singing began, my heart beat violently, for I was greatly interested in him.

I soon found I had no reason for uneasiness. He sang his two parts with the greatest correctness and the best taste imaginable, and, what was more, in a charming voice. I have rarely experienced a more agreeable surprise. After mass, he was highly complimented by the canons and musicians, whom he thanked in his usual jesting manner, but with perfect grace. M. le Maître embraced him heartily; I did the same; he saw that I was very glad, and this seemed to afford him pleasure.

The reader will assuredly agree with me that, after having become infatuated with Bâcle, who, when all is said and done, was nothing but a boor, it was only to be expected that I should be enchanted by Venture, a man of education, talent, intelligence, and worldly experience, who might be called an agreeable rake. This was just what happened to me, and which, I think, would have happened to any other young man in my position, the more easily in proportion as he possessed better judgment in recognising merit, and greater inclination to allow himself to be fascinated by it; for undoubtedly Venture possessed merit, and a merit very rare at his age – that of not being too eager to display his accomplishments. It is true that he boasted about many things which he did not understand at all; but of those things which he knew well, and these were by no means few, he said nothing – he waited for the opportunity of showing his knowledge, and when it came, he took advantage of it without exhibiting too much eagerness, which produced a great effect. As he stopped at each subject, without speaking of the rest, one could never tell when his knowledge was exhausted. Witty, droll, inexhaustible, seductive in conversation, always smiling and never laughing, he would say the rudest things in the most refined tone without ever giving offence. Even the most modest women were astonished at what they endured from him. It was useless for them to feel that they ought to be angry – they could not. He wanted nothing but loose women, and I do not believe that he was made to succeed with the sex, but he was certainly made to enliven immensely the society of those who enjoyed that good fortune. In a country where such agreeable accomplishments were duly esteemed and loved, he could not long remain limited to the sphere of a musician.

My liking for M. Venture, more reasonable in its cause, was also less extravagant in its effects than my friendship for M. Bâcle, although it was warmer and more lasting. I loved to see him, to listen to him; everything he did appeared to me charming, everything he said was an oracle to me; but my infatuation did not go so far that I could not have endured separation from him. I had in my neighbourhood a good safeguard against such extravagance. Besides, I felt that his principles, although they might be very good for him, were of no value to me; I wanted a different kind of pleasure, of which he had no idea, and of which I did not even venture to speak to him, as I felt sure that he would only have laughed at me. However, I would gladly have united this new attachment with that which already had possession of me. I spoke of him to mamma with transport; Le Maître spoke of him to her in terms of the highest praise. She consented that he should be introduced to her; but the meeting was altogether unsuccessful. He found her affected; she found him dissolute, and, being alarmed to think that I had formed so undesirable an acquaintance, she not only forbade me to bring him again, but painted in such lively colours the risks I ran with this young man, that I became a little more reserved in my intercourse with him, and, luckily for my morals and my understanding, we were soon separated.

M. le Maître had the taste of all the followers of his profession: he was fond of wine. At table, however, he was temperate; when working in his study, he was obliged to drink. His

maidservant knew him so well that, as soon as he arranged his
paper in order to compose, and took up his violoncello, his jug
and glass arrived the moment after, and the jug was replenished
from time to time. Without ever being completely drunk he was
always fuddled; this was really a pity, for he was essentially a
good fellow, and so playful that mamma always called him the
"Kitten." Unfortunately, he was fond of his talent, worked hard
and drank proportionately. This told upon his health, and, in the
end, upon his temper; he was sometimes suspicious and ready to
take offence. Incapable of rudeness, incapable of failing in
respect to anyone, he never used bad language, even to one of
his choir-boys; but neither was anyone allowed to fail in respect
to him, as was only fair. The misfortune was that he had too little
intelligence to distinguish manners and characters, and often
took offence at nothing.

The ancient Chapter of Geneva, into which formerly so many
princes and bishops esteemed it an honour to be admitted, has
lost in exile some of its ancient splendour, but has retained its
pride. In order to be admitted, it is still necessary to be a gentleman or doctor of Sorbonne; and if there is an excusable pride,
next after that which is derived from personal merit, it is that
which is derived from birth. Besides, all the priests, who have
laymen in their service, as a rule treat them with considerable
arrogance. It was thus that the canons often treated Le Maître.
The precentor especially, the Abbé de Vidonne, who in other
respects was extremely polite but too proud of his noble birth,
did not always treat him with the respect which his talents
deserved, and Le Maître could not endure this disdain. This
year, during Passion week, they had a more serious dispute than
usual at a regulation dinner given by the bishop to the canons, to
which Le Maître was always invited. The precentor showed him
some slight, and said something harsh to him, which he was
unable to stomach. He immediately resolved to run away the
next night, and nothing could dissuade him from this; although
Madame de Warens, to whom he went to say good-bye, did her
utmost to appease him. He could not forego the pleasure of
avenging himself upon his tyrants, by leaving them in the lurch
during the Easter festival, which was just the time when his

services were most needed. But what troubled him most was his
music, which he wanted to take with him – no easy task, for it
filled a tolerably heavy box which could not be carried under
the arm.

Mamma did what I should have done in her place, and should
do again. After many fruitless attempts to keep him back, seeing
that he had made up his mind to depart, whatever happened, she
devoted herself to assisting him as far as she possibly could. I
venture to say that it was her duty to do so. Le Maître had, so to
say, devoted himself entirely to her service. In reference to his
art, as well as other attentions, he was entirely at her command;
and the heartiness with which he carried out what she desired
attached a double value to his readiness to oblige. Consequently,
she only repaid a friend, on a critical occasion, for all that he had
done for her on many separate occasions during three or four
years, although she had a heart which, in order to repay such
obligations, had no need to be reminded that they were obligations. She sent for me and ordered me to follow Le Maître at
least as far as Lyons, and not to leave him as long as he needed
my assistance. She has since confessed to me that the desire of
separating me from Venture had been one of her chief considerations in this arrangement. She consulted Claude Anet, her
faithful servant, about the removal of the box. He was of
opinion that it would infallibly lead to discovery if we hired a
beast of burden in Annecy; that, as soon as it was dark, we ought
to carry the box ourselves a certain distance, and then hire an ass
in some village to convey it as far as Seyssel, where, being on
French territory, we should no longer run any risk. We followed
his advice; we set out the same night at seven o'clock, and
mamma, on pretence of paying my expenses, reinforced the
lightly-filled purse of the poor "Kitten" by a sum of money
which was very useful to him. Claude Anet, the gardener, and
myself carried the box as best we could as far as the first village,
where an ass relieved us; and the same night we reached Seyssel.

I believe that I have already observed that there are times
when I so little resemble myself, that one would take me for
another man of quite an opposite character. The following is
a case in point. M. Reydelet, *curé* of Seyssel, was canon of

St. Peter's, consequently acquainted with Le Maître, and one of the persons from whom it was most important that he should conceal himself. My advice, on the contrary, was that we should present ourselves to him, and, on some pretext or other, ask him for a night's lodging as if we were at Seyssel with the sanction of the Chapter. Le Maître liked the idea, which made his revenge ironical and amusing. We accordingly proceeded boldly to M. Reydelet's house, and were kindly received. Le Maître told him that he was going to Bellay, at the request of the bishop, to conduct the choir at the Easter festival, and that he expected to pass through Seyssel again in a few days; while I, to back up these lies, poured out a hundred others so unconcernedly, that M. Reydelet, finding me a nice-looking lad, took a fancy to me, and spoke to me in a most friendly manner. We were well entertained and well lodged. M. Reydelet did not know how to make enough of us; and we parted the best friends in the world, promising to stop longer on our return. We could scarcely wait till we were alone before we burst out laughing, and I declare that I do the same now, whenever I think of it; for I cannot imagine a piece of waggery better planned or more happily executed. It would have kept us in good spirits throughout the journey, had not Le Maître, who drank incessantly, and went from one tavern to another, been attacked two or three times by fits to which he was very liable, which strongly resembled epilepsy. These attacks alarmed me, and made me think how I could best get out of it.

We went on to Bellay to spend Easter, as we had told M. Reydelet; and, although we were not expected there, we were received by the choir-master, and joyfully welcomed by all. Le Maître had a reputation, and deserved it. The choir-master made a point of producing his best works, and endeavoured to obtain the approval of so experienced a critic; for Le Maître, besides being a connoisseur, was always fair, free from jealousy, and no flatterer. He was so superior to all these provincial choir-masters, and they were so well aware of it, that they looked upon him rather as their chief than as a brother professional.

After having spent four or five days very agreeably at Bellay, we set out again and continued our journey without any further adventures than those which I have just mentioned. When we arrived at Lyons, we put up at Notre Dame de Pitié; and, while we were waiting for the box (which, thanks to another lie, we had persuaded our kind patron, M. Reydelet, to put on board a vessel on the Rhône), Le Maître went to see his acquaintances, amongst others Father Caton, a Grey friar, of whom I shall have something to say later, and the Abbé Dortan, Comte de Lyon. Both received him kindly, but afterwards betrayed him, as will presently be seen; his good luck had become exhausted at M. Reydelet's.

Two days after our arrival at Lyons, as we were going through a little street not far from our inn, Le Maître was overtaken by one of his attacks, which was so violent that I was seized with affright. I cried out and shouted for help, gave the name of his inn, and begged someone to take him there; then while the crowd gathered round, eager to assist a man who had fallen senseless and foaming at the mouth in the middle of the street, he was abandoned by the only friend on whom he had a right to depend. I seized the moment when nobody was thinking of me; I turned the corner of the street and disappeared. Thank Heaven, I have finished this third painful confession! If I had many more of a similar kind to make, I should abandon the task I have commenced.

Of all the incidents I have related up to the present time some traces have remained in all the places where I have lived; those which I shall relate in the next book are almost entirely unknown. They are the greatest extravagances of my life, and it is fortunate that they have not led to worse results. But my head, raised to the pitch of a foreign instrument, was out of its proper key; it recovered it of itself, and I abandoned my follies, or at least only committed such as were more in agreement with my natural disposition. This period of my youth is the one of which I have the most confused idea. During this time scarcely anything occurred of sufficient interest to my heart for me to preserve a lively recollection of it; and it is almost unavoidable that, amidst so many wanderings backwards and forwards, so many successive changes, I should transpose times or places. I am writing entirely from memory, without notes, without materials to assist my recollection. There are events in my life

which are as fresh in my mind as if they had just happened; but
there are also gaps and voids, which I can only fill up by the aid
of a narrative which is as confused as the recollection of it which
has remained to me. It is, therefore, possible that I have sometimes made mistakes, and I may do so again, in unimportant
matters, up to the time when I possess surer information regarding myself; but, in all that is really of essential importance, I feel
sure of being an accurate and faithful chronicler, as I shall always
endeavour to be in everything – of that the reader may rest
assured.

As soon as I had left Le Maître, I made up my mind, and set
out again for Annecy. The reason and secrecy of our departure
had greatly interested me in the safety of our retreat; and this
interest, which entirely absorbed my attention, had for some
days diverted me from the thought of return; but as soon as a
feeling of security left me free from anxiety, the ruling passion
recovered its ascendancy. Nothing flattered or tempted me; my
only desire was to return to mamma. The warmth and tenderness of my attachment to her had uprooted from my heart all
imaginary projects, all the follies of ambition. I saw no other
happiness than that of living with her, and I never went a step
without feeling that I was removing further from this happiness.
I accordingly returned to her as soon as it was possible. My
return was so speedy, and my mind so distracted, that, although I
recall to mind all my other journeys with the liveliest pleasure,
I have not the slightest recollection of this; I remember nothing
about it, except my departure from Lyons and my arrival at
Annecy. I leave it to the reader to imagine whether this latter
period is ever likely to fade from my memory. On my arrival, I
no longer found Madame de Warens; she had set out for Paris.

I have never learnt the real secret of this journey. She would
have told me, I am convinced, if I had pressed her to do so; but
no one was ever less curious than myself about his friends'
secrets; my heart, occupied only with the present, is entirely
filled with it, and, except for past pleasures, which henceforth
form my only enjoyment, there is no empty corner in it for
anything that is past. From the little that she told me, I fancied
that, owing to the revolution at Turin, caused by the abdication

of the King of Sardinia,[1] she was afraid of being forgotten, and was anxious, with the assistance of the intrigues of M. d'Aubonne, to endeavour to obtain the same advantages at the French court, which, as she often told me, she would herself have preferred, because, in the midst of so many important affairs, one is not kept under such disagreeable surveillance. If this is true, it is surprising that, on her return, she was not regarded with greater disfavour, and that she has always drawn her pension uninterruptedly. Many believe that she was charged with some secret commission, either by the bishop, who had business at the French court and was obliged to undertake a journey thither himself, or by some even more powerful personage, who knew how to insure her a happy return. It is certain that, if this be the case, the ambassadress was not ill-chosen, and that, still young and beautiful, she possessed all the necessary qualifications for carrying out a negotiation successfully.

[1] Rousseau's memory seems to be at fault, for the abdication of Victor-Amadeus II did not in fact take place till nearly five months later.

BOOK IV

[1731–1732]

I ARRIVED at Annecy, where I no longer found her. Imagine my surprise and grief! Then, for the first time, my regret at having abandoned Le Maître in so cowardly a manner made itself felt. It became keener still, when I heard of the misfortunes that had befallen him. His box of music, which contained all his worldly goods, the precious box, which had cost such trouble to save, had been seized on its arrival at Lyons, in consequence of a letter, in which the Chapter had informed Comte Dortan of its secret removal. Le Maître in vain claimed his property, his means of livelihood, the work of his whole life. The ownership of the box was at least open to dispute; but the question was not raised. The matter was decided on the spot by the law of the stronger, and poor Le Maître thus lost the fruit of his talents, the work of his youth and the resource of his old age.

Nothing was wanting to the blow which fell upon me to make it overwhelming. But I was at an age when great sorrow takes little hold, and I soon found means of consolation. I expected soon to hear news of Madame de Warens, although I did not know her address and she was ignorant of my return; and, as for my desertion of Le Maître, all things considered, I did not find it so blameworthy. I had been of service to him in his flight; that was the only service I could render him. If I had remained with him in France, I could not have cured him of his illness, I could not have saved his box, I should only have doubled his expenditure without being able to help him. This was the light in which I then regarded the matter: I regard it differently now. A mean action does not torture us when we have just committed it, but long afterwards, when we recall it to mind; for the remembrance of it never dies.

In order to get news of mamma, the only thing I could do was to wait; for where could I look for her in Paris, and what means had I to make the journey? Annecy was the safest place to gain tidings of her whereabouts, sooner or later. I therefore remained where I was, but behaved very badly. I never called on the bishop, who had already assisted me, and might have assisted me further; my patroness was no longer near me, and I was afraid of being reprimanded by him for running away. Still less did I go to the seminary; M. Gros was no longer there. I visited none of my acquaintances; however, I should have liked to go and see the Intendant's wife, but was afraid to do so. I did worse than this; I found M. Venture again, of whom, in spite of my enthusiasm for him, I had not even thought since my departure. I found him resplendent, fêted throughout Annecy; the ladies fought for him. This success completely turned my head. I saw no one but Venture, who almost made me forget Madame de Warens. In order to profit by his lessons more easily, I proposed to him to share his lodgings; he agreed. He lodged at a shoe-maker's, a pleasant and amusing fellow, who in his *patois* never called his wife anything except *salopière* (slut), a name which she fully deserved. He often had quarrels with her, which Venture did his best to prolong, while pretending that he wanted to put a stop to them. Coldly, and in his Provençal dialect, he used words and expressions to them which produced the greatest effect; the scenes that took place were enough to make one burst with laughter. In this manner the mornings passed before we were aware of it; at two or three o'clock we took a modest lunch; Venture went to visit his friends, with whom he took dinner, while I went for a solitary walk, meditating upon his great advantages, admiring and envious of his rare talents, and cursing my unlucky star for not summoning me to an equally happy lot. How little I knew about it! my own life would have been a hundred times more delightful, if I had been less foolish, and had known better how to enjoy it!

Madame de Warens had only taken Anet with her; she had left Merceret behind, her maid of whom I have already spoken, and whom I found still occupying her mistress's room. Mademoiselle Merceret was a little older than myself, not pretty, but sufficiently agreeable; a good Fribourgeoise, free from vice, in whom I discovered no other failing except that at times she was somewhat insubordinate to her mistress. I went to see her pretty often; she was an old acquaintance, and the sight of her reminded me of another still dearer, for whose sake I loved her. She had several friends, amongst them a certain Mademoiselle Giraud, a Genevese, who, for my sins, took it into her head to take a fancy to me. She continually pressed Merceret to take me to see her, which I allowed her to do, because I was fond of her, and there were other young persons there whose company was very agreeable. As for Mademoiselle Giraud, who made up to me in every possible way, nothing could add to the aversion I felt towards her. When she put her withered black snout, filthy with snuff, near my face I could hardly keep from spitting on it. But I bore it patiently; besides, I enjoyed myself very much with all the girls, all of whom, either to pay court to Mademoiselle Giraud, or for my own sake, vied with one another in making much of me. In all this I saw nothing but friendship. Since then, I have sometimes thought that it only rested with myself to see something more; but it never occurred to me, I never even gave it a thought.

Besides, sempstresses, chambermaids, and shop girls had not much temptation for me; I wanted young ladies. Everyone has his fancies; this has always been mine, and my ideas on this point are not those of Horace.[1] However, it is certainly not the vanity of rank and position that attracts me; it is a well preserved complexion, beautiful hands, a charming toilet, a general air of elegance and neatness, better taste in dress and expression, a finer and better made gown, a nattier pair of shoes, ribbons, lace, better arranged hair – this is what attracts me. I should always prefer a girl, even of less personal attractions, if better dressed. I myself confess this preference is ridiculous; but my heart, in spite of myself, makes me entertain it.

Well! once again these advantages offered themselves, and it only rested with myself to profit by them. How I love, from time to time, to come suddenly upon the delightful moments of my youth! They were so sweet to me; they have been so brief, so rare, and I have enjoyed them so cheaply! Ah! the mere remembrance

---

[1] See Horace, *Satires*, Book I, no. 2, ll. 80–82: Nec magis huic inter niveos viridisque lapillos, *etc.* "The matron, in the snowy splendour of her pearls and the green of her emeralds, does not have a softer thigh or straighter leg than the courtesan."

of them brings back to my heart an unmixed pleasure which I sorely need to reanimate my courage and to sustain the weariness of my remaining years.

One morning, the dawn appeared so beautiful that I threw on my clothes and hurried out into the country to see the sun rise. I enjoyed this sight in all its charm; it was the week after the festival of St. John. The earth, decked in its greatest splendour, was covered with verdure and flowers; the nightingales, nearly at the end of their song, seemed to delight in singing the louder; all the birds, uniting in their farewell to spring, were singing in honour of the birth of a beautiful summer day, one of those beautiful days which one no longer sees at my age and which are unknown in the melancholy land[1] in which I am now living.

Without perceiving it, I had wandered some distance from the town; the heat increased, and I walked along under the shady trees of a little valley by the side of a brook. I heard behind me the sound of horses' hoofs and the voices of girls, who seemed in a difficulty, but, nevertheless, were laughing heartily at it. I turned round, and heard myself called by name; when I drew near, I found two young ladies of my acquaintance, Mademoiselle de Graffenried and Mademoiselle Galley, who, being poor horsewomen, did not know how to make their horses cross the brook. Mademoiselle de Graffenried was an amiable young Bernese, who, having been driven from her home in consequence of some youthful folly, had followed the example of Madame de Warens, at whose house I had sometimes seen her; but, as she had no pension, she had been only too glad to attach herself to Mademoiselle Galley, who, having conceived a friendship for her, had persuaded her mother to let her stay with her as her companion until she could find some employment. Mademoiselle Galley was a year younger than her companion, and better-looking; there was something about her more delicate and more refined; at the same time, she had a very neat and well-developed figure, the greatest charm a girl can possess. They loved each other tenderly, and their good nature could not fail to keep up this intimacy, unless some lover came

[1] Rousseau was at this time at Wootton, in Staffordshire.

to disturb it. They told me that they were on their way to Toune, an old château belonging to Madame Galley; they begged me to assist them to get their horses across, which they could not manage by themselves. I wanted to whip the horses, but they were afraid that I might be kicked and they themselves thrown off. I accordingly had recourse to another expedient. I took Mademoiselle Galley's horse by the bridle, and then, pulling it after me, crossed the brook with the water up to my knees; the other horse followed without any hesitation. After this, I wanted to take leave of the young ladies and go my way like a fool. They whispered a few words to each other, and Mademoiselle de Graffenried, turning to me, said, "No, no; you shan't escape us like that. You have got wet in serving us, and we owe it as a duty to our conscience to see that you get dry. You must come with us, if you please; we make you our prisoner." My heart beat; I looked at Mademoiselle Galley. "Yes, yes," added she, laughing at my look of affright; "prisoner of war. Get up behind her; we will give a good account of you." "But, mademoiselle," I objected, "I have not the honour of your mother's acquaintance; what will she say when she sees me?" "Her mother is not at Toune," replied Mademoiselle de Graffenried; "we are alone; we return this evening, and you can return with us."

The effect of electricity is not more rapid than was the effect of these words upon me. Trembling with joy, I sprang upon Mademoiselle de Graffenried's horse; and, when I was obliged to put my arm round her waist to support myself, my heart beat so violently that she noticed it. She told me that hers was beating too, since she was afraid of falling. In the situation in which I was, this was almost an invitation to me to verify the truth for myself; but I had not the courage; and, during the whole of the ride, my two arms surrounded her like a belt, which certainly held her tight, but never shifted its place for a moment. Many women who read this would like to box my ears – and they would not be wrong.

The pleasant excursion and the chatter of the young ladies made me so talkative that we were never silent for a moment until evening – in fact, as long as we were together. They had put me so completely at my ease, that my tongue was as eloquent as my eyes, although not in the same manner. For a few moments only, when I found myself alone with one or the other, the conversation became a little constrained; but the absent one soon returned, and did not allow us time to investigate the reason of our embarrassment.

When we reached Toune, after I had first dried myself, we breakfasted. Next, it was necessary to proceed to the important business of dinner. The young ladies from time to time left off their cooking to kiss the farmer's children, and their poor scullion looked on and smothered his vexation. Provisions had been sent from the town, and all that was requisite for a good dinner, especially in the matter of delicacies; but, unfortunately, the wine had been forgotten. This was no wonder, since the young ladies did not drink it; but I was sorry for it, since I had counted upon its assistance to give me courage. They also were annoyed, possibly for the same reason, although I do not think so. Their lively and charming gaiety was innocence personified; besides, what could the two of them have done with me? They sent all round the neighbourhood to try and get some wine, but without success, so abstemious and poor are the peasants of this canton. They expressed their regret to me; I said that they need not be so concerned about it, that they did not require wine in order to intoxicate me. This was the only compliment I ventured to pay them during the day; but I believe that the roguish creatures saw clearly enough that the compliment was sincere.

We dined in the farmer's kitchen, the two friends seated on benches on either side of the long table, and their guest between them on a three-legged stool. What a dinner! what an enchanting remembrance! Why should a man, when he can enjoy pleasures so pure and real at so little cost, try to find new ones? No supper at any of the *petites maisons* of Paris could be compared to this meal, not only for gaiety and cheerfulness, but, I declare, for sensual enjoyment.

After dinner we practised a little economy. Instead of drinking the coffee which remained over from breakfast, we kept it for our tea with the cream and cakes which they had brought with them; and, to keep up our appetites, we went into the orchard to finish our dessert with cherries. I climbed up the tree, and threw down bunches of fruit, while they threw the stones back at me through the branches. Once Mademoiselle Galley, holding out her apron and throwing back her head, presented herself as a mark so prettily, and I took such accurate aim, that I threw a bunch right into her bosom. How we laughed! I said to myself, If my lips were only cherries, how readily would I throw them into the same place!

The day passed in this manner in the most unrestrained enjoyment, which, however, never overstepped the limits of the strictest decency. No *double-entendre*, no risky jest was uttered; and this decency was by no means forced, it was perfectly natural, and we acted and spoke as our hearts prompted. In short, my modesty – others will call it stupidity – was so great, that the greatest liberty of which I was guilty was once to kiss Mademoiselle Galley's hand. It is true that the circumstances gave special value to this favour. We were alone, I was breathing with difficulty, her eyes were cast down; my mouth, instead of giving utterance to words, fastened upon her hand, which she gently withdrew after I had kissed it, looking at me in a manner that showed no irritation. I do not know what I might have said to her; her friend came into the room, and appeared to me distinctly ugly at that moment.

At last, they remembered that they ought not to wait till night before returning to the town. We only just had time to get back while it was daylight, and we hastened to set out in the same order as we came. If I had dared, I would have changed the order; for Mademoiselle Galley's looks had created a profound impression upon my heart; but I did not venture to say anything, and it was not for her to make the proposal. On the way, we said to ourselves that it was a great pity that the day was over; but, far from complaining that it had been too short, we agreed that we had possessed the secret of lengthening it by the aid of all the amusements with which we had known how to occupy it.

I left them almost at the spot where they had found me. With what regret we separated! with what delight we planned to meet again! Twelve hours spent together were for us as good as centuries of intimacy. The sweet remembrance of that day cost the young girls nothing; the tender union between us three was worth far livelier pleasures, which would not have suffered it to exist; we loved one another openly and without shame, and were ready to love one another always in the same manner. Innocence of character has its enjoyment, which is certainly equal to any other, since it knows no relaxation and never ceases. As for me, I know that the memory of so beautiful a day touches and charms me more, and goes straighter to my heart, than the recollection of any pleasures that I have ever enjoyed. I did not exactly know what I wanted with these two charming persons, but both of them interested me exceedingly. I do not say that, if I had had control of the arrangements, my heart would have been equally shared between them. I had a slight feeling of preference; I should have been quite happy to have Mademoiselle de Graffenried as a mistress; but, if it had depended entirely upon myself, I think I should have preferred her for an intimate friend. Be that as it may, it seemed to me, when I left them, that I could no longer live without them both. Who would have said that I was never to see them in my life again, and that our love of a day was to end there?

My readers will not fail to laugh at my love adventures, and to remark that, after lengthy preliminaries, even those which made greatest progress, end in a kiss of the hand. Oh, my readers, do not be mistaken! I have, perhaps, had greater enjoyment in my amours which have ended in a simple kiss of the hand, than you will ever have in yours, which, at least, have begun with that!

Venture, who had gone to bed very late the night before, came home soon after me. This time I did not feel as pleased as usual to see him, and I was careful not to tell him how I had spent the day. The young ladies had spoken of him somewhat contemptuously, and had seemed ill-pleased to know that I was in such bad hands; this did him harm in my estimation, and, besides, everything which drew my attention from them could not fail to be disagreeable. However, he soon brought me back to myself and to him, by speaking of my position. It was too critical to be able to continue. Although I spent very little, my purse was almost empty, and I was without resources. No news of mamma arrived; I did not know what to do, and I felt a cruel pang at seeing the friend of Mademoiselle Galley reduced to beggary.

Venture told me that he had spoken about me to the Juge-Mage[1] and that he would take me to dine with him on the following day; that he was a man who might be able to assist me through his friends, and a pleasant acquaintance to make, being a man of intelligence and education, and an agreeable companion who possessed talent himself and respected it in others; then, mingling together in his usual fashion the most serious matters with the most trifling frivolities, he showed me a pretty little couplet just arrived from Paris, set to an air out of one of Mouret's operas, which was being played at the time. This couplet had pleased M. Simon (the Juge-Mage) so much, that he wanted to compose another to the same tune to answer it; he had also told Venture to compose one, and the latter had been seized with the mad idea of making me compose a third, in order, as he said, that the couplets might be seen arriving on the next day like the sedan-chairs in the *Roman comique*.[2]

Being unable to sleep, I composed my couplet to the best of my abilities. Considering that they were the first verses that I had ever made, they were tolerable, even better, or, at any rate, more tasteful, than they would have been the day before, as the subject turned upon a tender situation, for which my heart was already sympathetic. I showed my couplet, in the morning, to Venture, who, thinking it pretty, put it in his pocket without telling me whether he had composed his own. We went to dine with M. Simon, who received us cordially. The conversation was animated, indeed, it could not have been anything else, when carried on by two intelligent and well-read men. As for me, I played my usual part; I listened and held my tongue. Neither of them said a word about the couplet; I said nothing either, and, as far as I know, mine was never mentioned.

M. Simon appeared satisfied with my behaviour; this was nearly all that he learned about me at this interview. He had

[1] The lieutenant of the seneschal, an important officer of the crown, who administered justice in the King's name.

[2] Allusion to Chapter VII of Scarron's *Roman comique* (1651–57), in which four horse-drawn litters arrive at a hostelry one after the other.

already seen me several times at mamma's house, without paying particular attention to me. It is from this dinner that I date my acquaintance with him, which proved useless as far as the object I had in view was concerned, but from which I afterwards gained other advantages, which cause me to remember him with pleasure.

I must not omit to say something about his personal appearance, of which, considering his magisterial capacity and the *bel esprit* on which he prided himself, it would otherwise be impossible for anyone to form an idea. His height was certainly not three feet. His legs, straight, thin, and tolerably long, would have made him look taller, if they had been vertical; but they formed an obtuse angle like those of a wide-opened pair of compasses. His body was not only short, but thin and in every way indescribably small. When naked, he must have looked like a grasshopper. His head, of ordinary size, with a well-formed face, noble features, and nice eyes, looked like a false head set upon a stump. He might have spared himself much expense in the matter of clothing, for his large wig alone covered him completely from head to foot.

He had two entirely different voices, which, when he spoke, continually mingled together, and contrasted in a manner which at first was very amusing, but soon became disagreeable. One was grave and sonorous; if I may say so, it was the voice of his head. The other – clear, sharp, and piercing – was the voice of his body. When he was very careful, spoke very deliberately, and husbanded his breath, he could always speak with his deep voice; but as soon as he became ever so little animated and spoke in a livelier tone, his accent resembled the whistling of a key, and he had the greatest difficulty in recovering his bass.

With the appearance which I have described, and which is not in the least exaggerated, M. Simon was polite, a great courtier, and careful in his dress even to foppishness. As he desired to make the most of his advantages, he liked to give audience in bed; for no one, who saw a fine head on the pillow, was likely to imagine that that was all. This sometimes caused scenes, which I am sure all Annecy still remembers.

One morning, when he was waiting for some litigants in, or rather upon, this bed, in a beautiful fine white nightcap, ornamented with two large knots of rose-coloured ribbon, a countryman arrived and knocked at the door. The maidservant had gone out. M. Simon, hearing the knock repeated, cried out, "Come in," and the word, spoken a little too vigorously, came out of his mouth with his shrill utterance. The man entered, looked to see where the woman's voice came from, and, seeing in the bed a woman's mob-cap and a top-knot, was going to retire with profound apologies. M. Simon became angry, and cried out in a still shriller voice. The countryman, confirmed in his idea and considering himself insulted, overwhelmed him with abuse, told him that he was apparently nothing but a prostitute, and that the Juge-Mage set anything but a good example in his house. M. Simon, full of fury, and having no other weapon but his chamberpot, was going to throw it at the poor man's head, when his housekeeper came in.

This little dwarf, although so cruelly treated by nature in regard to his person, had received compensation for this in his mental talents, which were naturally agreeable, and which he had carefully developed. Although he was said to be a tolerably good lawyer, he had no liking for his profession. He had thrown himself into polite literature, and had succeeded. He had, above all, acquired that brilliant superficiality, that gift of varied conversation which gives society its charm, even in the company of women. He knew by heart all the little characteristics of the *Anas*[1] and the like; he possessed the art of making the most of them, relating them to advantage and with an air of mystery, as if that which had taken place sixty years ago had been an anecdote of yesterday. He understood music, and sang agreeably with his man's voice – in short, he possessed many pretty accomplishments for a magistrate. By dint of long paying court to the ladies of Annecy, he had become the fashion amongst them: he was always in attendance upon them like a little *sapajou*.[2] He even

[1] Collections of memorable sayings of certain persons, and anecdotes connected with them, as Johnsoniana, Walpoliana. These titles originated in France.
[2] An American monkey: used figuratively in the sense of "an ugly little man".

pretended to have great success with women, which amused them exceedingly. A certain Madame d'Épagny said that the greatest favour for him was to be allowed to kiss a woman's knee.

As he had a knowledge of good literature and was very fond of talking about it, his conversation was not only amusing, but also instructive. Afterwards, when I had acquired a taste for study, I cultivated his acquaintance, and derived great advantage from it. I sometimes went from Chambéri, where I was at that time, to see him. He commended and encouraged my zeal, and gave me some good advice about my reading, by which I often benefited. Unfortunately, in this weakly body dwelt a very sensitive soul. Some years later, he had some trouble or other which so grieved him that he died of it. It was a pity; he was certainly a good little man, whom one began by laughing at and ended by loving. Although his life has had little to do with mine, yet as I have received some useful lessons from him, I thought I might, out of gratitude, dedicate a niche in my memory to him.

As soon as I was at liberty, I ran to the street where Mademoiselle Galley lived, flattering myself with the hope of seeing someone going in or out, or opening a window. Nothing, not even a cat, was to be seen; and all the time I was there the house remained as firmly closed as if it had never been inhabited. The street was narrow and deserted; the presence of a man attracted attention; from time to time someone passed, or went in or out of the neighbourhood. I was much troubled about my person; it seemed to me that they guessed why I was there; and this idea tormented me, for I have always preferred the honour and repose of those who were dear to me to my own pleasures.

At last, tired of playing the Spanish lover and having no guitar, I determined to write to Mademoiselle de Graffenried. I would rather have written to her friend, but I did not dare to do so; besides, it was more becoming to begin with the one to whom I owed the acquaintance of the other, and with whom I was more intimate. When my letter was finished, I took it to Mademoiselle Giraud, as had been agreed with the young ladies when we

parted. It was they who suggested this expedient. Mademoiselle
Giraud was a quilter, and, as she sometimes worked at Madame
Galley's, she had access to her house. The messenger, certainly,
did not appear to me well chosen: but I was afraid that, if I made
any difficulty about her, they would propose no other. Besides, I
did not dare to hint that she wanted to establish a claim of her
own upon me. I felt mortified that she should venture to think
that she was, in my eyes, of the same sex as those young ladies. In
short, I preferred this means of delivering my letter to none at
all, and took my chance.

At the first word Giraud guessed my secret; it was not
difficult. Even if a letter to be delivered to a young lady had
not spoken for itself, my silly and embarrassed air alone
would have betrayed me. It may be imagined that this commission did not afford her great pleasure; however, she undertook
it, and executed it faithfully. The next morning I ran to
her house, where I found my answer. How I hastened to
get outside, to read and kiss it to my heart's content – that
there is no need to tell; but there is all the more reason to
mention the manner in which Mademoiselle Giraud behaved,
in which she showed greater delicacy and reserve than
I should have expected from her. Sensible enough to perceive
that, with her thirty-seven years, her leveret's eyes, her snuff-
bedaubed nose, her shrill voice and her black skin, she stood a
bad chance against two young persons, full of grace and in all
the splendour of beauty, she resolved neither to betray nor to
assist them, and preferred to lose me rather than help them to
win me.

[1732.] – Merceret, not having received any tidings of her
mistress, had for some time thought of returning to Fribourg;
Mademoiselle Giraud made her decide to do so. She did
more; she gave her to understand that it would be right
that someone should take her back to her father, and proposed
myself. Little Merceret, who by no means disliked me
either, thought this idea a very good one. The same day
they spoke to me of it as a settled affair, and, as I found nothing
disagreeable in this manner of disposing of myself, I consented,
considering the journey as a matter of a week at most.

Giraud, who thought otherwise, arranged everything. I was obliged to confess the state of my finances. Provision was made for me; Merceret undertook to defray my expenses, and, to make up for the loss she thus incurred, it was agreed, at my entreaty, that her few belongings should be sent on in advance, and that we should make the journey slowly on foot. This was done.

I am sorry to be obliged to describe so many girls in love with me; but, as I have very little reason to be vain of the advantages I have gained from these amours, I think I may tell the truth without scruple. Merceret, younger and not so cunning as Giraud, never made such lively advances; but she imitated the tone of my voice and accent, repeated my words, showed me the attention which I ought to have shown to her, and, being naturally very timid, always took care that we slept in the same room; an intimacy which rarely stops at such a point in the case of a young man of twenty and a young woman of twenty-five who are travelling together.

On this occasion, however, such was the case. My simplicity was such that, although Merceret was not disagreeable to me, not only did the slightest attempt at gallantry never occur to my mind, during the whole journey, but I never even had the remotest idea of anything of the kind; and, even if the idea had occurred to me, I should have been too foolish to know how to take advantage of it. I could not imagine how a young man and a young woman could ever sleep together; I believed that it required ages to prepare for this terrible arrangement. If poor Merceret, when she offered to defray my expenses, reckoned upon some equivalent, she was deceived; we reached Fribourg exactly as we had left Annecy.

When we passed through Geneva, I did not go to see anyone; but I almost had a serious attack of illness on the bridges. I have never seen the walls of this happy city, never entered its gates, without feeling a certain heart-sinking, the result of excessive emotion. While the noble image of liberty elevated my soul, thoughts of equality, union, and gentleness of manners moved me even to tears, and inspired me with a lively regret at having lost all these blessings. How mistaken I was, and yet how naturally! I thought I saw all this in my native land, because I carried it in my heart.[1]

We were obliged to pass Nyon. Pass without seeing my good father! Had I been able to bring myself to do this, I should afterwards have died of grief. I left Merceret at the inn, and went at all risks to see him. Ah! how wrong I was to be afraid of him! When I approached him, his heart opened itself to those feelings of a father with which it was filled. How he wept while we embraced! He at first thought that I had returned to him. I told him my story and my resolution. He feebly opposed it. He pointed out to me the dangers to which I was exposing myself, and told me that the briefest follies were the best. For the rest, he did not feel the slightest temptation to detain me by force, and in that I am of opinion that he was right; but it is none the less certain that he did not do all that he might have done to bring me back, whether it was that he himself was of opinion that I ought not to retrace the step that I had already taken, or, perhaps, did not quite know what he could do with me at my age. I have since learned that he had formed a very unjust and entirely false, although very natural, opinion of my travelling companion. My step-mother, a good woman but rather mawkish, pretended to want to keep me to supper. I did not stay, but told them that I intended to stop longer with them on my return, and left in their charge my little bundle which I had sent by the boat and did not know what to do with. I set out early the next morning, pleased that I had had the courage to do my duty and had seen my father.

We arrived without accident at Fribourg. Towards the end of the journey, my companion's advances became less pronounced. After our arrival, she showed me nothing but coldness, and her father, who was not rolling in money, did not give me a very favourable reception; and I went to an inn to sleep. The following day I went to see them; they invited me to dinner; I accepted. Then we separated with dry eyes. In the evening I

---

[1] Rousseau's feelings towards his native city changed after its condemnation of *Emile*, and he would eventually renounce his citizenship. See Book XII, p. 653.

returned to my beershop, and left the place two days after my arrival, without exactly knowing which way I intended to go.

Here again was an incident in my life when Providence offered me exactly what I wanted, in order to spend my days in happiness. Merceret was a very good girl, certainly not brilliant or handsome, but neither was she ugly; she possessed little animation, and, but for occasional exhibitions of temper, which passed off with tears and never led to any stormy results, was very sensible. She was really attached to me; I might have married her without any difficulty, and followed her father's trade; my taste for music would have made me fond of it. I should have settled at Fribourg – a little town, not pretty, certainly, but inhabited by very good-natured people. I should, no doubt, have lost much pleasure, but I should have lived in peace to my last hour; and I, better than anyone else, ought to know that there was no reason for a moment's hesitation about such a bargain.

I returned, not to Nyon, but to Lausanne. I wanted to sate myself with the sight of this beautiful lake, which is there seen in its greatest extent. Few of the secret motives which have determined me to act have been more rational. Things seen at a distance are rarely powerful enough to make me act. The uncertainty of the future has always made me look upon plans, which need considerable time to carry them out, as decoys for fools. I indulge in hopes like others, provided it costs me nothing to support them; but if they require continued attention, I have done with it. The least trifling pleasure which is within my reach tempts me more than the joys of Paradise. However, I make an exception of the pleasure which is followed by pain; this has no temptation for me, because I love only pure enjoyments, and these a man never has when he knows that he is preparing for himself repentance and regret.

It was very necessary for me to reach some place, the nearer the better; for, having lost my way, I found myself in the evening at Moudon, where I spent the little money I had left, except ten kreutzers, which went the next day for dinner; and, in the evening, when I reached a little village near Lausanne, I entered an inn without a sou to pay for my bed, and not knowing what to do. Being very hungry, I put a good face upon the matter, and called for supper, as if I had been quite able to pay for it. I went to bed without thinking of anything, and slept soundly; and, after I had breakfasted in the morning and reckoned with my host, I wanted to leave him my waistcoat as security for the seven *batz*, which was the amount of my bill. This good fellow refused it; he said that, thanks to heaven, he had never stripped anyone; that he did not mean to begin for the sake of seven *batz*; that I could keep my waistcoat and pay him when I could. I was touched by his kindness, but less than I ought to have been, and less than I have been since, when I have thought of it again. I soon sent him his money, with thanks, by a messenger whom I could trust; but fifteen years afterwards, returning from Italy by way of Lausanne, I sincerely regretted to find that I had forgotten the name of the landlord and of the inn. I should certainly have gone to see him; it would have been a real pleasure to me to remind him of his act of charity, and to prove to him that it had not been ill-applied. The simple and unpretentious kindness of this worthy man appears to me more deserving of gratitude than services, doubtless more important, but rendered with greater ostentation.

When approaching Lausanne, I mused upon the straits in which I found myself, and thought how I might extricate myself without betraying my distress to my step-mother; and, in this pilgrimage on foot, I compared myself to my friend Venture on his arrival at Annecy. I was so heated with this idea that, without reflecting that I possessed neither his charm of manner nor his accomplishments, I took it into my head to play the little Venture at Lausanne, to give lessons in music, which I did not understand, and to say that I came from Paris, where I had never been. As there was no choir-school, in which I could have offered to assist, and as, besides, I was not such a fool as to venture amongst those who were acquainted with the art, I commenced to carry out my fine project by making inquiries for a small inn where I could live well and cheaply. I was recommended to a certain M. Perrotet, who took boarders. This Perrotet proved to be the best fellow in the world, and gave me a most hearty reception. I told him my petty lies, as I had prepared them. He promised to speak about me, and to try to get me some pupils, and said that he would not ask me for any money until I had earned some. His charge for board was five "white crowns,"[1] little enough, everything considered, for the accommodation, but a great deal for me. He advised me only to put myself on half-board at first; this meant some good soup, and nothing else, for dinner, but a good supper later. I agreed. Poor Perrotet let me have all this without payment, and with the best heart in the world, and spared no pains to be of use to me.

Why is it that, having found so many good people in my youth, I find so few in my later years? Is their race extinct? No; but the class in which I am obliged to look for them now, is no longer the same as that in which I found them. Among the people, where great passions only speak at intervals, the sentiments of nature make themselves more frequently heard; in the higher ranks they are absolutely stifled, and, under the mask of sentiment, it is only interest or vanity that speaks.

I wrote from Lausanne to my father, who forwarded my bundle, and gave me some excellent advice – of which I ought to have made better use. I have already noted moments of incomprehensible delirium, during which I was no longer myself. Here, again, is one of the most striking instances. In order to understand to what an extent I had lost my head, to what an extent I had, so to speak, *Venturised* myself, it is only necessary to consider how many extravagances I committed at one and the same time. Behold me a teacher of singing, without knowing how to decipher an air; for even had I profited by the six months spent with Le Maître, they would never have been sufficient; besides, I had been taught by a master, and that was enough to make me learn indifferently. A Parisian from Geneva, and a Catholic in a Protestant country, I considered I ought to change my name as well as my religion and my country. I always adhered as closely as possible to my great model. He had called himself Venture de Villeneuve; out of the name Rousseau I made the anagram Vaussore, and called myself Vaussore de Villeneuve. Venture knew how to compose, although he had

---

[1] Silver coins worth three francs.

said nothing about it; I, without any knowledge of this, boasted of my skill before all the world; and, without being able to score the most trifling vaudeville,[1] I gave myself out as a composer. This was not all; having been presented to M. de Treytorens, a professor of law, who was very fond of music and gave concerts at his house, I must needs give him a sample of my talents, and began to compose a piece for his concert with as much effrontery as if I knew how to set about it. I had the perseverance to work for a fortnight at this beautiful composition, to make a fair copy of it, to write out the parts, and distribute them with as much assurance as if it had been a masterpiece of harmony. Lastly, a thing which will hardly be believed although it is perfectly true, to crown this lofty production in a befitting manner, I added at the end a pretty minuet, which was sung in every street, and which, perhaps, everybody still recollects, the words of which were as follows:

> Quelle caprice!
> Quelle injustice!
> Quoi! ta Clarice
> Trahirait tes feux! etc.

Venture had taught me this air, with a bass accompaniment and other disgusting words, which had helped me to remember it. I accordingly added at the end of my composition this minuet and his bass, suppressing the words, and gave the whole out as my own, as fearlessly as if I had been talking to the inhabitants of the moon.

The company assembled to perform my piece. I explained to each how the time was to be taken, the manner of execution, and the signs of repetition of the parts. I was extremely busy. They spent five or six minutes in trying their voices and instruments, which seemed five or six centuries. At last all was ready; I gave five or six beats of "Attention!" with a beautiful roll of paper upon my conductor's desk. Silence having been obtained, I solemnly began to beat time, the performance commenced. . . .

---

[1] A *vaudeville* meant satirical verses composed to some well-known tune, for performance in popular theatres.

No, since the days of French opera, never has such a caterwauling been heard! Whatever they might have thought of my pretended talent, the effect was worse than anything that seemed to be expected. The musicians were ready to choke with laughter; the audience opened their eyes wide, and would gladly have stopped their ears, but did not know how. The musicians, who played the part of my executioners, wishing to amuse themselves, scraped horribly enough to split the drum of a deaf man's[1] ear. I had the hardihood to keep on without stopping, my forehead covered with large drops of sweat, but prevented by shame from running away and leaving them all in the lurch. By way of consolation, I heard those who were present whispering to themselves, or rather to me, "Intolerable! What mad music! What a witches' Sabbath!" Poor Jean Jacques! in this cruel moment, little did you think that one day, in the presence of the King of France and all his Court, your music would excite murmurs of applause and astonishment, and that, in all the boxes round you, charming women would whisper to themselves, "What enchanting music! What charming notes! All these airs go straight to the heart!"[2]

But what put everyone in good humour was the minuet. No sooner had a few notes been played, than I heard on all sides bursts of laughter. Everybody congratulated me on my refined taste; they assured me that this minuet would make a name for me, and that my composition deserved to be sung everywhere. I need not describe my anguish, nor confess that I well deserved it.

Next day, one of the musicians, named Lutold, came to see me, and was honest enough not to congratulate me on my success. The deep feeling of folly, shame and regret, despair at the position to which I was reduced, the impossibility of keeping my heart shut in my distress, made me open it to him. I let my tears flow freely; and, not content with confessing my ignorance, I told him everything, begging him to keep it a secret; he

[1] *Un quinze-vingt*: properly an inmate of the hospital at Paris, established for 300 *blind* men.
[2] He is referring to the first performance of his opera *Le Devin du village* at Fontainebleau in 1752 (see Book VIII, p. 400).

promised to do so, and kept his word in the manner that may be imagined. The same evening the whole of Lausanne knew who I was; and, what was remarkable, no one showed that he knew it, not even the good Perrotet, who in spite of everything, was not deterred from giving me board and lodging.

I lived, but my life was very melancholy. The results of my first appearance did not make Lausanne a very agreeable place for me to stay in. Pupils did not come in crowds; I did not even get a single girl to teach, and no one belonging to the town. I had in all two or three fat "Deutschers," whose stupidity was only equalled by my ignorance, who wearied me to death, and, in my hands, did not turn out very accomplished strummers. I was sent for to one house only, where a little serpent of a girl amused herself with showing me a quantity of music of which I could not read a note, and which she was spiteful enough afterwards to sing in the music-master's face, to show him how it ought to be executed. I was so little able to read an air at sight, that at the brilliant concert of which I have spoken, I was utterly unable to follow the performance even for a moment to find out whether the musicians were playing what I had before my eyes – the music which I had composed myself.

In the midst of these great humiliations I found sweet consolation in the news I received from time to time from my two charming friends. I have always found great power of consolation in their sex; and nothing soothes my dejection in times of affliction more than the feeling that an amiable person sympathises with me. The correspondence, however, came to an end soon afterwards, and was never renewed; but it was my fault. When I changed my place of abode, I forgot to give them my address; and, being compelled by necessity to think of nothing but myself, I soon forgot them altogether.

I have not spoken of poor mamma for some time; but it would be a mistake to think that I also forgot her. I never ceased to think of her and to long to find her again, not only to satisfy the needs of existence, but still more those of my heart. My devotion to her, lively and tender as it was, did not prevent me from loving others, but not in the same way. All alike owed my tenderness to their charms; but, whereas in the case of others these were the only cause of it, and it would have disappeared with them, mamma might have grown old and ugly, and I should have loved her as fondly as ever. My heart had completely transferred to her person the homage which it at first rendered to her beauty; and, whatever change she might have suffered, my feelings towards her could never have changed, provided that she had still remained herself. I knew very well that I owed her my gratitude; but in reality I did not think of that. Whatever she might have done for me or not, it would always have been the same. I loved her neither from a feeling of duty or self-interest, nor from motives of convenience; I loved her because I was born to love her. When I fell in love with any other woman, I admit that it distracted my attention, and I thought of her less frequently; but I thought of her with the same feelings of pleasure, and, whether in love or not, I never occupied my thoughts with her without feeling that there could never be any real happiness for me in life as long as I was separated from her.

Although I had not heard of her for so long, I never believed that I had lost her altogether, or thought it possible that she could have forgotten me. I said to myself: Sooner or later she will learn that I am a lonely wanderer, and will give me some sign of life; I shall find her again, of that I am certain. Meanwhile, it was a delight to me to live in her native country, to walk through the streets through which she had walked, past the houses in which she had lived – all by guess, for it was one of my foolish oddities that I could not bring myself to make inquiries about her, or even to mention her name, unless it was absolutely necessary. It seemed to me that I could not speak of her without betraying the feelings with which she inspired me, without my mouth revealing the secret of my heart, without in some way compromising her. I even believe that with this was mingled a certain feeling of alarm that someone might say something bad about her. The step she had taken had been freely commented upon, and her conduct discussed. For fear that they might not speak of her as I should have liked, I preferred to hear nothing at all said about her.

As my pupils did not take up much of my time, and her birthplace was only twelve miles from Lausanne, I spent three or four days in walking there, during which a feeling of most tender emotion never left me. The view of the Lake of Geneva and its delightful shores always possessed a special charm in my eyes which I cannot explain, and which consists not only in the beauty of the view, but in something still more attractive, which moves and touches me. Whenever I approach the Canton of Vaud, I am conscious of an impression in which the remembrance of Madame de Warens, who was born there, of my father who lived there, of Mademoiselle de Vulson who enjoyed the first fruits of my youthful love, of several pleasure trips which I made there when a child and, I believe, some other exciting cause, more mysterious and more powerful than all this, is combined. When the burning desire of this happy and peaceful life, which flees from me and for which I was born, inflames my imagination, it is always the Canton of Vaud, near the lake, in the midst of enchanting scenery, to which it draws me. I feel that I must have an orchard on the shore of this lake and no other, that I must have a loyal friend, a loving wife, a cow, and a little boat. I shall never enjoy perfect happiness on earth until I have all that. I laugh at the simplicity with which I have several times visited this country merely in search of this imaginary happiness. I was always surprised to find its inhabitants, especially the women, of quite a different character from that which I expected. How contradictory it appeared to me! The country and its inhabitants have never seemed to me made for each other.

During this journey to Vévay, walking along the beautiful shore, I abandoned myself to the sweetest melancholy. My heart eagerly flung itself into a thousand innocent raptures; I was filled with emotion, I sighed and wept like a child. How often have I stopped to weep to my heart's content, and, sitting on a large stone, amused myself with looking at my tears falling into the water!

At Vévay I lodged at *La Clef*, and, during the two days that I remained there without seeing anyone, I conceived an affection for this town which has followed me on all my journeys, and which, finally, made me fix the abode of the heroes of my romance there. I would say to all persons of taste and feeling: Go to Vévay, explore the country, contemplate the scenery, row on the lake, and then say if Nature has not made this beautiful country for a Julie, a Claire and a St. Preux; but do not expect to find them there!

I return to my history.

As I was a Catholic and professed to be one, I followed openly and without hesitation the faith which I had embraced. On Sundays, when it was fine, I went to mass at Assens, two leagues from Lausanne. I usually went in the company of other Catholics, particularly a Parisian embroiderer whose name I have forgotten. He was not a Parisian like myself, but a true Parisian from Paris, an arch-Parisian of the *bon Dieu*, good-natured as a child of Champagne. His love for his country was so great that he would not allow himself to have any doubts about my being a Parisian as well, for fear of losing the opportunity of talking about it. M. de Crouzas, the lieutenant-governor, had a gardener – who was also a Parisian, but not so good-natured – who considered the honour of his country compromised if anyone dared to claim it for his own when he had no right to do so. He questioned me with the air of a man who felt sure of catching me in a mistake, and then smiled maliciously. He once asked me what there was remarkable in the Marché-neuf. As may be imagined, I answered at random. Having lived twenty years in Paris, I ought by this time to know the city; and yet, if anyone were to ask me a similar question to-day, I should be equally at a loss for an answer, and my embarrassment might lead anyone to conclude that I have never been there. To such an extent is a person liable, even when he meets with the truth, to put his trust in misleading arguments.

I cannot say exactly how long I remained at Lausanne; I did not carry away from it very lively recollections. I only know that, finding myself unable to gain a livelihood, I went from there to Neufchâtel, where I spent the winter. I was more successful in the latter town; I got some pupils, and earned enough to settle with my good friend Perrotet, who had faithfully sent on my little bundle, although I still owed him a considerable sum.

I insensibly learned music by teaching it. My life was tolerably pleasant; a sensible man would have been content with it, but my restless heart wanted something more. On Sundays and other days when I was at liberty, I roamed the country and forests in the neighbourhood, ever wandering, musing, and sighing; and, when once out of the city, I never returned till the evening. One day, being at Boudry, I went into an inn to dine; I saw there a man with a long beard, a violet-coloured coat after the Greek style, a fur cap, of somewhat noble appearance and presence, who often had great difficulty in making himself understood, since he spoke an almost unintelligible jargon, which resembled Italian more than any other language. I understood nearly everything he said, and I was the only person who did. He could only express his meaning by making signs to the landlord and the country people. I said a few words to him in Italian, which he understood perfectly; he got up and embraced me with delight. The acquaintance was soon made, and from that moment I acted as his interpreter. His dinner was a good one, mine was barely tolerable; he invited me to share his, and I accepted without ceremony. Drinking and chattering, we became quite intimate, and at the end of the meal we were inseparable. He told me that he was a Greek prelate and Archimandrite of Jerusalem, and that he had been commissioned to make a collection in Europe for the restoration of the Holy Sepulchre. He showed me beautiful patents from the Czarina and the Emperor; he had several more from other sovereigns. He was well satisfied with the amount he had already collected, but he had found incredible difficulties in Germany, since he did not understand a word of German, Latin, or French, and was reduced to his Greek, Turkish, and the *lingua franca*, as his sole resource, which had not helped him much in the country in which he had made so bad a beginning. He proposed that I should accompany him as secretary and interpreter. Although I had just bought a new violet coat, which was not ill-suited to my new employment, I looked anything but smart, so that he thought it would be an easy matter to secure my services, and in this he was not mistaken. Our agreement was soon made; I asked nothing, and he promised much. Without security, without bond, without knowing anything about him, I submitted myself to his guidance, and the next morning behold me on my way to Jerusalem!

We commenced our journey with the Canton of Fribourg, where he did not do much. His episcopal rank did not allow him to play the beggar and collect money from private persons; but we presented his commission to the senate, who gave him a small sum. From there we went to Berne. We put up at the Falcon, at that time a good inn, where good company was to be found. The guests were numerous and the table well served. I had so long had to put up with bad fare, that I needed to recruit myself; I had the opportunity and made use of it. The worthy Archimandrite was himself very good company, lively, fond of the table, and conversed well with those who understood him. He was not without a certain amount of knowledge, and employed his Greek erudition with considerable taste. One day, while cracking nuts at dessert, he cut his finger very deeply; and as the blood poured forth in streams, he showed his finger to the company, and said, with a laugh, *Mirate, Signori; questo è sangue pelasgo.*[1]

At Berne my services were of some use to him, and I did not come off as badly as I had expected. I was more courageous and eloquent than I should have been on behalf of myself. But it was not so simple a matter as at Fribourg; lengthy and frequent conferences with the chief men of the State were necessary, and the examination of his papers was not the work of a day. At length, when everything was in order, he was admitted to an audience by the Senate. I went with him as his interpreter, and was ordered to speak. This was the last thing I had expected; it had never entered my head that, after long conferences with the individual members, it would be necessary to address the assembly in a body as if nothing had been said. Judge of my embarrassment! For a man as bashful as myself, to speak, not only in public but before the Senate of Berne, and to speak extempore, without having a single minute for preparation, was enough to annihilate me. And yet I did not even feel nervous. Briefly and clearly I explained the Archimandrite's commission. I praised the piety of those princes who had contributed to the collection he had come to make. In order to stir their excellencies to

---

[1] Admire, gentlemen; this is Pelasgian blood!

emulation, I said that no less was to be expected from their accustomed munificence; and then, having tried to prove that this good work was equally meritorious for all Christians without distinction of sect or creed, I ended by promising the blessings of Heaven to all those who should take part in it. I will not say that my speech made a great impression, but it was certainly to the taste of the audience, and, on leaving, the Archimandrite received a considerable donation, and, in addition, compliments upon the intelligence of his secretary, which I had the pleasing task of interpreting, although I did not venture to render them word for word. This is the only time in my life that I have ever spoken in public and in the presence of a sovereign, and perhaps, also the only time that I have spoken well and boldly. What a difference in the temperament of the same man! Three years ago, I went to Yverdun to see my old friend M. Roguin, and received a deputation, which came to thank me for some books which I had presented to the town library. The Swiss are great orators; they harangued me. I felt obliged to reply; but I was so embarrassed when I began to do so, and my head became so confused, that I stopped short and made myself ridiculous. Although naturally shy, I have sometimes shown confidence in my youth, never in my riper years. The more I have seen of the world, the less I have been able to conform to its manner.

On leaving Berne, we went to Soleure; for the Archimandrite intended to pass through Germany again and to return by way of Hungary or Poland, which was an enormously long round; but as his purse filled rather than emptied on the road, he had little fear of a roundabout way. As for me, it was a matter of indifference whether I was on horseback or on foot; and I should have desired nothing better than to travel in the same manner my whole life-time; but it was written that I should not go so far.

The first thing we did on our arrival at Soleure,[1] was to go and pay our respects to the French ambassador. Unfortunately

---

[1] The Swiss town of Soleure made a business of supplying mercenaries to the French army.

for my Bishop, this ambassador was the Marquis de Bonac, who had been ambassador at the Sublime Porte, and was bound to be well acquainted with everything concerning the Holy Sepulchre. The Archimandrite had a quarter of an hour's audience, to which I was not admitted, as the ambassador was acquainted with the *lingua franca* and spoke Italian at least as well as myself. When my Greek went out, I was going to follow him, but was detained; it was my turn next. Having given myself out as a Parisian, I was, as such, under his Excellency's jurisdiction. He asked me who I was, and exhorted me to tell the truth. I promised to do so, and asked him for a private audience, which was granted. He took me to his study, and shut the door. I threw myself at his feet and kept my word. I should not have confessed less, even if I had made no promise; for a continual need of opening my heart brings it every moment to my lips, and, having disclosed myself unreservedly to the musician Lutold, I was not likely to play the mysterious with the Marquis de Bonac. He was so satisfied with my little story, and the frankness with which I had unbosomed myself, that he took me by the hand, conducted me to his wife, and introduced me to her, at the same time giving her an outline of my story. Madame de Bonac received me kindly, and said that I must not be allowed to go with the Greek monk. It was decided that I should stay at the hotel, until they saw what could be done with me. I wished to go and say good-bye to my poor Archimandrite, for whom I had conceived a liking, but they would not allow me. He was informed that I had been detained, and, a quarter of an hour afterwards, I saw my little bundle arrive. M. de la Martinière, secretary to the embassy, was, in a manner, intrusted with the care of me. While showing me to the room which was intended for me, he said: "This room, in the time of the Comte du Luc, was occupied by a celebrated man of the same name as yourself;[1] it rests with yourself to supply his place in every respect, so that it may one day be said, Rousseau the first, Rousseau the second." This similarity, of which at that time I had little hopes, would have flattered my ambition less, if I had

---

[1] He was referring to the poet Jean-Baptiste Rousseau (1671–1741).

been able to foresee how heavy would be the price I should one day have to pay for it.

M. de la Martinière's words excited my curiosity. I read the works of the writer whose room I occupied; and, having regard to the compliment which had been paid me, and believing that I had a taste for poetry, I composed a cantata in praise of Madame de Bonac as a first attempt. This fancy did not last. From time to time I have written indifferent verses; it is a fairly good exercise, for practising oneself in elegant turns and improving one's prose; but I have never found sufficient attraction in French poetry to devote myself to it entirely.

M. de la Martinière wanted to see how I could write, and asked me to give him in writing the same details as I had given to the ambassador. I wrote him a long letter, which I hear has been preserved by M. de Marianne, who was for a long time attached to the embassy under the Marquis de Bonac, and has since succeeded M. de la Martinière during the ambassadorship of M. de Courteilles. I have asked M. de Malesherbes to try and get me a copy of this letter. If I can procure it through him or others, it will be found in the collection which is intended to accompany my Confessions.

The experience which I began to acquire by degrees moderated my romantic plans; for instance, I not only did not fall in love with Madame de Bonac, but I immediately saw that I had little chance of advancement in her husband's house. M. de la Martinière in office, and M. de Marianne waiting as it were to step into his shoes, left me nothing higher to hope for than the post of under-secretary, which was not excessively tempting to me. For this reason, when I was consulted as to what I should like to do, I showed a great desire to go to Paris. The ambassador liked the idea, which at least seemed likely to relieve him of me. M. de Merveilleux, secretary and interpreter to the embassy, said that his friend, M. Godard, a Swiss colonel in the service of France, was looking for a companion for his nephew, who was entering the service very early, and thought that I might suit him. With this idea, which was adopted without much consideration, my departure was settled; and I, who saw before me a journey, with Paris at the end of it, was highly delighted. They gave me some letters, a hundred francs for my travelling expenses, together with some very good advice, and I set out.

The journey took me a fortnight, which I may reckon amongst the happy days of my life. I was young, and in good health; I had sufficient money and abundant hopes; I travelled on foot and I travelled alone. That I should consider this an advantage would appear surprising, if the reader were not by this time familiar with my disposition. My pleasing chimeras kept me company, and never did my heated imagination give birth to any that were more magnificent. When anyone offered me an empty seat in a carriage, or accosted me on the road, I made a wry face when I saw that fortune overthrown, the edifice of which I reared during my walk. This time my ideas were warlike. I was going to be attached to a military man and to become a soldier myself; for it had been arranged that I should begin by being a cadet. I already saw myself in an officer's uniform, with a beautiful white plume. My breast swelled at this noble thought. I had a smattering of geometry and fortification; I had an uncle an engineer; I was, in a manner, a soldier born. My short sight was a slight obstacle, which, however, did not trouble me much; and I hoped, by dint of coolness and intrepidity, to supply this defect. I had read that Marshal Schomberg was very short-sighted; why should not Marshal Rousseau be the same? I grew so warm in pursuit of these foolish ideas, that I saw nothing but troops, ramparts, gabions, batteries, and myself, in the midst of fire and smoke, calmly giving my orders with my field-glass in my hand. However, when I passed through beautiful scenery, when I saw groves and rivulets, this touching sight made me sigh regretfully; in the midst of my glory, I felt that my heart was not made for such din and noise; and soon, without knowing how, I found myself in the midst of my beloved sheepfolds, renouncing for ever the toils of Mars.

How greatly did the entrance into Paris belie the idea I had formed of it! The external decorations of Turin, the beauty of its streets, the symmetry and regularity of the houses, had made me look for something quite different in Paris. I had imagined to myself a city of most imposing aspect, as beautiful as it was large, where nothing was to be seen but splendid streets and palaces of gold and marble. Entering by the suburb of St. Marceau, I saw nothing but dirty and stinking little streets, ugly black houses, a general air of slovenliness and poverty, beggars, carters, menders of old clothes, criers of decoctions and old hats. All this, from the outset, struck me so forcibly, that all the real magnificence I have since seen in Paris has been unable to destroy this first impression, and I have always retained a secret dislike against residence in this capital. I may say that the whole time, during which I afterwards lived there, was employed solely in trying to find means to enable me to live away from it.

Such is the fruit of a too lively imagination, which exaggerates beyond human exaggeration, and is always ready to see more than it has been told to expect. I had heard Paris so much praised, that I had represented it to myself as the ancient Babylon, where, if I had ever visited it, I should, perhaps, have found as much to take off from the picture which I had drawn of it. The same thing happened to me at the Opera, whither I hastened to go the day after my arrival. The same thing happened to me later at Versailles; and again, when I saw the sea for the first time; and the same thing will always happen to me, when I see anything which has been too loudly announced; for it is impossible for men, and difficult for Nature herself, to surpass the exuberance of my imagination.

To judge from the manner in which I was received by all those to whom I had letters, I thought my fortune was made. The person to whom I was specially recommended, and who received me with the least enthusiasm, was M. de Surbeck, who had left the service and was living in philosophic retirement at Bagneux, where I went to see him several times, and where he never offered me so much as a glass of water. I was better received by Madame de Merveilleux, the interpreter's sister-in-law, and by his nephew, an officer in the guards; mother and son not only received me kindly, but they gave me a standing invitation to their table, of which I often availed myself during my stay at Paris. Madame de Merveilleux seemed to me to have been handsome once; her hair was a beautiful black, and worn in ringlets on her forehead in the old-fashioned style. She still retained what does not perish with personal attractions: an agreeable mind. She appeared satisfied with mine, and did all she could to help me; but no one supported her, and I was soon undeceived in regard to the great interest which was apparently taken in me. I must, however, do justice to the French; they do not exhaust themselves so much in protestations as is said, and those they make are nearly always sincere; but they have a way of appearing to be interested in you, which is more deceptive than words. The coarse compliments of the Swiss can only impose upon fools. The manners of the French are more seductive, for the very reason that they are simpler; one would think that they are not telling you all they mean to do for you, in order to give you a more agreeable surprise. I will say more: they are not false in their professions; they are naturally obliging, kindly, benevolent, and even, whatever one may say, more sincere than any other nation; but they are fickle and flighty. The feelings which they express towards you are genuine; but these feelings are no sooner come than they are gone. When you converse with them, they are full of you; as soon as you are out of their sight, they forget you. Nothing is permanent in their hearts; with them everything is the work of the moment.

Thus I was greatly flattered, but little benefited. This Colonel Godard, to whose nephew I had been sent, turned out to be a frightful old miser, who, although rolling in riches, wanted my services for nothing, when he saw the distress I was in. He wanted me to be a sort of valet to his nephew, without wages, rather than a real tutor. As I was permanently attached to him, and thereby exempt from service, he said that I ought to live on my pay as a cadet – that is, as a soldier. He would scarcely consent to give me a uniform; he would have liked me to content myself with that of the regiment. Madame de Merveilleux, indignant at his proposals, herself persuaded me not to accept them; her son was of the same opinion. They looked for something else for me, but found nothing. In the meantime, I began to be pressed for money; a hundred francs, out of which I had paid the expenses of my journey, could not carry me very far. Fortunately, I received from the ambassador a small additional remittance which was very useful to me, and I think that he would not have abandoned me if I had had more patience; but I am unable to wait long for what I desire, or to solicit it. I lost heart, I appeared no more, and all was at an end. I had not forgotten my poor mamma; but how was I to find her? where was I to look for her? Madame de Merveilleux, who was acquainted with my story, had assisted me in my inquiries for a long time without success. At last, she informed me that Madame de Warens had left Paris more than two months ago, but that no one knew whether she had gone to Savoy or Turin, and that some said she had returned to Switzerland. This was enough to decide me to follow her, as I was sure that, wherever she was, I should find her in the country more easily than I had been able to do in Paris.

Before setting out, I exercised my new poetical talent in a letter to Colonel Godard, in which I abused him to the best of my power. I showed this scrawl to Madame de Merveilleux, who, instead of reproving me, as she ought to have done, was highly amused at my sarcasms; and so was her son, who, I fancy, had no great affection for M. Godard, and, indeed, I must confess that he was by no means an amiable person. I felt tempted to send him my verses; they encouraged me to do so. I made them up into a parcel addressed to him, and, as there was no city post in Paris at that time, I put it in my pocket and sent it to him from Auxerre as I passed through. I still sometimes laugh when I think of the wry face he must have made when he read this panegyric, in which he was described to the life. It began as follows: –

"Tu croyais, vieux pénard, qu'une folle manie
D'élever ton neveu m'inspirerait l'envie."[1]

This trifle – in truth, a poor production, but which was not wanting in wit, and showed a talent for satire – is, nevertheless, the only satirical composition which has proceeded from my pen. I have too little malice in my heart to make use of such a talent; but I think one may judge, from those polemics which I have written from time to time in my own defence, that, if I had

---

[1] You thought, you old sinner, that a mad folly would inspire me with a longing to bring up your nephew.

been of a quarrelsome disposition, my aggressors would seldom have had the laugh on their side.

What I most regret in regard to the details of my life which have escaped my memory, is that I never kept a diary of my travels. I have never thought so much, existed so much, lived so much, been so much myself, if I may venture to use the phrase, as in the journeys which I have made alone and on foot. There is something in walking which animates and enlivens my ideas. I can scarcely think when I remain still; my body must be in motion to make my mind active. The sight of the country, a succession of pleasant views, the open air, a good appetite, the sound health which walking gives me, the free life of the inns, the absence of all that makes me conscious of my dependent position, of all that reminds me of my condition – all this sets my soul free, gives me greater boldness of thought, throws me, so to speak, into the immensity of things, so that I can combine, select, and appropriate them at pleasure, without fear or restraint. I dispose of Nature in its entirety as its lord and master; my heart, roaming from object to object, mingles and identifies itself with those which soothe it, wraps itself up in charming fancies, and is intoxicated with delicious sensations. If, in order to render them permanent, I amuse myself by describing them by myself, what vigorous outlines, what fresh colouring, what power of expression I give them! All this, it is said, has been found in my works, although written in my declining years. Ah! if only one had seen the compositions of my early youth, those which I wrote during my travels, those which I sketched and have never written down! Then, why not write them? you will say. Why should I? I answer. Why deprive myself of the actual charms of enjoyment, in order to tell others that I did enjoy them? What did I care for readers, the public, or the whole world, while I was mounting to the skies? Besides, did I carry pens and paper with me? If I had thought of all that, nothing would have occurred to me. I did not foresee that I should have ideas; they come to me when it pleases them, not when it pleases me. They either do not come at all, or they come in crowds, and overwhelm me with their force and number. Ten volumes a day would not have been sufficient. When could I find time to write them? When I arrived at any town,

I thought of nothing but a good dinner; when I left it, of nothing but a good walk. I felt that a new paradise was waiting for me at the door. I thought only of going to find it.

I have never felt this so strongly as during the return journey of which I am speaking. On my way to Paris, my ideas were limited to what I was going to do there. I had thrown myself into the career which I thought lay before me, and should have gone through it with sufficient honour; but this career was not the one to which my heart summoned me, and the beings of reality injured the beings of imagination. Colonel Godard and his nephew ill suited a hero like myself. Thank Heaven! I was now freed from all these obstacles; I could plunge at will into the land of chimeras, for that alone lay before me. I went astray in it so completely, that several times I really lost my way; but I should have been very sorry to have taken a more direct route; for, having a presentiment that at Lyons I should again find myself on earth, I should have liked never to arrive there.

One day, amongst others, having purposely turned out of my way to get a nearer view of a spot which appeared worthy of admiration, I was so delighted with it, and went round it so often that, at last, I completely lost myself. After several hours of useless walking, tired, and dying of hunger and thirst, I entered a peasant's hut, not much to look at, but the only dwelling I saw in the neighbourhood. I expected to find it the same as in Geneva, or Switzerland, where all the well-to-do inhabitants are in a position to show hospitality. I begged him to give me dinner, and offered to pay for it. He offered me some skimmed milk and coarse barley bread, saying that that was all he had. I drank the milk with delight, and ate the bread, husks and all; but it was not very invigorating fare for a man exhausted by fatigue. The peasant, who examined me closely, estimated the truth of my story by my appetite, and immediately afterwards declared that he could see that I was a good and honourable young man,*[1]

* At that time, apparently, I did not have the sort of appearance that artists have given to me later. (R)
[1] In the second of his *Dialogues* Rousseau complains of certain portraits of himself which made him look as "abject, ridiculous and contemptible" as the descriptions of him in his enemies' books.

who had not come there to betray him for money. He opened
a little trapdoor near the kitchen, went down, and came up a
minute afterwards with a nice brown wheaten loaf, a very
tempting-looking ham, although considerably cut down, and a
bottle of wine, the sight of which rejoiced my heart more than all
the rest; to this he added a substantial omelette, and I made a
dinner such as none but a pedestrian ever enjoyed. When it came
to the question of payment, his uneasiness and alarm returned;
he would take none of my money, and refused it with singular
anxiety; and the amusing thing was that I could not imagine what
he was afraid of. At last, with a shudder, he uttered the terrible
words, "Revenue-officers and cellar-rats."[1] He gave me to
understand that he hid his wine on account of the excise, that
he hid his bread on account of the tax, and that he was a lost
man, if anyone had a suspicion that he was not starving. All that
he said to me on this subject, of which I had not the least idea,
made an impression upon me which will never be forgotten. It
was the germ of the inextinguishable hatred which subsequently
grew up in my heart against the oppression to which these
unhappy people are subject, and against their oppressors. This
man, although in good circumstances, did not dare to eat the
bread which he had obtained by the sweat of his brow, and could
only escape utter ruin by displaying the same poverty as prevailed around him. I left his house, equally indignant and
touched, lamenting the lot of these beautiful countries, upon
which Nature has only lavished her gifts to make them the prey
of barbarous farmers of taxes.

This is the only distinct recollection I have of the incidents of
this journey. The only other thing I remember is that, when near
Lyons, I was tempted to prolong my journey in order to visit the
banks of the Lignon, for, amongst the romances which I had
read with my father, "Astraea"[2] had not been forgotten, and
returned most frequently to my mind. I asked the way to Forez;
and, while talking with the landlady of an inn, was informed by

---

[1] *i.e.*, employees of the tax-farmers, so called because they inspected the
contents of cellars.
[2] The famous prose romance by Honoré d'Urfé, published 1607–27.

her that it was a good country for workmen, that there were many forges in it, and a considerable amount of work done in iron. This panegyric cooled my romantic curiosity at once, and it seemed incongruous to look for Dianas and Sylvanders amongst a tribe of blacksmiths. The good woman, who encouraged me in this manner, must have taken me for a journeyman locksmith.

I did not go to Lyons entirely without an object. As soon as I arrived, I went to the Chasottes to see Mademoiselle du Châtelet, a friend of Madame de Warens, to whom she had given me a letter when I went there with M. le Maître, so that it was an acquaintance already made. She informed me that her friend had, in fact, passed through Lyons, but that she did not know whether she had gone on as far as Piedmont; and that Madame de Warens herself, when she left, had been uncertain whether she would not have to stop in Savoy; that, if I desired, she would write for information, and that the best thing I could do would be to wait at Lyons till she had heard from her. I accepted her offer, but I did not venture to tell her that I was in a hurry for the answer, and that, as my small means were exhausted, I was not in a position to wait long for it. What restrained me was not any unfriendliness in her reception; on the contrary, she had been very cordial to me, and had treated me on a footing of equality, which deprived me of the courage to disclose my circumstances to her, and to come down from the *rôle* of an agreeable companion to that of a miserable beggar.

I seem to have a tolerably clear view of the sequence of events which I have described in this book. Nevertheless, I think that I recollect another voyage to Lyons belonging to this period, which I cannot fix, and during which I found myself in great straits. A little incident, which I find some difficulty in relating, will never allow me to forget it. One evening, I was sitting in Bellecour, after having partaken of a very light supper, musing how I should get out of my difficulties, when a man in a cap came and sat by my side. He looked like one of those silk-workers who, at Lyons, are called *taffetatiers*. He spoke to me; I answered him. After we had talked for about a quarter of an hour, with the same coolness and without any alteration in the tone of his voice, he proposed that we should amuse ourselves together. I waited for him to explain what amusement he meant, but, without another word, he made ready to give me a practical illustration. We were almost touching each other, and the night was not too dark to prevent me from seeing what he was going to do. He had no designs upon my person; at least, nothing seemed to show that he meditated anything of the kind, and the place would not have been adapted for it; just as he had told me, he only wanted each of us to amuse himself separately. This appeared to him so simple a matter, that it never occurred to him that I should not look upon it in the same light. I was so terrified at this disgraceful proposal, that, without replying, I got up in a hurry, and ran away as fast as I could, fancying the wretch was at my heels. I was so confused that, instead of making for my lodging, I ran in the direction of the quay, and did not stop till I had crossed the wooden bridge, trembling as if I had just committed a crime. I was addicted to the same vice; the recollection of this incident cured me of it for a long time.

During this journey I met with an adventure of an almost similar kind, but which exposed me to greater danger. Finding that my funds were nearly exhausted, I economised the miserable sum that remained. At first I took my meals less frequently at my inn; soon I gave up taking them there altogether, since, for five or six sous, I could satisfy myself quite as well at the tavern, as for twenty-five sous at the inn. As I no longer took my meals there, I did not feel justified in sleeping there, not that I was much in debt, but I was ashamed to occupy a bedroom without putting any profit into my landlady's pocket. It was beautiful weather. One very hot evening I decided to pass the night in the public square. I had already settled myself upon a bench, when an Abbé, who was passing by, saw me lying down, came up to me, and asked me if I had anywhere to sleep. I confessed the state of my affairs, and he seemed touched. He sat down by my side and we conversed. He was an agreeable talker; all he said gave me the highest possible opinion of him. When he saw that I was favourably inclined, he told me that he had not very extensive quarters himself; that he had only one room, but that he certainly would not leave me to sleep in the square; that it was too late to find a lodging, and he offered me half his bed for the night. I accepted his offer, for I already had hopes of finding in him a friend who might be useful to me. We went. He struck a light. His room seemed neat and clean, and he did the honours with great politeness. He took some cherries steeped in brandy out of a glass jar; we each ate two, and went to bed.

This man had the same tastes as my Jew of the hospice, but did not show them so brutally. Either because he knew that I should be heard and was afraid to force me to defend myself, or because he was really less determined in his designs, he did not venture to propose their accomplishment openly, and tried to excite without alarming me. Taught by my former experience, I soon understood what he wanted, and shuddered. Not knowing in what kind of house or in whose hands I was, I was afraid to make a noise for fear of being murdered. I pretended not to know what he wanted of me; but, appearing greatly annoyed at his caresses, and quite decided not to let them go on, I managed so well that he was obliged to restrain himself. Then I spoke to him with all the gentleness and firmness of which I was capable; and, without appearing to suspect anything, I excused my uneasiness on the score of my recent adventure, which I made a show of relating to him in terms so full of horror and disgust, that I believe I disgusted him, and he altogether abandoned his filthy designs. We spent the rest of the night quietly; he even gave me some good and sensible information; certainly he was a man of some intelligence, although a great rascal.

In the morning, the Abbé, not wishing to appear dissatisfied, spoke of breakfast, and asked one of his landlady's daughters, who was a pretty girl, to send some to him. She answered that she had no time. He turned to her sister, who did not deign to give him an answer. We still waited; no breakfast. At last, we went into these young ladies' room. They received the Abbé in a manner that was anything but cordial. I had still less reason to congratulate myself on my reception. The elder, turning round, stepped upon my toes with the pointed heel of her boot, where a very painful corn had obliged me to cut a hole in my shoe; the other abruptly pulled away from behind me a chair on which I was just going to sit down; their mother, while throwing water out of the window, splashed my face; wherever I sat down, they made me move that they might look for something. I had never in my life been so entertained. In their jeering and insulting looks I saw concealed rage, which I was so stupid as to fail to understand. Astounded, stupefied, and inclined to think they were all bewitched, I began to feel seriously alarmed, when the Abbé, who pretended to see and hear nothing, judging correctly that no breakfast was to be expected, decided to leave the house. I hastened to follow him, thinking myself lucky to escape from the three furies. As we were walking along, he proposed that we should go and have breakfast at the café. Although I was very hungry, I declined his offer, which he did not press me to accept, and we separated at the third or fourth turning. I was delighted to get out of sight of everything connected with that accursed house; and I believe that he was very glad to have taken me so far from it that I should have found great difficulty in recognising it. No similar adventures have ever happened to me either in Paris or any other city. They have given me so disagreeable an impression of the people of Lyons, that I have always looked upon this city as the most frightfully corrupt in all Europe.

The remembrance of the extremities to which I was there reduced, does not help to give me pleasant recollections of it. If I had been like anyone else, if I had possessed the art of borrowing and getting into debt at my inn, I should easily have got out of my difficulties; but in such matters my incapacity was equalled by my repugnance. To give an idea of the extent of both, it is enough to mention that, although I have spent nearly all my life in distressed circumstances, and have often been almost entirely without bread, I have never once been asked for money by a creditor without paying him at once. I have never been able to incur petty debts, and have always preferred to suffer than to owe money.

It was certainly suffering, to be reduced to spend the night in the streets, which was frequently my lot at Lyons. I preferred to spend the few sous I had left in buying bread than in paying for a lodging, because, after all, I ran less risk of dying of want of sleep than of hunger. The remarkable thing is that, in my miserable condition, I was neither melancholy nor uneasy. I did not feel the least anxiety about the future, and waited patiently for the

answer which Mademoiselle du Châtelet was sure to receive. At
night I lay in the open air, and, stretched on the ground or on
a bench, slept as calmly as upon a bed of roses. I remember,
especially, that I spent a delightful night outside the city, on a
road which ran by the side of the Rhône or Saône, I do not
remember which. Raised gardens, with terraces, bordered the
other side of the road. It had been very hot during the day; the
evening was delightful; the dew moistened the parched grass;
the night was calm, without a breath of wind; the air was fresh,
without being cold; the sun, having gone down, had left in the
sky red vapours, the reflection of which cast a rose-red tint upon
the water; the trees on the terraces were full of nightingales
answering one another. I walked on in a kind of ecstasy, abandoning my heart and senses to the enjoyment of all, only regretting, with a sigh, that I was obliged to enjoy it alone. Absorbed in
my delightful reverie, I continued my walk late into the night,
without noticing that I was tired. At last, I noticed it. I threw
myself with a feeling of delight upon the shelf of a sort of niche
or false door let into a terrace wall; the canopy of my bed was
formed by the tops of trees; a nightingale was perched just over
my head, and lulled me to sleep with his song; my slumbers were
sweet, my awaking was still sweeter. It was broad day; my eyes,
on opening, beheld the water, the verdure, a charming landscape. I got up and shook myself; and, feeling hungry, set out
gaily on my way to the city, resolved to spend the two small silver
pieces I still had left on a good breakfast. I was in such good
spirits, that I sang the whole way; I even remember that I sang
one of Batistin's cantatas, called *Les Bains de Thomery*, which
I knew by heart. Blessed be the good Batistin and his good
cantata, which procured me a better breakfast than I had reckoned upon, and a still better dinner, upon which I had not
reckoned at all! While walking and singing my best, I heard
someone behind me; I turned round, and saw an Antonine,[1]
who was following me, and seemed to be listening with pleasure
to my singing. He accosted me, greeted me, and asked me
whether I knew music. I replied, "A little," by which I meant

---

[1] The "Antonines" were a community of secularised monks.

him to understand, A great deal. He continued his questions. I told him part of my history. He asked me if I had ever copied music. "Often," I replied, which was true, for I had learned most by copying. "Well," said he, "come with me; I can give you something to do for a few days; in the meanwhile you shall want for nothing, but you must agree not to leave the room." I readily agreed, and followed him.

His name was Rolichon; he was very fond of music, which he knew well, and sang at some little concerts which he used to give with his friends. This was innocent and honourable enough; but his hobby was certainly degenerating into a mania, which he was partly obliged to conceal. He showed me to a little room, where I found a quantity of music which he had copied. He gave me some more to copy, particularly the cantata which I had sung, and which he was to sing himself in a few days. I remained there three or four days, copying all the time that I was not eating, for never in my life was I so hungry or better fed. He brought my meals himself from their kitchen, which must have been a good one, if the ordinary meals were as good as my own. In all my life I had never enjoyed my food so much; and I must also confess that these snacks came very opportunely, for I was as dry as a piece of wood. I worked almost as heartily as I ate, and that is saying a good deal. It is true that my accuracy did not equal my diligence. Some days afterwards, M. Rolichon met me in the street and told me that my score had rendered the music altogether impracticable, being so full of omissions, repetitions, and transpositions. I cannot deny that I chose the one profession for which I was least fitted. My notation was good and I copied very neatly; but the fatigue of a long task so bewilders me, that I spend more time in erasing than writing, and unless I compare the parts with the greatest carefulness, they always spoil the execution. Thus, in my endeavour to perform my task well, I performed it very badly; and, in my efforts at rapidity, I went all wrong. This, however, did not prevent M. Rolichon from treating me handsomely to the last; and, when I left him, he gave me a crown, which I by no means deserved, and which completely set me on my legs again; for, a few days afterwards, I heard of Madame de Warens, who was at Chambéri, and sent me some money to rejoin her, which I was only too delighted to do. Since then my finances have often been very low, but never to such an extent that I have been obliged to fast. I note this period of my life with a heart sensible of the care of Providence; it was the last time in my life that I ever suffered hunger and wretchedness.

I remained a week or so longer at Lyons, while Mademoiselle du Châtelet executed some trifling commissions for mamma. During this time I visited her more frequently than before, delighted to talk with her about her friend, and no longer distracted by the painful thoughts of my situation, or obliged to conceal it. Mademoiselle du Châtelet was neither young nor pretty, but was not wanting in comeliness; she was affable and familiar, and her mental endowments enhanced the value of this familiarity. She possessed that liking for moral observation which leads to the study of character; and it is to her that I originally owe the first impulse in this direction. She was fond of the romances of Le Sage, especially "Gil Blas"; she talked to me about it, and lent it to me; I read it with pleasure, but was not yet ripe for such literature; I wanted high-flown romances. In this manner I passed my time in her parlour with equal pleasure and profit; and it is certain that interesting and intelligent conversation with a woman of education and character are better calculated to form the understanding of a young man than all the pedantic philosophy that can be acquired from books. At the Chasottes I became acquainted with other boarders and their friends, amongst others Mademoiselle Serre, a young girl of fourteen, to whom I did not pay particular attention at the time, but with whom I fell violently in love eight or nine years later, and no wonder, for she was a charming girl.

Full of the expectation of soon seeing my good mamma again, I abandoned my dreams for awhile, and the real happiness which awaited me relieved me of the trouble of seeking for it in what was merely visionary. I not only found her again, but also, near her and by her assistance, a pleasant situation; for she informed me that she had found an occupation for me which she hoped would suit me, and one which would not take me far away from her. I exhausted my conjectures in trying to guess what this occupation might be, but it would have needed the gift of prophecy to guess aright. I had enough money to make the journey comfortably. Mademoiselle du Châtelet wanted me to take a horse; to this I would not agree, and I was right; I should have lost the enjoyment of the last journey I ever made on foot; for the excursions which I frequently made in the neighbour-hood of Motiers,[1] while I lived there, do not deserve the name.

It is a very remarkable fact, that my imagination is never more agreeably excited, than when my situation is the very reverse of agreeable, and that, on the contrary, it is less cheerful when all around me is cheerful. My obstinate nature is unable to bow to facts. It cannot beautify, it must create. Realities appear to it nothing more than they are; it can only embellish the objects of imagination. If I wish to depict the spring, it must be in winter; if I wish to describe a beautiful landscape, I must be surrounded by walls; and I have said a hundred times that, if I were ever imprisoned in the Bastille, I should draw the picture of Liberty. When setting out from Lyons, I saw only a pleasant future before me; I was – and I had every reason to be – as happy as I had been the reverse, when I set out from Paris. Nevertheless, during this journey, I did not enjoy those delight-ful reveries which had accompanied me before. My heart was light, and that was all. I drew near with emotion to the excellent friend whom I was going to see again, I tasted in advance, but without any feeling of intoxication, the happiness of living near her; I had always expected it; it seemed to me that there was nothing new for me in that. I felt anxious about my future occupation, as if that had been a great source of anxiety. My ideas were calm and gentle, instead of heavenly and enchanting. All material objects claimed my attention; I observed the sur-rounding country; I remarked the trees, the houses, the brooks; I took counsel with myself at the cross-roads; I was afraid of losing myself and did not do so. In a word, I was no longer in the clouds, I was just where I was, just where I was going, nowhere else.

In relating my journeys, as in making them, I do not know how to stop. My heart beat with joy when I drew near to my dear

[1] See Book XII, p. 633.

mamma, but I walked no faster. I like to walk at my ease, and to stop when I like. A wandering life is what I want. To walk through a beautiful country in fine weather, without being obliged to hurry, and with a pleasant prospect at the end, is of all kinds of life the one most suited to my taste. My idea of a beautiful country is already known. No flat country, however beautiful, has ever seemed so to my eyes. I must have mountain torrents, rocks, firs, dark forests, mountains, steep roads to climb or descend, precipices at my side to frighten me. I had this pleasure, and enjoyed it in all its charm, as I approached Chambéri. Not far from a precipitous mountain wall, called Le Pas de l'Échelle, below the military road cut out of the rocks, at the place called Chailles, a little stream rushes and foams in some fearful precipices, which it seems to have spent millions of ages in hollowing out. Along the side of the road is a parapet to prevent accidents, which enabled me to look down and be as giddy as I pleased; for the amusing thing about my taste for steep places is, that I am very fond of the feeling of giddiness which they give rise to, provided I am in a safe position. Leaning securely over the parapet, I stretched forward, and remained there for hours together, from time to time catching a glimpse of the foam and dark water, the roaring of which I heard in the midst of the screams of the ravens and birds of prey which flew from rock to rock, and from bush to bush, a hundred fathoms below me. In places where the slope was fairly even, and the brushwood was not too thick to allow stones to pass through, I collected from a distance a large number, as big as I could carry, and piled them up on the parapet; then, hurling them down, one after the other, I amused myself with watching them roll, rebound, and shiver into a thousand pieces, before reaching the bottom of the abyss.

Nearer Chambéri, I saw a similar sight, of a different kind. The road passes at the foot of the most beautiful cascade I have ever seen. The mountain is so steep, that the water falls away clear, in the shape of an arch, at a sufficient distance to allow a person to walk between it and the rock, sometimes even without being wetted; but, unless one is careful, it is easy to be deceived, as I was; for, owing to the immense height, the water divides and falls in a spray, and, if one goes only a little too near to this cloud, without at first noticing that he is getting wet, he is drenched in a moment.

At length I arrived; I saw her again. She was not alone. The Intendant-General was with her when I entered. Without a word, she took me by the hand and introduced me to him with that graceful manner which gained her the affection of all, saying: "Here is the poor young man, sir; deign to protect him as long as he deserves it, and I shall feel no further anxiety about him for the rest of his life." Then she turned to me; "My child," she said, "you belong to the King; thank Monsieur l'Intendant, who offers you the means to live." I opened my eyes wide and said nothing, without knowing exactly what to think of it; my growing ambition nearly turned my head, and already I saw myself a young Intendant. My fortune certainly did not prove as brilliant as I had expected from such a start; but, for the moment, it was enough to keep me, and that, for me, was a good deal. The state of the case was as follows:

King Victor Amadeus,[1] judging, from the issue of preceding wars and the state of his ancestral inheritance, that it would one day slip from his hands, did his utmost to exhaust it beforehand. A few years ago, having resolved to tax the Savoyard nobility, he had ordered a general land-register of the country to be made, in order to impose taxation on landed property and distribute it more fairly. The work, commenced in the father's time, was completed by the son. Two or three hundred persons, land-surveyors who were called geometricians, and writers who were called secretaries, were employed in the task, and mamma had secured me an appointment amongst the latter. The post, although not very lucrative, afforded me ample means to live upon in that country; the misfortune was, that the employment was only temporary, but it put me in a position to wait and look about me, and mamma had purposely endeavoured to secure for me the special protection of the Intendant, that I might be able to proceed to some more permanent employment, when my present work was finished.

[1] See *Biographies* (Sardinia), p. 714.

I entered upon my duties a few days after my arrival. The work was not difficult and I soon became familiar with it. Thus it came to pass, that, after four or five years of vagabondage, of folly, and suffering, since I had left Geneva, I began for the first time to earn a respectable living.

These lengthy details of my early youth will naturally have seemed puerile, and I regret it; although born a man in certain respects, I long remained a child, and in many respects I am one still. I have never promised to introduce a great character to the public; I have promised to describe myself as I am; and, in order to know me in my riper years, it is necessary to have known me well in my youth. Since, as a rule, objects make less impression upon me than the remembrance of them, and since all my ideas assume the form of the representations of objects in my mind, the first traits which have stamped themselves upon my mind have remained, and those which have since imprinted themselves there have rather combined with them than obliterated them. There is a certain sequence of mental conditions and ideas, which exercises an influence upon those which follow them, with which it is necessary to be acquainted, in order to pass a correct judgment upon the latter. I endeavour in all cases to develop the first causes, in order to make the concatenation of effects felt. I should like to be able to make my soul to a certain extent transparent to the eyes of the reader; and, with this object, I endeavour to show it to him from all points of view, to exhibit it to him in every aspect, and to contrive that none of its movements shall escape his notice, so that he may be able by himself to judge of the principles that produce them.

If I made myself responsible for the result, and said to him, Such is my character, he might think that, if I am not deceiving him, I am at least deceiving myself. But, in simply detailing to him everything that has happened to me, all my acts, thoughts, and feelings, I cannot mislead him, except wilfully, and even if I wished to do so, I should not find it easy. It is his business to collect these scattered elements, and to determine the being which is composed of them; the result must be his work; and if he is mistaken, all the fault will be his. But for this purpose it is not sufficient that my narrative should be true; it must also be exact. It is not for me to judge of the importance of facts; it is my duty to mention them all, and to leave him to select them. This is what I have hitherto aimed at with all my best endeavours, and in the sequel I will not depart from it. But the recollections of middle-age are always less vivid than those of early youth. I have begun by making the best possible use of the latter. If the former return to me with the same freshness, impatient readers will, perhaps, grow tired; but I myself shall not be dissatisfied with my work. I have only one thing to fear in this undertaking; not that I may say too much or what is not true, but that I may not say all, and may conceal the truth.

BOOK V

I THINK it was in 1732, as I have just related, I arrived at Chambéri, and commenced land-surveying in the King's service. I was nearly twenty-one years of age. For my age, my mind was sufficiently well formed; not so my powers of judgment, and I sorely needed instruction from those into whose hands I fell, in order to learn how to conduct myself sensibly; for my few years of experience had not been sufficient to cure me completely of my romantic fancies; and, in spite of all the sufferings I had endured, I knew as little of the world and mankind, as if I had never paid dearly for my knowledge of them.

I lived at home, that is to say, with mamma; but I never found my room at Annecy again. No garden, no brook, no landscape! The house which she occupied was dark and gloomy, and my room was the darkest and gloomiest in the house. A wall to look out upon, a blind alley instead of a street, very little air, light, or room; crickets, rats, rotten boards – all combined to make a by no means pleasant abode.[1] But I was in her house, I was near her; always at my desk, or in her room, I did not notice the ugliness of my own; I had no time to think of it. It will appear singular that she should have settled at Chambéri on purpose to live in this wretched house; but it was a piece of cleverness on her part, which I must not omit to explain. She very much disliked the idea of going to Turin, as she felt that, after the recent changes that had taken place there, and during the present excitement at the Court, it was not the right moment to present herself. However, her affairs required her presence; she was afraid of being forgotten or slandered, especially as she knew that the Comte de Saint-Laurent, Intendant-General of Finance, was not favourably disposed towards her. He had an old house at Chambéri, badly built, and so disagreeably situated, that it was always empty; she took it, and settled there. This plan succeeded better than a journey to Turin; her pension was not

---

[1] The house, 13 rue de Boigne (previously rue des Portiques), still stands.

discontinued, and from that time the Comte de Saint-Laurent was always one of her best friends.

I found her household arrangements much the same as before, and the faithful Claude Anet still with her. I believe I have already stated that he was a peasant from Montru,[1] who, in his childhood, used to gather herbs in Jura to make Swiss tea, and whom she had taken into her service on account of his knowledge of drugs, finding it convenient to have a lackey who understood them. He was so passionately fond of the study of plants, and she encouraged his taste so strongly, that he became a real botanist, and, if he had not died young, might have made himself a name in this department of science, equal to that which he deserved as an honest man. Being serious, even grave, and older than myself, he became to me a kind of mentor, who kept me from many follies; for he inspired me with respect, and I never ventured to forget myself in his presence. He made the same impression on his mistress, who knew his good sense, uprightness, and unshaken devotion to herself, and repaid it in kind. Claude Anet was, undoubtedly, no ordinary man and the only man of his kind that I have ever seen. Slow, sedate, thoughtful, prudent in his behaviour, cold in manner, laconic and sententious in his utterances, when under the influence of his passions he was a prey to a violent impetuosity, which he never showed, but which inwardly devoured him, and never caused him to commit a folly in his life, except one, and that a terrible one – he took a dose of poison. This tragic event took place shortly after my arrival; nothing but this made me aware of the intimacy between him and his mistress; for, unless she had told me herself, I should never have suspected it. If devotion, zeal, and loyalty can deserve such a recompense, it was certainly due to him; and the fact that he never abused her confidence proves that he was worthy of it. Their disputes, which were rare, always ended amicably, with the exception of one, which did not terminate so happily. His mistress, in a passion, said something insulting to him; unable to endure the affront, he took counsel with his despair, and finding a bottle of laudanum ready to hand, he swallowed it, and then went quietly to bed, never expecting to wake again. Luckily Madame de

[1] *i.e.*, Montreux.

Warens, uneasy and agitated herself, while wandering about the house, found the empty bottle, and guessed the rest. She flew to his assistance, with shrieks that attracted my attention. She confessed everything, implored my assistance, and with much difficulty succeeded in making him bring up the opium. Witnessing this scene, I marvelled at my stupidity in never having entertained the least suspicion of the connection of which she informed me. But Claude Anet was so discreet, that keener observers than myself might well have been deceived. The reconciliation was of such a nature that I was greatly affected by it; and, from that time, my esteem for him being increased by a feeling of respect, I became in a manner his pupil, which was by no means to my disadvantage.

However, it was not without pain that I discovered that another could live with her on terms of greater intimacy than myself. I had never even thought of desiring such a position for myself; but it was hard for me to see it filled by another, and my feeling was a very natural one. Notwithstanding, instead of conceiving an aversion to him who had robbed me of her, I actually found that my attachment to her extended itself to him. Before all things I desired her happiness; and, since he was necessary to it, I was content that he should be happy likewise. On his part, he entered completely into his mistress's views, and conceived a sincere friendship for the friend whom she had chosen. Without claiming the authority over me to which his position entitled him, he naturally exercised that which his superior intelligence gave him over mine. I never ventured to do anything of which he appeared to disapprove, and he only disapproved of what was bad. Thus we lived in a union which made us all happy, and which could only be dissolved by death. One of the proofs of the excellent character of this admirable woman is, that all those who loved her loved one another. Jealousy, even rivalry, submitted to the predominant feeling which she inspired, and I have never seen any of those who surrounded her ill-disposed towards one another. Let my readers pause a moment at this panegyric, and if they can think of any other woman of whom they can say the same, I advise them to attach themselves to her, if they value their repose.

Here commences, from the time of my arrival at Chambéri to my departure from Paris in 1741, a period of eight or nine years, during which I shall have few events to relate, because my life was as simple as it was pleasant. This uniformity was exactly what I most wanted to complete the formation of my character, which continual troubles had prevented from becoming settled. During this precious interval, my miscellaneous and disconnected education acquired consistency, and made me what I have never ceased to be, amidst all the storms which awaited me. This development was imperceptible and slow, accompanied by few events worth recording; but, nevertheless, it deserves to be followed out and described.

At first, I was almost entirely occupied with my work; the ties of the desk left me scarcely any time to think of anything else. The little time I had free was spent with my good mamma; and, not having even sufficient leisure to read, I felt no inclination to do so. But when my duties, having become a kind of routine, occupied my mind less, the feeling of restlessness returned. Reading again became necessary, and, as if the desire for it had always been heightened when it was difficult to satisfy, it would have again become a passion with me, as at my master's, had not other inclinations interfered and diverted my attention from it.

Although we did not require a very profound knowledge of arithmetic for our calculations, we required enough to sometimes cause me some trouble. To overcome this difficulty, I bought some books on arithmetic, and learned the subject well, for I learned it alone. Practical arithmetic is of wider extent than one imagines, when strict accuracy is aimed at. There are calculations of extraordinary length, in which I have sometimes seen skilled geometricians go wrong. Reflection, combined with practice, gives clear ideas, and then one discovers short methods, the invention of which is flattering to one's self-complacency, while their accuracy satisfies the mind, and which lend a charm to a task thankless in itself. I threw myself into it with such success that no problem, which was capable of being solved by figures alone, gave me any difficulty; and even now, when all that I have known daily fades from my memory, this accomplishment in part still remains, after an interval of thirty years. A few days ago, when I made a journey to Davenport,[1] being present at my host's house when his children were having their arithmetic lesson, I worked out, without a mistake and with incredible pleasure, an extremely complicated calculation. It seemed to me, as I set down my figures, that I was still at Chambéri in my happy days. What a distant recollection!

The colouring of the maps of our geometricians had also given me a taste for drawing. I bought some colours, and began to paint flowers and landscapes. It was a pity that I found I possessed but little talent for this art, for I was entirely devoted to it. I could have spent whole months in the midst of my crayons and pencils without going out. As this occupation occupied too much of my attention, they were compelled to drag me away from it. It is always the same with all the pursuits to which I begin to devote myself; they grow upon me, become a passion, and soon I see nothing else in the world but my favourite amusement. Age has not cured me of this fault, it has not even diminished it; even while I write this, I sit like an old twaddler, infatuated with another study, which is useless to me and of which I understand nothing, which even those who have devoted themselves to it during their youth, are obliged to give up at the age when I want to begin it.

At that time, it would have been in its right place. The opportunity was favourable, and I had some temptation to make use of it. The satisfaction that I saw in Anet's eyes, when he came home loaded with new plants, two or three times nearly made me go out botanising with him. I am almost certain that, if I had only gone once, I should have been captivated by it, and I should, perhaps, now be a famous botanist; for I know no study in the world better suited to my natural tastes than that of plants; and the life which I have now been leading for ten years in the country is hardly anything but a continual botanising, although certainly without purpose, or progress; but, at that time, having no idea of the science of botany, I conceived a kind of contempt – even of aversion – for it, and only considered it an occupation fit for an apothecary. Mamma, who was very fond of it, made no other use

---

[1] Davenport Park in Cheshire, home of Richard Davenport, who had lent Rousseau and Thérèse their house in Wootton.

of it herself; she only looked for common plants, such as she could make use of in her remedies. In this manner, botany, chemistry, and anatomy, confused in my mind under the general term medicine, only served to provide me throughout the day with a subject for humorous sarcasms, and, from time to time, brought upon me a box on the ears. Besides, a different and most opposite taste gradually developed itself in me, and soon supplanted all the others, I mean music. I must certainly have been born for this art, since I began to love it from my earliest childhood, and it is the only one that I have loved constantly at all times. The remarkable thing is, that an art, for which I was intended by Nature, has nevertheless cost me so much trouble to learn, and that my progress in it has been so slow, that, although I have practised it all my life, I have never been able to sing with any certainty at sight. What at that time made this study particularly a pleasure, was that I could pursue it together with mamma. With very different tastes in other respects, we found in music a bond of union, which I gladly made use of. She made no objection; I was at that time almost as advanced as she was; after two or three attempts we could decipher an air. Sometimes, when I saw her busy round a furnace, I used to say: "Mamma, here is a charming duet, which seems to me just the thing to make your drugs smell of *empyreuma*."[1] "On my honour," she would reply, "if you make me burn them, I will make you eat them." While the dispute was going on, I pulled her to her piano, where we soon forgot everything else; the extract of juniper or absinthe was reduced to powder; she smeared my face with it — and how delightful it all was!

It will be seen that, with little time to spare, I had many things to employ it. One amusement, however, was worth all the rest.

We lived in a dungeon so stifling, that we were sometimes obliged to go and get some fresh air in the country. Anet persuaded mamma to rent a garden in one of the suburbs, to rear plants. Attached to this garden was a pretty little rustic house, which was decently furnished, and a bed put up in it. We often had dinner, and I sometimes slept there. Imperceptibly, I became infatuated with this little retreat.

[1] Technical term for "burning".

I took a few books there and a number of prints; I spent part
of my time in decorating it, and preparing an agreeable surprise
for mamma when she walked out there. I sometimes left
her, that I might busy my mind with her, and think of her with
greater pleasure; this was another whim, which I can neither
excuse nor explain, but which I acknowledge, since it was really
the case. I remember that Madame de Luxembourg once
spoke jestingly to me of a man, who used to leave his mistress
in order to write to her. I told her that I might very well have
been that man, and I might have added that I had sometimes
acted like him. However, when I was with mamma, I never felt
it necessary to leave her, in order to love her more; for, *tête-à-tête*
with her, I felt as completely at my ease as if I had been alone,
which I have never felt in the presence of anyone else, man
or woman, however much attached to them I may have
been. But she was so often surrounded by people who were by
no means congenial to me, that a feeling of annoyance and
weariness drove me to my refuge, where I could enjoy her as
I wanted her, without fear of being followed by troublesome
visitors.

In this manner, my time being divided between work,
pleasure, and instruction, I led a life of sweetest repose.
Europe, however, was not so calm as myself. France and
the Emperor had just declared war;[1] the King of Sardinia[2] had
taken part in the quarrel, and the French army was marching
through Piedmont to invade Milanese territory. One column
passed through Chambéri, amongst others the regiment of
Champagne, the colonel of which was the Duc de la
Trémouille, to whom I was presented. He was lavish in his
promises, and I am quite certain that he never once thought of
me again. Our little garden was situated just at the end of the
suburb through which the troops entered, so that I could enjoy

---

[1]   The War of the Polish Succession (1733–35) arose over rival candidatures
for the throne of Poland, after the death of Augustus II; the Emperor and
Russia supported Augustus's son, whereas France, in alliance with Spain and
the King of Sardinia, supported Louis XV's father-in-law, Stanislaus Leczinski.
War was declared on 8 October 1733, and the French army immediately
crossed the Alps to join the Sardinian forces.
[2]   [Sardinia, kings of] See *Biographies*, p. 714.

to my heart's content the pleasure of seeing them pass, and I was as eager for the success of this war as if I had had the greatest interests at stake in it. Hitherto it had not entered my head to think about public affairs; and I began to read the newspapers for the first time, but with such partiality for France, that my heart beat with joy when it gained the least success, while its reverses afflicted me as much as if they had overtaken myself. If this folly had only been transitory, I should not consider it worth speaking of; but it has become so rooted in my heart without any sufficient reason, that when, later, at Paris, I played the part of the enemy of tyrants and the proud republican, I felt, in spite of myself, a secret predilection for this very nation I found servile, and for the government which I pretended to condemn. The amusing thing was that, being ashamed of an inclination so opposed to my principles, I never dared to confess it to anyone, and I rallied the French on their defeats, while my heart bled for them more than their own. I am certainly the only man who, living in the midst of a people who treated him well and whom he worshipped, has assumed amongst them an air of contempt. On my part, this inclination is so disinterested, so powerful, so lasting, and so invincible, that, even after my departure from France, after the storm which its government, magistrates, and writers have vied with one another in stirring up against me, and since it has become the fashion to overwhelm me with undeserved abuse, I have been unable to cure myself of my folly. I love them in spite of myself, in spite of their ill treatment of me. Seeing the decadence of England, which I predicted in the midst of its triumphs, now already beginning, I let myself nurse the mad hope that the French nation, victorious in its turn, will one day perhaps come and rescue me from the sad captivity in which I live.[1]

I have long endeavoured to discover the reason of this partiality, and have been unable to find it anywhere except in the occasion that produced it. A growing taste for literature gave me a fondness for French books, their authors, and the country

[1] Rousseau, who is writing this at Wootton in Staffordshire near the end of 1766, had convinced himself that there was a plot to hold him captive in England.

of these authors. At the moment when the French army was marching past, I read Brantôme's "Great Captains." My head was full of the Clissons, Bayards, Lautrecs, Colignys, Montmorencys, and Trimouilles, and I loved their descendants as the inheritors of their virtues and their courage. In each regiment that passed I thought I beheld again those famous black bands which had formerly performed such heroic deeds in Piedmont. In short, I connected with what I saw the ideas which I drew from my books; my continuous reading, still confined to French authors, nourished my affection for their country, and finally converted it into a blind infatuation, which nothing has been able to overcome. I have later had occasion to remark in the course of my journeys that this impression was not peculiar to myself, and that, exercising more or less influence in all countries upon that part of the nation which loves reading and cultivates literature, it counter-balanced the general hatred inspired by the conceited manners of the French. Their romances, more than their men, win the hearts of the women of all countries, their dramatic masterpieces attract the young to their theatres. The fame of the theatres of Paris draws crowds of strangers, who return home their enthusiastic admirers. In short, the excellent taste displayed in their literature captivates the minds of all those who have any mind: and, during the war which ended so disastrously for them, I have seen their authors and philosophers uphold the honour of the French name, so tarnished by its warriors.

I was, then, an ardent Frenchman, and this made me a news-monger. I went with the crowd of gapers to the market-place, to wait for the post; and, sillier than the ass in the fable,[1] I was very anxious to know what master's saddle I should have the honour to carry; for at that time it was declared that we should belong to France, and that Savoy would be exchanged for the territory of Milan. However, it must be admitted that I had some reason for anxiety; for, if this war had turned out badly for the allies, mamma's pension would have been in danger. But I had full confidence in my good friends; and, this time, in spite of the surprise of M. de Broglie, my confidence was not

[1] See La Fontaine's fable "The Old Man and the Donkey".

deceived, thanks to the King of Sardinia, whom I had never thought of.[1]

While there was fighting in Italy, there was singing in France. Rameau's operas began to make a stir, and gave a lift to his theoretical works, which, by reason of their obscurity, were within the reach of only a few capacities. Having accidentally heard his "Treatise on Harmony" mentioned, I had no rest till I had procured the book. By another accident I fell ill. The malady was an inflammation, which was very violent during the short time it lasted, but my restoration to health was tedious, and I was unable to go out for a month. During this period, I worked at, I devoured my "Treatise on Harmony"; but it was so long, so diffuse, and so badly arranged, that I felt it would take me a considerable time to study and disentangle it. I suspended my efforts, and refreshed my eyes with music. The cantatas of Bernier, which I practised, were never out of my mind. I learned four or five of them by heart, amongst others, *The Sleeping Cupids*, which I have never seen again since then, and which I still remember almost perfectly, and also *Cupid Stung by a Bee*, a very pretty cantata by Clérambault, which I learned almost at the same time.

To confirm my passion, a young organist, called the Abbé Palais, arrived from Val-d'Aost, a good musician, a good fellow, and an excellent accompanist. I made his acquaintance, and we immediately became inseparable. He had been the pupil of an Italian monk, a fine organist. He spoke to me of his principles of music, which I compared with those of my Rameau; I filled my head with harmony, accompaniments, and chords. My ear required training for all that, and I proposed to mamma to give a little concert every month, to which she agreed. I was so full of this concert, that, day and night, I thought of nothing else; and it really occupied a considerable part of my time to arrange the music, the accompanists, and instruments, to write out the parts, and so forth. Mamma sang; Père Caton – of whom I have already spoken, and of whom I shall have occasion to speak

[1] In September 1734 the French commander the Comte de Broglie was surprised in his sleep by the Imperial troops and nearly taken prisoner, being saved by the King of Sardinia.

again – sang also; M. Roche, a dancing-master, and his son played the violin; M. Canavas, a Piedmontese musician, who was employed in the Survey, and has since married and settled at Paris, played the violoncello; the Abbé Palais accompanied on the piano, and I had the honour of conducting with my baton. It may be imagined how delightful it was! Not quite like the concerts at M. de Treytorens's, but nearly so.

This little concert given by Madame de Warens, a new convert, who lived, as was reported, on the King's charity, gave offence to the band of devotees; but for many worthy people it was an agreeable amusement. It would not easily be guessed whom I placed at the head of these on this occasion. It was a monk, but a monk, talented and even amiable, whose later misfortunes keenly affected me, and whose memory, connected as it is with that of my happy days, is still dear to me. The monk in question was Père Caton, a Franciscan, who, conjointly with Comte Dortan, had caused the music of the poor "Kitten" to be confiscated at Lyons, which was not the most worthy incident in his life. He was a Bachelor of Sorbonne; he had lived a long time in the highest circles in Paris, and was an especial favourite with the Marquis d'Antremont, at that time Sardinian ambassador. He was tall, well built, with a full face and prominent eyes, black hair, which curled naturally over his forehead, and a manner at once noble, frank, and modest; his appearance was simple and pleasing, without the hypocritical or impudent attitude of a monk, or the haughty demeanour of a man of fashion, although he was one; he displayed only the assurance of an honourable man, who, without blushing for his cloth, respects himself and always feels himself in his proper place in honourable company. Although he was not very learned for a doctor, he was very accomplished for a man of the world; and, never eager to display his knowledge, he made use of it so opportunely, that he was credited with more than he really possessed. Having lived much in society, he had paid more attention to agreeable accomplishments than to solid learning. He was witty, wrote verses, talked well, sang better, had a fine voice, and played the organ and piano. This was more than enough to make him sought after, as indeed he was; but so little did this cause him to neglect the duties of his position, that, in spite of jealous rivals, he was chosen *Définiteur*[1] of his province, in other words, one of the highest dignitaries of the order.

Père Caton made mamma's acquaintance at the Marquis d'Antremont's. He heard our concerts spoken of, and expressed a desire to take part in them; he did so, and made them delightful. We soon became attached by our mutual taste for music, which, with both of us, was a lively passion, the only difference being that he was really a musician, while I was only a bungler. We used to go and play in his room together with Canavas and the Abbé Palais, and sometimes, on feast days, we had music on his organ. We often shared his little table at dinner; for – a thing surprising in a monk – he was liberal, profuse, and fond of the pleasures of the table without being a glutton. On our concert days, he stayed to supper with mamma. These suppers were very gay and very pleasant. We spoke as we thought, and sang duets; I was in my element, and displayed my wit and humour; Père Caton was delightful, mamma was adorable; the Abbé Palais, with his deep voice, was the butt of all. Sweet moments of youthful folly; how long is it since you have departed?

As I shall have no further occasion to speak of this poor Père Caton, let me finish his melancholy story in a few words. The other monks, jealous, or rather, furious, at seeing in him good qualities and a refinement of manners which had nothing in common with monastic debauchery, conceived a violent hatred for him, since he was not as hateful as themselves. Their leaders combined against him, and stirred up the inferior monks who envied his position, and who had hitherto not dared to look at him. They heaped a thousand insults upon him, deprived him of his office, took away his room, which he had furnished with taste, although quite simply, and banished him I know not whither; at last, these wretches so overwhelmed him with insults, that his honourable and justly proud soul was unable to withstand them; and he who had been the delight of the most agreeable society, died of grief on a miserable bed, in some cell or dungeon, regretted and lamented by all the worthy people

[1] Assessor to the head of his order.

who had known him and found no other fault in him, except that of being a monk.

Living in this manner, I soon became entirely absorbed by music, and found it impossible to think of anything else. I never went to my desk willingly; the restraint and constant hard work made it an unendurable torture, and at last I expressed a wish to throw up my employment, in order to devote myself entirely to music. It may be imagined that this folly on my part did not escape opposition. To leave a respectable situation and a certain salary in order to run after uncertain pupils, was too foolish a plan to meet with mamma's approval. Even if my future success should prove as great as I imagined, it was fixing very humble limits to my ambition, to confine myself for life to the position of a musician. She, whose plans for me were all ambitious, and who no longer judged me entirely in accordance with M. d'Aubonne's verdict,[1] was sorry to see me seriously occupied with a talent which she regarded as unprofitable, and often repeated to me the provincial saying, which is less applicable in Paris, "He who sings and dances well, has a profession which does not lead to much." On the other hand, she saw me carried away by an irresistible inclination; my passion for music was becoming a regular madness, and there was reason to fear that my work might suffer from my distractions, and that this might cause me to be dismissed, which would be far worse than voluntary resignation. Again, I pointed out to her that my employment was only temporary, that I should be obliged to do something for a livelihood, and that it was far safer to acquire by practice a thorough knowledge of the art to which my tastes inclined me and which she had chosen for me, than to put myself at the mercy of patrons, or to try something fresh which might not succeed, and might leave me, when I was too old to learn, without the means of earning my bread. At last, I extorted her consent more by dint of importunities and caresses than arguments which she considered satisfactory. I immediately ran to M. Coccelli, general manager of the Survey, to resign my appointment, as proudly as if I had performed a most heroic

[1] For M. d'Aubonne's discouraging verdict on Rousseau see Book III, p. 118–19.

action; and I voluntarily resigned my situation, without cause, reason, or excuse, with as much and even greater joy than I had accepted it less than two years before.

This step, utterly foolish as it was, procured for me in the country a certain consideration which was useful to me. Some imagined that I possessed means which I did not possess; others, seeing me entirely devoted to music, estimated my talents by the sacrifice that I had made, and believed that, with so much passion for this art, I must really possess a superior knowledge of it. In the country of the blind the one-eyed are kings; I passed for a good master, since all the rest were bad. Besides, since I really possessed a certain taste for singing, and was also favoured by my age and personal appearance, I soon had more lady pupils than were necessary to make up the pay I had received as a clerk.

It is certain that, as far as a pleasant life was concerned, it would not have been possible for anyone to pass more rapidly from one extreme to the other. At the Survey, occupied for eight hours daily with the most disagreeable employment, amongst people still more disagreeable, shut up in a gloomy office, poisoned by the breath and perspiration of a number of clods, most of them dirty and unkempt, I was sometimes so overcome by the exertion, smell, restraint and weariness, that I felt quite giddy. In place of this, I was suddenly launched into the fashionable world, admitted and sought after in the best houses, everywhere graciously received, caressed, and fêted; amiable young ladies, gaily dressed, awaited my arrival, and received me with eagerness; I saw nothing but enchanting objects, I smelt nothing but the perfume of roses and orange-flowers, found nothing but singing, gossip, laughter and amusement; I only left one house to find the same in another. It will be agreed that, the other advantages being equal, there could be no hesitation in the choice. I was so satisfied with mine, that I never once repented it, and I do not regret it even now, when I weigh in the scale of reason the actions of my life, and am free from the not very sensible motives which led me to make it.

This was almost the only time that I was not deceived in my expectations, when I only obeyed my inclinations. The affable and sociable disposition, the easy-going temperament of the inhabitants of this country rendered my intercourse with the world agreeable, and the liking I then conceived for it has clearly proved to me that, if I do not like society, it is society's fault rather than mine.

It is to be regretted that the Savoyards are not rich, or, perhaps, it would be still more to be regretted if they were; for, such as they are, they are the best and most sociable people that I know. If there is a little city in the world where it is possible to enjoy the pleasures of life in agreeable and safe intercourse, it is Chambéri. The noble families of the province, who assemble there, have only enough to live on, not enough to advance themselves; and, being unable to indulge in ambitious projects, are obliged to follow the counsel of Cineas.[1] In youth, they devote themselves to military service, and return to spend their old age in peace at home. Honour and reason have an equal share in this distribution of their lives. The women are beautiful, without having any need to be so; they possess all those qualities which can give beauty its value, and even supply its place. It is remarkable that I, whose profession brought me into contact with so many young girls, do not remember to have ever seen one in Chambéri who was not charming. It will be said that I was inclined to find them so, and there may be some truth in that; but I had no need to add anything of my own. In truth, I cannot think of my young pupils without pleasure. Why, when I mention here the most amiable of them, can I not reinstate them and myself together in those happy times which we then enjoyed, those sweet and innocent moments, which we spent together? The first was Mademoiselle de Mellarède, my neighbour, the sister of M. Gaime's pupil. She was a lively brunette, full of tender vivacity and grace, and free from thoughtlessness. Like most girls of her age, she was rather thin; but her bright eyes, her slender figure, and her attractive manner needed no fulness to add to her charm. I used to go to her in the morning, when she was generally in deshabille, without any headdress except her hair, carelessly pinned up and set off by a few flowers which she placed there on my arrival, and which were taken off

[1] In his *Life* of Pyrrhus, King of Epirus, Plutarch tells how Cineas warned the King against ambition.

when I left, for her hair to be dressed. I am more afraid of a pretty young woman in deshabille than of anything else in the world; I should fear them a hundred times less in full dress, as Mademoiselle de Menthon, to whose house I went in the afternoon, always was. She made upon me an equally pleasing but entirely different impression. Her hair was very light; she was very slight, very shy, and very fair; her voice was clear, correct, and melodious, but she was afraid of employing its full compass. She had a scar on her bosom where she had been scalded by some boiling water, which was only partly hidden by a neckerchief of blue chenille. This mark sometimes drew my attention to the place, and, in a short time, no longer on account of the scar. Mademoiselle de Challes, another of my neighbours, was fully developed, tall, well made, and rather stout. She had been very pretty, but was no longer a beauty; but she deserves notice on account of her graceful manners, even temper, and good disposition. Her sister, Madame de Charly, the prettiest woman in Chambéri, no longer learned music, but I gave lessons to her daughter, who was still quite young, and whose growing beauty gave promise of equalling that of her mother, had she not unfortunately been somewhat red-haired. At the Convent of the Visitation I gave lessons to a young French lady, whose name I have forgotten, but who deserves a place in the list of my favourite pupils. She had adopted the slow and drawling tones of the nuns, and in this drawling tone made some very witty remarks, which seemed quite out of harmony with her manner. For the rest, she was idle, not caring to take pains to show her wit, which was a favour she did not grant to everyone. It was only after a month or two, during which I had given her lessons and she had been very idle, that she bethought herself of this expedient to make me more punctual, a thing which I have never been able to persuade myself to be. I liked my lessons while I was giving them; but I did not like the idea of being obliged to attend, or being tied to time; restraint and subjection of any kind are to me at all times unbearable; they would make me hate even pleasure itself. It is said that, amongst the Mahommedans, a man goes through the streets at daybreak, ordering husbands to do their duty to their wives. I should be a poor Turk at that hour.

I also had some pupils among the middle classes, amongst others, one who was the indirect cause of a change in my relations, of which I have to speak, since I must tell everything. She was a grocer's daughter, named Mademoiselle Lard; a perfect model for a Greek statue, and whom I should quote as the most beautiful girl I have ever seen, if true beauty could exist without life and soul. Her indifference, coldness, and want of feeling were almost incredible. It was as impossible to please as it was to annoy her; and I am convinced that, if any man had made an attempt upon her virtue, she would have allowed him to succeed, not from inclination, but from sheer stupidity. Her mother, who did not wish to run the risk, never left her for a moment. In having her taught singing, in providing her with a young master, she did all she could to rouse her, but without success. While the master tried to fascinate the daughter, the mother tried to fascinate the master, with equally bad success. Madame Lard united with her natural vivacity all the sprightliness which her daughter should have possessed. She was a lively, pretty little woman, although her features were somewhat irregular and marked with the small-pox. She had small, fiery eyes, which were rather red, and nearly always sore. Every morning, on my arrival, I found my coffee and cream ready; the mother never failed to salute me with a hearty kiss on the lips, which I should have liked to return to the daughter, merely out of curiosity to see how she would have taken it. All this was done so simply and naturally, that, even when M. Lard was there, the kissing and caressing went on as usual. He was a good fellow, the true father of his daughter, whom his wife never deceived, since she had no need to do so.

I submitted to all these caresses with my usual stupidity, treating them simply as tokens of friendship. Sometimes they became troublesome, for lively Madame Lard always exacted her rights, and if, in the course of the day, I had passed the shop without stopping, it would have created a disturbance. When I was in a hurry, I was obliged to go round by another street; for I well knew that it was not so easy a matter to get out of her house as to enter it.

Madame Lard showed me too much attention for me to show none to her. These attentions touched me greatly. I spoke about them to mamma, as something which was no secret; and, even if there had been any mystery, I should have spoken to her all the same, for it would have been impossible for me to keep a secret of any kind from her; my heart was as open before her as in the sight of heaven. She did not consider the matter quite as harmless as I did. She saw advances where I had only seen friendship; she thought that, if Madame Lard made it a point of honour not to leave me as great a fool as she had found me, she would somehow or other succeed in making herself understood, and, apart from the consideration that it was not fair that another woman should undertake the instruction of her pupil, she had motives, which were more worthy of her, in a desire to protect me from the snares to which my age and calling exposed me. At the same time, a more dangerous snare was set for me, which I indeed escaped, but which showed her that the dangers, which continually threatened me, rendered necessary all the measures of protection which she could employ.

The Comtesse de Menthon, the mother of one of my pupils, was a woman of great wit, and had the reputation of being equally malicious. It was reported that she had caused several quarrels, amongst others, one which had had fatal consequences for the house of Antremont. Mamma was sufficiently intimate with her to be acquainted with her character; having quite innocently taken the fancy of someone upon whom Madame de Menthon had designs, mamma was charged by her with the offence of the preference shown towards her, although she had neither sought nor accepted it; and, from that time, Madame de Menthon sought to do her rival several ill turns, none of which succeeded. By way of sample, I will relate one of the most laughable. They were together in the country, with several gentlemen of the neighbourhood, amongst whom was the suitor in question. Madame de Menthon one day told one of these gentlemen that Madame de Warens was very affected, and she had no taste, dressed badly, and kept her bosom covered like a tradesman's wife. "As for the last point," answered the gentleman, who was fond of a joke, "she has her reasons for it; I know she has a scar on her breast, just like an ugly rat, so perfectly natural that it looks as if it was moving." Hatred, like love, causes credulity. Madame de Menthon resolved to make capital out of this discovery; and one day, when mamma was playing cards with the lady's ungrateful favourite, she seized the opportunity to step behind her rival, and, almost upsetting her chair, cleverly turned back her neckerchief; but, instead of the large rat, the gentleman saw something very different, which it was easier to see than to forget, and this was certainly not what the lady had intended.

I was not calculated to attract Madame de Menthon, who only liked to see brilliant company around her; nevertheless, she paid me some attention, not on account of my personal appearance, about which she certainly did not trouble herself, but because of my supposed wit, which might have made me serviceable to her. She had a lively taste for satire, and was fond of composing songs and verses upon those who displeased her. If she had found me sufficiently gifted to assist her in composing her verses, and sufficiently obliging to write them, between us we should soon have turned Chambéri upside down. These lampoons would have been traced back to their source; Madame de Menthon would have got out of it by sacrificing me, and I should, perhaps, have been imprisoned for the rest of my life, as a reward for playing the Apollo of the ladies.

Happily, nothing of the kind happened. Madame de Menthon kept me to dinner two or three times, to make me talk, and found that I was only a fool. I was conscious of this myself, and sighed over it, envying the accomplishments of my friend Venture, whereas I ought to have been grateful to my stupidity for saving me from danger. I continued her daughter's singing-master, and nothing more; but I lived peacefully, and was always welcome in Chambéri, which was far better than being considered a wit by her, and a serpent by everybody else.

Be that as it may, mamma saw that, in order to rescue me from the perils of my youth, she must treat me as a man, which she immediately proceeded to do, but in the most singular manner that ever occurred to a woman in similar circumstances. I found her manner more serious, and her utterances more moral than usual. The playful gaiety, which was usually mingled with her advice, was all at once succeeded by a sustained gravity, neither familiar nor severe, which seemed to pave the way for an explanation. After having in vain asked myself the reason of this change, I asked her, which was just what she expected. She proposed a walk in the little garden on the following day; the next morning found us there. She had taken precautions that we should be left undisturbed all day, and employed the time in preparing me for the kindness which she wished to show me, not, as another woman would have done, by artifices and coquetry, but by language full of feeling and good sense, better calculated to instruct than to seduce me, which appealed rather to my heart than my senses. But, however admirable and useful the words she addressed to me may have been, although they were anything but cold and mournful, I did not listen to them with all the attention they deserved, and did not impress them on my memory, as I should have done at any other time. The manner in which she began, the appearance of careful prepara- tion had disquieted me; while she was speaking, I was dreamy and distracted, thinking less of what she was saying than of what she wanted; and, as soon as I understood, which was by no means easy, the novelty of the idea, which had never once entered my head all the time I had been living with her, it so completely took possession of me, that I was no longer in a state to pay attention to what she said to me. I only thought of her, and did not listen to her.

Most instructors are liable to the perverse idea, which I have not avoided myself in my "Émile," of making young people attentive to that which they desire to impress upon them, by revealing to them the prospect of something in the highest degree attractive. Struck by the object held before him, a young man devotes his attention to that exclusively, and, leaping lightly over your introductory discourses, makes straight for the goal towards which you are leading him too slowly for his liking. If it be desired to make him attentive, he must not be allowed to go too far ahead; and it was just in this particular that mamma showed her want of judgment. With characteristic singularity, which accorded with her systematic mind, she took the superfluous precaution of attaching conditions; but, as soon as I saw their reward, I no longer listened to them, and hastened to agree to everything. I even doubt whether there is a man in the world sufficiently honest and courageous to make a bargain in a similar case, or a woman capable of pardoning him, if he ventured to do so. In consequence of the same singularity, she attached to the agreement the most solemn formalities, and gave me eight days to think over them, which, like a hypocrite, I assured her I did not require; for, to crown the singularity of the whole affair, I was really glad of the respite, so greatly had the novelty of these ideas struck me, and so disordered did I feel the state of my own to be, that I wanted time to set them in order.

It will be imagined that those eight days seemed eight centuries to me; on the contrary, I could have wished that they had really lasted as long. I do not know how to describe my condition; it was a kind of fright mingled with impatience, during which I was so afraid of what I longed for, that I sometimes seriously endeavoured to think of some decent way of avoiding the promised happiness. Consider my ardent and lascivious temperament, my heated blood, my heart intoxicated with love, my vigorous health, my age. Remember that, in this condition, thirsting after women, I had never yet touched one; that imagination, need, vanity, and curiosity, all combined to devour me with the burning desire of being a man and showing myself one. Add to this, above all – for it must never be forgotten – that my tender and lively attachment to her, far from diminishing, had only become warmer every day, that I was never happy except with her; that I never left her except to think of her; that my heart was full, not only of her goodness and amiability, but of her sex, her form, her person; in a word, of her, under every aspect in which she could be dear to me. Do not imagine, that, because she was ten or twelve years older than myself, she had either grown old, or appeared so to me. During the five or six years since the first sight of her had so enchanted me, she had really altered very little, and, in my eyes, not at all. She had always appeared charming to me, and, at that time, everyone still considered her so. Her figure alone had become a little stouter. In other respects, it was the same eye, the same complexion, the same bosom, the same features, the same beautiful fair hair, the same cheerfulness, even the voice was the same, the silvery voice of youth, which always made so deep an impression upon me, that, even now, I cannot hear without emotion the tones of a pretty girlish voice.

What I had to fear in the expectation of possessing one who was so dear to me, was naturally the anticipation of it, and the inability to control my desires and imagination sufficiently to remain master of myself. It will be seen that, at an advanced age, the mere idea of certain trifling favours which awaited me in the company of the person I loved, heated my blood to such a degree that it was impossible for me to make with impunity the short journey which separated me from her.[1] How then was it that, in the flower of my youth, I felt so little eagerness for the first enjoyment? How was it that I could see the hour approach with more pain than pleasure? How was it that, instead of the rapture which should have intoxicated me, I almost felt repugnance and fear? There is no doubt that, if I had been able to escape my happiness with decency, I should have done so with all my heart. I have promised singularities in the history of my attachment to her; this is surely one which would never have been expected.

The reader, already disgusted, is doubtless of opinion that, being already possessed by another man, she degraded herself in my eyes by distributing her favours, and that a feeling of disesteem cooled those with which she had inspired me. He is mistaken. This distribution was certainly very painful to me, as much in consequence of a very natural feeling of delicacy as because I really considered it unworthy of her and myself; but it never altered my feelings towards her, and I can swear that I never loved her more tenderly than when I had so little desire to possess her. I knew too well her modest heart and her cold temperament to think for a moment that sensual pleasure had anything to do with this abandonment of herself; I was perfectly convinced that nothing but anxiety to save me from dangers that were otherwise almost inevitable and to preserve me entirely for myself and my duties, caused her to violate a duty which she did not regard in the same light as other women, as will be shown later. I pitied her and pitied myself. I should have liked to say to

[1] See Book IX, p. 477.

her: "No, mamma, it is not necessary; I will answer for myself without that." But I did not dare to do so – first, because it was not a thing to say, and, in the second place, because in the main I felt that it was not true, and that, in reality, there was only *one* woman who could protect me against other women and secure me against temptations. Without desiring to possess her, I was very glad that she prevented me from desiring the possession of other women, to such an extent did I look upon everything as a misfortune which would draw me away from her. Our long-continued and innocent intercourse, far from weakening my feelings for her, had strengthened them, but, at the same time, had given them a different turn, which made them more affectionate, more tender perhaps, but also less sensual. Having so long called her mamma, having enjoyed with her the intimacy of a son, I had become accustomed to look upon myself as one. I believe that this was really the cause of the little eagerness I felt to possess her, although she was so dear to me. I well remember that my early feelings, without being livelier, were more sensual. At Annecy, I was intoxicated; at Chambéri, I was no longer so. I still loved her as passionately as possible; but I loved her more for her own sake than for my own, or, at least, I sought happiness with her, rather than enjoyment; she was for me more than a sister, more than a mother, more than a friend, even more than a mistress; and for that very reason she was not a mistress for me. In short, I loved her too well to desire to possess her; that is most clearly prominent in my ideas.

The day, more dreaded than wished for, at length arrived. I promised everything, and kept my word. My heart sealed all my vows, without desiring their reward. However, I obtained it. For the first time I found myself in the arms of a woman, a woman whom I adored. Was I happy? No; I tasted pleasure. A certain unconquerable feeling of melancholy poisoned its charm; I felt as if I had been guilty of incest. Two or three times, while pressing her in ecstasy to my arms, I wetted her bosom with my tears. She, on the other hand, was neither sad nor excited; she was tender and calm. As she was by no means sensual and had not looked for enjoyment, she felt no gratification, and never experienced remorse.

I repeat it: all her faults were due to her errors, none to her passions. She was well born, her heart was pure, she loved propriety; her inclinations were upright and virtuous, her taste was refined; she was formed for an elegance of manners which she always loved but never followed, because, instead of listening to her heart, which always guided her aright, she listened to her reason, which guided her wrongly; for when the latter is led astray by false principles, these are always belied by its real feelings; but, unfortunately, she rather prided herself on her philosophy, and the morals which she drew from it corrupted those which her heart dictated.

M. de Tavel, her first lover, was her instructor in philosophy, and the principles which he taught her were those which he found necessary, in order to seduce her. Finding her attached to her husband, devoted to her duties, always cold, calculating, and inaccessible to sensual feelings, he endeavoured to reach her by sophistries, and succeeded in convincing her that the duties, to which she was so attached, were so much catechism-nonsense, intended solely for the amusement of children; that the union of the sexes was in itself a matter of the greatest indifference; that conjugal fidelity was merely an apparent obligation, the inner morality of which only had reference to public opinion; that the husband's repose was the only rule of duty which the wife need respect, so that secret acts of unfaithfulness, being nothing to him against whom they were committed, were equally nothing to the conscience; in short, he persuaded her that the thing was nothing in itself, that only scandal called it into existence, and that every woman who appeared virtuous owed it to that alone. In this manner the wretch attained his object, by corrupting the mind of a child whose heart he had been unable to corrupt. He was punished for it by an all-devouring jealousy, being convinced that she treated him as he had persuaded her to treat her husband. I do not know whether he was mistaken in this. The minister Perret was supposed to have been his successor. All I know is, that the cold temperament of this young woman, which ought to have protected her against this system, was just what subsequently prevented her from abandoning it. She could not conceive that anyone should attach such importance to that which possessed no importance for her. She never honoured by the name of virtue an abstinence which cost her so little.

She hardly ever misused these false principles for her own sake; but she misused them for the sake of others, and that in consequence of another maxim almost equally false, but more in harmony with the goodness of her heart. She always believed that nothing attached a man so strongly to a woman as possession; and, although her love for her friends was only friendship, it was a friendship so tender, that she employed all possible means at her disposal to attach them more strongly to her. The remarkable thing is, that she nearly always succeeded. She was so truly amiable, that, the greater the intimacy in which one lived with her, the more one found fresh reasons for loving her. Another thing worthy of notice is that, after her first weakness, she rarely bestowed her favours except upon the unfortunate; persons of distinction spent their labour upon her in vain; but, if she once began to feel sympathy for a man, he must have been little deserving of love if she did not end by loving him. If she sometimes chose those who were unworthy of her, the blame rested, not on any low inclinations, which were far removed from her noble heart, but only on her too generous, too kindly, too compassionate, and too feeling disposition, which she did not always control with sufficient judgment.

If some false principles led her astray, how many admirable ones did she possess, to which she always remained constant! By how many virtues did she make up for her weaknesses, if those errors can be so called, with which the senses had so little to do! The same man, who deceived her in one point, instructed her admirably in a thousand others; and, as her passions were not so unruly as to prevent her from following her reason, she took the right path when her sophisms did not mislead her. Her motives, even in her errors, were praiseworthy; owing to her mistaken ideas, she might do wrong, but she was incapable of doing so wilfully. She abhorred duplicity and lying; she was just, fair, humane, disinterested, faithful to her word, her friends, and the duties which she regarded as such, incapable of revenge or hatred, without the least idea that there was any merit in forgiveness. Finally, to return to those qualities which less admit of excuse, without knowing how to estimate the value of her favours, she never made a common trade of them; she was lavish of them, but she never sold them, although she was always at her wit's end how to live; and I venture to assert, that if Socrates could esteem Aspasia,[1] he would have respected Madame de Warens.

I know beforehand, that, when I ascribe to her a sensitive disposition and a cold temperament, I shall, as usual, be accused of contradiction, and with as much reason. It may be that Nature was wrong, and that this combination ought not to have existed; I only know that it did exist. All who have known Madame de Warens, many of whom are still alive, know well that this was the case. I will even venture to add, that she never knew but *one* real pleasure in life – to procure enjoyment for those whom she loved. Anyone is at liberty to judge of that as he pleases, and learnedly prove that it is not true. My duty is to state the truth, not to make people believe it.

By degrees I became acquainted with all I have just said in the course of the conversations which succeeded our union, and which alone rendered it delightful. She had been right in hoping that her complaisance would be useful to me; I derived great advantages from it as regards my instruction. Hitherto, she had only spoken to me of myself alone as if she had been talking to a child. She now began to treat me as a man, and spoke to me of herself. All that she said to me was so interesting, and I felt so touched by it, that, when I reflected, I derived greater advantage from these confidences than from her instructions. When we truly feel that the heart speaks, our own opens to receive its confidences, and all the morality of a pedagogue will never be worth the tender and loving chatter of a clever woman, who has gained our affection.

The intimate terms on which I lived with her afforded her the opportunity of forming a more favourable estimate of me than before; she was of opinion that, in spite of my awkward manner, I was worth being trained for the world, and that, if I one day appeared on a certain footing, I should be in a position to make my way. With this idea, she devoted herself, not only to forming

[1] The story of Socrates and Aspasia is told in Plutarch's *Life* of Pericles.

my judgment, but also my appearance and manners, in order to
make me amiable as well as estimable; and, if it is true that worldly
success is compatible with virtue – which for my part I do not
believe – I am at least convinced, that there is no other way to
such an end than that which she had taken and wished to teach
me. For Madame de Warens understood mankind, and understood, in a high degree, the art of dealing with them without
falsehood and without indiscretion, without deceiving or
offending them. But she taught this art rather by her character
than by her lessons; she knew better how to practise than explain
it, and I was of all men in the world the least capable of learning it.
Thus her efforts in this direction were nearly all labour lost, as
well as the trouble she took to provide me with fencing and
dancing-masters. Although supple and of a good figure, I could
never learn to dance a minuet. Owing to my corns, I had contracted the habit of walking on my heels, of which Roche could
never cure me; and, in spite of my active appearance, I have never
been able to jump an ordinary ditch. It was worse at the fencing-
school. After three months' instruction I was still obliged to
confine myself to parrying, without being able to deliver an
attack; my wrist was not supple enough, or my arm sufficiently
firm, to hold my foil, whenever my master chose to make it fly
out of my hand. In addition to this, I had a mortal aversion to this
exercise, and to the master who attempted to teach me. I could
never have believed that a man could be so proud of being able to
kill another. In order to bring his commanding genius within my
reach, he always explained himself by comparisons drawn from
music, about which he knew nothing. He discovered striking
analogies between a thrust in tierce and carte and the musical
intervals of the same name. When he intended to make a feint, he
told me to look out for a *dièse*,[1] because a *dièse* was formerly called
a *feinte*; when he had knocked the foil out of my hand, he used to
say, with a grin, that it was a *pause*. In short, I have never in my life
beheld a more insufferable pedant than this wretched fellow with
his plumes and his leather stomacher.

I consequently made little progress in these exercises, which I
soon gave up from sheer disgust; but I succeeded far better in a

[1] Mus., sharp.

more useful art — that of being content with my lot, and not desiring one more brilliant, for which I began to feel that I was not born. Entirely devoted to the desire of making mamma's life happy, I always felt greater pleasure in her company; and, when I was obliged to leave her and hurry into the town, in spite of my passion for music, I began to feel the restraint imposed upon me by my lessons.

I do not know whether Claude Anet was aware of the intimacy of our relations. I have reason to believe that it did not escape his notice. He was very quick-witted, but very discreet; he never said what he did not think, but he did not always say what he thought. Without giving me the least hint that he knew about it, he seemed to show by his conduct that he did. This conduct was certainly not due to any lowness of disposition, but to the fact that, having adopted his mistress's principles, he could not disapprove if she acted in accordance with them. Although no older than she was, he was so mature and serious, that he looked upon us almost as two children, who deserved to be indulged, and both of us regarded him as a man worthy of respect, whose esteem we had to conciliate. It was not until she had been unfaithful to him, that I understood the extent of the attachment that she felt for him. Since she knew that I only felt, thought and breathed through her, she showed me how much she loved him, in order that I might feel the same affection for him, and she laid less stress upon her friendship than upon her esteem for him, since this was the feeling which I was capable of sharing most fully. How often did she move our hearts, and make us embrace with tears, at the same time telling us that we were both necessary to her happiness in life! Let not those women who read this laugh maliciously. With her peculiar temperament, there was nothing suspicious about this necessity; it was solely the necessity of her heart.

Thus a companionship was established between us, of which there is, perhaps, no other example upon earth. All our wishes, cares, and inclinations were in common; none of them went beyond our little circle. The habit of living together, to the exclusion of the rest of the world, became so strong, that if, during the course of our meals, one of the three was absent, or a fourth came in, everything was upset, and, in spite of our special bonds of attachment, our *tête-à-têtes* were not so sweet as our party of three. What prevented all restraint between us was an extreme mutual confidence, and what prevented weariness was the fact that we were all constantly employed. Mamma, always planning and always active, allowed neither of us to be idle; and, besides, we each of us had enough to do on our own account, to keep our time fully occupied. In my opinion, want of occupation is equally the scourge of society and solitude. Nothing narrows the mind more, nothing begets more nothings – gossip, tittle-tattle, bickering, and lies – than for people to be eternally shut up, opposite one another, in the same room, reduced, for the want of anything else to do, to the necessity of chattering incessantly. When everyone is busy, people only speak when they have something to say; but, when doing nothing, they are absolutely obliged to keep talking, which is the most wearisome and the most dangerous kind of constraint. I even venture to go further and maintain that, in order to make company really agreeable, not only must everybody be doing something, but something that requires a certain amount of attention. Knitting is as bad as doing nothing; and it takes as much trouble to amuse a woman who is knitting, as one who is sitting with her arms folded. Embroidering is different; she is sufficiently occupied to fill up the intervals of silence. What is disgusting and ridiculous, is to see, in the meantime, a dozen overgrown hobble-de-hoys get up, sit down again, walk backwards and forwards, turn round on their heels, move the porcelain chimney-ornaments about, and rack their brains in order to keep up an inexhaustible flow of words – a charming occupation truly! Such people, whatever they may do, will always be a burden to themselves and others. When I was at Motiers, I used to go to my neighbours' houses to make stay-laces; if I went back into the world, I should always carry a cup and ball in my pocket, and amuse myself with it all day, to avoid being obliged to speak when I have nothing to say. If everyone did the same, men would become less spiteful, their intercourse would become safer, and, in my opinion, more agreeable. In short, let wits laugh if they please, but I maintain that the only lesson of morality within the reach of the present generation is the morality of the cup and ball.

Besides, we were not allowed much time for taking precautions against *ennui* when by ourselves; the crowds of troublesome visitors caused us too much weariness to allow us to feel any when we were left to ourselves. The feeling of impatience, with which they had formerly inspired me, had not diminished, and the only difference was, that I had less time to abandon myself to it. Poor mamma had not lost her old fancy for schemes and systems; on the contrary, the more pressing her domestic embarrassments became, the more she abandoned herself to visionary projects, in order to meet them; the smaller her present resources, the greater she imagined them in the future. Advancing years only strengthened her in this folly; and, in proportion as she lost the taste for the pleasures of the world and youth, she supplied its place by a mania for secrets and schemes. The house was never free from quacks, manufacturers, alchemists, and promoters of all kinds, who flung millions about them, and ended by being in want of a crown-piece. None of them left her empty-handed; and it has always amazed me, how she was able to support such extravagant expenditure without exhausting her means and the patience of her creditors.

The scheme with which she was most occupied at the time of which I am speaking, and which was not the most unreasonable that she had formed, was to establish at Chambéri a royal botanical garden with a paid demonstrator; it will be guessed for whom this post had already been designed. The position of this town, in the midst of the Alps, was excellently adapted for botanical purposes; and mamma, who always tried to assist one scheme by another, combined with it the idea of a college of pharmacy, which really seemed likely to be very useful in so poor a country, where apothecaries are almost the only medical men. The retirement of Grossi, the royal physician in ordinary, to Chambéri, after the death of King Victor, seemed to her to be very favourable to this idea, or, perhaps, suggested it. However that may be, she laid herself out to flatter Grossi, who was by no means an easy subject; he was certainly the most sarcastic and brutal fellow that I have ever known. The reader will be able to judge of his character by two or three specimens of it, which I will mention.

One day, he was in consultation with some other physicians, one of whom had been summoned from Annecy, and was the patient's usual medical attendant. This young man, who possessed little tact for a physician, ventured to disagree with Grossi's opinion. The latter, by way of reply, simply asked him when he was going back, which way he meant to go, and by what conveyance he travelled. The other, having satisfied Grossi on these points, asked him in his turn whether he could do anything for him. "Nothing, nothing," said Grossi, "except that I intend to sit at a window while you are passing, to have the pleasure of seeing an ass riding on horseback." He was as mean as he was wealthy and hard-hearted. One of his friends once asked him to lend him some money on good security. "My friend," said he, seizing his arm and grinding his teeth, "if St. Peter himself came down from heaven to borrow ten pistoles from me, and offered me the Trinity as sureties, I would not lend them to him." One day, being invited to dinner with Comte Picon, Governor of Savoy, who was a very religious man, he arrived before the time; and his Excellency, who was busy telling his beads, proposed the same amusement to him. Not knowing exactly what to answer, he made a fearful grimace and knelt down; but he had scarcely recited two *Aves*, when, unable to endure it any longer, he hastily got up, took his stick, and went off without saying a word. Comte Picon ran after him, crying, "M. Grossi! M. Grossi! stop, stop! there is an excellent red partridge on the spit!" "Monsieur le Comte," replied the other, turning round, "I would not stay if you were to set a roasted angel before me." Such was the chief physician, M. Grossi, whom mamma took in hand, and succeeded in taming. Although extremely busy, he was in the habit of coming to see her very frequently, conceived a friendship for Anet, showed that he thought highly of his learning, spoke of him in terms of esteem, and, what one would not have expected from such a bear, treated him with studious respect, to obliterate the impressions of the past. For, although Anet was no longer on the footing of a servant, it was known that he had formerly been one, and it needed nothing less than the example and authority of the chief physician, to make people treat him in a manner which they would certainly not have adopted from anyone else. Claude Anet, with his black coat, well-combed wig, serious and respectable demeanour, prudent and careful behaviour, a tolerably extensive knowledge of botany and medicine, and the support of the head of the Faculty, might reasonably have hoped to fill the place of Demonstrator Royal of plants, if the idea of the establishment had been carried out; and, in fact, Grossi had approved of the plan, had taken it up, and only waited an opportunity to lay it before the Court, when the conclusion of peace should allow it to give attention to useful things, and leave some money at its disposal to provide for the necessary expenses.

But this project, the carrying out of which would probably have plunged me into the study of botany, for which, as it appears to me, I was born, failed in consequence of one of those unexpected accidents which overthrow the best concerted plans. I was fated to become by degrees an example of human misery. It was as if Providence, who summoned me to these great trials, with its own hand removed every obstacle which might have prevented me from encountering them. In an excursion which Anet had made to the top of the mountains to look for genipi, a rare plant which only grows upon the Alps and which M. Grossi wanted, the poor fellow got so hot that he was attacked by a pleurisy, which the genipi was unable to cure, although it is said to be a specific for that complaint; and, notwithstanding all the skill of Grossi, who was certainly a very clever man, in spite of the unremitting care and attention of his good mistress and myself, he died in our arms on the fifth day, after suffering the most cruel agonies, during which he had no spiritual exhortations but mine, which I lavished upon him with such outbursts of grief and fervour, that, if he had been able to understand me, they must have afforded him some consolation. Thus I lost the most faithful friend I have had in my life; an uncommon and estimable man, in whom Nature took the place of education, who, in his position as a servant, nourished in his heart all the virtues of great men, and who, in order to show himself one of them to all the world, perhaps wanted nothing except a longer life and a different position.

The next day, I was speaking of him to mamma with the most lively and sincere affliction; when suddenly, in the midst of our conversation, the vile and unworthy thought came across my mind, that I should inherit his wardrobe, particularly a nice black coat, which had caught my fancy. I thought of this, and consequently gave utterance to my thought; for when I was with her, to think and speak was the same thing for me. Nothing made her feel more keenly the loss which she had sustained than this contemptible and hateful remark, disinterestedness and nobility of soul being qualities for which the deceased had been preeminently distinguished. The poor woman, without answering a word, turned away from me and began to cry. Dear and precious tears! They were understood, and all made their way into my heart, from which they washed away even the last traces of so contemptible and unworthy a thought. Never again, since that time, has a similar thought entered it.

This loss caused mamma as much harm as sorrow. From this moment, her affairs went from bad to worse. Anet had been very exact and methodical, and kept his mistress's house in good order. His vigilance was feared, and extravagance was checked. Even mamma herself was afraid of his censure, and curtailed her expenses. She was not satisfied with his attachment, she wished to preserve his esteem, and she dreaded the just reproach which he sometimes ventured to utter, that she was squandering not only her own property, but that of others as well. I thought as he did, and even said so; but I had not the same influence over her, and my words did not make the same impression upon her as his. When he was no more, I was obliged to take his place, for which I had as little capacity as inclination; consequently, I filled it badly. I was not sufficiently careful, I was very shy; though grumbling to myself, I let everything go on as it liked. Besides, although I had gained the same confidence, I had not the same authority. I saw the disorder, I sighed over it, I complained of it, but no one paid any attention to me. I was too young and too lively to have a right to be sensible; and, when I wanted to interfere and play the censor, mamma gave me two or three playful slaps on the cheek, called me her little Mentor, and obliged me to resume the part which suited me.

The profound conviction of the distress into which her unlimited extravagance was bound, sooner or later, to plunge her, made an impression upon me, which was so much the stronger, as, being now the overseer of her household, I was able to judge for myself of the difference between her income and expenses, in which the balance was in favour of the latter. It is from this period that I date the tendency to avarice, which I have always felt since then. I have never been foolishly extravagant except by fits and starts; but, until then, it never troubled me whether I had little or much money. I now began to pay attention to this, and to look after my purse. I became miserly from a very excellent motive; for, in truth, my only thought was, how to save something for mamma against the time of the crash which I saw coming. I was afraid that her creditors would confiscate her pension, or that it might be altogether discontinued; and I imagined, with my narrow ideas, that my little savings would then be of great service to her. But, in order to save anything, and, above all, to keep it, it was necessary for me to hide it from her; for, while she was hard pressed for money, it would never have done for her to know of the existence of my little hoard. I accordingly looked about for various hiding-places, where I stored a few *louis*, intending to increase the store from time to time, until the moment when I intended to lay it at her feet. But I was so awkward in the choice of my hiding-places, that she always found them out; and then, in order to let me know that she had done so, she removed the money which I had deposited and replaced it by a larger sum in different coinage. Then, feeling quite ashamed, I put my little treasure into the common purse, and she never failed to lay it out in clothes or other articles for my use, such as a silver-hilted sword, a watch, or something of the kind.

Convinced that I should never succeed in saving much money, and that, after all, it would only be of very little use to her, I at last felt that there was nothing else to be done, in view of the disaster which I feared, except for me to secure a position, which would enable me to provide for her myself, as soon as she ceased to provide for me and found herself reduced to want. Unfortunately, I built my plans upon my own inclinations, and foolishly persisted in looking for my fortune in music; feeling *motifs* and melodies rising in my head, I thought that, as soon as I should be in a position to make use of them, I should become a celebrated man, a modern Orpheus, whose notes could not fail to attract all the wealth of Peru. As I now began to read music fairly well, the question was, how I was to learn composition. The difficulty was to find anyone to teach me; for I did not expect to be able to teach myself with the assistance of my Rameau alone; and, since Le Maître's departure, there was no one in Savoy who knew anything about harmony.

Here will be seen another of those inconsistencies of which my life is full, and which have often led me directly away from the object I had in view, even when I thought that I was making straight for it. Venture had often spoken to me of the Abbé Blanchard, his composition-master, a man of great merit and talents, who at the time was music-master of Besançon Cathedral, and now occupies the same post in the Chapel of Versailles. I determined to go to Besançon and take lessons from the Abbé Blanchard; and this idea seemed to me so sensible, that I succeeded in making mamma look upon it in the same light. She immediately set about getting ready my little outfit with the extravagance she displayed in everything. Thus, with the object of preventing her bankruptcy and repairing in the future the consequences of her extravagance, I began at the outset by putting her to an expenditure of eight hundred francs; I hastened her ruin, in order to put myself in a position to prevent it. Foolish as this conduct may have been, the illusion was complete on my part and even on hers. We were both of us convinced – I, that I was working for her benefit: she, that I was working for my own.

I had counted upon finding Venture still at Annecy, and intended to ask him for a letter of introduction to the Abbé Blanchard. He was no longer there. I could learn nothing more, and was obliged to content myself with a mass composed by himself, written in four parts, which he had left for me. With this recommendation, I set out for Besançon, by way of Geneva,

where I paid a visit to my relations, and through Nyon, where I
saw my father, who received me as usual and undertook to send
on my trunk, which, as I was on horseback, arrived after myself.
I reached Besançon. The Abbé received me kindly, promised to
teach me, and offered to help me in any way he could. When we
were ready to begin, I received a letter from my father, informing
me that my trunk had been seized and confiscated at Rousses, a
French custom-house on the Swiss frontier. Alarmed at this
news, I made use of the acquaintances whom I had made at
Besançon, to find out the reason of this confiscation; for, being
certain that I had nothing contraband, I could not imagine what
excuse there was for it. At last I discovered the reason, and it was
so curious that I must relate it.

At Chambéri I had made the acquaintance of an old
Lyonnese, named Duvivier, a very worthy fellow, who, under
the Regency, had been employed at the passport-office, and, for
want of occupation, had come to assist in the land-survey. He
had lived in the fashionable world; he possessed talents and
some knowledge, was kind-hearted and courteous; he understood music; and, as we worked in the same room, we had
become attached to each other by preference in the midst of
the unlicked cubs around us. He had correspondents at Paris,
who kept him supplied with those little trifles, those ephemeral
publications, which circulate, one knows not why, and die, one
knows not how, of which no one thinks any further after they
have ceased to be spoken of. As I sometimes took him to dine
with mamma, he treated me with a certain amount of respect,
and, to make himself agreeable, endeavoured to inspire me with
a taste for such twaddle, for which I have always felt such
disgust, that I have never in my life read any of it myself.
Unhappily, one of these cursed papers had been left in the
breast-pocket of a new coat which I had worn two or three
times, to prevent its seizure by the custom-house officers. This
paper contained an insipid Jansenist parody of the beautiful
scene in Racine's *Mithridates*; I had not read ten lines of it, and
had forgotten to take it out of my pocket. This was the reason of
the confiscation of my property. The tax-collectors, at the head
of the inventory of my trunk, drew up an imposing report, in

which, assuming that the document was brought from Geneva in order to be printed and distributed in France, they launched out into pious invectives against the enemies of God and the Church, and into praises of those who, by their pious watchfulness, had prevented this infernal project from being carried out. No doubt they also found that my shirts smelt of heresy, for, on the strength of this terrible paper, everything was confiscated, and I never received any account or news of my poor outfit. The revenue-officers, to whom I applied, required so many informations, proofs, vouchers, and memorials that, after losing myself a thousand times in the mazes of this labyrinth, I was obliged to give up everything. I genuinely regret that I have not kept the report drawn up by the officials of Rousses; it would have figured with distinction amongst the collection which is to accompany this work.

This loss made me return at once to Chambéri, without having learned anything with the Abbé Blanchard; and, after weighing everything carefully, and seeing that misfortune pursued me in all my undertakings, I resolved to attach myself entirely to mamma, to share her lot, and no longer to trouble myself to no purpose about a future on which I had no influence. She received me as if I had brought back treasures, gradually supplied the loss of my wardrobe, and my misfortune, sufficiently great for us both, was forgotten almost as soon as it overtook us.

Although it had cooled my ardour for music, I still continued to study my Rameau; and, by dint of repeated efforts, I at length succeeded in understanding it, and made some trifling attempts at composition, the success of which encouraged me. The Comte de Bellegarde, son of the Marquis d'Antremont, had returned from Dresden after the death of King Augustus. He had lived a long time at Paris, and was passionately fond of music, especially Rameau's. His brother, the Comte de Nangis, played the violin; the Comtesse de la Tour, their sister, sang a little. All this made music the fashion at Chambéri, and what may be called public concerts were introduced there, which I was at first asked to direct; but it soon became clear that this was beyond my powers, and other arrangements were made. I still continued, however, to compose some little pieces of my own, amongst others a cantata, which met with great approval. It was not a well-executed piece of work, but it was full of new airs and effects, which were not expected from me. These gentlemen could not believe that I, who read music so indifferently at sight, could be capable of composing anything tolerable, and felt certain that I had taken the credit of someone else's work. In order to settle the matter, M. de Nangis came to see me one morning and brought a cantata by Clérambault, which he told me he had transposed to suit his voice, and for which another bass was required, since the original could no longer be played in consequence of the transposition. I told him that it would involve considerable labour, and that it could not be finished on the spot. He thought this was only an excuse, and pressed me to write, at least, the bass of a recitative. I did so, badly, I have no doubt, since, in order to do anything well, I must be free and unrestrained; but, at least, I wrote it according to the rules, and, as he was present, he could have no doubt that I knew the elements of composition. I did not, therefore, lose my pupils, but it somewhat cooled my ardour for music, to see that they could give a concert without my assistance.

It was about this time that peace was concluded, and the French army recrossed the Alps. Several officers came to visit mamma, amongst others the Comte de Lautrec, colonel of the Orleans regiment, afterwards Plenipotentiary at Geneva, and subsequently Marshal of France, to whom she presented me. After hearing her account of me, he appeared to take a great interest in me, and made me several promises, which he never remembered till the last year of his life, when I no longer needed his assistance. The young Marquis de Sennecterre, whose father was at the time ambassador at Turin, passed through Chambéri at the same time. He dined with Madame de Menthon. I happened to be dining there the same day. After dinner, the conversation turned upon music, which he knew well. The opera of *Jephtha* was at that time something new; he spoke of it and it was brought to him. He made me shudder by proposing that we should go through the opera together, and opened the book just at the famous piece for the double chorus:

"La terre, l'enfer, le ciel même,
Tout tremble devant le Seigneur."[1]

He asked me, "How many parts will you take? I will take these six." I was not yet accustomed to French forwardness, and, although I had sometimes stammered out the score, I did not understand how one man could take six parts at once, or even two. I have found nothing more difficult in practising music, than skipping lightly from one part to the other, and keeping my eye on a whole score at once. From the manner in which I evaded this attempt, M. de Sennecterre must have been inclined to think that I did not understand music. It was, perhaps, in order to clear up his doubts on the point, that he suggested to me to compose the score of a song which he wanted to give to Mademoiselle de Menthon. I could not refuse. He sang the song, and I wrote down the music, without asking him to repeat it too often. He afterwards read it, and found that it was correctly scored. He had noticed my embarrassment and seemed pleased to make the most of my trifling success. It was, however, in reality, a very simple matter. In the main, I had a very considerable knowledge of music; I only needed that first rapid glance, which I have never possessed in any single thing, and which can only be acquired in music by constant practice. Anyhow, I felt thankful for his honourable efforts to efface from the minds of others, as well as my own, the trifling disgrace which I had suffered; and, twelve or fifteen years later, when I met him at different houses in Paris, I was frequently tempted to remind him of this incident, and to show him that I had not forgotten it. But he had lost his sight since then, and I was afraid to renew his regrets, by reminding him of the use he had formerly made of it, and I held my tongue.

I now come to the moment which connects my past with my present existence. Some friendships, which have lasted from that time to this, are very dear to me. They have often caused me to regret that happy obscurity, when those who called themselves my friends were really such, and loved me for myself,

---

[1] "Earth, hell and even Heaven,/Everything trembles before the Lord": chorus from the opera *Jepthé* by Pellegrin, to music by Monteclair.

from pure goodwill, not from the vanity of being intimate with a well-known man, or from the secret desire of thus finding more opportunity of injuring him.

It is from this period that I date my acquaintance with my old friend Gauffecourt, who has always remained true to me, in spite of the efforts of others to take him away from me. Always? Alas, no! I have just lost him. But his affection for me only ended with his life; our friendship only ended at his death. M. de Gauffecourt was one of the most amiable men who have ever existed. It was impossible to see him without loving him, or to live with him without becoming devotedly attached to him. I have never seen more frank or more kindly features, or an expression which showed greater calmness, feeling and intelligence, or inspired greater confidence. However reserved a man might be, it was impossible for him to help being, at first sight, as familiar with him as if he had known him for twenty years. I myself, who found it so hard to feel at ease with strangers, was at home with him from the first moment. His manner, his way of speaking, his conversation were in perfect accord with his features. The tone of his voice was clear, full, well modulated, a fine bass, sonorous and powerful, which filled the ear and penetrated to the heart. It is impossible to imagine a gentler or more uniform cheerfulness, simpler or more unaffected grace, more natural or more tastefully cultivated talents. Add to this a loving heart – a little too affectionate towards all the world – a character too ready to oblige without discretion, serving his friends zealously, or rather making friends of people whom he was able to serve, capable of managing his own affairs very cleverly, while warmly promoting the interests of others. Gauffecourt was the son of a humble watchmaker, and had himself followed his father's trade. But his personal appearance and merits summoned him to another sphere, into which he was not slow to enter. He made the acquaintance of M. de la Closure, the French Resident at Geneva, who took a fancy to him. He procured him other acquaintances at Paris who proved useful to him, and by their influence he secured the right of supplying the salt at Valais, which brought him in an income of twenty thousand francs. His good fortune, which was amply sufficient, ended there as far as men were concerned; but, in regard to women, it was a great struggle; he had to choose, and made what choice he thought best. It was a rare and most honourable point about him, that, having connections with persons in all ranks of life, he was everywhere beloved and sought after by all, without ever incurring anyone's hatred or jealousy; and I believe that he died without ever having had a single enemy. Happy man! He went every year to the baths at Aix, the resort of the best society of the neighbouring countries. Intimate with all the nobility of Savoy, he came from Aix to Chambéri to visit the Comte de Bellegarde and his father the Marquis d'Antremont, at whose house mamma made his acquaintance and introduced me to him. This acquaintance, which did not seem destined to lead to anything, and was broken off for several years, was renewed on an occasion which I will afterwards relate, and became a genuine attachment. This is enough to justify me in speaking of a friend with whom I have been so closely connected; but, even if I had no personal interest in remembering him, he was so amiable a man and born under so lucky a star, that, for the credit of the human race, I should always think his memory worth preserving. Certainly, this charming man had his faults like others, as will be afterwards seen; but, if he had not had any, he would, perhaps, have been less amiable. To make him as attractive as possible, it was necessary that he should sometimes require to be pardoned.

Another connection of the same period is not yet entirely extinct, and still tempts me with the hope of earthly happiness, which dies so hard in the heart of man. M. de Conzié, a Savoyard gentleman, at that time young and amiable, took it into his head to learn music, or rather to make the acquaintance of him who taught it. With considerable intelligence and a taste for polite acquirements, M. de Conzié combined a gentleness of character which made him very fascinating, and I also easily made myself attractive to people in whom I found such a disposition. Our friendship was soon formed.* The germs of literature and

* I have seen him since, and found him entirely changed. What a mighty magician is M. Choiseul! None of my old acquaintances has been proof against his powers of transformation. (R)

philosophy, which were beginning to stir in my head and only waited for a little care and encouragement to develop themselves completely, found them in him. M. de Conzié had little talent for music, which was a good thing for me; for the lesson hours were devoted to everything else but singing scales. We breakfasted, talked, and read new publications, but never said a word about music. Voltaire's correspondence with the Crown Prince of Prussia was at that time causing some stir; we frequently conversed about these two celebrated men, one of whom, who had only lately ascended the throne, already gave promise of what he was soon to become, while the other, as vilified as he is now admired, caused us to lament sincerely the misfortune by which he seemed to be pursued, and which is so often the heritage of great minds. The prince had enjoyed little happiness in his youth; and Voltaire seemed born never to enjoy any. The interest which we took in both extended to everything connected with them. Nothing that Voltaire wrote escaped us. The pleasure which these readings afforded me inspired me with the desire of learning to write elegantly, and of attempting to imitate the beautiful colouring of this author, which enchanted me. Some time afterwards his "Philosophical Letters" appeared. Although certainly not his best work, it was that which most attracted me to study, and this growing taste was never extinguished from that time.

But the moment had not yet come for me to devote myself to it entirely. I still had a somewhat fickle disposition, a desire for rambling, which had been restrained rather than eradicated, and which was fostered by our manner of living at Madame de Warens's, which was too noisy to suit my solitary disposition. The crowd of strangers who swarmed around her from all directions, and my conviction that they were only seeking, each in his own way, to deceive her, made my life at home a regular torture. Since I had taken the place of Claude Anet in his mistress's confidence, I attentively followed the condition of her affairs, and saw them going from bad to worse in a most alarming manner. A hundred times I had remonstrated, begged, pressed and entreated her, but always in vain. I had thrown myself at her feet, and represented to her, as forcibly as I was able, the catastrophe which threatened her; I had strongly advised her to curtail her expenses, and to begin with me; to undergo a little privation while she was still young, rather than, by continually increasing her debts and the number of her creditors, to expose herself to their annoyance and to poverty in her old age. Touched by the sincerity of my zeal, she became affected like myself, and made me the finest promises in the world. But, the moment some worthless fellow arrived, all was forgotten. After a thousand proofs of the uselessness of my remonstrances, what was left for me to do but to turn my eyes away from the mischief which I could not prevent? I withdrew from the house, the door of which I was unable to guard; I made little excursions to Nyon, Geneva and Lyons, which distracted my attention from my secret trouble, while at the same time they increased the cause of it owing to the expense. I can swear that I would joyfully have put up with any kind of retrenchment, if mamma would really have profited by such saving; but, feeling convinced that the money I denied myself would only find its way into the pockets of swindlers, I abused her generosity in order to share it with them, and, like a dog returning from the slaughter-house, carried off my bit from the piece which I had not been able to save.

I never lacked excuses for all these journeys; mamma herself would have supplied me with them in abundance, having so many engagements, negotiations, affairs and commissions in all parts, which required a trustworthy agent to execute them. She desired nothing better than to send me away; I was always ready to go; the result of this could only be a wandering kind of life. These journeys afforded me the opportunity of making acquaintances, who proved either agreeable or useful to me. At Lyons, M. Perrichon, whom I reproach myself for not having cultivated sufficiently, considering the kindness he showed me; at Grenoble, Madame Deybens and the wife of the President of Bardonanche, a woman of great intelligence, who would have shown me especial favour, if I had had the opportunity of seeing her oftener; at Geneva, the French Resident, M. de la Closure, who often spoke to me of my mother, who still retained a hold upon his heart, in spite of death and time; the two Barillots, whose father, who called me his grandson, was a most agreeable companion and one of the worthiest persons I have ever known. During the troubles of the Republic, these two citizens took opposite sides; the son, that of the people, the father, that of the authorities; and when fighting began in 1737, happening to be at Geneva, I saw father and son leave the same house with arms in their hands, the former to go to the town hall, the latter to his headquarters, certain of finding themselves, two hours later, face to face, with the chance of cutting each other's throat. This terrible sight made so deep an impression upon me, that I took an oath never to take part in any civil war, and never to defend liberty at home by force of arms, either in my own person or by my approval, if I ever entered upon my rights as a citizen. I can prove that I kept my oath on a difficult occasion, and it will be found – at any rate I hope so – that my restraint was not without its value.[1]

But I had not yet arrived at that first fermentation of patriotism which Geneva in arms excited in my heart. How far I was removed from it may be judged from a very serious fact which reflects upon myself, which I have forgotten to mention in its proper place, but which ought not to be omitted.

My uncle, Bernard, some years ago, had crossed over to Carolina, to superintend the building of the city of Charlestown, the plan of which he had designed, and died there shortly afterwards. My poor cousin had also died in the service of the King of Prussia, and thus my aunt lost her son and husband almost at the same time. These losses somewhat revived her friendship for her nearest surviving relative, who happened to be myself. Whenever I went to Geneva, I stayed with her, and amused myself with rummaging through and turning over the books and papers which my uncle had left. Amongst them I found several curious things, together with some letters, of the existence of which certainly no one had any suspicion. My aunt, who attached little value to these papers, would have allowed me to take them all away, if I had wanted to do so. I contented myself with two or three books annotated by my grandfather Bernard, the minister, amongst others a quarto

[1] See Book XII, p. 669.

edition of the posthumous works of Rohault, the margin of which was full of excellent remarks, which gave me a fondness for mathematics. This book has remained with those of Madame de Warens; I have always regretted that I did not keep it. Besides these books, I took five or six manuscript pamphlets, and one printed one, written by the famous Micheli Ducret, a man of great talent, learned and enlightened, but too revolutionary in his ideas. He was cruelly treated by the Council of Geneva, and recently died in the fortress of Arberg, in which he had been imprisoned for many years, in consequence, it is said, of having been mixed up in the Bernese conspiracy.

This pamphlet was a judicious criticism of the extensive and absurd plan of fortification which has partly been carried out at Geneva, and is the laughing-stock of experts who do not know the secret purpose which the Council had in carrying out this magnificent enterprise. M. Micheli, who had been excluded from the fortification-commission for having found fault with the plan, imagined that he, as a member of the Two Hundred, and even as a citizen, might venture to express his opinion at greater length; this he did in the pamphlet in question, which he was imprudent enough to get printed, although he did not publish it; for he only had a sufficient number of copies struck off to send to the Two Hundred, which were all seized at the post-office by order of the Senate. I found the pamphlet amongst my uncle's papers, together with the reply which he had been commissioned to make to it, and I took both away with me. I had taken this journey soon after leaving the Survey, and I was still on good terms with the advocate Coccelli, who was at the head of it. Some time afterwards, the Director of Customs took it into his head to ask me to stand godfather to his child, with Madame de Coccelli as godmother. This compliment turned my head; and proud of being so closely connected with the advocate, I tried to put on an air of importance, to appear worthy of so great an honour.

With this idea, I thought I could do nothing better than show him Micheli's printed pamphlet – which was really a curiosity – to prove to him that I belonged to the important personages of Geneva who were acquainted with State secrets. However, with a kind of semi-reserve which I should find it difficult to account for, I did not show him my uncle's reply to the pamphlet, perhaps because it was in manuscript, and nothing but printed matter was worth the advocate's attention. However, he had so strong an opinion of the value of the document, which I had been foolish enough to intrust to him, that I was never able to get it back or ever to see it again; and, convinced of the useless-ness of my efforts, I made a merit of the matter, and changed the theft into a present. I do not doubt for a moment that he made the most of this pamphlet, although it was more curious than useful, at the Court of Turin, and that, somehow or other, he took care to reimburse the money which it was naturally sup-posed he must have spent in getting possession of it. Happily, of all possible future contingencies, one of the least likely is that the King of Sardinia will ever besiege Geneva. But, as it is not impossible, I shall always reproach myself for my foolish vanity in having revealed the weaknesses of that place to its most inveterate enemy.

In this manner I passed two or three years, my attention divided between music, magisteries, schemes, and journeys; wandering incessantly from one thing to another; wanting to settle down to something, without knowing what, but gradually being drawn towards study, associating with men of letters, hearing literature discussed, even sometimes venturing to join in the discussion myself; rather adopting the terminology of books than understanding their contents. In my journeys to Geneva, I occasionally called upon my good old friend M. Simon, who encouraged my growing eagerness by entirely fresh news from the republic of letters, taken from Baillet or Colomiés. At Chambéri I also frequently saw a Jacobin, a professor of physics, a good-natured friar, whose name I have forgotten, who often performed little experiments which amused me extremely. From his directions, and with the assist-ance of the "Mathematical Recreations" of Ozanam, I tried to make some sympathetic ink. With this object, having filled a bottle more than half full with quicklime, orpiment and water, I corked it tightly. Almost immediately it began to effervesce violently. I ran to uncork the bottle, but was too late; it burst in my face like a bomb. I swallowed so much chalk and orpiment that it nearly killed me. I could not see for more than six weeks, and this taught me not to dabble again in experimental physics, without any knowledge of the elements of the science.[1]

This event proved very detrimental to my health, which for some time had been sensibly deteriorating. I do not understand how it was that, although I had a good constitution, and did not indulge in any excesses, I visibly declined. I am pretty strongly built and broad-chested, and my lungs must have ample room to play; notwithstanding, I was short of breath, had a feeling of oppression, sighed involuntarily, had palpitation of the heart, and spat blood; a slow fever supervened, from which I have never been entirely free. How can one fall into such a state in the flower of one's age, without any internal injury, without having done anything to destroy health?

It is sometimes said that the sword wears out the scabbard. That is my history. My passions have made me live, and my passions have killed me. What passions? will be asked. Trifles, the most childish things in the world, which, however, excited me as much as if the possession of Helen or the throne of the universe had been at stake. In the first place – women. When I possessed one, my senses were calm; my heart, never. The needs of love devoured me in the midst of enjoyment; I had a tender mother, a dear friend; but I needed a mistress. I imagined one in her place; I represented her to myself in a thousand forms, in order to deceive myself. If I had thought that I held mamma in my arms when I embraced her, these embraces would have been no less lively, but all my desires would have been extinguished; I should have sobbed from affection, but I should never have felt any enjoyment. Enjoyment! Does this ever fall to the lot of man? If I had ever, a single time in my life, tasted all the delights of love in their fulness, I do not believe that my frail existence could have endured it; I should have died on the spot.

Thus I was burning with love, without an object; and it is this state, perhaps, that is most exhausting. I was restless, tormented by the hopeless condition of poor mamma's affairs, and her imprudent conduct, which were bound to ruin her completely at

[1] Rousseau, believing he was dying, dictated a will at this time.

no distant date. My cruel imagination, which always anticipates misfortunes, exhibited this particular one to me continually, in all its extent and in all its results. I already saw myself compelled by want to separate from her to whom I had devoted my life, and without whom I could not enjoy it. Thus my soul was ever in a state of agitation; I was devoured alternately by desires and fears.

Music was with me another passion, less fierce, but no less wasting, from the ardour with which I threw myself into it, from my persistent study of the obscure treatises of Rameau, from my invincible determination to load my rebellious memory with them, from my continual running about, from the enormous heap of compilations which I got together and often spent whole nights in copying. But why dwell upon permanent fancies, while all the follies which passed through my inconstant brain – the transient inclinations of a single day, a journey, a concert, a supper, a walk to take, a novel to read, a comedy to see, everything that was entirely unpremeditated in my pleasure or business, became for me so many violent passions, which, in their ridiculous impetuosity, caused me the most genuine torment? The imaginary sufferings of Cleveland,[1] which I read of with avidity and constant interruption, have, I believe, afflicted me more than my own.

At Chambéri there was a Genevese, named M. Bagueret, who had been employed by Peter the Great at the Russian Court; he was one of the greatest rascals and greatest fools that I have ever seen, always full of schemes as mad as himself, who flung millions about like rain and thought nothing of an extra cipher. This man, who had come to Chambéri on account of some law-suit before the Senate, got hold of mamma, as was only to be expected, and in return for the ciphers which he generously lavished upon her, drew her few crowns, one by one, out of her purse. I disliked him; he saw it – never a difficult matter in my case – and left no kind of meanness untried, in order to gain my favour. He took it into his head to propose to teach me chess, which he himself played a little. I tried it, almost against my inclination; and, after I had learnt the moves indifferently, I

---

[1] Prévost's *Cleveland* concerns a supposed natural son of Oliver Cromwell, who becomes king of a tribe of American Indians.

made such rapid progress that, before the end of the first sitting, I was able to give him the rook which at first he had given me. That was enough; I was mad for chess from that moment. I bought a chess-board and a "Calabrois";[1] I shut myself up in my room, and spent days and nights in trying to learn all the openings by heart, in stuffing them into my head by force, and in playing by myself without rest or relaxation. After two or three months of this praiseworthy occupation and these incredible efforts, I went to the café, thin, sallow, and almost stupid. I tried my hand, I played again with M. Bagueret; he beat me once, twice, twenty times; all the different combinations had become mixed up in my head, and my imagination was so enfeebled, that I saw nothing but a cloud before my eyes. Whenever I wished, with the help of Philidor or Stamma, to practise myself in studying different games, the same thing happened to me; and, after exhausting myself with fatigue, I found myself weaker than before. For the rest, whether I gave up chess for a time, or endeavoured to improve myself by constant practice, I never made the slightest progress after the first sitting, and always found myself just where I was when it was over. I might practise for thousands of generations and not be able to do more than give Bagueret the rook, and nothing else. Time well employed! you will say; and I employed not a little of it in this way. I did not finish the first attempt, until I no longer had strength to continue it. When I left my room, I looked like a corpse, and, if I had continued to live in the same manner, I should certainly not have remained long above ground. It will be admitted that it is difficult, especially in the ardour of youth, for such a disposition to allow the body to enjoy continued good health.

The decline in my health affected my temper and moderated the ardour of my imagination. Feeling myself weaker, I became quieter, and lost, in some degree, my mania for travelling. I remained more at home, and was attacked, not by ennui, but by melancholy; my passions were succeeded by hysteria; my languor changed to sadness; I wept and I sighed about nothing; I felt life slipping away from me before I had enjoyed it. I sighed

[1] A treatise by a famous Italian chess-player, Gioachino Greco, known as "Le Calabrois"; he lived in the time of Louis XIV.

over the state in which I was leaving my poor mamma; over the state into which I saw her ready to fall. I can assert that my only regret was at leaving her, and leaving her in so lamentable a condition. At length, I became really ill. She nursed me more tenderly than any mother ever nursed her child; and this was beneficial to herself, since it diverted her from schemes, and kept away the promoters of them. How sweet would death have been if it had come then! If I had not enjoyed many of the good things of life, I had felt but few of its sorrows. My peaceful soul would have departed without that cruel feeling of the injustice of mankind, which poisons both life and death. I should have had the consolation that I was surviving myself in the better half of me; it could hardly have been called death. Had it not been for the uneasiness I felt concerning her lot, I could have died as easily as I could have fallen asleep; and my very uneasiness was connected with an affectionate and tender object, which softened its bitterness. I said to her: "My whole being is in your hands; make it happy." Two or three times, when I was worse than usual, I got up during the night and dragged myself to her room, to give her advice upon her conduct, which I may say was thoroughly correct and sensible, but in which my sympathy for her was more marked than anything else. As if tears had been food and medicine, those which I shed by her side, sitting on her bed, holding her hands in mine, seemed to give me strength. The hours slipped away in these nightly conversations, and I left her, feeling better than when I entered; calm and content with the promises which she had made me, with the hopes with which she had inspired me, I went to sleep, peace in my heart, and resigned to Providence.

After I have had so many reasons to hate life, after all the storms which have shaken my existence, and only make it a burden to me, may God grant that the death which is to end it may not be more cruel than it would have been to me at that moment!

By her unremitting attention and watchfulness, and incredible exertions she saved me; and it is certain that she alone could have done so. I have little faith in the medicine of physicians, but a great deal in that of true friends; those things on which our happiness depends are always more salutary than anything else. If there is such a thing as a delightful sensation in life, it is that which we felt when we were restored to each other. Our mutual attachment was not increased, that was impossible; but it assumed a more intimate form which I cannot explain, more touching in its great simplicity. I became entirely her work, entirely her child, more so than if she had been really my mother. We began, without thinking of it, to be inseparable, to share, as it were, our existence in common; and feeling that we were not only necessary, but sufficient, for each other, we accustomed ourselves to think of nothing that was foreign to us, to limit our happiness and all our desires to that possession of each other, which was, perhaps, unique of its kind amongst human beings, which, as I have said, was not love, but a more real possession, which, without being dependent upon the senses, sex, age or personal appearance, was concerned with all that which makes one what one is, and which one can only lose by ceasing to exist.

How came it that this delightful crisis did not bring happiness for the rest of her days and mine? It was not my fault; I can console myself with the conviction of that. Neither was it hers, at least, not wilfully. It was written that the ineradicable tendency of my disposition should soon reassert its sway. But this fatal recoil did not take place all at once. There was, thank Heaven, an interval – a short and precious interval – which did not end through any fault of mine, and which I cannot reproach myself with having badly employed.

Although cured of my serious complaint, I had not recovered my strength. My chest was still weak; some traces of fever remained, and made me languid. I desired nothing except to end my days near her who was so dear to me, to support her in her good resolutions, to make her feel what constituted the real charm of a happy life, to make her life such, as far as it depended on me. But I saw, I even felt, that the continual solitude of our intercourse in a dull and gloomy house would end in becoming equally dull and gloomy. The remedy presented itself as it were of its own accord. Mamma had prescribed milk for me, and wanted me to go into the country to take it. I consented, provided she went with me. That was enough to determine her; the only question to be decided was, where we should go. The garden in the suburb could not be properly called country – surrounded by houses and other gardens, it did not possess the charm of a rustic retreat. Besides, after Anet's death, we had given up the garden for the sake of economy, since we no longer had any desire to rear plants, and other considerations caused us to feel but little regret for that retreat.

Taking advantage of the dislike, which I discovered she felt towards the town, I proposed to her to leave it altogether, and to settle in pleasant solitude, in some little house, at a sufficient distance from the town to baffle troublesome visitors. She would have done so, and the resolution, which her good angel and mine suggested to me, would probably have assured us a happy and peaceful life, until death should have separated us. But we were not destined for such a lot. Mamma was fated to experience all the miseries of want and discomfort, after having passed her life in abundance, to enable her to quit it with less regret; while I, overwhelmed with misfortune of all kinds, was destined one day to serve as a warning to all who, inspired solely by love of justice and the public welfare, and trusting to the strength of their innocence alone, have the courage to tell the truth openly to the world, without the support of cabals, and without having formed a party to protect them.

An unfortunate apprehension kept her back. She did not dare to leave her uncomfortable house, for fear of displeasing the landlord. "Your plan of retirement," she said, "is charming, and I like it very much; but in such retirement we should have to live. If I leave my prison, I run the risk of losing my bread; and, when this fails us in the woods, we shall be obliged to return again to town to look for it. To lessen the chance of being obliged to do so, do not let us leave the town altogether. Let us pay this trifling annuity to the Comte de St. Laurent, that he may leave me mine. Let us look for some retreat, far enough from the town to allow us to live in peace, and near enough for us to return to it whenever it is necessary." This was what we did. After looking about a little, we settled upon Les Charmettes, an estate belonging to M. de Conzié, close to Chambéri, but as retired and solitary as if it had been a hundred leagues away. Between two rather high hills, there is a little valley extending from north to south, at the bottom of which a stream of water runs amongst the trees and pebbles. Along this valley, half-way up the hill, there are some scattered houses, a very pleasant retreat for anyone who is fond of a somewhat wild and retired asylum. Having looked at two or three of these houses, we at last chose the nicest, which belonged to a gentleman in the army, named Noiret. The house was very habitable. In front was a garden with a terrace, above that, a vineyard, and below, an orchard; facing it was a little forest of chestnut-trees, and a fountain close by; higher up on the mountain were pasture meadows; in short, everything requisite for the little country establishment we intended to set up. As far as I can remember times and dates, we took possession of it towards the end of the summer of 1736. I was delighted the first night we slept there. "Oh, mamma," said I to my dear friend, while I embraced her with tears of tenderness and joy, "this is the abode of happiness and innocence. If we do not find both here, it will be useless to look for them anywhere else."

BOOK VI

[1736]

Hoc erat in votis; modus agri non ita magnus,
Hortus ubi et tecto vicinus iugis aquae fons,
Et paulum silvae super his foret.

I cannot add:

                              Auctius atque
Di melius fecere.[1]

But no matter; I had no need of more; I did not even need any
property at all; the enjoyment of it was enough for me, and I
have long ago said and felt, that the proprietor and the possessor
are often two very different persons, even if one leaves husbands
and lovers out of the question.

I Iere begins the brief happiness of my life; here approach the
peaceful, but rapid moments which have given me the right to
say, *I have lived*. Precious and regretted moments! begin again for
me your delightful course; and, if it be possible, pass more slowly
in succession through my memory, than you did in your fugitive
reality. What can I do, to prolong, as I should like, this touching
and simple narrative, to repeat the same things over and over
again, without wearying my readers by such repetition, any more
than I was wearied of them myself, when I recommenced the life
again and again? If all this consisted of facts, actions, and words,
I could describe, and in a manner, give an idea of them; but how
is it possible to describe what was neither said nor done, nor
even thought, but enjoyed and felt, without being able to assign
any other reason for my happiness than this simple feeling? I got
up at sunrise, and was happy; I walked, and was happy; I saw
mamma, and was happy; I left her, and was happy; I roamed the
forests and hills, I wandered in the valleys, I read, I did nothing, I
worked in the garden, I picked the fruit, I helped in the work of

---

[1]   Horace, *Satires*, II, 6, II. 1–4: "This is what I prayed for: a piece of land not
so very large, where there would be a garden, and near the house a spring of
fresh water, and a little wood besides." "The gods have blessed me with more
than I deserve".

the house, and happiness followed me everywhere – happiness, which could not be referred to any definite object, but dwelt entirely within myself, and which never left me for a single instant.

Nothing that occurred to me during that delightful period, nothing that I did, said, or thought, during all the time it lasted, has escaped my memory. Preceding and subsequent periods only come back to me at intervals; I recall them unequally and confusedly; but I recall this particular period in its entirety, as if it still existed. My fancy, which, during my youth, always looked ahead, and now always looks back, compensates me by these charming recollections for the hope which I have lost for ever. I no longer see anything in the future to tempt me; only the reminiscences of the past can flatter me, and these remi- niscences of the period of which I speak, so vivid and so true, often make my life happy, in spite of my misfortunes.

I will mention one single instance of these recollections, which will enable the reader to judge of their liveliness and accuracy. The first day we set out to pass the night at Les Charmettes, mamma was in a sedan-chair, and I followed on foot. The road was somewhat steep, and, being rather heavy and afraid of tiring her bearers, she got down about half-way, intend- ing to finish the rest of the journey on foot. During the walk, she saw something blue in the hedge, and said to me, "Look! there is some periwinkle still in flower." I had never seen any periwinkle, I did not stoop down to examine it, and I am too near-sighted to distinguish plants on the ground, when standing upright. I merely cast a passing glance at it, and nearly thirty years passed before I saw any periwinkle again, or paid any attention to it. In 1764, when I was at Cressier with my friend Du Peyrou,[1] we were climbing a hill, on the top of which he has built a pretty *salon*, which he rightly calls Belle-Vue. I was then beginning to botanise a little. While ascending the hill, and looking amongst the bushes, I exclaimed with a cry of joy, "Ah! there is some periwinkle!" as in fact it was. Du Peyrou observed my delight, without knowing the cause of it; he will learn it, I hope, one day,

[1] [Du Peyrou] See *Biographies*, p. 709.

when he reads these words. The reader may judge, from the impression which so trifling a circumstance made upon me, of the effect produced by everything which has reference to that period.

In the meantime, the country air did not restore me to my former state of health. I was sickly, and grew worse. I could not take milk, and was obliged to give it up. At that time hydropathy was the rage, as a cure for every complaint. I rushed into it with so little discretion, that it nearly put an end, not to my ailments, but to my life. Every morning, when I got up, I went to the spring with a large goblet, and, walking about, drank about two bottlefuls without stopping. I entirely gave up drinking wine at my meals. The water which I drank was rather hard and difficult to pass, like most mountain waters. In short, I managed so well, that in less than two months I completely ruined my stomach, which had hitherto been excellent, and I recognised that I could no longer hope to be cured, as I was totally incapable of digesting anything. At the same time, an accident occurred to me, as curious in itself as in its results, which will only end with my life.

One morning, when I was no worse than usual, while lifting the top of a little table upon its stand, I became conscious of a sudden and almost incomprehensible disturbance in my whole body. I cannot compare it better than with a kind of storm, which arose in my blood, and in a moment gained the mastery over all my limbs. My veins began to beat so violently that I not only felt, but even heard it, especially the beating of the carotid arteries. This was accompanied by a loud noise in my ears, of three, or rather, four kinds; a dull and heavy buzzing, a more distinct murmur like that of running water, a sharp whistling sound, and the beating which I have just described, the pulsations of which I could easily count, without feeling my pulse or touching my body with my hands. This internal noise was so loud, that it deprived me of my hitherto keen faculties of hearing, and made me not altogether deaf, but hard of hearing, as I have continued to be from that day.

My surprise and affright may easily be imagined. I looked upon myself as dead; I took to my bed, and the physician was sent for; trembling with fear, I told him my case, which

I considered hopeless. I believe he thought the same, but he acted as became his profession. He strung together a series of lengthy explanations of which I understood nothing; then, in consequence of his sublime theory, he commenced, *in anima vili*, the experimental cure which he was pleased to try. It was so painful, so disgusting, and produced so little effect, that I soon became tired of it; and, at the end of a few weeks, finding myself neither better nor worse, I left my bed and resumed my ordinary occupations, although the beating of my arteries and the buzzing in my ears still continued, and, in fact, have never left me for a moment from that day, that is to say, for thirty years.

Hitherto I had been a great sleeper. The total inability to sleep, by which all these symptoms have been accompanied, even to the present day, finally convinced me that I had not long to live. This conviction at first calmed my anxiety to recover. As I could not prolong my life, I resolved to get as much as possible out of the few years or months that remained to me; and this I was enabled to do, thanks to a special favour of Nature, which, notwithstanding my melancholy condition, gave me exemption from the pain by which it would naturally have been accompanied. I was inconvenienced by the noise, but it caused me no suffering; the only habitual inconveniences by which it was attended were, inability to sleep at night, and a perpetual shortness of breath, not, however, amounting to asthma, and which only made itself felt when I attempted to run or exert myself more than usual.

This accident, which should have killed my body, only killed my passions; and I bless Heaven every day for the happy effect which it produced upon my soul. I can certainly say that I never began to live, until I looked upon myself as a dead man. While estimating at their true value the things I was going to leave, I began to occupy my thoughts with nobler cares, as if in anticipation of the duties I should soon have to fulfil, and which until then I had seriously neglected. I had often burlesqued religion after my own fashion, but I had never been entirely without it. It was easier for me to hark back to this subject, so melancholy for so many, but so sweet for one who can find in it a source of hope and consolation. On this occasion, mamma was far more useful to me than all the theologians in the world could have been.

As she always reduced everything to a system, she had not failed to treat religion in the same manner. Her system of religion was made up of ideas of the most different kinds, some very sensible, others very foolish, of feelings connected with her character, and of prejudices arising from her education. As a rule, believers make God like themselves; the good represent him as good, the wicked, as wicked; malicious and bilious devotees see nothing but hell, because they would like to see the whole world damned; while loving and gentle souls do not believe in the existence of such a place. I have never been able to recover from my astonishment at finding the good Fénélon speak of it in his "Telemachus," as if he sincerely believed in it; but I hope that he lied then, for, after all, however truthful a man may be, he is obliged to lie sometimes – when he is a Bishop. Mamma did not lie to me; and her soul, free from gall and bitterness, which could not imagine a vindictive and ever-wrathful God, saw only mercy and compassion, where devotees see nothing but retributive justice and punishment. She often used to say that, if God were to be strictly just towards us, it would not be justice on His part, since He has not made us such as to require it, and would in such a case require from us more than He has given. The curious thing was that, while not believing in hell, she still believed in purgatory. The reason of this was that she did not know what to do with the souls of the wicked, feeling unable either to damn them or to put them with the good until they had become good themselves. In fact, it must be confessed that, both in this world and the next, the wicked are always a source of considerable embarrassment.

Another of her curious ideas was the following. It is obvious that the whole doctrine of original sin and redemption is destroyed by this system, that the foundations of ordinary Christianity are shaken, and that Catholicism, at any rate, cannot exist. Mamma, however, was a good Catholic, or professed to be one, and certainly in all good faith. It seemed to her that people were accustomed to explain the Scriptures too literally and too harshly. All that we read in them about eternal torments was, according to her, to be taken only as a threat or in a figurative sense. The death of Jesus Christ appeared to her an example of truly divine charity, to teach men to love God and one another in the same manner. In a word, true to the religion which she had adopted, she accepted in all sincerity its entire profession of faith; but, when it came to a discussion of each article, it was manifest that her belief was quite different from that of the Church to which she always professed submission. In reference to this, she displayed a simplicity of heart, and a frankness which was more eloquent than petty cavillings, and which frequently embarrassed even her confessor,[1] from whom she concealed nothing. "I am a good Catholic, and desire always to remain one," she used to say to him; "I submit with my whole heart to the decisions of Holy Mother Church. I am not mistress of my belief, but I am mistress of my will, which I control without reserve, and am prepared to believe everything. What more can you ask of me?"

Even had no Christian morality existed, I believe she would have followed its principles, since they harmonised so completely with her character. She did all that was prescribed; but she would have done it just the same, even if it had not been prescribed. In unimportant matters she liked to show her obedience; and, if it had not been permitted, even if she had been ordered, to eat meat on fast-days, she would have fasted in order to please God, without any regard for considerations dictated by prudence. But all these principles of morality were subordinated to the principles of M. de Tavel, or rather, she declared that she found nothing contradictory therein. She would have slept every day with twenty men with a calm conscience, and without feeling any more scruple than desire in the matter. I know that many devotees are not more scrupulous on this point, but the difference is that, while they are led astray by their passions, she was only misled by her sophisms. In the course of the most touching, I even venture to say the most edifying, conversations, she would have been able to allude to this matter without any alteration of tone or manner, and without thinking that she was in the least inconsistent. She would even, if necessary, have

[1] See p. 259, where he is named as Father Hemet.

interrupted such a conversation to speak of the subject, and would have been able to resume it as calmly as before, so intimate was her conviction that the whole matter was only a principle of social economy, which every intelligent person was at liberty to interpret, apply, or reject, according to his or her view of the matter, without the least danger of offending God. Although I certainly did not share her opinion upon this point, I confess that I never ventured to contradict her, since I was ashamed of the lack of politeness which such conduct on my part would have forced me to exhibit. I might, certainly, have endeavoured to establish a rule for others, and attempted to make an exception in my own case; but, not only was her temperament a sufficient protection against the abuse of her principles, but I knew that she was not a woman to be easily deceived, and, if I had claimed exception for myself, I should only have left it for her to grant it to anyone else who might be agreeable to her. Besides, I only mention this inconsistency incidentally by the side of the rest although it has never had much influence upon her conduct, and at that time, had none at all; but I have promised to give a faithful account of her principles, and I wish to fulfil this promise. Let me now return to myself.

As I found in her all the principles which I needed in order to fortify my soul against the terrors of death and its consequences, I drew upon this source of confidence with perfect security. I became more closely attached to her than I had ever been: I should have liked to hand over to her entirely the life which I felt was ready to leave me. The result of this redoubled attachment to her, of the conviction that I had only a short time to live, of the profound tranquillity with which I contemplated my future state, was a calm, even sensual frame of mind – even of enjoyment – which, while it allayed all those passions, which remove our hopes and fears to a distance, permitted me to enjoy, without anxiety or trouble, the few days which remained to me. Another thing helped to make them more agreeable: the endeavour to foster her taste for country life by every amusement that I could think of. While I made her fond of her garden, her poultry-yard, her pigeons, and her cows, I myself acquired a

liking for them all, and these trifling occupations, which filled up
my day without disturbing my tranquillity, did me more good
than the milk and all other remedies employed to keep my poor
machine in order, and even repaired it as far as was possible.

The vintage and the gathering of the fruit amused us for the
remainder of this year, and made us more and more attached to
country life, amongst the good people by whom we were surrounded. We were very sorry to see the approach of winter, and
went back to town as if we had been going into exile – myself
especially, since I did not think that I should live to see the spring
again, and believed that I was saying good-bye to Les
Charmettes for the last time. Before I left, I kissed the ground
and the trees, and turned back several times as I went on my way.
As I had long given up my pupils, and lost my taste for the
amusements and society of the town, I never went out, and
never saw anybody, except mamma and M. Salomon, who had
recently become her physician and mine, an honourable and
intelligent man, a strong Cartesian,[1] who talked sensibly about
the system of the world, and whose agreeable and instructive
conversation did me more good than all his prescriptions. I have
never been able to endure the silly and nonsensical padding of
ordinary conversation, but serious and useful discourse always
affords me great pleasure, and I never refuse to take part in it. I
took great delight in M. Salomon's conversation; it seemed to
me that, while in his company, I was acquiring a foretaste of that
higher knowledge, which was reserved for my soul, when it had
lost the fetters which confined it. My predilection for him
extended to the subjects which he discussed, and I began to
look for books which might help me to understand him better.
Those which combined devotion and science were most suitable
for me, particularly those of the Oratory and Port-Royal,[2] which
I began to read, or rather, to devour. I came across one written
by Father Lamy, entitled "Entretiens sur les Sciences," a kind of
introduction to the knowledge of those books which treated of
them. I read and re-read it a hundred times, and resolved to
make it my guide. At last, I felt myself, in spite of, or rather by
reason of, my condition, gradually and irresistibly attracted to

[1] A follower of the doctrines of Descartes.   [2] The school of the Jansenists.

study, and, while looking upon each day as my last, I studied with
as great eagerness as if I had been destined to live for ever. I was
told that this was injurious to me. I believe that it was beneficial,
not only to my mind, but also to my body; for this occupation,
to which I passionately devoted myself, became so delightful
to me, that I no longer thought of my sufferings, and was much
less affected by them. It is certainly true that nothing afforded me
any real relief; but, as I felt no acute pain, I became accustomed
to languor and sleeplessness, to thought instead of action, and,
at last, I came to look upon the slow and gradual decay of my
powers as an unavoidable process, which death alone could
arrest.

Not only did this opinion release me from all idle and earthly
cares, but it also delivered me from the annoyance of the various
remedies to which, hitherto, I had been obliged to submit, in
spite of myself. Salomon, convinced that his drugs could not
cure me, spared me the unpleasantness of taking them, and was
content to soothe poor mamma's grief with some of those
harmless prescriptions which deceive the sick man with hopes
and keep up the reputation of the physician. I gave up strict diet,
began to take wine again, and, as far as my strength allowed me,
led the life of a man in perfect health, temperate in everything,
but denying myself nothing. I even went out sometimes, and
began to visit my acquaintances again, especially M. de Conzié,
whose society I found very agreeable. In short, whether it was
that I thought it a fine thing to keep on learning till my last hour,
or that some slight hope of life still remained concealed at the
bottom of my heart, the expectation of death, far from diminishing my taste for study, seemed rather to enliven it, and I made
great haste to pick up a little knowledge for the next world, as if I
had believed that in it I should only possess such knowledge as I
took with me. I became fond of the bookshop of a M. Bouchard,
frequented by several men of letters; and, as the spring, which I
had never expected to live to see, was close at hand, I looked out
some books to take to Les Charmettes, in case I should have the
good fortune to return there.

I had this good fortune, and I made the best use of it. The joy
with which I beheld the first buds is indescribable. To me it was

like a resurrection in Paradise to see the spring again. No sooner had the snow begun to melt than we left our dungeon, and arrived at Les Charmettes soon enough to hear the first notes of the nightingale. From that time I no longer thought of dying; and it is really remarkable, that I have never had any serious illness in the country. I have suffered much there, but have never been confined to my bed. I have often said, when feeling more than usually unwell: "When you see me at the point of death, carry me under the shade of an oak. I promise you that I shall get well again." Although still weak, I resumed my country occupations, but to an extent proportionate to my powers. I was truly grieved not to be able to see after the garden alone; but after half a dozen digs with the spade, I was quite out of breath, the sweat poured down my face, and I felt quite exhausted. When I stooped, my palpitations increased, and the blood flew to my head with such violence that I was obliged to stand upright immediately. Compelled to confine myself to less fatiguing occupations, I undertook, amongst other things, the care of the pigeon-house, to which I became so strongly attached, that I often spent several hours in succession there without feeling a moment's weariness. The pigeon is a very timid creature, and difficult to tame. However, I succeeded in inspiring mine with such confidence that they followed me everywhere, and allowed me to catch them whenever I wanted. I could not show myself in the garden or court without immediately finding two or three of them on my arms and head; and at last, in spite of the pleasure this afforded me, this following became so troublesome to me, that I was obliged to discourage their excessive familiarity. I have always found singular pleasure in taming animals, especially such as are shy and wild. It appeared to me delightful to inspire them with a confidence which I have never abused. I desired their fondness for me to be perfectly unrestricted.

I have mentioned that I took some books with me; but I made use of them in a manner less calculated to instruct than to overwhelm me. The false idea which I entertained of things caused me to believe that, in order to read a book with profit, it was necessary to possess all the preliminary knowledge which it presupposed. I had no suspicion that very frequently the author himself did not possess it, and that he extracted it from other books as he required it. Possessed by this foolish idea, I was detained every moment, and obliged to run incessantly from one book to another: sometimes, before I had reached the tenth page of the work I wanted to study, I should have been obliged to exhaust the contents of whole libraries. However, I followed this senseless method so persistently that I lost an enormous amount of time, and my head became so confused that I almost lost the power of seeing or comprehending anything. Happily, I at last perceived that I was on the wrong track, which was leading me astray in an interminable labyrinth, and I left it before I was quite lost in it.

The first thing that strikes anyone who has a genuine taste for learning, however slight, when he devotes himself to it, is the close connection of the sciences, which causes them to attract, support, and throw light upon each other, so that one cannot dispense with the other. Although the human intellect is not capable of mastering all, and one must always be regarded as the principal object of study, yet, without some idea of the rest, a man often finds himself in the dark in his own particular branch. I felt that what I had undertaken was good and useful in itself, and that all that was necessary was a change of method. Taking the encyclopaedia[1] first, I had divided it into its different branches. I saw that I should have done exactly the opposite; that I ought to have taken each branch separately and followed it up to the point at which all unite. Thus, I returned to the ordinary synthetical method, but like a man who knows what he is about. In this, meditation supplied the place of knowledge, and a very natural reflection helped me on the right road. Whether I lived or died, I had no time to lose. A man who, at the age of five-and-twenty, knows nothing and wishes to learn everything, is bound to make the best use of his time. Not knowing at what point destiny or death might arrest my zeal, I desired, in any case, to get an idea of everything, in order to discover the special bent of my natural abilities, and also to judge for myself what was worthy of cultivation.

In the execution of this plan I found another advantage which had not occurred to me — that of economising my time.

[1] By "encyclopaedia" Rousseau means the "chain of sciences".

I certainly cannot have been born for study, for continuous application tires me to such an extent, that I am utterly unable to devote more than half an hour together to the close study of the same subject, especially when following another's train of thought; for it has sometimes happened that I have been able to devote myself to my own ideas longer, and even with tolerable success. When I have read a few pages of an author who must be read carefully, my mind wanders from him, and is lost in the clouds. If I persist, I exhaust myself to no purpose; I become dazed, and cease to see anything. But if different subjects follow each other, even without interruption, one relieves me from the other, and, without feeling the need of any relaxation, I follow them more easily. I profited by this observation in my plan of study, and I combined them in such a manner that I was busy the whole day without ever fatiguing myself. It is true that rural and domestic occupations afforded me useful distractions; but, in my increasing zeal, I soon found means to spare time from these to devote to study, and to busy myself with two kinds of things at the same time, without thinking that the result in each case was less satisfactory.

In these trifling details, which afford me delight, and with which I often weary my reader, I nevertheless exercise a reserve which he would scarcely suspect unless I took care to inform him. Here, for example, I remember with delight all the various attempts I made to distribute my time in such a manner as to derive from it as much pleasure and profit as possible; and I can say that this period, during which I lived in retirement and always in ill-health, was the period of my life during which I was least idle and least wearied. Two or three months were thus spent in trying the bent of my mind, and in enjoying, in the most beautiful season of the year, and in a spot which it rendered delightful, the charm of life, the value of which I so well appreciated, – the charm of an unrestrained and sweet companionship, if such a name can be given to a union so perfect, and of the wonderful knowledge which I proposed to acquire; for it seemed to me as if I already possessed it, or rather, it was still better, since the pleasure of learning counted for much in my happiness.

I must pass over these attempts, which were all a source of enjoyment to me, but are too simple to be satisfactorily expressed. I repeat, true happiness cannot be described; it can only be felt, and felt the more, the less it can be described, since it is not the result of a number of facts, but is a permanent condition. I often repeat myself, but I should do so still more if I said the same thing as often as it occurs to me. When my frequently-changed manner of life had at last adopted a regular course, it was distributed as nearly as possible in the following manner.

I got up every day before sunrise; I climbed through a neighbouring orchard to a very pretty path above the vineyard which ran along the slope as far as Chambéri. During my walk I offered a prayer, which did not consist merely of idle, stammering words, but of a sincere uplifting of the heart to the Creator of this delightful Nature, whose beauties were spread before my eyes. I never like to pray in a room: it has always seemed to me as if the walls and all the petty handiwork of man interposed between myself and God. I love to contemplate Him in His works, while my heart uplifts itself to Him. My prayers were pure, I venture to say, and for that reason deserved to be heard. I only asked for myself and for her, who was inseparably associated with my wishes, an innocent and peaceful life, free from vice, pain, and distressing needs; the death of the righteous, and their lot in the future. For the rest, this act of worship consisted rather of admiration and contemplation than of requests, for I knew that the best means of obtaining the blessings which are necessary for us from the giver of all true blessings, was to deserve, rather than to ask for, them. My walk consisted of a tolerably long round, during which I contemplated with interest and pleasure the rustic scenery by which I was surrounded, the only thing of which heart and eye never tire. From a distance I looked to see if it was day with mamma. When I saw her shutters open, I trembled with joy and ran towards the house; if they were shut, I remained in the garden until she awoke, amusing myself by going over what I had learned the evening before, or by gardening. The shutters opened, I went to embrace her while she was still in bed, often still half asleep; and this embrace, as pure as it was tender, derived from its very innocence a charm which is never combined with sensual pleasure.

We usually took *café au lait* for breakfast. This was the period of the day when we were most undisturbed, and chatted most at our ease. We usually sat a considerable time over our breakfast, and from that time I have always had a great liking for this meal. I infinitely prefer the fashion of the Swiss and English, with whom breakfast is really a meal at which all the family assemble, to that of the French, who breakfast separately in their rooms, or, most commonly, take no breakfast at all. After an hour or two of conversation, I went to my books till dinner. I began with some philosophical treatise, such as the Logic of Port-Royal, Locke's Essay, Malebranche, Leibniz, Descartes, &c. I soon observed that all these authors nearly always contradicted each other, and I conceived the fanciful idea of reconciling them, which fatigued me greatly, and made me lose considerable time. I muddled my head without making any progress. At last, abandoning this plan, I adopted one that was infinitely better, to which I attribute all the progress which, in spite of my want of talent, I may have made; for it is certain that I never had much capacity for study. As I read each author, I made a practice of adopting and following up all his ideas, without any admixture of my own or of those of anyone else, and without ever attempting to argue with him. I said to myself: "Let me begin by laying up a store of ideas, no matter whether they be true or false, provided only they are definite, until my head is sufficiently equipped with them to be able to select and compare them." I know that this method is not without its inconveniences; but it has answered my purpose of self-instruction. After I had spent some years in thinking exactly as others thought, without, so to speak, reflecting, and almost without reasoning, I found myself in possession of a fund of learning sufficient to satisfy myself, and to enable me to think without the assistance of another. Then, when travelling and business matters deprived me of the opportunity of consulting books, I amused myself by going over and comparing what I had read, by weighing everything in the scale of reason, and, sometimes, by passing judgment upon my masters. I did not find that my critical faculties had lost their vigour owing to my having begun to exercise them late; and, when I published my own ideas, I have never been accused of being a servile disciple, or of swearing *in verba magistri*.[1]

From these studies I proceeded to elementary geometry, beyond which I never advanced, although I persistently attempted, in some degree, to overcome my weakness of memory by dint of retracing my steps hundreds of times, and by incessantly going over the same ground. I did not like Euclid, whose object is rather a chain of proofs than the connection of ideas. I preferred Father Lamy's "Geometry," which from that time became one of my favourite works, and which I am still able to read with pleasure. Next came algebra, in which I still took Father Lamy for my guide. When I was more advanced, I took Father Reynaud's "Science of Calculation"; then his "Analysis Demonstrated," which I merely skimmed. I have never got so far as to understand properly the application of algebra to geometry. I did not like this method of working without knowing what I was doing; and it appeared to me that solving a geometrical problem by means of equations was like playing a tune by simply turning the handle of a barrel-organ. The first time that I found by calculation, that the square of a binomial was composed of the square of each of its parts added to twice the product of those parts, in spite of the correctness of my multiplication, I would not believe it until I had drawn the figure. I had considerable liking for algebra, in so far as it dealt with abstract quantities; but, when it was applied to space and dimensions, I wanted to see the operation explained by lines; otherwise I was entirely unable to comprehend it.

After this came Latin. I found this my most difficult task, and I have never made much progress in it. At first I began with the Port-Royal method, but without result. Its barbarous verses disgusted me, and my ear could never retain them. The mass of rules confused me, and when learning the last, I forgot all that had preceded it. A man who has no memory does not want to study words; and it was just in order to strengthen my memory that I persisted in this study, which I was finally obliged to abandon. I

[1] "By the words of a master": an allusion to the disciples of Pythagoras, who slavishly reproduced the ideas of their master.

was sufficiently acquainted with the construction to be able to read an easy author with the help of a dictionary. I kept to this plan with tolerable success. I limited myself to translations, not written, but mental. By dint of continual practice, I was able to read the Latin authors with tolerable ease, but I have never been able to speak or write in that language, which frequently caused me embarrassment, when I found myself, I know not how, enrolled a member of the society of men of letters. Another disadvantage resulting from this method of learning is, that I have never learned prosody, still less the rules of versification. However, in my desire to feel the harmony of the language in verse as well as prose, I made great efforts to succeed in this; but I am convinced that it is impossible without the aid of a master. After I had learned the structure of the easiest of all verses, the hexameter, I had sufficient patience to scan nearly the whole of Virgil, marking the feet and quantities; then, when I afterwards had any doubt whether a syllable was long or short, I referred to my Virgil. It may easily be conceived that this made me commit many errors, in consequence of the licence allowed by the rules of versification. But, if there is an advantage in self-instruction, there are also great disadvantages, especially the incredible amount of labour necessary. This I know better than anyone else.

Before noon I left my books, and, if dinner was not ready, I paid a visit to my friends the pigeons, or worked in the garden until it was. When I heard myself called, I was very glad to run to table, provided with an excellent appetite; for it is a remarkable thing that, however ill I may be, my appetite never fails. We dined very pleasantly, talking of our affairs, until mamma was able to eat. Two or three times a week, when it was fine, we took our coffee in a cool and shady arbour behind the house, which I had decorated with hops, which made it very agreeable during the heat. We spent some little time in looking at our vegetables and flowers, and in talking about our mode of life, which heightened the enjoyment of it. I had another little family at the bottom of the garden – some bees. I rarely failed to visit them, and mamma often accompanied me. I took great interest in their work: it amused me immensely to see them returning from their foraging expeditions, their little legs often so loaded that they could scarcely move. At first my curiosity made me too inquisitive, and I was stung two or three times; but at last they got to know me so well, that they let me go as close to them as I pleased; and, however full their hives were, when they were ready to swarm, I had them all round me, on my hands and on my face, without ever getting stung. All animals rightly distrust human beings; but when they once feel sure that they do not mean to hurt them, their confidence becomes so great that a man must be worse than a barbarian to abuse it.

I returned to my books, but my afternoon occupations deserved less to be called work and study than recreation and amusement. I have never been able to endure close application in my room after dinner, and, generally speaking, any effort during the heat of the day is painful to me. However, I occupied myself with reading without study, without restraint, and almost without any system. My most regular occupations were history and geography; and, as these did not require any great effort of mind, I made as much progress as was possible, considering my weak memory. I tried to study Father Pétau,[1] and plunged into the obscurities of chronology; but I was disgusted by the critical portion of it, which is most intricate, and by preference I took up the study of the exact measurement of time and the course of the heavenly bodies. I should also have become fond of astronomy, if I had had the necessary appliances; but I was obliged to content myself with a few elementary principles, learnt from books, and some crude observations which I made with a telescope, merely to learn the general idea of the situation of the heavenly bodies; for my shortsightedness does not allow me to distinguish the stars clearly with the naked eye. In regard to this, I remember an adventure which has often made me laugh since. I had bought an astronomical chart, in order to study the constellations. I fastened this chart to a frame, and, when the nights were clear, I went into the garden, and placed my frame on four stakes about my own height, with the chart turned downwards. In order to prevent the wind from blowing out my candle, I put it in a pail, which I placed between the four

[1] The Jesuit Denis Pétau was author of *Tabulae chronologicae* (1628), which became popular in French translation.

stakes on the ground. Then, looking alternately at the map with my eyes and the stars with my telescope, I practised myself in distinguishing the constellations and the individual stars. I think I have mentioned that M. Noiret's garden was in the form of a terrace, so that everything that took place could be seen from the road. One evening, some peasants, who were passing by at rather a late hour, saw me, most comically attired, busy at my work. The dim light, which fell upon my chart, without their being able to see where it came from, since it was hidden from their eyes by the edges of the pail, the four stakes, the large sheet of paper covered with figures, the frame, and the movements of my telescope, which kept appearing and disappearing, gave an air of witchcraft to the whole proceeding, which terrified them.

My dress was not calculated to reassure them. A broad-brimmed hat over my cap, and a short, wadded night-dress belonging to mamma, which she had forced me to put on, presented to their eyes the appearance of a real sorcerer; and, as it was nearly midnight, they had no doubt that a witches' meeting was going to commence. Feeling little curiosity to see any more, they ran away in great alarm, woke up their neigh-bours to tell them of the apparition they had seen, and the story spread so quickly that, on the following day, everyone in the neighbourhood knew that a witches' gathering had been held in M. Noiret's garden. I do not know what would have been the result of this rumour, had not one of the peasants, who had been a witness of my incantations, carried a complaint on the same day to two Jesuits,[1] who often came to see us, and who, without knowing what it was all about, in the meantime disabused them of the idea. They told us the story; I told them the origin of it, and we enjoyed a hearty laugh over it. However, it was decided, for fear of its being repeated, that for the future I should take my observations without the assistance of a light, and that I should consult my chart at home. Those who have read, in my "Letters from the Mountain," of my Venetian magic, will, I hope, find that sorcery had long been my vocation.[2]

---

[1] See p. 259 for more about these Jesuits.

[2] In *Lettres écrites de la montagne* (1764) Rousseau describes a species of conjuring-trick or divination which he used to practise when a Secretary at the Venice embassy.

Such was my life at Les Charmettes, when I was not occupied with country pursuits, to which I always gave the preference, and in anything which was not beyond my strength I worked like a peasant; but it is true that my extreme weakness allowed me little merit on this point, except that of good intentions. Besides, I wanted to do two different things at once, and consequently did neither well. I had resolved to acquire a good memory by violent measures, and persisted in my attempts to learn a great deal by heart. With this object, I always carried some book with me, which I studied and repeated to myself while at work, with incredible pains. I cannot understand how it was that my persistency in these useless and continued efforts did not end by reducing me to a state of stupidity. I must have learnt and relearnt at least twenty times the Eclogues of Virgil, and yet I do not know a single word of them. I have lost or dismembered numbers of books through the habit of carrying them about with me everywhere, in the pigeon-house, in the garden, in the orchard, and in the vineyard. While occupied with something else, I put my book down at the foot of a tree or on a hedge; I always forgot to take it up again, and, at the end of a fortnight, I frequently found it rotted away, or eaten by ants and snails. This eagerness for learning became a mania which drove me nearly stupid, so incessantly was I employed with muttering something or other to myself.

The writings of Port-Royal and the Oratory, which I read most frequently, had made me half a Jansenist, and, in spite of all my trust in God, their harsh theology sometimes frightened me. The dread of hell, which hitherto had had little terror for me, gradually disturbed my peace of mind, and, if mamma had not calmed my uneasiness, this terrible doctrine would have upset me altogether. My confessor, who was also hers, did his best to keep me in a comfortable frame of mind. This confessor was a Jesuit, named Father Hemet, a good and wise old man, whose memory I shall always revere. Although a Jesuit, he was as simple as a child; and his morality, rather gentle than lax, was exactly what I needed to counterbalance the gloomy impressions of Jansenism. This simple old man and his companion, Father Coppier, often came to see us at Les

Charmettes, although the road was very rough and the journey long for persons of their age. Their visits did me great good: may God recompense their souls! for they were too old at the time for me to suppose that they are still alive. I also went to see them at Chambéri. I gradually became quite at home in their house; their library was at my disposal. The memory of this happy time is so closely connected with my recollection of the Jesuits, that I love the one for the sake of the other; and, although I have always considered their doctrines dangerous, I have never been able to bring myself to hate them cordially.

I should much like to know, whether the same childish ideas ever enter the hearts of other men as sometimes enter mine. In the midst of my studies, in the course of a life as blameless as a man could have led, the fear of hell still frequently troubled me. I asked myself: "In what state am I? If I were to die this moment, should I be damned?" According to my Jansenists, there was no doubt about the matter; but, according to my conscience, I thought differently. Always fearful, and a prey to cruel uncertainty, I had recourse to the most laughable expedients to escape from it, for which I would unhesitatingly have anyone locked up as a madman if I saw him doing as I did. One day, while musing upon this melancholy subject, I mechanically amused myself by throwing stones against the trunks of trees with my usual good aim, that is to say, without hardly hitting one. While engaged in this useful exercise, it occurred to me to draw a prognostic from it to calm my anxiety. I said to myself: "I will throw this stone at the tree opposite; if I hit it, I am saved; if I miss it, I am damned." While speaking, I threw my stone with a trembling hand and a terrible palpitation of the heart, but with so successful an aim that it hit the tree right in the middle, which, to tell the truth, was no very difficult feat, for I had been careful to choose a tree with a thick trunk close at hand. From that time I have never had any doubt about my salvation! When I recall this characteristic incident, I do not know whether to laugh or cry at myself. You great men, who are most certainly laughing, may congratulate yourselves; but do not mock my wretchedness, for I swear to you that I feel it deeply.

However, these troubles and alarms, perhaps inseparable from piety, were not lasting. As a rule I was tolerably calm, and the impression which the idea of a speedy death produced upon my soul was not so much one of sadness as of peaceful resignation, which even had its charm. I have just found, amongst some old papers, a kind of exhortation addressed to myself, in which I congratulated myself upon dying at an age when a man feels sufficient courage in himself to look death in the face, and without having undergone any great sufferings, either bodily or mental, during the course of my life. My judgment was only too correct! a presentiment made me afraid of living only to suffer. It seemed as if I foresaw the destiny which awaited me in my old age. I have never been so near wisdom as during those happy days. Without great remorse for the past, free from all anxiety regarding the future, my dominant feeling was the enjoyment of the present. The devout, as a rule, possess a small amount of very lively sensuality, which gives a flavour of rapturous enjoyment to the innocent pleasures which are permitted to them. The worldly look upon this as a crime on their part, I do not know why, – or rather, I know quite well; they envy in others the taste for simple pleasures which they have lost themselves. This taste I had, and I found it delightful to satisfy it with a quiet conscience. My heart, still fresh, abandoned itself to everything with a childish pleasure, or rather, if I may venture to say so, with angelic rapture; for, in truth, these quiet enjoyments possess the serene charm of the joys of Paradise. Dinners on the grass at Montagnole, suppers in the arbour, the gathering of the fruit, the vintage, the evenings spent in assisting our people to pull off the fibres of hemp – all these were so many festivals for us, which afforded mamma as much pleasure as myself. Solitary walks possessed a still greater charm, because the heart had greater freedom of expansion. Amongst others, I remember one which marks an epoch in my memory, which we took on one St. Louis's day, after whom mamma was named. We set out alone, early in the morning, after having heard mass read by a Carmelite at day-break in a chapel attached to the house. I had proposed that we should stroll about the opposite side of the valley, which we had never yet visited. We had sent our provisions on ahead, for the excursion was to last all day. Mamma, although somewhat stout and fat, was a fairly good walker. We wandered from hill to hill, from thicket to thicket, sometimes in the sun and frequently in the shade, resting now and again, forgetting ourselves for hours, talking of ourselves, our union, and our happy lot, and offering up prayers for its continuance, which were not heard. Everything seemed in a conspiracy to enhance the happiness of that day. A shower of rain had recently fallen; there was no dust; the brooks were full of running water. A slight, fresh breeze stirred the leaves; the air was pure, the horizon cloudless; the sky was as serene as our hearts. We took our dinner at a peasant's house, and shared it with his family, who showered upon us heartfelt blessings. What good people these poor Savoyards are! After dinner, we reached the shade of some tall trees, where mamma amused herself with botanising amongst the underwood, while I collected some dry sticks to boil our coffee. Mamma pointed out to me a thousand curious things in the structure of the flowers which I had picked for her on the way, which greatly delighted me, and should have inspired me with a taste for botany; but the time for that was not yet come – I was too fully occupied by other studies. I was struck by an idea which diverted my mind from flowers and plants. My frame of mind, all that we said and did on that day, all the objects which had struck my attention, recalled to me the dream which I had had at Annecy seven or eight years before, of which I have given an account in its proper place. The resemblance was so striking that, when I thought of it, I was moved to tears. In a transport of emotion I embraced my dear friend. "Mamma, mamma," I said passionately, "this day has long been promised to me; I can imagine no greater happiness. My joy, thanks to you, is at its height. May it never decline; may it last as long as I feel its charm; it will never end except with my life!"

Thus passed my happy days; happier, since I saw nothing which could disturb them, and I only conceived it possible for them to end when my own end came. Not that the source of my anxiety was completely exhausted; but I found that it took a different course, which I did my best to direct towards useful objects, that it might carry its remedy with it. Mamma was naturally fond of the country, and this taste did not cool while she was with me. She gradually conceived a liking for country pursuits. She endeavoured to make her property a source of profit, and she took pleasure in making a practical use of her knowledge of such matters. Not content with the land belonging to the house, she rented a field or a meadow. Directing her love of enterprise towards agriculture, she soon bid fair to become a regular farmer, instead of remaining idle at home. I was not particularly pleased to see her enlarging her sphere of occupation, and I opposed it as much as I could, feeling convinced that she would always be disappointed, and that her generous and extravagant disposition would always cause the expenditure to exceed the receipts. However, I consoled myself with the thought that these receipts would amount to something, and would help her to live. Of all the schemes she could possibly have thought of, this appeared to me the least ruinous, and without expecting any profit from it as she did, I saw in it a continuous occupation, which would protect her from unlucky undertakings and the machinations of swindlers. For this reason, I was eager to regain sufficient health and strength to enable me to watch over her affairs and to be her foreman or head workman; and the exercise, which this obliged me to take, often took me away from my books and diverted my thoughts from my condition, so that my health was naturally improved.

[1737–1741.] – The following winter Barillot returned from Italy. He brought me some books; amongst others, the "Bontempi" and the "Cartella della Musica," which gave me a taste for the history of music and the theoretical investigation of this beautiful art. Barillot remained with us some time; and, as I had attained my majority some months ago,[1] it was agreed that, in the following spring, I should go to Geneva to claim my mother's fortune, or, at least, the share that came to me, until it should be discovered what had become of my brother. This plan was carried out as had been arranged: I went to Geneva, where I was joined by my father. He had for some time been in the habit of visiting the place without anyone molesting him, although the decree against him was still in force; but, as he was esteemed for

[1] *i.e.*, had reached the age of 25.

his courage and respected for his honesty, it was pretended that his little affair was forgotten; and the magistrates, busy with the grand scheme, which soon afterwards burst forth in all its glory, did not desire to irritate the *bourgeoisie* prematurely, by reminding them of their former partisanship at an inopportune moment.

I was afraid of difficulties being raised in consequence of my change of religion, but found none. The laws of Geneva are in this respect not so severe as those of Berne, where anyone who changes his religion loses, not only his status, but his property as well. My claims were not disputed, but the inheritance itself, for some reason or other which I do not know, was reduced to a very small sum. Although it was almost certain that my brother was dead, there was no legal proof of this. I had not sufficient title to claim his share, and I willingly left it to help to support my father, who, as long as he lived, enjoyed the use of it. As soon as the legal formalities were concluded and I received my money, I laid out part of it in books, and flew to lay the rest at mamma's feet. During the journey my heart beat with joy, and, at the moment when I placed this money in her hands, I was a thousand times happier than when it was placed in mine.[1] She received it with the simplicity of all beautiful souls, who, finding no difficulty in such actions themselves, are not astonished when they see them performed by others. The money was laid out almost entirely upon myself, with the same simplicity. It would have been employed in exactly the same manner, if it had come from any other source.

Meanwhile, my health was not completely re-established; on the contrary, I was visibly wasting away. I was as pale as a corpse and thin as a skeleton. The beating of my veins was terrible; the palpitations of my heart were more frequent. I continually suffered from shortness of breath, and my weakness at length became so great that I could scarcely move. I could not walk fast without a feeling of suffocation; I could not stoop without turning giddy; I could not lift the smallest weight; and I was forced to remain inactive, the greatest torment for a man as restless as I was. There is no doubt that my illness was, to a great extent, attributable to vapours. This, which is the ailment of

[1] He received 6,500 florins, roughly equivalent to 3,000 French *livres*.

privileged people, was mine. The tears which I often shed without any cause for weeping, my lively alarm at the rustling of a leaf or the chirping of a bird, my changeable disposition amidst the calm of a most happy life – all these were indications of that weariness of happiness, which, so to speak, leads to an extravagant sensibility. We are so little formed for happiness in this world, that of necessity the soul or the body must suffer, when they do not suffer together, and a happy condition of the one nearly always injures the other. When I might have enjoyed life heartily, the decaying machinery of my body prevented me without anyone being able to localise the cause of the evil. Later, my body, in spite of my declining years and very real and painful sufferings, appears to have regained its strength, in order to feel my sufferings more keenly; and, while I am writing these words, weak and almost sixty years of age, overwhelmed by pains of every description, I feel that I possess more life and strength for suffering than I possessed for enjoyment in the flower of my age and in the bosom of the truest happiness.

By way of reducing myself completely, after having read a little philosophy, I began the study of anatomy, and took a survey of the number and working of the individual parts which composed my bodily machine. Twenty times a day I was prepared to feel the whole out of gear. Far from being astonished at finding myself in a dying condition, I only felt surprised that I was still able to live, and I believed that every complaint of which I read the description was my own. I am convinced that, if I had not been ill, this fatal study would have made me so. Finding in each complaint the symptoms of my own, I thought that I was suffering from all; and thereby contracted one, which was still more cruel than all the rest, and from which I thought I was free, – an eager desire to be cured, which it is difficult for a man to escape, when once he begins to read medical books. By dint of research, reflection, and comparison, I came to the conclusion that the foundation of my malady was a polypus of the heart, and Salomon himself seemed struck by this idea. These suppositions should reasonably have confirmed me in my previous resolutions. But this was not the case. I exerted all my mental powers to discover how polypus of the heart could be healed, resolved to undertake this marvellous cure. Anet, during a journey which he made to Montpellier, to visit the botanical gardens and the demonstrator, M. Sauvages, had been told that M. Fizes had cured such a polypus. Mamma remembered this, and mentioned it to me. This was enough to inspire me with a longing to go and consult M. Fizes. The hope of being cured restored my courage, and gave me strength to undertake the journey. The money which I had brought from Geneva furnished the means; and mamma, far from attempting to dissuade me, encouraged me to go. Behold me, then, on my way to Montpellier! I had no need to go so far to find the physician I required. As riding fatigued me too much, I took a carriage at Grenoble. At Moirans five or six other carriages arrived, one after the other, after my own. This time it was, in truth, the story of the sedan-chairs.[1] Most of these carriages formed part of the equipage of a newly-wedded bride, whose name was Madame du Colombier. She was accompanied by another lady, Madame de Larnage, who was younger and not so good-looking, but equally amiable, who intended to proceed from Romans, where Madame du Colombier was stopping, to the town of St. Andiol, near the Pont-Saint-Esprit. Considering my well-known shyness, it will not be imagined that I readily made the acquaintance of these elegant ladies and their suite; but at last, as I travelled by the same route, stopped at the same inns, and, under penalty of being considered a regular boor, was obliged to appear at the same table, it became impossible for me to avoid making the acquaintance. I did so, and even sooner than I could have wished, for all this bustle was ill-suited to a sick man, especially one of my temperament. But curiosity makes these roguish creatures so insinuating, that, in order to make a man's acquaintance, they begin by turning his head. This is what happened to me. Madame du Colombier was too closely surrounded by young dandies to have time to make advances to me, and besides, it was not worth while, since we were soon to separate; but Madame de Larnage, who was not so beset by admirers, had to make provision for her journey. It was Madame de Larnage who undertook my conquest; and, from that time, *it*

1 [*brancards*] See p. 148.

was good-bye to poor Jean Jacques, or rather to my fever, hysteria, and polypus – good-bye to everything, when in her company, with the exception of certain palpitations of the heart, which remained, and of which she showed no inclination to cure me. The bad state of my health was our first subject of conversation. They saw that I was ill; they knew that I was going to Montpellier; and my appearance and manners must have made it clear that I was no profligate, for it was evident, from what followed, that they did not suspect that I was going there in order to be cured of the effects of debauchery. Although ill-health is no great recommendation amongst women, it made me interesting in the eyes of these ladies. In the morning they sent to know how I was, and invited me to take chocolate with them; and asked me how I had passed the night. On one occasion, in accordance with my praiseworthy habit of speaking without thinking, I answered that I did not know. This answer made them think that I was mad. They examined me more closely, and this examination did me no harm. I once heard Madame du Colombier say to her friend: "He has no manners, but he is amiable." This word greatly encouraged me, and caused me to act up to it.

As we became more intimate, I was obliged to speak about myself; to say who I was, and where I came from. This caused me some embarrassment, for I clearly saw that the word "convert" would ruin me in polite society and amongst ladies of fashion. I do not know what curious whim prompted me to pass myself off as an Englishman. I gave myself out as a Jacobite. I called myself Dudding, and they called me Mr. Dudding. A confounded Marquis de Torignan, who was with us, an invalid like myself, and old and ill-tempered into the bargain, took it into his head to enter into conversation with Mr. Dudding. He talked to me about King James, the Pretender, and the old Court of Saint-Germain. I was on thorns: I knew nothing about them, except the little I had read in Count Hamilton and the newspapers; but I made such good use of my scanty knowledge that I got out of it pretty well. Luckily, no one thought of asking me about the English language, of which I did not understand a single word.

We got on exceedingly well together, and looked forward with regret to our separation. We travelled at a snail's pace by day. One Sunday we found ourselves at Saint-Marcellin. Madame de Larnarge wanted to attend mass, and I accompanied her, which nearly spoilt my game. I behaved during service as I had always been in the habit of doing. From my modest and reserved behaviour she concluded that I was a devotee, which gave her the worst possible opinion of me, as she confessed to me two days later. It required great efforts of gallantry on my part to efface this unfavourable impression; or rather, Madame de Larnage, like a woman of experience, not being easily discouraged, was willing to run the risk of making advances to see how I would extricate myself. She made them so freely and in such a manner that, since I thought nothing of my personal appearance, I believed she was laughing at me. In this ridiculous idea, there was no kind of folly that I did not commit: I was worse than the Marquis du Legs.[1] Madame de Larnage stood her ground; tried to tempt me so often and spoke so tenderly to me, that a wiser man than myself would have found difficulty in taking it all seriously. The more she persisted, the more she confirmed me in my belief; and what tormented me still more was, that I became seriously enamoured of her. I said, with a sigh, to myself and to her: "Ah! if all you say were only true, I should be the happiest of men." I believe that my raw simplicity only piqued her fancy, and that she was unwilling to acknowledge a defeat.

We had left Madame du Colombier and her suite at Romans. We continued our journey, slowly and most agreeably, – Madame de Larnage, the Marquis de Torignan, and myself. The Marquis, although an invalid and a grumbler, was a decent fellow, but was not best pleased at seeing other people enjoying themselves without being able to do so himself.[2] Madame de Larnage took so little trouble to conceal her fancy for me, that he

[1] A character in Marivaux's comedy, who is in love for the first time, and, being of an exceedingly timid disposition, is afraid to make a declaration; while the character of the Countess is exactly the opposite. The plot turns on a legacy (*legs*): hence the name.

[2] *Manger son pain à la fumée du rôti*: literally, "To eat bread when he could smell roast meat."

perceived it sooner than I did myself, and his malicious sarcasms should at least have given me the confidence which I did not venture to draw from the lady's advances, had I not imagined, in a spirit of perversity, of which I alone was capable, that they had come to an understanding to amuse themselves at my expense. This foolish idea at last completely turned my head, and made me play the utter simpleton in a situation in which my heart, being really smitten, might have instructed me to act a far more distinguished part. I cannot understand how it was that Madame de Larnage was not disgusted with my sullenness, and did not dismiss me with utter contempt. But she was a clever woman, who understood the people she had to deal with, and saw clearly that there was more silliness than lukewarmness in my behaviour.

She at last succeeded, with some difficulty, in making herself understood. We had reached Valence in time for dinner, and, according to our praiseworthy custom, remained there for the rest of the day. We put up outside the town, at Saint-Jacques. I shall never forget this inn or the room which Madame de Larnage occupied. After dinner she wanted to go for a walk. She knew that the Marquis was not fond of walking. It was a plan to secure for herself a *tête-à-tête*, which she had resolved to make the most of, for there was no more time to be lost, if any was to be left to make use of. We walked round the town, along the moats. I recommenced the long story of my complaints, to which she replied so tenderly, sometimes pressing my arm to her heart, that only stupidity like mine could have prevented me from being convinced that she spoke seriously. The unaccountable thing was, that I myself was greatly affected. I have said that she was amiable; love made her charming; it restored all the brightness of her early youth, and she managed her advances so cunningly, that she would have seduced a man of the greatest experience. I was very ill at ease, and frequently on the point of taking liberties; but the fear of offending or displeasing her, and the still greater dread of being derided, laughed at, mocked, of providing an anecdote for the table, and being complimented upon my courage by the merciless Marquis, kept me back and made me feel irritated at my foolish bashfulness, and at my inability to overcome it, while I reproached myself with it. I was on the rack. I had already abandoned my timid language,[1] the absurdity of which I felt, now that I was so well on the road; but as I did not know how to act or what to say, I held my tongue and looked sulky. In a word, I did everything that was calculated to bring upon me the treatment which I feared. Happily, Madame de Larnage was more humane. She abruptly interrupted the silence by putting her arm round my neck, while, at the same time, her mouth, pressed upon my own, spoke too clearly for me to have any further doubt. The crisis could not have occurred at a more happy moment. I became amiable. It was time. She had given me the confidence, the want of which has always prevented me from being natural. For once I was myself: never have my eyes, my senses, my heart and my mouth spoken so well; never have I repaired my errors so completely; and if this little conquest had cost Madame de Larnage some trouble, I had reason to believe that she did not regret it.

If I were to live a hundred years, I could never think of this charming woman without delight. I use the word charming, because, although she was neither young nor beautiful, and yet neither old nor ugly, there was nothing in her face to prevent her intellect and grace from exercising their full effect. In complete contrast to other women, her least freshness was in her face, and I believe that the use of rouge had ruined it. She had reasons for her easy virtue: it was the best way in which she could assert all her charms. It was possible to look at her without loving her; it was impossible to possess her without adoring her. This seems to me to prove that she was not always so lavish of her favours as she was with me. Her advances to me had been too sudden and lively to be excusable; but her heart at least had as much to do with it as her senses, and, during the brief and delicious period which I spent with her, I had reason to believe, from the forced moderation which she imposed upon me, that, although sensual and voluptuous, she thought more of my health than her own pleasure.

[1] *Mes propos de Céladon*: "My Celadonic way of speaking." Céladon was one of the characters in the "Astrée," a celebrated romance by Honoré d'Urfé (1568–1625), and came to be used for a devoted but bashful lover.

The understanding between us did not escape the Marquis. He did not, however, leave off chaffing me, but, on the contrary, treated me more than ever as a bashful lover, a martyr to his lady's cruelty. Not a word, not a smile, not a look escaped him, which could have made me suspect that he had found us out; and I should have believed that he had been deceived by us, had not Madame de Larnage, who was keener than I was, told me that this was not the case, but that he was a chivalrous man; and, indeed, no one could have shown more polite attention, or behaved more courteously than he always did, even towards myself, with the exception of his raillery, especially after my success. He perhaps attributed the credit of it to me, and considered me not such a fool as I had appeared to be. He was mistaken, as has been seen: but no matter, I profited by his mistake; and it is true that, since I now had the laugh on my side, I endured his epigrams with good heart and grace, and sometimes retorted, even happily, proud to be able to exhibit, in the presence of Madame de Larnage, the wit with which she had credited me. I was no longer the same man.

We were in a country and a season of good cheer; and, thanks to the Marquis, we enjoyed it to the full. I could have dispensed with his extending his attentions even to our bedrooms; but he always sent his lackey to engage them in advance, and this rascal, either on his own responsibility or by the Marquis's instructions, always took a room for him next to Madame de Larnage, while I was poked away at the other end of the house. But this caused me little embarrassment, and only added piquancy to our rendezvous. This delightful life lasted four or five days, during which I was intoxicated with the sweetest pleasures. They were unadulterated and lively, without the least alloy of pain, the first and only pleasures of the kind that I have enjoyed; and I can only say that I owe it to Madame de Larnage that I shall not leave the world without having known the meaning of pleasure.

If my feeling for her was not exactly love, it was at least so tender a return for the love which she showed for me, it was a sensuality so burning in its satisfaction, and an intimacy so sweet in its intercourse, that it had all the charm of passion without that delirium which turns the brain and spoils enjoyment. I have only felt true love once in my life, and it was not with her. Nor did I love her as I had loved, and still loved, Madame de Warens; but for that very reason the possession of her afforded me a hundred times greater enjoyment. With mamma, my pleasure was always disturbed by a feeling of sadness, by a secret feeling of oppression at the heart, which I found difficult to overcome. Instead of congratulating myself upon possessing her, I reproached myself with degrading her. With Madame de Larnage, on the contrary, I was proud of my manhood and my happiness, and abandoned myself with confident joy to the satisfaction of my desires. I shared the impression which I produced upon hers. I was sufficiently master of myself to regard my triumph with as much self-complacency as pleasure, and to derive from it the means of redoubling it.

I do not remember where the Marquis, who belonged to the district, left us; but we were alone when we reached Montélimar, where Madame de Larnage made her maid get into my carriage, while I travelled in her own. I can assure you that in this manner we did not find the journey tedious, and I should have found it difficult to describe the country through which we passed. She was detained at Montélimar three days on business, during which, however, she only left me for a quarter of an hour to pay a visit, which brought her in return some importunate and pressing invitations, which she was by no means disposed to accept. She pleaded indisposition, which did not, however, prevent us from walking together alone every day in the most beautiful country and under the most beautiful sky in the world. Oh, those three days! I have had reason to regret them sometimes! I have never enjoyed their like again!

Travelling amours cannot last. We were obliged to separate, and I confess that it was time: not that I was surfeited, or anything like it; I became more attached to her every day; but, in spite of her discretion, I had little left except goodwill, and, before we separated, I wished to enjoy that little, which she submitted to, by way of precaution against the young ladies of Montpellier. We beguiled our regrets by forming plans to meet again. It was decided that I should continue the treatment, which did me considerable good, and spend the winter at Saint-Andiol under her superintendence. I was to stay only five or six weeks at Montpellier, to allow her time to arrange the necessary preliminaries, to prevent scandal. She gave me full instructions about what it was necessary for me to know, what I was to say, and the manner in which I was to behave. Meanwhile, we were to write to each other. She spoke to me long and seriously about the care of my health, advised me to consult some clever physicians, to follow their instructions carefully, and took upon herself to make me carry out their directions, however strict they might be, as long as I was with her. I believe that she spoke sincerely, for she loved me. Of this she gave me numerous proofs, more reliable than her favours. From my style of travelling, she judged that I was not rolling in money; and, although she herself was by no means well off, she wanted to make me share the contents of her purse, which she had brought pretty well filled from Grenoble, and I had the greatest difficulty in making her accept my refusal. At last I left her, my heart full of her, and leaving, as I believe, a true attachment for myself in her own.

I finished my journey, while going over it again in my memory from the beginning, and for the moment I was very well content to sit in a comfortable carriage and dream at my ease of the pleasures which I had enjoyed and of those which were promised to me. I thought of nothing but Saint-Andiol, and the delightful life which awaited me there. I saw nothing but Madame de Larnage and her surroundings: the rest of the world was nothing to me: even mamma was forgotten. I employed myself in arranging in my head all the details into which Madame de Larnage had entered, in order to give me beforehand an idea of her house, her neighbourhood, her friends, and her manner of life. She had a daughter, of whom she had often spoken to me in terms of most lavish affection. This daughter was in her sixteenth year, lively, charming, and amiable. Madame de Larnage had promised me that I was sure to be a great favourite with her. I had not forgotten the promise, and I was very curious to see how Mademoiselle de Larnage would behave towards her mamma's good friend. Such were the subjects of my reveries from Pont-Saint-Esprit to Remoulin. I had been told to go and see the Pont du Gard, and did not fail to do so. It was the first Roman work that I had seen. I expected to see a monument worthy of the hands which had erected it; for once, and for the only time in my life, the reality surpassed the expectation. Only the Romans could have produced such an effect.

The sight of this simple, yet noble, work produced the greater impression upon me, as it was situated in the midst of a desert, where silence and solitude bring the object into greater prominence, and arouse a livelier feeling of admiration; for this pretended bridge was nothing but an aqueduct. One naturally asks what strength has transported these enormous stones so far from any quarry, and united the arms of so many thousands of men in a spot where not one of them dwells. I went through the three storeys of this superb building, within which a feeling of respect almost prevented me from setting foot. The echo of my footsteps under these immense vaults made me imagine that I heard the sturdy voices of those who had built them. I felt myself lost like an insect in this immensity. I felt, in spite of my sense of littleness, as if my soul was somehow or other elevated, and I said to myself with a sigh, "Why was I not born a Roman?" I remained there several hours in rapturous contemplation. I returned, distracted and dreamy, and this dreaminess was not favourable to Madame de Larnage. She had been careful to warn me against the girls of Montpellier, but not against the Pont du Gard. One never thinks of everything!

At Nîmes I went to see the amphitheatre. It is a far more magnificent work than the Pont du Gard, but it made far less impression upon me; either the latter had exhausted my powers of admiration, or the former, being situated in the midst of a town, was less calculated to arouse them. This vast and splendid circus is surrounded by ugly little houses, and the arena is filled with other houses, still smaller and uglier, so that the aspect of the whole produces a confused and incongruous effect, in which regret and indignation stifle pleasure and surprise. Since then I have seen the Circus at Verona, which is far smaller and less imposing, but is kept and preserved with the greatest possible neatness and cleanliness, and for that very reason produced upon me a more forcible and agreeable impression. The

French take care of nothing, and have no respect for monuments. They are all eagerness to undertake anything, but do not know how to finish, or keep it in repair when it is finished.

I was so changed, and my sensuality, which had been roused to activity, was awakened to such a degree, that I remained for a whole day at the Pont du Lunel, in order to enjoy its good cheer with the other visitors. This inn, the most famous in Europe, at that time deserved its reputation. Its proprietors had known how to take advantage of its excellent position, in order to keep it abundantly supplied with choice provisions. It was really curious to find, in a lonely and isolated house in the middle of the country, a table furnished with salt and freshwater fish, excellent game, choice wines, served with the attention and civility which is only found in the houses of the great and wealthy – all for thirty-five *sous* a head. But the Pont du Lunel did not long remain on this footing, and, by presuming too much on its reputation, at length lost it altogether.

During my journey I had quite forgotten that I was ill: I remembered it when I arrived at Montpellier. My attacks of hysteria were certainly cured, but all my other ailments remained; and, though familiarity made me less sensitive to them, they were enough to make anyone, who was suddenly attacked by them, fancy himself at death's door. In fact, they were more alarming than painful, and caused more suffering of the mind than of the body, the destruction of which they seemed to announce. Hence, while distracted by violent passions, I thought no more of the state of my health; but, as my complaints were not imaginary, I became aware of them again as soon as I recovered my coolness. I then began to think seriously of Madame de Larnage's advice, and the object of my journey. I consulted the most famous physicians, particularly M. Fizes, and, by way of excessive precaution, boarded with a doctor. He was an Irishman, named Fitzmorris, who took in a considerable number of medical students; and what made his house more comfortable for a resident patient was, that he was satisfied with a moderate fee for board, and charged his boarders nothing for medical attendance. He undertook to carry out M. Fizes's regulations, and to look after my health. As far as diet was concerned, he acquitted himself admirably: none of his boarders suffered from indigestion; and, although I am not very sensible to privations of this kind, the opportunities of drawing comparison were so near, that I could not help sometimes thinking to myself that M. de Torignan was a better purveyor than M. Fitzmorris. However, as we were not absolutely starved, and the young students were very cheerful, this way of living really did me good, and prevented me from falling into my former state of depression. I spent the morning in taking medicines, especially some waters, which I believe came from Vals, although I am not certain, and in writing to Madame de Larnage; for the correspondence continued, and Rousseau undertook to fetch his friend Dudding's letters. At noon I took a walk to La Canourge with one of our young messmates, all of whom were very good lads; after which we assembled for dinner. When this meal was over, most of us engaged in an important occupation until evening: we went a little way out of town to play two or three games of mall for our afternoon tea.[1] I did not play myself, as I possessed neither the requisite strength nor skill, but I betted on the result. In this manner, interested in my wager, I followed our players and their balls across rough and stony roads, and enjoyed agreeable and healthy exercise, which suited me admirably. We took our tea at an inn outside the city. I need not say that these meals were very lively; but I may add that there was nothing improper about them, although the landlord's daughters were very pretty. M. Fitzmorris, who was a great player himself, was our president; and I can declare that, in spite of the bad reputation of the students, I found more decency and propriety amongst these young men than it would have been easy to find amongst an equal number of grown-up men. They were noisy rather than licentious, merry rather than profligate, and I become so easily accustomed to any manner of life, when it is voluntary, that I could have desired nothing better than a continuance of it. Amongst the students were several Irish, from whom I tried to learn a few words of English, in anticipation of Saint-Andiol; for the time of my departure was close at hand. Madame de Larnage importuned me by every

[1]   *Goûter*: a light meal between dinner and supper.

post, and I prepared to obey her. It was clear that my physicians, who did not understand my complaint at all, regarded it as existing only in my imagination, and, under those circumstances, treated me with their China-root, their waters, and their whey. Physicians and philosophers, differing entirely from theologians, only admit that to be true which they are able to explain, and make their understanding the measure of what is possible. These gentlemen understood nothing about my complaint: therefore I was not ill at all; for of course doctors knew everything. I saw that they were only trying to humbug me and make me waste my money; and as I thought that their substitute at Saint-Andiol would do that just as well as they, but in a more agreeable manner, I resolved to give her the preference, and, with this wise resolution, I left Montpellier. I set out towards the end of November, after a stay of six weeks or two months in that city, where I left behind me a dozen *louis d'or*, without any benefit either to my health or understanding, with the exception of a course of anatomy which I commenced under M. Fitzmorris, and which I was obliged to give up, owing to the fearful stench of the bodies which were dissected, and which I found it impossible to endure.

Feeling very ill at ease concerning the resolution that I had taken, I began to reflect upon it as I continued my journey towards the Pont-Saint-Esprit, which was the road to Chambéri as well as Saint-Andiol. The remembrance of mamma and her letters, although she did not write to me so often as Madame de Larnage, again aroused in my heart the remorse which I had stifled during the first part of my journey, and which, on my return, became so keen that, counterbalancing the love of pleasure, it put me in a condition to listen to reason alone. In the first place, in the rôle of adventurer which I was again going to play, I might be less fortunate than I had been on the previous occasion: it only needed, in the whole of Saint-Andiol, a single person who had been in England, or who was acquainted with the English manners or language, to expose me. Madame de Larnage's family might take a dislike to me and treat me with discourtesy. Her daughter, of whom, in spite of myself, I thought more than I ought to have done, also caused me considerable uneasiness. I trembled at the idea of falling in love with her, and this very apprehension half finished the business. Was I, by way of repaying the mother's kindness, to attempt to lead the daughter astray, to enter upon a most detestable connection, to bring dissension, dishonour, scandal, even hell itself into her house? This idea horrified me; I firmly resolved to resist and defeat myself, if this wretched inclination made itself felt. But why expose myself to such a struggle? What a miserable state of things would it be to live with the mother, of whom I was tired, and to be burning with love for the daughter, without daring to disclose the state of my feelings! What necessity was there deliberately to seek such a position, to expose myself to misfortunes, affronts and remorse, for the sake of pleasures, the greatest charm of which I had exhausted in advance? for it is certain that my fancy had lost its early vivacity. The taste for pleasure was still there, but not passion. With these thoughts were mingled reflections upon my situation and my duty, and thoughts of that good and generous mamma, whose debts, already heavy, were increased by my foolish expenditure, who drained her purse for my sake and whom I was so unworthily deceiving. This reproach became so lively that it finally turned the scale. When I had nearly reached the Pont-Saint-Esprit, I resolved to hasten past Saint-Andiol without stopping. I carried out this resolution courageously, with a few sighs, I confess, but also with the inward satisfaction that, for the first time in my life, I could say to myself: "I have a right to think well of myself; I know how to prefer my duty to my pleasure." This was the first real advantage for which I had to thank my studies; they had taught me to reflect and compare. After the virtuous principles which I had so recently adopted, after the rules of wisdom and virtue which I had drawn up for myself and which I had felt such pride in following, a feeling of shame at being so little consistent with myself, of giving the lie to my own maxims so soon and so emphatically, gained the victory over pleasure. Perhaps pride had as much to do with my resolution as virtue; but, if this pride is not virtue itself, its effects are so similar that it is excusable to confound them.

One of the good results of virtuous actions is, that they elevate the soul and incline it to attempt something even better;

for so great is human weakness, that we must reckon amongst virtuous actions abstention from the evil which we are tempted to commit. As soon as I had taken my resolution, I became another man, or rather, I became the man I had formerly been, whom the intoxication of the moment had caused to disappear. Full of good sentiments and good resolutions, I continued my journey with the intention of expiating my error, thinking only of regulating my future conduct by the laws of virtue, of devoting myself unreservedly to the service of the best of mothers, of vowing to her a loyalty equal to my attachment, and of listening to no other call but that of my duties. Alas! the sincerity of my return to virtue appeared to promise a different destiny; but my own was already written and begun, and at the moment when my heart, full of love for all that was good and honourable, saw nothing but innocence and happiness before it, I was approaching the fatal moment which was destined to drag behind it the long chain of my misfortunes.

My impatience to reach home made me travel faster than I had intended. I had sent a letter to mamma from Valence, to inform her of the day and hour of my arrival. As I was half a day in advance, I spent that time at Chaparillan, in order to arrive exactly at the moment I had fixed. I wanted to enjoy to the full the pleasure of seeing her again. I preferred to put it off a little, in order to add to it the pleasure of being expected. This precaution had always proved successful: I had always found my arrival celebrated by a kind of little holiday; I expected as much on this occasion, and these attentions, which I felt so much, were worth the trouble of procuring.

I arrived, then, punctual to the moment. When I was still some distance off, I looked ahead in the hope of seeing her on the road; my heart beat more violently, the nearer I approached. I arrived out of breath, for I had left my carriage in town; I saw no one in the court, at the door, or at the window. I began to feel uneasy and afraid that some accident had happened. I entered: everything was quiet: some workmen were eating in the kitchen: there were no signs that I was expected. The maid appeared surprised to see me: she knew nothing about my coming. I went upstairs; at last I saw her, my dear mamma, whom I loved so

tenderly, so deeply and so purely; I ran up to her, and
threw myself at her feet. "Ah!" said she, embracing me,
"you are back again then, little one! have you had a pleasant
journey? how are you?" This reception somewhat surprised me.
I asked her whether she had received my letter. She answered,
"Yes." "I should not have thought so," I said, and the explanation ended there. A young man was with her. I remembered
having seen him in the house before I left, but now he seemed
established there, as in fact he was. In a word, I found my place
filled.

This young man belonged to the Vaud country; his father,
named Vintzenried, was keeper, or, as he called himself, Captain
of the Castle of Chillon. The son was a journeyman wig-maker,
and was travelling the country in pursuit of his calling, when he
first presented himself to Madame de Warens, who received him
kindly, as she received all travellers, especially those from her
own country. He was tall, fair-haired, insipid, tolerably well set
up, with a face as dull as his intellect, and spoke like a *beau
Léandre,*[1] mingling all the airs and tastes of his calling with the
long story of his conquests, and, according to his own account,
mentioning only half the marchionesses with whom he had
slept, and boasting that he had never dressed a pretty woman's
head without decorating the husband as well. Vain, foolish,
ignorant and insolent, he was in other respects the best fellow
in the world. Such was the substitute who replaced me during
my absence and the companion who was offered to me after my
return.

If souls, when freed from their earthly bonds, still look down
from the bosom of the eternal light upon that which takes place
upon this earth, pardon me, dear and honoured shade, if I show
no more favour to your faults than my own, but unveil both
equally before the reader's eyes! I must and will be as true for you
as for myself: you will always have much less to lose than I. Ah!
how your amiable and gentle character, your inexhaustible goodness of heart, your frankness, and all your admirable qualities
atone for your weaknesses, if simple errors of judgment deserve

[1]   One of the stock characters of Italian comedy, a fop who takes great pride
in his personal appearance, and is fond of displaying his ribbons and lace.

that name! You erred, but you were free from vice; your conduct was blameworthy, but your heart was always pure.

The new-comer had shown himself zealous, diligent and careful in carrying out her numerous little commissions, and had appointed himself foreman of her labourers. As noisy as I was quiet, he was seen and heard everywhere at once, at the plough, in the hay-loft, in the wood-house, in the stable, in the farm-yard. Gardening was the only thing he neglected, because the work was too quiet, and afforded no opportunity for making a noise. His great delight was to load and drive a waggon, to saw or chop wood: he was always to be seen with an axe or pick in his hand, running, hustling, and shouting with all his might. I do not know how many men's work he did, but he made noise enough for ten or a dozen. All this noise and bustle imposed on my poor mamma: she thought that in this young man she had found a treasure to assist her in business matters. In order to attach him to her, she employed all the means she thought likely to produce this result – not forgetting that on which she placed most reliance.

The reader must have gained some knowledge of my heart, and of its truest and most constant feelings, especially those which brought me back to her at this moment. What a sudden and complete upset of my whole being! To judge of it, let the reader put himself in my place. I saw all the happy future which I had depicted to myself vanish in a moment. All the dreams of happiness which I had so fondly cherished disappeared, and I, who from my youth had never considered my existence except in connection with hers, for the first time found myself alone. This moment was frightful! those which followed were all gloomy. I was still young, but the pleasant feeling of enjoyment and hope which animates youth, deserted me for ever. From that time my sensible being was half dead. I saw nothing before me but the melancholy remains of an insipid life: and, if now and again an image of happiness floated lightly across my desires, this happiness was no longer that which was peculiarly my own: I felt that, even if I succeeded in obtaining it, I should still not be really happy.

I was so simple, and my confidence was so great that, in spite of the new-comer's familiar tone, which I looked upon as one of the results of mamma's easy-going disposition, which attracted everyone towards her, I should never have suspected the real reason of it, unless she had told me herself; but she hastened to make this avowal with a frankness which might well have increased my rage, if my heart had been capable of it. She herself considered it quite a simple matter, reproached me with my carelessness in the house, and appealed to my frequent absences, as if her temperament had been such that it required the void to be filled as quickly as possible. "Ah, mamma," I said to her, with a heart wrung with grief, "what do you dare to tell me? What a reward for such devotion as mine! Have you so often saved my life, only in order to deprive me of that which made it dear to me? It will kill me, but you will regret my loss." She replied, with a calmness calculated to drive me mad, that I was a child, that people did not die of such things, that I should lose nothing, that we should be equally good friends, equally intimate in all respects, and that her tender attachment to me could neither diminish nor end except with her own life. In short, she gave me to understand that all my privileges would remain the same, and that, while sharing them with another, I should not find them in any way curtailed. Never did the purity, truth and strength of my attachment for her, never did the sincerity and uprightness of my soul make itself more plainly felt than at that moment. I threw myself at her feet, and, shedding floods of tears, clasped her knees. "No, mamma," I exclaimed, half distracted, "I love you too deeply to degrade you; the possession of you is too precious for me to be able to share it with another; the regrets which I felt when you first bestowed yourself upon me have increased with my affection; I cannot retain possession of you at the same price. I shall always worship you: remain worthy of it: I have still greater need to respect than to possess you. I resign you to yourself; to the union of our hearts I sacrifice all my pleasures. I would rather die a thousand times than seek an enjoyment which degrades one whom I love."

I remained true to this resolution, with a steadfastness worthy, I venture to say, of the feeling which had produced it. From that moment I only regarded this dear mamma with the eyes of a real son; and I must observe that, although my resolution did not meet with her private approbation, as I perceived only too clearly, she never attempted to make me abandon it, either by insinuating proposals, caresses, or any of those clever allurements which women so well know how to make use of without committing themselves, and which are rarely unsuccessful.

Compelled to seek for myself a lot independent of her, and unable even to think of one, I soon fell into the other extreme, and sought it entirely in her. There I sought it so completely that I almost succeeded in forgetting myself. The ardent desire to see her happy, at whatever cost, absorbed all my affections. It was useless for her to separate her happiness from mine; I looked upon it as my own, in spite of her.

Thus, together with my misfortunes, those virtues began to develop, the seeds of which were sown at the bottom of my heart, which had been cultivated by study, and only waited for the leaven of adversity in order to bear fruit. The first result of this disinterestedness was the removal from my heart of all feeling of hatred and envy against him who had supplanted me. On the contrary, I desired in all sincerity to become intimate with this young man, to form his character, to educate him, to make him sensible of his happiness, to make him worthy of it, if possible, and, in a word, to do for him all that Anet had formerly done for me in similar circumstances. But our dispositions were not alike. Although gentler and better informed than Anet, I possessed neither his coolness nor firmness, nor that force of character which inspires respect, and which would have been necessary to insure success. Still less did I find in this young man the qualities which Anet had found in me: docility, attachment, gratitude, and, above all, the consciousness that I needed his attention, and the eager desire of profiting by it. All these qualities were wanting. He whom I wanted to educate considered me as nothing more than a tiresome pedant, who could do nothing else but chatter. On the other hand, he admired himself as a person of importance in the house; and, estimating the services he thought he rendered by the noise he made about them, he looked upon his axes and picks as infinitely more useful than all my old books. In a certain sense, he was right; but, starting from that, he gave himself airs enough to make anyone die with laughter. With the peasants he attempted to play the country gentleman. He soon treated me in the same way, and even mamma herself. As the name Vintzenried did not appear sufficiently distinguished, he abandoned it for that of M. de Courtilles, by which name he was afterwards known at Chambéri, and in Maurienne, where he married.

In a word, this illustrious person soon became everything in the house, and I myself nothing. If I had the misfortune to displease him, it was mamma, not I, whom he scolded. For this reason, the fear of exposing her to his brutal behaviour rendered me subservient to all his wishes; and, whenever he chopped wood – an occupation of which he was inordinately proud – I was obliged to stand by, an idle spectator and quiet admirer of his prowess. His disposition was not, however, altogether bad. He loved mamma because no one could help loving her; he showed no aversion even for me; and, in his calmer moments, he sometimes listened to us quietly enough, and frankly owned that he was only a fool, and, immediately afterwards, proceeded to commit fresh follies. In addition to this, his understanding was so limited and his tastes so low, that it was difficult to reason, and almost impossible to feel at ease with him. Not content with the possession of a most charming woman, he added, by way of seasoning, that of an old, red-haired, toothless waiting-woman, whose disgusting services mamma had the patience to endure, although it quite upset her. I observed this new intrigue, and was beside myself with indignation; but at the same time I perceived something else, which affected me still more deeply, and dispirited me more than anything else which had as yet occurred. This was a growing coldness in mamma's behaviour towards me.

The privation which I had imposed upon myself, and of which she had pretended to approve, is one of those things which women never pardon, however they pretend to take it; not so much for the sake of that of which they are themselves deprived, as by reason of the feeling of indifference which they consider it implies. Take the most sensible, the most philo-sophical, the least sensual woman: the most unpardonable crime that a man, for whom in other respects she cares nothing, can be guilty of towards her, is not to enjoy her favours when he has the chance of doing so. There can be no exception to this rule, since a sympathy, at once so natural and so deep, was impaired in her in consequence of an abstinence, the only motives of which were virtue, attachment, and esteem. From that moment, I no longer found in her that intimacy of hearts which had always afforded the sweetest enjoyment to my own. She no longer unbosomed herself to me, except when she had occasion to complain of the new-comer. When they were on good terms, I was rarely admitted to her confidence. At length, by degrees, she became entirely estranged from me. She still seemed pleased to see me, but no longer found my company indispensable; even had I passed whole days without seeing her, she would not have noticed it.

Insensibly I felt myself isolated and alone in that house of which I had formerly been the soul, and in which I led, so to speak, a double life. I gradually accustomed myself to disregard all that took place in it, and even kept aloof from those who dwelt in it. In order to spare myself continual torment, I shut myself up with my books, or wept and sighed to my heart's content in the midst of the woods. This life soon became unendurable. I felt that the personal presence of a woman who was so dear to me, while I was estranged from her heart, only aggravated my sorrow, and that I should feel the separation from her less cruelly if I no longer saw her. I therefore resolved to leave the house. I told her so, and, far from offering any opposition, she approved of it. She had a friend at Grenoble, named Madame Deybens, whose husband was a friend of M. de Mably, the *Grand-Prévot* of Lyons. M. Deybens suggested to me that I should undertake the education of M. de Mably's children. I accepted the post, and set out for Lyons, without causing, almost without feeling, the slightest regret at a separation, the mere idea of which would formerly have caused us both the most deadly anguish.

I possessed almost sufficient knowledge for a tutor, and believed that I had the necessary qualifications. During the year which I spent at M. de Mably's, I had ample time to undeceive myself. My naturally gentle disposition would have made me well adapted for this profession, had not a violent temper been mingled with it. As long as all went well, and I saw that my trouble and attention, of which I was not sparing, were successful, I was an angel; but, when things went wrong, I was a devil. When my pupils did not understand me, I raved like a madman; when they showed signs of insubordination, I could have killed them, which was not the way to make them either learned or well-behaved. They were two in number, of very different dispositions. One, between eight and nine years old, named Sainte-Marie, had a pretty face, was fairly intelligent, lively, giddy, playful, and mischievous, but his mischief was always good-humoured. The younger, Condillac, who seemed almost stupid, was idle and lazy, as obstinate as a mule, and incapable of learning anything. It may be imagined that, between the two, I had my work cut out. With the aid of patience and coolness I might, perhaps, have succeeded; but, as I possessed neither, I made no progress, and my pupils turned out very badly. I did not lack assiduity, but I wanted evenness of temper, and, above all, tact. I only knew three means to employ, which are always useless and frequently ruinous to children; sentiment, argument, anger. At one time, with Sainte-Marie, I was moved to tears, and attempted to arouse similar emotions in him, as if a child could have been capable of genuine feeling. At another time I exhausted myself in arguing with him, as if he had been able to understand me; and, as he sometimes made use of very subtle arguments, I seriously thought that he must be intelligent, because he knew how to argue. The little Condillac was still more troublesome, since he understood nothing, never made an answer, and was never affected by anything. His obstinacy was immovable, and he never enjoyed anything more than the triumph of putting me in a rage. Then, indeed, he was the wise man and I was the child. I recognised all my faults, and was conscious of them. I studied my pupils' characters, and fathomed them successfully; and I do not believe that I was ever once taken in by their artifices. But what advantage was it to me to see the evil, if I did not know how to apply the remedy? Although I saw through everything, I prevented nothing, and succeeded in nothing, and everything that I did was exactly what I ought not to have done.

I was hardly more successful in regard to myself than my pupils. Madame Deybens had recommended me to Madame de Mably, and had requested her to form my manners and to give me the tone of society. She took some pains about it, and wanted to teach me how to do the honours of her house; but I showed myself so awkward, I was so bashful and so stupid, that she became discouraged, and gave me up. This, however, did not prevent me falling in love with her, after my usual manner. I managed to make her perceive it, but I never dared to declare my passion. She was never disposed to make advances, and all my ogling glances and sighs were in vain, so that I soon wearied of them, seeing that they led to nothing.

While with mamma, I had completely lost my inclination for petty thefts, because, since everything was mine, I had nothing to steal. Besides, the lofty principles which I had laid down for myself ought to have made me for the future superior to such meannesses, and certainly they have usually done so; but this was not so much the result of my having learned to overcome my temptations as of having cut them off at the root, and I very much fear that I should steal, as in my childhood, if exposed to the same desires. I had a proof of this at M. de Mably's, where, although surrounded by trifles which I could easily have pilfered, and which I did not even look at, I took it into my head to long for a certain light, white Arbois wine, which was very agreeable, and for which a few glasses I had drunk at table had given me a strong liking. It was a little thick. I prided myself upon my skill in clearing wine. This particular brand was intrusted to me. I cleared it, and, in doing so, spoiled it, but only to look at, for it still remained pleasant to drink, and I took the opportunity of occasionally appropriating a few bottles to drink at my ease by myself. Unfortunately, I have never been able to drink without eating. How was I to manage to get bread? It was impossible for me to lay by a store; to have sent the lackeys to buy it would have betrayed me, and would at the same time have been almost an insult to the master of the house. I was afraid to buy any myself. How could a fine gentleman, with a sword by his side, go into a baker's shop to buy a piece of bread? At length, I recollected the last resource of a great princess, who, when told that the peasants had no bread, replied: "Then let them eat *brioche*."[1] But what trouble I had to get it! I went out alone for this purpose, and sometimes traversed the whole town, passing thirty pastrycooks' shops before entering one. It was necessary that there should be only one person in the shop, and this person's features had to be very attractive, before I could make up my mind to take the plunge. But, when once I had secured my dear little cake, and, shutting myself up carefully in my room, fetched my bottle of wine from the bottom of a cupboard, what delightful little drinking-bouts I enjoyed all by myself, while reading a few pages of a novel, for I have always had a fancy for reading while eating, if I am alone; it supplies the want of society. I devour alternately a page and a morsel. It seems as if my book were dining with me.

I have never been dissolute or sottish: in fact, I have never been drunk in my life. Thus, my petty thefts were not very indiscreet. However, they were discovered: the bottles betrayed me. No notice was taken of it, but I no longer had the management of the cellar. In all this M. de Mably behaved honourably and sensibly. He was a very upright man, who, beneath a manner as harsh as his office, concealed a really gentle disposition and rare goodness of heart. He was shrewd, just, and what would not have been expected in an officer of the *Maréchaussée*,[2] even kindly. Sensible of his indulgence, I became more attached to him, and this made me remain longer in his house than I should otherwise have done. But, at length, disgusted with a profession for which I was ill-adapted, and with a very troublesome situation, which had nothing agreeable for me, after a year's trial, during which I had spared no pains, I resolved to leave my pupils, feeling convinced that I should never succeed in bringing them up properly. M. de Mably saw this as well as I did. However, I do not think that he would ever have taken upon

---

[1] "Let them eat cake", the remark attributed to Marie-Antoinette, is apocryphal: it had already been attributed to Louix XV's daughter Victorine and perhaps to others.
[2] Mounted police, replaced by the *gendarmerie* in 1791.

himself to dismiss me, if I had not spared him the trouble, and such excessive condescension in such a case I cannot certainly approve of.

What made my present situation still more insupportable, was the comparison I continually drew with that which I had left: the remembrance of my dear Charmettes, of my garden, of my trees, of my fountain, of my orchard, and, above all, of her for whom I felt I was born, who was the life and soul to everything. When I thought again of our pleasures and our innocent life, my heart was seized by a feeling of oppression and suffocation, which deprived me of the courage to do anything. A hundred times I felt violently tempted to set out instantly on foot and return to Madame de Warens. If I could only see her once again, I felt that I should have been content to die on the spot. At length I could no longer resist those tender remembrances, which called me back to her at any cost. I said to myself that I had not been sufficiently patient, obliging, or affectionate; that, if I exerted myself more than I had hitherto done, I might still live happily with her on terms of tender friendship. I formed the most beautiful plans in the world, and burned to carry them out.

I left everything, I renounced everything, I set out, I flew, and, arriving in all the transports of my early youth, found myself again at her feet. Ah! I should have died for joy, if I had found again in her reception, in her eyes, in her caresses, or, lastly, in her heart, one quarter of that which I had formerly found there, and which I myself still brought back to her.

Alas for the terrible illusions of human life! She received me with the same excellent heart, which could only die with her; but I sought in vain the past which was gone, never to return. I had scarcely remained with her half an hour, when I felt that my former happiness was gone for ever. I found myself again in the same disconsolate situation from which I had been obliged to flee, without being able to fix the blame on anyone; for, at bottom, Courtilles was not a bad fellow, and he seemed more glad than annoyed to see me again. But how could I bear to be a supernumerary with her for whom I had been everything, and who would never cease to be everything for me? How could I live as a stranger in the house of which I felt myself the child?

The sight of the objects which had witnessed my past happiness made the comparison still more painful. I should have suffered less in another house. But the sight of so many sweet remembrances, continually revived, only irritated the consciousness of my loss. Consumed by idle regrets, abandoned to the blackest melancholy, I resumed my old manner of life and remained alone, except at meal-times. Shut up with my books, I sought to find in them some useful distraction; and, feeling that the danger, which I had so long dreaded, was imminent, I racked my brains anew, in the endeavour to find in myself a means to provide against it, when mamma's resources should be exhausted. I had so managed her household affairs, that at least things did not grow worse; but, since I had left her, everything was changed. Her steward was a spendthrift. He wanted to make a show with a fine horse and carriage. He was fond of playing the noble in the eyes of the neighbours, and was continually undertaking something about which he knew nothing. Her pension was swallowed up in advance, the quarterly payments were mortgaged, the rent was in arrears, and debts accumulated. I foresaw that her pension would soon be seized, and perhaps discontinued altogether. In a word, I saw nothing but ruin and disasters ahead, and the moment appeared so close, that I felt all its horrors by anticipation.

My dear little room was my only recreation. After a prolonged search for remedies against my mental anxiety, I bethought myself of looking about for a remedy against the troubles which I foresaw; and, returning to my old ideas, I suddenly began to build fresh castles in the air, in order to extricate my poor mamma from the cruel extremities into which I saw her on the point of falling. I did not feel myself sufficiently learned, and I did not believe that I was sufficiently talented, to shine in the republic of letters, or to make a fortune by that means. A new idea, which occurred to me, inspired me with the confidence which the mediocrity of my talents could not give me. I had not given up the study of music when I left off teaching it; on the contrary, I had studied the theory of it sufficiently to consider myself learned in this department of the art. Whilst reflecting upon the trouble I had found in learning to read the notes, and the great difficulty I still felt in singing at sight, I began to think that this difficulty might be due to the nature of the case as much as to my own incapacity, especially as I knew that no one finds it an easy task to learn music. On examining the arrangement of the musical signs, I found them frequently very badly invented. I had long thought of denoting the scale by figures, to obviate the necessity of always drawing the lines and staves when the most trifling air had to be written. I had been hindered by the difficulties of the octaves, the time, and the values of the notes. This idea again occurred to me, and, on reconsidering it, I saw that these difficulties were not insurmountable. I carried it out successfully, and was at length able to note any music whatever by my figures with the greatest exactness, and also, I may say, with the greatest simplicity. From that moment, I considered my fortune made; and, in my eagerness to share it with her to whom I owed everything, I thought of nothing but setting out for Paris, feeling no doubt that, when I laid my scheme before the Academy, I should cause a revolution. I had brought a little money back from Lyons; I sold my books. In a fortnight my resolution was taken and carried out.

At last, full of the magnificent hopes which had inspired me, being ever and at all times the same, I started from Savoy with my system of music, as I had formerly started from Turin with my heron-fountain.

Such have been the errors and faults of my youth. I have related the history of them with a fidelity of which my heart approves. If, later, I have honoured my riper years with any virtues, I should have declared them with the same frankness, and such was my intention. But I must stop here. Time may lift many a veil. If my memory descends to posterity, perhaps it will one day learn what I had to say; then it will be understood why I am silent.[1]

---

[1] After a quarrel with his executor du Peyrou at the Château de Trye in November 1767, Rousseau seems for the moment to have decided to proceed no further with his *Confessions*.

PART THE SECOND
BOOK VII

[1741]

AFTER two years of silence and patience, in spite of my resolutions, I again take up my pen. Reader, suspend your judgment upon the reasons which force me to do so; you cannot judge of them until you have read the story of my life.

You have seen my peaceful youth pass away in a tolerably uniform and agreeable manner, without great disappointments or remarkable prosperity. This absence of extremes was in great part the result of my passionate but weak disposition, which, more easily discouraged than prompt to undertake, only quitted its state of repose when rudely shocked, but fell back into it again from weariness and natural inclination; and which, while keeping me away from great virtues, and still further from great vices, led me back steadily to the indolent and peaceful life for which I felt Nature intended me, and never permitted me to attain to greatness in anything, either good or bad. What a different picture I shall soon have to draw! Destiny, which for thirty years favoured my inclinations, during a second thirty thwarted them, and this continued opposition between my position and inclinations will be seen to have produced monstrous errors, unheard-of misfortunes, and all the virtues that can render adversity honourable, with the exception of strength of character.

The first part of my Confessions was written entirely from memory, and I must have made many mistakes in it. As I am obliged to write the second part also from memory, I shall probably make many more. The sweet remembrances of my best years, passed in equal innocence and tranquillity, have left me a thousand charming impressions, which I love to recall incessantly. It will soon be seen how different are the recollections of the remainder of my life. To recall them renews their bitterness. Far from increasing the painfulness of my situation by these melancholy retrospects, I put them away from me as much as possible, and frequently succeed so well, that I am unable to recall them even when it is necessary. This capacity for easily forgetting misfortunes is a consolation, which Heaven has bestowed upon me amidst those afflictions which destiny was one day fated to heap upon my head. My memory, which only revives the recollection of agreeable things, is the happy counterpoise of my fearful imagination, which causes me to foresee only a cruel future.

All the papers which I have collected to fill the gaps in my memory and to guide me in my undertaking, have passed into other hands, and will never return to mine. I have only one faithful guide upon which I can depend; the chain of the feelings which have marked the development of my being, and which will remind me of the succession of events, which have been either the cause or the effect of these feelings. I find it easy to forget my misfortunes, but I cannot forget my faults, still less my virtuous feelings, the recollection of which is too precious ever to be effaced from my heart. I may omit or transpose facts, I may make mistakes in dates, but I cannot be deceived in regard to what I have felt or what my feelings have prompted me to do; and this is the chief subject under discussion. The real object of my Confessions is, to contribute to an accurate knowledge of my inner being in all the different situations of my life. What I have promised to relate, is the history of my soul; I need no other memoirs in order to write it faithfully; it is sufficient for me to enter again into my inner self as I have hitherto done.

Very luckily, however, there is an interval of six or seven years concerning which I possess trustworthy information in a collection of copies of certain letters, the originals of which are in the hands of M. du Peyrou. This collection, which ends with the year 1760, embraces the whole period of my stay at the "Hermitage" and my great quarrel with my so-called friends – a memorable epoch of my life, which was the origin of all my other misfortunes. In regard to any original letters of more recent date, which I may perhaps have preserved, and which are only few in number, instead of copying and adding them to this collection, which is too voluminous for me to hope to be able to conceal it from the watchful eyes of my Arguses, I will copy them into this work itself, when they seem to me to afford any elucidation of

facts, either in my favour or against me; for I have no fear that
the reader, forgetting that I am writing my Confessions, will ever
imagine that I am writing my Apologia; but neither must he
expect that I shall keep silence regarding the truth, when it
speaks in my favour.

Besides, this truth is all that this second part has in common
with the first, and the only advantage it can claim over it is, the
greater importance of the facts related. With this exception, it
cannot fail to be inferior to it in every respect. I wrote the first
part with pleasure and gratification, and at my ease, at Wootton
or in the Castle of Trye.[1] All the memories which I had to recall
were for me so many fresh enjoyments. I turned back to them
incessantly with renewed pleasure, and I was able to revise my
descriptions until I was satisfied with them, without feeling in
the least bored. At the present time, my failing memory and
enfeebled brain unfit me for almost every kind of work. I only
undertake my present task under compulsion, with a heart
oppressed by grief. It offers me nothing but misfortunes, treachery, perfidy, melancholy and heartrending recollections. I would
give anything in the world to be able to bury in the darkness of
time what I have to say; and, while constrained to speak in spite
of myself, I am also obliged to hide myself, to employ cunning,
to endeavour to deceive, and to lower myself to conduct utterly
at variance with my nature. The roof under which I am has eyes,
the walls around me have ears. Beset by spies and watchful and
malevolent overlookers, uneasy and distracted, I hurriedly
scribble a few disjointed sentences, which I have scarcely time
to read over, still less to correct. I know that, in spite of the
barriers set up around me in ever-increasing numbers, my enemies are still afraid that the truth may find some loophole
through which to escape. How am I to set about bringing it to
the light? I am making the attempt with little hope of success. It
will be easily understood, that this is not the material out of
which pleasant pictures are made, or such as is calculated to give
them an attractive colouring. I therefore give notice to those
who intend to read this portion of my work that, in the course of
their reading, nothing can guarantee them against weariness,

[1] In the department of the Oise, belonging to the Prince of Conti.

unless it be the desire of completing their knowledge of a man, and a sincere affection for truth and justice.

At the conclusion of the first part of my Confessions, I was setting out, much against my wish, for Paris, having left my heart at Les Charmettes, where I had built my last castle in the air, intending one day to return and lay at the feet of mamma, restored to her former self, the riches I should have gained, and reckoning upon my system of music as a sure road to fortune.

I stayed a little time at Lyons, to visit my acquaintances, to get some letters of introduction for Paris, and to sell my geometrical books which I had taken with me. Everybody received me kindly. M. and Madame de Mably were glad to see me again, and invited me to dinner several times At their house I made the acquaintance of the Abbé de Mably, as I had previously made that of the Abbé de Condillac, both of whom were on a visit to their brother. The Abbé de Mably gave me some letters for Paris, amongst them one for M. de Fontenelle, and another for the Comte de Caylus. I found them both very agreeable acquaint ances, especially the former, who, up to the time of his death, never ceased to show me marks of friendship, and, when we were alone, gave me good advice, of which I ought to have made better use.

I saw M. Bordes again, an old acquaintance of mine, who had often assisted me with the greatest willingness and with genuine pleasure. On this occasion I found him just the same. It was he who assisted me in disposing of my books, and himself gave me, or procured from others, strongly-worded letters of introduction for Paris. I saw the Intendant again, for whose acquaintance I was indebted to M. Bordes, who also procured me an introduction to the Duc de Richelieu, who was staying in Lyons at the time. M. Pallu presented me to him; he received me kindly, and told me to come and see him in Paris, which I did several times; but the acquaintance of this distinguished personage, of which I shall frequently have to speak in the sequel, has never been of the least use to me.

I again saw David the musician, who had assisted me in my distress on one of my previous journeys. He had lent or given me a cap and a pair of stockings, which he has never asked for, and which I have never returned to him, although we have often seen each other since then. However, I afterwards made him a small present, of nearly equal value. I should be able to speak more favourably of myself, if it were a question of what I ought to have done; but it is a question of what I have done, which unfortunately is not the same thing.

I again saw the noble and generous Perrichon, who again behaved towards me with his accustomed munificence. He gave me the same present as he had formerly given to "Gentil-Bernard";[1] he paid for my seat in the *diligence*. I again saw Surgeon Parisot, the best and most benevolent of men; I again saw his dear Godefroi, whom he kept for ten years, whose gentle disposition and goodness of heart were almost her only merits, but whom no one could see for the first time without sympathy or leave without emotion, for she was in the last stages of consumption, of which she soon afterwards died. Nothing shows a man's true inclinations better than the character of those whom he loves.* Whoever had seen the gentle Godefroi, had made the acquaintance of the worthy Parisot.

Although I was greatly indebted to all these worthy people, I afterwards neglected them all, not certainly from ingratitude, but owing to my unconquerable idleness, which has often made me appear ungrateful. The remembrance of their kindnesses has never left my heart, but it would have been easier for me to prove my gratitude by deeds than to express it continually in words. Regularity in correspondence has always been beyond my strength: as soon as I begin to feel slack, shame and a feeling

---

[1] A French poet (1710–1775). The name "Gentil" was given to him by Voltaire.

* Unless he is at the outset deceived in his choice, or the character of the woman to whom he has formed an attachment subsequently changes, in consequence of a combination of extraordinary circumstances, which is not absolutely impossible. If this principle were admitted without modification, Socrates would have to be judged by his wife Xantippe, and Dion by his friend Calippus, a judgment which would be the most unfair and the most misleading that has ever been passed. Further, let no one make any insulting application of it to my wife. She is certainly more narrow-minded and more easily deceived than I had imagined; but her pure, excellent and generous character deserves all my esteem, which it will enjoy as long as I live. (R)

of embarrassment in repairing my fault make me aggravate it, and I leave off writing altogether. I have therefore kept silence, as if I had forgotten them. Parisot and Perrichon took no notice at all, and I always found them the same; but, twenty years later, in the case of M. Bordes, it will be seen how far the self-complacency of a wit can make him carry his vengeance, when once he fancies himself slighted.

Before I leave Lyons, I must not forget to mention an amiable person, whom I saw again with greater pleasure than ever, and who left in my heart most tender remembrances. This was Mademoiselle Serre, of whom I have spoken in the first part of this work, and whose acquaintance I had renewed while I was with M. de Mably. As I had more time to spare on the present occasion, I saw more of her, and conceived a most lively attachment to her. I had some reason to believe that she herself was not unfavourably disposed towards me; but she treated me with a confidence which kept me from the temptation to abuse it. She had no means, neither had I. Our positions were too much alike for us to become united, and, with the views which I then entertained, marriage was far from my thoughts. She told me that a young merchant, M. Genève, seemed desirous of paying his addresses to her. I saw him once or twice in her company. He had the reputation of being, and appeared to me to be, an honourable man. Feeling convinced that she would be happy with him, I wanted him to marry her, as he afterwards did, and, in order not to disturb their innocent affection, I made haste to depart, offering up heartfelt prayers for the happiness of this charming young lady, which, alas! were only listened to for a short time on this earth: for I afterwards heard, that she died after she had been married two or three years. Filled with tender regrets throughout my journey, I felt, and have often felt since then, when I think of it again, that, even if the sacrifices which are made to duty and virtue are painful to make, they are well repaid by the sweet recollections which they leave at the bottom of the heart.

On my previous journey I had seen Paris in an unfavourable aspect. On the present occasion I saw it from a correspondingly brilliant point of view, not, however, in the matter of lodgings, for, upon the recommendation of M. Bordes, I put up at the Hôtel St. Quintin, in the Rue des Cordiers, near the Sorbonne; I had a wretched room, in a wretched street and a wretched hotel, in which, however, several distinguished persons had stayed, such as Gresset, Bordes, the Abbés de Mably and de Condillac and several others, none of whom, unfortunately for me, were any longer there; but I made the acquaintance of a certain M. de Bonnefond, a young country-squire, who was lame, fond of litigation, and set up for a purist. Through him I made the acquaintance of M. Roguin, now my oldest friend, who introduced me to the philosopher Diderot, of whom I shall soon have much to say.

I arrived at Paris in the autumn of 1741, with fifteen *louis d'or* in my pocket, my comedy of *Narcissus*, and my musical scheme, as my sole resource. I had therefore little time to lose in trying to lay them out to the best advantage. I hastened to make use of my letters of introduction. A young man, who arrives in Paris with a pretty good appearance and advertises himself by his talents, is always sure of being well received, as I was. This procured me certain pleasures, but did not materially assist me. Only three of the persons to whom I had letters were of use to me – M. Damesin, a Savoyard gentleman, at that time the equerry, and, I believe, the favourite of the Princesse de Carignan; M. de Boze, Secretary of the Academy of Inscriptions and keeper of the King's collection of medals; and Père Castel, a Jesuit, the inventor of the *clavecin oculaitre*.[1] All these introductions, except that to M. Damesin, had been given to me by the Abbé de Mably.

M. Damesin provided for my most urgent need by introducing me to M. de Gasc, President[2] of the Parliament of Bordeaux, who was a very good player on the violin, and also to the Abbé de Léon, who was then living in the Sorbonne, a young and amiable nobleman, who died in the prime of life, after having cut a brilliant figure in the world for a brief period, under

---

[1] A keyboard instrument employing colours instead of musical notes and, in theory, capable of performing colour "symphonies" and "sonatas". Its inventor, the genial and eccentric Jesuit Father Castel (1688–1757), wrote extensively about it and made one or two not very successful attempts to design a working model.

[2] *President à mortier*, that is, who wore the *mortier*, or round black-velvet cap.

the name of the Chevalier de Rohan. Both of them took a fancy to learn composition; and I gave them a few months' lessons, which to some extent replenished my purse, which was almost empty. The Abbé de Léon conceived a friendship for me, and wanted me to be his secretary: but, as he was by no means rich, and could only offer me a salary of 800 francs, I felt obliged, to my regret, to refuse his offer, as the sum would not have been sufficient to pay for my board and lodging and clothes.

M. de Boze received me very kindly. He had a taste for learning, and was himself a learned man, but somewhat pedantic. Madame de Boze might have been his daughter; she was brilliant and affected. I sometimes dined at his house, and it would have been impossible for anyone to be more awkward and confused than I was in her presence. Her free and easy manner intimidated me, and made my own more ridiculous. When she handed me a dish, I put out my fork and modestly took a morsel of what she offered me; whereupon she returned to her lackey the dish which she had intended for me, at the same time turning round to hide her laughter. She had no suspicion that there was, nevertheless, something in the country-bumpkin's head. M. de Boze presented me to his friend M. de Réaumur, who dined with him every Friday, when the Academy of Sciences held its meeting. He spoke to him of my scheme, and of my wish to submit it to the Academy for examination. M. de Réaumur undertook to bring my proposal forward, and it was accepted. On the day appointed, I was introduced and presented by M. de Réaumur; and on the same day, the 22nd of August, 1742, I had the honour of reading before the Academy the Essay which I had prepared for the purpose. Although this illustrious assembly was certainly very imposing, I felt much less nervous than in the presence of Madame de Boze, and I managed to get through my reading and examination with credit. The Essay was well received, and I was complimented upon it, which equally surprised and flattered me, for I did not imagine that, in the opinion of an Academy, anyone who did not belong to it could possess common sense. The commission appointed to examine me consisted of MM. de Mairan, Hellot and De Fouchy, all three certainly persons of ability, but not one was sufficiently acquainted with music, at least, to be competent to judge of my scheme.

[1742.] – In the course of my conferences with these gentlemen, I became convinced, with as much certainty as surprise, that if learned men are sometimes less prejudiced than others, they cling more closely, by way of revenge, to those prejudices which they do entertain. However weak, however false for the most part their objections were – and although I answered them timidly, I confess, and in ill-chosen terms, but yet with decisive arguments – I never once succeeded in making myself understood or in satisfying them. I was always astounded at the readiness with which, by the help of a few sonorous phrases, they refuted without having understood me. They discovered, somewhere or other, that a monk named Souhaitti had already conceived the idea of denoting the scale by figures. This was enough to make them uphold that my system was not new. That may be; for although I had never heard of Souhaitti – although his method of writing the seven notes of plain-song, without paying any attention to the octaves, in no respect deserved to be compared with my simple and convenient invention for noting all imaginable kinds of music, without difficulty, by means of numbers – keys, rests, octaves, measures, time, and value of the notes, of which Souhaitti had never even thought – nevertheless, it was quite true that, as far as the elementary designation of the seven notes is concerned, he was the first inventor. But they not only attributed to this primitive invention more importance than it deserved, but did not stop there; and, as soon as they attempted to speak of the fundamental principles of the system, they did nothing else but talk nonsense. The greatest advantage of my system was, that it did away with transpositions and keys, so that the same piece could be noted and transposed at will into whatever key one pleased, by means of the supposed change of a single initial letter at the beginning of the air. These gentlemen had heard it said by Parisian strummers that the method of playing a piece of music by transposition was worthless. Starting from this, they turned the most distinct advantage of my system into an insuperable objection against it, and they came to the decision that my system of notation was good for vocal, but unsuitable for instrumental, music, instead of deciding, as they should have done, that it was good for vocal and better for instrumental music. As the result of their report, the Academy granted me a certificate full of high-flown compliments, between the lines of which it was easy to read that, as a matter of fact, it considered my system to be neither new nor useful. I did not feel under any obligation to adorn with such a document my work entitled, "A Treatise on Modern Music," in which I made my appeal to the public.

I had reason to observe on this occasion how, even in the case of a person of limited intelligence, an exclusive but thorough knowledge of anything is more likely to enable him to judge of it correctly than all the learning acquired by scientific culture, unless it is combined with a special study of the subject in question. The only solid objection which could be made to my system was made by Rameau. No sooner had I explained it to him than he saw its weak side. "Your signs," he said, "are very good, in so far as they determine simply and clearly the value of the notes, accurately represent the intervals, and always show the simple way in the double notes – things which the ordinary system does not do; they are bad, in that they require a mental operation, which cannot always follow the rapidity of the execution. The position of our notes," he continued, "is represented to the eye without the assistance of this operation. When two notes, one very high and the other very low, are united by a series of intermediate notes, I can see at the first glance the gradual progress from one to the other; but according to your system, in order to make sure of this series, I am obliged to spell through all your figures in succession; a general glance is unable to supply any deficiency." The objection appeared to me unanswerable, and I immediately admitted the force of it; although it is simple and striking, it is one that only great experience in the art could suggest, and it is not to be wondered at that it occurred to none of the members of the Academy, but it is to be wondered at that all these great scholars, who know so many things, so little understand that each should only pass judgment upon matters connected with his own special branch of study.

My frequent visits to my examining board and other Academicians put it within my reach to make the acquaintance of all the most distinguished literary men in Paris; thus their acquaintance was already made when, later, I suddenly found myself enrolled amongst them. For the moment, entirely absorbed in my musical system, I persisted in my design of bringing about a revolution in the art, and by this means attaining to a celebrity which, when acquired in the fine arts in Paris, is always accompanied by fortune. I shut myself up in my room and worked with indescribable zeal for two or three months, in order to revise the pamphlet which I had read before the Academy, and make it into a work fit for publication. The difficulty was to find a publisher who would accept my manuscript, as some outlay would have been necessary for the new characters, and publishers are not in the habit of throwing their money at the heads of beginners, although it seemed to me only fair, that my work should bring me back the bread which I had eaten while I was writing it.

Bonnefond found me the elder Quillau, who made an agreement with me on terms of half profits, without reckoning the privilege,[1] for which I had to pay myself. The aforesaid Quillau managed the affair so badly, that the money I paid for my privilege was wasted, and I never made a farthing by my publication, which probably enough had only a small sale, although the Abbé Desfontaines had promised to push it, and the other journalists had spoken fairly well of it.

The greatest impediment to a trial of my system was the fear that, if it were not adopted, the time spent in learning it would be lost. My reply to this was, that practice in my method of notation would make the ideas so clear that, in learning music by means of the ordinary signs, time would still be gained by commencing with mine. To put it to the test, I gave lessons in music for nothing to a young American lady, named Mademoiselle des Roulins, whose acquaintance I had made through M. Roguin. In three months she was able to read any kind of music according to my notation, and even to sing at sight, better than myself, any

---

[1] *Privilege*: the exclusive right granted by the King to a publisher to print a work.

piece that did not present too many difficulties. This success was striking, but did not become known. Anyone else would have filled the newspapers with it; but, although I possessed some talent for making useful discoveries, I was never capable of turning them to account.

Thus my heron-fountain was again broken; but, on this second occasion, I was thirty years old, and I was in the streets of Paris, where one cannot live for nothing. The resolution which I came to in this extremity will astonish none but those who have not attentively read the first part of these Memoirs.

After the great and fruitless exertions I had recently made, I needed a little rest. Instead of abandoning myself to despair, I quietly abandoned myself to my usual idleness and the care of Providence; and, in order to give the latter time to do its work, I proceeded to consume, in a leisurely manner, the few *louis* which I still had left. I regulated the expense of my careless pleasures, without entirely giving them up. I only went to the café every other day, and to the theatre twice a week. As for money spent on women, there was no need for retrenchment, for I have never in my life laid out a *sou* in this manner, except on one occasion, of which I shall have to speak presently.

The calmness, delight and confidence with which I abandoned myself to this indolent and solitary life, although I had not sufficient means to continue it for three months, is one of the peculiarities of my life and one of the oddities of my character. The great need of sympathy which I felt, was the very thing which deprived me of the courage to show myself; and the necessity of paying visits to people made them so unendurable, that I even gave up going to see the Academicians and other men of letters, with whom I was already on more or less intimate terms. Marivaux, the Abbé de Mably, and Fontenelle were almost the only persons whom I still continued to visit. I even showed my comedy of *Narcisse* to the first. He was pleased with it, and was kind enough to touch it up. Diderot,[1] who was not so old, was about my own age. He was fond of music, and acquainted with the theory of it; we talked about it, and he also spoke to me of his own literary projects.

[1] [Diderot] See *Biographies,* p. 708.

This resulted in a most intimate connection between us, which lasted fifteen years, and would probably have still continued, if I had not, unfortunately, and by his own fault, been thrown into the same profession as himself.

No one would guess how I employed this brief and precious interval, which still remained to me before I was compelled to beg my bread. I learned by heart passages from the poets which I had already learnt a hundred times and forgotten. Every morning, about ten o'clock, I used to walk in the Luxembourg Gardens with a Virgil or Rousseau[1] in my pocket, and, until dinner-time, I recommitted to memory a sacred ode or an eclogue, without being discouraged by the fact that, while going over the task of the day, I was sure to forget what I had learnt the day before. I remembered that, after the defeat of Nicias at Syracuse, the Athenian prisoners supported themselves by reciting the poems of Homer. The lesson which I drew from this specimen of erudition, in order to prepare myself against poverty, was to exercise my admirable memory in learning all the poets by heart.

I possessed an equally solid expedient in chess, to which I regularly devoted my afternoons at the Café Maugis, on the days when I did not go to the theatre. I there made the acquaintance of M. de Légal, M. Husson, Philidor, and all the great chess-players of the day, without making any progress myself. However, I had no doubt that in the end I should become a better player than any of them; and this, in my opinion, was enough for my support. Whenever I became infatuated with any fresh folly, I always reasoned about it in the same manner. I said to myself, "Anyone who excels in something, is always sure of being sought after. Let me, therefore, excel in something, no matter what: I shall be sought after; opportunities will present themselves, and my own merits will do the rest." This childishness was not the sophism of my reason, but of my indolence. Frightened at the great and rapid efforts which would have been necessary to make me exert myself, I endeavoured to flatter my idleness, and concealed its disgrace from myself by arguments worthy of it.

[1] Jean Baptiste Rousseau, the French lyric poet.

Thus, I quietly waited until my money should be exhausted; and I believe that I should have come to my last *sou* without any further uneasiness, had not Father Castel, whom I sometimes went to see on my way to the café, roused me from my lethargy. He was mad, but, after all, a good fellow. He was sorry to see me wasting my time and abilities without doing anything. He said to me, "Since musicians and savants will not sing together with you, change your string and try the women; perhaps you will succeed better in that quarter. I have spoken about you to Madame de Beuzenval; go and see her, and mention my name. She is a good woman, who will be pleased to see a countryman of her son and husband. At her house you will meet her daughter, Madame de Broglie, who is a clever and accomplished woman. Madame Dupin is another lady to whom I have spoken of you; take your work to her; she is anxious to see you and will receive you kindly. No one can do anything in Paris without the women; they are like the curves, of which clever people are the asymptotes; they constantly approach, but never touch."

After having repeatedly put off these terrible tasks, I at length summoned up courage and went to call upon Madame de Beuzenval, who received me affably. Madame de Broglie happening to enter the room, she said to her, "My daughter, this is M. Rousseau, of whom Father Castel spoke to us." Madame de Broglie complimented me upon my work, and, conducting me to her piano, showed me that she had paid some attention to it. Seeing that it was nearly one o'clock, I wanted to retire, but Madame de Beuzenval said to me, "It is a long way to your quarter; stop and dine here." I needed no pressing. A quarter of an hour later I understood, from something she said, that the dinner to which she invited me was in the servants' hall. Although Madame de Beuzenval was undoubtedly a very good woman, she was of limited understanding, and, too full of her illustrious Polish nobility, had little idea of the respect due to talent. Even on this occasion, she judged me more by my manner than by dress, which, although simple, was very respectable, and by no means indicated a man who ought to be invited to dine at the servants' table. I had too long forgotten the way there, to desire to learn it again. Without showing all the

annoyance I felt, I told Madame de Beuzenval that I remembered
I was obliged to return to my quarter on business, and I again
prepared to leave. Madame de Broglie went up to her mother and
whispered a few words in her ear, which had their effect. Madame
de Beuzenval rose to detain me, and said, "I hope you will do us
the honour of dining *with us*." Believing that to show pride would
be to play the fool, I stayed. Besides, Madame de Broglie's kindness had touched me, and rendered her attractive to me. I was
very glad to dine with her, and I hoped that, when she knew me
better, she would have no cause to regret having procured me this
honour. The President of Lamoignon, a great friend of the family,
dined there on the same occasion. Like Madame de Broglie, he
was familiar with the small-talk jargon of Paris, which consisted
of *petits mots* and delicate little allusions. In this poor Jean Jacques
had little chance of shining. I had the good sense not to try to play
the wit, when Minerva was not agreeable, and I held my tongue.
Would that I had always been as wise! – I should not be in the
abyss in which I find myself to-day.

I was deeply grieved at my own dulness, and also because I was
unable to justify, in the eyes of Madame de Broglie, what she had
done in my behalf. After dinner, I bethought myself of my usual
resource. I had in my pocket a letter in verse, which I had written
to Parisot[1] during my stay at Lyons. This fragment was not
wanting in fire, to which I added by my manner of reciting, and
I moved all three to tears. Whether my own vanity or the truth
made me so interpret it, I thought I saw that Madame de Broglie's
eyes said to her mother, Well, mamma, was I wrong in telling you,
that this man was more fitted to dine with you than with your
waiting-women? Until this moment my heart had been somewhat heavy, but after I had thus avenged myself, I was satisfied.
Madame de Broglie pushed her favourable opinion of me a little
too far, and believed that I should cause a sensation in Paris and
become a favourite with the ladies. To guide my inexperience,
she gave me the "Confessions of the Comte de —."[2] "This

[1] Gabriel Parisot (1680–1762), surgeon at the Hôtel-Dieu in Lyons.
[2] By Charles Pinot de Duclos (1704–72), the novelist and Academician.
Rousseau became very friendly with him and only began to have suspicions of
him after his death. This note, a later addition to the *Confessions*, tallies with one
in his *Dialogues*, in which he explicitly accuses Duclos of treachery.

book," said she to me, "is a Mentor, of which you will have need in the world; you will do well to consult it sometimes." I have kept this copy for more than twenty years, out of a feeling of gratitude to the hand from which I received it, although I often laugh at the opinion which this lady appeared to entertain of my capacities for gallantry. Directly I had read the work, I desired to gain the friendship of the author. This inspiration was justified by the event. He is the only true friend I have had amongst men of letters.*

From that time, I felt confident that Madame de Beuzenval and Madame de Broglie, considering the interest they had shown in me, would not long leave me without resources, and I was not mistaken. Let me now speak of my introduction to Madame Dupin,[1] the consequences of which were more lasting.

As is well known, Madame Dupin was the daughter of Samuel Bernard and Madame Fontaine. There were three sisters, who might be called the three Graces – Madame de la Touche, who ran away to England with the Duke of Kingston; Madame d'Arty, the mistress and, what was more, the friend, the only true friend, of the Prince de Conti – a woman worthy to be adored as much for the gentleness and goodness of her charming character as for her pleasant wit and the unalterable cheerfulness of her disposition; lastly, Madame Dupin, the most beautiful of the three, and the only one of them who has never been reproached with any irregularity of conduct. She was the reward of the hospitality of M. Dupin, upon whom her mother bestowed her, together with a post as farmer-general of taxes and an immense fortune, out of gratitude for the kindly manner in which he had received her in his province. When I saw her for the first time, she was still one of the most beautiful women in Paris. She received me while she was dressing herself. Her arms were bare, her hair dishevelled, and her dressing-gown disarranged. Such an introduction was quite new to me; my poor

* I was so long and so firmly convinced of this, that it was to him that I intrusted the manuscript of my Confessions after my return to Paris. The distrustful Jean Jacques has never been able to believe in treachery and falsehood until he has been their victim. (R)

[1] [Dupin] See *Biographies*, p. 709.

head could not stand it; I was troubled and confused; in short, I fell madly in love with her.

My confusion did not appear to create a bad impression: she took no notice of it. She received the book and the author kindly, spoke to me about my system like one who knew all about it, sang, accompanied herself on the piano, made me stay to dinner, and gave me a seat at table by her side. This was more than enough to turn my head completely, and it did so. She gave me permission to call upon her, which permission I used and abused. I went to her house nearly every day, and dined there two or three times a week. I was dying to declare myself, but did not dare. Several reasons increased my natural shyness. The entry into a wealthy house was an open door to fortune; in my present position, I was unwilling to run the risk of shutting it against myself. Madame Dupin, with all her amiability, was serious and cold; I found nothing in her behaviour sufficiently encouraging to embolden me. Her house, which at that time was as brilliant as any in Paris, was the rendezvous of a society, which, if it had only been a little less numerous, would have contained the pick of all persons of distinction. She was fond of gathering around her all who made any stir in the world – great personages, men of letters, and handsome women. Only dukes, ambassadors and knights of the blue ribbon[1] were seen at her house. Madame la Princesse de Rohan, Madame la Comtesse de Forcalquier, Madame de Mirepoix, Madame de Brignolé and Lady Hervey might be considered her friends. M. de Fontenelle, M. de Fourmont, M. de Bernis, M. de Buffon, M. de Voltaire, the Abbé de Saint-Pierre and the Abbé Sallier were members of her circle and were invited to her table. If her reserved manner did not attract a large number of young people, the society which assembled at her house was the more select and, consequently, more imposing; and the poor Jean Jacques could not flatter himself with the idea of making a brilliant figure in the midst of such surroundings. I therefore did not venture to speak, but, being unable to keep silence any longer, I ventured to write. She

[1] Knights of the Holy Ghost, so called from the colour of the ribbon worn by them. But *cordons bleus* may simply mean here "distinguished persons" generally.

kept the letter for two days without saying anything to me about it. On the third day she returned it to me, with a few words of admonition, spoken in a tone of coldness which froze my blood. I tried to speak, the words died upon my lips; my sudden passion was extinguished with my hope, and, after a formal declaration of my love, I continued to visit her as before, without saying a word more, even with my eyes.

I believed that my folly was forgotten: I was wrong. M. de Francueil,[1] her step-son, was about the same age as myself and his step-mother. He was witty, and a man of handsome person, who might have looked high. It was reported that he aspired to the favours of Madame Dupin, perhaps simply because she had procured him a very ugly but at the same time very gentle wife, and lived in perfect harmony with both. M. de Francueil admired talent in others and cultivated it. Music, which he understood well, was a bond of union between us. I saw him frequently, and became intimate with him. Suddenly, he gave me to understand that Madame Dupin found my visits too frequent, and requested me to discontinue them. Such a compliment would not have been out of place when she gave me back my letter; but, eight or ten days after, without any further apparent reason for it, it seemed to me inopportune. What made the situation still more curious was, that I was made no less welcome at M. and Madame de Francueil's house than before. However, I went there less frequently; and I should have discontinued my visits altogether, had not Madame Dupin, actuated by another unforeseen caprice, begged me to undertake for eight or ten days the charge of her son, who was changing his tutor, and was left to himself during the interval. I spent these eight days in a state of torture, which nothing but the pleasure of obeying Madame Dupin could render endurable; for poor Chenonceaux already displayed the evil disposition which nearly brought dishonour upon his family, and caused his death in the Isle de Bourbon. As long as I was with him, I prevented him from doing harm to himself or others, and that was all; besides, it was no easy task, and I would not have undertaken it for eight days longer, even had Madame offered herself by way of payment.

[1] [Francueil] See *Biographies*, p. 710.

M. de Francueil conceived a friendship for me: we worked together, and began a course of chemistry with Rouelle.[1] In order to be near him, I left my Hôtel St. Quentin, and went to lodge at the Tennis Court in the Rue Verdelet, which adjoins the Rue Plâtrière, where M. Dupin lived. In consequence of a neglected cold, I was attacked by an inflammation of the lungs, of which I nearly died. During my youth I frequently suffered from inflammatory diseases, pleurisy, and, especially, quinsy, to which I was very subject, and others, of which I need not here give a list, which have all brought me sufficiently near death to familiarise me with its appearance. During the period of convalescence, I had time to reflect upon my condition and to lament my timidity, my weakness, and my indolence, which, in spite of the fire by which I felt myself inflamed, left me to vegetate in mental idleness at the gate of misery. The day before I fell ill, I had gone to see an opera by Royer, which was being played at the time, the name of which I have forgotten. In spite of my prejudice in favour of the talents of others, which has always made me so mistrustful of my own, I could not prevent myself from thinking the music feeble, cold, and wanting in originality. I even sometimes said to myself: It seems to me that I could do better than that. But the awe-inspiring idea I had formed of the composition of an opera, the importance which I heard specialists attach to such an undertaking, immediately discouraged me, and made me blush for having ventured to entertain the idea. Besides, where was I to find anyone who would be willing to supply me with the words and to take the trouble to cast them according to my liking? These ideas of music and an opera returned to me during my illness, and in my feverish delirium I composed songs, duets, and choruses. I am certain that I composed two or three pieces, *di prima intenzione*,[2] which perhaps would have been worthy of the admiration of the masters, if they had heard them performed. If it were only possible to keep a record of the dreams of one sick of the

[1] Guillaume-François Rouelle (1703–70) was Demonstrator at the Royal botanic garden. His lecture-courses on chemistry enjoyed an international reputation.
[2] Impromptu.

fever, what great and lofty things would sometimes be seen to result from his delirium!

The same subject occupied my attention also during my convalescence, but I was calmer. After long, and often involuntary, thinking about the matter, I determined to satisfy myself, and to attempt to compose an opera, words and music, without any assistance from others. This was not altogether my first attempt. At Chambéri I had composed a tragic opera, entitled *Iphis and Anaxarete*, which I had had the good sense to throw into the fire. At Lyons I had composed another, *The Discovery of the New World*, which, after I had read it to M. Bordes, the Abbé de Mably, the Abbé Trublet and others, I treated in the same manner, although I had already written the music of the prologue and the first act, and David, when he saw the music, had told me that it contained passages worthy of Buononcini.[1]

This time, before putting my hand to the work, I gave myself time to think over my plan. I sketched an epic ballet, with three different subjects, in three separate acts, each set to music of a different character, and taking for the subject of each the amours of a poet, I called the opera *Les Muses Galantes*. My first act, in the powerful style, was Tasso; the second, in the tender style, was Ovid; the third, entitled Anacreon, was intended to breathe the gaiety of the dithyramb. I first tried my skill on the first act, and devoted myself to it with a zeal which, for the first time, enabled me to taste the charm of enthusiasm in composition. One evening, just as I was going to enter the opera-house, I felt myself so overmastered and tormented by my ideas, that I put my money back into my pocket, ran home and shut myself in. I went to bed, having first drawn the curtains close to prevent the daylight entering, and there, entirely abandoning myself to the poetical and musical inspiration, in seven or eight hours I rapidly composed the greater part of the act. I may say that my love for the Princess of Ferrara — for I was Tasso for the moment — and my noble and haughty feelings in the presence

---

[1] There were three famous Italian musicians of this name, a father and his two sons. The younger son, who stayed some time in England, had the greatest reputation.

of her unjust brother, made me pass a night a hundred times more delightful than if I had spent it in the arms of the Princess herself. In the morning, only a very small portion of what I had composed remained in my head; but this little, almost obliter-ated by weariness and sleep, nevertheless bore evidence of the vigour of the whole, of which it only represented the remains.

This time I did not carry on my work to any great extent, as I was diverted from it by other matters. While I was attached to the house of Dupin, Madame de Beuzenval and Madame de Broglie, whom I still saw occasionally, had not forgotten me. The Comte de Montaigu, a captain in the guards, had just been appointed ambassador at Venice. He owed his ambassadorship to Barjac, to whom he assiduously paid court. His brother, the Chevalier de Montaigu, *gentilhomme de la manche*[1] to the Dauphin, was acquainted with these two ladies, and with the Abbé Alary, of the French Academy, whom I also saw sometimes. Madame de Broglie, knowing that the ambassador was looking out for a secretary, proposed me. We entered into negotiations. I asked fifty *louis*[2] as salary, which was little enough for a post in which it was necessary to keep up an appearance. He only offered a hundred *pistoles*,[2] and I was to pay my own travelling expenses. The proposal was ridiculous. We were unable to come to terms. M. de Francueil, who did his utmost to prevent me from going, in the end prevailed. I remained, and M. de Montaigu departed, taking with him another secretary, named M. Follau, who had been recommended to him at the Foreign Office. No sooner had they arrived at Venice than they quarrelled. Follau, seeing that he had to do with a madman, left him in the lurch; and M. de Montaigu, having no one but a young abbé named de Binis, who wrote under the secretary's instruction, and was not in a position to fill the place, was obliged to have recourse to me again. The chevalier, his brother, a man of intelligence, by giving me to understand that there were certain privileges connected with the post of secretary, succeeded in inducing me to accept the

[1] Noblemen who attended on French princes in their youth. They were called "Gentlemen of the sleeve" because etiquette forbade them to take their royal charge by the hand.
[2] A *louis* was then worth 24 francs, a *pistole* ten.

thousand francs. I received twenty *louis* for my travelling expenses, and set out.

[1743–1744.] – At Lyons, I should have liked to take the route by way of Mont Cenis, in order to pay a passing visit to my poor mamma; but I went down the Rhône, and took ship at Geneva for Toulon, on account of the war and for the sake of economy, and also in order to procure a passport from M. de Mirepoix, at that time commander in Provence, to whom I had been directed. M. de Montaigu, finding himself unable to do without me, wrote me letter after letter to hasten my journey. An incident delayed it.

It was the time of the plague at Messina.[1] The English fleet was anchored there, and visited the felucca on which I was. On our arrival at Genoa, after a long and tedious passage, we were subjected to a quarantine of twenty-one days. The passengers were allowed the choice of performing it on board or in the lazaretto, where we were warned that we should find nothing but the four walls, since there had been no time to furnish it. All chose the felucca except myself. The insupportable heat, the confined space, the impossibility of taking exercise, and the vermin on board, made me prefer the lazaretto at all hazards. I was conducted into a large two-storeyed building, absolutely bare, in which I found neither windows, nor table, nor bed, nor chair not even a stool to sit upon, nor a bundle of straw to lie on. They brought me my cloak, my travelling bag, and my two trunks; the heavy doors with huge locks were shut upon me, and I remained at liberty to walk as I pleased, from room to room and from storey to storey, finding everywhere the same solitude and the same bareness.

In spite of all this, I did not regret having chosen the lazaretto in preference to the felucca; and, like a second Robinson Crusoe, I began to make the same arrangements for my twenty-one days as I should have done for my whole life. At first, I had the amusement of hunting the lice which I had picked up in the felucca. When, after frequent changes of clothing and linen, I had at length succeeded in getting myself clean, I proceeded to furnish the room which I had chosen. I made myself a good

[1] The plague, brought to Messina from the Levant, cost 40,000 lives.

mattress out of my waistcoats and shirts, some sheets out of a number of napkins which I sewed together, a blanket out of my dressing-gown, a pillow out of my cloak rolled up. I made a seat of one of my trunks laid flat, and a table of the other set on end. I took out an inkstand and some paper; and arranged about a dozen books which I had by way of a library. In short, I made myself so comfortable that, with the exception of windows and curtains, I was almost as well lodged in this absolutely bare lazaretto as in my Tennis-Court in the Rue Verdelet. My meals were served with much ceremony. Two grenadiers, with fixed bayonets, accompanied them; the staircase was my dining-room, the landing did duty for a table, the bottom step for a seat, and, as soon as my dinner was served, they retired, after having rung a bell, to inform me that I might sit down to table. Between my meals, when I was not reading, writing, or working at my furnishing, I went for a walk in the Protestant cemetery, which served me as a courtyard, or I ascended a turret, from which I could see the ships entering and leaving the harbour. In this manner I spent fourteen days; and I could have spent the whole twenty-one there without a moment's weariness, had not M. de Jonville, the French ambassador, to whom I managed to send a letter saturated with vinegar, perfumed, and half-burnt, procured me a remission of eight days, which I spent at his house, where, I confess, I found myself more comfortably lodged than at the lazaretto. He treated me with very great kindness. Dupont, his secretary, was a good fellow, who introduced me to several houses, both in Genoa and in the country, where we were agreeably entertained. We became very good friends, and kept up a correspondence for a long time afterwards. I had a pleasant journey through Lombardy. I visited Milan, Verona, Brescia, and Padua, and at length reached Venice, where the ambassador was impatiently expecting me.

I found heaps of despatches from the Court and the other ambassadors, of which he had been unable to read the parts written in cypher, although he possessed the key. As I had never worked in any office, and had never in my life seen a government cypher, I was at first afraid of finding myself perplexed; but I found that nothing could be more simple, and in less than a week I had deciphered the whole, which certainly was not worth the trouble, for the embassy at Venice has seldom much to do, and, besides, the government would not have cared to intrust the most trifling negotiation to a man like M. de Montaigu. Until my arrival he had found himself in great difficulties, since he did not know how to dictate or to write legibly. I was very useful to him; he was aware of it, and treated me well. He had another reason for this. After the departure of his predecessor, M. de Froulay, who had gone out of his mind, the French consul, M. le Blond, had taken over the affairs of the embassy, and even after the arrival of M. de Montaigu, continued to manage them until he had familiarised the latter with the routine. M. de Montaigu, in his jealousy at the performance of his duties by another, although he himself was incapable of them, conceived an aversion to the consul, and, as soon as I arrived, deprived him of the functions of ambassadorial secretary, in order to hand them over to me. These functions being inseparable from the title, he told me to assume it. As long as I remained with him, he never sent anyone, except myself, under this name to the Senate or persons sent by it to confer with him, and really, it was very natural that he should prefer to have as ambassadorial secretary a person attached to himself than a consul or office-clerk appointed by the Court.

This made my situation tolerably agreeable and prevented his noblemen, who, like his pages and most of his people, were Italians, from disputing precedence with me in the house. I successfully made use of the authority attached to it to maintain his *droit de liste*, that is to say, the freedom of his quarter, against the attempts which were several times made to infringe it, and which his Venetian officers were unwilling or unable to resist. But I never allowed banditti to take refuge there, although I might thereby have gained considerable profit, which his Excellency would not have disdained to share.

He even presumed to lay claim to part of the perquisites of the secretaryship, which were called the *chancellerie*. Although it was in time of war, a number of passports had to be made out. For each of these passports a sequin[1] was paid to the secretary who

[1] Worth from 9 to 12 francs.

drew out and countersigned them. All my predecessors had been in the habit of demanding this sequin from Frenchmen and foreigners alike. This practice appeared to me unfair, and, although I was not a Frenchman, I abolished it in the case of the French; but I exacted my perquisite so rigorously from everyone else that, when the Marquis Scotti, the brother of the favourite of the Queen of Spain, had sent a messenger to me for a passport without my perquisite, I sent to ask him for it – a piece of audacity which the revengeful Italian did not forget. As soon as the reform which I had introduced in regard to the taxing of passports became known, nothing but crowds of pretended Frenchmen presented themselves in order to procure them, who, in a fearful jargon, called themselves Provençals, Picards and Burgundians. As I have a tolerably keen ear, I was rarely taken in, and I do not believe that a single Italian ever did me out of my sequin, or that a single Frenchman paid it. I was foolish enough to tell M. de Montaigu, who knew nothing about anything, of what I had done. The word sequin made him open his ears, and, without expressing any opinion upon the suppression of the fees for the French, he demanded that I should settle with him on account of the others, promising me other equivalent advantages in return. Indignant at this meanness, rather than influenced by feelings of self-interest, I scornfully rejected his proposal. He persisted; I grew warm. "No, monsieur," I said to him in a decided tone, "let your Excellency keep what belongs to you, and leave me what is mine; I will never give up a *sou*." When he saw that he could gain nothing by this means, he adopted another plan, and had the effrontery to say to me that since I drew the perquisites of his *chancellerie*, it was only fair that I should bear the expenses of it. I did not care to squabble about such a trifle, and from that time I provided my own ink, paper, sealing-wax, candles, ribbon and even the seal, which I had repaired, without receiving a farthing from him by way of reimbursement. This did not prevent me from making over a small share of the fees to the Abbé de Binis, who was a good fellow, and never attempted to claim it. If he was civil to me, I was equally straightforward with him, and we always got on very well together.

I found the performance of my duties less difficult than I had expected, seeing that I had no experience, and was associated with an ambassador who was equally inexperienced, whose ignorance and obstinacy, in addition, seemed to delight in thwarting everything that good sense and some little knowledge suggested to me as likely to be useful for the King's service and his own. His most sensible act was to form a connection with the Marquis de Mari, the Spanish ambassador, a clever and shrewd person, who could have led him by the nose if he had been so minded, but who, out of consideration for the common interests of the two Courts, usually gave him good advice, which was rendered useless by M. de Montaigu, who always intruded some of his own ideas when carrying it out. The only thing they had to do in common was to induce the Venetians to observe neutrality. The latter, who continually protested their faithful observance of it, nevertheless publicly supplied the Austrian troops with ammunition, and even with recruits, under the pretence that they were deserters. M. de Montaigu, who, I believe, desired to gain the goodwill of the Republic, in spite of my representations, invariably made me give assurances in all his despatches that there was no fear that the Venetians would ever violate the conditions of neutrality. The obstinacy and stupidity of this poor man made me every moment write and commit absurdities, of which I was obliged to be the agent since he so desired it, but which sometimes rendered the performance of my duties unendurable and even almost impracticable. For instance, he insisted that most of his despatches to the King and the Minister should be written in cypher, although neither the one nor the other contained anything at all which rendered such a precaution necessary. I represented to him that, between Friday, when the despatches from the Court arrived, and Saturday, when our own were sent off, there was not sufficient time for so much writing in cypher and the large amount of correspondence which I had to get ready for the same courier. He discovered an admirable plan: this was, to begin on Thursday to write the answers to the despatches which were due on the following day. This idea appeared to him so happy that, in spite of all I could say as to the impossibility and absurdity of carrying it out, I was obliged to resign myself to it. For the rest of the time that I remained with him, after having kept note of a few words uttered by him at random during the week, and of some trifling pieces of information which I picked up here and there, provided with these scanty materials, I never failed to bring him on Thursday morning the rough draft of the despatches which had to be sent off on Saturday, with the exception of a few hurried additions or corrections which were rendered necessary by the despatches which arrived on Friday, to which ours were intended to be the reply. Another very amusing whim of his, which made his correspondence indescribably ridiculous, was to send back each item of news to its source, instead of making it follow its course. He sent the news from the Court to M. Amelot, the news from Paris to M. de Maurepas, the news from Sweden to M. d'Havrincourt, the news from St. Petersburg to M. de la Chetardie; and sometimes he sent back to each of these the news which came from him, after I had slightly altered it. As he only glanced through the despatches to the Court, out of all that I put before him to sign, and signed those to the other ambassadors without reading them, this gave me a little more liberty to revise the latter in my own way, and at least I made the information cross. But it was impossible for me to give a sensible turn to the important despatches. I thought myself lucky when it did not occur to him to interlard them with some impromptu lines out of his own head, which obliged me to return, in order to transcribe, in all haste, the despatch adorned with this new piece of imbecility, which was obliged to be honoured with the cypher, otherwise he would not have signed it. I was often tempted, out of regard for his reputation, to cypher something different from what he had dictated, but feeling that nothing could justify such a breach of good faith, I let him rave at his own risk, content with frankly expressing my opinion, and, at any rate, fulfilling my duty while I was in his service.

This I always did with an honesty, a zeal, and a courage which deserved on his part a different reward from that which I received in the end. It was time that I should for once be what Heaven, who had bestowed upon me a happy disposition, and what the education, which I had received from the best women, and that which I had given myself, had intended me to be, and that I was then. Left to myself, without friends, without advisers, without experience, in a foreign land, in the service of a foreign nation, surrounded by a crowd of rascals, who, for the sake of their own interest and in order to remove the stumbling-block of a good example, urged me to imitate them – in spite of all this, far from doing anything of the kind, I faithfully served France, to whom I owed nothing, and, as was only right, her ambassador even more faithfully, in all that depended upon myself. Irreproachable in a position which was sufficiently open to observation, I deserved and obtained the esteem of the Republic and of all the ambassadors with whom we cor-responded, and the affection of all the French residents in Venice, not even excepting the consul, whom, to my regret, I supplanted in the performance of duties which I knew rightly belonged to him, and which brought me more trouble than pleasure.

M. de Montaigu, completely under the control of the Marquis Mari, who did not trouble himself about the details of his duty, neglected his own to such an extent, that the French who lived in Venice would never have known that there was a French ambassador resident in the city, had it not been for me. Being always dismissed without a hearing, whenever they sought his protection, they became disgusted, and none of them were ever seen in his suite or at his table, to which, in fact, he never invited them. I frequently took it upon myself to do what he ought to have done: I did all I could for the French who applied to him or me. In any other country I would have done more, but as, by reason of my official capacity, I could not see anyone who held any position, I was frequently obliged to refer to the consul, who, being settled in the country with his family, was obliged to be careful, which prevented him from doing as much as he would have liked. Sometimes, however, when he hung back and did not venture to speak, I was emboldened to take danger-ous steps, which generally proved successful. I remember one instance which even now makes me laugh. It would hardly be suspected that it is to me that the theatre-goers of Paris are indebted for Coralline and her sister Camille; but nothing is more true. Veronese, their father, had accepted an engagement for himself and his children in the Italian company, and, after having received 2,000 francs for travelling expenses, instead of starting for France, quietly entered into an engagement at the *théâtre de Saint-Luc** in Venice, where Coralline, although quite a child, attracted large audiences. M. le Duc de Gesvres, as lord high chamberlain, wrote to the ambassador to claim the father and daughter. M. de Montaigu handed me the letter, and simply said "See to this," without giving me any further instructions. I went to M. le Blond, and begged him to speak to the patrician to whom the theatre belonged, who was, I believe, a Giustiniani, and persuade him to dismiss Veronese, as being engaged in the King's service. Le Blond, who was not very eager to accept the commission, performed it badly. Giustiniani had recourse to various subterfuges, and Veronese was not discharged. I felt annoyed. It was the time of the Carnival. I took a domino and a mask and rowed to the palace Giustiniani. All who saw my gondola arrive with the ambassador's livery were astounded; such a thing had never been seen in Venice. I entered, and ordered myself to be announced as "a lady in a mask." As soon as I was introduced, I removed my mask and announced myself. The senator turned pale, and stood astounded. "Monsieur," I said to him in Venetian, "I regret to trouble your Excellency with this visit, but you have at your theatre a man named Veronese, who is engaged in the King's service, who has been claimed from you, but without success. I come to demand him in His Majesty's name." This brief speech took effect. No sooner had I left, than Giustiniani ran to give an account of the incident to the State Inquisitors, who reprimanded him severely. Veronese was dismissed the same day. I sent him a message that, if he did not start in a week, I would have him arrested, and he set out without delay.

On another occasion, by my own efforts and almost without anyone's assistance, I extricated the captain of a merchant ship from a difficulty. He was a Marseillais, named Olivet. I have forgotten the name of the ship. A quarrel had broken out

* I am not sure that it was not *Saint-Samuel.* I never can remember proper names. (R)

between his crew and the Slavonians in the service of the Republic. Acts of violence had been committed, and the vessel had been placed under such strict embargo that no one, with the exception of the captain, was allowed to go on board or leave it without permission. He appealed to the ambassador, who told him to go to the devil. Next he applied to the consul, who told him that it was not a commercial matter, and that he could not interfere. At his wits' end, he came to me. I represented to M. de Montaigu, that he ought to allow me to present a note on the subject to the Senate. I do not know whether he gave me permission, and whether I did so, but I well remember that, as my attempts proved ineffectual and the embargo was not removed, I resolved upon a course of action which proved successful. I inserted an account of the affair in a despatch to M. de Maurepas, although I had great difficulty in persuading M. de Montaigu to allow it to stand. I knew that our despatches, although they were hardly worth the trouble, were opened at Venice. I had proof of this: for I found passages from them reproduced word for word in the "Gazette" – a breach of faith of which I had vainly endeavoured to induce the ambassador to complain. My object, in speaking of this annoying circumstance in the despatch, was to make use of the curiosity of the Venetians, in order to frighten them and induce them to release the vessel; for if it had been necessary to wait for an answer from the Court upon the matter, the captain would have been ruined before it arrived. I did more. I went on board to question the crew. I took with me the Abbé Patizel, chancellor of the consulate, who only accompanied me with reluctance, for all these poor creatures were greatly afraid of offending the Senate. Being unable to go on board, on account of the prohibition, I remained in my gondola and drew up my report, interrogating all the crew in a loud voice, one after the other, and framing my questions in such a manner as to obtain replies which might be to their advantage. I wanted to induce Patizel to put the questions and draw up the report himself, which, in fact, was more his business than mine, but he refused. He never said a word, and would scarcely consent to sign the report after me. However, this somewhat bold course proved successful, and the vessel was released long before the minister's answer arrived. The captain wanted to make me a present. Without showing any displeasure, I slapped him on the shoulder and said, "Capitaine Olivet, do you think that a man who does not demand from the French the fee for passports, which he finds established as a right, is likely to sell them the protection of the King?" He asked me at least to dine on board. I accepted the invitation, and took with me Carrio, the secretary to the Spanish embassy, an amiable and talented man, who has since held a similar position at Paris, as well as that of *chargé d'affaires*, and with whom I had formed an intimacy, after the manner of our ambassadors.

I should have been happy if, when I was doing all the good I was able to do with the most absolute disinterestedness, I had known how to introduce sufficient order and accuracy into all my trifling affairs, so as to avoid being taken in myself and serving others at my own expense! But, in positions such as that which I held, in which the slightest mistakes are not without consequences, I exhausted all my attention in the effort not to commit any errors detrimental to my service. In all that concerned the essential duties of my office, I was to the last most regular and exact. With the exception of a few errors, which excessive haste caused me to make in cyphering, of which M. Amelot's clerks once complained, neither the ambassador nor anyone else had ever to reproach me with carelessness in the performance of any of my duties, which was remarkable for a man so careless and thoughtless as I am: but I was sometimes forgetful and careless in the conduct of special commissions which I undertook, and my love of justice always made me take the blame upon myself of my own accord, before anyone thought of making a complaint. I will merely mention one instance, which has reference to my departure from Venice, and of which I subsequently felt the effects in Paris.

Our cook, named Rousselot, had brought from France an old two-hundred-franc bill, which a wig-maker of his acquaintance had received from a Venetian noble, Zanetto Nani, in payment for some wigs supplied. Rousselot brought this bill to me, and begged me to see whether anything could be made out of it by arrangement. I knew, and he knew, also, that it is the regular practice of Venetian nobles never to pay debts contracted in a foreign country when once they have returned home; if any attempt is made to compel them to do so, they wear out the unhappy creditor with so many delays, and put him to such expense, that he becomes disheartened, and finally abandons his claim altogether, or accepts the most trifling composition. I asked M. le Blond to speak to Zanetto, who acknowledged the bill, but refused to pay. After a long struggle he promised to pay three sequins. When Le Blond took him the bill, the three sequins were not ready, and there was nothing for it but to wait. During the interval occurred my quarrel with M. de Montaigu and my retirement from his service. I left the ambassador's papers in perfect order, but Rousselot's bill could not be found. M. le Blond assured me that he had returned it to me. I knew his honourable character too well to doubt his word, but I was utterly unable to recall to mind what had become of the bill. As Zanetto had acknowledged the debt, I begged Le Blond to try and get the three sequins by giving him a receipt, or to induce him to renew the bill in duplicate; but Zanetto, when he knew that the bill was lost, refused to do either. I offered the three sequins to Rousselot out of my own pocket, in order to discharge the bill. He refused to take them, and told me to arrange the matter with the creditor in Paris, whose address he gave me. But the wig-maker, who knew what had happened, demanded his bill or payment in full. In my indignation, what would I not have given to find the accursed bill! I paid the two hundred francs myself, and that at a time when I was greatly pressed for money. Thus, the loss of the bill procured for the creditor payment of the debt in full, whereas if, unfortunately for him, it had been found, he would have experienced a difficulty in getting the ten crowns promised by his Excellency Zanetto Nani.

The capacity for my employment, which I believed I possessed, made my work agreeable; and, with the exception of the society of my friend Carrio, and the excellent Altuna (of whom I shall speak presently), the very innocent recreations of the theatre and the Piazza di San Marco, and a few visits which we nearly always paid together, I found my only pleasure in the performance of my duties. Although my work was not very laborious, especially as I had the assistance of the Abbé de Binis, I was always tolerably busy, since our correspondence was very extensive and war was going on. Every day I worked for the greater part of the morning, and on post-days sometimes until midnight. I devoted the remainder of my time to the study of the profession which I was entering upon, and in which I hoped, in consequence of my successful *début*, to be appointed to a more lucrative post. In fact, there was only one opinion concerning me, beginning with that of the ambassador, who was thoroughly satisfied with my services, and never made a single complaint. His subsequent rage arose from the fact that, finding that my complaints were not listened to, I demanded my discharge. The ambassadors and ministers of the King, with whom we were in correspondence, paid him compliments upon the efficiency of his secretary, which ought to have been flattering to him, but which produced quite the contrary effect in his perverse head. One compliment, in particular, which he received on a special occasion, he never forgave me. The circumstances deserve explanation.

He was so little capable of imposing any constraint upon himself, that even on Saturday, the day on which nearly all the couriers left, he could not wait till the work was finished before going out; and, incessantly urging me to finish the despatches for the King and the ministers, he hurriedly signed them and ran off I know not whither, generally leaving the rest of the letters unsigned. This obliged me, when there was nothing but news, to throw them into the form of a bulletin; but when it was a question of affairs relating to the service of the King, someone was obliged to sign them, and I did so. I did this in the case of an important despatch, which we had just received from M. Vincent, the King's *chargé d'affaires* at Vienna. This was at the time when the Prince de Lobkowitz was marching to Naples, and the Comte de Gages carried out that memorable retreat, the finest military achievement of the century, which attracted too little attention in Europe. The information that reached us was, that a man, of whom M. Vincent sent us the description, was setting out from Vienna, with the intention of secretly passing by way of Venice to the Abruzzi, in order to bring about a rising of the people in that quarter, on the approach of the Austrians. In the absence of M. de Montaigu, who took no interest in anything, I sent on to M. le Marquis de l'Hôpital this information, which was so opportune, that it is perhaps to the much-abused Jean Jacques that the house of Bourbon owes the preservation of the kingdom of Naples.

The Marquis de l'Hôpital, as was proper, thanked his colleague, and spoke to him about his secretary and the service which he had just rendered to the common cause. The Comte de Montaigu, who had to reproach himself with carelessness in the matter, thought that he saw in this a reproof intended for himself, and spoke to me somewhat angrily about it. I had had occasion to do the same for the Comte de Castellane, ambassador at Constantinople, although in a less important matter. As there was no other communication with Constantinople except the couriers sent by the Senate, from time to time, to its Baile,[1] notice of the departure of these couriers was given to the French ambassador, in order that he might take the opportunity of writing to his colleague, if he thought fit. This notice was usually given a day or two beforehand, but so little was thought of M. de Montaigu, that it was considered sufficient to send to him an hour or two before the courier's departure, merely for form's sake, so that I frequently had to write the despatch in his absence. M. de Castellane, in replying, made honourable mention of me. M. de Jonville, at Genoa, did the same: and each token of their good opinion of me became a fresh cause for grievance.

I confess that I did not try to avoid the opportunity of making myself known, but neither did I seek it unbecomingly. It appeared to me only fair that I should look for the natural reward of valuable services, that is to say, the esteem of those who are in a position to estimate and reward them. I do not know whether my assiduity in the fulfilment of my duties afforded the ambassador a legitimate reason for complaint, but I certainly know that it was the only complaint that he uttered up to the day of our separation.

[1] The title of the Venetian ambassador at Constantinople.

His house, which he had never put upon a proper footing, was always full of rabble. The French were badly treated; the Italians had the upper hand; and, even amongst them, those good servants who had long been attached to the embassy were all rudely discharged, amongst them his first gentleman, who had already held that position with the Comte de Fronlay, whose name, I believe, was the Comte Peati, or something very like it. The second gentleman, whom he had chosen himself, was a bandit from Mantua, by name Domenico Vitali, whom the ambassador intrusted with the care of his house, and who, by dint of toadying and sordid stinginess, gained his confidence and became his favourite, to the detriment of the few honest persons who were still around him, and of the secretary who was at their head. The honest eye of an upright man always makes rogues uneasy. This alone would have been enough to make him hate me, but there was yet another reason for his hatred, which aggravated it considerably. I must state what this reason was, and I am willing to be condemned if I was wrong.

According to long-established custom, the ambassador had a box at each of the five theatres. Every day at dinner he named the theatre to which he intended to go; I had the next choice, and his gentlemen disposed of the other boxes between them. As I went out, I took the key of the box which I had chosen. One day, as Vitali was not there, I commissioned the lackey who attended upon me to bring me my key to a house which I named to him. Vitali, instead of sending me the key, said that he had disposed of it. I was the more incensed, as the footman gave me an account of his errand before everybody. In the evening, Vitali tried to utter a few words of apology, to which I refused to listen. "Sir," said I to him, "you will come to-morrow, at a stated time, to the house in which I received the insult, and will make your apologies to me in the presence of those who witnessed it; otherwise, the day after to-morrow, whatever happens, I declare that either you or I will leave this house." My resolute tone inspired him with respect. He came to the house at the appointed time, and apologised publicly, in an abject manner worthy of him; but he laid his plans at leisure, and, while cringing to me in public, in secret he worked so successfully in true Italian fashion, that, although he could not persuade the ambassador to dismiss me, he obliged me to resign my position myself.

Such a wretch was certainly not capable of understanding me, but he knew enough of me to serve his own ends. He knew that I was good-natured and mild to excess in enduring involuntary injustice, proud and hasty when insulted with malice afore-thought, a lover of decency and dignity on proper occasions, and no less exacting in the respect that was due to me, than careful in showing to others the respect that I owed to them. He resolved to take advantage of this to disgust me, and succeeded. He turned the house upside down, and banished from it the regularity, subordination, order, and decency, which I had endeavoured to maintain there. An establishment without a woman at its head requires a somewhat severe discipline, in order to introduce the rule of decency which is inseparable from dignity. He soon made ours a house of dissoluteness and debauchery, a haunt of rogues and profligates. Having procured the dismissal of the second gentleman, he bestowed his place upon another pimp like himself, who kept a public brothel at the "Maltese Cross"; and these two rascals, who understood each other perfectly, were as shameless as they were insolent. With the exception of the ambassador's room, and even that was not in very good order, there was not a corner in the house endur-able for a respectable man.

As his Excellency did not take supper, the gentlemen and myself had a special meal, of which the Abbé de Binis and the pages also partook. In the commonest beershop one would have been served with more cleanliness and decency, and provided with cleaner table-linen and better food. We had nothing but one small dirty tallow candle, pewter plates, and iron forks. I might have endured what went on in private; but I was deprived of my gondola. Of all the ambassadorial secretaries, I was the only one who was obliged to hire one or to go on foot; and I was only attended by his Excellency's servants when I went to the Senate. Besides, all that went on in the house was known in the city. All the ambassador's officials cried out loudly. Domenico, who was the sole cause of all, cried the loudest, since he knew well that the indecent manner in which we were treated affected me more than all the rest. I was the only person in the house who said nothing outside, but I complained loudly to the ambassador, not only of what went on, but also of himself; and he, being secretly urged on by his evil genius, daily put some new affront upon me. Being obliged to spend a considerable sum in order to keep on a level with my colleagues, and to live in a manner befitting my position, I could not save a *sou* out of my salary; and, when I asked him for money, he talked to me of his esteem and of his confidence in me, as if that ought to have been enough to fill my purse and provide for all my wants.

These two bandits at length succeeded in completely turning their master's head, which was already weak enough. They ruined him by continual dealings in old curiosities, and induced him to conclude bargains, in which he was always taken in, but which they persuaded him were marvels of sharpness. They made him rent a palace on the Brenta for twice as much as it was worth, and shared the surplus with the proprietor. The rooms were inlaid with mosaic, and adorned with pillars and columns of beautiful marble, after the fashion of the country. M. de Montaigu had all this covered with a magnificent fir panelling, for the simple reason that the rooms in Paris are wainscoted in this manner. For a similar reason, he was the only ambassador in Venice who deprived his pages of their swords and his footmen of their sticks. Such was the man who, perhaps for the same reason, took a dislike to me, solely because I served him faithfully.

I patiently endured his neglect, his brutality and ill-treatment as long as I thought I saw in it only bad temper, and no signs of hatred; but as soon as I saw that the design had been formed of depriving me of the consideration I deserved for my faithful services, I determined to resign my post. The first proof of his ill-will which I received was on the occasion of a dinner, which he intended to give to the Duke of Modena and his family, who were at Venice, at which he informed me that I could not be present. I answered, with some annoyance but without anger, that, as I had the honour of dining there every day, if the Duke of Modena, when he arrived, required that I should not be present, it would be a point of honour for his Excellency and a duty for me, not to yield to his request. "What!" said he, in a rage, "does my secretary, who is not even a gentleman, claim to dine with a Sovereign, when my gentlemen do not?" "Yes, sir," I replied; "the post with which your Excellency has honoured me confers such high rank upon me, as long as I hold it, that I even take precedence of your gentlemen or those who call themselves such, and I am admitted where they cannot appear. You are aware that, on the day when you make your public entry, I am required by etiquette and immemorial custom to follow you in state robes, and have the honour of dining with you in the palace of St. Mark; and I do not see why a man, who is allowed and required to dine in public with the Doge and Senate of Venice, should not be allowed to dine in private with the Duke of Modena." Although my argument was unanswerable, the ambassador would not give in; but we had no occasion to renew the dispute, for the Duke of Modena did not come to dinner.

From that time he never ceased to cause me annoyance, and to treat me with injustice, by doing his utmost to deprive me of the trifling privileges attached to my post, in order to hand them over to his dear Vitali; and I am sure that, if he had dared to send him to the Senate in my place, he would have done so. He usually employed the Abbé de Binis to write his private letters in his study; he commissioned him to write an account of the affair of Capitaine Olivet to M. de Maurepas, in which, without making any mention of me, who alone had interfered in the matter, he even deprived me of the honour of the report, of which he sent him a duplicate, and gave the credit of it to Patizel, who had not said a single word. He wanted to annoy me and please his favourite, without, however, getting rid of me. He felt that it would not be so easy to find a successor to me as to M. Follau, who had already spread abroad what kind of a man he was. A secretary who knew Italian was absolutely necessary to him, on account of the answers from the Senate; one who was able to write all his despatches, and manage all his affairs without his interference; who combined with the merit of serving him faithfully the meanness of playing the agreeable to his contempt-ible gentlemen. He accordingly desired to keep me and mortify me at the same time, by keeping me far from my country and his own, without money to return; and he would perhaps have succeeded if he had set about it more prudently. But Vitali, who had other views, and wanted to force me to make up my mind, succeeded. As soon as I saw that I was wasting my trouble, that the ambassador regarded my services as crimes, instead of being grateful to me for them, that I had nothing more to look for, as long as I was with him, but annoyance in the house and injustice outside, and that, amidst the general discredit which he had brought upon himself, the harm he attempted to do me might injure me more than his good offices could benefit me, I made up my mind and asked permission to resign, giving him time, however, to provide himself with another secretary. Without saying yes or no, he continued to behave as before. Seeing that matters did not improve, and that he took no steps to find another secretary, I wrote to his brother and, telling him my reasons, begged him to obtain my dismissal from his Excellency, adding that, in any case, it was impossible for me to remain. I waited for some time, but received no answer. I was beginning to feel greatly embarrassed, when the ambassador at length received a letter from his brother. It must have been very outspoken, for, although he was subject to most violent outbreaks of rage, I never saw him so furious before. After a torrent of horrible abuse, not knowing what else to say, he accused me of having sold the key of his cypher. I began to laugh, and asked him, scoffingly, if he thought that there was in all Venice a man who would be fool enough to give him a crown for it. This answer made him foam with rage. He made a pretence of calling his servants, as he said, to throw me out of the window. Until then I had been very quiet, but, at this threat, anger and indignation got the mastery of me in my turn. I rushed to the door, and, having drawn the bolt which fastened it inside, I gravely went up to him and said, "No, Monsieur le Comte, your people shall not interfere in this matter; be good enough to allow it to be settled between ourselves." This action on my part and my demeanour calmed him at once; his whole attitude betrayed surprise and alarm. When I saw that he had recovered from his frenzy, I bade him adieu in a few words, and then, without waiting for him to answer, I opened the door, left the room, and walked quietly through the ante-room in the midst of his people, who rose as usual, and who, I really believe, would rather have assisted me against him than him against me. Without going up to my room again, I immediately went downstairs, and left the palace, never to enter it again.

I went straight to M. le Blond to tell him what had taken place. He was not much surprised; he knew the man. He kept me to dinner. The dinner, though impromptu, was splendid. All the French in Venice who were of any importance were present. There was not a single person at the ambassador's. The consul related my case to the company. At the recital, all cried out with one voice, but not in favour of his Excellency. He had not settled my account, and had not given me a *sou*; and, reduced to a few *louis* which I had in my purse, I did not know how I was to pay the expenses of my return. Everyone offered me the use of his purse. I borrowed twenty sequins from M. le Blond, and the same amount from M. de Saint-Cyr, with whom, next after him, I was most intimate. I thanked the others, and, until I left, I lodged with the chancellor of the consulate, in order to prove to the public, that the nation had no share in the unjust behaviour of the ambassador. The latter, enraged at seeing me fêted in my misfortune, while he, in spite of being an ambassador, was neglected, lost his head altogether and behaved like a madman. He so far forgot himself as to present a written memorial to the Senate demanding my arrest. The Abbé de Binis having given me a hint of this, I decided to remain another fortnight, instead of leaving on the second day, as I had intended. My conduct had been seen and approved. I was universally esteemed. The Seigneurie did not even condescend to reply to the ambassador's extravagant memorial, and informed me, through the consul, that I could remain in Venice as long as I pleased, without troubling myself about the vagaries of a madman. I continued to visit my friends. I went to take leave of the Spanish ambassador, who received me very kindly, and of the Comte de Finochietti, the Neapolitan minister, whom I did not find at home. I wrote to him, however, and received a most courteous reply from him. At last I set out, and, in spite of my difficulties, I left no other debts than the loans of which I have just spoken, and about fifty crowns, which I owed to a merchant named Morandi, which Carrio undertook to pay, and which I have never returned to him, although we have often seen each other since then. As for the two loans, I punctually repaid them as soon as it was in my power to do so.[1]

I must not leave Venice without saying a few words about the famous amusements of this city, or, at least, the small share of them which I enjoyed during my stay. The reader has seen how little I sought after the pleasures of youth, or, at least, those which are so called. My tastes underwent no alteration at Venice, but my occupations, which would have prevented me from seeking them, gave a greater relish to the simple pleasures which I allowed myself. Foremost and most delightful of these was the company of persons of distinction, such as MM. le Blond, de Saint-Cyr, Carrio, Altuna, and a Forlan[2] gentleman, whose name, to my great regret, I have forgotten, and whose amiability I cannot recall without emotion: of all the men whose acquaintance I have ever made, he was the one whose heart most resembled my own. We had also become intimate with two or three witty and well-educated Englishmen, who were as passionately fond of music as ourselves. All these gentlemen had their wives or female friends or mistresses; the latter were nearly all women of education, at whose houses music and dancing took place. A little gambling also went on; but our lively tastes, talents, and fondness for the theatre rendered this amusement insipid. Gambling is only the resource of those who do not know what to do with themselves. I had brought with me from Paris the national prejudice against Italian music, but Nature had also endowed me with that fine feeling against which such prejudices are powerless. I soon conceived for this music the passion which it inspires in those who are capable of judging it correctly. When I heard the barcarolles,[3] I discovered that I had never heard singing before; and I soon became so infatuated

---

[1]   There is a mass of detail on this quarrel in surviving letters from Montaigu and Rousseau and in the Venetian archives.

[2]   *i.e.*, from Frioul.

[3]   Gondoliers' songs. The gondoliers were given free seats at the opera-house and theatres.

with the opera that, tired of chattering, eating, and playing in the boxes, when I only wanted to listen, I often stole away from the company in order to find another seat, where, quite alone, shut up in my box, in spite of the length of the performance, I abandoned myself to the pleasure of enjoying it, without being disturbed, until it was over. One day, at the theatre of St. Chrysostom, I fell asleep more soundly than I could have done in my bed. The noisy and brilliant airs failed to wake me; but it would be impossible to describe the delightful sensation produced upon me by the sweet harmony and angelic music of the air which finally aroused me. What an awaking! what rapture! what ecstasy, when I opened, at the same moment, my eyes and my ears! My first idea was to believe myself in Paradise. This delightful piece, which I still recollect, and which I shall never forget while I live, began as follows:

> "Conservami la bella
> Che si m' accende il cor."

I wanted to have the music. I procured it and kept it for a long time, but it was not the same on paper as in my memory. The notes were certainly the same, but it was not the same thing. This divine air can only be performed in my head, as it was really performed at the time when it awoke me.

The music, which, according to my taste, is far superior to that of the opera, and which has not its like, either in Italy or the rest of the world, is that of the *scuole*. The *scuole* are charitable institutions, founded for the education of young girls without means, who are subsequently portioned by the Republic either for marriage or for the cloister. Amongst the accomplishments cultivated in these young girls music holds the first place. Every Sunday, in the church of each of these *scuole*, during Vespers, motets are performed with full chorus and full orchestra, composed and conducted by the most famous Italian masters, executed in the latticed galleries by young girls only, all under twenty years of age. I cannot imagine anything so voluptuous, so touching as this music. The abundant art, the exquisite taste of the singing, the beauty of the voices, the correctness of the execution – everything in these delightful concerts contributes to produce an impression which is certainly not "good style," but against which I doubt whether any man's heart is proof. Carrio and myself never missed going to Vespers in the Mendicanti,[1] and we were not the only ones. The church was always full of amateurs; even operatic singers came to form their taste after these excellent models. What drove me to despair was the confounded gratings, which only allowed the sounds to pass through, and hid from sight the angels of beauty, of whom they were worthy. I could talk of nothing else. While speaking about it one day, at M. le Blond's, he said, "If you are so curious to see these young girls, it is easy to satisfy you. I am one of the directors of the institution. I will take you to a collation with them." I did not give him a moment's peace until he kept his word. When we entered the saloon which confined these longed-for beauties I felt an amorous trembling, which I had never before experienced. M. le Blond presented these famous singers to me one after the other, whose names and voices were all that I knew about them. Come, Sophie . . . she was a horrible fright. Come, Cattina . . . she had only one eye. Come, Bettina . . . she was disfigured by small-pox. Hardly one of them was without some noticeable defect. The cruel wretch laughed at my painful surprise. Two or three, however, appeared passable; they only sang in the chorus. I was in despair. During the collation we teased them, and they became quite lively. Ugliness does not exclude certain graces, which I found they possessed. I said to myself, they could not sing so delightfully without soul; they must possess one. At last, the feeling with which I regarded them was so altered that I left the room almost in love with all these ugly creatures. I hardly ventured to return to their Vespers: I had reason to feel that the danger was over. I continued to find their singing delicious, and their voices lent such a fictitious charm to their faces that, as long as they were singing, I persisted in thinking them beautiful, in spite of my eyes.

Music in Italy costs so little, that it is not worth while for anyone who is fond of it to deprive himself of it. I hired a piano,

[1] One of the four Venetian *ospitali*. These establishments had *scuole* where young women were taught music and singing.

and for a crown I engaged four or five symphonists to come to my rooms, with whom, once a week, I practised the pieces which had afforded me most pleasure at the opera. I also made them try some symphonies from my *Muses galantes*. Either because they really pleased, or because he wanted to flatter me, the ballet-master of St. John Chrysostom asked me for two of them, which I had the pleasure of hearing performed by this admirable orchestra; they were danced by a little Bettina, a pretty and amiable girl, who was kept by one of our friends, a Spaniard named Fagoaga, at whose house we often spent the evening.

As for women, it is not in a city like Venice that a man abstains from them. Have you no confessions to make on this point? someone may ask. Yes, I have something to tell, and I will make this confession as frankly as the rest.

I have always disliked common prostitutes; however, at Venice there was nothing else within my reach, since my position excluded me from most of the distinguished houses in the city. M. le Blond's daughters were very amiable, but very reserved: besides, I had too much respect for their father and mother even to think of desiring them.

A young person named Mademoiselle de Catanéo, daughter of the agent of the King of Prussia, would have been more to my taste; but Carrio was in love with her – even marriage had been talked of. He was well-to-do, while I had nothing; his salary was a hundred *louis*, mine only a hundred *pistoles*: and, not to mention that I had no wish to poach on a friend's preserves, I knew that a man had no right to enter upon affairs of gallantry with a poorly-filled purse, wherever he was, especially in Venice. I had not lost the pernicious habit of satisfying my wants, and, being too much occupied to feel keenly those which the climate causes, I lived nearly a year in Venice as chastely as I had lived in Paris, and I left it at the end of eighteen months, without having had anything to do with women, except twice, in consequence of special opportunities, which I will mention.

The first was provided for me by that honourable gentleman Vitali, some time after the formal apology which I forced him to make to me. At table, the conversation turned upon the amusements of Venice. The company reproached me for my indifference to the most piquant of all, and extolled the graceful manners of the Venetian women, declaring that they had not their equals in the world. Domenico said that I must make the acquaintance of the most amiable of all; he expressed himself ready to introduce me, and assured me that I should be delighted with her. I began to laugh at this obliging offer, and Count Peati, an old man of high character, said, with greater frankness than I should have expected from an Italian, that he considered me too sensible to allow myself to be taken to see a woman by my enemy. In fact, I had neither the intention nor the inclination; but, in spite of this, by one of those inconsistencies which I can hardly understand myself, I ended by allowing myself to be dragged there, against my inclination, heart and reason, and even against my will, simply from weakness and shame of exhibiting mistrust, and, in the language of the country, *per non parer troppo coglione.*[1] The *padoana*, to whose house we went, was good-looking, even handsome, but her beauty was not of the kind that pleased me. Domenico left me with her. I sent for *sorbetti*, asked her to sing to me, and, at the end of half an hour, I put a ducat on the table, and prepared to go. But she was so singularly scrupulous, that she refused to take it without having earned it, and, with equally singular foolishness, I satisfied her scruples. I returned to the palace, feeling so convinced that I had caught some complaint, that the first thing I did was to send for the physician and ask him to give me some medicine. Nothing can equal the feeling of depression from which I suffered for three weeks, without any real inconvenience, or the appearance of any symptoms to justify it. I could not imagine that it was possible to get off unscathed from the embraces of the *padoana*. Even the physician had the greatest trouble imaginable to re-assure me. He only succeeded by persuading me that I was formed in a peculiar manner, which lessened the chance of infection; and, although I have perhaps exposed myself to this risk less than any other man, the fact that I have never suffered in this respect seems to prove that the physician was right. However, this belief has never made me imprudent; and, if

[1] In order not to appear too great a blockhead.

Nature has really bestowed this advantage upon me, I can declare that I have never abused it.

My other adventure, although with a woman also, was of a very different kind, both in its origin and consequences. I had mentioned that Capitaine Olivet invited me to dinner on board, and that I took with me the secretary of the Spanish embassy. I expected a salute of cannon. The crew received us, drawn up in line, but not a grain of priming was burnt. This mortified me greatly, on account of Carrio, who I saw was a little annoyed at it. Certainly, on merchant ships, people by no means as important as ourselves were received with a salute of cannon, and besides, I thought that I had deserved some mark of distinction from the captain. I was unable to conceal my feelings, a thing which I have never been able to do; and although the dinner was a very good one, and Olivet did the honours admirably, I began it in an ill-humour, eating little, and speaking still less.

When the first health was drunk, I expected at least a volley. Nothing of the kind! Carrio, who read my thoughts, laughed to see me sulking like a child. Before the dinner was half over, I saw a gondola approaching. "Faith!" said the captain to me, "take care of yourself; here comes the enemy." I asked him what he meant, and he answered with a jest. The gondola lay to, and I saw a dazzlingly beautiful young woman step out, coquettishly dressed and very nimble. In three bounds she was in the cabin and seated at my side, before I perceived that a place had been laid for her. She was a brunette of twenty years at the most, as charming as she was lively. She could only speak Italian. Her accent alone would have been enough to turn my head. While eating and chatting, she fixed her eyes upon me, and then, exclaiming, "O holy Virgin! O my dear Brémond, how long is it since I saw you!" she threw herself into my arms, pressed her lips close to mine, and squeezed me almost to suffocation. Her large, black, Oriental eyes darted shafts of fire into my heart, and although surprise at first caused me some disturbance, my amorous feelings so rapidly overcame me that, in spite of the spectators, the fair enchantress was herself obliged to restrain me. I was intoxicated, or rather delirious. When she saw me worked up to the pitch she desired, she moderated her caresses, but not her liveliness; and, when she thought fit to explain to us the true or pretended reason of her forwardness, she told us that I was the very image of one M. de Brémond, a director of the Tuscan custom-house; that she had been, and still was, madly in love with him; that she had left him, because she was a fool; that she took me in his place; that she wanted to love me, since it suited her; that, in like manner, I must love her as long as it suited her, and, when she left me in the lurch, bear it patiently, as her dear Brémond had done. No sooner said than done. She took possession of me as if I had belonged to her, gave me her gloves to take care of, her fan, her veil, and her headgear. She ordered me to go here and there, to do this and that, and I obeyed. She told me to send back her gondola, because she wanted to use mine, and I did so. She told me to change places with Carrio, because she had something to say to him, and I did so. They talked together for a long time in a low voice, and I did not disturb them. She called me: I went back to her. "Listen, Zanetto," she said to me; "I do not want to be loved in French fashion; indeed, it would lead to no good. The moment you are tired, go. But do not stop half-way, I warn you." After dinner we went to see the glass manufactory at Murano. She bought several little knicknacks, which without ceremony she left us to pay for; but she everywhere gave away in gratuities much more than we spent altogether. From the carelessness with which she threw away her money and allowed us to throw away our own, it was easy to see that she attached no value to it. When she demanded payment for herself, I believe it was more out of vanity than greed. She was flattered by the price men put upon her favours.

In the evening, we escorted her back to her apartments. While we were talking, I noticed two pistols on her dressing-table. "Ah!" said I, taking one up, "here is a beauty-spot box of new manufacture; may I ask what it is used for? I know you have other weapons, which fire better than these." After some pleasantries of the same kind, she said, with an ingenuous pride which made her still more charming, "When I am good-natured to those for whom I have no affection, I make them pay for the weariness which they cause me; nothing can be fairer; but, although I endure their caresses, I will not endure their insults, and I shall not miss the first man who shall show himself wanting in respect to me."

When I left her, I made an appointment for the next day. I did not keep her waiting. I found her in *vestito di confidenza*, which is only known in southern countries, and which I will not amuse myself with describing, although I remember it only too well. I will only say that her ruffles and tucker were edged with a silk border, ornamented with rose-coloured bows, which appeared to me to set off a very beautiful skin. I discovered later that this was the fashion at Venice; and the effect is so charming, that I am surprised that it has never been introduced into France. I had no idea of the pleasures which awaited me. I have spoken of Madame de Larnage, in the transport which the recollection of her sometimes still awakens in me; but how old, ugly, and cold she was, compared to my Zulietta! Do not attempt to imagine the charms and graces of this bewitching girl; you would be far from the truth. The young virgins of the cloister are not so fresh, the beauties of the harem are not so lively, the houris of paradise are not so piquant. Never was such sweet enjoyment offered to the heart and senses of mortal man. Ah, if I had only known how to taste of it in its full completeness, at least, for a single moment! I tasted it, it is true, but without charm; I dulled all its delights; I killed them, as it were, intentionally. No! Nature has not created me for enjoyment. She has put into my wretched head the poison of that ineffable happiness, the desire for which she has planted in my heart.

If there is one circumstance in my life which well describes my character, it is that which I am about to relate. The vividness with which at this moment I recall the purpose of my book will, in this place, make me forget the false feeling of delicacy which would prevent me from fulfilling it. Whoever you may be, who desire to know the inmost heart of a man, have the courage to read the next two or three pages; you will become thoroughly acquainted with Jean Jacques Rousseau.

I entered the room of a courtesan as if it had been the sanctuary of love and beauty; in her person I thought I beheld its divinity. I should never have believed that, without respect and esteem, I could have experienced the emotions with which she inspired me. No sooner had I recognised, in the preliminary familiarities, the value of her charms and caresses than, for fear of losing the fruit of them in advance, I was anxious to make haste to pluck it. Suddenly, in place of the flame which consumed me, I felt a deathly chill run through my veins; my legs trembled under me; and, feeling ready to faint, I sat down and cried like a child.

Who would guess the reason of my tears, and the thoughts that passed through my head at that moment? I said to myself: This object, which is at my disposal, is the masterpiece of nature and love; its mind and body, every part of it perfect; she is as good and generous as she is amiable and beautiful. The great ones of the world ought to be her slaves; sceptres ought to be laid at her feet. And yet she is a miserable street-walker, on sale to everybody; a merchant captain has the disposal of her; she comes and throws herself at my head, mine, although she knows that I am poor, while my real merits, being unknown to her, can have no value in her eyes. In this there is something incomprehensible. Either my heart deceives me, dazzles my senses, and makes me the dupe of a worthless slut, or some secret defect, with which I am unacquainted, must destroy the effect of her charms, and render her repulsive to those who would otherwise fight for the possession of her. I began to look for this defect with a singular intensity of mind, and it never occurred to me that the possible consequences of having anything to do with her might possibly have something to do with it. The freshness of her skin, her brilliant complexion, her dazzlingly white teeth, the sweetness of her breath, the general air of cleanliness about her whole person, so completely banished this idea from my mind, that, being still in doubt as to my condition since my visit to the *padoana*, I rather felt qualms of conscience as to whether I was in sufficiently good health for her, and I am quite convinced that I was not deceived in my confidence.

These well-timed reflections so agitated me that I shed tears. Zulietta, for whom this was certainly quite a novel sight under the circumstances, was astounded for a moment; but, after having walked round the room and looked in her glass, she understood, and my eyes convinced her, that dislike had nothing to do with this whimsical melancholy. It was an easy matter for her to drive it away, and to efface the slight feeling of shame; but, at the moment when I was ready to sink exhausted upon a bosom, which seemed to permit for the first time the contact of a man's hand and mouth, I perceived that she had only one nipple. I smote my forehead, looked attentively and thought I saw that this nipple was not formed like the other. I immediately began to rack my brains for the reason of such a defect, and, feeling convinced that it was connected with some remarkable natural imperfection, by brooding so long over this idea, I saw, as clear as daylight, that, in the place of the most charming person that I could picture to myself, I only held in my arms a kind of monster, the outcast of nature, of mankind and of love. I pushed my stupidity so far as to speak to her about this defect. At first she took it as a joke, and said and did things in her frolicsome humour, which were enough to make me die of love; but as I was unable to conceal from her that I still felt a certain amount of uneasiness, she at last blushed, adjusted her dress, got up, and, without saying a word, went and seated herself at the window. I wanted to sit by her side, but she moved, sat down on a couch, got up immediately afterwards, and, walking about the room and fanning herself, said to me in a cold and disdainful tone, "Zanetto, lascia le donne, et studia la matematica."[1]

Before I left, I begged her to grant me another interview on the following day. She postponed it till the third day, adding, with an ironical smile, that I must want rest. I spent this interval very ill at ease, my heart full of her charms and graces, sensible of my folly, with which I reproached myself, regretting the moments which I had so ill employed, which it had only rested with myself to make the sweetest moments of my life, awaiting with the most lively impatience the time when I might repair their loss, but, nevertheless, still uneasy, in spite of myself, how I should reconcile the perfections of this adorable girl with her unworthy manner of life. I ran – I flew to her at the appointed hour. I do not know whether her ardent temperament would have been more satisfied with this visit. Her pride at least would have been flattered: and I enjoyed in anticipation

[1] Give up the ladies, and study mathematics.

the delight of proving to her, in every respect, that I knew how to repair my errors. She spared me the test. The gondolier, whom I sent to her apartments on landing, informed me that she had set out for Florence on the previous evening. If I had not felt my whole love for her when I had her in my arms, I felt it cruelly now, when I had lost her. My foolish regret has never left me. Amiable and enchanting as she was in my eyes, I could have consoled myself for the loss of her; but I confess that I have never been able to console myself for the thought that she only carried away a contemptuous recollection of me.

Such were my two adventures. The eighteen months which I spent at Venice have left me no more to tell, with the exception of a merely projected amour. Carrio, who was very fond of women, tired of always visiting those who belonged to others, took it into his head to keep one himself; and, as we were inseparable, he proposed to me an arrangement, common enough in Venice, that we should keep one between us. I agreed. The difficulty was to find one with whom we should run no risk. He was so industrious in his researches, that he unearthed a little girl between eleven and twelve years of age, whom her unworthy mother wanted to sell. We went together to see her. My compassion was stirred at the sight of this child. She was fair and gentle as a lamb; no one would have taken her for an Italian. Living costs little at Venice. We gave the mother some money, and made arrangements for the daughter's keep. She had a good voice, and, in order to provide her with a means of livelihood, we gave her a spinet and engaged a singing master for her. All this scarcely cost us two *sequins* a month, and saved more in other expenses; but, as we were obliged to wait until she was of a riper age, this was sowing a long time before we could reap. However, we were content to pass our evenings, to chat and play innocently with this child, and amused ourselves perhaps more agreeably than if we had possessed her, so true is it that what most attaches us to women is not so much sensuality, as a certain pleasure which is caused by living with them. My heart became insensibly attached to the little Anzoletta, but this attachment was paternal. My senses had so little to do with it that, in proportion as it increased, the possibility of allowing them to have any influence in like manner diminished. I felt that I should have dreaded connection with this child, after she had grown up, as an abominable incest. I saw that the worthy Carrio's feelings, unknown to himself, took the same direction. We procured for ourselves, without thinking of it, pleasures as delightful, though very different from those we had originally contemplated; and I am convinced that, however beautiful she might have grown, far from being the corrupters of her innocence, we should have been its protectors. The subsequent change in my affairs, which took place shortly afterwards, did not leave me time to take part in this good work, and I have nothing for which to commend myself in this matter except the inclinations of my heart. Let me now return to my journey.

My first intention, on leaving M. de Montaigu, was to retire to Geneva, until happier circumstances should have removed the obstacles which prevented me from rejoining my poor mamma. But the stir which our quarrel had caused, and the ambassador's folly in writing to the Court about it, made me resolve to go there in person to give an account of my own conduct and to lodge a complaint against that of a madman. From Venice I communicated my resolution to M. du Theil, who, after M. Amelot's death, had been provisionally charged with the conduct of foreign affairs. I set out immediately after my letter, travelling by way of Bergamo, Como, and Duomo d'Ossola, and crossing the Simplon. Arrived at Sion, M. de Chaignon, the French *chargé d'affaires*, gave me a most kindly reception; at Geneva M. de la Closure did the same. I there renewed my acquaintance with M. de Gauffecourt, from whom I had to receive some money. I had passed through Nyon without seeing my father; not that it did not cost me a severe pang, but I had been unable to make up my mind to present myself to my step-mother after my ill-luck, feeling sure that she would condemn me unheard. Duvillard, an old friend of my father, reproached me severely for this neglect. I explained the reason of it, and, in order to repair it without exposing myself to the risk of meeting my step-mother, I hired a carriage, and we went to Nyon together and got down at the inn. Duvillard went to fetch my poor father, who came in all haste to embrace me. We supped together, and, after having spent a most delightful evening, I returned on the following morning to Geneva with Duvillard, to whom I have always felt grateful for the kindness which he showed me on this occasion.

My shortest route was not by way of Lyons, but I wanted to pass through it, in order to satisfy myself in regard to a very mean trick of M. de Montaigu. I had had a small chest sent to me from Paris, containing a gold-embroidered waistcoat, some pairs of ruffles, and six pairs of white silk stockings; that was all. On his own proposal, I ordered this chest, or rather box, to be added to his luggage. In the apothecary's bill, which he wanted to make me take in payment of my salary, and which he had written out himself, he had set down the weight of this box, which he called a bale, as eleven hundredweight, and had charged the carriage of it to me at an enormous rate. Thanks to the exertions of M. Boy de la Tour, to whom I had been recommended by his uncle, M. Roguin, it was proved, from the custom-house registers of Lyons and Marseilles, that the bale in question only weighed forty-five pounds, and that the carriage had been charged accordingly. I added this authentic extract to M. de Montaigu's bill, and, armed with this and other evidence equally strong, I repaired to Paris, full of impatience to make use of it. During the whole of this long journey, I had little adventures at Como in Valais, and other places. Amongst other things, I saw the Borromean Islands, which are worth describing; but time presses – I am surrounded by spies, and I am obliged to accomplish, inefficiently and in haste, a task which would require peace of mind and leisure which I do not enjoy. Should Providence ever deign to cast its eyes upon me, and at last grant me a less troubled existence, I am determined to employ it in recasting this work, if possible, or, at least, in adding a supplement, which, I feel, it greatly needs.*

The report of my story had preceded me; and, on my arrival, I found that everyone, both in the offices and in public, was scandalised at the ambassador's follies. But, in spite of this, in spite of the public outcry in Venice, in spite of the unanswerable proofs which I produced, I was unable to obtain justice. In fact,

* I have now abandoned this idea. (R)

far from getting either satisfaction or reparation, I was even left to the tender mercies of the ambassador for my salary, simply because, not being a Frenchman, I had no claim to the protection of the nation, and it was a private matter that concerned only our two selves. Everyone agreed with me that I was insulted, injured, and unfortunate; that the ambassador was outrageously foolish, cruel, and unjust, and that the whole affair was a lasting disgrace to him. But – he was the ambassador; I was only the secretary. Good order, or that which is so called, required that I should not obtain justice, and I did not obtain it. I imagined that, by continued complaints, and by publicly treating this fool as he deserved, I should at last make people tell me to hold my tongue, which was just what I was waiting for, since I was firmly resolved not to obey until I had obtained justice. But at that time there was no Minister of Foreign Affairs. Others permitted, even encouraged, me to make an outcry, and joined in the chorus; but the matter never proceeded further, until at length, tired of being always in the right, and never obtaining justice, I became disheartened, and let it drop.

The only person who received me coldly, and from whom I should least have expected this unfair treatment, was Madame de Beuzenval. With her head full of the privileges conferred by rank and nobility, she could not understand that an ambassador could ever be wrong in his dealings with his secretary. The manner of her reception was in accord with this prejudice. I was so annoyed at it that, after leaving her house, I wrote to her one of the strongest and most violent letters that I have perhaps ever written, and I never went to her house again. Father Castel made me more welcome, but, at the bottom of his Jesuitical wheedling, I saw that he followed faithfully one of the grand principles of his society – always to sacrifice the weaker to the stronger. The lively consciousness of the justice of my cause and my natural pride did not allow me to endure this partisanship patiently. I gave up visiting Father Castel, and, consequently, the Jesuits, amongst whom I knew no one but himself. Besides, the tyrannical and intriguing disposition of his colleagues, so different from the amiability of good Father Hemet, caused me to feel such an aversion to their society, that, since then, I have never seen any of them except Father Berthier, whom I met two or three times at M. Dupin's, together with whom he was working with all his might at the refutation of Montesquieu.

Let me finish, once for all, what I still have to say concerning M. de Montaigu. I had told him, in the course of our disputes, that he did not want a secretary, but a lawyer's clerk. He followed this advice, and actually engaged, as my successor, a real attorney, who, in less than a year, robbed him of twenty or thirty thousand *livres*. He dismissed him, and had him imprisoned; discharged his gentlemen in a manner that caused great scandal; quarrelled with everyone; put up with affronts that a lackey would not have endured; and at last, by his repeated acts of folly, succeeded in getting himself recalled and sent into retirement in the country. Amongst the reprimands which he received from the Court, his affair with me was apparently not forgotten. At any rate, shortly after his return, he sent his *maître d'hôtel* to me to settle my account and give me some money, which I sorely needed at the time, for my debts at Venice – debts of honour, if there ever were such – weighed heavily upon my mind. I seized the opportunity which was afforded me of discharging them, together with Zanetto Nani's bill. I took what was offered to me, paid all my debts, and, although this left me as penniless as before, I was relieved from a burden which had become unendurable to me. Since then, I never heard a word about M. de Montaigu until his death, which I learned through the newspapers. Heaven rest the poor man! He was as fit for the trade of an ambassador as, in my youth, I had been for that of an attorney. However, it had only rested with him to have maintained himself honourably with my assistance, and to have ensured my speedy promotion in the position for which the Comte de Gouvon had designed me in my youth, and which, by my own exertions at a more advanced age, I had qualified myself to fulfil.

The justice and uselessness of my complaints left in my mind the seeds of indignation against our foolish civil institutions, whereby the real welfare of the public and true justice are always sacrificed to an apparent order, which is in reality subversive of all order, and of which the only effect is, to bestow the sanction of public authority upon the oppression of the weak and the injustice of the strong. Two causes prevented these seeds from developing at that time, as they did afterwards. In the first place, it was a matter that concerned myself: and private interest, which has never produced anything great or noble, cannot draw from my heart the divine flights which only the purest love of the just and the beautiful can produce; in the second place, the charm of friendship moderated and calmed my anger by the ascendancy of a gentler feeling. At Venice I had made the acquaintance of a Biscayan, a friend of my friend Carrio, and a person who deserved the friendship of every honourable man. This amiable young man, endowed with every accomplishment and virtue, had just travelled through Italy in order to cultivate a taste for the fine arts, and, thinking that he had nothing further to learn, intended to return direct to his own country. I told him that the arts were merely the recreation of a genius like his, which was made to cultivate the sciences; and I advised him, in order to acquire a taste for these, to take a journey to Paris and stay there for six months. He believed what I said, and, on my arrival at Paris, I found him waiting for me. His apartments were too large for him; he offered to share them with me, and I accepted. I found him full of enthusiasm for the higher branches of knowledge. Nothing was beyond his powers of comprehension; he devoured and digested everything with marvellous rapidity. How he thanked me for having provided him with this nourishment for his mind, which was tormented by a thirst after knowledge, without his being aware of it himself! What treasures of knowledge and virtue did I find in this vigorous soul! I felt that this was the friend I needed; we became intimate. Our tastes were not the same; we were always disputing. Both obstinate, we could never agree on a single subject. Notwithstanding, we were unable to separate; and, although we perpetually contradicted each other, neither of us would have wished the other to be different.

Ignacio Emmanuel de Altuna was one of those rare individuals, whom Spain alone produces, too seldom for her own glory. He was not a man of the violent national passions common to his countrymen; the idea of revenge was as far from his mind as the desire of it from his heart. He was too proud to be vindictive, and I have often heard him say, with great *sang-froid*, that no living man could offend him. He was gallant without being tender; he played with women as if they had been pretty children; he amused himself with his friends' mistresses, but I never knew him to have one himself or even to desire it. The flames of the virtue which consumed his heart never suffered the passions of desire to become excited.

After his travels, he married, died young, and left children; and I am as convinced as I am of my own conscience, that his wife was the first and only woman with whom he enjoyed the pleasures of love. Outwardly, he was devout, like a Spaniard; in his heart he had the piety of an angel. With the exception of myself, he is the only tolerant person I have ever seen in my life. He never asked anyone what his religious views were. It made little difference to him whether his friend was a Jew, Protestant, Turk, bigot, or atheist, provided he was an honest man. Obstinate and headstrong in matters of little importance, the moment religion, or even morality, became the subject of discussion, he drew back, held his tongue, or simply said, "I have only myself to answer for." It is incredible that so elevated a mind could be associated with an attention to detail carried to minuteness. He divided and settled in advance the occupations of his day, by hours, quarters, and minutes, and he adhered so scrupulously to this arrangement, that, if the hour struck while he was in the middle of a sentence, he would have shut the book without finishing it. Each of these portions of time, thus broken up, was set apart for a different occupation; reflection, conversation, divine service, Locke, telling his beads, visiting, music, painting; no pleasure, temptation, or desire to oblige, was permitted to interrupt this arrangement; only a duty to be fulfilled could have done so. When he gave me the list of his distribution of time, in order that I might follow it, I began by laughing, and ended with tears of admiration. He never bored others, or suffered them to bore him; he was somewhat abrupt with those who, out of politeness, attempted to do so. He was hottempered, but not sulky. I have often seen him in a passion, but never angry. Nothing could be more cheerful than his disposition. He knew how to make and take a joke; he was even brilliant in this respect, and had a talent for epigram. When anyone roused him, he was loud and noisy, and his voice could be heard at a distance; but, whilst he exclaimed loudly, one could see him smile, and, in the midst of his excitement, he would utter some pleasantry, which made everyone burst out laughing. He had neither the phlegmatic disposition nor the complexion of a Spaniard. His skin was white, his cheeks ruddy, his hair light brown, almost fair. He was tall and well-built; his body was a worthy habitation for his soul.

This man, wise in heart as in understanding, was a man of the world, and was my friend. This is my only answer to those who are not. We became so intimate, that we formed the intention of spending our lives together. It was agreed that, in a few years, I should go and live with him on his estate at Ascoytia. All the details of this plan were arranged between us the day before he left. Nothing was wanting, except that which does not depend upon men in the best-concerted plans. Later events, my misfortunes, his marriage, and, lastly, his death, separated us for ever. One would feel inclined to say, that only the dark schemes of the wicked succeed; that the innocent projects of the good are hardly ever fulfilled.

Having felt the inconvenience of dependence, I firmly resolved never to expose myself to it again. Having seen the ambitious projects, which circumstances had caused me to form, overthrown almost at their birth, discouraged from again entering the career, which I had begun so successfully, and from which, notwithstanding, I had just been driven, I resolved never to attach myself to anyone again, but to remain independent, by making the best use of my talents, the extent of which I was at last beginning to appreciate, and of which I had hitherto entertained too modest an opinion. I resumed work at my opera, which had been discontinued owing to my journey to Venice, and in order to devote myself to it with less interruption, after Altuna's departure, I returned to my old lodgings at the Hôtel St. Quentin, which was situated in an unfrequented quarter of the city, close to the Luxembourg, and was better suited for quiet work than the noisy Rue St. Honoré. There, the only real consolation, which Heaven has afforded me in my misery, and which alone renders it endurable, awaited me. As this is no passing acquaintance, I must enter in some detail upon the manner in which it was formed.

We had a new landlady, who came from Orleans. To help her with the linen, she had a young girl from her native place, about twenty-two or twenty-three years of age, who, like the landlady, took her meals with us. This girl, whose name was Thérèse le Vasseur, was of respectable family, her father being an official at the Orleans mint, and her mother engaged in business. The family was a large one, and, as the mint stopped working, the father found himself without resources, while the mother, who had become bankrupt, managed her affairs badly, gave up business, and came to Paris with her husband and daughter, who, by her own exertions, supported all three.

The first time I saw this girl appear at table, I was struck by her modest behaviour, and, still more, by her lively and gentle looks, which, in my eyes, at that time appeared incomparable. The company at table, besides M. de Bonnefond, consisted of several Irish priests, Gascons, and others of the same description. Our hostess herself had led an irregular life. I was the only person who spoke and behaved decently. They teased the girl, I took her part, and immediately their railleries were turned against me. Even if I had not felt naturally inclined towards this poor girl, a feeling of compassion, even of opposition, would have aroused my sympathy. I have always admired decency in words and manners, especially in the opposite sex. I openly avowed myself her champion. I saw that she was touched by my sympathy, and her looks, enlivened by gratitude which she dared not express, were thereby rendered more eloquent.

She was very bashful, and so was I. The intimacy, which this similarity of disposition seemed to keep at a distance, was, however, very speedily formed. The landlady, who perceived it, became furious, and her brutal behaviour gained me greater favour with the little one, who, having no one in the house except myself to help her, was grieved to see me go out, and sighed for her protector's return. The relation of our hearts, and the similarity of our disposition, soon exercised their usual effect. She thought that she saw in me an honourable man, and she was not mistaken. I thought that I saw in her a feeling, simple girl, free from coquetry, and I was not deceived either. I declared to her beforehand that I would never forsake her, but that I would never marry her. Love, esteem, and simple sincerity secured my triumph, and it was because her heart was tender and virtuous, that I was happy without being too audacious.

Her fear that it would annoy me not to find in her that which she believed I expected, delayed my happiness more than anything else. I saw that she was disturbed and confused before she gave herself up to me, anxious to make herself understood, and yet afraid to explain herself. Far from suspecting the real cause of her embarrassment, I quite wrongly attributed it to another, the idea of which was highly insulting to her character. Believing that she intended me to understand that my health might be endangered, I was greatly perplexed, and, although this did not restrain my feelings, for several days it poisoned my happiness. As neither of us understood the other, our conversations on the subject were so many riddles and ridiculous misunderstandings. She was inclined to believe that I was utterly mad, and I hardly knew what to think of her. At last we came to an explanation. She confessed to me with tears that she had once misconducted herself in the early years of her womanhood, when a cunning seducer had taken advantage of her ignorance. As soon as I understood her, I uttered a cry of joy. "Virginity!" I cried; "Paris is the right place, twenty is the right age to look for it! Ah, my Thérèse! I am only too happy to possess you, modest and healthy, and not to find what I never looked for."

At first I had only sought amusement; I now saw that I had found more and had gained a companion. A little intimacy with this excellent girl, a little reflection upon my situation, made me feel that, while thinking only of my pleasures, I had done much to promote my happiness. To supply the place of my extinguished ambition, I needed a lively sentiment which should take complete possession of my heart. In a word, I needed a successor to mamma. As I should never live with her again, I wanted someone to live with her pupil, in whom I might find the simplicity and docility of heart which she had found in me. I felt it necessary that the gentle tranquillity of private and domestic life should make up to me for the loss of the brilliant career which I was renouncing. When I was quite alone, I felt a void in my heart, which it only needed another heart to fill. Destiny had deprived me of, or, at least in part, alienated me from, that heart for which Nature had formed me. From that moment I was alone; for with me it has always been everything or nothing. I found in Thérèse the substitute that I needed. Thanks to her, I lived happily, as far as the course of events permitted. At first I tried to improve her mind, but my efforts were useless. Her mind is what Nature has made it; culture and teaching are without influence upon it. I am not ashamed to confess that she has never learnt how to read properly, although she can write fairly well. When I went to live in the Rue Neuve-des-Petits-Champs, opposite my windows, at the Hôtel de Pontchartrain there was a clock. For more than a month I did my utmost to teach her how to tell the time by it, but, even now, she can hardly do so. She has never been able to give the names of the twelve months of the year in correct order, and does not know a single figure, in spite of all the trouble I have taken to teach her. She can neither count money nor reckon the price of anything. The words which she uses in speaking are often the very opposite of those which she means. I once made a dictionary of the phrases she used, to amuse Madame de Luxembourg, and her absurd mistakes have become famous in the society in which I lived. But this person, so limited in understanding – so stupid, if you will – is a most excellent adviser in cases of difficulty. Frequently, in Switzerland, in England, and in France, at the time of the misfortunes which befell me, she saw what I did not see myself, gave me the best advice to follow, rescued me from dangers into which I was rushing blindly, and, in the presence of ladies of the highest rank, of princes and the great ones of the world, her opinions, her good sense, her answers, and her behaviour have gained for her the esteem of all, and for me, compliments upon her good qualities which I felt convinced were sincere.

When we are with those we love, sentiment nourishes the mind as well as the heart, and we have little need to search for ideas elsewhere. I lived with my Thérèse as pleasantly as with the most brilliant genius in the world. Her mother, who prided herself on having been formerly brought up with the Marquise de Monpipeau, tried to play the wit, and wanted to undertake the mental guidance of her daughter, and, by her craftiness, spoiled the simplicity of our intercourse. The annoyance which her importunity caused me made me, in some degree, get over the foolish shame, which prevented me from venturing to show myself with Thérèse in public, and we took little walks together in the country, where we had little collations which were delightful to me. I saw that she loved me sincerely, and this increased my affection for her. This sweet intimacy made up for everything. I no longer felt any concern about the future, or, at least, I only thought of it as a prolongation of the present. I only desired to make sure that it would last.

This attachment rendered all other recreation superfluous and insipid. I never went out except to visit Thérèse; her place of abode became almost my own. This retired life proved so favourable to my work that, in less than three months, my opera, words and music, was finished, and nothing remained to be added, except some accompaniments and a few tenor notes.[1] This drudgery wearied me exceedingly. I proposed to Philidor to undertake it in return for a share of the profits. He came twice and put in a few notes in the act of "Ovid"; but he was unable to tie himself to a task which required such unremitting application, on the chance of remote and even doubtful profit. He did not come again, and I finished my task myself.

My opera being ready, the next thing was to make some money by it, which was a far more difficult task. It is impossible for a man who lives a solitary life to succeed in Paris. I thought of making my way with the aid of M. de la Poplinière, to whom I had been introduced by Gauffecourt on my return from Geneva. M. de la Poplinière was the Maecenas of Rameau; Madame de la Poplinière was his most humble pupil; Rameau was completely master in that house. Supposing that he would be glad to give his support to the work of one of his disciples, I wanted to show him mine. He refused to look at it, saying that he could not read scores; it was too fatiguing. La Poplinière suggested that it might

[1] *Remplissages*: the parts between bass and treble.

be possible to get him to listen to it, and offered to get an orchestra together to perform selections. I desired nothing better. Rameau grumblingly consented, repeating incessantly that the composition of a man, who had not been brought up to the profession, and who had learnt music entirely by himself, must be something fine. I hastened to copy out in parts five or six of the best passages. I had about ten instrumentalists, Albert, Bérard, and Mademoiselle Bourdonnais being the vocalists. As soon as the overture commenced, Rameau, by his extravagant praises, intended to make it understood that the work could not be my own composition. He exhibited signs of impatience at every passage; but, after a counter-tenor song, the execution of which was robust and powerful, and the accompaniment brilliant, he could no longer contain himself; he addressed me with a brutality which gave universal offence, and declared that part of what he had just heard was the work of a consummate master of the art, while the rest was by an ignorant fellow, who did not even understand music. It is true that my work, uneven and irregular, was sometimes sublime and sometimes insipid, as must be the work of everyone who only elevates himself by flashes of genius, without the support of scientific training. Rameau declared that he saw in me only a contemptible plagiarist, without talent or taste. The company present, and particularly the master of the house, thought differently. M. de Richelieu, who at that time, as is well known, was a frequent visitor, heard of my work, and wished to hear the whole of it played, intending, if it pleased him, to have it performed at Court. It was performed with full chorus and orchestra, at the King's expense, at the house of M. Bonneval, manager of the Court amusements.[1] Francœur directed the performance, and the effect was surprising. The Duke was never tired of loudly expressing his approval; and, at the end of a chorus in the act of "Tasso," he got up from his seat, came over to me, shook me cordially by the hand, and said, "M. Rousseau, that is a delightful harmony! I have never heard anything finer; I will have it performed at Versailles." Madame de la Poplinière, who was

[1] *Intendant des menus (plaisirs)*: lit. Manager of the expenses connected with Court ceremonies, festivals, and theatrical and other performances.

present, did not say a word. Rameau, although invited, had refused to come. The next day Madame de la Poplinière received me very ungraciously at her toilette, pretended to depreciate my work, and told me that, although a little false glitter had dazzled M. de Richelieu at first, he had recovered himself, and she advised me not to build any hopes upon my opera. The Duke arrived shortly afterwards, and spoke to me in quite a different tone, flattered me upon my talents, and seemed still disposed to get my work performed before the King. "Only the act of 'Tasso' would not be permitted at Court," said he; "you must write another instead of it." These words alone were enough to make me go and shut myself up in my room; and in three weeks I had composed another act in place of "Tasso," the theme of which was "Hesiod inspired by one of the Muses." I found means to introduce into the act part of the history of the development of my talents and of the jealousy with which Rameau had been pleased to honour them. In the new act, the flight was less gigantic and better sustained than in "Tasso." The music was equally grand and the composition far superior, and, if the other two acts had been equal to this, the whole piece might have been represented with success; but, while I was putting the last touches upon it, another undertaking interrupted its execution.

[1745–1747.] – During the winter after the battle of Fontenoy, several fêtes took place at Versailles, and several operas were performed at the Théâtre des Petites-Écuries. Amongst these was Voltaire's drama, *La Princesse de Navarre*, set to music by Rameau, which had just been revised and the title changed to *Les Fêtes de Ramire*. This change of subject rendered several alterations necessary in the *divertissements*,[1] both in the words and music. The question was, to find someone capable of performing this two-fold task. Voltaire and Rameau being in Lorraine, where they were both engaged on the opera of *Le Temple de la Gloire*, and consequently unable to give their attention to it, M. de Richelieu thought of me, and proposed to me that I should undertake the task; and, in order that I should be better able to judge what there was to be done, sent me the poem and the

---

[1] The incidental songs and dances.

music separately. Before all, I was unwilling to touch the words without the author's consent, and I wrote to him on the subject a very polite and even respectful letter, as was only proper, and received the following answer, the original of which is to be found in the packet of papers, docketed A, No. 1:

"December 15th, 1745.

"Sir, – Two accomplishments, which have hitherto always been separate, are united in you. These are two good reasons why I should esteem and endeavour to love you. I am sorry, for your own sake, that you should employ these accomplishments upon a work which is none too worthy of you. Some months ago, M. de Richelieu gave me strict orders to compose, at a moment's notice, a trifling and poor sketch of some insipid and unfinished scenes, which were to be adapted to *divertissements* utterly unsuited to them. I obeyed most scrupulously. I worked very rapidly and very badly. I sent the miserable skit to M. de Richelieu, feeling sure that he would not make use of it, or that I should have to correct it. Happily it is in your hands; you may do exactly what you please with it; I have entirely put it out of my sight. I have no doubt that you have corrected all the errors which must have occurred in the hasty composition of a simple sketch, and that you have filled in all that was wanting.

"I remember that, amongst other stupid blunders, I have forgotten to explain, in the scenes which connect the *divertissements*, how the Princess Grenadine is suddenly transported from a prison into a garden or palace. As it is not a magician, but a Spanish nobleman, who gives the festival in her honour, it seems to me that nothing ought to take place by enchantment. I beg you, Sir, to look at this passage again, of which I have only a confused idea. See if it is necessary that the prison should open, and our princess be conducted from it to a beautiful gilded and varnished palace, already prepared for her. I know that all this is very wretched stuff, and that it is beneath the dignity of a thinking being to make a serious business of such trifles; but, since it is our duty to displease as little as possible, we must employ as much reason as we are able, even upon a miserable opera *divertissement*.

"I entirely depend upon you and M. Ballod, and I trust soon to have the honour of thanking you, and of assuring you, Sir, how I have the honour to be," &c. &c.

There is nothing to cause surprise in the excessive politeness of this letter, compared with the almost rude tone of those which I have since then received from him. He thought that I was high in favour with M. de Richelieu, and his well-known courtly suppleness obliged him to show great politeness towards a new-comer, until he had become better acquainted with the measure of his importance.

Authorised by M. de Voltaire, and relieved from considering Rameau at all in the matter, since his only object was to injure me, I set to work, and in two months my task was executed. The poetry was a mere trifle; my only endeavour was to prevent the difference of style being noticed, and I was presumptuous enough to believe that I was successful. The music cost me more time and labour; besides being obliged to compose several introductory pieces, amongst others the overture, the whole of the recitative, which devolved upon me, presented very great difficulties, since I was obliged to connect, often in a few lines, and by means of very rapid modulations, symphonies and choruses in very different keys; for, in order that Rameau might not be able to accuse me of having spoilt his airs, I was determined not to alter or transpose a single one. The recitative was a success. It was well accented, full of vigour, and above all, admirably modulated. The idea of the two great men, with whom I had the honour to be thus associated, had elevated my genius, and I can say that, in this thankless and inglorious task, of which the public could not even be informed, I nearly always kept myself up to the level of my models.

The piece, as revised by me, was rehearsed at the grand theatre of the Opera. Of the three authors I alone was present. Voltaire was away from Paris, and Rameau either did not come, or kept himself hidden.

The words of the first monologue were very melancholy. It began as follows:

"O mort! viens terminer les malheurs de ma vie."

I had been obliged to set it to appropriate music; and yet it was just this upon which Madame de la Poplinière founded her criticism, and accused me, with considerable bitterness, of having composed a funeral anthem. M. de Richelieu judiciously began by inquiring who had written the words of the monologue. I showed him the manuscript which he had sent me, which proved that it was Voltaire. "In that case," said he,

"Voltaire alone is to blame." During the rehearsal, all my work was disapproved of by Madame de la Poplinière, and defended by M. de Richelieu. But in the end I found the opposition too strong, and it was notified to me, that I should have to make several alterations in my work, in regard to which it would be necessary to consult M. Rameau. Deeply grieved at such a result, instead of the praise which I had expected and certainly deserved, I returned home heart-broken. Worn out with fatigue, and consumed by grief, I fell ill, and for six weeks I was unable to leave my room.

Rameau, who was commissioned to make the alterations indicated by Madame de la Poplinière, sent to ask me for the overture of my great opera, in order to substitute it for that which I had just composed. Luckily, I perceived the trick and refused. As there were only four or five days before the representation, he had no time to compose a fresh overture, and was obliged to leave mine as it was. It was in the Italian style, at that time quite unknown in France. Nevertheless, it gave satisfaction and I heard, through M. de Valmalette, the King's *maître d'hôtel*, the son-in-law of M. Mussard, a relative and friend of mine, that musical enthusiasts had expressed themselves well satisfied with my work, and that the general public had not been able to distinguish it from Rameau's. But the latter, in concert with Madame de la Poplinière, took measures to prevent anyone from knowing that I had anything at all to do with it. On the books of the words, which were distributed amongst the spectators, and in which the authors' names are always given, Voltaire alone was mentioned. Rameau preferred the suppression of his own name to seeing mine associated with it.

As soon as I was able to go out, I resolved to call upon M. de Richelieu. It was too late; he had just set out for Dunkirk, where he was to direct the embarkation of the troops for Scotland.[1] When he returned, in order to justify my idleness, I said to myself that it was too late. As I never saw him again, I lost the

---

[1] The Young Pretender had landed in Scotland in July 1745, and by the secret Treaty of Fontainbleau of 24 October 1745 Louis XV pledged him military assistance. The intended invasion, ill-managed by the Duc de Richelieu, had, however, to be abandoned.

honour which my work deserved, and the fee which it ought to have brought me; while I never received the least return, or rather compensation for my time, my trouble, my vexation, my illness, and the expense which it entailed. Nevertheless, I have always thought that M. de Richelieu was himself well-disposed towards me, and entertained a favourable opinion of my abilities; but my ill-luck and Madame de la Poplinière combined prevented him from giving effect to his goodwill.

I was quite unable to understand the dislike with which I was regarded by this woman, whom I had done my utmost to please, and to whom I paid court regularly. Gauffecourt explained the reasons for it. "In the first place," said he, "her friendship for Rameau, whose avowed patroness she is, and who will brook no rival; and, in the second place, an original sin, which condemns you in her eyes, and which she will never forgive – the fact that you are a Genevese." In regard to this, he told me that the Abbé Hubert, who also came from Geneva, and was the sincere friend of M. de la Poplinière, had done his utmost to prevent him from marrying this woman, whose character he knew well, and that, after the marriage, she had sworn implacable hatred against him and all the Genevese as well. "Although M. de la Poplinière is well-disposed towards you," he added – "this I know to be a fact – do not reckon upon his support. He is very fond of his wife; she hates you; she is mischievous and cunning. You will never do any good in that house." I took the hint.

The same Gauffecourt also rendered me a very essential service about this time. I had just lost my worthy father; he was about sixty years of age.[1] I did not feel this loss as keenly as I should have done at another time, when the difficulties of my situation occupied my attention less. During his lifetime, I had never attempted to claim the remainder of my mother's property, and had allowed him to draw the trifling interest it produced. After his death, I no longer felt any scruples about the matter, but the want of legal proof of my brother's death caused a difficulty which Gauffecourt undertook to remove, and did so, with the aid of the good offices of De Lolme, the advocate. As I had pressing need of this small addition to my finances, and the

[1] Rousseau's father died on 9 May 1747, his age being in fact 75.

result was so uncertain, I waited for definite information with
the liveliest impatience.

One evening, on entering my lodgings, I found the letter
which was bound to contain it; I took it up, in order to open
it, with an impatient trembling, of which I inwardly felt ashamed.
"What!" said I contemptuously to myself, "shall Jean Jacques
suffer himself to be overcome by self-interest and curiosity?" I
immediately put back the letter on the mantelpiece, undressed,
went quietly to bed, slept better than usual, and got up rather late
the next day, without thinking any more about my letter. While
dressing, I caught sight of it, opened it leisurely, and found a bill
of exchange inside. Many pleasant feelings entered my mind at
once; but the liveliest of all was the consciousness of my victory
over myself. I could mention a number of similar instances in
the course of my life, but I am too pressed for time to relate
everything. I sent a little of the money to poor mamma, regretting with tears the happy time when I should have laid the whole
at her feet. All her letters showed signs of her distress. She sent
me heaps of recipes and secret remedies, which she declared
would make my fortune and her own. Already the thought of her
wretchedness contracted her heart and narrowed her mind. The
small sum which I was able to send her fell into the hands of the
rascals by whom she was surrounded. She derived no benefit
from anything. I was disgusted at the idea of sharing what
I myself sorely needed with these wretches, especially after the
fruitless attempts which I made to get her out of their hands, as
will be afterwards related.

Time slipped away, and the money with it. We were two, even
four in number, or, to speak more correctly, seven or eight; for,
although Thérèse was disinterested to a degree almost unexampled, her mother was by no means the same. As soon as
she found herself somewhat improved in circumstances –
thanks to my attention – she sent for her whole family to
share the fruits of it. Sisters, sons, daughters, grand-daughters
– all came, with the exception of her eldest daughter, who was
married to the manager of the carriage service at Angers. All that
I did for Thérèse was turned by her mother to the benefit of
these starvelings. As I had not to do with a covetous person, and

was not under the influence of a foolish passion, I committed no follies. Content to keep Thérèse decently, but without luxury, protected against pressing needs, I consented to her handing over to her mother all that she was able to earn by her own exertions, nor did I limit myself to that; but, by a fatality which always pursued me, while mamma was plundered by the rascals who surrounded her, Thérèse was preyed upon by her family, and I could render no assistance in either case which benefited her for whom it was intended. It was curious that Madame le Vasseur's youngest child – the only one who had not received a marriage portion – was the only one who supported her father and mother, and that, after having long endured the blows of her brothers and sisters, and even of her nieces, this poor girl was now plundered by them, without being able to offer a better resistance to their thefts than formerly to their blows. Only one of her nieces, named Goton Leduc, was of a tolerably amiable and gentle disposition, although she was spoiled by the example and lessons of the others. As I frequently saw them together I gave them the names which they gave to each other. I called the niece my niece, and the aunt my aunt, and both called me uncle. Hence the name of "aunt" by which I continued to call Thérèse, and which my friends sometimes repeated by way of a joke.

It will easily be understood that, in such a situation, I had not a moment to lose before attempting to extricate myself from it. Supposing that M. de Richelieu had forgotten me, and no longer expecting anything from the Court, I made some attempts to get my opera accepted in Paris; but I encountered difficulties which it required considerable time to overcome, and I became more hard pressed every day. I resolved to offer my little comedy of *Narcisse* to the Italian theatre. It was accepted, and I was given a free pass to the theatre, which pleased me greatly, but this was all. I could never get my piece performed, and at length, tired of paying court to comedians, I turned my back upon them. At length I had recourse to the last expedient which remained, and the only one which I ought to have adopted. While visiting at M. de la Poplinière's house, I had kept away from M. Dupin's. The two ladies, although related, were not on good terms, and never visited. There was no intercourse between the two houses – Thieriot alone was at home in both. He was commissioned to endeavour to bring me back to M. Dupin. M. de Francueil at that time was studying natural history and chemistry, and was making a collection. I believe that his ambition was to be elected a member of the Academy of Sciences. With this object he wanted to write a book, and he thought that I might be useful to him in this undertaking. Madame Dupin, who also contemplated a book, had almost similar views in regard to me. They would have liked to engage me as a kind of secretary, to be shared between them; and this was the object of Thieriot's exhortations. I required, as a preliminary, that M. de Francueil should employ his own and Jelyote's influence to get my piece rehearsed at the opera. He consented. The *Muses galantes* was at first rehearsed several times at the Magasin,[1] and afterwards at the Grand Theatre. There was a large audience at the general rehearsal, and several pieces were warmly applauded. Nevertheless, during the performance – very badly conducted by Rebel – I felt myself that the piece would not be accepted, and, indeed, that it could not be presented to the public without great alterations. Accordingly I withdrew it without saying a word, and without exposing myself to the risk of rejection; but I clearly saw, from several indications, that, even if the work had been perfect, it would not have passed. M. de Francueil had certainly promised to get it rehearsed, not to secure its acceptance. He scrupulously kept his word. I have always fancied, on this and several other occasions, that neither he nor Madame Dupin were particularly anxious that I should acquire a certain reputation in the world, perhaps for fear that, when their own works appeared, it might be supposed that they had grafted their talents upon mine. However, as Madame Dupin had always entertained a very moderate idea of my abilities, and never employed me except to write at her dictation, or to undertake purely learned researches, this reproach, especially as far as she was concerned, might have been unjust.

[1747–1749.] – This last failure completely discouraged me. I abandoned every prospect of fame and promotion; and, without

---

[1] The place where scenery and costumes were stored. It was in the rue Nicaise, and it also housed a school of music (ancestor of the *Conservatoire*).

thinking further of my real or fancied talents, which were of such little service to me, I devoted my time and trouble to providing for the support of myself and my dear Thérèse, in a manner which might be agreeable to those who undertook to assist me in doing so. I accordingly attached myself entirely to Madame Dupin and M. de Francueil. This did not place me in a very affluent position, for the 800 or 900 *francs* which I received for the first two years was hardly sufficient for my most pressing needs, as I was obliged to rent a furnished room in their neighbourhood, in a somewhat expensive quarter, and to pay for another lodging quite at the other end of Paris, at the top of the Rue Saint-Jacques, where I went nearly every evening to supper, whatever the state of the weather might be. I soon got into the way of my new occupation, and even began to like it. I became interested in chemistry, and went through several courses at M. Rouelle's, together with M. de Francueil, and we proceeded, to the best of our ability, to fill quires of paper with our scribblings upon this science, of which we scarcely knew the elements.[1] In 1747 we went to spend the autumn in Touraine, at the Château of Chenonceaux, a Royal mansion upon the Cher, built by Henri II for Diana of Poitiers, whose monogram may still be seen there, and which is now in the possession of M. Dupin, a farmer-general. We enjoyed ourselves greatly in this beautiful place; we lived well, and I became as fat as a monk. We had a good deal of music. I composed several trios, full of vigour and harmony, of which I shall perhaps speak in my supplement, if I ever write one. We played comedies. I wrote one, in three acts, entitled *l'Engagement téméraire*, which will be found amongst my papers, and has no other merit than that of great liveliness. I also composed some other trifles, amongst them a piece in verse, called *l'Allée de Sylvie*, from a walk in the park, on the banks of the Cher. This did not, however, interrupt my chemical studies, or the work which I was doing for Madame Dupin.

While I was growing fat at Chenonceaux, my poor Thérèse was increasing in size at Paris for another reason; and, on my return, I found the work which I had commenced in a more

[1] The Ms. of Rousseau's *Institutions chimiques* survived and has been published.

forward condition than I had expected. Considering my position, this would have thrown me into the greatest embarrassment, had not some table companions furnished me with the only means of getting out of the difficulty. This is one of those essential pieces of information which I cannot give with too much simplicity, because, if I were to offer any explanation, I should be obliged either to excuse or to inculpate myself, and in this place I ought not to do either the one or the other.

During Altuna's stay at Paris, instead of going to an eating-house, we usually took our meals in our neighbourhood, nearly opposite the *cul-de-sac* of the Opera, at the house of one Madame la Selle, a tailor's wife, whose dinners were indifferent, but her table was always in request, on account of the good and respectable company which resorted there; no one was admitted unless he was known, and it was necessary to be introduced by one of the regular guests. Commandeur de Graville, an old rake, full of wit and politeness, but filthy in his language, lodged there, and attracted a jovial and brilliant company of young officers in the guards and musketeers; Commandeur de Nonant, protector of all the girls employed at the Opera, daily brought all the news from that haunt of vice; M. Duplessis, a retired lieutenant-colonel, a good and respectable old man; and Ancelet,* an officer in the musketeers, maintained a certain amount of order amongst these young people. The house was also frequented by merchants, financiers, and purveyors, but polite and honourable men, distinguished in their profession, M. de Besse, M. de Forcade, and others whose names I have forgotten. In short, good company of all classes was to be met there, with the

* It was to this Ancelet that I gave a little comedy of mine, entitled *Les Prisonniers de Guerre*, which I had written after the disasters of the French in Bavaria and Bohemia, but which I never ventured to show or acknowledge, for the singular reason that the King, France, and the French people have perhaps never been more highly or sincerely praised than in this piece; and, avowed Republican and censurer of the Government as I was, I did not dare to confess myself the panegyrist of a nation, whose principles were all exactly the opposite of my own. More grieved at the misfortunes of France than even the French themselves, I was afraid of being taxed with flattery and cowardice, on account of the expressions of sincere attachment, the date and origin of which I have mentioned in the first part of this work, and which I was ashamed to make public. (R)

exception of abbés and lawyers, whom I never saw there, and it was agreed that members of those professions were never to be introduced. The company, fairly numerous, was very gay without being noisy, and many broad stories were told, which, however, were free from vulgarity. Old de Graville, with all his risky stories, never lost his old-fashioned courtly politeness, and no indecency ever escaped his lips which was not so witty that any woman would have pardoned it. He gave the tone to the whole table; all these young people related their adventures of gallantry with equal freedom and grace; and there was no lack of stories of girls, as there was a stock of them close at hand, since the passage leading to Madame la Selle's house also led to the shop of Madame Duchapt, a famous dressmaker, who at the time employed some very pretty girls, with whom our gentlemen used to go and chat before or after dinner. I should have amused myself like the rest, if I had been bolder. I only needed to go in as they did, but I never ventured. As for Madame de la Selle, I often went to dine at her house after Altuna had left. I there heard a number of amusing anecdotes, and also gradually adopted, thank Heaven! not the morals, but the principles which I found established. Honourable people injured, husbands deceived, women seduced, secret accouchements, these were the most ordinary topics; and he who contributed most to the population of the Foundling Hospital was always most applauded. I caught the infection; I formed my manner of thinking upon that which I saw prevalent amongst very amiable and, in the main, very honourable people. I said to myself, "Since it is the custom of the country, one who lives here may follow it." Here was the expedient for which I was looking. I cheerfully resolved to adopt it, without the least scruples on my own part; I only had to overcome those of Thérèse, with whom I had the greatest trouble in the world to persuade her to adopt the only means of saving her honour. Her mother, who, in addition, was afraid of this new embarrassment in the shape of a number of brats, supported me, and Thérèse at last yielded. We chose a discreet and safe midwife, one Mademoiselle Gouin, who lived at the Pointe Saint-Eustache, to take care of this precious charge; and when the time came, Thérèse was taken to her house by her mother for her accouchement. I went to see her several times, and took her a monogram, which I had written on two cards, one of which was placed in the child's swaddling clothes, after which it was deposited by the midwife in the office of the hospital in the usual manner. The following year the same inconvenience was remedied by the same expedient, with the exception of the monogram, which was forgotten. On my side there was no more reflection, no greater approval on the mother's; she obeyed with a sigh. Later, all the vicissitudes which this fatal conduct produced in my manner of thinking, as well as in my destiny, will become apparent; for the present, let us keep to this first period. Its consequences, as cruel as they were unforeseen, will force me to return to it only too frequently.[1]

Here I will mention my first acquaintance with Madame d'Epinay,[2] whose name will frequently recur in these Memoirs. Her maiden name was Mademoiselle d'Esclavelles, and she had just married M. d'Epinay, son of M. de Lalive de Bellegarde, farmer-general. Her husband, like M. de Francueil, was musical. She also was musical, and devotion to the art led to a great intimacy between the three. M. de Francueil introduced me to Madame d'Epinay, who sometimes invited me to supper. She was amiable, witty, and talented, and certainly a very desirable acquaintance. But she had a friend, Mademoiselle d'Ette, who was supposed to be very spiteful, and lived with the Chevalier de Valory, who did not enjoy a good reputation either. I believe that the society of these two people did harm to Madame d'Epinay, who, although of a very exacting disposition, was endowed by Nature with qualities admirably adapted to regulate or counterbalance its extravagances. M. de Francueil partly inspired her with the friendship he himself entertained for me, and confessed his relations with her, which, for this reason, I would not speak of here, had they not become public property, and even reached the

---

[1] A great deal has been written about Rousseau's children, and the question has been raised (1) whether he was in fact their father (2) whether, if he were not, he was aware of it (3) whether the whole story of the children might not be a fabrication. The investigations made at the Foundlings' Hospital in 1761 by his friend the Duchesse de Luxembourg bore no fruit, and the same is true of later ones.

[2] [Epinay] See *Biographies*, p. 710.

ears of M. d'Epinay himself. M. de Francueil made singular revelations to me concerning this lady, which she never mentioned to me herself, and of which she never thought I had been informed. I never opened, and never will open, my lips on the subject, to her or anyone else. All these confidential communications from one quarter and another rendered my situation very embarrassing, especially with Madame de Francueil, who knew me sufficiently well not to distrust me, although I was intimate with her rival. As well as I was able, I consoled this poor lady, whose husband certainly did not return the love which she felt for him. I listened to these three persons separately, and kept their secrets so faithfully, that not one of the three ever extracted from me any of the secrets of the other two, while at the same time I did not conceal from either of the women my attachment to her rival. Madame de Francueil, who wanted to make use of me in several ways, had to put up with a formal refusal, and Madame d'Epinay, who on one occasion wanted to intrust me with a letter for Francueil, not only met with a similar denial, but I plainly declared that, if she wanted to drive me from her house for ever, she had only to propose the same thing to me again. I must, however, do justice to Madame d'Epinay. Far from showing herself displeased with my conduct, she spoke in the highest terms of it to Francueil, and made me as welcome as ever. In this manner, amidst the stormy relations between these three persons, whom I had to manage most carefully, upon whom I in a manner depended, and to whom I was sincerely attached, I retained to the end their friendship, their esteem, and their confidence, while I behaved with gentleness and complaisance, but always with uprightness and firmness. In spite of my awkwardness and stupidity, Madame d'Epinay would take me with her to the gaieties at La Chevrette, a château near Saint-Denis belonging to M. de Bellegarde. There was a stage there, on which performances were frequently given. A part was given to me, which I studied for six months without intermission, but when the piece was performed, I had to be prompted in it from beginning to end. After this trial, no more parts were offered to me.[1]

[1]   The play was Rousseau's own *L'Engagement téméraire*. He played the part of Carlin.

The acquaintance of Madame d'Epinay also procured me that of her step-sister, Mademoiselle de Bellegarde, who soon afterwards became Comtesse de Houdetot.[1] When I first saw her, it was just before her marriage, and she conversed with me for a long time with that charming familiarity which is natural to her. I found her very amiable; but I was far from foreseeing that this young person would one day decide the destiny of my life, and was fated to drag me down, although innocently, into the abyss in which I find myself to-day.

Although, since my return from Venice, I have not spoken of Diderot, or my friend Roguin, I had not neglected either, and with the former especially I had daily grown more and more intimate. He had a Nanette, just as I had a Thérèse: this was a further point of agreement between us. But the difference was, that my Thérèse, who was at least as good-looking as his Nanette, was of a gentle disposition and an amiable character, calculated to gain the attachment of an honourable man, while his Nanette, who was a regular shrew and a fish-hag, exhibited no redeeming qualities which could compensate, in the eyes of others, for her defective education. However, he married her, which was very praiseworthy, if he had promised to do so. As for myself, having made no promise of the kind, I was in no hurry to imitate him.

I had also become connected with the Abbé de Condillac,[2] who, like myself, was unknown in the literary world, but was destined to become what he is at the present day. I was, perhaps, the first who discovered his abilities, and estimated him at his proper value. He also seemed to have taken a fancy to me; and while, shut up in my room in the Rue Jean-Saint-Denis, near the Opera, I was composing my act of *Hesiode*, he sometimes dined with me *tête-à-tête*, and we shared the expenses. He was at that time engaged upon his "Essai sur l'Origine des Connaissances humaines," his first work. When it was finished, the difficulty was to find a bookseller to take it. The booksellers of Paris are always arrogant and hard towards a new author, and metaphysics, which was not much in fashion at the time, did not

[1] [Houdetot] see *Biographies*, p. 712.
[2] [Condillac] See *Biographies*, p. 708.

offer a very attractive subject. I spoke of Condillac and his work
to Diderot, and introduced them to each other. They were made
to suit each other, and did so. Diderot induced Durant the
bookseller to accept the Abbé's manuscript, and this great
metaphysician received for his first book – and that almost as
a favour – one hundred crowns, and even that he would perhaps
not have received but for me. As we lived at a great distance
from one another,[1] we all three met once a week at the Palais-
Royal, and dined together at the Hôtel du Panier Fleuri. These
little weekly dinners must have been exceedingly agreeable to
Diderot, for he, who nearly always failed to keep his other
appointments, never missed one of them. On these occasions
I drew up the plan of a periodical, to be called *Le Persifleur*, to be
written by Diderot and myself alternately. I sketched the outlines of the first number, and in this manner became acquainted
with D'Alembert,[2] to whom Diderot had spoken of it. However,
unforeseen events stopped the way, and the project fell into
abeyance.

These two authors had just undertaken the "Dictionnaire
Encyclopédique," which at first was only intended to be a kind
of translation of Chambers's,[3] almost like that of James's
"Dictionary of Medicine,"[4] which Diderot had just finished.
The latter wanted to secure my assistance in this second enterprise, and proposed that I should undertake the musical part of
it. I consented, and completed it very hastily and indifferently, in
the three months which were allowed to myself, and all the other
collaborators in the work. But I was the only one who was ready
at the time appointed. I handed him my manuscript, which I had
had copied by one of M. de Francueil's lackeys, named Dupont,
who wrote a very good hand, paying him ten crowns out of my
own pocket, for which I have never been reimbursed. Diderot,

[1] Rousseau was living in the rue Platrière, near Les Halles. Diderot was
living in the rue de la Vieille Estrapade, in the Latin quarter.

[2] [Alembert] See *Biographies*, p. 707.

[3] The *Cyclopaedia, or Universal Dictionary of the Arts and Sciences* of the Scottish
encyclopaedist Emphraim Chambers, published in 1728 (ancestor of the
present *Chambers's Encyclopaedia*).

[4] Diderot had helped to translate the voluminous *Medicinal Dictionary* of
Robert James, first published in 1743 45.

on the part of the booksellers, promised me some remuneration, which neither of us ever mentioned again to the other.

The undertaking was interrupted by his imprisonment. His "Pensées philosophiques" had brought upon him a certain amount of annoyance, which led to no further consequences. It was different with his "Lettre sur les Aveugles," which contained nothing that deserved censure except a few personal allusions, at which Madame Dupré de Saint-Maur and M. de Réaumur took offence, and for which he was confined in the donjon of Vincennes.[1] It is impossible to describe the anguish which my friend's misfortune caused me. My melancholy imagination, which always exaggerates misfortune, became alarmed. I thought that he would be imprisoned for the rest of his life; I nearly went mad at the idea. I wrote to Madame de Pompadour, entreating her to procure his release, or to get me imprisoned with him. I received no answer to my letter; it was too unreasonable to produce any effect, and I cannot flatter myself that it contributed to the subsequent alleviation of the hardships of poor Diderot's confinement. Had its severity continued without relaxation, I believe that I should have died of despair at the foot of this accursed donjon. Besides, even if my letter produced but little effect, neither did I myself claim much merit for it, for I only mentioned it to one or two people, and never to Diderot himself.

[1] The *Parlement* of Paris had, in July 1746, ordered Diderot's freethinking *Pensées philosophiques* to be burnt. On 24 July 1749 he was arrested and incarcerated in the royal prison of Vincennes, where he remained till 3 November.

BOOK VIII

[1749]

I HAVE been obliged to pause at the end of the preceding book. With the present book commences, in its first origin, the long chain of my misfortunes.

Having lived in two of the most brilliant houses in Paris, I had made some acquaintances, in spite of my want of tact; amongst others, at Madame Dupin's, the young hereditary prince of Saxe-Gotha and Baron de Thun, his tutor; at M. de Poplinière's, M. Seguy, a friend of Baron de Thun, who was known in the literary world by his beautiful edition of Rousseau. The Baron invited M. Seguy and myself to spend a day or two at Fontenay-sous-Bois, where the Prince had a country house. We accepted the invitation. While passing Vincennes, I felt so distressed at the sight of the donjon, that the Baron perceived the effects of my emotion on my countenance. At supper the Prince spoke of Diderot's confinement. The Baron, in order to make me speak, accused the prisoner of imprudence, which I myself displayed by the impetuosity with which I defended him. This excess of zeal was excused in a man who was inspired by attachment to an unfortunate friend, and the conversation took another turn. Two Germans, belonging to the Prince's suite, were present: M. Klüpfel, a man of great ability, his chaplain, who afterwards supplanted the Baron, and became his tutor; and a young man named Grimm,[1] who held the post of reader until he could find some other place, and whose modest equipment showed how urgent was his need for finding something of the kind. From that same evening, Klüpfel and myself formed an acquaintance which soon ripened into friendship. My acquaintance with M. Grimm did not advance so rapidly; he kept himself in the background, and gave no signs of the boastfulness which he afterwards displayed when he became prosperous. At dinner the next day the conversation turned upon music; he spoke well upon the subject. I was delighted when I heard that he was able to accompany on the piano. After dinner, some music was sent

[1] [Grimm] See *Biographies*, p. 711.

for, and we amused ourselves for the rest of the day on the Prince's piano. In this manner began that friendship, at first so pleasant to me, and in the end so fatal, of which, from this time forth, I shall have so much to say.

On my return to Paris, I received the agreeable news that Diderot had been released from the donjon, and confined to the château and park of Vincennes on parole, with permission to see his friends. How painful it was to me not to be able to run to him on the spot! But I was detained for two or three days at Madame Dupin's by duties which I could not neglect, and, after what seemed three or four centuries of impatience, I flew into my friend's arms. O indescribable moment! He was not alone; D'Alembert and the treasurer of the Sainte-Chapelle were with him. When I entered, I saw no one except him. I made a single bound, I uttered a single cry; I pressed my face to his; I embraced him closely without an utterance, except that of my tears and sighs; I was choked with tenderness and joy. The first thing he did, after leaving my arms, was to turn towards the ecclesiastic and say to him: "You see, sir, how my friends love me!" Completely overcome by my emotion, I did not at that time think of this manner of turning it to advantage; but, when occasionally reflecting upon it afterwards, I have always thought that this would not have been the first idea that would have occurred to me had I been in Diderot's place.

I found him greatly affected by his imprisonment. The donjon had made a terrible impression upon him, and, although he was comfortable at the castle and allowed to walk where he pleased in a park that was not even surrounded by walls, he needed the society of his friends, to avoid giving way to melancholy. As I was certainly the one who had most sympathy with his sufferings, I believed that I should also be the one whose presence would be most consoling to him, and, in spite of very pressing engagements, I went at least every other day, alone or with his wife, to spend the afternoon with him.

The summer of 1749 was excessively hot. Vincennes is reckoned to be two leagues distant from Paris. Being unable to afford a conveyance, I set out at two o'clock in the afternoon on foot, when I was alone, and walked fast, in order to get there sooner. The trees on the road – always lopped after the fashion of the country[1] – hardly afforded any shade, and often, exhausted by heat and fatigue, I threw myself on the ground, being unable to walk any further. In order to moderate my pace, I bethought myself of taking a book with me. One day I took the *Mercure de France*, and, while reading as I walked, I came upon the subject proposed by the Academy of Dijon as a prize essay for the following year: "Has the progress of the arts and sciences contributed more to the corruption or purification of morals?"

From the moment I read these words, I beheld another world and became another man. Although I have a lively recollection of the impression which they produced upon me, the details have escaped me since I committed them to paper in one of my four letters to M. de Malesherbes. This is one of the peculiarities of my memory which deserves to be mentioned. It only serves me so long as I am dependent upon it. As soon as I commit its contents to paper it forsakes me, and when I have once written a thing down, I completely forget it. This peculiarity follows me even into music. Before I learned it, I knew a number of songs by heart. As soon as I was able to sing from notes, I could not retain a single one in my memory, and I doubt whether I should now be able to repeat, from beginning to end, a single one of those which were my greatest favourites.

What I distinctly remember on this occasion is, that on my arrival at Vincennes I was in a state of agitation bordering upon madness. Diderot perceived it. I told him the reason, and read to him the Prosopopoea of Fabricius,[2] written in pencil, under an oak-tree. He encouraged me to allow my ideas to have full play, and to compete for the prize.[3] I did so, and from that moment I was lost. The misfortunes of the remainder of my life were the inevitable result of this moment of madness.

[1] Foreign visitors frequently complained of the French passion for clipped trees.

[2] Soliloquy of the famous Roman general, introduced by Rousseau in his essay.

[3] According to one account it was Diderot who actually advised Rousseau to take the adverse view, but it seems more likely he merely said "You can be trusted to take the line that nobody else will".

With inconceivable rapidity, my feelings became elevated to the tone of my ideas. All my petty passions were stifled by the enthusiasm of truth, liberty and virtue; and the most astonishing thing is, that this fervour continued in my heart for more than four or five years, in a higher degree, perhaps, than has ever been the case with the heart of any other man.

I worked at this Essay in a very curious manner, which I have adopted in almost all my other works. I devoted to it the hours of the night when I was unable to sleep. I meditated in bed with my eyes shut, and turned and re-turned my periods in my head with incredible labour. Then, when I was finally satisfied with them, I stored them up in my memory until I was able to commit them to paper; but the time spent in getting up and dressing myself made me forget everything, and when I sat down in front of my paper I could recall scarcely anything of what I had composed. I conceived the idea of making Madame le Vasseur my secretary. I had taken lodgings for her, her husband and her daughter, nearer to my own; and she, in order to save me the expense of a servant, came every morning to light my fire and attend to my little wants. When she came, I dictated to her from my bed the result of my labours of the preceding night; and this plan, to which I have long adhered, has saved me from forgetting much.

When the Essay was finished I showed it to Diderot, who was pleased with it, and suggested a few corrections. This production, however, although full of warmth and vigour, is altogether destitute of logic and arrangement. Of all the works that have proceeded from my pen, it is the weakest in argument and the poorest in harmony and proportion; but, however great a man's natural talents may be, the art of writing cannot be learnt all at once.

I sent off the work without mentioning it to anyone, with the exception, I fancy, of Grimm, with whom I began to be on most intimate terms after he went to live with the Comte de Frièse. He had a piano, which formed our meeting-place, and at which I spent in his company all my spare moments, singing Italian airs and *barcarolles*, without break or intermission from morning till evening, or, rather, from evening till morning; and whenever I was not to be found at Madame Dupin's I was sure to be found at Grimm's, or, at least, in his company, either on the promenade or at the theatre. I gave up going to the Comédie Italienne, where I had a free pass, but which he did not care for, and paid to go to the Comédie Française, of which he was passionately fond. At length I became so powerfully attracted to this young man, and so inseparable from him, that even poor "aunt" was neglected – that is to say, I saw less of her, for my attachment to her has never once wavered during the whole course of my life.

This impossibility of dividing the little spare time I had in accordance with my inclinations, renewed more strongly than ever the desire, which I had long since entertained, of having only one establishment for Thérèse and myself; but the obstacle presented by her numerous family and, above all, want of money to buy furniture, had hitherto prevented me. The opportunity of making an effort to provide a home presented itself, and I seized it. M. de Francueil and Madame Dupin, feeling that 800 or 900 *francs* a year could not be sufficient for me, of their own accord raised my salary to fifty *louis*; and, in addition, Madame Dupin, when she heard that I wanted to furnish my own rooms, gave me some assistance. With the furniture which Thérèse already had, we put all together, and, having rented some small rooms in the Hôtel de Languedoc, in the Rue de Grenelle-Saint-Honoré,[1] kept by very respectable people, we settled there as comfortably as we could, and we lived there quietly and agreeably for seven years, until I removed to the Hermitage.

Thérèse's father was a good old man, of a very peaceful disposition and terribly afraid of his wife, upon whom he had bestowed the name of "Criminal Lieutenant,"[2] which Grimm afterwards jestingly transferred to the daughter. Madame le Vasseur was not lacking in intelligence, that is to say, in address; she even prided herself on her politeness and distinguished manners; but she had a confidential wheedling tone, which

[1] Rousseau and Thérèse moved early in 1750 to a fourth-floor apartment in the hôtel de Languedoc, in the place des Deux Ecus, at the intersection of the present rue de Louvre and rue Jean-Jacques Rousseau.

[2] *Lieutenant Criminel*: a former magistrate of the Châtel (the name of two old courts, civil and criminal) of Paris.

was unendurable to me. She gave her daughter bad advice, tried
to make her dissemble with me, and cajoled my friends, separately, at the expense of one another, and at my own; in other
respects, she was a fairly good mother, because she found it
worth her while to be, and she concealed her daughter's faults,
because she profited by them. This woman, whom I loaded with
care, attention, and little presents, and whose affection I was
exceedingly anxious to gain, by reason of my utter inability to
succeed, was the only cause of trouble in my little establishment;
for the rest, I can say that, during these six or seven years, I
enjoyed the most perfect domestic happiness that human weakness can permit. My Thérèse's heart was that of an angel;
intimacy increased our attachment, and we daily felt more and
more how perfectly we were made for each other. If our
pleasures could be described, their simplicity would appear
ridiculous; our walks, *tête-à-tête*, outside the city, where I spent
my eight or ten *sous* magnificently in some beer-house; our little
suppers at the open window, at which we sat opposite each
other on two low chairs placed upon a trunk which filled up the
breadth of the window-niche. In this position, the window
served us as a table, we breathed the fresh air, we could see the
surrounding country and the passers-by, and, although we were
on the fourth storey, we could look down upon the street
while we ate. Who could describe, who could feel the charm
of these meals, at which the dishes consisted of nothing more
than a quartern loaf of coarse bread, a few cherries, a morsel of
cheese, and half a pint of wine, which we shared between us?
Friendship, confidence, intimacy, tranquillity of mind, how
delicious are your seasonings! Sometimes we remained there
till midnight, without thinking of it or suspecting how late it
was, until the old lady informed us. But let us leave these details,
which must appear insipid or ridiculous. I have always felt and
declared, that it is impossible to describe true enjoyment.

At the same time I indulged in a somewhat coarser enjoyment, the last of the kind with which I have to reproach myself. I
have mentioned that Klüpfel, the minister, was of an amiable
disposition; my relations with him were nearly as intimate as
with Grimm, and became equally confidential. They sometimes

shared my table. These meals, somewhat more than simple, were enlivened by the witty and broad jokes of Klüpfel and the humorous Germanisms of Grimm, who had not yet become a purist.

Sensuality did not preside at our little orgies; its place was supplied by gaiety, and we were so well satisfied with each other that we were unable to separate. Klüpfel had furnished a room for a little girl, who, notwithstanding, was at everybody's disposal, since he was unable to keep her by himself. One evening, as we were entering the *café*, we met him coming out to go and sup with her. We rallied him; he revenged himself gallantly by taking us to share the supper, and then rallied us in turn. The poor creature appeared to me to be of a fairly good disposition, very gentle, and little adapted for her profession, for which an old hag, whom she had with her, dressed her as well as she was able. The conversation and the wine enlivened us to such a degree that we forgot ourselves. The worthy Klüpfel did not desire to do the honours of his table by halves, and all three of us, in turn, went into the adjoining room with the little one, who did not know whether she ought to laugh or cry. Grimm has always declared that he never touched her, and that he remained so long with her simply in order to amuse himself at our impatience. If he really did not touch her, it is not likely that he was prevented by any scruples, since, before going to live with the Comte de Frièse, he lived with some girl in the same quarter of Saint-Roch.

I left the Rue des Moineaux,[1] where this girl lived, feeling as ashamed as Saint-Preux, when he left the house where he had been made drunk, and I had a vivid remembrance of my own story when writing his. Thérèse perceived, from certain indications, and, above all, from my confused air, that I had something to reproach myself with; I relieved my conscience of the burden by making a prompt and frank confession. In this I did well; for,

[1] The rue des Moineaux corresponded to the portion of the present Avenue de l'Opéra between the rue Saint-Roch and the rue Sainte-Anne. In *La Nouvelle Héloïse* (Part II, Letter 26) the penitent Saint-Preux tells Julie how some Swiss friends in Paris took him to a disreputable dinner-party, where he drank too much and woke to find himself in bed with one of his women fellow-guests.

the next morning, Grimm came in triumph to her, to give her an exaggerated account of my offence, and since that time he has never failed spitefully to remind her of it. This was the more inexcusable in him, since I had freely and voluntarily taken him into my confidence and had the right to expect from him that he would not give me cause to repent it. I never felt so much as on this occasion the goodness of my Thérèse's heart, for she was more indignant at Grimm's conduct than offended at my unfaithfulness, and I only had to submit to tender and touching reproaches on her part, in which I did not detect the slightest trace of anger.

This excellent girl's good-heartedness was equalled by her simplicity of mind. Nothing more need be said; however, I may be permitted to mention an example of it, which I recollect. I had told her that Klüpfel was preacher and chaplain to the Prince of Saxe-Gotha. In her estimation a preacher was so extraordinary a person that, oddly confounding two most dis-similar ideas, she got it into her head to take Klüpfel for the Pope. I thought she was mad when she told me, for the first time, on my return home, that the Pope had called to see me. I made her explain herself, and made all haste to go and tell the story to Grimm and Klüpfel, whom we ever afterwards called Pope, and gave the name of Pope Joan to the girl in the Rue des Moineaux. Our laughter was inextinguishable, and almost choked us. Those who have made me say, in a letter which they have been pleased to attribute to me, that I have only laughed twice in my life, were not acquainted with me at that time or in my youthful days; otherwise, this idea would certainly never have occurred to them.

[1750–1752.] – In the following year (1750) I heard that my Essay, of which I had not thought any more, had gained the prize at Dijon. This news awoke again all the ideas which had suggested it to me, animated them with fresh vigour, and stirred up in my heart the first leavening of virtue and heroism, which my father, my country, and Plutarch had deposited there in my infancy. I considered that nothing could be grander or finer than to be free and virtuous, above considerations of fortune and the opinion of mankind, and completely independent. Although false shame and fear of public disapproval at first prevented me from living in accordance with my principles, and from openly insulting the maxims of my age, from that moment my mind was made up, and I delayed carrying out my intention no longer than was necessary for contradiction to irritate it and render it victorious.

While philosophising upon the duties of man, an event occurred which made me reflect more seriously upon my own. Thérèse became pregnant for the third time. Too honest towards myself, too proud in my heart to desire to belie my principles by my actions, I began to consider the destination of my children and my connection with their mother, in the light of the laws of nature, justice, and reason, and of that religion – pure, holy and eternal, like its author – which men have polluted, while pretending to be anxious to purify it, and which they have converted, by their formulas, into a mere religion of words, seeing that it costs men little to prescribe what is impossible, when they dispense with carrying it out in practice.

If I was wrong in my conclusions, nothing can be more remarkable than the calmness with which I abandoned myself to them. If I had been one of those low-born men, who are deaf to the gentle voice of Nature, in whose heart no real sentiment of justice or humanity ever springs up, this hardening of my heart would have been quite easy to understand. But is it possible that my warm-heartedness, lively sensibility, readiness to form attachments, the powerful hold which they exercise over me, the cruel heartbreakings I experience when forced to break them off, my natural goodwill towards all my fellow-creatures, my ardent love of the great, the true, the beautiful, and the just; my horror of evil of every kind, my utter inability to hate or injure, or even to think of it; the sweet and lively emotion which I feel at the sight of all that is virtuous, generous, and amiable; is it possible, I ask, that all these can ever agree in the same heart with the depravity which, without the least scruple, tramples underfoot the sweetest of obligations? No! I feel and loudly assert – it is impossible. Never, for a single moment in his life, could Jean Jacques have been a man without feeling, without compassion, or an unnatural father. I may have been mistaken, never hardened. If I were to state my reasons, I should say too much. Since they were strong enough to mislead me, they might mislead many others, and I do not desire to expose young people, who may read my works, to the danger of allowing themselves to be misled by the same error. I will content myself with observing, that my error was such that, in handing over my children to the State to educate, for want of means to bring them up myself, in deciding to fit them for becoming workmen and peasants rather than adventurers and fortune-hunters, I thought that I was behaving like a citizen and a father, and considered myself a member of Plato's Republic. More than once since then, the regrets of my heart have told me that I was wrong; but, far from my reason having given me the same information, I have often blessed Heaven for having preserved them from their father's lot, and from the lot which threatened them as soon as I should have been obliged to abandon them. If I had left them with Madame d'Epinay or Madame de Luxembourg, who, from friendship, generosity, or some other motive, expressed themselves willing to take charge of them, would they have been happier, would they have been brought up at least as honest men? I do not know; but I do know that they would have been brought up to hate, perhaps to betray, their parents; it is a hundred times better that they have never known them.

My third child was accordingly taken to the Foundling Hospital, like the other two. The two next were disposed of in the same manner, for I had five altogether. This arrangement appeared to me so admirable, so rational, and so legitimate, that, if I did not openly boast of it, this was solely out of regard for the mother; but I told all who were acquainted with our relations. I told Grimm and Diderot. I afterwards informed Madame d'Epinay, and, later, Madame de Luxembourg, freely and voluntarily, without being in any way obliged to do so, and when I might easily have kept it a secret from everybody; for Gouin was an honourable woman, very discreet, and a person upon whom I could implicitly rely. The only one of my friends to whom I had any interest in unbosoming myself was M. Thierry, the physician who attended my poor "aunt" in a dangerous confinement. In a word, I made no mystery of what I did, not only because I have never known how to keep a secret from my friends, but because I really saw no harm in it. All things considered, I chose for my children what was best, or, at least, what I believed to be best for them. I could have wished, and still wish, that I had been reared and brought up as they have been.

While I was thus making my confessions, Madame le Vasseur on her part did the same, but with less disinterested views. I had introduced her and her daughter to Madame Dupin, who, out of friendship for me, did them a thousand kindnesses. The mother confided her daughter's secret to her. Madame Dupin, who is good-hearted and generous, whom she never told how attentive I was to provide for everything, in spite of my moderate means, herself made provision for her with a generosity which, by her mother's instructions, the daughter always kept a secret from me during my stay in Paris, and only confessed to me at the Hermitage, after several other confidences. I did not know that Madame Dupin, who never gave me the least hint of it, was so well informed. Whether Madame de Chenonceaux, her daughter-in-law, was equally well informed, I do not know; but Madame de Francueil, her step-daughter, was, and was unable to hold her tongue. She spoke to me about it the following year, after I had left their house. This induced me to address a letter to her on this subject, which will be found in my collections, in which I have set forth those reasons for my conduct, which I was able to give without compromising Madame le Vasseur and her family, for the most decisive of them came from that quarter, and upon them I kept silence.

I can rely upon the discretion of Madame Dupin and the friendship of Madame de Chenonceaux; I felt equally sure in regard to Madame de Francueil, who, besides, died long before my secret was noised abroad. It could only have been disclosed by those very people to whom I had confided it, and, in fact, it was not until after I had broken with them, that it was so disclosed. By this single fact they are judged. Without desiring to acquit myself of the blame which I deserve, I would rather have it upon my shoulders than that which their malice deserves. My fault is great, but it was due to error; I have neglected my duties, but the desire of doing an injury never entered my heart, and the feelings of a father cannot speak very eloquently on behalf of children whom he has never seen; but, to betray the confidence of friendship, to violate the most sacred of all agreements, to disclose secrets poured into our bosoms, deliberately to dishonour the friend whom one has deceived, and who still respects us while leaving us – these are not faults; they are acts of meanness and infamy.

I have promised my confession, not my justification; therefore I say no more on this point. It is my duty to be true; the reader's to be just. I shall never ask more from him than that.

The marriage of M. de Chenonceaux made his mother's house still more pleasant to me, owing to the accomplishments of his young wife – a very amiable person, who appeared to take especial notice of me amongst M. Dupin's secretaries. She was the only daughter of Madame la Vicomtesse de Rochechouart, a great friend of the Comte de Frièse, and, consequently, of Grimm, who was attached to him. It was I, however, who introduced him to his daughter; but, as their dispositions did not agree, the acquaintance did not last long, and Grimm, who from that time only had eyes for that which was solid, preferred the mother, who belonged to the great world, to the daughter, who desired friends on whom she could rely and who were agreeable to her, who were neither mixed up in any intrigues nor sought to gain credit amongst the great. Madame Dupin, not finding in Madame de Chenonceaux all the docility which she expected from her, made her house very dull for her, and Madame de Chenonceaux, proud of her own merits, and perhaps also of her birth, preferred to renounce the pleasures of society, and to remain almost alone in her room, than to bear a yoke for which she felt she was not adapted. This species of exile increased my attachment for her, from the natural inclination which attracts me towards the unfortunate. I found in her a metaphysical and thoughtful mind, although at times somewhat sophistical. Her conversation, which was by no means that of a young woman just leaving the convent, was very attractive to me; and yet she was not twenty years of age. Her complexion was dazzlingly fair. Her figure would have been dignified and beautiful, if she had carried herself better. Her hair, which was ashen-grey and of rare beauty, reminded me of my dear mamma's in her youth, and caused a lively emotion in my heart. But the strict principles which I had just laid down for myself, and which I was resolved to act up to at all cost, protected me against her and her charm. During a whole summer I spent three or four hours every day alone with her, solemnly teaching her arithmetic, and wearying her with my everlasting figures, without ever uttering a single word of gallantry or casting a glance of admiration upon her. Five or six years later, I should have been neither so wise nor so foolish; but it was destined that I should only love truly once in my life, and that the first and last sighs of my heart should be given to another than her.

Since I had lived at Madame Dupin's, I had always been satisfied with my lot, without showing any desire to see it improved. The increase in my salary, due to her and M. de Franceuil together, was quite voluntary on their part. This year, M. de Francueil, whose friendship for me increased daily, wanted to make my position somewhat more comfortable and less precarious. He was Receiver-General of Finance. M. Dudoyer, his cashier, was old, well to do, and anxious to retire. M. de Francueil offered me his place; and, in order to make myself fit to take it, I went for a few weeks to M. Dudoyer's house, to receive the necessary instructions. But, whether it was that I had little talent for this occupation, or that Dudoyer, who seemed to me to have someone else in his eye as his successor, did not instruct me in good faith, my acquisition of the knowledge required was slow and unsatisfactory, and I was never able to get into my head the state of accounts, which perhaps had been purposely muddled. However, without having grasped the intricacies of the business, I soon acquired sufficient knowledge of its ordinary routine to undertake the general management. I even commenced its duties. I kept the ledgers and the cash; I paid and received money, and gave receipts; and although I had as little inclination as ability for such employment, advancing years made me more sensible: I determined to overcome my dislike, and to devote myself entirely to my duties. Unfortunately, just as I was beginning to get used to them,

M. de Francueil went away on a short journey, during which I remained in charge of his cash, which at that time, however, did not amount to more than 25,000 or 30,000 francs. The care and anxiety which this deposit caused me convinced me that I was not made for a cashier, and I have no doubt that the impatience with which I awaited his return contributed to the illness which subsequently attacked me.

I have already mentioned, in the first part of this work, that I was almost dead when I was born. A defective formation of the bladder caused, during my childhood, an almost continual retention of urine; and my aunt Suzon, who took care of me, had the greatest difficulty in keeping me alive. However, she at length succeeded: my robust constitution at length gained the upper hand, and my health improved so much during my youth that, with the exception of the attack of languor which I have described, and the frequent necessity of making water, which the least heating of the blood always rendered a matter of difficulty, I reached the age of thirty without feeling my early infirmity at all. The first touch of it which I had was on my arrival at Venice. The fatigue of the journey, and the fearful heat which I had suffered, brought on a constant desire to make water and an affection of the kidneys, which lasted till the beginning of the winter. After my visit to the *padoana*, I looked upon myself as a dead man, and yet I never suffered the slightest inconvenience from it. After having exhausted myself more in imagination than in reality for my Zulietta, I was in better health than ever. It was only after Diderot's confinement that the overheating, caused by my journeys to Vincennes during the fearful heat, brought on a violent pain in the kidneys, and since that time I have never recovered my health completely.

At the time of which I am speaking, having perhaps overtired myself with my distasteful work at the confounded office, I became worse than before, and was confined to my bed for five or six weeks in the most melancholy condition that can be imagined. Madame Dupin sent the celebrated Morand to see me, who, in spite of his cleverness and delicacy of touch, caused me incredible suffering, and could never get to probe me. He advised me to consult Daran, who managed to introduce his bougies, which were more flexible, and afforded me some relief; but, when giving Madame Dupin an account of my condition, he declared that I had less than six months to live.

This verdict, which I afterwards heard, caused me to reflect seriously upon my condition, and upon the folly of sacrificing the repose and comfort of my few remaining days to the slavery of an employment for which I felt nothing but aversion. Besides, how could I reconcile the strict principles which I had just adopted with a situation which harmonised so ill with them? Would it not have been very bad taste in me, cashier of a Receiver-General of Finance, to preach disinterestedness and poverty? These ideas fermented so strongly in my head together with the fever, and combined so powerfully, that from that time nothing could uproot them, and, during the period of my recovery, I quietly determined to carry out the resolutions which I had made during my delirium. I renounced for ever all plans of fortune and promotion. Resolved to pass my few remaining days in poverty and independence, I employed all my strength of mind in breaking away from the bonds of the opinion of the world, and in courageously carrying out everything which appeared to me to be right, without troubling myself about what the world might think of it. The obstacles which I had to overcome, the efforts which I made to triumph over them, are incredible. I succeeded as much as was possible, and more than I had myself hoped. If I had been as successful in shaking off the yoke of friendship as that of public opinion, I should have accomplished my purpose, perhaps the greatest, or, at any rate, the most conducive to virtue, that a mortal has ever conceived; but, while I trampled underfoot the senseless judgments of the common herd of the so-called great and wise, I suffered myself to be subjugated and led like a child by so-called friends, who, jealous of seeing me strike out a new path by myself, thought of nothing but how to make me appear ridiculous, and began by doing their utmost to degrade me, in order to raise an outcry against me. It was the change in my character, dating from this period, rather than my literary celebrity, that drew their jealousy upon me; they would perhaps have forgiven me for distinguishing myself in the art of writing; but they could not forgive me for setting an example in my change of life, which seemed likely to cause them inconvenience. I was born for friendship; my easy and gentle disposition found no difficulty in cherishing it. As long as I was unknown to the world, I was loved by all who knew me, and had not a single enemy; but, as soon as I became known, I had not a single friend. This was a great misfortune; it was a still greater one that I was surrounded by people who called themselves my friends, and who only made use of the privileges which this name allowed them to drag me to my ruin. The sequel of these memoirs will reveal this odious intrigue; at present I only point out its origin; my readers will soon see the first link forged.

In the state of independence in which I intended to live, it was necessary, however, to find means of subsistence. I bethought myself of a very simple plan: copying music at so much a page. If a more solid employment would have fulfilled the same end, I should have adopted it; but as I had taste and ability for this, and as it was the only occupation which would provide my daily bread without personal dependence, I was satisfied with it. Believing that I no longer had need of foresight, and silencing the voice of vanity, from cashier to a financier I became a copyist of music. I thought I had gained greatly by the choice, and I have so little regretted it, that I have never abandoned this employment except under compulsion, and then only to resume it as soon as I was able.

The success of my first Essay made it easier for me to carry out this resolution. After it had gained the prize, Diderot undertook to get it printed. While I was in bed he wrote me a note, informing me of its publication and the effect it had produced. "It has gone up like a rocket," he told me; "such a success has never been seen before." This voluntary approval of the public, in the case of an unknown author, gave me the first real assurance of my ability, as to which, in spite of my inner feelings, I had until then always been doubtful. I saw the great advantage I might derive from it in view of the resolution which I was on the point of carrying out, and I judged that a copyist of some literary celebrity would not be likely to suffer from want of work.

As soon as my resolution was taken and confirmed, I wrote a note to M. de Francueil to inform him of it, thanking him and Madame Dupin for all their kindness, and asking for their custom. Francueil, quite unable to understand the note, and believing that I was still delirious, came to me in all haste, but he found my mind so firmly made up that he was unable to shake my resolution. He went and told Madame Dupin and everyone else that I had gone mad. I let him do so, and went my way. I commenced my reformation with my dress. I gave up my gold lace and white stockings, and put on a round wig. I took off my sword and sold my watch, saying to myself with incredible delight, "Thank Heaven, I shall not want to know the time again!" M. de Francueil was kind enough to wait some time before he found a successor to me. At last, when he saw that my mind was made up, he gave my post to M. d'Alibard, formerly tutor to the young Chenonceaux, known in the botanical world for his "Flora Parisiensis."*

In spite of the strictness of my sumptuary reform, I did not at first extend it to my linen, which was good, and of which I had a large stock – the remains of my Venetian outfit – and for which I had a special fondness. I had considered it so much a matter of cleanliness that I ended by making it a matter of luxury, which was certainly expensive. Someone was kind enough to deliver me from this servitude. On Christmas Eve, while the women-folk were at vespers, and I was at the "spiritual concert,"[1] the door of a garret in which all our linen was hung up after a wash, which was just finished, was broken open. Everything was stolen, amongst other things, forty-two fine linen shirts belonging to me – the principal part of my linen wardrobe. From the description given by the neighbours of a man who had been seen to leave the hotel carrying some bundles, Thérèse and myself suspected her brother, who was known to be a worthless fellow. The mother indignantly repudiated the suspicion, but it was

* I have no doubt that Francueil and his associates now give a totally different account of all this, but I appeal to what he said about it at the time, and for a long time afterwards, to all his acquaintances, until the conspiracy was formed. Men of good sense and honour cannot have forgotten his words. (R)

[1] At which only religious music was heard, and which, on certain days, was a substitute for secular concerts.

confirmed by so many proofs that we could not abandon it, in spite of her indignation. I did not venture to make strict inquiries for fear of discovering more than I might have liked. The brother never showed himself again, and at last disappeared altogether. I deplored Thérèse's misfortune and my own in being connected with so mixed a family, and I urged her more strongly than ever to shake off a yoke so dangerous. This adventure cured me of my passion for fine linen, and from that time I have only worn shirts of very common material, more in keeping with the rest of my dress.

Having thus completed my reforms, my only anxiety was to make them solid and lasting, by doing my utmost to root out of my heart everything which was still liable to be affected by public opinion; everything which, from fear of censure, might turn me aside from that which was good and reasonable in itself. In consequence of the stir which my Essay created, my resolution also made a sensation and brought me employment, so that I commenced my new profession with tolerable success. Nevertheless, several causes prevented me from succeeding as well as I might have done in other circumstances. In the first place, my bad health. My recent attack left after-effects which prevented me from ever regaining my former state of health: and it is my belief that the physicians, to whose treatment I intrusted myself, did me as much harm as my illness. I consulted, in succession, Morand, Daran, Helvétius, Malouin and Thierry, all very learned men, and my personal friends. Each treated me in his own way, afforded me no relief, and considerably weakened me. The more I submitted to their treatment, the yellower, thinner, and weaker I became. My imagination, which they terrified, judged of my condition by the effect of their drugs, and only set before my eyes a continuous succession of sufferings before my death – retention of urine, gravel, and stone. All the remedies which afford relief to others – ptisans, baths, and bleeding – only aggravated my sufferings. Finding that Daran's bougies, the only ones which had any effect, and without which I thought I could not live, only afforded me momentary relief, I proceeded, at great expense, to lay in an enormous stock of them, so that, in case of Daran's death, I might always have some for use. During the eight or ten years in which I made such constant use of them I must have spent at least fifty *louis*. It will be readily imagined that a treatment so expensive, painful, and troublesome distracted me from my work, and that a dying man is not very eager about earning his daily bread.

Literary occupations were equally prejudicial to my daily work. No sooner had my Essay appeared, than the defenders of literature fell upon me as if by common consent. Indignant at the sight of so many Messieurs Josse,[1] who did not even understand the question, attempting to decide like masters, I took up my pen and treated some of them in such a manner that they no longer had the laugh on their side. One M. Gautier, from Nancy, the first who fell under my lash, was roughly abused in a letter to Grimm. The second was King Stanislaus[2] himself, who did not disdain to enter the lists with me. The honour which he did me obliged me to change the tone of my answer. I adopted one that was more serious, but equally emphatic, and, without failing in respect towards the author, I completely refuted his work. I knew that a Jesuit, Father Menou, had had a hand in it. I trusted to my judgment to distinguish the work of the Prince from that of the monk; and, mercilessly attacking all the Jesuitical phrases, I brought into prominence, as I went along, an anachronism which I believed could only have proceeded from the pen of his reverence. This composition, which, for some reason or other, has made less stir than my other writings, is, in its way, unique. In it I seized the opportunity of showing the public, how a private individual could defend the cause of truth, even against a sovereign. It would be difficult to adopt, at the same time, a more dignified and respectful tone than that which I adopted in my answer to him. I was fortunate enough to have to deal with an adversary for whom I felt sincere esteem, which I could exhibit without servile adulation; this I did with tolerable success, and always in a dignified manner. My friends, alarmed on my behalf,

[1] M. Josse was one of the characters in Molière's *L'Amour médecin*. The saying, "Vous êtes orfèvre, Monsieur Josse," is used to remind a man that he is personally interested in the success of anything which he strongly recommends or supports.

[2] [Stanislaus] See *Biographies*, p. 714.

thought they already saw me in the Bastille. I never once had any such fear, and I was right. This worthy Prince, after he had seen my reply, said, "I have had enough of it; I will have nothing more to do with it." Since then I have received from him various marks of esteem and kindness, some of which I shall have to mention presently; and my composition quietly circulated throughout France and Europe, without anyone finding anything in it to censure.

Shortly afterwards, I had another opponent, whom I had not expected, the same M. Bordes[1] of Lyons, who, ten years previously, had shown me much friendship, and rendered me several services. I had not forgotten him, but had neglected him from simple laziness; and I had not sent him my writings, since I had had no convenient opportunity of getting them delivered to him. I was wrong; he attacked me, certainly with politeness, and I answered in the same tone. He made a more decided rejoinder, which drew from me a final answer, after which he remained silent. But he became my most violent enemy, profited by the time of my misfortunes to write a most fearful libel against me, and took a journey to London on purpose to do me harm there.

All these polemics took up a great deal of my time, which was lost to my copying, without any advantage to the cause of truth, or profit to my purse. Pissot, who was my publisher at the time, gave me very little for my brochures, and often nothing at all; for instance, I never received a *sou* for my first Essay; Diderot gave it to him for nothing. I was obliged to wait a long time, and extract the little remuneration which he gave me, *sou* by *sou*. In the meantime, my copying was a failure. I carried on two trades, which was the way to fail in both.

They were contradictory in another way – the different mode of life which they forced me to adopt. The success of my first writings had made me the fashion. The position which I had taken up aroused curiosity; people were anxious to make the

[1] Charles Bordes (1711–81) was a native of Lyons, and in 1741 Rousseau had addressed a verse *Epistle* to him, praising the industriousness and prosperity of the Lyonnais. Bordes delivered a *Discourse* attacking Rousseau's views before the Academy of Lyons in May 1751, and it was published in the *Mercure* in December. He later went to live in England.

acquaintance of the singular man, who sought no one's society, and whose only anxiety was to live free and happy after his own fashion; this was sufficient to make this an impossibility for him. My room was never free from people who, under different pretexts, came to rob me of my time. Ladies employed a thousand artifices to get me to dine with them. The more I offended people, the more obstinate they became. I could not refuse everybody. While I made a thousand enemies by my refusals, I was incessantly a slave to my desire to oblige; and, however I managed, I never had an hour to myself during the day.

I then discovered that it is by no means so easy as one imagines to be poor and independent. I wanted to live by my profession; the public would not have it. They invented a thousand ways of indemnifying me for the time which they made me lose. Presents of all kinds were always being sent to me. Soon I should have been obliged to show myself like Punch, at so much a head. I know no slavery more cruel and degrading than that. I saw no remedy for it, except to refuse all presents, great and small, and to make no exception in favour of anyone. The only effect of this was to increase the number of the donors, who desired to have the honour of overcoming my resistance, and of compelling me to be under an obligation to them, in spite of myself. Many, who would not have given me a crown if I had asked for it, never ceased to importune me with their offers, and to avenge themselves when they found them rejected, charged me with arrogance and ostentation, in consequence of my refusal.

It will easily be understood that the resolution which I had taken, and the system which I desired to follow, were not at all to the liking of Madame le Vasseur. All the daughter's disinterestedness was unable to prevent her from following the instructions of her mother; and the *gouverneuses*, as Grimm used to call them, were not always as firm in their refusal as I was. Although many things were concealed from me, I saw enough to convince me that I did not see everything, and this tormented me, not so much on account of the charge of connivance, which I readily foresaw would be made, as by the cruel thought that I could never be master of my own household, or even of myself.

I begged, entreated, and got angry – all in vain. Mamma gave me the reputation of an eternal grumbler and a surly boor. Continual whisperings with my friends went on; all was mystery and secrecy in my household; and, to avoid exposing myself to perpetual storms, I no longer ventured to make inquiries about what was going on. To deliver myself from all this disturbance would have needed a firmness of which I was incapable. I knew how to make a noise, but not how to act. They allowed me to speak and went their way.

These continual upsets and the daily importunities to which I was subjected at length made my apartments and my stay at Paris very unpleasant. When my ill-health permitted me to go out, and I did not allow myself to be dragged hither and thither by my acquaintances, I used to go for a solitary walk, during which, dreaming of my grand system, I jotted down some ideas on paper with the aid of a pocket-book and pencil, which I always carried about with me. In this manner the unforeseen unpleas-antnesses of a condition which I had chosen for myself threw me entirely into a literary career, by way of escaping from them; and this is the reason why, in all my early works, I introduced the bitterness and ill-humour which caused me to write them.

Another circumstance contributed to this. Thrown, in spite of myself, into the great world, without possessing its manners, and unable to acquire or conform to them, I took it into my head to adopt manners of my own, which might enable me to dispense with them. Being unable to overcome my foolish and disagree-able shyness, which proceeded from the fear of offending against the rules of polite society, I resolved, in order to give myself courage, to trample them underfoot. Shame made me cynical and sarcastic. I affected to despise the politeness which I did not know how to practise. It is true that this rudeness, in harmony with my new principles, became ennobled in my mind and assumed the form of dauntless virtue; and on this lofty basis, I venture to assert, it supported itself longer and more success-fully than would naturally have been expected from an effort so contrary to my disposition. However, in spite of the reputation for misanthropy, which my outward appearance and some happy remarks gained for me in the world, it is certain that, in private, I always sustained my part badly. My friends and acquaintances led this unsociable bear like a lamb, and, limiting my sarcasms to unpalatable but general truths, I was never capable of saying a single discourteous word to anyone whatsoever.

The *Devin du Village* made me quite the fashion, and soon there was not a man in Paris more sought after than myself. The history of this piece, which was an epoch in my life, is mixed up with that of the connections which I had formed at that time. In order that the sequel may be rightly understood, I must enter into details.

I had a tolerably large number of acquaintances, but only two chosen friends, Diderot and Grimm. Owing to the desire which I always feel, to bring together all who are dear to me, I was so devoted a friend of both, that it was unavoidable that they should soon become equally devoted to each other. I brought them together; they suited each other, and soon became more intimate with each other than with me. Diderot had acquaintances without number; but Grimm, being a foreigner and a newcomer, had his to make. I desired nothing better than to assist him. I had introduced him to Diderot; I introduced him to Gauffecourt. I took him to Madame de Chenonceaux, to Madame d'Epinay, to the Baron d'Holbach, with whom I found myself connected, almost in spite of myself. All my friends became his; that was simple enough. But none of his ever became mine; this was not so intelligible. While he lived with the Comte de Frièse, he often invited us to dine with him, but I have never received any proof of friendship from the Comte de Frièse or the Comte de Schomberg, his relative, who was very intimate with Grimm, or from any other person, male or female, with whom Grimm had any connection through their means. The only exception was the Abbé Raynal, who, although his friend, also proved himself mine, and, when I needed it, placed his purse at my disposal with a rare generosity. But I had known the Abbé long before Grimm himself, and I had always entertained a great regard for him since he had behaved to me in a most delicate and honourable manner, in a matter certainly of little importance, but which I never forgot.

The Abbé Raynal was certainly a warm friend. He gave me a proof of this about this time in a matter that concerned Grimm, with whom he was very intimate. Grimm, after having long been on very friendly terms with Mademoiselle Fel, suddenly took it into his head to conceive a violent passion for her, and wanted to supplant Cahusac. The young lady, priding herself upon her constancy, showed her new admirer the door. The latter took the matter in a tragic light, and had a fancy that it would be his death. He suddenly began to suffer from the strangest illness that has perhaps ever been heard of. He passed days and nights in a state of continued lethargy, his eyes wide open, his pulse regular, but without speaking, eating, or stirring, sometimes seeming to hear, but never answering, even by signs; in other respects, he was free from agitation, pain or fever, and lay as if he had been dead. The Abbé Raynal and myself took it in turns to watch him, the Abbé, being stronger and in better health, by night, and myself by day; he was never left alone, and neither of us ever quitted him before the other had come to take his place. The Comte de Frièse, being alarmed about him, brought Senac to see him, who, after a careful examination, declared that there was nothing the matter with the patient, and did not even prescribe for him. My anxiety about my friend made me carefully observe the physician's countenance, and I saw him smile as he left the room. Nevertheless, Grimm remained for several days without moving, without taking broth or anything else, except some preserved cherries which I laid upon his tongue from time to time, and which he eagerly swallowed. One fine morning, he got up, dressed himself, and resumed his ordinary occupations, without ever saying anything either to me, or, as far as I know, to the Abbé, or anyone else, about this singular lethargy, or of the attention and care which we had bestowed upon him as long as it lasted.

This adventure, nevertheless, made a considerable stir; and it would really have been a wonderful story, if the cruelty of an opera-girl had caused a man to die of despair. This violent passion made Grimm the rage; he was soon looked upon as a prodigy of love, friendship, and devotion in every respect. This reputation caused him to be run after and fêted in the great world, which separated him from me, who had never been anything to him but a makeshift. I saw that he was on the point of being entirely estranged from me. This was very distressing to me, for all the lively feelings, of which he made such a show, were just those which I entertained for him, although I did not make such a noise about it. I was glad that he should succeed in the world, but I should have wished him to do so without, at the same time, forgetting his friend. I said to him one day, "Grimm, you are neglecting me; I forgive you. When the first intoxication of noisy success has produced its effect, and you begin to perceive its emptiness, I hope that you will come back to me: you will always find me the same. For the present, do not put yourself out; I leave you to do as you please, and will wait for you." He told me that I was right, made his arrangements accordingly, and went his own way so completely, that I only saw him in the company of our mutual friends.

Our chief meeting-place, before he became so closely connected with Madame d'Epinay, was the Baron d'Holbach's[1] house. This Baron was the son of a self-made man, who possessed an ample fortune, which he used nobly. He received at his house men of letters and learning, and, by his own knowledge and accomplishments, was well able to hold his own amongst them. Having been long intimate with Diderot, he had sought my acquaintance through him, even before my name became known. A natural repugnance for a long time prevented me from meeting his advances. One day he asked me the reason, and I said to him, "You are too wealthy." He persisted, and finally prevailed. My greatest misfortune has ever been inability to resist flattery, and I have always regretted yielding to it.

Another acquaintance, which ripened into friendship as soon as I had a reason to claim it, was that of M. Duclos. Several years had elapsed since I had seen him, for the first time, at La Chevrette, at the house of Madame d'Epinay, with whom he was on intimate terms. We only dined together, and he returned the same day; but we conversed for a few moments after dinner. Madame d'Epinay had spoken to him of me and my opera of *Les*

[1] [d'Holbach] See *Biographies*, p. 711.

Muses Galantes. Duclos, who was gifted with too great talent himself not to value those who possessed it, became prepossessed in my favour, and had invited me to go and see him. In spite of my early inclination, which was strengthened by acquaintance, my timidity and want of energy kept me back as long as I had no other passport to him except his courtesy; but, encouraged by my first success and his praises, which were repeated to me, I went to call upon him, and he returned my call. In this manner commenced the connection between us, which will always cause me to regard him with affection, and to which, as well as the testimony of my own heart, I owe the knowledge, that uprightness and honour may sometimes be combined with literary culture.

Many other connections less lasting, which I here pass over, were the result of my early successes, and continued until curiosity was satisfied. I was a man who was so soon understood, that, after the first day, there was nothing more to be seen in me. One lady, however, who at that time sought my acquaintance, was more constant to me than any of the rest. This was Madame la Marquise de Créqui, niece of the Bailli de Froulay, the Maltese ambassador, whose brother had preceded M. de Montaigu in the embassy at Venice, and whom I had gone to see on my return from that city. Madame de Créqui wrote to me; I called upon her, and she conceived a friendship for me. I sometimes dined at her house, where I met several men of letters; amongst others, M. Saurin, the author of "Spartacus," "Barneveldt," and other works, who afterwards became my bitterest enemy, for no other reason that I can imagine, except that I bear the name of a man whom his father had persecuted disgracefully.[1]

It will be seen that, for a copyist who ought to be occupied with his business from morning till evening, I had numerous distractions, which prevented my daily work from being very lucrative, and myself from paying sufficient attention to what I had to do, for me to do it well. I thus lost more than half the time I had left in erasing or scratching out mistakes, or beginning my

[1] *i.e.*, the poet Jean-Baptiste Rousseau, about whom Saurin's father Joseph wrote some scurrilous verses.

work again on a fresh sheet of paper. This constant interruption made Paris daily more intolerable to me, and I eagerly seized every opportunity of going into the country. I went several times to spend a few days at Marcoussis,[1] where Madame le Vasseur knew the vicar, at whose house we so arranged matters that he found himself at no disadvantage. Once Grimm went with us.* The vicar had a good voice and sang well; and, although not a musician, could learn his part with ease and accuracy. We spent the time in singing the trios which I had composed at Chenonceaux. I also wrote two or three new ones, to the words which Grimm and the vicar put together as well as they could. I cannot help regretting these trios, which were written and sung in moments of pure joy, and which I have left at Wootton with all my music. Mademoiselle Davenport has, perhaps, already made curl-papers of them; but they were worth preserving, and are mostly written in a very good counterpoint. It was after one of these little excursions, when I was delighted to see "aunt" at her ease and very cheerful, and had also enjoyed myself very much, that I wrote to the vicar a letter in verse, hastily dashed off and a very poor composition, which will be found amongst my papers.[2]

Nearer Paris, I found another place of refuge, very much to my taste, with M. Mussard, a countryman, relative, and friend, who had made a charming retreat for himself at Passy, where I have spent many peaceful moments. M. Mussard was a jeweller, a man of good sense, who, after having made a comfortable fortune in his business, married his only daughter to M. de Valmalette, the son of an exchange broker, and *maître d'hôtel* to the King, and prudently left trade and business in his old age, in order to enjoy an interval of repose and enjoyment between the

[1] Marcoussis is a village in Seine-et-Oise, about 17 miles south of Paris.

* Since I have here omitted to mention a trifling, but memorable adventure which I had with the aforesaid Grimm, one morning when we were to dine at the Fountain of Saint-Vandrille, I will not return to it; but, on subsequent reflection, I concluded that, in the bottom of his heart, he was already hatching the conspiracy which he afterwards carried out with such marvellous success. (R)

[2] Rousseau addressed a verse *Epistle*, a diatribe against Paris, to the vicar of Marcoussis in 1751. The fontaine de Sainte-Wandrille lies a few miles NW of the village.

worries of life and his death. The worthy Mussard, a real practical philosopher, lived, free from cares, in a very nice house,
which he had built for himself, standing in a very pretty
garden which he had planted with his own hands. While digging
up the terraces of this garden, he found fossil shells in such
quantities, that his lively imagination saw nothing but shells in
the natural world, and he at last sincerely believed that the
universe consisted of nothing but shells, and remains of shells,
and that the whole earth was nothing but so much shell sand.
Thinking of nothing but this fact and his wonderful discoveries,
he became so excited with these ideas, that they would soon
have turned to a system in his head, that is to say, to madness,
had not death – fortunately for his reason, but unfortunately for
his friends, who were much attached to him, and found at his
house a most agreeable refuge – removed him from them by a
most strange and painful disease. This was a constantly growing
tumour in the stomach, which for a long time prevented him
from eating before the reason was discovered, and which, after
several years of suffering, caused his death from sheer starvation.
I can never recall without the greatest anguish the last days of
this unfortunate and worthy man, who still heartily welcomed
Lenieps and myself, the only friends whom the sight of the
sufferings which he endured did not drive away from him until
his last hour, who, as I say, was reduced to devouring with his
eyes the repast which he caused to be set before us, scarcely able
to swallow a few drops of weak tea, which he was obliged to
bring up the next moment. But, before these days of suffering,
how many agreeable hours did I spend at his house with the
select circle of his friends! At the head of these I place the Abbé
Prévost, an amiable and simple person, whose heart inspired his
writings, which deserved to be immortalised, and who, neither in
his disposition nor in society, showed any traces of the sombre
colouring which characterised his works; Procope the physician,
a little Aesop, who was a great ladies' man; Boulanger, the
famous posthumous author of "Le Despotisme Oriental," and
who, I believe, extended Mussard's theories on the age of the
world. Amongst his lady friends were Madame Denis, Voltaire's
niece, who at that time was simple and unaffected, and made no

pretence to be a wit; Madame Vanloo, who was certainly no beauty, but was charming and sang like an angel; and Madame de Valmalette herself, who also sang, and who, although very thin, would have been very amiable if she had made less pretence of being so. These made up nearly the whole of M. Mussard's friends; their society would have been very agreeable to me, had not his conchylomania been even more agreeable; and I can say that for six months or more I worked in his study with as much pleasure as himself.

He had for a long time insisted that the waters of Passy would be beneficial to me, and strongly advised me to come to his house and drink them. In order to get away from the noisy crowd of the city for a little while, I at last gave in, and spent eight or ten days at Passy, which did me more good because I was in the country, than because I took the waters. Mussard played the violoncello, and was passionately fond of Italian music. One evening we had a long conversation about it before going to bed, especially about the *opera buffa,* which we had both seen in Italy, and with which we had both been delighted. During the night, being unable to sleep, I began to ponder how it would be possible to give an idea of this kind of drama in France, for the *Amours de Ragonde*[1] had not the least resemblance to it. In the morning, while walking and drinking the waters, I hastily made up a few specimens of verse, and set them to the airs which came into my head as I composed them. I scribbled down the whole in a kind of vaulted *salon* at the top of the garden, and, at tea, I could not refrain from showing these airs to Mussard and Mademoiselle Duvernois, his house keeper, who was really a most excellent and amiable young woman. The three pieces which I had sketched were the first monologue, *J'ai perdu mon serviteur*, the air of the *Devin du village, L'Amour croît s'il s'inquiète,* and the last duet, *A jamais, Colin, je t'engage,* &c. I so little thought that it was worth the trouble of going on with it that, had it not been for the applause and encouragement of both, I should have thrown my scraps of paper into the fire and thought nothing more about it, as I had often done with other pieces which were at least as good; but I

[1] Comédie-ballet (1742) by Philippe Néricault, known as Destouches.

felt so encouraged, that in six days my drama was finished,
with the exception of a few lines, and all the music sketched
out, so that I had nothing more to do in Paris except to add a
little recitative and fill up the tenor parts. I finished the whole
so quickly, that in three weeks my scenes were copied out fairly
and fit for representation. The only thing remaining was the
divertissement, which was not composed until a long time
afterwards.

[1752.] – The composition of this work had so excited me that
I had a great desire to hear it, and I would have given all I
possessed to have seen it performed, as I should have liked, with
closed doors, as Lulli is said to have once had *Armide* performed
before himself alone. As it was not possible for me to enjoy this
pleasure except in company with the public, I was obliged to get
my piece accepted at the Opera in order to hear it.
Unfortunately, it was in a style entirely new, to which the ears of
the public were quite unaccustomed; and, besides, the failure
of the *Muses galantes* made me expect the like for the *Devin*, if
I presented it in my own name. Duclos helped me out of the
difficulty, and undertook to get the piece tried without disclosing
the author. To avoid betraying myself, I did not attend the
rehearsal, and the "little violins"* themselves, who conducted,
were ignorant of the composer's name, until the general
approval had attested the excellence of the work. All who
heard it were so delighted, that, the next day, nothing else was
talked of in all circles. M. de Cury, manager of Court entertain-
ments, who had been present at the rehearsal, asked for the
piece, in order that it might be performed at Court. Duclos, who
knew my intentions, and thought that I should have less control
over my piece at the Court than in Paris, refused to deliver it.
Cury demanded it by virtue of his office. Duclos persisted in his
refusal, and the dispute between them became so lively that, one
day, at the Opera, they would have gone out together to fight a
duel, unless they had been separated. Cury wanted to treat with
me. I left the decision with Duclos, and Cury was obliged to
apply again to him. M. le Duc d'Aumont interfered. At length

---

* These were the names given to Rebel and Francœur, who, from their youth,
had been in the habit of going from house to house to play the violin. (R)

Duclos thought it right to yield to authority, and the piece was given up in order to be played at Fontainebleau.[1]

The part to which I had devoted most attention, and in which I had made the greatest departure from the beaten track, was the recitative. Mine was accented in an entirely new manner and kept time with the delivery[2] of the words. This horrible innovation was not allowed to stand, for fear of shocking the ears of those who followed each other like a flock of sheep. I consented that Francueil and Jelyotte should compose another recitative, but I refused to have anything to do with it myself.

When everything was ready and the day fixed for the performance, it was proposed to me that I should take a journey to Fontainebleau, to be present at the last rehearsal, at any rate. I went with Mademoiselle Fel, Grimm, and, I think, the Abbé Raynal, in one of the Royal carriages. The rehearsal was tolerable; I was better satisfied with it than I had expected to be. The orchestra was a powerful one, consisting of those of the Opera and the Royal band. Jelyotte played Colin; Mademoiselle Fel, Colette; Cuvilier, the Devin (soothsayer). The choruses were from the Opera. I said little. Jelyotte had arranged everything, and I did not desire to have any control over his arrangements; but, in spite of my Roman air, I was as bashful as a schoolboy amongst all these people.

On the following day, when the rehearsal was to take place, I went to breakfast at the *Café du Grand Commun*, which was full of people, talking about the rehearsal of the previous evening, and the difficulty there had been in getting in. An officer who was present said that he had found no difficulty, gave a long account of the proceedings, described the author, and related what he had said and done; but what astounded me most in his long description, given with equal confidence and simplicity, was that there was not a word of truth in it. It was perfectly clear to me, that the man who spoke so positively about this rehearsal had never been present, since he had before his eyes the author, whom he pretended he had observed so closely, and did not recognise him. The most remarkable thing about this incident

---

[1] The first performance took place on 18 October 1752.
[2] *Débit*: a term specially applied to the manner in which a recitative is sung.

was the effect which it produced upon me. This man was somewhat advanced in years; there was nothing of the coxcomb or
swaggerer about him, either in his manner or tone; his countenance was intelligent, while his cross of Saint-Louis showed that
he was an old officer. In spite of his unblushing effrontery, in
spite of myself, he interested me; while he retailed his lies I
blushed, cast down my eyes, and was on thorns; I sometimes
asked myself whether it might not be possible to think that he
was mistaken, and really believed what he said. At last, trembling
for fear that someone might recognise me and put him to shame,
I hurriedly finished my chocolate without saying a word, and,
holding my head down as I passed him, I left the *café* as soon as
possible, while the company were discussing his description of
what had taken place. In the street, I found that I was bathed in
perspiration; and I am certain that, if anyone had recognised and
addressed me by name before I left, I should have exhibited all
the shame and embarrassment of a guilty person, simply from
the feeling of humiliation which the poor fellow would have
experienced, if his lies had been detected.

I now come to one of the critical moments of my life, in
which it is difficult to confine myself to simple narrative, because
it is almost impossible to prevent even the narrative bearing the
stamp of censure or apology. However, I will attempt to relate
how, and from what motives I acted, without adding an expression of praise or blame.

On that day I was dressed in my usual careless style, with a
beard of some days' growth and a badly combed wig.
Considering this want of good manners as a proof of courage,
I entered the hall where the King, the Queen, the Royal Family,
and the whole Court were presently to arrive. I proceeded to
take my seat in the box to which M. de Cury conducted me; it
was his own – a large stage box, opposite a smaller and higher
one, where the King sat with Madame de Pompadour.
Surrounded by ladies, and the only man in front of the box, I
had no doubt that I had been put there on purpose to be seen.
When the theatre was lighted up, and I found myself, dressed in
the manner I was, in the midst of people all most elegantly
attired, I began to feel ill at ease. I asked myself whether I was

in my right place, and whether I was suitably dressed. After a few moments of uneasiness, I answered "Yes," with a boldness which perhaps was due rather to the impossibility of drawing back than to the force of my arguments. I said to myself: I am in my place, since I am going to see my own piece performed; because I have been invited; because I composed it solely for that purpose; because, after all, no one has more right than myself to enjoy the fruit of my labour and talents. I am dressed as usual, neither better nor worse. If I again begin to yield to public opinion in any single thing, I shall soon become its slave again in everything. To be consistent, I must not be ashamed, wherever I may be, to be dressed in accordance with the condition of life which I have chosen for myself. My outward appearance is simple and careless, but not dirty or slovenly. A beard in itself is not so, since it is bestowed upon us by Nature, and, according to times and fashions, is sometimes even an ornament. People will consider me ridiculous, impertinent. Well, what does it matter to me? I must learn how to put up with ridicule and censure, provided they are not deserved. After this little soliloquy, I felt so encouraged that I should have behaved with intrepidity, if it had been necessary. But, whether it was the effect of the presence of the ruler, or the natural disposition of those near me, I saw nothing in the curiosity, of which I was the object, except civility and politeness. This so affected me, that I began to be uneasy again about myself and the fate of my piece, and to fear that I might destroy the favourable impressions which showed only an inclination to applaud me. I was armed against their raillery; but their kindly attitude, which I had not expected, so completely overcame me, that I trembled like a child when the performance began.

I soon found I had no reason for uneasiness. The piece was very badly acted, but the singing was good, and the music well executed. From the first scene, which is really touching in its simplicity, I heard in the boxes a murmur of surprise and applause hitherto unheard of at similar performances. The growing excitement soon reached such a height, that it communicated itself to the whole audience, and, in the words of Montesquieu, "the very effect increased the effect." In the scene between the two good little people, this effect reached its highest point. There is never any clapping when the King is present: this allowed everything to be heard, and the piece and the author were thereby benefited. I heard around me women, who seemed to me as beautiful as angels, whispering and saying to each other in low tone, "Charming! delightful! every note speaks to the heart!" The pleasure of affecting so many amiable persons moved me to tears, which I was unable to restrain during the first duet, when I observed that I was not the only one who wept. For a moment I felt anxious, when I recalled the concert at M. de Treytorens's.[1] This reminiscence produced upon me the same effect as the slave who held the crown over the head of a Roman general in his triumphal procession, but it did not last long, and I soon abandoned myself, completely and without reserve, to the delight of tasting the sweets of my success. And yet I am sure that at this moment I was much more affected by sensual impulse than by the vanity I felt as an author. If none but men had been present, I am convinced that I should not have been consumed, as I was, by the incessant desire of catching with my lips the delightful tears which I caused to flow. I have seen pieces excite more lively transports of admiration, but never so complete, so delightful, and so moving an intoxication, which completely overcame the audience, especially at a first performance before the Court. Those who saw it on this occasion can never have forgotten it, for the effect was unique.

The same evening, M. le Duc d'Aumont sent word to me to present myself at the château on the following day at eleven o'clock, when he would present me to the King. M. de Cury, who brought me the message, added that he believed that it was a question of a pension, the bestowal of which the King desired to announce to me in person.

Will it be believed, that the night which succeeded so brilliant a day was for me a night of anguish and perplexity? My first thought, after that of this presentation, was a certain necessity, which had greatly troubled me on the evening of the performance, and had frequently obliged me to retire, and might

---

[1] [Treytorens] See Book IV, pp. 158–9.

trouble me again on the next day, in the gallery or the King's apartments, amongst all the great people, while waiting for His Majesty to pass. This infirmity was the chief cause which prevented me from going into society, or from staying in a room with ladies when the doors were closed. The mere idea of the situation in which this necessity might place me, was enough to affect me to such an extent, that it made me feel ready to faint, unless I should be willing to create a scandal, to which I should have preferred death. Only those who know what this condition is, can imagine the horror of running the risk of it.

I next pictured myself in the King's presence and presented to His Majesty, who condescended to stop and speak to me. On such an occasion, tact and presence of mind were indispensable in answering. Would my accursed timidity, which embarrasses me in the presence of the most ordinary stranger, abandon me when I found myself in the presence of the King of France? would it suffer me to select, on the spur of the moment, the proper answer? It was my desire, without abandoning the austerity of tone and manner which I had assumed, to show that I was sensible of the honour which so great a monarch bestowed upon me. It was necessary that I should convey some great and useful truth in words of well-selected and well-deserved eulogy. To be able to prepare a happy answer beforehand, it would have been necessary to know exactly what he might say to me; and, even had this been possible, I felt perfectly certain that I should not be able to recollect in his presence a single word of all that I had previously thought over. What would become of me at this moment, before the eyes of all the Court, if, in my embarrassment, some of my usual silly utterances were to escape my lips? This danger alarmed, frightened, and made me tremble so violently, that I resolved, at all hazards, not to expose myself to it.

I lost, it is true, the pension, which was in a manner offered to me; but, at the same time, I escaped the yoke which it would have imposed upon me. Adieu truth, liberty, and courage! How could I, from that time forth, have dared to speak of independence and disinterestedness? I could only flatter or keep my mouth closed if I accepted this pension; and besides, who would guarantee the payment of it? What steps should I have had to take, how many people I should have been obliged to solicit! It would have cost me more trouble and far more unpleasantness to keep it, than to do without it. Consequently, in renouncing all thoughts of it, I believed that I was acting in a manner quite consistent with my principles, and sacrificing the appearance to the reality. I communicated my resolution to Grimm, who had nothing to say against it. To others I alleged my ill-health as an excuse, and I left the same morning.

My departure caused some stir, and was generally censured. My reasons could not be appreciated by everybody; it was much easier to accuse me of a foolish pride, and this more readily allayed the jealousy of all who felt they would not have acted like myself. The following day, Jelyotte wrote me a note, in which he gave me an account of the success of my piece and of the great fancy which the King himself had conceived for it. "All day long," he informed me, "his Majesty is continually singing, with the most execrable voice in his kingdom, and utterly out of tune, *J'ai perdu mon serviteur; j'ai perdu tout mon bonheur.*" He added that, in a fortnight, a second performance of the *Devin* was to be given, which would establish in the eyes of all the public the complete success of the first.

Two days later, as I was going to supper at Madame d'Epinay's, about nine o'clock in the evening, a coach passed me at the door. Someone inside made a sign to me to get in. I did so; the person was Diderot. He spoke to me about the pension more warmly than I should have expected a philosopher to speak on such a subject. He did not regard my unwillingness to be presented to the King as an offence; but he considered my indifference about the pension as a terrible crime. He said to me that, even if I was disinterested on my own account, I had no right to be so in regard to Madame le Vasseur and her daughter; that I owed it to them to neglect no honourable means, within my reach, of providing for their support; and as, after all, it could not be said that I had refused this pension, he insisted that, since there appeared a disposition to bestow it upon me, I ought to ask for it and obtain it, at any cost. Although I felt touched by his zeal, I was unable to approve of his principles, and we had a lively discussion on the subject, the first which had ever occurred between us. All our subsequent disputes were of the same kind, he dictating to me what he maintained I ought to do, while I as firmly refused, because I did not believe it was my duty.

It was late when we separated. I wanted to take him with me to supper at Madame d'Epinay's, but he would not go; and, in spite of the efforts which the desire of bringing together those whom I regard with affection caused me to make from time to time, to induce him to visit her – I even went so far as to take her to his door, which he refused to open to us – he always declined to see her, and never spoke of her except with great contempt. It was only after my disagreement with both that they became intimate, and that he began to speak of her with respect.

From that time Diderot and Grimm seemed to make it their object to set the *gouverneuses*[1] against me, by giving them to understand that, if they were not better off, it was entirely my fault, and that they would never do any good with me. They tried to induce them to leave me, and promised them, through Madame d'Epinay's interest, a licence to sell salt, or a tobacconist's shop, and I know not what besides. They even tried to drag Duclos and Holbach into their alliance, but the former persistently refused to join them. At the time I had some notion of their intrigues, but I only learned them clearly a long time afterwards, and I often had reason to lament the blind and indiscreet zeal of my friends, who, in endeavouring to reduce me, in my ill-health, to a state of most melancholy isolation, imagined that they were doing their utmost to make me happy by the very means which, beyond all others, were most adapted to make me utterly miserable.

[1753.] – In the following carnival, the *Devin* was played at Paris, and, during the interval, I had time to compose the overture and *divertissement*. The latter, as it was designed and engraved, was intended to keep up a sustained and connected action from one end of the piece to the other, which, in my judgment, gave opportunities for very agreeable tableaux. But, when I proposed this idea at the Opera, I was not even listened to, and I was obliged to patch together songs and dances in the

[1] A half contemptuous term for the "women-folk."

ordinary manner. The result was that the *divertissement*, although full of charming ideas, which certainly did not damage the effect of the scenes, only enjoyed a very moderate success. I struck out Jelyotte's recitative and restored my own in its original form as it is engraved; and this recitative, somewhat Frenchified, I confess – that is to say, drawled out by the actors – far from offending anyone, was as successful as the music, and was considered, even by the people, equally well composed. I dedicated my piece to M. Duclos, who had taken it under his protection, and declared that this should be my only dedication. However, I wrote a second with his consent; but he must have thought himself still more honoured by the exception than if I had written none at all.

I could relate a number of anecdotes about this piece, but more important matters which I must mention do not allow me time to dwell upon them here; I may, perhaps, on a future occasion return to them in a supplement. One, however, I must mention, which may have reference to all that follows. I was one day looking over the Baron d'Holbach's music in his study. After I had looked through a number of pieces of different kinds, he showed me a collection of pieces for the piano, and said, "These were written especially for me; they are very tasteful, and well-suited for singing. No one is acquainted with them, or shall ever see them, except myself. You ought to select one, and introduce it into your *divertissement*." As I already had in my mind far more subjects for airs and symphonies than I could ever make use of, I cared very little about his. However, he pressed me so earnestly that, to oblige him, I selected a shepherd's song, which I abridged and altered into a trio, for the entry of Colette's companions. Some months afterwards, while the *Devin* was still running, on going into Grimm's rooms, I found a number of people round his piano, from which he hastily got up on my arrival. Looking mechanically at his music-stand, I saw the identical collection of Baron d'Holbach, open exactly at the piece which he had pressed me to take, while assuring me that it should never leave his hands. Some time afterwards, I saw the same collection open on M. d'Epinay's piano, one day when there was some music at his house. Neither Grimm nor anyone else ever spoke to me about this air, and I should have said nothing about it myself, if it had not been rumoured, some time afterwards, that I was not the author of the *Devin du Village*. As I was never a great instrumentalist, I am convinced that, had it not been for my "Dictionary of Music,"[1] it would at last have been said that I knew nothing about the subject.*

Some time before the *Devin du Village* was performed, some Italian comedians had arrived at Paris, and were ordered to play at the Opera. The effect which they were destined to produce could not be foreseen. Although they were detestable, and the orchestra, at that time very ill-trained, mutilated to its heart's content the pieces which they performed, they nevertheless fatally injured the French Opera. The comparison of the two kinds of music, heard the same day at the same theatre, opened the French ears; none of them could endure their drawling music after the lively and pronounced accentuation of the Italian; as soon as the comedians had finished, everyone left the house. It was found necessary to change the order of representation, and to put off the performance of the comedians to the last. *Églé*, *Pygmalion*, and *Le Sylphe* were played; nothing held its ground. The *Devin du Village* alone could bear comparison, and was listened to with pleasure, even after the *Serva padrona*.[2] When I composed my interlude, I had my head full of these pieces, and borrowed my ideas from them; but I was far from suspecting that my piece would be criticised by the side of them. If I had been a plagiarist, how many thefts would then have been detected, and how eagerly would they have been pointed out! But nothing of the kind was discovered; all attempts to find in my music the slightest reminiscence of any other were in vain; and all my songs, when compared with the supposed originals, were found to be as new as the character of the music which I had created. If Mondonville or Rameau had been forced to submit to such a test, they would not have escaped without being torn to shreds. The comedians gained

[1] Rousseau published a *Dictionary of Music* in 1767. Debates as to the authenticity of his musical works continued even after his death.
* I could not foresee that, in spite of the "Dictionary," this would really be said of me. (R)
[2] Opéra-comique by Pergolesi, first performed in 1733. It enjoyed peculiar prestige in the "Queen's corner", *i.e.*, among the champions of Italian music.

some very ardent support for Italian music. Paris was divided into two parties, more violently opposed than if it had been a matter of religion or of an affair of State. One, the more numerous and influential, composed of the great, the wealthy, and the ladies, supported the French music; the other, more lively, more proud, and more enthusiastic, was composed of real connoisseurs, persons of talent, and men of genius. This little group assembled at the Opera, under the Queen's box. The other party filled the rest of the pit and house; but its chief meeting-place was under the King's box. This was the origin of these celebrated party names, "King's corner" and "Queen's corner." The dispute, as it became more animated, gave rise to several brochures. If the "King's corner" attempted to be witty, it was ridiculed by the "Petit Prophète";[1] if it attempted to argue, it was crushed by the "Lettre sur la musique Française." These two little pamphlets, by Grimm and myself respectively, are all that have survived the quarrel; all the rest are already forgotten.

But the "Petit Prophète," which, in spite of my denial, was for a long time attributed to me, was taken as a joke, and did not bring the least annoyance upon its author, whereas the "Lettre sur la musique" was taken seriously and roused against me the whole nation, which considered itself insulted in its music. A description of the incredible effect of this brochure would be worthy of the pen of Tacitus. It was the time of the great quarrel between Parliament and clergy.[2] The Parliament had just been

[1] *Le Petit prophète de Boemischbroda*, an anonymous satirical pamphlet by Melchior Grimm, published in January 1753 and relating the amazement of a penniless student of Prague when transported by miraculous agency to the Paris opera-house. In his *Letter on French Music*, published in November 1753, Rousseau argued that the French had never had a decent music and never could have.

[2] During 1753 the quarrel between the Paris *Parlement* and the King, and the parallel quarrel between the Parlementarians, who were predominantly Jansenist in sympathies, and the Jesuits, who were in favour at Court, had revived with great bitterness. The orthodox clergy had been refusing the last rites to declared Jansenists, and *Parlement* had been bringing legal proceedings against them for doing so; ordered by the King to stop all such proceedings, *Parlement* had refused to sit or to perform its judicial duties. The King had thereupon sent its members into exile by *lettre de cachet*, and by the time of Rousseau's *Letter* he was attempting to abolish *Parlement* altogether and replace it with a royal chamber.

banished; the ferment was at its height; everything pointed to an approaching outburst. From the moment the brochure appeared, all other quarrels were at once forgotten; nothing was thought of, except the perilous condition of French music, and the only outburst was against myself. It was such that the nation has never quite recovered from it. At Court, the only doubt was whether the Bastille or exile should be the punishment; and the Royal warrant of arrest would have been drawn up, had not M. de Voyer shown the ridiculous aspect of the affair. Anyone who sees it stated that this brochure possibly prevented a revolution in the State will believe that he is dreaming. It is, however, an actual truth, which all Paris can still attest, since it is at the present day no more than fifteen years since this singular incident took place.

Although my liberty was not attacked, I was unsparingly insulted, and even my life was in danger. The Opera orchestra entered into an honourable conspiracy to assassinate me when I left the theatre. Being informed of this, I only attended the Opera more frequently than before, and it was not until a long time afterwards that I learned that M. Ancelet, an officer in the Musketeers, who was friendly disposed towards me, had prevented the plot from being carried out, by causing me to be protected, unknown to myself, when I left the theatre. The city had recently taken over the management of the Opera. The first exploit of the *Prévôt des Marchands*[1] was to deprive me of my free pass, in the most uncivil manner possible, by publicly refusing me admission when I presented myself, so that I was obliged to take a ticket for the amphitheatre to avoid the mortification of going back. The injustice was the more outrageous, as the only recompense I had stipulated for, when I gave up my rights in the piece, was a free pass for life; for, although this was a privilege which all authors enjoyed – and I had thus a double claim to it – I nevertheless expressly stipulated for it in M. Duclos's presence. It is true that fifty *louis* were sent to me through the treasurer of the Opera by way of honorarium, which I had not asked for; but, besides that these fifty *louis* were not even equal to the amount which was due to me according to the regulations, this payment

[1] [*Prévôt des marchands*] *i.e.*, the chief municipal officer.

had nothing to do with the right of admission, which had been formally stipulated for, and which was entirely independent of it. In this behaviour there was such a combination of injustice and brutality, that the public, although at the height of its animosity against me, was nevertheless unanimously disgusted at it, and many, who had insulted me on the previous evening, cried out loudly on the following day in the house, that it was a shame to deprive an author in this manner of his right of admission, which he had well deserved and which he was even entitled to claim for two persons. So true is the Italian proverb, *Ognun' ama la giustizia in casa d'altrui.*

Under these circumstances, I had only one course to take – to demand the return of my work, since the recompense agreed upon was withheld. I wrote to that effect to M. d'Argenson, who had control of the Opera, adding to my letter an unanswerable memorandum. Letter and memorandum both remained unanswered, and produced no effect. This unjust man's silence wounded me deeply, and did not tend to increase the very moderate opinion which I had always entertained of his character and ability. Thus the Opera kept my piece and defrauded me of the recompense for which I had surrendered my rights in it. Between the weak and the strong, this would be called robbery; between the strong and the weak, it is simply called the appropriation of what belongs to one's neighbour.

As for the pecuniary profits of this work, although it did not bring me in a quarter of what it would have brought in in the hands of another, they were, nevertheless, large enough to enable me to live upon them for several years, and to make up for the continued ill-success of my copying. I received a hundred *louis* from the King, fifty from Madame de Pompadour for the performance at Bellevue, at which she herself took the part of Colin, fifty from the Opera, and five hundred *francs* from Pissot for the engraving, so that this interlude, which cost me no more than five or six weeks' work, in spite of my ill-luck and stupidity brought me in almost as much as my "Émile," on which I spent twenty years of meditation and three years of labour. But I paid dearly for the pecuniary ease which this piece procured me by the endless annoyance which it brought upon me. It was the germ of the secret jealousies, which did not break out until long afterwards. From the time of its success, I no longer found in Grimm, Diderot, or, with few exceptions, in any of the men of letters with whom I was acquainted, the cordiality, the frankness, or pleasure in my society, which I believed I had hitherto found in them. As soon as I appeared at the Baron's, the conversation ceased to be general. Those present collected in small groups and whispered together, so that I was left alone, without knowing whom to speak to. For a long time I endured this mortifying neglect, and, finding that Madame d'Holbach, who was gentle and amiable, always received me kindly, I put up with her husband's rudeness as long as it was possible. One day, however, he attacked me without reason or excuse, and with such brutality – in the presence of Diderot, who never said a word, and of Margency, who has often told me since then, that he admired the gentleness and moderation of my answers – that at last, driven away by this unworthy treatment, I left his house, resolved never to enter it again. However, this did not prevent me from always speaking respectfully of himself and his house; while he never expressed himself in regard to me in other than most insulting and contemptuous terms. He never spoke of me except as the little *cuistre*,[1] without, however, being able to point to a single wrong of any kind which I had ever done to him or anyone in whom he took an interest. This was the manner in which he fulfilled my predictions and my fears. As for myself, I believe that my friends would have forgiven me for writing books – even excellent books – because such a reputation was attainable by themselves; but they were unable to forgive me for having composed an opera, or for its brilliant success, because not one of them was capable of following the same career, or aspiring to the same honour. Duclos alone, superior to such jealousy, seemed to become even more attached to me. He introduced me to Mademoiselle Quinault, by whom I was treated with as much attention, politeness, and friendliness as I had found wanting at the Baron's house.

While the *Devin* was being played at the Opera, its author was also discussed at the Comédie Française, but somewhat less favourably. Having vainly attempted, during seven or eight

---

[1] Corresponding somewhat to a "college scivitor."

years, to get my *Narcisse* performed at the Italian Opera, I became
disgusted with this theatre, since the actors performed so badly
in French pieces, and I should have been glad to get my piece
accepted at the Comédie Française rather than at the Italian
Opera. I mentioned my wish to La Noue, the comedian, whose
acquaintance I had made, and who, as is well known, was an
author and an accomplished man. He was pleased with *Narcisse*,
and undertook to get it performed anonymously; meanwhile, he
procured me a pass, which was a great pleasure to me, since I
have always preferred the Théâtre Français to the other two. The
piece was received with applause, and performed without
the author's name being given; but I have reason to believe
that the actors and many others were not ignorant who it was.
Mesdemoiselles Gaussin and Grandval played the love-parts;
and although in my opinion the performance showed a lack of
intelligence generally, it could not be called absolutely bad.
However, I was surprised and touched by the indulgence of the
public, who had the patience to listen quietly from beginning to
end, and even to allow it to be performed a second time, without
exhibiting the least signs of impatience. As for myself, I was so
bored with the first, that I could not sit out to the end. I left the
theatre and went into the Café de Procope, where I found Boissy
and others, who had probably been as much bored as myself.
There I cried *peccavi*, and, humbly or proudly, confessed myself
the author of the piece, and spoke of it as everyone thought of it.
This public confession of the authorship of a piece which had
failed was received with much astonishment, and caused me little
pain. I even found a certain satisfaction to my *amour-propre* in the
courage with which I had made it; and I believe that, on this
occasion, there was more pride in speaking, than there would
have been false shame in keeping silence. However, as there was
no doubt that the piece, although spoilt at the performance,
would bear reading, I had it printed, and, in the preface, which
is one of my best productions, I began to express my principles a
little more freely than I had hitherto done.

I soon had an opportunity to disclose them unreservedly in a
work of greater importance; for it was, I think, in this year (1753)
that the "Origin of Inequality amongst Mankind" appeared as

the subject proposed for discussion by the Academy of Dijon. Struck by this great question, I felt surprised that this Academy had ventured to propose it; but since it had had the courage to do so, I thought I might have the courage to discuss it, and undertook the task.

In order to consider this great subject at my ease, I went to Saint-Germain, on a seven or eight days' journey, with Thérèse, our hostess, who was a good sort of woman, and one of her friends. I count this trip as one of the most agreeable in my life. It was very fine weather: the good women took all the trouble and expense upon themselves. Thérèse amused herself with them, while I, relieved from all anxiety, joined them at mealtimes, and diverted myself without having anything to trouble me. The remainder of the day, I buried myself in the forest, where I sought and found the picture of those primitive times, of which I boldly sketched the history. I demolished the pitiful lies of mankind; I dared to expose their nature in all its nakedness, to follow the progress of time and of the things which have disfigured this nature; and, comparing the man, as man has made him, with the natural man, I showed him, in his pretended perfection, the true source of his misery. My soul, uplifted by these sublime considerations, ascended to the Divinity; and, seeing my fellow creatures following blindly the path of their prejudices, their errors, their misfortunes, and their crimes, I cried aloud to them with a feeble voice which they could not hear, "Fools, who continually complain of Nature, learn that you bring all your misfortunes upon yourselves."

The result of these meditations was the "Essay on Inequality," a work which was more to Diderot's taste than any of my other writings. He gave most useful advice concerning it,* but it only found few readers in Europe who understood it, and none of the latter ever chose to speak of it. It was written to compete for the prize, so I sent it in, feeling certain beforehand that it would

---

* At the time when I wrote these words, I had no suspicion of Diderot's and Grimm's great conspiracy; otherwise I should easily have seen how the former abused my confidence, in order to give my writings the harsh tone and air of gloominess which ceased to be found in them when he no longer guided me. The description of the philosopher who contrives to harden himself against the complaints of a man in distress by stopping up his ears, is in his style; and he had

be unsuccessful, as I knew well that the prizes of Academies were not intended for works of the kind.

This excursion and occupation were beneficial to my health and temper. Several years before, tortured by my retention of urine, I had put myself unreservedly into the physicians' hands, and they, without alleviating my sufferings, had exhausted my strength and undermined my constitution. After my return from Saint-Germain, I found myself stronger and better. I took the hint, and determined to recover or die without the assistance of physicians or drugs. I said good-bye to them for ever, and began to live without any fixed rules, remaining quiet when I could not walk, and walking as soon as I was strong enough to do so. Life in Paris, amongst pretentious people, was little to my taste; the cabals of men of letters, their shameful quarrels, their lack of candour as exhibited in their books, the haughty airs they gave themselves in society, were all so hateful to me and so anti-pathetic, I found so little gentleness, open-heartedness, and frankness, even in the society of my friends, that, disgusted with this tumultuous life, I began to long earnestly for residence in the country; and, as I saw no prospect of my profession allowing me to settle there, I hastened to spend in it at least the few hours which I had to spare. For several months, at first after dinner, I used to go for a walk by myself in the Bois de Boulogne, to think over subjects for future works, and did not return till nightfall.

[1754–1756.] – Gauffecourt, with whom I was at that time extremely intimate, found himself obliged to make a journey to Geneva on business, and proposed to me to accompany him; I consented. As I was not well enough to be able to dispense with the care of the *gouverneuse*, it was decided that she should go with us, and that her mother should look after the house. Having made all our arrangements, we all three set out together on the 1st of June, 1754.

---

supplied me with several others, even still stronger, which I could never bring myself to use. But, as I attributed to his confinement in the donjon of Vincennes this melancholy tinge, which may be found again, in considerable proportions in his "Clairval,"[1] it never occurred to me to suspect any evil intention. (R)

[1]   Rousseau's mistake for "Dorval," name of the hero of Diderot's play *Le Fils naturel*.

I must mention this journey as the period of the first experience which, in the course of a life of forty-two years, gave a shock to the confidence of my naturally unsuspicious disposition, to which I had always abandoned myself without reserve and without inconvenience. We had a hired carriage, which conveyed us by very short daily stages without changing horses. I often got down and walked. We had scarcely performed half the journey, when Thérèse showed the greatest repugnance to remaining alone in the carriage with Gauffecourt, and when, in spite of her entreaties, I wanted to get down, she did the same, and walked with me. For some time I scolded her for this whim, and even opposed it so strongly, that she felt obliged to declare the reason for her conduct. I thought that I was dreaming, I fell from the clouds, when I heard that my friend de Gauffecourt, more than sixty years old, gouty, impotent, and worn out by a life of pleasure and dissipation, had been doing his utmost, since we had started, to corrupt a person who was no longer young or beautiful, and who belonged to his friend, and that by the lowest and most disgraceful means, even going so far as to offer her money, and attempting to excite her passions by reading a disgusting book to her and showing her the disgraceful pictures of which it was full. Thérèse, in a fit of indignation, once threw his villainous book out of the carriage; and she told me that, the very first day, when I had gone to bed before supper with a very violent headache, he had employed all the time, during which he was alone with her, in attempts and actions more worthy of a satyr or he-goat than of an honourable man, to whom I had confided myself and my companion. What a surprise! what an entirely new cause of grief for me! I, who had until then believed that friendship was inseparable from all the amiable and noble sentiments which constitute all its charm, for the first time in my life found myself compelled to couple it with contempt, and to withdraw my confidence and esteem from a man whom I loved, and by whom I believed myself to be loved! The wretch concealed his disgraceful conduct from me; and, to avoid exposing Thérèse, I found myself compelled to conceal my contempt from him, and to keep hidden, in the bottom of my heart, feelings which he was never to know. Sweet and holy illusion of friendship! Gauffecourt was the first to lift thy veil before my eyes. How many cruel hands since then have prevented it from covering thy face again!

At Lyons I left Gauffecourt, to take the road through Savoy, as I could not bring myself to be so near mamma again, without seeing her once more. I saw her again – my God! in what a condition! How low had she fallen! What was left of her former virtue? Could it be the same Madame de Warens, once so brilliant, to whom M. Pontverre, the *curé*, had sent me? How my heart was torn! The only resource I could see for her was, that she should leave the country. I reiterated, earnestly but in vain, the entreaties which I had several times addressed to her in my letters, begging her to come and live quietly with me, and let me devote my life and Thérèse's to make her own happy. Clinging to her pension, from which, although it was regularly paid, she had for a long time drawn nothing, she refused to listen to me. I gave her a small portion of my money, much less than I ought to have given, much less than I should have given her, if I had not felt certain, that she would not have spent a *sou* upon herself. During my stay in Geneva, she took a journey to Chablais, and came to see me at Grange-Canal. She had no money to continue her journey. I had not as much with me as she wanted, and sent it to her by Thérèse an hour later. Poor mamma! Let me mention one more proof of her goodness of heart. Her sole remaining jewel was a little ring; she took it from her finger and placed it upon that of Thérèse, who immediately replaced it, at the same time kissing and bathing in her tears that noble hand. Ah! then would have been the moment to pay my debt! I ought to have left all and followed her, to have never left her until her last hour, to have shared her lot, whatever it might have been. I did nothing of the kind. Occupied with another attachment, I felt the tie which bound us loosened, for want of any hope of being able to make it of any use to her. I wept over her, but did not follow her. Of all the stings of conscience that I have ever felt, this was the sharpest and most lasting. My conduct deserved the terrible punishment which since then has never ceased to overwhelm me; I hope it may have atoned for my ingratitude, which, indeed, showed itself in my conduct, but has wounded my heart too deeply for it ever to have been the heart of an ungrateful man.

Before I left Paris, I had sketched the dedication of my "Essay on Equality." I finished it at Chambéri, and dated it from that place, thinking it better, in order to avoid all unpleasantness, not to date it either from France or Geneva. On my arrival in this city, I gave myself up to the republican enthusiasm which had led me there. This enthusiasm was increased by the reception I met with. Fêted and made much of by all classes, I abandoned myself entirely to patriotic zeal, and, ashamed of being excluded from my rights as a citizen by the profession of a religion different from that of my fathers, I resolved publicly to return to the latter. As the Gospel was the same for every Christian, and as the essential part of the doctrine only differed in the attempts of different people to explain what they were unable to understand, I said to myself that, in each country, it was the right of the Sovereign alone to define the manner of worship and to settle this unintelligible dogma, and that it was consequently the duty of every good citizen to accept the dogma and to follow the manner of worship prescribed by the law. Constant association with the encyclopaedists, far from shaking my faith, had strengthened it, in consequence of my natural aversion to quarrels and schism. The study of man and the universe had everywhere shown me the final causes and the intelligence which directed them. The reading of the Bible, especially the Gospels, to which I had for several years devoted myself, had taught me to despise the low and foolish interpretations given to the teaching of Jesus Christ by persons utterly unworthy of understanding it. In a word, philosophy, while firmly attaching me to what was essential in religion, had released me from the petty and rubbishy forms with which it has been obscured. Believing that, for an intelligent man, there could not be two ways of being a Christian, I also believed that all religious form and discipline, in each country, came under the jurisdiction of the law. From this reasonable, social, and pacific principle, which has brought upon me such cruel persecutions, it followed that, if I desired to become a citizen, I ought to be a Protestant, and to return to the religion of my country. I accordingly determined to do so. I even submitted to the instructions of the pastor of the parish, in which I was staying, which was outside the city. I only desired not to be obliged to appear before the consistory. However, the ecclesiastical law was definite in regard to this; but they were kind enough to make an exemption in my favour, and a commission of five or six members was appointed to receive my profession of faith in private. Unfortunately, Perdriau, the minister, a mild and amiable man, with whom I was on friendly terms, took it into his head to tell me that they were delighted at the idea of hearing me speak in this little assembly. The expectation of this so alarmed me, that, after having studied, night and day, for three weeks, a little speech which I had prepared, I became so confused at the moment when I had to deliver it, that I was unable to utter a single word of it, and, at this meeting, I behaved like the most stupid schoolboy. The members of the commission spoke for me; I answered "Yes" and "No" like a fool; after which I was admitted to the Communion, and reinstated in my rights as a citizen. I was enrolled as such in the list of the civic guards, who are paid by the citizens and full burgesses only, and I attended an extraordinary general council, to receive the oath from the syndic[1] Mussard. I was so touched by the kindness shown to me on this occasion by the Council and consistory, and by the courteous and polite behaviour of all the magistrates, ministers, and citizens, that, persuaded by the persistent entreaties of the excellent Deluc, and influenced still more by my own inclinations, I decided only to return to Paris to break up my establishment, arrange my little business matters, find a situation for Madame le Vasseur and her husband or provide for their wants, and then to return with Thérèse and settle at Geneva for the rest of my life.

This resolution once taken, I suspended all serious occupations, in order to enjoy myself with my friends, until it was time to set out for Paris. Of all my amusements, that which pleased me most was rowing round the lake with Deluc, his daughter-in-law, his two sons, and my Thérèse. We spent seven days in this excursion, in the most beautiful weather. I preserved the liveliest recollection of the spots which had delighted me at the other

[1] Head of a corporation.

end of the lake, and which I described some years later in the "Nouvelle Héloïse."

The principal connections which I formed at Geneva, beside the Delucs whom I have mentioned, were: the young minister Vernes, whose acquaintance I had already made in Paris, and of whom I had a better opinion than he afterwards justified; M. Perdriau, at that time a country pastor, now professor of *belles-lettres*, whose pleasant and agreeable society I shall ever regret, although he has since thought it the proper thing to break off the acquaintance; M. Jalabert, professor of physics, since then counsellor and syndic, to whom I read my "Essay on Inequality" (omitting the dedication), with which he appeared delighted; Professor Lullin, with whom I kept up a correspondence up to the time of his death, and who even commissioned me to purchase some books for the library; Professor Vernet, who turned his back upon me, like the rest of the world, after I had shown him proofs of attachment and friendship, which ought to have touched him, if a theologian could be touched by anything; Chappuis, clerk and successor to Gauffecourt, whom he desired to supplant, and who was soon afterwards supplanted himself; Marcet de Mézières, an old friend of my father, who had also shown himself mine, but who, after having formerly deserved well of his country, became a dramatic author and candidate for the Two Hundred, changed his opinions, and made himself ridiculous before his death. But the acquaintance from whom I hoped most was Moultou — a young man whose talents and ardent spirit aroused the greatest expectations. I have always felt an affection for him, although his conduct towards myself has often been suspicious, and he is on intimate terms with my bitterest enemies; but, notwithstanding all this, I cannot prevent myself from looking upon him as one day destined to become the defender of my memory, and the avenger of his friend.

In the midst of these amusements, I neither lost the taste for my solitary walks, nor discontinued them. I frequently took long rambles on the shores of the lake, during which my brain, accustomed to work, did not remain idle. I worked up the outline of my "Institutions Politiques," of which I shall have to speak presently. I projected a "Histoire du Valais" — a tragedy in prose, the subject of which was nothing less than Lucretia, by which I hoped to crush the scoffers, although I ventured to introduce this unfortunate woman on the stage again at a time when she was no longer possible at any French theatre. I also tried my hand at Tacitus, and made a translation of the first book of the Histories, which will be found amongst my papers.

After four months' stay at Geneva, I returned to Paris in October, avoiding Lyons, so as not to meet Gauffecourt. As I did not intend to return to Geneva until the following spring, I resumed, during the winter, my usual habits and occupations, the chief of which was the correction of the proofs of my "Discourse on Inequality," which was being published in Holland by Rey,[1] whose acquaintance I had recently made at Geneva. As this work was dedicated to the Republic, and this dedication might be displeasing to the Council, I waited to see the effect it produced at Geneva before I returned there. The result was not favourable to me; and this dedication, which had been dictated solely by the purest patriotism, made enemies for me in the Council, and brought upon me the jealousy of some of the citizens. M. Chouet, at that time chief syndic, wrote me a polite, but cold, letter, which will be found in my collection (Packet A, No. 3). From private individuals, amongst others Deluc and Jalabert, I received a few compliments, and that was all; I did not find that a single Genevese really thanked me for the hearty zeal which was to be found in the work. This indifference shocked all those who observed it. I remember that, one day, at Clichy, when I was dining with Madame Dupin in company with Crommelin, minister of the Republic, and M. de Mairan, the latter openly declared that the Council owed me a reward and public honours for this work, and that it would disgrace itself if it failed to do its duty. Crommelin, who was a dark and vulgarly spiteful little man, did not venture to make any answer in my presence, but he made a frightful grimace, which caused Madame Dupin to smile. The only advantage, besides the satisfaction it afforded my heart, which I obtained from this work, was the title of "citizen," which was bestowed upon me by my

---

[1] [Rey] See *Biographies*, p. 713.

friends and afterwards by the public, which I afterwards lost from having deserved it too well.

However, this ill-success would not have kept me from carrying out my intention of retiring to Geneva, had not motives, which had greater influence over my heart, contributed to this result. M. d'Epinay, being desirous of adding a wing which was wanting to the château of La Chevrette, went to extraordinary expense to finish it. One day, having gone, in company with Madame d'Epinay, to see the works, we continued our walk a quarter of a league further, as far as the reservoir of the waters of the park, which adjoined the forest of Montmorency, where there was a pretty kitchen-garden, attached to which was a small and very dilapidated cottage, called the Hermitage. This solitary and agreeable spot had struck my attention when I saw it for the first time before my journey to Geneva. In my transport, I let fall the exclamation, "Ah, madam, what a delightful place to live in! Here is a refuge ready made for me." Madame d'Epinay did not take much notice of my words at the time; but, on this second visit, I was quite surprised to find, in place of the old ruins, a little house almost entirely new, very nicely arranged, and very habitable for a small establishment of three persons. Madame d'Epinay had had the work carried out quietly and at very trifling expense, by taking some materials and some of the workmen from the château. When she saw my surprise, she said, "There, Mr. Bear, there is your asylum; you chose it; friendship offers it to you. I hope that it will put an end to your cruel idea of separating from me." I do not believe that I have ever felt more deeply or more delightfully touched; I bathed with my tears the beneficent hand of my friend; and, if I was not vanquished from that moment, I was sorely shaken in my resolution. Madame d'Epinay, who was unwilling to be beaten, became so pressing, employed so many different means, and so many persons, in order to get over me – even enlisting Madame le Vasseur and her daughter in her service – that she finally triumphed over my resolutions. Abandoning the idea of settling in my native country, I decided, and promised, to live in the Hermitage; and, while the building was getting dry, she undertook to see after the furniture, so that all was ready for occupation the following spring.

One thing which greatly contributed to confirm my resolution, was the fact that Voltaire had settled in the neighbourhood of Geneva.[1] I knew that this man would cause a revolution there; that I should find again in my own country the tone, the airs, and the manners which drove me from Paris; that I should have to maintain a perpetual struggle; and that no other choice would be left to me, except to behave either as an insufferable pedant, or as a coward and a bad citizen. The letter which Voltaire wrote to me about my last work caused me to hint at my apprehensions in my reply; the effect which it produced confirmed them. From that moment I looked upon Geneva as lost, and I was not mistaken. I ought perhaps to have defied the storm, if I had felt that I was capable of doing so. But what could I, timid, and a poor speaker, have done unaided against one who was arrogant, wealthy, supported by the credit of the great, brilliantly eloquent, and already the idol of the women and young men? I was afraid of exposing my courage uselessly to danger; I only listened to the voice of my naturally peaceable disposition, and my love of tranquillity which, if it deceived me then, still deceives me at the present day in this particular. By retiring to Geneva, I should have spared myself great misfortunes; but I doubt whether, with all my ardent and patriotic zeal, I should have done anything great or serviceable to my country.

Tronchin,[2] who, nearly about the same time, settled at Geneva, came to Paris some time afterwards to play the quack, and brought away some of its treasures. On his arrival, he came to see me with the Chevalier de Jancourt. Madame d'Epinay was very anxious to consult him privately, but it was difficult to get through the crowd. She had recourse to me, and I induced him to go and see her. Thus, under my auspices, they commenced a connection, which, later, they strengthened at my expense. Such

[1] Voltaire and his niece Mme Denis took up residence at Les Délices, near Geneva, in March 1755. Voltaire, in a letter (which he later published) acknowledging a copy of Rousseau's *Second Discourse*, thanked him for his "new book against the human race."

[2] [Tronchin] See *Biographies*, p. 715.

has ever been my lot; no sooner have I brought together separate friends of my own, than they have infallibly combined against me. Although, in the conspiracy, which the Tronchins from that time entered into, to reduce their country to a state of servitude, they must all have felt a mortal hatred towards me, the doctor for a long time continued to show me proofs of his goodwill. He even wrote to me after his return to Geneva, offering me the post of honorary librarian. But my mind was made up, and this offer did not shake my resolution.

At this time I returned to M. d'Holbach. The reason for my visit was the death of his wife, which had taken place during my stay at Geneva. Madame Francueil had also died during the same interval. Diderot, when informing me of the death of Madame d'Holbach, spoke of the husband's deep affliction. His grief touched my heart, and I myself regretted this amiable woman. I wrote to M. d'Holbach a letter of condolence. The sad event made me forget all his injustice; and, when I returned from Geneva, and he himself came back from a tour through France, which he had made in company with Grimm and some other friends to divert his thoughts from his sorrow, I went to visit him, and continued to do so until my departure for the Hermitage. When it became known in his circle that Madame d'Epinay, with whom he was not yet acquainted, was preparing a dwelling-place for me, sarcasms fell upon me thick as hail; it was said that, unable to live without the flattery and amusements of the city, I could not endure to remain even a fortnight in solitude. Conscious of my real feelings, I let them say what they pleased, and went my way. Nevertheless, M. d'Holbach helped me to find a place for good old Le Vasseur,* who was over eighty years of age, and whose wife, feeling the burden too heavy for her, continually begged me to relieve her of it. He was put into a poorhouse, where his great age, and his grief at finding himself separated from his family,

---

* Here is an instance of the tricks which my memory plays me. Long after writing this, I have just learnt, while talking with my wife about her good old father, that it was not M. d'Holbach, but M. de Chenonceaux, at that time one of the Committee of the Hôtel Dieu, who procured him the place. I had so completely forgotten him, and had so lively a recollection of M. d'Holbach, that I could have sworn that it had been he. (R)

brought him to the grave almost as soon as he was admitted. His wife and children felt but little regret for him, but Thérèse, who loved him fondly, has never consoled herself for his loss, and has never forgiven herself for allowing him, when so near his end, to finish his days at a distance from her.

About the same time, I received a visit which I little expected, although from an old acquaintance. I speak of my friend Venture who surprised me one fine morning, when he was the last person I was thinking of. He had a companion with him. How changed he appeared to be! Instead of his former graceful manners, I only found in him a general air of dissipation, which prevented me from opening my heart to him. Either my eyes were no longer the same, or debauchery had stupefied his intellect, or else all his early brilliancy had depended upon the brilliancy of youth, which he no longer possessed. I treated him almost with indifference, and we parted rather coolly. But, after he had left, the remembrance of our former intimacy so vividly recalled the recollections of my own youth, so delightfully and so completely devoted to the angelic woman who was now no less changed than himself, the little incidents of that happy time, the romantic day's journey to Toune, spent so innocently and delightfully in the company of the two charming girls whose only favour had been a kiss of the hand, which, nevertheless, had left behind such lively, touching and lasting regret; all the delightful transports of a young heart, which I had then felt in all their force, and which I thought were gone for ever; all these tender reminiscences made me weep for my past youth and its delights, henceforth lost for me. Ah! how I should have wept over their tardy and melancholy return, if I had foreseen the sorrow they were to cost me!

Before I left Paris, during the winter which preceded my retirement, I enjoyed a pleasure quite after my own heart, which I tasted in all its purity. Palissot, a member of the Academy of Nancy, who was known for some plays which he had written, had just had one performed at Lunéville, before the King of Poland. He evidently hoped to gain favour by introducing, in this piece, a man who had ventured to cross pens with the King. Stanislaus, who was a generous man and not fond of satire, was indignant that anyone should venture to introduce personalities in his presence. M. le Comte de Tressan wrote, by this Prince's orders, to d'Alembert and myself, to inform me that it was His Majesty's intention to procure the expulsion of Palissot from the Academy. In reply, I earnestly entreated M. de Tressan to intercede with the King in Palissot's favour. He was pardoned, and M. de Tressan, when informing me of it in the King's name, added that the incident would be inserted in the records of the Academy. I replied that this would rather be inflicting a perpetual punishment than granting a pardon. At last, by dint of entreaties, I succeeded in obtaining a promise, that the whole affair should be kept out of the records, and that no trace of it should appear in public. The promise was accompanied, both on the part of the King and of M. de Tressan, by protestations of esteem and regard, which flattered me exceedingly; and I felt on this occasion, that the esteem of those, who are so worthy of it themselves, produce in the soul a feeling far sweeter and nobler than that of vanity. I have inserted in my collection the letters of M. de Tressan, together with my replies. The originals will be found in Bundle A, Nos. 9, 10 and 11.

I quite feel that, if these Memoirs ever see the light, I am here perpetuating the memory of an incident, all traces of which I desired to efface; but I have handed down many other incidents to posterity with equal reluctance. The great object of my undertaking, which is ever before my eyes, the indispensable duty of carrying it out in its fullest extent, will not permit me to be turned aside from my purpose by unimportant considerations, which would divert me from my object. In my singular and unique situation, I owe too much to truth to owe anything further to anyone else. In order to know me well, one must know me in all my aspects, both good and bad. My Confessions are necessarily connected with those of many others. I make both with equal frankness in all that relates to myself, as I do not think that I am bound to treat anyone else with greater consideration than myself, although I should certainly like to do so. I desire to be always just and truthful, to say as much good of others as I can, only to speak evil when it concerns myself, and when I am compelled to do so. Who, in the position in which I have been placed by the world, has the right to demand more from me? My Confessions are not written to appear during my lifetime, or that of the persons concerned in them. If I were the master of my own destiny and of that of this work, it should not see the light until long after my death and their own. But the efforts, which the dread of truth causes my powerful oppressors to make, in order to efface all traces of it, force me to do all that the most scrupulous fairness and the strictest sense of justice allow me, in order to preserve these traces. If the remembrance of me were destined to die with me, rather than compromise anyone, I would, without a murmur, endure an unjust and momentary ignominy; but, since my name is destined to live, it is incumbent upon me to endeavour to hand down with it the remembrance of the unfortunate man who bore it – such as he really was, not such as his unjust enemies incessantly endeavour to represent him.

BOOK IX

I w a s so impatient to take up my abode in the Hermitage, that I could not wait for the return of fine weather; and, as soon as my new home was ready, I hastened to betake myself thither, amidst the loud ridicule of the Holbachian clique, who openly predicted that I should not be able to endure three months' solitude, and that they would soon see me returning to confess my failure and live in Paris as they did. I myself, who had been for fifteen years out of my element, and now saw that I was on the point of returning to it, took no notice of their raillery. Ever since I had been thrown into the world against my will, I had not ceased to regret my dear Charmettes, and the blissful life which I had led there. I felt that I was born for the country and retirement; it was impossible for me to live happily anywhere else. At Venice, amidst the bustle of public business, in the position of a kind of diplomatic representative, in my proud hopes and schemes of promotion; at Paris – in the whirl of high society, in the sensual enjoyment of suppers, in the brilliant spectacles of the theatre, in the cloud of vain-glory which surrounded me – the recollection of my groves, brooks, and solitary walks was ever present to distract and sadden me, to draw from me sighs of longing and regret. All the toil to which I had been able to subject myself, all the ambitious schemes which, by fits and starts, had roused my zeal, had no other end in view but that of one day enjoying the happy country ease, to which at that moment I flattered myself I had attained. Without having acquired the respectable independence which I considered could alone lead me to it, I considered that, owing to my peculiar position, I was able to dispense with it, and to reach the same end by quite a different road. I had no income whatever; but I had a name, I possessed ability. I was temperate and had freed myself from the most expensive wants, which are satisfied in obedience to popular opinion. Besides, although indolent, I could work hard when I chose; and my indolence was not so much that of a confirmed idler as of an independent person, who only cares to work when he is in the humour for it. My copying was neither a brilliant nor a lucrative employment, but it was certain. The world approved of my courage in having chosen it. I could always feel sure of work, and, if I worked hard, of earning sufficient to live upon. Two thousand *francs*, the remains of the profits of the *Devin du Village* and my other writings, was a sufficient capital to keep me from being pushed for money for some time, and several works which I had in hand promised me, without being obliged to draw upon the booksellers, a sufficient addition to my funds to enable me to work comfortably without over-exerting myself and even to employ to advantage the leisure of my walks. My little household, consisting of three people, who were all usefully employed, was not very expensive to keep up. In short, my resources, which corresponded to my wants and desires, bade fair to promise me lasting happiness in the life which my inclination had chosen for me.

I might have thrown myself entirely into the most lucrative path, and, instead of lowering my pen to copying, I might have devoted it entirely to writings, which, in the flight which I had taken, and which I felt myself capable of continuing, might have enabled me to live in opulence, even in luxury, if only I had been disposed to combine, in the smallest degree, an author's tricks with carefulness to produce good books. But I felt that writing for bread would soon have stifled my genius and destroyed my talents, which were more those of the heart than of the pen, and arose solely from a proud and elevated manner of thinking, which alone could support them. Nothing great, nothing vigorous can proceed from a pen that is entirely venal. Necessity, perhaps avarice, might have led me to write with greater rapidity than excellence. If the need of success had not plunged me into cabals, it might have made me strive to say what might please the multitude, rather than what was true and useful, and instead of a distinguished author which I might possibly become, I should have ended in becoming nothing but a mere scribbler. No, no! I have always felt that the position of an author is not and cannot be distinguished or respectable, except in so far as it is not a profession. It is too difficult to think nobly, when one thinks only in order to live. In order to be able and to venture to utter great truths, one must not be dependent upon success. I threw my books amongst the public with the sure consciousness of having spoken for the general good, without caring for anything else. If the work was rejected, so much the worse for those who refused to profit by it. As for myself, I did not need their approval in order to live; my profession would support me, if my books did not sell; and it was just this which made them sell.

It was on the 9th of April, 1756, that I left Paris, never to live in a city again, for I do not reckon the brief periods for which I afterwards stayed in Paris, London and other cities, only when passing through them, or against my will. Madame d'Epinay took us all three in her carriage; her farmer took charge of my small amount of luggage, and I was installed in my new home the same day. I found my little retreat arranged and furnished simply, but neatly and even tastefully. The hand which had attended to these arrangements conferred upon them in my eyes an inestimable value, and I found it delightful to be the guest of my friend, in a house of my own choice, which she had built on purpose for me. Although it was cold, and there was still some snow on the ground, the earth was beginning to show signs of vegetation: violets and primroses could be seen, the buds were beginning to open on the trees, and the night of my arrival was marked by the first song of the nightingale, which made itself heard nearly under my window, in a wood adjoining the house. When I awoke, after a light sleep, forgetting my change of abode, I thought that I was still in the Rue de Grenelle, when suddenly this warbling made me start, and in my delight I exclaimed, "At last all my wishes are fulfilled!" My first thought was to abandon myself to the impression caused by the rural objects by which I was surrounded. Instead of beginning to set things in order in my new abode, I began by making arrangements for my walks; there was not a path, not a copse, not a thicket, not a corner round my dwelling, which I had not explored by the following day. The more I examined this charming retreat, the more I felt that it was made for me. This spot, solitary rather than wild, transported me in spirit to the end of the world. It possessed those impressive beauties which are

rarely seen in the neighbourhood of cities; no one, who had
suddenly been transported there, would have believed that he
was only four leagues from Paris.

After having devoted some days to my rustic enthusiasm, I
began to think about putting my papers in order and distributing
my occupations. I set aside my mornings for copying, as I had
always done, and my afternoons for walking, armed with my
little note-book and pencil; for, as I had never been able to write
or think freely, except *sub divo*,[1] I felt no temptation to change
my method, and I reckoned that the forest of Montmorency,
which was almost at my door, would in future be my study. I had
several works already begun, and I went over them again. I was
magnificent enough in my schemes; but, amidst the bustle of the
city, they had hitherto made but little progress. I counted upon
being able to devote a little more attention to them when
I should have less to distract me. I think that I have fairly
fulfilled this expectation; and, for a man who was often ill,
often at La Chevrette, Épinay, Eaubonne and the Château of
Montmorency, often beset in his own house by curious idlers,
and always busy half the day in copying, if one counts and
considers the work which I produced during the six years
spent at the Hermitage and Montmorency, I am convinced
that it will be agreed that, if I lost my time during this period,
it was at least not wasted in idleness.

Of the different works which I had on the stocks, the one
which I had long had in my head, at which I worked with the
greatest inclination, to which I wished to devote myself all my
life, and which, in my own opinion, was to set the seal upon my
reputation – was my "Institutions Politiques." Thirteen or fourteen years ago, I had conceived the idea of it, when, during my
stay at Venice, I had had occasion to observe the faults of its
much-vaunted system of government. Since then, my views had
become greatly enlarged by the historical study of morals. I had
come to see that everything was radically connected with poli-
tics, and that, however one proceeded, no people would be
other than the nature of its government made it; thus this
great question of the best government possible appeared to

_____
[1] In the open air.

me to reduce itself to the following: What kind of government is best adapted to produce the most virtuous, the most enlightened, the wisest, and, in short, the best people, taking the word "best" in its widest signification? I thought that I perceived that this question was very closely connected with another, very nearly, although not quite the same. What is the government which, from its nature, always keeps closest to the law? This leads to the question, What is the law? and to a series of questions equally important. I saw that all this led me on to great truths conducive to the happiness of the human race, above all, to that of my country, in which I had not found, in the journey I had just made thither, sufficiently clear or correct notions of liberty and the laws to satisfy me; and I believed that this indirect method of communicating them was the best suited to spare the pride of those whom it concerned, and to secure my own forgiveness for having been able to see a little further than themselves.

Although I had been already engaged five or six years upon this work, it was still in a very backward state. Books of this kind require meditation, leisure, and tranquillity. Besides, I worked at it, as the saying is, *en bonne fortune*,[1] without communicating my intention to anyone, not even to Diderot. I was afraid that it might appear too foolhardy, considering the age and country in which I wrote, and that the alarm of my friends would embarrass me in its execution.* I was not yet sure whether it would be finished in time, and in such a manner as to admit of its being published during my lifetime. I wished to be able to devote to my subject, without restraint, all the efforts which it demanded of me; for I felt convinced that, as I had no satirical vein, and never desired to be personal, I should always be free from blame, if fairly judged. I naturally desired to employ to the full

[1] Secretly.

* It was the prudent strictness of Duclos in particular that inspired me with this apprehension. As for Diderot, somehow or other, all my conversations with him always tended to make me more satirical and caustic than I was naturally inclined to be. This very circumstance hindered me from consulting him in regard to an undertaking, in which I desired to employ nothing but the force of argument, without the least trace of irritation or party-feeling. The tone which I adopted in this work may be gathered from that of the "Contrat Social," which is taken from it. (R)

the right of thinking, which was mine by birth, but always in such a manner as to show respect towards the government under which I lived, without ever disobeying its laws; and, while extremely careful not to violate the law of nations, I by no means intended to renounce the advantages it afforded, owing to any considerations of fear. I even confess that, as a stranger and living in France, I found my position advantageous for speaking the truth boldly. I knew well that, if I continued, as I intended, to have nothing printed in the State without permission, I was under no responsibility to anyone as regarded my principles and their publication in any other country. I should have been less independent even at Geneva, where the authorities had the right to criticise the contents of my writings wherever they might have been printed. This consideration had greatly contributed to make me yield to the entreaties of Madame d'Epinay, and to abandon my intention of settling at Geneva. I felt, as I have stated in my "Émile," that, unless a man is a born intriguer, he must by no means compose his books in the bosom of his country, if he desires to devote them to its welfare.

What made me feel still happier was, that I was persuaded that the Government of France, without perhaps regarding me with a very favourable eye, would make it a point of honour, if not to protect me, at least to leave me unmolested. This appeared to me a very simple, but, nevertheless, very clever stroke of policy – to make a merit of tolerating what could not be prevented, since, if I had been driven from France, which was all the authorities had a right to do, my books would have been written just the same, and perhaps with less reserve; whereas, by leaving me undisturbed, they would keep the author as surety for his works; and, further, would abolish prejudices deeply rooted in the rest of Europe, by gaining the reputation of having an enlightened respect for the rights of nations.

Those who judge, from the result, that my confidence deceived me, may be deceived themselves. In the storm which has overwhelmed me my books have served as an excuse, but it was against myself personally that the attack was directed. They cared little about the author, but were eager to ruin Jean Jacques;

and the worst thing that could be found in my writings, was the honour which they might possibly pay me. But let us not anticipate the future. I do not know whether this mystery – for such it still is to me – will subsequently be cleared up in the eyes of my readers. I only know that, if my publicly-declared principles had deserved to bring upon me the treatment I have suffered, I should have become its victim sooner, since the treatment of all my writings, in which these principles are unfolded, with the greatest hardihood, not to say audacity, appeared to have produced its effect even before my retirement to the Hermitage, without it having occurred to anyone, I will not say to pick a quarrel with me, but even to hinder the publication of the work in France, where it was sold as openly as in Holland. Afterwards the "Nouvelle Héloïse" appeared with no greater difficulty, and, I venture to say, with the same approval; and, what seems almost incredible, the profession of faith of this same Héloïse is exactly the same as that of the Savoyard Vicar. All that is outspoken in the "Contrat Social" had formerly appeared in the "Discours sur l'Inégalité." All that is outspoken in "Émile" had formerly appeared in "Julie." But these outspoken passages created no outcry against the two earlier works, therefore it could not have been they which created it against the latter.

Another undertaking, much of the same nature, the idea of which had occurred to me later, occupied my attention more at this moment. This was "Selections" from the works of the Abbé de Saint-Pierre, of whom I have hitherto been unable to speak, having been carried away by the thread of my narrative. The idea had been suggested to me, after my return from Geneva, by the Abbé de Mably, not directly, but through the intervention of Madame Dupin, who had a sort of interest in getting me to take it up. She was one of the three or four pretty women of Paris whose spoilt child the old Abbé had been; and, if she had not decidedly enjoyed the preference, she had at least shared it with Madame d'Aiguillon. She preserved for the memory of the good old man a feeling of respect and affection which did honour to both, and her vanity would have been flattered by seeing the still-born works of her friend brought to life again by her secretary. These works themselves, however, contained some excellent things, but so badly expressed, that it was a wearisome undertaking to read them; and it is astonishing that the Abbé, who regarded his readers merely as grown-up children, should, nevertheless, have addressed them as men, to judge by the little trouble he took to gain a hearing from them. With this idea the task had been proposed to me, as useful in itself, and very suitable for a man who was an industrious worker, but idle as an originator, who, finding the effort of thinking very fatiguing, preferred, in things which were to his taste, to elucidate and advance the ideas of another to creating ideas of his own. Besides, as I did not confine myself to the part of a mere translator, I was not prohibited from sometimes thinking for myself; and I was at liberty to give my work such a form, that many important truths might find their way into it under the mantle of the Abbé de Saint-Pierre with less risk than under my own. In addition, the undertaking was no light one; it was a question of nothing less than reading, thinking over, and making selections from twenty-three volumes, diffuse, confused, full of prolixities, repetitions, and narrow or false views, amongst which it was necessary to fish out some few that were great and lofty, which gave one the courage to endure the painful task. I myself was often on the point of relinquishing it, if I could have drawn back with decency – but, by accepting the Abbé's manuscripts, which were given to me by his nephew the Comte de Saint-Pierre, at the entreaty of Saint-Lambert, I had in a manner pledged myself to make use of them, and it was necessary for me either to return them, or to endeavour to turn them to account. It was with the latter intention that I had brought these manuscripts to the Hermitage, and it was the first work to which I intended to devote my spare time.

I contemplated a third work, the idea of which was due to certain observations which I had made upon myself; and I felt the more encouraged to undertake it, as I had reason to hope that I might produce a book really useful to mankind, even one of the most useful that could be offered to it, if the execution worthily corresponded to the plan which I had sketched for myself. The observation has been made, that most men, in the course of their lives, are frequently unlike themselves, and seem transformed into quite different men. It was not to establish a truth so well known that I desired to write a book; I had a newer and even more important object. This was to investigate the causes of these changes, confining myself to those which depended on ourselves, in order to show how we might ourselves control them, in order to make ourselves better and more certain of ourselves. For it is unquestionably more difficult for an honourable man to resist desires, already fully formed, which he ought to overcome, than it is to prevent, change or modify these same desires at the fountain-head, supposing him to be in a position to trace them back to it. A man resists temptation at one time because he is strong; another time, he yields to it because he is weak; if he had been the same as before, he would not have yielded.

While examining myself, and endeavouring to find, in the case of others, upon what these different conditions of being depended, I discovered that they depended in great part upon the impression which external objects had previously made upon us, and that we, being continually modified by our senses and our bodily organs, exhibited, without perceiving it, the effect of these modifications of ourselves, in our ideas, our feelings, and even in our actions. The numerous and striking observations which I had collected were unassailable, and, from their physical principles, seemed to me well adapted to furnish an external rule of conduct, which, being altered according to circumstances, might place or keep the mind in the condition most favourable to virtue. From how many errors would the reason be preserved, how many vices would be strangled at their birth, if mankind knew how to compel the animal economy to support the moral order, which it so frequently disturbs! Different climates, seasons, sounds, colours, darkness, light, the elements, food, noise, silence, movement, repose – all affect the bodily machine, and consequently the mind; all afford us a thousand opportunities, which will almost infallibly enable us to govern those feelings in their first beginnings, by which we allow ourselves to be dominated. Such was the fundamental idea which I had already sketched upon paper, and from which I expected, in the case of well-disposed persons, who, loving virtue sincerely, mistrust their weakness, a surer effect, inasmuch as it appeared easy to me to make of it a book as agreeable to read as it was to write. However, I have made but little progress in the work, the title of which was *La Morale Sensitive*, or *Le Matérialisme du Sage*. Distractions, the cause of which the reader will soon learn, prevented me from giving it attention, and he will also learn what was the fate of my sketch, which is more closely connected with my own than it might appear.

Besides all this, I had for some time contemplated a system of education, to which Madame de Chenonceaux, who trembled for her son's future, as the result of the education which he was receiving from his father, had begged me to give attention. The power of friendship caused this subject, although less to my taste in itself, to claim my attention more than all the rest. For this reason this is the only project, amongst all those which I have just mentioned, that I have carried out. The object which I proposed to myself in this work should, in my opinion, have brought the author a different reward. But let us not here anticipate this melancholy topic. I shall have only too much reason to speak of it in the sequel.

All these various projects afforded me material for meditation during my walks, for, as I believe I have already said, I can only think while walking: as soon as I stop, I can think no longer; my brain can only move with my feet. However, I had taken the precaution of providing myself with an indoor task for rainy days. This was my "Dictionary of Music"; the scattered, mutilated, and raw materials of which made it necessary to rewrite the work almost entirely. I bought some books which I required for the purpose. I had spent two months in making extracts from a number of others which I borrowed from the King's library, and some of which I was even allowed to take with me to the Hermitage. These were my materials for compiling indoors, when the weather did not allow me to go out, or when I was tired of my copying. This arrangement suited me so well, that I adhered to it both at the Hermitage and at Montmorency, and even, subsequently, at Motiers, where I finished this work while continuing others; and I always found a real relaxation in a change of occupation.

I followed for some time, with tolerable exactness, the distribution of time that I had marked out for myself, and was very well satisfied with it; but, when the fine weather brought back Madame d'Epinay more frequently to Épinay or La Chevrette, I found that attentions, which at first did not cost me much, but which I had not reckoned upon, greatly upset my other arrangements. I have already said that Madame d'Epinay had some very amiable qualities; she was very devoted to her friends and served them most zealously; and, as she spared neither time nor trouble, she certainly deserved that they should show her some attentions in return. Hitherto I had fulfilled this duty without feeling that it was one; but at last I discovered that I had loaded myself with a chain, the weight of which only friendship prevented me from feeling: I had made the burden heavier by my dislike of crowded rooms. Madame d'Epinay availed herself of this to make a proposal, which seemed to suit me well, and suited her even better; this was that she should let me know when she would be alone, or nearly so. I consented, without foreseeing to what I was binding myself. The consequence was, that I no longer visited her when it was convenient to me, but when it suited her, so that I was never sure of having a whole day at my disposal. This tie considerably spoiled the pleasure which my visits to her had formerly afforded me. I found that the freedom which she had so often promised me, was only granted to me on condition that I never made use of it; and, when once or twice I attempted to do so, it gave occasion to so many messages, so many notes and such apprehensions concerning my health, that I plainly saw that nothing but being completely confined to my bed could excuse me from running to her at the first intimation of her wishes. I was obliged to submit to this yoke. I submitted, and with tolerably good grace for so bitter an enemy of dependence as I was, since my sincere attachment to her prevented me in great measure from feeling the chain which accompanied it. She also filled up in this manner, more or less, the void which the absence of her usual circle left in her amusements. It was for her a very poor stop gap, but it was better than complete solitude, which was unbearable to her. However, she was able to fill it much more easily after she began to try her hand at literature, and took it into her head to write, no matter how, romances, letters, comedies, tales, and such trifles. But what amused her was not so much writing as reading them; and if she by chance managed to scribble two or three consecutive pages, it was absolutely necessary for her to feel sure of having at least two or three favourable hearers, when she had completed this enormous task. I rarely had the honour of being one of the chosen, except by the favour of another. By myself, I was hardly ever considered at all in anything, not only in the society of Madame d'Epinay, but in that of M. d'Holbach, and wherever Grimm set the fashion. This complete insignificance suited me perfectly well, except in a *tête-à-tête*, when I did not know what attitude to assume, as I did not venture to talk about literature, of which I was not competent to judge, nor about gallantry, since I was too bashful, and I feared, more than death itself, the ridiculous appearance of an old beau. Besides, this idea never occurred to me when with Madame d'Epinay, and would perhaps never have occurred to me once in my life, even had I spent it altogether in her society; not that I had any personal repugnance to her – on the contrary, I perhaps loved her too much as a friend, to be able to love her as a lover. It gave me pleasure to see her and to talk with her. Her conversation, although agreeable enough in society, was dull in private; my own, which was by no means fluent, was not much assistance to her. Ashamed of a too lengthy silence, I strained every nerve to enliven the interview; and, although it often tired me, it never wearied me. I was very glad to show her trifling attentions, to give her little brotherly kisses, which did not appear to excite her sensuality any more than my own, and that was all. She was very thin, very pale, her breast was as flat as my hand. This defect alone would have been sufficient to chill me; my heart and senses have never been able to see a woman in one who has no breasts; and other reasons, which it would be useless to mention, always caused me to forget her sex.

Having thus made up my mind to an inevitable servitude, I resigned myself to it without resistance, and found it, at least during the first year, less burdensome than I should have expected. Madame d'Epinay, who usually spent the whole summer in the country, only spent part of the summer of this year there, either because her affairs required her to be more at Paris, or because the absence of Grimm rendered her stay at La Chevrette less agreeable. I profited by the intervals of her absence, or when she had much company, to enjoy my solitude with my good Thérèse and her mother in a manner which made me thoroughly appreciate it. Although for some years I had visited the country pretty frequently, I had rarely enjoyed it; and those excursions, always taken in the company of pretentious persons, and always spoiled by a feeling of restraint, only whetted my appetite for country pleasures, and, the nearer the glimpse I had of them, the more I felt the want of them. I was so weary of salons, waterfalls, groves, flower-gardens, and their still more wearisome exhibitors; I was so tired of stitching, pianos, sorting wool, making bows, foolish witticisms, insipid affectations, trifling story-tellers, and big suppers that, when I caught a glimpse of a simple thorn-bush, a hedge, a barn, or a meadow; when I inhaled, while passing through a hamlet, the fragrance of a savoury chervil omelette; when I heard from a distance the rustic refrain of the *bisquières*,[1] I wished all rouge, furbelows, and ambergris[2] at the devil; and, regretting the goodwife's homely dinner and the native wine, I should have been delighted to slap the face of M. le chef and M. le maître, who forced me to dine at my usual supper-hour, and to sup at a time when I am usually asleep; above all, I should have liked to slap MM. les laquais, who devoured with their eyes the morsels I ate, and, if I was not prepared to die of thirst, sold me their master's adulterated wine at ten times the price I should have paid for wine of a better quality at an inn.

Behold me, then, at last, in my own house, in a pleasant and solitary retreat, able to spend my days in the independent, even, and peaceful life, for which I felt that I was born. Before describing the effect of this situation, so new to me, upon my heart, it behoves me to recapitulate its secret inclinations, that

---

[1] Female goatherds   [2] Used for perfume

the progress of these new modifications may be better followed up in its origin.

I have always considered the day which united me to my Thérèse as that which determined my moral being. I needed an attachment, since that which should have sufficed me had been so cruelly broken. The thirst for happiness is never quenched in man's heart. Mamma was growing old and degraded. It was clear to me that she could never again be happy in this world. Thus, the only thing left for me was to seek for a happiness which should be my own, since I had for ever lost all hope of sharing hers. I drifted for some time from one idea, from one plan, to another. My voyage to Venice would have plunged me into public affairs, if the man with whom I was to be connected had been possessed of common sense. I am easily discouraged, especially in difficult and long-winded undertakings. My ill-success in this disgusted me with all others; and since, in accordance with my old maxim, I looked upon distant objects as decoys for fools, I determined to live henceforth without any fixed plan, as I no longer saw anything in life which might have tempted me to exert myself.

It was just at that time that we became acquainted. The gentle character of this good girl appeared to me so well suited to my own, that I united myself to her by means of an attachment which neither time nor wrongs have been able to lessen, and everything which ought to have broken it has only increased it. The strength of this attachment will be seen in the sequel, when I lay bare the wounds and pangs with which she has rent my heart during the height of my misery, without a word of complaint to anyone ever escaping me, until the moment when I am writing these lines.

When it becomes known that, after having done all and braved everything, to avoid being separated from her, after having lived with her for twenty-five years, in spite of destiny and mankind, I finally married her in my old age, without any expectation or solicitation on her part, without any engagement or promise on my own, it will be believed that a mad love, which turned my head from the first day, gradually led me on to the last extravagance; and it will be the more readily believed, when the special and weighty reasons, which should have prevented me from ever doing such a thing, also become known. What then will the reader think, when I declare to him, in all the sincerity which he must now recognise as part of my character, that, from the first moment when I saw her up to this day, I never felt the least spark of love for her; that I no more desired her possession than that of Madame de Warens, and that the sensual needs, which I satisfied in her person, were only for me those of sexual impulse, without being in any way connected with the individual? He will perhaps believe that, being constituted differently from other men, I was incapable of feeling love, since it did not enter into the feelings which attached me to those women who have been most dear to me. Patience, reader! the fatal moment is approaching, when you will be only too rudely undeceived.

I repeat myself; I know it; but it is unavoidable. The first, the greatest, the most powerful, the most irrepressible of all my needs was entirely in my heart; it was the need of a companionship as intimate as was possible; it was for that purpose especially that I needed a woman rather than a man, a female rather than a male friend. This singular want was such, that the most intimate corporal union had been unable to satisfy it; I should have wanted two souls in the same body; without that, I was always conscious of a void. I thought that the moment had come, when I should feel it no longer. This young person, amiable by reason of a thousand excellent qualities, and, at that time, even by her personal appearance, which was without a trace of unnaturalness or coquetry, would have confined my whole existence in herself, if I had been able to confine hers to me, as I had hoped. I had nothing to fear from men; I am certain that I am the only man she ever truly loved, and her passions were so cool, that she rarely felt the want of other men, even when I had ceased to be one to her in this respect. I had no family; she had one; and this family, the members of which were all of a far different character from herself, was not such that I could ever have regarded it as my own. This was the first cause of my unhappiness. What would I not have given to have been able to make myself her mother's child! I tried all I could to do so, but never succeeded. It was useless for me to attempt to unite all our interests; it was impossible. She always created interests different from mine, set them in opposition to mine, and even to those of her daughter, which were already identical with them. She and her other children and grandchildren became so many leeches, and the least injury they did to Thérèse was that of robbing her. The poor girl, who was accustomed to give in, even to her nieces, allowed herself to be robbed and ruled without saying a word; and it pained me to see that, while I exhausted my money and good advice in vain, I could do nothing to assist her. I tried to get her away from her mother; but she always opposed it. I respected her opposition, and esteemed her the more for it; but this refusal was none the less prejudicial to her interests and my own. Devoted to her mother and the rest of her family, she belonged more to them than to me, even more than to herself. Their greed was not so ruinous to her as their advice was pernicious; in short, if, thanks to her love for me and her naturally good disposition, she was not completely their slave, she was sufficiently so to prevent, in great part, the effect of the good principles which I endeavoured to instil into her, and to cause us always to remain two, in spite of all my efforts to the contrary.

Thus it came to pass that, notwithstanding a sincere and mutual attachment, upon which I had bestowed all the tenderness of my heart, the void in this heart was never completely filled. Children, who might have effected this, were born to us; but this only made matters worse. I shuddered at the thought of handing them over to the care of this badly brought up family, to be brought up even worse. The risks of bringing up at the Foundling Hospital were far less. This reason for the resolution which I took, stronger than all those which I stated in my letter to Madame de Francueil,[1] was, however, the only one which I did not venture to tell her. I preferred to remain not completely cleared from so grave a reproach, in order to spare the family of a person whom I loved. But it may be judged, from the behaviour of her miserable brother, whether, in spite of anything that may be said about it, I should have been justified in exposing my children to the risk of receiving a similar education to his.

[1]   [Letter to Mme de Francueil] See Book VIII, p. 381.

Being unable to enjoy to the full this intimate intercourse of which I felt the need, I sought to supplement it in a manner which, although it did not completely fill the void, caused me to feel it less. For want of a friend, who should be entirely devoted to me, I needed friends whose impulse might overcome my indolence. For this reason I cultivated and strengthened my relations with Diderot and the Abbé de Condillac, entered into fresh and still closer relations with Grimm, and, in the end, owing to the unlucky Essay, the history of which I have related, I found myself thrown back, without any idea of it, upon literature, which I thought I had abandoned for ever.

My first appearance led me by a new path into another intellectual world, the simple and lofty economy of which I was unable to look upon without enthusiasm. My continued attention to it soon convinced me, that there was nothing but error and folly in the doctrine of our philosophers, and misery and oppression in our social arrangements. Deluded by my foolish pride, I thought that I was born to destroy all these illusions, and, believing that, in order to gain a hearing, it was necessary for my manner of life to harmonise with my principles, I adopted the singular course which I have not been permitted to continue, in which I set an example for which my pretended friends have never forgiven me, which at first made me ridiculous, and would have ended by making me respectable, if it had been possible for me to persevere in it.

Hitherto I had been good; from that moment I became virtuous, or, at least, intoxicated with virtue. This intoxication had commenced in my head, but had passed on into my heart. The noblest pride sprang up therein on the ruins of uprooted vanity. I pretended nothing; I became really what I seemed; and, for the four years at least, during which this state of effervescence lasted in all its force, there was nothing great or beautiful, which a man's heart could contain, of which I was not capable between heaven and myself. This was the origin of my sudden eloquence, of the truly celestial fire which inflamed me and spread over my first writings, and which for forty years had not emitted the least spark, since it was not yet kindled.

I was truly transformed; my friends and acquaintances no longer recognised me. I was no longer the shy, bashful rather than modest man, who did not venture to show himself or utter a word, whom a playful remark disconcerted, whom a woman's glance caused to blush. Audacious, proud, undaunted, I carried with me everywhere a confidence, which was firmer in proportion to its simplicity, and had its abode rather in my soul than in my outward demeanour. The contempt for the manners, principles, and prejudices of my age, with which my deep meditations had inspired me, rendered me insensible to the raillery of those who possessed them, and I pulverised their trifling witticisms with my maxims, as I should have crushed an insect between my fingers. What a change! All Paris repeated the penetrating and biting sarcasms of the man who, two years before and ten years afterwards, never knew how to find the thing he ought to say, nor the expression he ought to use. Anyone who endeavours to find the condition of all others most contrary to my nature will find it in this. If he desires to recall one of those brief moments in my life during which I ceased to be myself, and became another, he will find it again in the time of which I speak; but, instead of lasting six days or six weeks, it lasted nearly six years, and would, perhaps, have lasted until now, had it not been for the special circumstances which put an end to it, and restored me to Nature, above which I had attempted to elevate myself.

This change began as soon as I had left Paris and the sight of the vices of the great city ceased to keep up the indignation with which it had inspired me. As soon as I lost sight of men, I ceased to despise them; as soon as I lost sight of the wicked, I ceased to hate them. My heart, little adapted for hatred, only caused me to deplore their wretchedness, from which it did not distinguish their wickedness. This gentler, but far less lofty, frame of mind soon dulled the burning enthusiasm which had so long carried me away, and, without anyone perceiving it, even without perceiving it myself, I became again shy, courteous, and timid; in a word, the same Jean Jacques as I had been before.

If this revolution had merely restored me to myself, and had gone no further, all would have been well; but, unfortunately, it went much further, and carried me away rapidly to the other extreme. From that time my soul, in a state of agitation, no longer kept its centre of gravity, and its oscillations, ever renewed, always destroyed it. I must describe at some length this second revolution – the terrible and fatal epoch of a destiny without example among mankind.

As we were only a party of three in our retreat, leisure and solitude naturally increased the intimacy of our intercourse. This was what occurred in the case of Thérèse and myself. We spent some delightful hours together under the shady trees, more delightful than any I had ever enjoyed before. She herself appeared to appreciate it more than she had hitherto done. She opened her heart to me without reserve, and told me things about her mother and her family, which she had been strongminded enough to conceal from me for a long time. Both had received from Madame Dupin a number of presents intended for me, which the cunning old woman, to save me annoyance, had appropriated for herself and her other children, without leaving any for Thérèse, whom she strictly forbade to say anything to me about them – a command which the poor girl obeyed with an obedience which is almost incredible.

A thing which surprised me still more, was the discovery that, besides the secret conversations which Diderot and Grimm had frequently held with both, in order to estrange them from me, but which had failed in their object owing to the opposition of Thérèse, both of them had since then held frequent secret conferences with her mother, without her knowing anything of what was brewing between them. She only knew that sundry little presents played a part in it; that there were little journeys to and fro, which they attempted to conceal from her, of the reason of which she was completely ignorant. At the time when we left Paris, Madame le Vasseur had long been in the habit of calling upon Grimm two or three times a month, and spending some time there with him in private conversation, on which occasions even his servant was always sent out of the room.

I judged that the motive of all this was no other than the same scheme into which they had attempted to make the daughter enter, by promising to procure for them, through Madame d'Epinay's influence, a licence to retail salt, or a tobacco-shop; in a word, by tempting them with the prospect of gain. They had represented to these women that, as I was not in a position to do anything for them, I could not do anything for myself either, on account of them. As I saw nothing in all this but good intentions, I was not absolutely annoyed with them. Only the secrecy revolted me, especially on the part of the old woman, who, in addition, daily showed herself more toadying and wheedling in her manner towards me, which, however, did not prevent her from incessantly reproaching her daughter in private with being too fond of me and telling me everything, saying that she was a fool, and would find herself taken in in the end.

This woman possessed in the highest degree the art of killing two birds with one stone, of concealing from one what she received from another, and from me, what she received from all. I might have pardoned her for her avarice, but I could not forgive her dissimulation. What could she have to conceal from me – from me, whose happiness she so well knew depended almost entirely upon her daughter's happiness and her own? What I had done for her daughter, I had done for myself, but what I had done for her deserved some acknowledgement on her part; she at least should have been grateful to her daughter for it, and should have loved me also out of love for her who loved me. I had rescued her from utter misery; from me she received the means of existence, to me she owed all those acquaintances whom she so well knew how to make use of. Thérèse had long supported her by her own exertions, and was now supporting her with bread supplied by me. She owed all to this daughter, for whom she had done nothing, while her other children, on whom she had bestowed marriage portions, and for whom she had ruined herself, far from helping to support her, devoured her substance and my own. It seemed that, under these circumstances, she should have regarded me as her only friend, as her most reliable protector, and, far from keeping me in the dark as to my own affairs, far from joining in a plot against me in my own house, should have faithfully informed me of everything that might concern me when she learned it sooner than I did. In what light, then, could I regard her deceitful and mysterious conduct? Above all, what was I to think of the sentiments with which she endeavoured to inspire her daughter? What monstrous ingratitude must have been the mother's, when she sought to instil it into the daughter!

All these considerations finally alienated my heart so completely from this woman, that I could no longer look upon her without contempt. However, I never ceased to treat the mother of the partner of my life with respect, and to show her in everything almost the consideration and esteem of a son; but I must admit that I never cared to remain long in her company, and I am ill able to put restraint upon myself.

This, again, is one of the brief moments of my life, in which I have been almost within sight of happiness, without being able to attain to it, although through no fault of my own. If this woman had been of good character, we should, all three, have been happy to the end of our days; the last survivor would alone have deserved pity. Instead of this, the reader will see the development of events, and be able to judge whether I could have altered it.

Madame le Vasseur, seeing that I had gained ground in her daughter's heart while she had lost it, endeavoured to recover it; and, instead of regaining my esteem through the daughter, attempted to alienate her from me altogether. One of the means that she employed was to invoke the assistance of her family. I had begged Thérèse not to invite any of them to the Hermitage, and she had promised not to do so. They were invited in my absence, without consulting her, and they then made her promise to say nothing to me about it. When the first step was taken, the rest was easy. When a person once keeps anything secret from one whom he loves, he soon feels no scruple about concealing everything from him. As soon as I was at La Chevrette, the Hermitage was full of people, who enjoyed themselves tolerably well. A mother has always great influence over a daughter of good disposition; nevertheless, in spite of all her efforts, the old woman could never induce Thérèse to enter into her views, or persuade her to join the conspiracy against me. As for herself, she made up her mind irrevocably. As she saw, on the one side, her daughter and myself, at whose house she could live and that was all; and, on the other, Diderot, Grimm, d'Holbach, and Madame d'Epinay, who promised much and gave something, it never entered her head that she could possibly be in the wrong in company with a farmer-general's wife and a Baron. If I had been more observant, I should have seen, from that moment, that I was nourishing a serpent in my bosom; but my blind confidence, which nothing had as yet diminished, was such that it never even occurred to me, that anyone could wish to injure a person who deserved to be loved. While I saw a thousand conspiracies formed around me, all I could complain of was the tyranny of those whom I called my friends, and whose only object, as I imagined, was to force me to be happy in their own fashion rather than in my own.

Although Thérèse refused to enter into the conspiracy with her mother, she again kept her secret. Her motive was praiseworthy; I will not undertake to decide whether she did well or ill. Two women who have secrets are fond of chattering together about them. This brought them closer together; and Thérèse, by dividing her attentions, sometimes caused me to feel that I was alone, for I could no longer regard as a society the relations between us three. Then it was that I felt keenly the mistake which I had committed, at the beginning of our connection, in not having taken advantage of the pliability which was the result of her affection, to improve her mind and furnish her with a store of knowledge, which by drawing us closer together in our retirement, would have filled up her time and my own agreeably, and prevented us from ever noticing the length of a *tête-à-tête*. Not that our conversation ever flagged, or that she showed any signs of weariness during our walks; but we had not a sufficient number of ideas in common to make a great stock. We could no longer speak incessantly of our plans, which henceforth were limited to plans of enjoyment. The objects around us inspired me with reflections which were beyond her comprehension. An attachment of twelve years had no longer need of words; we knew each other too well to be able to find anything fresh. The only resource left was gossip, scandal, and feeble jokes. It is in solitude especially that one feels the advantage of living with someone who knows how to think. I had no need of this resource to amuse myself in her society; but she would have needed it, in order to be able always to amuse herself in mine. The worst thing was, that we were obliged to hold our interviews secretly; her mother, who had become a nuisance to me, forced me to look out for opportunities. I felt under retraint in my own house – this is saying everything. The atmosphere of love ruined simple friendship. We enjoyed an intimate intercourse without living in intimacy.

As soon as I thought I observed that Thérèse sometimes sought excuses to avoid the walks which I proposed to her, I ceased to propose them, without being annoyed with her for not finding as much pleasure in them as myself. Pleasure does not depend upon the will. I was sure of her affection, and that was enough for me. As long as my pleasures were hers, I enjoyed them with her; when this was not the case, I preferred her contentment to my own.

Thus it happened that, half deceived in my expectation, leading a life after my own inclination, in a spot which I had chosen for myself, with a person who was dear to me, I nevertheless at length found myself almost isolated. What I still lacked prevented me from enjoying what I possessed. In the matter of happiness and enjoyment, I must have all or nothing. It will afterwards be seen why I have considered this explanation necessary. I now resume the thread of my narrative.

I believed that I possessed a veritable treasure in the manuscripts which the Comte de Saint-Pierre had given me. On examining them more attentively, I found that they were little more than the collection of his uncle's printed works, corrected and annotated by his own hand, together with a few trifling fragments which had never been published. His writings on moral subjects confirmed me in the idea which some letters from him, which Madame de Créqui had shown me, had given me, that he possessed much greater talent than I had imagined; but, after a thorough examination of his political works, I found nothing but superficial views, or schemes, useful indeed, but rendered impracticable by the idea which the author could never get rid of, that men acted in accordance with their lights rather than their passions. The high opinion of modern learning which he entertained had caused him to adopt this false principle of wisdom brought to perfection, the foundation of all his proposed institutions, and the origin of all his political sophisms. This singular man, an honour to his age and his kind – the only man perhaps who, since the human race has existed, has had no other passion than that of reason – nevertheless wandered from one error to another in all his systems, in his desire to make men like himself, instead of taking them as they are, and as they will continue to be. He laboured only for imaginary beings, while believing that he was working for his contemporaries.

Recognising all this, I found myself somewhat embarrassed as to the form I should give to my work. By allowing the author's visionary ideas to remain undisturbed, I should render no service; by refuting them rigorously, I should be guilty of discourtesy, since the delivery of his manuscripts, which I had accepted and even asked for, imposed upon me the obligation of treating their author honourably. I finally decided upon the course of action which appeared to me most becoming, most judicious, and most useful: this was, to present the author's and my own ideas separately, and, with this object, to enter into his views, to elucidate them, to enlarge them, and to omit nothing which could secure them full appreciation.

My work, therefore, was to be composed of two entirely separate parts. The one was intended to explain, in the manner I have just indicated, the different schemes of the author; in the other, which was not intended to appear until the first had produced its effect, I should have brought my judgment to bear upon these same schemes, which, I confess, might certainly have exposed them sometimes to the fate of the sonnet of the "Misanthrope." At the commencement of the whole work I intended to give a life of the author, for which I had collected a quantity of sufficiently good material, which I flattered myself I should be able to make use of without spoiling. I had seen the Abbé de Saint-Pierre two or three times in his old age, and the respect which I had for his memory was a guarantee to me that, upon the whole, M. le Comte would not be dissatisfied with the manner in which I treated his relation.

I made my first attempt upon the "Paix perpetuelle," the most important and the most elaborate of all the works which made up the collection; and, before I began my reflections upon it, I had the courage to read absolutely everything that the Abbé had written upon this fine subject, without once allowing myself to be discouraged by its prolixity and repetitions. As the public has seen this abstract, I have nothing to say about it. The judgment which I passed upon it has never been printed, and I do not know if it ever will be; but it was written at the same time. I next went on to the "Polysynodie," or "Plurality of Councils," a work written in the Regent's time, to support the form of administration which he had introduced, which led to the expulsion of the Abbé from the French Academy, in consequence of certain attacks upon the preceding administration, which irritated the Duchesse de Maine and the Cardinal de Polignac. I finished this work in the same manner as the preceding, both abstract and judgment; but I stopped there, as I did not intend to finish this undertaking, which I ought never to have commenced.

The consideration which caused me to abandon it presented itself naturally, and it is surprising that it never occurred to me before. Most of the Abbé's writings consisted of or contained critical observations upon certain aspects of the French system of government, and some of them were so outspoken, that he had reason to congratulate himself upon escaping scot-free. But, in the ministerial offices, he had always been looked upon as a sort of preacher rather than as a serious politician, and he was allowed to say what he pleased, because it was well known that nobody would listen to him. If I had succeeded in getting him a hearing, the case would have been different. He was a Frenchman, I was not; and, if I repeated his censures, even in his own name, I ran the risk of being asked rudely, but with perfect justice, what I was interfering with. Luckily, before going too far, I saw the handle I was about to give to others against myself, and I speedily withdrew. I knew that, living alone in the midst of men, all more powerful than myself, I should never be able, in spite of all that I could do, to shelter myself from any injury they might choose to inflict upon me. There was only one thing that depended upon myself: to make it impossible for them, should they desire to injure me, to do so without injustice. This principle, which made me give up the Abbé de Saint-Pierre, has frequently caused me to renounce far more cherished schemes. Those who are always ready to look upon misfortune as a crime, would be greatly surprised if they knew the pains I have taken, all my life through, to prevent anyone being able to say to me with truth, in time of my misfortune: "You have well deserved it."

The relinquishment of this work left me for some time undecided as to what I should undertake next; and this interval of idleness was my ruin, since it gave me time to direct my thoughts towards myself, for lack of anything outside to claim my attention. I no longer had any schemes for the future to amuse my imagination; it was not even possible for me to form any, since my present situation was exactly that in which all my desires were united; I could imagine no more, and yet my heart was still conscious of a void. My condition was the more cruel, as I saw none that could be preferred to it. I had centred my tenderest affection upon a person after my own heart, who returned it.

I lived with her without restraint, and, so to say, as I pleased. Nevertheless, a secret feeling of oppression never left me, whether I was with her or away from her. While possessing her, I felt that she was still not mine; and the mere idea that I was not all in all to her, caused her to seem hardly anything to me.

I had friends of both sexes, to whom I was attached by the purest friendship and the most perfect esteem. I counted upon the truest return of these feelings on their part, and it never even occurred to me ever once to doubt their sincerity; yet this friendship was more painful to me than agreeable, owing to their obstinacy, even their affectation, in opposing all my inclinations, tastes, and manner of life. It was enough for me to seem to desire anything which concerned myself alone, and which did not depend upon them, in order to see them all immediately combine to force me to renounce it. This obstinate desire to control me absolutely in all my fancies – which was the more unjust as, far from attempting to control theirs, I did not even take the trouble to make myself acquainted with them – became so cruelly burdensome to me, that at last I never received a letter from them without feeling, when I opened it, a certain alarm, which was only too well justified by the perusal of it. I thought that, in the case of people who were all younger than myself, and who all stood in sore need themselves of the good advice which they lavished upon me, it was treating me too much like a child. "Love me," said I to them, "as I love you; as for the rest, do not interfere with my affairs, any more than I interfere with yours. That is all I ask of you." If they have granted me one of these two requests, it has certainly not been the latter.

I had a retired abode in a charming solitude. Master within my own four walls, I could live there in my own fashion, without being subjected to anyone's control. But this abode imposed upon me certain duties which were pleasant to fulfil, but indispensable. My liberty was altogether precarious. In a position of greater subjection than if I had been under orders, I could not help being so by inclination. When I got up, I could never once say to myself: I will spend this day as I please. Besides being dependent upon Madame d'Epinay's arrangements, I had still a more importunate claim upon me – that of the public and chance visitors. The distance of my residence from Paris did not prevent the daily arrival of crowds of idlers, who, not knowing what to do with their own time, wasted mine without the slightest scruple. When I least expected it, I was mercilessly assailed, and I rarely made agreeable plans for spending the day without finding them upset by the arrival of some unexpected visitor.

In short, amidst the blessings which I had most eagerly longed for, finding no pure enjoyment, I returned by fits and starts to the unclouded days of my youth, and I sometimes cried, with a sigh, to myself, "Ah! this is not Les Charmettes!"

The recollections of the different periods of my life led me to reflect upon the point which I had reached, and I saw myself, already in my declining years, a prey to painful evils, and believed that I was approaching the end of my career, without having enjoyed in its fulness scarcely one single pleasure of those for which my heart yearned, without having given scope to the lively feelings which I felt it had in reserve, without having tasted or even sipped that intoxicating pleasure which I felt was in my soul in all its force, and which, for want of an object, always found itself kept in check, and unable to give itself vent in any other way but through my sighs.

How came it to pass that I, a man of naturally expansive soul, for whom to live was to love, had never yet been able to find a friend entirely devoted to myself, a true friend – I, who felt admirably adapted to be one myself? How came it to pass that, with feelings so easily set on fire, with a heart full of affection, I had never once been inflamed with the love of a definite object? Consumed by the desire of loving, without ever having been able to satisfy it completely, I saw myself approaching the portals of old age, and dying without having lived.

These melancholy but touching reflections caused me to turn my thoughts towards myself with a regret which was not without its pleasure. It seemed to me that destiny owed me something which it had not yet granted me. Why had I been born with delicate faculties, if they were to remain unemployed to the end? The consciousness of my inner value, while calling forth the feeling of having been unfairly depreciated, in some degree compensated for it, and caused me to shed tears which it was a pleasure to me to allow to flow.

I pursued these reflections in the most beautiful season of the year, in the month of June, in cool groves, amidst the song of the nightingale and the purling of brooks. Everything combined to plunge me again into that too seductive indolence, to which I was naturally inclined, but from which the hard and austere frame of mind, to which a long period of inner ferment had brought me, should have delivered me once and for all. Unhappily, I went on to recall the dinner at the Château of Toune, and my meeting with those two charming girls at the same season of the year, and in a spot almost like that where I was at the moment. This recollection, rendered still more charming by the breath of innocence which pervaded it, brought back others of the same kind. Presently, I saw gathered round me all the objects which had touched my heart with emotion during my youth – Mademoiselle Galley, Mademoiselle de Graffenried, Mademoiselle de Breil, Madame Basile, Madame de Larnage, my young pupils, even the piquant Zulietta, whom my heart can never forget. I saw myself surrounded by a seraglio of houris and by my old acquaintances, the liveliest desire for whom was no new sensation for me. My blood became heated and inflamed, my head swam, in spite of my hairs already growing grey: and the serious citizen of Geneva, the austere Jean Jacques, close upon his forty-fifth year, suddenly became again the love-sick shepherd. The intoxication which seized me, although so sudden and extravagant, was, notwithstanding, so strong and lasting, that nothing less than the unforeseen and terrible crisis of the unhappiness into which it plunged me would have been able to cure me of it.

However, this intoxication, to whatever point it was carried, did not go so far as to make me forget my age and my position, flatter me with the idea that I could still inspire love, or make me attempt to communicate this devouring, but barren fire, by which, from childhood, I felt my heart in vain consumed. I did not hope, I did not even desire it; I knew that the time for love was over; I was too keenly conscious of the ridicule heaped upon elderly beaux, to expose myself to it, and I was not the man to become presumptuous and self-confident in my declining years, after having so rarely displayed such qualities during my best days. Besides, as a friend of peace, I should have dreaded domestic storms, and I loved Thérèse too sincerely, to expose her to the annoyance of seeing me entertain livelier feelings for others than those with which she herself inspired me.

What did I do on this occasion? The reader must have already guessed, if he has hitherto followed me with the least attention. The impossibility of grasping realities threw me into the land of chimeras, and, seeing nothing in existence which was worthy of my enthusiasm, I sought nourishment for it in an ideal world, which my fertile imagination soon peopled with beings after my own heart. This resource was never so welcome to me or so fruitful. In my continued ecstasies, I intoxicated myself with full draughts of the most delightful sensations that have ever entered the heart of man. I entirely forgot the human race, and created for myself societies of perfect beings, heavenly alike in their beauties and virtues; trusty, tender, and loyal friends such as

I never found in this world below. I found such pleasure in soaring into the empyrean, in the midst of the charming objects by which I was surrounded, that I passed the hours and days in it without taking count of them, and, forgetting everything else, no sooner had I hastily eaten a morsel of food, than I burned to escape, in order to run to my groves again. When ready to set out for my world of enchantment, if I saw some wretched mortals arrive who came to keep me back upon earth, I was unable to conceal or restrain my annoyance, and, losing control over myself, I gave them so rude a reception, that it might almost have been called brutal. This only increased my reputation as a misanthrope, whereas it would have gained for me a very different one, if the world had read my heart better.

At the height of my greatest exaltation, I was suddenly pulled back like a kite by the string, and restored to my place by Nature, assisted by a smart attack of my complaint. I employed the only remedy which afforded me relief, that is to say, the bougies, which put a stop to my celestial amours; for, besides that a man is seldom amorous when he is suffering, my imagination, which is animated in the open air and under the trees, languishes and dies in a room and under the rafters of a ceiling. I have often regretted that Dryads did not exist; it would most assuredly have been amongst them that I should have found the object of my attachment.

Other domestic disturbances occurred at the same time to increase my annoyance. Madame le Vasseur, while paying me the most effusive compliments, was doing her utmost to alienate her daughter from me. I received letters from my old neighbourhood, in which I was informed that the worthy old woman, without my knowledge, had contracted debts in the name of Thérèse, who knew it, but said nothing to me about it. That I had to pay them annoyed me much less than their having been kept a secret from me. How could she, from whom I had never kept a secret, keep one from me? Can one conceal anything from those whom one loves? The Holbachian clique, finding that I never went to Paris, began to be seriously afraid that I was comfortable in the country, and that I should be foolish enough to remain there. Then began those intrigues, the object of which was to get me back, indirectly, to the city. Diderot, who did not want to show himself so soon, began by detaching Deleyre from me, whom I had made acquainted with him, and who received and handed on to me the impressions which Diderot desired to give him, without perceiving their real purpose.

Everything seemed in league to tear me from my delightful and foolish reveries. Before I had recovered from my attack of illness, I received a copy of the poem on the destruction of Lisbon,[1] which I supposed was sent to me by the author. This put me under the obligation of writing to him, and saying something about his composition. This I did in a letter which was printed a long time afterwards without my consent, as will be mentioned later.

Surprised to hear this poor man, overwhelmed, so to speak, by fame and prosperity, declaim bitterly against the miseries of this life, and declare everything to be bad, I formed the senseless plan of bringing him to himself again, and proving to him that everything was good. Voltaire, while always appearing to believe in God, has never really believed in anything but the Devil, since his pretended God is nothing but a malicious being, who, according to him, finds no pleasure except in doing injury. The absurdity of this doctrine, which is obvious, is particularly revolting in a man loaded with blessings of every kind, who, from the bosom of happiness, endeavours to reduce his fellows to despair by the fearful and cruel picture of all the calamities from which he is himself exempt. I, who had a better right to count and weigh the evils of human life, examined them impartially, and proved to him that Providence is acquitted of responsibility in regard to every single one, and that they all have their origin in man's abuse of his faculties, rather than in the nature of things themselves. I treated him in this letter with all possible regard, consideration, delicacy, and, I venture to say, respect. But, as I knew how easily his self-love was irritated, I did not send the letter to himself, but to Dr. Tronchin, his physician and

[1] The great Lisbon earthquake took place on 1 November 1755, and Voltaire's pessimistic poem on "The Lisbon disaster" reached Rousseau, via their mutual friend Charles Duclos, in July 1756. He replied in a "Letter on Providence" dated 18 August. *Candide* did not appear until three years or so later.

friend, with full authority to deliver or suppress it, whichever he thought best. Tronchin gave him the letter. Voltaire, in reply, wrote me a few lines to the effect that, as he was ill and also nurse to someone else, he would defer his answer to another occasion, and said not a word about the subject. Tronchin, who sent this letter to me, enclosed it in one from himself, in which he expressed little esteem for the person who had handed it to him.

I have never published, or even shown, these two letters, since I am not fond of making a show of such petty triumphs; the originals will be found in my collection (Bundle A, Nos. 20 and 21). Since then, Voltaire has published the answer which he promised me, but never sent. It is no other than the romance of "Candide," of which I cannot speak, because I have not read it.

All these distractions ought to have cured me completely of my fantastic amours, and they were perhaps a means offered me by Heaven to prevent their fatal consequences; but my unlucky star was in the ascendant, and I had scarcely begun to go out again, when my heart, my head, and my feet again took the same paths. I say the same, in certain respects; for my ideas, a little less exalted, this time remained upon earth, but made so dainty a selection of everything amiable that could be found, that this selection was hardly less chimerical than the imaginary world, which I had abandoned.

I represented to myself love and friendship, the two idols of my heart, under the most enchanting forms. I took delight in adorning them with all the charms of the sex which I had always adored. I imagined two female friends, rather than two of my own sex, because if an instance of such friendship is rarer, it is at the same time more amiable. I bestowed upon them two analogous, but different, characters; two faces, not perfect, but after my taste, lighted up by kindliness and sensibility. I made one dark, the other fair; one lively, the other gentle; one prudent, the other weak, but with so touching a weakness, that virtue seemed to gain by it. I gave to one a lover, whose tender friend the other was, and even something more; but I admitted no rivalry, no quarrelling, no jealousy, because it is difficult for me to imagine painful feelings, and I did not wish to mar this charming picture by anything which degraded Nature. Smitten by my two charming models, I identified myself with the lover and the friend as far as it was possible for me; but I made him young and amiable, bestowing upon him, in addition, the virtues and defects which I was conscious of in myself.

In order to place my characters in the midst of suitable surroundings, I successively passed in review the most beautiful spots that I had seen in the course of my travels. But I found no woodland sufficiently delightful, no landscape sufficiently moving, to satisfy my taste. The valleys of Thessaly might have satisfied me, if I had seen them; but my imagination, tired of inventing, wanted some actual spot which might serve as a foundation, and create for me an illusion as to the reality of the inhabitants whom I intended to place there. For a long time I thought of the Borromean Islands,[1] the charming aspect of which had delighted me; but I found too much ornament and artificiality there. However, a lake was absolutely necessary, and I ended by choosing that one, on the shores of which my heart has never ceased to wander. I fixed upon that part of the shore, where my wishes had long placed my residence, in the imaginary happiness to which my destiny has limited me. The birthplace of my poor mamma still possessed a special charm for me. The contrast of natural situations, the richness and variety of the landscape, the magnificence, the majesty of the whole, which enchants the senses, moves the heart, and elevates the soul, finally decided me, and I established my young *protégés* at Vévai. This was all I imagined at the moment; the remainder was not added until later.

For a long time I confined myself to this indefinite plan, because it was sufficient to fill my fancy with agreeable objects, and my heart with feelings, upon which it loves to feed itself. These fictions, by their constant recurrence, at length assumed greater consistency, and fixed themselves in my brain under a definite shape. It was then that it occurred to me to give expression upon paper to some of the situations which they offered me, and, recalling all the feelings of my youth, to give play, to a certain extent, to the desire of loving, which I had never been able to satisfy, and by which I felt myself devoured.

[1] In the Lago Maggiore.

At first, I scribbled upon paper a few scattered letters, without sequence or connection; and when I wanted to put them together, I was often greatly embarrassed. What seems almost incredible, but is nevertheless perfectly true, is that the first two parts were written almost entirely in this manner, without my having formed any definite plan, and without my foreseeing that I should one day be tempted to make a regular work of it. Thus it will be seen, that these two parts, composed too late of materials which were not shaped for the place which they occupy, are full of wordy padding, which is not found in the others.

In the height of my reveries, I received a visit from Madame d'Houdetot, the first she had ever paid me in her life, but which, unfortunately, was not the last, as will be seen later. The Comtesse d'Houdetot was the daughter of the late M. de Bellegarde, farmer-general, and sister of M. d'Epinay and MM. de Lalive and de la Briche, both of whom were afterwards introducers of ambassadors.[1] I have mentioned how I became acquainted with her before she was married. Since then, I never saw her except at the festivities at La Chevrette, at Madame d'Epinay's, her sister-in-law. Having frequently spent several days with her, both at Épinay and at La Chevrette, I not only found her always very amiable, but I fancied that I perceived that she was favourably disposed towards myself. She was fond of walking with me; we were both of us good walkers, and our conversation never flagged. However, I never visited her in Paris, although she asked, and even pressed me to do so. Her connection with M. de Saint-Lambert,[2] with whom I was becoming intimate, rendered her still more interesting to me; and it was in order to bring me news of this friend, who at the time was, I believe, at Mahon,[3] that she came to the Hermitage.

This visit somewhat resembled the commencement of a romance. She lost her way. Her coachman had left the road at a place where it turned off, and tried to cross straight from the mill at Clairvaux to the Hermitage; her carriage stuck in the mud

[1]   Certain persons whose duty it was to conduct ambassadors and foreign princes to an audience with the Sovereign or head of the State.

[2]   [Saint-Lambert] See *Biographies*, p. 714.

[3]   The siege by the French of Fort Mahon at Minorca (May 1756) was one of the first events of the Seven Years' War.

at the bottom of the valley; she decided to get out and finish the journey on foot. Her thin shoes were soon wet through; she sank in the mire; her servants had the greatest trouble imaginable to extricate her, and at last she reached the Hermitage in a pair of boots, making the air ring with shouts of laughter, in which I joined when I saw her arrive. She was obliged to change all her clothes; Thérèse provided for her wants, and I persuaded her to put aside her dignity, and join us in a rustic collation, at which she greatly enjoyed herself. It was late, and she remained only a short time; but the meeting was so cheerful that she was delighted, and seemed disposed to come again. However, she did not carry out her intention until the following year; but alas! this delay was not of the least avail to protect me.

I spent the autumn in an occupation which no one would suspect – that of protecting M. d'Epinay's fruit. The Hermitage was the reservoir for the park of La Chevrette; there was a garden enclosed by walls, planted with espaliers and other trees, which supplied M. d'Epinay with more fruit than his kitchen-garden at La Chevrette, although three-quarters of it was stolen. Not to be an entirely useless guest, I undertook the management of the garden and the superintendence of the gardener. All went well until the fruit season; but, in proportion as it ripened, I found that it disappeared, without knowing what became of it. The gardener assured me that the dormice ate it all. I accordingly waged war upon the dormice, and destroyed a large number of them; but the fruit disappeared all the same. I kept watch so carefully, that at length I discovered that the gardener himself was the chief dormouse. He lived at Montmorency, and used to come from there in the evening, with his wife and children, to take away the stores of fruit which he had put aside during the day, and which he offered for sale in the Paris market as openly as if he had had a garden of his own. This wretch, whom I loaded with kindnesses, whose children Thérèse clothed, and whose father, who went out begging, I almost supported, robbed us with equal ease and effrontery, since not one of us three was sufficiently watchful to put a stop to it; and, in a single night, he succeeded in emptying my cellar, which I found completely stripped on the following morning. As long as he only seemed to devote his attention to me, I bore it all; but, as I wished to render an account of the fruit, I was obliged to denounce the thief. Madame d'Epinay asked me to pay him, discharge him, and look out for another gardener, which I did. As this rascal prowled round the Hermitage every night, armed with a large iron-tipped stick like a club, and accompanied by other vagabonds of his own sort, in order to reassure the women-folk, who were terribly alarmed at him, I made his successor sleep at the Hermitage; and, as even this failed to quiet their fears, I sent to ask Madame d'Epinay for a gun, which I gave to the gardener to keep in his room, with instructions only to make use of it in case of necessity, if an attempt was made to break open the door or scale the garden wall, and only to fire a discharge of powder, simply to frighten the thieves. These were assuredly the least measures of precaution which a man in ill-health, who had to pass the winter in the midst of the forest, alone with two nervous women, could have taken for the common safety. Lastly, I procured a little dog to serve as sentinel. When Deleyre came to see me during that time, I told him my story, and joined him in laughing at my military preparations. On his return to Paris, he tried in his turn to amuse Diderot with an account of them; and this was how the Holbachian clique learned that I seriously intended to pass the winter at the Hermitage. This consistency on my part, which they could never have imagined, quite disconcerted them; and, in the meantime, until they could think of some other annoyance to render my stay unpleasant,* they separated from me, through Diderot, this same Deleyre, who at first considered my precautions quite natural, and ended by calling them contrary to my principles and worse than ridiculous, in some letters in which he overwhelmed me with sarcasms, sufficiently biting to offend me, if I had been in the humour. But at that time, steeped in

* At the present moment, I marvel at my stupidity in not having seen, when I was writing this, that the annoyance, which the Holbachians felt when they saw me go to stay in the country, was chiefly due to the fact that they no longer had Madame le Vasseur at hand, in order to guide them in their system of intrigues at fixed places and times. This idea, which occurs to me too late, completely explains the strangeness of their conduct, which is inexplicable under any other supposition. (R)

affectionate and tender sentiments, and susceptible of no others, I regarded his bitter sarcasms as nothing but a joke, and looked upon him as merely silly, when anyone else would have considered him a madman. Thus those who prompted him lost their trouble on this occasion, and I passed the winter without being in the least disturbed.

By dint of care and watchfulness, I succeeded so well in protecting the garden that, although the yield of fruit was almost entirely a failure this year, the result was triple that of the preceding year. I certainly spared no pains to preserve it. I even accompanied the consignments which I sent to La Chevrette and Épinay, and carried some baskets myself. I remember that "aunt" and myself once carried one that was so heavy that, to avoid succumbing under the load, we were obliged to rest every dozen steps, and arrived bathed in perspiration.

[1757.] – When the bad weather began again, and I was confined to the house, I tried to resume my stay-at-home occupations, but found it impossible. I saw everywhere nothing but my two charming friends, their friend, their surroundings, the country in which they lived, the objects which my fancy created or embellished for them. I no longer belonged to myself for a single moment. My delirium never left me. After several fruitless attempts to banish all these imaginary creations from my mind, I became at last completely seduced by them, and all my efforts were thenceforth devoted to reducing them to some sort of order and coherence, in order to work them up into a kind of romance.

I was chiefly embarrassed by the shame which I felt at contradicting myself so openly and so boldly. After the strict principles which I had just laid down with so much noise, after the austere maxims which I had preached so strongly, after the biting invectives which I had launched against the effeminate books which breathed nothing but love and tenderness, could anything more unexpected or more shocking be imagined, than to see me, all at once, enrol myself with my own hand amongst the authors of those books which I had so strongly censured? I felt this inconsistency in all its force. I reproached myself with it, I blushed for it, I was vexed with myself for it; but all this was

unable to bring me back to reason. Completely enthralled, I was
forced to submit to the yoke at all risks, and to make up my mind
to brave public opinion, except in regard to considering later,
whether I should decide to show my work or not: for I did not as
yet suppose that I should ever determine to publish it.

Having taken this resolution, I threw myself heartily into my
reveries, and, after repeatedly turning them over and over in my
head, I at last sketched the kind of plan, with the execution of
which the public is acquainted. This was certainly the best
advantage that could be derived from my follies: the love of
the good, which has never left my heart, turned them naturally
towards useful objects, which might have been productive of
moral advantage. My voluptuous pictures would have lost all
their grace, if the gentle colouring of innocence had been wanting in them. A weak girl is an object of pity, which may be
rendered interesting by love, and which is frequently not less
amiable; but who can endure without indignation the sight of
fashionable manners? What can be more revolting than the
pride of an unfaithful wife, who, openly trampling under foot
all her duties, nevertheless claims that her husband should be
deeply grateful for the favour which she grants him – of being
kind enough not to allow herself to be caught in the act? Perfect
beings do not exist; the lessons which they give are too far
remote from us. But – that a young person, born with a heart
equally tender and virtuous, while still unwedded, should allow
herself to be overcome by love, and, when wedded, should find
strength to overcome it in her turn and become virtuous again –
if anyone should tell you that this picture is, on the whole,
scandalous and unprofitable, he is a liar and a hypocrite: do
not listen to him.

Besides morality and conjugal fidelity, which are radically
connected with all social order, I had another and deeper object
in view – harmony and public peace, an object greater and
perhaps more important in itself, and certainly so at the
moment. The storm aroused by the "Encyclopédie," far from
subsiding, was at that time at its height. The two parties, let loose
against each other with desperate frenzy, were more like mad
wolves ready to tear each other to pieces in their rage, than

Christians and philosophers desirous of mutually enlightening, convincing, and leading each other back into the way of truth. It may almost be said that nothing was wanting on either side but active leaders of sufficient importance, for the quarrel to degenerate into civil war; and God only knows what would have been the result of a civil war waged on behalf of religion, in which the most cruel intolerance was in the main the same on both sides. A born enemy of all party spirit, I had frankly told some hard truths to both parties, to which they had paid no attention. I bethought myself of another expedient, which, in my simplicity, I considered admirable: this was to soften their mutual hatred by destroying their prejudices, and to point out to each party the merits and virtues of the other as worthy of public esteem and the respect of all mankind. This by no means sensible scheme, which assumed good faith amongst men, and which led me into the mistake with which I reproached the Abbé de Saint-Pierre, met with the success which it deserved: it entirely failed to reconcile the two parties, and only brought them together again in order to overwhelm me. Meanwhile, until experience had shown me my folly, I devoted myself to it, I venture to say, with a zeal worthy of the motive which inspired me, and I sketched the two characters of Wolmar and Julie in a state of rapture, which made me hope that I should succeed in making both amiable, and, what is more, by means of each other.

Satisfied with having roughly sketched my plan, I returned to the situations of detail which I had marked out. The result of the form in which I arranged them was the two first parts of *Julie*, which I wrote and made a fair copy of during the winter months with indescribable pleasure, using the finest gilt-edged paper, blue and silver writing-sand to dry the ink, and blue ribbon to fasten my manuscript; in short, nothing was sufficiently elegant or refined for the charming girls, with whom, like another Pygmalion, I was infatuated. Every evening, by the fireside, I read and read again these two parts to the women-folk. The daughter, without saying a word, and moved to tenderness, joined her sobs to mine; the mother, finding no compliments in it, understood nothing of it, remained quiet, and contented herself with repeating to me, during the intervals of silence, "That is very fine, sir."

Madame d'Epinay, uneasy at knowing that I was alone in winter, in the middle of the forest, in a lonely house, frequently sent to inquire after me. I had never received such genuine proofs of her friendship, and my own feelings towards her never responded to them with greater warmth. Amongst these proofs, I should be wrong to omit to state that she sent me her portrait, and asked me to tell her how she could procure mine, which had been painted by Latour, and exhibited at the Salon. Nor ought I to omit another mark of her attention, which will appear laughable, but is a feature in the history of my character, by reason of the impression which it produced upon me. One day, when it was freezing very hard, I opened a parcel which she had sent, containing several things which she had undertaken to procure for me, and found in it a little under-petticoat of English flannel, which she informed me she had worn, out of which she desired me to make myself a waistcoat. The style of her note was charming, full of tenderness and simplicity. This mark of attention, which was more than friendly, appeared to me so tender, as if she had stripped herself to clothe me, that, in my emotion, I kissed the note and the petticoat with tears. Thérèse thought that I had gone mad. It is singular that, of all the marks of friendship lavished upon me by Madame d'Epinay, not one has ever moved me so much, and, even since the rupture between us, I have never thought of it without emotion. I kept her little note for a long time, and I should still have it in my possession, if it had not shared the fate of all my other letters of that period.

Although the difficulty I had in making water gave me little rest during the winter, and, for part of the time, I was obliged to use probes, yet, on the whole, it was the most enjoyable and most quiet time that I had spent since my arrival in France. For the four or five months, during which the bad weather secured me still further from the interruptions of unexpected visitors, I enjoyed, more than I ever had or have done before or since, this independent, even, and simple life, the enjoyment of which only increased its value, without any other society than that of the two women in reality, and that of the two cousins in idea. It was at that time, especially, that I congratulated myself more and more every day upon the resolution which I had had the good sense to take, without paying heed to the outcries of my friends, who were annoyed to see me delivered from their tyranny; and, when I heard of the attempt of a madman,[1] when Deleyre and Madame d'Epinay informed me in their letters of the disturbance and agitation prevailing in Paris, I heartily thanked Heaven for having kept me at a distance from those spectacles of horror and crime, which would only have fed and sharpened the bilious temperament, which the sight of public disturbances stirred up within me; whereas now, seeing myself surrounded by nothing but smiling and peaceful objects in my retreat, my heart was entirely given up to amiable feelings. I here record with satisfaction the course of the last peaceful moments which I have been permitted to enjoy. The spring which followed this calm winter saw the germs of the misfortunes which I have still to describe burst forth, in the series of which will be found no similar intervals, in which I have had time to take breath.

I think, however, that I remember that, during this interval of peace, and even in the depths of my solitude, I did not remain altogether undisturbed by the Holbachians. Diderot stirred up some annoyances against me, and, unless I am very much mistaken, it was during this winter that the "Fils Naturel"[2] appeared, of which I shall have to speak presently. Not to mention that, for reasons which will subsequently appear, very few trustworthy records of that period have been preserved, even those which I have been permitted to keep are very inaccurate in regard to dates. Diderot never dated his letters. Madame d'Epinay and Madame d'Houdetot only put the day of the week, and Deleyre usually did the same. When I wanted to arrange these letters in order, I was obliged to grope in the dark and to supply the omissions by uncertain dates, upon which I cannot rely. Therefore, as I am unable to fix with certainty the date of the commencement of these quarrels, I prefer to

---

[1] On 4 January 1757 the valet Damiens attacked Louis XV with a knife at Versailles.

[2] Diderot's first play, *Le Fils naturel*, was published in February 1757.

relate afterwards, in a single section, all that I can recollect about them.

The return of spring had redoubled my tender frenzies, and in my erotic transports I had composed for the last parts of *Julie* several letters which have a flavour of the rapturous frame of mind in which I wrote them. I may mention, amongst others, that which deals with the Elysium and the walk along the shores of the lake, which, if I rightly recollect, are at the end of the fourth part. If anyone can read these two letters, without feeling his heart softened and melted by the same emotion which dictated them to me, he had better shut the book; he is incapable of judging of matters of sentiment.

Exactly at the same time, I had a second unexpected visit from Madame d'Houdetot. In the absence of her husband, who was a captain in the *Gendarmerie*, and of her lover, who was also in the service, she had come to Eaubonne, in the midst of the valley of Montmorency, where she had taken a very nice house. It was from there that she made a second excursion to the Hermitage. On this occasion, she came on horseback, dressed in men's clothes. Although I am not fond of such masquerades, I was charmed with the air of romance in this particular case, and this time – it was love. As it was the first and only time in my life, and its consequences have stamped it indelibly upon my recollection with terrible force, I must be permitted to enter with some detail into the matter.

Madame la Comtesse d'Houdetot was approaching her thirtieth year, and was by no means handsome. Her face was pitted with small-pox, her complexion was coarse, she was short-sighted, and her eyes were rather too round, but, notwithstanding, she looked young, and her features, at once lively and gentle, were attractive. She had an abundance of luxuriant black hair, which curled naturally, and reached down to her knees. Her figure was neat, and all her movements were marked by awkwardness and grace combined. Her wit was both natural and agreeable; gaiety, lightheartedness, and simplicity were happily united in it. She overflowed with delightful sallies of wit, which were perfectly spontaneous, and which often fell from her lips involuntarily. She possessed several agreeable accomplishments, played the piano, danced well, and composed very pretty verses. As for her character, it was angelic; gentleness of soul was the foundation of it; and, with the exception of prudence and strength, all the virtues were combined in it. Above all, she was so completely to be trusted in her intercourse, and was so loyal to those with whom she associated, that even her enemies had no need to conceal themselves from her. By her enemies, I mean those men, or, rather, those women who hated her; for, as for herself, her heart was incapable of hatred, and I believe that this similarity of disposition greatly contributed to inspire me with passion for her. In the confidences of the most intimate friendship, I have never heard her speak ill of the absent, not even of her sister-in-law. She was unable either to disguise her thoughts from anyone, or to repress any of her feelings: and I am quite convinced that she spoke of her lover even to her husband, as she spoke of him to her friends, acquaintances, and everybody, without distinction. Lastly, what proves unquestion ably the purity and sincerity of her excellent disposition is, that, being subject to fits of most remarkable absence of mind, she was often guilty of the most ridiculous indiscretions, which were in the highest degree imprudent, as far as she was herself concerned, but which were never offensive to others.

She had been married very young and against her inclinations to the Comte d'Houdetot, a man of position and a gallant soldier, but a gambler and a shuffler, and a person of but few amiable qualities, whom she had never loved. She found in M. de Saint-Lambert all the good qualities of her husband, together with others that were more agreeable   intellect, virtue, and talent. If one can excuse anything in the manners of the age, it is undoubtedly an attachment, which is refined by its duration, honoured by its effects, and only cemented by mutual esteem.

As far as I have been able to judge, she came to see me a little from her own inclination, but more from a desire to please Saint-Lambert, who had exhorted her to do so, and was right in believing that the friendship, which was beginning to be formed between us, would make this society agreeable to all three. She knew that I was aware of their relations, and, being able to speak of him to me without restraint, it was natural that she should find my society agreeable. She came; I saw her. I was intoxicated with love without an object. This intoxication enchanted my eyes; this object became centred in her. I saw my Julie in Madame d'Houdetot, and soon I saw only Madame d'Houdetot, but invested with all the perfections with which I had just adorned the idol of my heart. To complete my intoxication, she spoke to me of Saint-Lambert in the language of passionate love. O contagious power of love! When I listened to her, when I found myself near her, I was seized with a delightful shivering, which I have never felt when with anyone else. When she spoke, I felt myself overcome by emotion. I imagined that I was interesting myself only in *her* feelings, when my own were similar. I swallowed in deep draughts the contents of the poisoned cup, of which as yet I only tasted the sweetness. At last, without either of us perceiving it, she inspired me with all those feelings for herself which she expressed for her lover. Alas! it was very late, it was very hard for me, to be consumed by a passion, as violent as it was unfortunate, for a woman whose heart was full of love for another!

In spite of the extraordinary emotions which I had felt in her presence, I did not at first understand what had happened to me. It was not until she had left me that, when I attempted to think of Julie, I was surprised to find that I could think of nothing but Madame d'Houdetot. Then the scales fell from my eyes; I understood my misfortune, I groaned over it, but I did not foresee its results. I hesitated for a long time how I should behave towards her, as if real love left anyone sufficiently rational to be able to act in accordance with the result of such deliberations. I had not made up my mind, when she came again and took me by surprise. On this occasion, I understood the state of things. Shame, the companion of evil, made me speechless. I trembled before her, not venturing to open my mouth or lift my eyes. I was inexpressibly troubled, and she must have seen it. I resolved to confess it, and to leave her to guess the reason. This would be telling her the truth plainly enough.

If I had been young and attractive, and Madame d'Houdetot had shown herself weak, I should here blame her conduct. Nothing of the kind; I can only applaud and admire it. The course she took was equally generous and prudent. She could not suddenly give up my acquaintance without telling Saint-Lambert the reason, for he had himself persuaded her to visit me. This would have exposed two friends to the risk of a rupture, and, perhaps, of a public scandal, which she desired to avoid. She esteemed me and wished me well. She pitied my folly, and, without flattering, lamented it, and endeavoured to cure me of it. She was very glad to be able to keep for herself and her lover a friend whom she valued. Nothing gave her more pleasure than to speak of the close and happy intimacy which we might form between us, as soon as I should have recovered my senses. She did not, however, altogether confine herself to these friendly exhortations, and, when necessary, did not spare the harsher reproaches which I had so well deserved.

I spared myself even less. As soon as I was alone, I came to myself again. I was calmer for having spoken. Love, when it is known to her who inspires it, becomes more endurable. The energy with which I reproached myself for the love which I felt, must have cured me of it, if it had been possible. I summoned to my aid all the most powerful arguments I could think of, to stifle it. My moral sense, my feelings, my principles, the shame, the disloyalty, the crime, the abuse of a trust confided to me by friendship, and, lastly, the absurdity, at my age, of being inflamed with a most extravagant passion for one whose heart, already engaged, could neither make me any return, nor permit me to entertain the least hope – a passion, besides, which, far from having anything to gain by constancy, became more unbearable from day to day: I thought of all these.

Who would believe that the last consideration, which should have added weight to all the rest, was the one which weakened their force? What scruples, said I to myself, need I entertain in regard to a folly by which I am the only sufferer? Am I a young gallant of whom Madame d'Houdetot should feel alarmed? Would it not be said, to judge from my conceited remorse, that my gallantry, my manner, and my personal appearance were on the way to lead her astray? O poor Jean Jacques! love on to your heart's content, with a perfectly safe conscience, and have no fear that your sighs will ever injure Saint-Lambert.

My readers have seen that I was never presuming, even in my youth. This way of thinking was in keeping with the bent of my mind; it flattered my passion; it was sufficient to make me abandon myself to it unreservedly, and even laugh at the irrelevant scruples, which I thought I had created rather out of vanity than in accordance with the dictates of reason. What a lesson for honest souls, whom vice never attacks openly, but whom it finds the means to surprise, ever hiding itself under the mask of some sophism – frequently, of some virtue!

Guilty without remorse, I soon became so without measure: and I beg the reader to observe how my passion followed the track of my disposition, to drag me finally into the abyss. At first, it assumed a humble attitude, to reassure me; and then, in order to encourage me, pushed this humility to mistrust. Madame d'Houdetot, without relaxing her efforts to recall me to my duty and reason, without ever flattering my folly for a moment, treated me in other respects with the greatest gentleness, and assumed towards me a tone of the tenderest friendship. This friendship would have been enough for me, I declare, if I had believed it to be sincere; but, as I found it too pronounced to be true, I proceeded to get the idea into my head that love, which was from this time forth so ill-suited to my age and general appearance, had degraded me in the eyes of Madame d'Houdetot; that, in the extravagance of her youth, she only desired to amuse herself with me and my superannuated passions; that she had taken Saint-Lambert into her confidence, and that, indignation at my disloyalty having brought him over to her views, there was an understanding between them to turn my head completely, and then to laugh at me. This folly, which had caused me, at twenty-six years of age, to make a fool of myself with Madame de Larnage, whom I did not know, would have been excusable in me, at the age of forty-five, in the case of Madame d'Houdetot, if I had not known that she and her lover were both too honourable to indulge in so cruel an amusement.

Madame d'Houdetot continued to pay me visits, which I was not slow to return. Like myself, she was fond of walking: we took long walks in an enchanted country. Content to love her, and to venture to declare it, my situation would have been most delightful, had not my extravagant folly completely destroyed its charm. At first, she utterly failed to understand the silly petulance with which I received her tenderness; but my heart, which has ever been incapable of concealing any of its emotions, did not long leave her in ignorance of my suspicions. She tried to treat them as a joke; but this expedient was unsuccessful. Violent attacks of rage would have been the result: she accordingly altered her tone. Her compassionate gentleness remained unshaken. She reproached me in a manner which cut me to the heart; she exhibited, in regard to my unjust apprehensions, an uneasiness which I abused. I demanded proof that she was not laughing at me. She saw that there was no other way of reassuring me. I became pressing; the matter was a delicate one. It is surprising – it is, perhaps, unique – that a woman, who had ventured to go so far as to hesitate should have got out of the affair so well. She refused me nothing that the most tender friendship could grant. She granted nothing that could expose her to the charge of infidelity, and I had the humiliation of seeing that the flames, which the slightest favours on her part kindled in my heart, never threw the slightest spark into her own.

I have said, somewhere, that one must grant nothing to the senses, when one desires to refuse them something. In order to see how this maxim was falsified in the case of Madame d'Houdetot, and how completely she was justified in her self-dependence, it will be necessary to enter into the details of our long and frequent *tête-à-têtes*, and to describe them, in all their liveliness, during the four months which we spent together, in the course of an intimacy almost unprecedented between two friends of opposite sexes, who confine themselves within the limits beyond which we never went. Ah! if it was so late before I felt true love, my heart and senses paid dearly for the arrears! How great are the transports one must feel, by the side of a dearly-loved object of affection, who returns our love, when even a love which is unrequited can inspire those which it does!

But I am wrong in speaking of an unrequited love; to some extent mine was returned; it was equal on both sides, although it was not mutual. We were both intoxicated with love; she for her lover, I for her. Our sighs, our delightful tears mingled together.

Tender confidants, our feelings were so closely connected, that it was impossible that they should not unite in something; and yet, amidst this dangerous intoxication, she never forgot herself for a moment; as for myself, I protest, I swear that if, sometimes carried away by my senses, I attempted to make her unfaithful, I never truly desired it. The vehemence of my passion of itself kept it within bounds. The duty of self-denial had exalted my soul. The splendour of all the virtues adorned in my eyes the idol of my heart; to have soiled its divine image would have been its annihilation. I might have committed the crime; it has been committed a hundred times in my heart; but – to degrade my Sophie! could that ever have been possible? No, no! I told her so myself a hundred times. Had it been in my power to satisfy myself, had she abandoned herself to me of her own accord, I should, except in a few brief moments of delirium, have refused to be happy at such a cost. I loved her too dearly to desire to possess her.

It is nearly a league from the Hermitage to Eaubonne; on my frequent visits, I sometimes passed the night there. One bright moonlight evening, after having supped together, we went for a walk in the garden. At the bottom of this garden there was a rather large copse, through which we made our way to a pretty grove, adorned with a cascade, the idea of which she had carried out at my suggestion. Immortal souvenir of innocence and bliss! It was in this grove that, seated by her side on a grassy bank, under an acacia in full bloom, I found, to express the feelings of my heart, language that was really worthy of them. For the first and only time in my life I was sublime, if one may so call all the amiability and seductive charm that the tenderest and most ardent love can inspire in a man's heart. What intoxicating tears I shed upon her knees! What tears I caused her to shed in spite of herself! At last, in an involuntary transport, she exclaimed, "Never, no, never was a man so amiable; never did a lover love like you! But your friend Saint-Lambert is listening to us. My heart cannot love twice." I sighed; and was silent; I embraced her – what an embrace! But that was all. For six months she had lived alone, that is to say, far from her lover and her husband; during three of these months I saw her nearly every day, and Love was always with us. We had supped alone; we were alone, in a grove, beneath the light of the moon; and, after two hours of the liveliest and tenderest conversation, she left, in the middle of the night, this grove and the arms of her friend, as free from guilt, as pure in heart and person as she had entered it. Reader, weigh all these circumstances: I will add no more.

At the same time, let no one imagine that, on this occasion, my senses left me as undisturbed as in the presence of Thérèse or mamma. I have already said that this time it was love – love in all its force and in all its frenzy. I will not describe the agitation, the shivering, the palpitation, the convulsive movements, or the faintness of the heart, which I felt continually. The reader can judge of it from the impression which her image alone produced upon me. I have said that it was a considerable distance from the Hermitage to Eaubonne. I went past the hills of Andilly, which are delightful. As I walked, I dreamed of her whom I was going to see, of the tender reception, of the kiss which awaited me on my arrival. This kiss alone, this fatal kiss, even before I received it, inflamed my blood to such a degree that I felt dizzy, my eyes swam, I was blinded; my trembling knees could no longer support me; I was obliged to stop and sit down; my whole bodily machinery was utterly out of gear; I felt ready to faint. Aware of the danger, I tried, when I set out again, to distract my attention and to think of something else. I had scarcely gone twenty yards, when the same recollections and their incidental results returned to the attack, and I found it impossible to shake them off. In spite of all my efforts, I do not believe that I ever succeeded in accomplishing this journey alone, without paying the penalty. I arrived at Eaubonne, weak, exhausted, and worn out, scarcely able to stand upright. The moment I saw her, I was completely reinvigorated. By her side, I felt nothing but the importunity of an inexhaustible and ever useless vigour. On the road, within sight of Eaubonne, there was a pleasant terrace called Mont Olympe, where we sometimes met. If I arrived first, I had to wait for her. How painful was this waiting! In order to divert my attention, I attempted to write notes with my pencil, which I might have written with my purest blood. I was never able to finish a single one that was legible. When she found one in the niche which we had agreed upon, all she could read in it was the truly deplorable state I was in when I wrote it. This state, and, above all, its continuance during three months of excitement and self-restraint, so exhausted me that I did not recover for several years, and, finally, brought on a rupture, which I shall carry with me, or which will carry me with it, into the grave. Such was the only amorous enjoyment of the man of the most inflammable temperament, but, at the same time, of the most retiring disposition that Nature has perhaps ever produced. Such were the last happy days that have been permitted to me upon earth. I now commence the long series of the misfortunes of my life, which was seldom, if ever, interrupted.

Throughout the course of my life, as has been seen, my heart, transparent as crystal, has never been able to conceal, even for a moment, any feelings at all lively which may have taken refuge in it. The reader can judge whether I found it possible to conceal for long my affection for Madame d'Houdetot. Our intimacy was patent to everybody; we made no secret or mystery of it : it was not of a kind to require it; and, as Madame d'Houdetot had the tenderest friendship for me, of which she made no reproach, while I felt for her an esteem, the full justice of which no one knew better than myself, we afforded – she, by her frankness, absence of mind, and thoughtlessness; I, by my truthfulness, awkwardness, pride, impatience, and impetuosity – in our delusive security, more opportunity for attack than we should have done if we had been guilty. We went together to La Chevrette, we frequently met there, sometimes even by appointment. We lived there as usual, walking alone every day while talking of our love, our duties, our friend, our innocent schemes, in the park, opposite Madame d'Epinay's apartments, beneath her windows, from which she continually watched us, and, thinking herself defied, glutted her heart, by means of her eyes, with rage and indignation.

All women possess the art of concealing their anger, especially when it is strong. Madame d'Epinay, who was violent but deliberate, possesses this art in an eminent degree. She pretended to see nothing, to suspect nothing; and, while she redoubled her care and attention to me, and almost flirted with me, she at the same time pretended to overwhelm her sister-in-law with rudeness and marks of contempt, with which she appeared to wish to inspire me as well. It may be imagined that she did not succeed; but I was on the rack. Torn by contradictory feelings, while at the same time I felt touched by her tenderness, I had difficulty in restraining my anger, when I saw her wanting in respect to Madame d'Houdetot. The angelic gentleness of the latter enabled her to endure everything without complaining, even without resenting it. Besides, she was frequently so absent-minded, and always so little sensitive to such things, that half the time she did not even notice it.

I was so taken up with my passion, that, seeing nothing but Sophie – this was one of Madame d'Houdetot's names – I did not even notice that I had become the talk of the whole household and of the visitors. Baron d'Holbach, who, as far as I know, had never before been to La Chevrette, was one of the latter. If I had been as mistrustful as I afterwards became, I should have strongly suspected Madame d'Epinay of arranging this visit, in order to afford him the gratification of the amusing spectacle of the amorous citizen. But at that time I was so stupid, that I did not even see what was glaringly obvious to everyone. However, all my stupidity did not prevent me from finding the Baron more contented and jovial than usual. Instead of scowling at me, he discharged at me a volley of witticisms, of which I understood nothing. I opened my eyes wide without answering; Madame d'Epinay was obliged to hold her sides to restrain her laughter; I could not make out what was the matter with them. As the limits of jest were not yet exceeded, the best thing I could have done, if I had understood, would have been to join in it. But it is true that, amidst all the Baron's mocking joviality, it was easy to perceive the light of a spiteful joy in his eyes, which would perhaps have made me uneasy, if I had noticed it as much at the time, as I afterwards did when I recalled it to mind.

One day, when I went to see Madame d'Houdetot at Eaubonne, on her return from one of her journeys to Paris, I found her sad, and saw that she had been crying. I was obliged to restrain myself, since Madame de Blainville, her husband's sister, was present; but, as soon as I had a moment to myself, I told her of my uneasiness. "Ah!" she said, with a sigh, "I am much afraid that your follies will deprive me of all peace for the rest of my life. Saint-Lambert has been informed, and wrongly informed. He does me justice, but he is annoyed, and, what is worse, he does not tell me all. Happily, I have made no secret of our friendship, which was formed under his auspices. My letters, like my heart, were full of you; I have concealed nothing from him except your insensate love, of which I hoped to cure you, and which, although he does not mention it, I can see that he considers a crime on my part. Someone has done us an ill turn, and wronged me; but never mind. Let us either break off our acquaintance, or do you behave yourself as you ought. I do not wish to have anything more to conceal from my lover."

This was the first moment when I was sensible of the shame of seeing myself humiliated, through the consciousness of my offence, in the presence of a young woman, whose reproaches I felt to be just, and whose Mentor I ought to have been. The indignation which this caused me to feel against myself might perhaps have been strong enough to overcome my weakness, had not the tender compassion with which its victim inspired me again softened my heart. Alas! was that the moment to be able to harden it, when it overflowed with tears which penetrated it from all directions? This tenderness soon changed to anger against the vile informers, who had only seen the evil of a criminal but involuntary feeling, without believing, or even suspecting, the honourable sincerity of heart which redeemed it. We did not long remain in doubt as to the hand which had dealt the blow.

We both of us knew that Madame d'Epinay corresponded with Saint-Lambert. It was not the first storm which she had raised against Madame d'Houdetot; she had made countless attempts to get him away from her, and the past success of some of these attempts made Madame d'Houdetot tremble for the future. In addition, Grimm, who I believe had followed M. de Castries to the army, was in Westphalia, as well as Saint-Lambert; and they sometimes saw each other. Grimm had made some advances to Madame d'Houdetot, which had been unsuccessful. This so annoyed him that he gave up visiting her. One can imagine the *sang-froid* with which, considering his well-known modesty, he received the supposition that she preferred a man older than himself, and of whom, since he had been admitted to the society of the great, he only spoke as his *protégé*.

My suspicions of Madame d'Epinay became certainties, when I heard what had happened at home. While I was at La Chevrette, Thérèse often came there to bring my letters or to do certain things for me which my ill-health rendered necessary. Madame d'Epinay had asked her whether Madame d'Houdetot and myself corresponded. When she told her that we did, Madame d'Epinay pressed her to hand Madame d'Houdetot's letters to her, assuring her that she would seal them up again so cleverly that it would not be noticed. Thérèse, without letting it be seen how shocked she was at this proposal, and even without informing me, contented herself with taking greater precautions to conceal the letters which she brought me – a very wise precaution, for Madame d'Epinay had her watched when she came, and, waiting for her as she passed, on several occasions carried her boldness so far as to feel in her bib. She did more: she invited herself one day, together with M. de Margency, to dinner at the Hermitage, for the first time since I had lived there, and took advantage of the moment when I was walking with Margency, to go into my study with the mother and daughter, and begged them to show her Madame d'Houdetot's letters. If the mother had known where they were, they would certainly have been handed to her, but, luckily, only the daughter knew, and she declared that I had not kept any of them. This was a falsehood, beyond dispute, most honourable, loyal, and generous, while to have told the truth would have been simply an act of treachery. Madame d'Epinay, seeing that she could not seduce her, attempted to rouse her jealousy by reproaching her with her good-nature and blindness. "How can you," she said to her, "fail to perceive that their connection is a criminal one? If, in spite of all you can see for yourself with your own eyes, you still want further proofs, assist in what you must do to obtain them: you say that he tears up Madame d'Houdetot's letters as soon as he has read them; well, then! pick up the pieces carefully, and give them to me; I will put them together again." Such were the lessons which my friend gave to my companion.

Thérèse had the discretion to say nothing to me for a long time about all these attempts; but at last, seeing my embarrassment, she felt bound to tell me all, so that, knowing with whom I had to deal, I might take steps to protect myself against the treachery which was intended against me. My indignation and fury were indescribable. Instead of dissembling with Madame d'Epinay, as she had done with me, and employing counterplots, I abandoned myself without restraint to my natural impetuosity, and, with my usual thoughtlessness, broke out openly. My imprudence may be gauged by the following letters, which sufficiently show how each of us proceeded on this occasion:

LETTER FROM MADAME D'EPINAY (PACKET A, No. 44).

"What is the reason that I do not see you, my dear friend? I am uneasy about you. You promised me faithfully that you would confine yourself to going backwards and forwards from the Hermitage. Upon that, I left you to do as you pleased; but no, you have let a week go by. Unless I had been told that you were well, I should think that you were ill. I expected you yesterday or the day before, but I see no signs of you. My God! what can be the matter with you? You have no business, you can have nothing to annoy you either: for I flatter myself that you would have come at once to confide in me. You must be ill, then. Relieve my anxiety immediately, I beg you. Adieu, my dear friend. May this 'Adieu' bring a 'Good morning' from you."

ANSWER.

"Wednesday Morning.

"I cannot yet say anything to you. I am waiting until I am better informed, as I shall be, sooner or later. Meanwhile, rest assured that accused innocence will find a defender sufficiently zealous to give the slanderers, whoever they may be, some cause for repentance."

SECOND LETTER FROM MADAME D'EPINAY (PACKET A, No. 45).

"Do you know that your letter alarms me? What does it mean? I have read it more than five-and-twenty times. In truth, I do not understand it. I can only learn from it that you are uneasy and tormented, and that you are waiting until you are so no longer, before speaking to me about it. My dear friend, is this what we agreed? What has become of our friendship, our confidence? and how have I lost it? Are you angry with me or because of me? In any case, come this evening, I entreat you. Remember that you promised, not a week ago, to keep nothing on your mind, but to let me know of it at once. My dear friend, I rely upon that confidence. . . . Stay! I have just read your letter again. I do not understand it any better, but it makes me tremble. You seem to me painfully agitated. I wish I could calm you; but as I do not know the reason of your uneasiness, I do not know what to say to you, except that I shall be as unhappy as yourself until I have seen you. If you are not here by six o'clock this evening, I shall start to-morrow for the Hermitage, whatever kind of weather it is, and whatever my state of health, for I can no longer endure this uneasiness. Good day, my dear, good friend. At all risks, I venture to tell you, without knowing whether I need do so or not, to try and take care of yourself and arrest the progress which solitude allows uneasiness to make. A fly becomes a monster. I have often experienced it."

ANSWER.

"Wednesday Evening.

"I can neither come to see you nor receive your visit, as long as my present uneasiness continues. The confidence of which you speak no longer exists, and it will not be easy for you to regain it. At present, I see in your eagerness nothing but the desire of extracting from the confessions of another some advantage which may promote your views. My heart, so ready to unbosom itself to another which opens to receive it, shuts its doors in the face of slyness and cunning. I recognise your usual adroitness in the difficulty which you find in understanding my letter. Do you believe me simple enough to think that you have not understood it? No, but I shall know how to overcome your cunning by frankness. I am going to explain myself more clearly, in order that you may comprehend me still less.

"Two lovers, firmly united and worthy of each other's love, are dear to me; I expect that you will not understand whom I mean unless I tell you their names. I assume that attempts have been made to part them, and that I have been made use of to inspire one of them with jealousy. The choice is not very clever, but it appeared convenient for malicious purposes; and it is you whom I suspect of these designs. I hope that this makes matters clearer.

"So then the woman, whom I esteem above all others, with my knowledge, would have the infamy of dividing her heart and her person between two lovers, and I the disgrace of being one of these two wretches? If I knew that, for a single moment in your life, you could have entertained such thoughts of her and me, I should hate you to my dying day; but I only accuse you of having said, not of having thought it. I do not understand, in such a case, which of the three you have desired to injure; but, if you love tranquillity, you should dread being so unfortunate as to succeed. I have neither concealed from you, nor from her, how much evil I see in certain connections; but I desire that they should be put an end to by means as honourable as the feelings which originally formed them, and that an illicit love should be changed into an eternal friendship. Should I, who never injured anyone, be made the innocent means of doing harm to my friends? No; I would never forgive you; I should become your irreconcilable enemy. Your secrets alone should be respected; for I will never be disloyal.

"I do not imagine that my present embarrassment can last long. I shall soon know whether I am mistaken. Then I shall perhaps have a great injury to repair, and I shall never have done anything in my life with greater goodwill. But, do you know how I shall repair my errors during the short time which I have still to spend near you? By doing what no one but myself will do; by telling you frankly what the world thinks of you, and the breaches in your reputation which you have to repair. In spite of all the pretended friends by whom you are surrounded, when you see me depart, you may say farewell to truth; you will never find anyone else to tell it to you."

THIRD LETTER FROM MADAME D'EPINAY (PACKET A, No. 46).

"I did not understand your letter of this morning; I told you so, because it was the truth. I understand that of this evening. Do not be afraid that I shall ever answer it; I am only too anxious to forget it; and although you excite my pity, I have been unable to resist the bitterness with which it fills my soul. I employ slyness and cunning against you! I accused of the blackest of infamies! Good-bye; I regret that you have – good-bye; I do not know what I am saying – good-bye. I should be only too glad to forgive you. Come when you like; you will meet with a better reception than your suspicions would entitle you to. You can spare yourself the trouble of thinking about my reputation. It matters little to me what it is. My conduct is good; that is enough for me. I may add, that I am absolutely ignorant of what has happened to the two persons who are as dear to me as to you."

This last letter delivered me from one terrible embarrassment and plunged me into another, which was almost as great. Although all these letters and answers had been delivered with extraordinary rapidity in the course of a single day, this interval had been long enough to allow a break in my transports of fury, and to give me time to reflect upon my monstrous imprudence. Madame d'Houdetot had impressed upon me, more strongly than anything else, the necessity of remaining calm; of leaving her the responsibility of extricating herself; and of avoiding, especially at the moment, all noise and actual rupture; yet I, by the most open and monstrous insults, was on the point of completely filling with rage the heart of a woman, who was already only too much inclined towards it! Naturally, I could only expect, on her part, an answer so proud, disdainful, and contemptuous, that it would leave me no alternative, unless I behaved like an utter coward, but to leave her house immediately. Happily, her cleverness was greater than my rage. She avoided, by the tone of her answer, reducing me to this extremity. But it was absolutely necessary for me either to leave the house or to go and see her at once; one or the other was unavoidable. I decided upon the latter, feeling greatly embarrassed as to the attitude I should adopt in the explanation, which I foresaw would have to be made. How could I extricate myself without compromising Madame d'Houdetot or Thérèse? And woe to her whom I should name! There was nothing which the vengeance of an implacable and intriguing woman did not cause me to apprehend for her upon whose head it might fall. It was to prevent this misfortune that I had only spoken of suspicions in my letters, to avoid being compelled to produce my proofs. It is true that this made my outbursts the more inexcusable, since no mere suspicion justified me in treating a woman, especially one who was my friend, as I had just treated Madame d'Epinay. But here commences the grand and noble task, which I have worthily fulfilled, of expiating my secret faults and weaknesses, by taking upon myself the responsibility of more serious faults, of which I was incapable, and of which I never was guilty.

I had not to endure the attack which I had feared, and got off with a simple fright. When I approached her, Madame d'Epinay flung her arms round my neck, and burst into tears. This unexpected reception, on the part of an old friend, touched me greatly, and I also wept freely. I said a few words to her, which did not mean much: she said a few to me, which meant still less, and that was all. Dinner was served; we took our seats at the table, where, in the expectation of the explanation, which I thought was only put off until after supper, I cut a very poor figure; for I am so overcome by the slightest uneasiness which takes possession of me, that I cannot conceal it even from the most unobservant. My embarrassed manner should have inspired her with courage; however, she did not risk it. There was as little explanation after supper as before. There was none on the next day either; and our silent *tête-à-têtes* were filled up with indifferent matters or a few polite words on my part, in which, while expressing myself to the effect that I could not yet say anything about the foundation for my suspicions, I protested with all sincerity that, if they proved unfounded, my whole life would be devoted to repairing their injustice. She did not exhibit the least curiosity to know exactly what these suspicions were, or how they had occurred to me; and our reconciliation, both on her part and my own, was entirely limited to our embrace when we met. Since she alone was the injured party, at least in form, it seemed to me that it was not my business to desire an explanation which she herself did not desire, and I returned home as I had left. In other respects my relations with her remained unaltered, I soon almost entirely forgot the quarrel, and foolishly believed that she had forgotten it herself, because she no longer seemed to remember it.

As will presently be seen, this was not the only annoyance which my own weakness brought upon me; but I also suffered others, equally annoying, which I had certainly not brought upon myself, and which were caused solely by the desire of others to tear me away from my solitude, by dint of tormenting me in it.* These annoyances came upon me from Diderot and the Holbachian clique. Since my establishment at the Hermitage, Diderot had never ceased to harass me, either himself or through Deleyre; and I soon saw, from the jests of the latter upon my walks in the forest, with what delight they had travestied the hermit as an amorous shepherd. But it was not a question of this in my encounter with Diderot, the cause of which was more serious. After the publication of the "Fils Naturel," he had sent me a copy of it, which I had read with the interest and attention which one naturally bestows on the works of a friend. On reading the kind of poetical prose dialogue

* That is to say, the desire of tearing the old woman away from it, whose services were necessary in arranging the conspiracy. It is astonishing that, during the whole of this long storm, my stupid confidence in others prevented me from understanding that it was not I, but she, whom they wanted to see in Paris again. (R)

which he had added to it, I was surprised, and even somewhat saddened, to find in it, amongst several discourteous but endurable remarks directed against those who live a solitary life, the following harsh and bitter sentence, without anything to tone it down: "Only the wicked are alone."[1] This sentence is, it appears to me, ambiguous, and capable of two interpretations, one quite true, the other equally false; since it is impossible for a man who is and who desires to be alone, to be able or desirous to injure anyone, and therefore he cannot be wicked. The sentence in itself therefore required an explanation; it required it still more on the part of an author who, when he wrote the sentence, had a friend who was living in retirement and solitude. It appeared to me shocking and dishonourable that, when publishing it, he should either have forgotten this solitary friend, or that, if he had remembered him, he should not have made, at least in the general statement, the honourable and just exception which he owed not only to this friend, but to the many respected philosophers, who, in all ages, have sought peace and tranquillity in retirement, and of whom, for the first time since the existence of the world, an author permits himself, by a single stroke of the pen, to make so many villains without distinction.

I was tenderly attached to Diderot, I esteemed him sincerely, and I reckoned upon the same feelings on his part with perfect confidence. But, worn out by his unwearying obstinacy in eternally opposing me in my tastes, inclinations, manner of living, in fact, in everything which concerned myself alone; disgusted at seeing a man younger than myself attempting to control me absolutely like a child; sick of his readiness in making promises, and his carelessness in fulfilling them; weary of so many appointments made and broken on his part, and of his fancy for continually making fresh ones, only to be broken again; tired of waiting for him in vain three or four times a month, on days fixed by himself, and of dining alone in the evening, after having gone as far as Saint-Denis to meet him, after waiting for him the whole day, my heart was already full of his continued want of consideration. The last instance appeared to me more serious,

[1] The line "Il n'y a que le méchant qui soit seul" is in fact spoken by Constance to the hero Dorval in the play itself (Act IV, Scene 3).

and wounded me still more deeply. I wrote to him to complain of it, but with a gentleness and emotion which caused me to drench the paper with my tears; and my letter was touching enough to have drawn tears from him. No one would guess how he replied upon the matter; here is his answer word for word (Packet A, No. 33):

"I am very glad that my work has pleased you, that it has affected you. You are not of my opinion concerning hermits; say as much good of them as you please, you will be the only one in the world of whom I shall think it; and yet I should be able to say a good deal on the matter, if I could say it to you without offending you. A woman of eighty years of age! etc. Someone has told me of a phrase from a letter of Madame d'Epinay's son, which must have pained you greatly, or else I do not know you thoroughly."

I must explain the two last phrases of this letter.

At the beginning of my stay at the Hermitage, Madame le Vasseur did not seem comfortable, and appeared to find it too lonely. Her remarks on the subject were repeated to me, and I offered to send her back to Paris if she preferred it, to pay for her lodging there, and to look after her just as if she were still with me. She refused my offer, declared that she was very well satisfied with the Hermitage, and that the country air did her good, which it was easy to see was true, for she seemed to grow younger, and was in far better health than at Paris. Her daughter even assured me that she would have been, on the whole, very sorry if we had left the Hermitage, which really was a charming residence; that she was very fond of pottering about in the garden and in the orchard, of which she had the management, and that she had only said what she had been told to say, to try and induce me to return to Paris.

This attempt having proved unsuccessful, they endeavoured to obtain, by appealing to my scruples, the result which my readiness to oblige had not produced; they declared that it was a crime on my part to keep the old woman there, far from the assistance which she might need at her age, without considering that she and many other old people, whose life is prolonged by the healthy air of the country, might procure this assistance from

Montmorency, which was close to my doors — as if Paris had been the only place in which there were old people, and it was impossible for them to live anywhere else. Madame le Vasseur, who was a large and very ravenous eater, was subject to overflows of bile and violent attacks of diarrhœa, which lasted several days, and acted as a remedy. At Paris she took nothing for them, and let Nature take its course. She did the same at the Hermitage, since she knew well that she could do nothing better. Never mind; because there were no physicians and apothecaries in the country, to leave her there showed a wish for her death, although she was in very good health there. Diderot ought to have fixed the age at which it is no longer permitted, under penalty of being charged with manslaughter, to allow old people to live out of Paris.

This was one of the two monstrous accusations, in regard to which he made no exception in my case, in his statement that "Only the wicked are alone"; and this was the meaning of his pathetic exclamation and the etcetera which he so kindly added, "A woman of eighty years of age! etc."

I thought I could not reply to this reproach better than by referring to Madame le Vasseur herself. I asked her to write quite simply and naturally to Madame d'Epinay and tell her what her opinion was. To put her completely at her ease, I did not even ask to see her letter, and I showed her the following, which I wrote to Madame d'Epinay, in reference to an answer which I had decided to make to a still harsher letter from Diderot, and which she had prevented me from sending.

"*Thursday.*

"Madame le Vasseur is going to write to you, my good friend. I have asked her to tell you frankly what she thinks. To put her entirely at her ease, I have told her that I do not want to see her letter, and I beg you to tell me nothing about its contents.

"I will not send my letter, since you oppose it; but as I feel grievously offended, it would be a baseness and a falsehood, which I cannot permit myself, to allow that I am wrong. The Gospel certainly orders him who receives a blow on one cheek to offer the other, but not to ask for pardon. Do you remember the man in the comedy, who exclaims, while dealing blows with his stick, 'That is the part of the philosopher'?

"Do not flatter yourself that you can prevent him from coming in the present bad weather. His anger will give him the time and strength which friendship refuses him, and it will be the first time in his life that he has come on the day he has promised. He will do his utmost to come and repeat, with his own mouth, the insults which he has heaped upon me in his letters. I will endure them with the utmost patience. He will return to Paris to be ill; and, as usual, I shall be a very hateful person. But what can I do? I must endure it.

"But, can you help admiring the cleverness of this man, who wanted to come and take me in a coach to Saint-Denis to dinner, and to bring me back; and who, a week afterwards,[1] finds that his finances do not allow him to visit the Hermitage except on foot? It is not absolutely impossible, to adopt his language, that this is the tone of sincerity; but, in this case, a strange alteration in the state of his finances must have taken place in the course of a week.

"I share your grief at your mother's illness; but you see that your sorrow is not nearly as great as mine. It causes less suffering to see those whom one loves, ill, than to see them cruel and unjust.

"Adieu, my good friend; this is the last time that I shall speak to you about this unfortunate affair. You speak to me of going to Paris with a coolness and indifference, which, at any other time, would rejoice me greatly."

I informed Diderot of what I had done in regard to Madame le Vasseur, at Madame d'Epinay's own suggestion; and as she chose, as may be imagined, to remain at the Hermitage, where she was very comfortable, always had company, and found her life very agreeable, Diderot, no longer knowing what crime to charge me with, construed this very precaution on my part into one, as well as Madame le Vasseur's continued stay at the Hermitage, although it had been her own choice, and it had only rested, and still rested with her, to return to Paris to live, with the same assistance from me as she received at my house.

Such is the explanation of the first reproach in Diderot's letter, No. 33. The explanation of the second is contained in his letter, No. 34:

" 'The man of letters'[2] must have written to you, that there were twenty poor wretches on the rampart[3] dying of cold and hunger, and waiting for the farthing you used to give them. This is a sample of our

---

[1] Packet A No. 34.
[2] A name jokingly bestowed by Grimm upon Madame d'Epinay's son.
[3] [rampart] A place of public resort in Paris.

small-talk — and if you were to hear the rest, it would amuse you as much as this."

Here is my answer to this terrible argument, of which Diderot seemed so proud:

"I believe that I replied to the 'man of letters,' that is to say, the son of a farmer-general, that I did not pity the poor whom he had seen upon the rampart, waiting for my farthing; that he had apparently amply compensated them for its loss; that I had appointed him my substitute; that the poor of Paris would have no reason to complain of the exchange; but that I could not easily find an equally good one for those of Montmorency, who had much greater need of it. There is here a good and worthy old man, who, after having worked all his life, can work no longer, and is dying of hunger in his old age. My conscience is better satisfied with the two sous which I give him every Monday, than with the hundred farthings which I should have distributed to all the beggars on the rampart. You are amusing, you philosophers, when you regard all the inhabitants of cities as the only people with whom your duty bids you concern yourselves. It is in the country that one learns to love and serve humanity; one only learns to despise it in cities."

Such were the singular scruples, which led a man of intelligence to the folly of seriously making a crime of my absence from Paris, and made him attempt to prove to me, by my own example, that it was impossible for anyone to live outside the city without being wicked. At the present day I cannot understand how I was so foolish as to answer him and to feel annoyed, instead of laughing in his face as my only reply. However, Madame d'Epinay's decisions and the clamours of the Holbachian clique had so blinded people's minds in her favour, that I was generally considered to be wrong in the matter, and Madame d'Houdetot herself, who was an enthusiastic admirer of Diderot, wanted me to go and see him in Paris, and make all the first advances towards a reconciliation, which, sincere and complete as it was on my part, did not last long. The triumphant argument, which she made use of to influence my heart was, that Diderot, at this moment, was unhappy. Besides the storm aroused against the "Encyclopédie," he had at that time to endure another, even more violent, caused by his piece, which, in spite of the little account prefixed by him at the commencement, he was accused of having taken entirely from Goldoni.

Diderot, even more sensitive to criticism than Voltaire, was overwhelmed. Madame de Graffigny had even had the spitefulness to circulate the report that I had taken this opportunity to break off my acquaintance with him. I considered that it would be just and generous publicly to demonstrate the contrary, and I went to spend two days, not only in his company, but at his house. This was my second journey to Paris since my settlement at the Hermitage. I had taken the first in order to hasten to poor Gauffecourt, who had an attack of apoplexy, from which he has never quite recovered, during which I never left his bedside until he was out of danger.

Diderot received me cordially. How many wrongs can a friend's embrace wipe out! What resentment, after that, can still remain in the heart? We entered into few explanations. There is no need of it in a case of mutual abuse. There is only one thing to be done – to forget it. There had been no underhand proceedings, at least as far as I knew; it was not the same as with Madame d'Epinay. He showed me the outline of the "Père de Famille." "That," said I to him, "is the best defence of the 'Fils Naturel.' Remain silent, work this piece out carefully, and then suddenly fling it at your enemies' head as your only reply." He did so, and found the plan successful. I had sent him the first two parts of *Julie* nearly six months before, asking for his opinion of them. He had not yet read them. We read a portion of them together. He found it all *feuillet*; that was the word he used, meaning that it was overloaded with words and full of padding. I had already felt this myself; but it was the babbling of delirium; I have never been able to correct it. The last parts are different. The fourth especially, and the sixth, are masterpieces of diction.

On the second day after my arrival, he insisted upon taking me to supper at M. d'Holbach's. We could never manage to agree. I even wanted to break the agreement concerning the manuscript on Chemistry,[1] as I was indignant at being under an obligation for it to such a man. Diderot was completely victorious. He swore that M. d'Holbach had a most sincere affection

---

[1] It would seem that d'Holbach had commissioned Rousseau to see a translation of some German chemical treatise through the press for him.

for me; that I must excuse his manner, which was the same to everybody, and from which his friends had to suffer more than anyone. He represented to me that to refuse the proceeds of this manuscript, after having accepted it two years before, would be an insult to the donor, which he had not deserved; that this refusal might even be misinterpreted, as a secret reproach to him for having been so long in fulfilling the agreement. "I see d'Holbach every day," he added; "I know his inner self better than you do. If you had not reason to be satisfied with it, do you think your friend capable of advising you to act meanly?" In short, with my usual weakness, I allowed myself to be overcome, and we went to supper with the Baron, who received me in his usual manner; but his wife received me coldly, and almost rudely. I no longer recognised the amiable Caroline who, before she was married, showed me so many marks of goodwill. Long before, I had fancied that I perceived that, since Grimm had been a constant visitor at the house of Aine, I was no longer regarded with so favourable an eye.

While I was in Paris, Saint-Lambert arrived on leave. As I knew nothing of it, I did not see him until after my return to the country, at first at La Chevrette, and afterwards at the Hermitage, where he came with Madame d'Houdetot to ask me to invite him to dinner. It may be imagined how pleased I was to receive them; but I was still more pleased to see the good understanding between them. Rejoiced that I had not disturbed their happiness, I felt happy in it myself; and I can swear that, during the whole course of my mad passion, but especially at this moment, even if I had been able to take Madame d'Houdetot from him, I should not have wished, and I should not even have felt tempted to do so. I found her so amiable, so devoted to Saint-Lambert, that I could hardly imagine that she might have been equally devoted in her love for myself; and, without desiring to disturb their union, all that I had most truly desired from her in my delirium, was that she should allow herself to be loved. In short, however violent the passion with which I had been inflamed for her, I felt it as delightful to be the confidant as the object of her affections, and I have never for a moment regarded her lover as my rival, but always as my friend.

It will be said that this was not yet actual love. So be it; but then, it was more.

As for Saint-Lambert, he behaved honourably and judiciously. As I was the only guilty party, I alone was punished, and that even mercifully. He treated me severely, but amicably; and I saw that I had lost something of his esteem, but nothing of his friendship. I consoled myself, since I knew that it would be easier for me to regain the former than the latter, and that he was too sensible to confound an involuntary and momentary weakness with a radical vice. If, in all that had taken place, there had been errors on my part, they were trifling ones. Was it I who had sought his mistress? Was it not he who had sent her to me? Was it not she who had sought me? Could I have avoided seeing her? What could I do? They alone had done the mischief, and I had been the one to suffer from it. In my place, he would have done just as I did, perhaps worse; for, in short, however faithful, however estimable Madame d'Houdetot may have been, she was a woman. He was very often absent; the opportunities were frequent, the temptations were great, and it would have been very difficult for her always to defend herself with equal success against a more enterprising lover. It was certainly a great thing for her and for me, in such a situation, that we had been able to fix the limits, which we never permitted ourselves to overstep.

Although, in the bottom of my heart, I could produce sufficiently honourable testimony in my favour, appearances were so much against me, that the unconquerable feeling of shame, by which I was always dominated, gave me, in his presence, the appearance of a guilty person, and he often abused it in order to humiliate me. A single incident will make our mutual relations clear. After dinner I read to him the letter which I had written to Voltaire the year before, and which he had heard spoken of. He went to sleep while I was reading it; and I, formerly so proud, now so foolish, did not venture to discontinue reading, and read on while he snored. Thus did I humble myself; thus did he avenge himself; but his generosity never permitted him to do so except when we three were alone.

After he went away again, I found Madame d'Houdetot greatly altered in her behaviour towards me. I was as surprised as if I ought not to have expected it. I was more affected by it than I ought to have been, and this caused me much suffering. It seemed that everything by which I expected to be cured only plunged deeper into my heart the arrow which I had at length rather broken off than pulled out.

I was resolved to conquer myself completely, and to leave nothing undone to change my foolish passion into a pure and lasting friendship. With this object, I had formed the most admirable plans in the world, which I needed Madame d'Houdetot's assistance in carrying out. When I attempted to speak to her, I found her absent and embarrassed. I felt that she had ceased to feel any pleasure in my society, and I saw clearly that something had taken place which she did not want to tell me, and which I have never learnt. This change, of which I was unable to obtain an explanation, tortured me cruelly. She asked me to return her letters: I returned them all, with a fidelity which, to my great mortification, she for a moment doubted. This doubt was another unexpected pang for me, as she must have well known. She did me justice, but not immediately. I understood that the examination of the packet which I had returned to her had made her conscious of her injustice. I even saw that she reproached herself, and this gave me a certain advantage again. She could not take back her own letters without returning mine. She told me that she had burnt them; in my turn, I ventured to doubt it, and I confess that I doubt it still. No; one does not throw such letters into the fire.[1] The letters in *Julie* have been considered burning. Good heavens! what would have been thought of mine? No, no; a woman capable of inspiring such a passion will never have the courage to burn the proofs of it. But neither do I fear that she has ever misused them. I do not believe her capable of it; and besides, I had taken measures to prevent it. The foolish, but lively fear of being ridiculed had made me commence this correspondence in a tone which protected the contents of my letters from being communicated to

[1] Rousseau's letters to Sophie were in fact burnt, though it is not certain when or by whom.

others. I even carried the familiar tone which I adopted in them so far as to *thee* and *thou* her, but in such a manner that she certainly could not have been offended. Certainly, she complained of it several times, but without success. Her complaints only aroused my suspicions, and, besides, I could not bring myself to draw back. If these letters are still in existence, and should one day see the light, it will be known how I have loved.

The pain which Madame d'Houdetot's coldness caused me, and the certainty that I had not deserved it, caused me to take the singular course of complaining about it to Saint-Lambert himself. While waiting to see the result of my letter on the subject, I plunged into the distractions to which I ought to have had recourse sooner. Some festivities took place at La Chevrette, for which I composed the music. The pleasure of distinguishing myself in the eyes of Madame d'Houdetot, by the display of a talent which she admired, spurred my energies; and another circumstance contributed to arouse them, namely, the desire of showing that the author of the *Devin du Village* understood music; for I had long since perceived that someone was secretly working to make this seem doubtful, at least in regard to composition. My first appearance in Paris, the tests to which I had there been subjected on different occasions, at M. Dupin's and M. de la Poplinière's; the quantity of music which I had composed during fourteen years in the midst of the most famous artists, under their very eyes; and lastly, the opera of the *Muses Galantes*, even that of the *Devin*, a motet which I had written for Mademoiselle Fel, and which she had sung at the "spiritual concert," the numerous discussions on this beautiful art which had taken place between myself and its greatest masters – all these proofs should have prevented or dissipated any such doubt. It existed, however, even at La Chevrette, and I saw that M. d'Epinay was not free from it. Without appearing to be aware of it, I undertook to compose a motet for him for the dedication of the chapel of La Chevrette, and I asked him to supply me with words chosen by himself. He commissioned de Linant, his son's tutor, to write them. De Linant composed some words suitable to the occasion, and, a week after they were given to me, the motet was finished. This time, spite was my Apollo, and never did richer music leave my hands. The words began with: "Ecce sedes hic Tonantis."* The pomp of the opening was in keeping with the words, and the whole motet was so beautiful that everyone was struck with admiration. I had written for a large orchestra. D'Epinay got together the best instrumentalists. Madame Bruna, an Italian singer, sang the motet, and was excellently accompanied. The motet was so successful that it was afterwards given at the "spiritual concert," at which, in spite of the secret intrigues and the poorness of the execution, it was twice heartily applauded. For M. d'Epinay's birthday, I supplied the idea of a kind of piece, half drama, half pantomime, which Madame d'Epinay composed, and for which I also wrote the music. Grimm, on his arrival, heard of my musical successes; an hour later, nothing more was said about them; but, at any rate, as far as I know, there was no longer any question of my knowledge of composition.

No sooner was Grimm at La Chevrette, where already I was not very comfortable, than he made my stay completely unendurable by putting on airs, which I had never seen exhibited by anyone before, and of which I had not even an idea. The day before his arrival, I was turned out of the best visitor's-room, which I was occupying, next to Madame d'Epinay's; it was got ready for Grimm, and another, in a more remote part of the house, was given to me. "See," said I to Madame d'Epinay with a laugh, "see how the new-comers turn out the old." She appeared embarrassed; and I understood the reason for this better in the evening, when I learned that, between her room and that which I was leaving, there was a secret door of communication, which she had not thought it worth while to show me. Her relations with Grimm were no secret to anybody, neither in her own house nor in public, nor even to her husband; however, far from admitting it to me, her confidant in secrets of far greater importance, and which she knew were perfectly safe with me, she stoutly denied it. I understood that this reserve was due to Grimm, who, although he was the depositary of all my secrets, was unwilling that I should have any of his own in my keeping.

* I have since heard that these words were by de Santeuil, and that M. de Linant had quietly appropriated them (R)

However much my former feelings, which were not yet extinguished, and the man's real merits, prejudiced me in his favour, these feelings were not proof against the efforts he took to destroy them. He received me in the style of the Comte de Tuffière;[1] he hardly condescended to return my greeting; he never addressed a single word to me, and soon cured me of addressing any to him, by never answering me at all. He took precedence everywhere, and held first place, without ever paying any attention to me. I could have let that pass, if he had not displayed an offensive affectation. A single incident out of a thousand will explain what I mean. One evening, Madame d'Epinay, feeling slightly unwell, told the servants to bring her something to eat upstairs to her room, where she intended to have her supper by the side of the fire. She asked me to go upstairs with her, which I did. Grimm came up afterwards. The little table was already laid, but only for two. Supper was brought in; Madame d'Epinay took her seat on one side of the fire. M. Grimm took an easy chair, settled himself in the other corner, drew up the little table between them, unfolded his napkin, and proceeded to eat, without saying a single word to me. Madame d'Epinay blushed, and, to induce him to apologise for his rudeness, offered me her own place. He said nothing, and did not even look at me. As I was unable to get near the fire, I decided to walk up and down the room, until they brought me a plate. At last, he allowed me to sup at the end of the table, away from the fire, without making the slightest apology to me, his senior, in ill-health, an older acquaintance of the family, who had introduced him to the house, the honours of which he ought even to have shown to me, as the favourite of the lady of the house. All his behaviour to me was very much after the same pattern. He did not treat me exactly as his inferior; he looked upon me as a perfect nonentity. I found it hard to recognise the former *cuistre* who, in the Prince of Saxe-Gotha's establishment, felt himself honoured by a look from me. I found it still harder to reconcile this profound silence, and this insulting haughtiness, with the tender friendship which he boasted he entertained for me, in the presence of these who he knew entertained it for me themselves.

[1]   One of the characters in *Le Glorieux*, a comedy by Destouches (1732).

It is true that he rarely gave any signs of it, except to sympathise with my pecuniary position, of which I never complained, or to compassionate my melancholy lot, with which I was quite content, or to lament that I so harshly rejected the beneficent attentions which he declared he was eager to show me. It was by artifices like this that he caused his tender generosity to be admired, my ungrateful misanthropy to be censured, and imperceptibly accustomed everyone to imagine, that the relations between a protector like himself and an unfortunate creature like me could only be, on the one side, benefits, and, on the other, obligations, without supposing, even as a remote possibility, a friendship between two equals. As for myself, I have vainly tried to discover in what respect I could be under an obligation to this new patron. I had lent him money, he had never lent me any; I had nursed him during his illness, he hardly ever came to see me during mine; I had introduced him to all my friends, he had never introduced me to one of his; I had sung his praises with all my might, he . . . if he sang my praises, it was less publicly, and in quite a different manner. He has never rendered or even offered to render me any service of any kind. How then was he my Maecenas? how was I his *protégé*? This was beyond my powers of comprehension, and it still remains so.

It is true that, more or less, he was arrogant with everybody, but with no one so brutally as with myself. I remember that, on one occasion, Saint-Lambert was on the point of throwing his plate at his head, when he ventured to give him the lie publicly at table, by saying rudely, "That is not true." To his naturally sarcastic tone, he united the conceit of an upstart, and his continual impertinence even made him ridiculous. Intercourse with great people had led him to assume airs which one only sees in the least sensible amongst them. He never summoned his lackey except with an "Eh!" – as if my fine gentleman did not know which of his numerous attendants was on duty. When he gave him a commission to execute, he threw the money on the ground, instead of putting it into his hand. At last, forgetting altogether that he was a man, he treated him with such disgusting contempt and cruel disdain on every occasion that the poor lad, who was a very good fellow, whom Madame d'Epinay had given him, left his service, without any other cause of complaint than the impossibility of enduring such treatment. He was the La Fleur of this new Glorieux. As foppish as he was vain, with his large, dull eyes and his flabby face, he pretended to have great success with the ladies; and, after his farce with Mademoiselle Fel, he was considered by numbers of the fair sex to be a man of deep feeling. This had made him the fashion and had given him a taste for feminine neatness. He began to play the dandy: his toilet became a serious matter. Everybody knew that he made up, and I, who at first refused to believe it, began to be convinced, not only by his beautiful complexion and by the fact of finding some pots of cosmetic on his dressing-table, but because one morning, on entering his rooms, I found him brushing his nails with a little brush made for the purpose, an occupation which he proudly continued in my presence. I argued that a man who could spend two hours every morning in brushing his nails might very well employ a few minutes in filling up the wrinkles in his skin with cosmetic. The worthy Gauffecourt, who was no fool, had humorously nicknamed him "Tiran le Blanc."[1]

All this was merely ridiculous, but very antipathetic to my character, and at last made me suspicious of his. I could scarcely believe that a man, whose head was so turned, could have his heart in the right place. He prided himself, more than anything else, upon his sensibility of soul and vigorous energy of feeling. How did that agree with those defects, which are peculiar to little minds only? How could the lively and continuous flights, which a feeling heart takes in pursuit of things outside it, allow him time to busy himself with such petty cares for his little person? Why, good heavens! one who feels his heart inflamed by this heavenly fire seeks to pour it forth, and to display his inner self. He would be eager to show his heart upon his face; he will never think of any other cosmetics.

I remembered the compendium of his morality, which Madame d'Epinay had told me of, and which she had adopted.

---

[1] *i.e.*, "the white tyrant". *Tirant-lo-Blanch* was the title of an ancient Catalan romance of chivalry, very popular in France in a translation by the Comte Caylus. Gauffecourt or Rousseau evidently intended a hit at Grimm's white face-powder.

This consisted of one single article, namely, that the sole duty of man is, to follow in everything the inclinations of his heart. This code of morality, when I heard of it, afforded me terrible material for thought, although at that time I only looked upon it as a witticism. But I soon saw that this principle was really his rule of conduct, and, in the sequel, I had only too convincing proof of it at my own expense. It is the inner doctrine, of which Diderot has so often spoken to me, but of which he has never given me any explanation.

I remembered the frequent warnings that I had received, several years before, that the man was false, that he was only playing at sentiment, and that, above all, he had no affection for me. I recollect several little incidents, which M. de Francueil and Madame de Chenonceaux had related to me on that point; neither of them had any esteem for him, and both ought to have known him well, since Madame de Chenonceaux was the daughter of Madame de Rochechouart, the intimate friend of the late Comte de Friese, and M. de Francueil, who was at that time very intimate with the Vicomte de Polignac, had lived much in the Palais-Royal[1] just at the time when Grimm began to secure a footing there. All Paris heard of his despair after the death of the Comte de Friese. It was a question of keeping up the reputation which he had gained after the cruel treatment he had experienced from Mademoiselle Fel, the humbug of which I should have seen through better than anyone else, if I had not been so blind. He had to be dragged to the Hôtel Castries, where, abandoning himself to the most deadly affliction, he played his part worthily. Every morning he went into the garden to weep at his ease, holding before his eyes his handkerchief drenched with tears, as long as he was in sight of the hôtel; but as soon as he turned round into a certain narrow street, persons of whom he had no suspicion saw him immediately put his handkerchief in his pocket and pull out a book. He was seen to do this more than once, and the fact soon became public property in Paris, and was almost as soon forgotten. I had forgotten it myself; a fact, which concerned myself, reminded me of it. I

---

[1] [Palais-Royal] Residence of the Duc d'Orléans, for whom Grimm worked as a secretary.

was in bed, at death's door, in the Rue de Grenelle; he was in the country. One morning he came to see me, quite out of breath, and declared that he had only just arrived. A minute afterwards, I learned that he had arrived the day before, and that he had been seen in the theatre the same day.

A thousand little incidents of this kind came back to me; but something which I was surprised that I had not observed sooner, struck me most of all. I had introduced Grimm to all my friends without exception; they had all become his. I was so inseparable from him, that I should hardly have cared to continue visiting at a house to which he had not the entry. Only Madame de Créqui refused to admit him, and from that time I also almost entirely discontinued my visits to her. Grimm, on his part, made other friends, both on his own initiative and also through the Comte de Friese. Of all those friends, not a single one ever became mine. He never said a word to me, to induce me at least to make their acquaintance; and, of all those whom I sometimes met at his rooms, not one ever showed me the least goodwill, not even the Comte de Friese, with whom he lived, and with whom it would consequently have been very pleasant to me to form a connection, nor the Comte de Schomberg, his relation, with whom Grimm was even more intimate.

More than this: my own friends, whom I made his own, and who had all been devotedly attached to me before they made his acquaintance, showed a sensible alteration in their feelings and behaviour towards me, after they had made it. He never introduced one of his friends to me. I introduced him to all mine, and he ended by depriving me of them all. If such are the results of friendship, what will be the results of hatred?

Diderot himself, at the outset, warned me several times that Grimm, upon whom I bestowed such confidence, was not my friend. Subsequently, he altered his tone, when he himself had ceased to be a friend.

The manner in which I had disposed of my children had required no one's assistance. However, I informed my friends of it, simply for the sake of informing them, in order not to appear better in their eyes than I really was. These friends were three in number: Diderot, Grimm, and Madame d'Epinay.

Duclos, who was the most worthy of my confidence, was the only one whom I did not inform. However, he knew it. From whom? I do not know. It is hardly probable that Madame d'Epinay was guilty of this breach of confidence, for she well knew that, by imitating it, if I had been capable of doing so, I could have cruelly avenged myself. There remain Grimm and Diderot, at that time so closely united in many things – especially against myself – that it is more than probable that they were both guilty. I would wager that Duclos, to whom I did not reveal my secret, and who was consequently in no way bound to silence, was the only one who faithfully kept it.

Grimm and Diderot, in their scheme of getting the women-folk away from me, had done their utmost to induce him to enter into their plans; but he always scornfully refused. It was not until later that I learned from him all that had taken place between them in the matter; but I learned enough at the time from Thérèse to see that, in the whole affair, there was some secret design, and that they were anxious to dispose of me, if not against my will, at least without my knowledge; or that they certainly wished to make use of these two persons as their tools in some secret design. In all this there was certainly something very dishonourable. The opposition of Duclos proves it beyond contradiction. Let him who pleases believe that it was friend-ship.

This pretended friendship was as disastrous to me at home as outside. The long and frequent conversations with Madame le Vasseur, for several years past, had perceptibly altered her feel-ings towards me, and this alteration was most certainly not favourable to me. What, then, was the subject of discussion during these singular *tête-à-têtes*? Why this deep mystery? Was the conversation of this old woman sufficiently agreeable for it to be considered such a piece of good fortune, or sufficiently import-ant to make such a mystery about it? During the three or four years that these conferences lasted, they had appeared to me ridiculous; but, when I reconsidered them, I began to wonder at them. This feeling of wonder would have ended in uneasiness, if I had known at the time what this woman was plotting against me.

In spite of Grimm's pretended zeal for me, of which he boasted so loudly outside, and which was difficult to reconcile with the tone which he assumed towards me in my presence, I gained nothing by it, from any point of view, and the pity which he pretended to feel for me served less to benefit than to humiliate me. He even, as far as lay in his power, deprived me of the benefits of the profession which I had chosen for myself, by depreciating my abilities as a copyist. I admit that in that he spoke the truth, but it was not his place to do so. He clearly showed that he did not intend it as a joke, by employing another copyist himself, and taking away from me all the customers he could. One would have said that his object was to make me dependent upon him and his interest for my subsistence, and to exhaust my resources until I should be reduced to such a condition.

All things being taken into consideration, my reason at last imposed silence upon my former prejudice in his favour, which still made itself heard. I came to the conclusion that his character was, at least, very suspicious; and, as for his friendship, I decided that it was false. Accordingly, having made up my mind not to see him again, I informed Madame d'Epinay of my determination, which I justified by several unanswerable reasons, which I have now forgotten.

She strongly opposed this determination, without exactly knowing what reply to make to the reasons which had decided me. She had not yet come to an understanding with him; but, on the following day, instead of entering into a verbal explanation with me, she sent me a very cleverly-worded letter, which they had drawn up together, in which, without entering into details, she excused him on the ground of his reserved disposition, and, imputing it as a crime to me that I had suspected him of treachery towards his friend, exhorted me to become reconciled to him. This letter shook my determination. In a conversation which subsequently took place between us, when I found her better prepared than she had been the first time, I allowed myself to be completely vanquished; I persuaded myself that I might have judged wrongly, and that, in this case, I had really committed a grave wrong towards a friend, which it was my duty to repair. In short, as I had several times already done in the case of Diderot and the Baron d'Holbach, partly of my own accord and partly through weakness, I made all those advances which I had a right to demand: I went to see Grimm, like a second George Dandin,[1] to apologise for offences of which he had been guilty against myself; always under the mistaken conviction, which all my life long has caused me to abase myself before my pretended friends, that there is no hatred so strong that it cannot be disarmed by gentleness and good behaviour; whereas, on the contrary, the hatred of the wicked is only strengthened by the impossibility of finding anything to justify it, and the consciousness of their own injustice is only an additional grievance against him who is the victim of it. Without going further than my own history, I have a strong proof of this axiom in the conduct of Grimm and Tronchin, who became my two most implacable enemies, of their own inclination, for their own pleasure, out of sheer caprice, without being able to quote a single instance of any kind in which I had done either of them wrong,* and whose rage increases daily, like that of the tiger, from the ease with which they are able to glut it.

I expected that Grimm, confused by my condescension and advances, would receive me with open arms and the tenderest affection. As a fact, he received me like a Roman Emperor, with an unparalleled haughtiness. I was utterly unprepared for this reception. Embarrassed at having to play a part so ill-suited to me, in a few words I timidly explained the object of my visit. Before taking me back into favour, he delivered, with great dignity, a long harangue which he had prepared, containing a list of his numerous and rare virtues, especially in matters of friendship. He dwelt for some time upon a circumstance, which at first struck me considerably – that he always kept the same friends. While he was speaking, I said to myself that it would be cruel on my part to make myself the only exception to this rule.

[1]   See Molière's comedy *George Dandin* (1668), Act I, Scene 6.
*   It was not until later that I nicknamed the latter "Jongleur" (juggler), long after his declaration of hostility and the cruel persecution which he stirred up against me at Geneva and elsewhere. I even soon suppressed the name when I saw that I was entirely his victim. I consider mean and paltry vengeance unworthy of my heart, and hatred never sets foot in it. (R)

He returned to this so frequently and with such affectation, that he at last made me think that, if in this he only listened to the feelings of his heart, he would show himself less struck by this sentiment which he so freely expressed, and that he was making use of it as a trick which might serve his purpose of self-advancement. Hitherto I had been in the same case: I had always kept all my friends; since my earliest childhood I had not lost a single one, except by death, and yet I had never made it a subject of reflection; it was not a principle which I had laid down for myself. Since we both had this advantage in common, what right had he to boast of it as peculiar to himself, unless he already designed to deprive me of it? He devoted himself to the task of humiliating me by proving that our mutual friends preferred him to me. I was as well aware as he was of this preference; the question was, how he had obtained it. By superior merits or address, by exalting himself, or by endeavouring to humiliate me? At last, when he had put between us, to his heart's content, all the distance which could attach value to the favour which he intended to grant me, he bestowed upon me the kiss of peace in a slight embrace, which resembled the *accolade* which the King bestows upon newly-created knights. I fell from the clouds; I was amazed; I did not know what to say; I could not utter a single word. The whole scene had the appearance of a reprimand given by a master to a pupil, when he lets him off a flogging. I never think of it without feeling how deceptive are judgments founded upon appearances, to which the vulgar attach such weight, and how frequently audacity and pride are on the side of the guilty, shame and embarrassment on the side of the innocent.

We were reconciled; this was at least a relief to my heart, which is always mortally distressed by a quarrel. It may be imagined that such a reconciliation produced no alteration in his manners; it simply deprived me of the right of complaining of them. Accordingly, I resolved to endure everything, and to say nothing.

So many annoyances, one after another, threw me into a state of depression, which scarcely left me strength to regain command of myself. Without any reply from Saint-Lambert, neglected by Madame d'Houdetot, no longer venturing to open my heart to anyone, I began to fear that, in making friendship the idol of my heart, I had wasted my life in sacrificing to chimeras. In proof of this, out of all my friendships, there only remained two men, who had retained my full esteem, and whom my heart could trust: Duclos, whom I had lost sight of since my retirement to the Hermitage, and Saint-Lambert. I believed that I could only repair my injustice towards the latter by opening my heart to him unreservedly; and I resolved to make a full and complete confession to him, in everything which did not compromise his mistress. I have no doubt that this resolution was another snare set by my passion, in order to keep me closer to it; but it is certain that I should have thrown myself unreservedly into her lover's arms, that I should have submitted myself completely to his guidance, and that I should have pushed my frankness as far as it could go. I was ready to write a second letter to him, to which I felt sure that he would reply, when I learned the melancholy reason of his silence in regard to the first. He had been unable to endure the fatigues of the campaign to the end. Madame d'Epinay informed me that he had just had a stroke of paralysis; and Madame d'Houdetot, whose affliction at last made her ill herself, and who was not in a fit state to write to me immediately, sent me word, two or three days later, from Paris, where she was at that time, that he intended to be removed to Aix-la-Chapelle, to take the baths. I do not say that this melancholy news afflicted me as much as her; but I doubt whether the sorrow which it caused me was less painful than her grief and tears. Sorrow at knowing him to be in such a condition, aggravated by the apprehension that uneasiness might have contributed to it, touched me more than all that hitherto happened to me; and I felt, to my cruel sorrow, that I could not find, in my own self-esteem, the strength which I needed in order to support such grief. Happily, this generous friend did not long leave me in such a state of depression; in spite of his illness, he did not forget me, and I soon learned from himself that I had ill-judged his feelings and condition. But it is time to proceed to the great and sudden change in my destiny, the catastrophe which has divided my life into two parts, so different from each other, and which, from a very trifling cause, has drawn such terrible effects.

One day, when I least expected it, Madame d'Epinay sent for me. When I entered the room, I observed, in her eyes and manner, an appearance of embarrassment, which was the more striking to me as it was unusual, since no one in the world knew better than she how to control her features and movements. "My friend," said she, "I am leaving for Geneva; my chest is in a bad state, my health is breaking up so rapidly that I must go and consult Tronchin, even if I have to neglect everything else." This resolution, so abruptly taken, at the commencement of bad weather, astonished me the more, as, when I left her thirty-six hours before, not a word had been said about it. I asked her whom she intended to take with her. She told me that she meant to take her son and M. de Linant, and then added, in an indifferent tone, "And won't you come too, my dear bear?" As I did not believe that she spoke seriously, since she knew that, in the time of year upon which we were just entering, I was hardly in a fit state to leave my room, I spoke jestingly of the advantage of one sick person being accompanied by another. She herself did not seem to have meant the proposition seriously, and nothing more was said about it. During the rest of my visit, we spoke of nothing but the preparations for her journey, into which she threw herself with great energy, as she had made up her mind to start in a fortnight.

I did not need much penetration to understand that there was a secret reason for this journey which was not being told me.[1] This secret, which was a secret to me alone in the house, was discovered the very next day by Thérèse, to whom Teissier, the *maître d'hôtel*, who had heard it from the lady's-maid, revealed it. Although I am under no obligation to Madame d'Epinay to keep the secret, since I did not learn it from her, it is too closely connected with those which she did confide to me, for me to be able to make any distinction. On this point, therefore, I will say nothing. But these same secrets, which never have been, and never will be revealed by me, either by word of mouth or the pen, have become known to too many, for it to be possible that

[1] He is evidently hinting that Mme d'Epinay was pregnant by her lover Grimm.

they can have remained unknown to any of Madame d'Epinay's associates.

Being aware of the true motive of this journey, I should have recognised the secret instigation of the hand of an enemy, in the attempt to make me the chaperon of Madame d'Epinay; but, as she had not pressed me at all to accompany her, I persisted in regarding the attempt as not seriously intended, and I merely laughed at the fine figure that I should have cut, if I had been foolish enough to undertake the charge. Besides, she gained considerably by my refusal, for she succeeded in persuading her husband himself to accompany her.

A few days afterwards I received the following letter from Diderot. This letter, merely folded in two, so that anyone could easily read its contents, was addressed to me, "Care of Madame d'Epinay," and intrusted to M. de Linant, the tutor of the son and the confidant of the mother.

LETTER FROM DIDEROT (PACKET A, No. 52).

"I am born to love you and to cause you annoyance. I hear that Madame d'Epinay is going to Geneva, and I do not hear it said that you accompany her. My friend, if you are satisfied with Madame d'Epinay, you must go with her; if you are dissatisfied, you must go all the more readily. Are you over-burdened with the weight of the obligations under which she has laid you? here is an opportunity of partly discharging them and of lightening your burden. Will you find another opportunity in your life of showing your gratitude to her? She is going into a country where she will be as if she had fallen from the clouds. She is ill; she will need amusement and distraction. Winter, too! Consider, my friend. The objection on the score of your health may be far stronger than I think it is; but, are you worse to-day than you were a month ago, and than you will be at the beginning of spring? Will you make the journey, three months hence, more comfortably than now? For myself, I declare to you that, if I could not endure the carriage, I would take a stick and follow her. Then, are you not afraid that your behaviour may be misinterpreted? You will be suspected either of ingratitude or of some other secret motive. I am well aware that, whatever you do, you will always have the testimony of your conscience on your side; but is this testimony sufficient by itself, and is it allowed to neglect, up to a certain point, that of other men? Besides, my friend, I write this letter in order to discharge an obligation to you as well as to myself. If it displeases you, throw it in the fire, and think no more of it than if it had never been written. I salute, love, and embrace you."

I trembled with rage, and felt so utterly astounded while reading this letter, that I could scarcely finish it; but this did not prevent me from observing how cleverly Diderot affected a gentler, more flattering, and more polite tone than in any of his other letters, in which he at most addressed me as "my dear," without condescending to call me "friend." I easily perceived the indirect means by which this letter had reached me: the address, style, and the way in which it arrived, betrayed the roundabout manner of proceeding clumsily enough; for we usually corresponded through the post or the Montmorency messenger, and this was the first and only time that he made use of the present method of communication.

When my first transports of indignation permitted me to write, I hastily threw off the following reply, which I immediately took from the Hermitage, where I was at the time, to La Chevrette, to show it to Madame d'Epinay, to whom, in my blind passion, I intended to read it, as well as Diderot's letter.

"My dear friend, you cannot know either the extent of my obligations to Madame d'Epinay, or how far they are binding, or whether she has really need of me on her journey, or wishes me to accompany her, or whether it is possible for me to do so, or the reasons I may have for refusing. I do not object to discuss all these points with you; but, in the meantime, you must admit that to dictate to me so positively what I ought to do, without being in a position to judge, is, my dear philosopher, to talk nonsense. The worst thing about it is, that I see that the opinion is not your own. Not to mention that I am little disposed to allow myself to be led by a third or fourth person under your name, I find in these indirect acts a certain amount of underhandedness, which ill suits your frankness, which, for both our sakes, you will do well to avoid for the future.

"You express yourself afraid that my conduct may be misinterpreted; but I defy a heart like yours to venture to think ill of mine. Others would perhaps speak better of me, if I were more like them. Heaven preserve me from gaining their approval! Let the wicked spy upon me and interpret my conduct as they please. Rousseau is not a man to fear them, or Diderot a man to listen to them.

"You wish me to throw your letter in the fire if it displeases me, and to think no more about it. Do you think that what comes from you can be so easily forgotten? My dear friend, you hold my tears, in the pain which you cause me, as cheap as my life and health, in the care which you exhort me to take. If you could correct yourself of this, your friendship would be so much the sweeter to me, and I should be so much the less to be pitied."

On entering Madame d'Epinay's room, I found Grimm with her, which delighted me. I read to them, in a loud and clear voice, my two letters, with an intrepidity of which I should not have believed myself capable, and, when I had finished, I added a few remarks which did not belie it. I saw that this unexpected audacity on the part of a man usually so timid astonished and astounded them both. They did not answer a word. Above all, I saw that arrogant man cast down his eyes, not venturing to meet the angry flashes from my own; but, at the same instant, in the bottom of his heart, he was vowing my destruction, and I am positive that they agreed upon it before they parted.

It was about this time that I at last received, through Madame d'Houdetot, Saint-Lambert's letter (Packet A, No. 57), dated from Wolfenbuttel, a few days after his accident, written in answer to mine, which had been greatly delayed on the road. This reply afforded me some consolation, which I greatly needed at that moment, in the proofs of esteem and friendship of which it was full, and which gave me the courage and strength to deserve them. From that moment I did my duty; but it is certain that, if Saint-Lambert had shown himself less sensible, less generous, less a man of honour, I should have been lost beyond recall.

The weather became bad, and people were beginning to leave the country. Madame d'Houdetot informed me of the day on which she intended to come and say good-bye to our valley, and made an appointment to meet me at Eaubonne. It so happened that it was the day on which Madame d'Epinay was leaving La Chevrette for Paris, in order to make her final preparations for her journey. Fortunately, she set out in the morning, and I still had time, after leaving her, to go and dine with her sister-in-law. I had Saint-Lambert's letter in my pocket, and read it several times as I walked along. It acted as a shield against my weakness. I made and kept the resolution to see in Madame d'Houdetot nothing but my friend and my friend's mistress; and I spent four or five hours in her company, *tête-à-tête*, in a delightful calm, infinitely preferable, even in the matter of enjoyment, to the

attacks of burning fever which I had hitherto felt in her presence. As she knew only too well that my heart was unchanged,
she was grateful for the efforts I had made to control myself; it
increased her esteem for me, and I had the pleasure of seeing
that her friendship for me was not extinguished. She informed
me of the speedy return of Saint-Lambert, who, although he had
almost recovered from his attack, was no longer in a condition
to endure the fatigues of war, and was leaving the service in
order to live quietly with her. We formed the charming plan of
an intimate companionship between us three, and we had reason
to hope that the execution of this plan would be lasting in its
results, seeing that all the feelings which can unite upright and
feeling hearts were the foundation of it, and we combined, in our
three selves, sufficient talents and knowledge to render any
foreign elements unnecessary. Alas! while abandoning myself
to the prospect of so charming a life, I little thought of that
which awaited me.

We afterwards spoke of my relations with Madame d'Epinay.
I showed her Diderot's letter, together with my answer; I told
her all the circumstances connected with it, and informed her of
my resolution to leave the Hermitage. She vigorously opposed it,
and with arguments which were all-powerful with my heart. She
declared that she would have much liked me to go with her to
Geneva, as she foresaw that she would inevitably be compromised by my refusal; indeed, Diderot's letter seemed to announce
it beforehand. However, as she knew my reasons as well as
myself, she did not insist upon this point; but she begged me
at any price to avoid scandal, and to palliate my refusal by
reasons sufficiently plausible to remove the unjust suspicion
that she had anything to do with it. I told her that it was no
easy task that she was imposing upon me; but that, being
resolved to atone for my offences, even at the cost of my
reputation, I desired to give the preference to hers, as far as
honour would allow me to go. It will soon be seen whether
I knew how to keep my promise.

I can swear that, far from my unfortunate passion having lost
any of its force, I never loved my Sophie so fondly, so tenderly,
as on that day. But Saint-Lambert's letter, my sense of duty, and

horror of treachery, made such an impression upon me that, during the whole of the interview, my senses left me completely at peace in her company, and I was not even tempted to kiss her hand. At parting, she kissed me before her servants. This kiss, so different from those which I had sometimes stolen from her beneath the trees, was a guarantee to me that I had regained command over myself. I am nearly certain that, if my heart had had time to strengthen itself without interruption, three months would have been more than enough to cure me completely.

Here end my personal relations with Madame d'Houdetot: relations, of which every man has been able to judge by appearances according to the nature of his own heart, but in which the passion with which this amiable woman inspired me, the liveliest passion that a man has perhaps ever felt, will always be honoured in Heaven's sight and our own, by the rare and painful sacrifices which we both made to duty, honour, love and friendship. We had too high an opinion of each other to be able to degrade ourselves easily. We must have been utterly unworthy of esteem to make up our minds to lose a mutual regard of such great value; and the energy of our feelings, which might have made us guilty, was the very thing which prevented us from becoming so.

Thus, after a long friendship for the one of these two women, and a deep affection for the other, I took farewell of both on the same day: of one, never to see her again in my life; of the other, only to see her twice more, upon occasions of which I shall afterwards speak.

After their departure, I found myself greatly embarrassed how to fulfil so many urgent and contradictory obligations, the result of my follies. If I had been in my natural position, after the proposal of the journey to Geneva had been made and I had declined it, I need only have remained quiet, and there would have been nothing more to be said. But I had foolishly made of it a matter which could not remain where it was, and I could only avoid further explanation by leaving the Hermitage, which I had just promised Madame d'Houdetot not to do, at least for the present. Besides, she had asked me to make my excuses for my refusal to my so-called friends, to prevent it being laid to her charge. And yet I could not declare the real reason without insulting Madame d'Epinay, to whom I certainly owed some gratitude, after all that she had done for me. After carefully considering everything, I found myself confronted by the cruel but unavoidable alternatives, of showing disrespect to Madame d'Epinay, Madame d'Houdetot, or myself: I chose the last. I chose it boldly, unreservedly, without shuffling, and with a generosity which surely deserved to expiate the offences which had reduced me to such an extremity. This sacrifice, which my enemies perhaps expected, and by which they have known how to profit, has caused the ruin of my reputation, and, thanks to their efforts, has robbed me of the esteem of the public; but it has restored to me my own, and has consoled me in my misfortunes. This is not the last time, as will be seen, that I have made similar sacrifices, nor the last time that they have been taken advantage of to overwhelm me.

Grimm was the only one who appeared to have taken no part in this affair; and it was to him that I resolved to address myself. I wrote a long letter to him, in which I exposed the absurdity of wishing me to look upon it as my duty to take the journey to Geneva, the uselessness of it, even the embarrassment I should have been to Madame d'Epinay, and the inconveniences which would have resulted to myself. In this letter, I could not resist the temptation of letting him see that I was well informed, and that it seemed to me singular that anyone should expect me to undertake the journey, while he himself was considered exempt, and his name was not even mentioned. This letter, in which, owing to its being impossible for me to state my reasons outright, I was often obliged to wander from the point, might have presented the appearance of guilt to the general public; but it was a model of prudence and discretion for those who, like Grimm, were well acquainted with the facts, which I did not mention in it, and which fully justified my conduct. I did not even shrink from exciting a further prejudice against myself, by foisting Diderot's advice upon my other friends, in order to hint that Madame d'Houdetot had thought the same, as in fact was the case, and by avoiding to mention that, in consequence of my arguments, she had changed her opinion. There was no better way of clearing her from the suspicion of connivance on her part, than by seeming to be dissatisfied with her conduct in this respect.

This letter concluded with an exhibition of confidence by which any other man would have been touched. While I exhorted Grimm to consider my reasons well, and afterwards to inform me of his opinion, I gave him to understand that his advice, whatever it might be, would be followed. Such was really my intention, even if he had declared himself in favour of my going. As M. d'Epinay had undertaken to be his wife's escort on the journey, my company would have assumed quite a different aspect: whereas, at first, it was I who was asked to undertake this duty, and there was no question of M. d'Epinay until I had refused.

Grimm did not reply for some time. His answer was curious. I will here give a copy of it (see Packet A, No. 59):

"Madame d'Epinay's departure is put off; her son is ill, and she is obliged to wait until he has recovered. I will think over your letter. Stay quietly at your Hermitage. I will let you know my opinion in time. As she will certainly not leave for some days, there is no hurry. Meanwhile, if you think fit, you can make your offers to her, although that appears to me a matter of indifference. For, as I know your position as well as you know it yourself, I have no doubt that she will reply to them as she ought. It seems to me that the only thing to be gained by it is, that you will be able to say to those who urge you, that, if you do not go, it will not be for want of having offered your services. Besides, I do not see why you think it absolutely necessary that the philosopher should be the speaking-trumpet of all the world; and why do you imagine, because his advice is that you should go, that all your friends are of the same opinion? If you write to Madame d'Epinay, her answer may serve as a reply to all those friends, since you set such great store upon replying to them. Adieu. I salute Madame le Vasseur and the 'Criminal.' "*

Greatly astonished by the perusal of this letter, I anxiously endeavoured to find out what it might mean, but in vain. What! instead of sending me a simple answer to my letter, he takes time to think over it, as if the time he had already taken had not been

* M. le Vasseur was in the habit of calling his wife, who ruled him rather strictly, the "Criminal-Lieutenant." Grimm, in jest, gave the same name to the daughter, and, for shortness, afterwards omitted the second word. (R)

enough! He even informs me of the state of suspense in which he desires to keep me, as if it were a question of a difficult problem which had to be solved, or as if it was important to him to deprive me of every means of clearly understanding his feelings, until the moment when he should be pleased to declare them to me! What could be the meaning of all these precautions, this delay, this secrecy? Is this the way to respond to confidence? Does this look like honourable and upright behaviour? I sought in vain for some favourable interpretation of his conduct; I found none. Whatever his intention might be, his position made it easy for him to carry it out, if it was hostile to myself, while my own made it impossible for me to put any obstacle in his way. A favourite in the house of a great Prince, with many acquaintances in the world, a man who gave the tone to the society in which we moved, whose oracle he was, he was able, with the help of his usual cleverness, to arrange all his machinery as he pleased; whereas I, alone in my Hermitage, far from all, without anyone to advise me, without communication with the outside world, could do nothing but wait and remain quiet. All I did was to write to Madame d'Epinay, about her son's illness, as polite a letter as could possibly be, but in which I did not walk into the snare of offering to accompany her on her journey.

After long waiting, in a state of cruel anxiety, into which this barbarous man had plunged me, I heard, eight or ten days later, that Madame d'Epinay had set out, and I received a second letter from him. It contained only seven or eight lines, which I did not read through . . . It proclaimed a rupture, but in terms such as only the most infernal hate can dictate, and which, from his eagerness to make them offensive, seemed almost silly. He forbade me to enter his presence as he might have warned me off his estates. His letter, to make it appear ridiculous, only needed to be read with greater calmness. Without copying it, without even reading it to the end, I sent it back to him immediately with the following note:

"I refused to listen to my just suspicions. Too late I understand your character.

"This, then, is the letter which you wanted time to think over. I send it back to you; it is not for me. You can show mine to all the world, and hate me without concealment: that will be one falsehood less on your part."

The permission which I gave him to show my preceding letter referred to a passage in his own, from which the reader will be enabled to judge of the profound adroitness with which he acted throughout the whole affair.

I have said that, in the opinion of the uninitiated, my letter might have afforded many opportunities for attacking me. He was delighted to see it; but how was he to take advantage of it without compromising himself? If he showed the letter, he exposed himself to the reproach of abusing his friend's confidence.

To relieve himself from this embarrassment, he determined to break off his relations with me in the most cutting manner possible, and to make me feel, in his letter, the favour which he did me by not showing mine. He felt quite certain that, in my indignant anger, I should reject his pretended discretion, and allow him to show my letter to everybody. This was exactly what he wanted, and everything turned out as he had planned. He sent my letter all round Paris, together with remarks of his own, which, however, did not prove so successful as he had expected. It was not considered that the permission to show my letter, which he had known how to extort from me, exempted him from reproach, for having so lightly taken me at my word in order to injure me. People kept asking what personal wrong I had done to him that could justify so violent a hatred. At last they came to the conclusion that, even if they had been of such a nature as to oblige him to break with me, friendship, even though extinguished, still had rights which he ought to have respected. But, unfortunately, Paris is frivolous. Impressions of the moment are soon forgotten. The unfortunate man who is absent is neglected; the prosperous man inspires respect by his presence. The game of intrigue and wickedness continues, and is renewed; and its effects, unceasingly reviving, soon efface the past.

This was the way in which this man, after having so long deceived me, at last threw off the mask, convinced that, in the state to which he had brought matters, he no longer needed it.

Relieved from all apprehension of being unjust towards this wretch, I left him to his own reflections, and ceased to think of him. Eight days after the receipt of his letter, I received from Geneva an answer from Madame d'Epinay to my former letter (Packet B, No. 10). I saw, from the tone which she assumed for the first time in her life, that both, reckoning upon the success of their plans, were acting in concert, and that, looking upon me as a man lost beyond all hope of safety, they intended to devote themselves from that time forth, without any risk, to the pleasure of completely crushing me.

In fact, my condition was most deplorable. I saw all my friends leaving me, without my knowing how or why. Diderot, who boasted of alone remaining faithful to me, and who had, for three months past, promised to pay me a visit, never came at all. The winter now began to make itself felt, and, with it, attacks of my usual complaints. My constitution, although vigorous, had been unable to sustain the conflicts of so many contradictory passions. I was in a state of exhaustion, which left me neither strength nor courage to resist anything. Even if my promises, even if the continued remonstrances of Diderot and Madame d'Houdetot had allowed me to leave the Hermitage at this moment, I did not know either where to go or how to drag myself there. I remained stupid and motionless, without power to think or act. The mere idea of taking a step, of writing a letter, of saying a word, made me shudder. However, I could not leave Madame d'Epinay's letter unanswered, without confessing that I deserved the treatment with which she and her friend overwhelmed me. I decided to communicate my feelings and resolutions to her, not doubting for a moment that the feelings of humanity, generosity, propriety, and the good qualities which I believed I had recognised in her, in spite of those that were bad, would make her hasten to agree with me. My letter was as follows:

"THE HERMITAGE, *November 23rd,* 1757.

"If one could die of grief, I should not be alive now. But at last I have made up my mind. All friendship between us is over, madam; but that which no longer exists still preserves its rights, which I know how to respect. I have by no means forgotten your kindness towards me, and you can reckon upon all the gratitude which a man can feel for one whom he can no longer love. All further explanation would be useless: I keep my own conscience, and refer you to your own.

"I wanted to leave the Hermitage, and I ought to have done so. But people tell me I must remain here until spring; and since my friends desire it, I will remain until then, if you consent to it."

After this letter had been written and despatched, my only thought was to remain quiet at the Hermitage, take care of my health, endeavour to recover my strength, and make arrangements to leave in the spring, without creating any disturbance or openly proclaiming the rupture. But this was not what M. Grimm and Madame d'Epinay reckoned upon, as will be seen directly.

A few days later, I at last had the pleasure of receiving from Diderot the visit which he had so often promised, and as often failed to keep his word.[1] It could not have occurred at a more opportune moment; he was my oldest friend; he was almost the only friend I had left; under these circumstances, my delight at seeing him may be imagined. My heart was full; I poured its contents into his. I enlightened him upon many facts which had been kept from him, or had been disguised or invented. I told him what I felt justified in telling him of all that had taken place. I made no pretence of concealing from him what he knew only too well – that a love, as unfortunate as it was foolish, had been the instrument of my destruction; but I never admitted that Madame d'Houdetot knew of it, or, at least, that I had declared it to her. I told him of Madame d'Epinay's unworthy artifices to intercept the very innocent letters written to me by her sister-in-law. I desired that he should learn these details from the lips of the persons whom she had attempted to seduce. Thérèse gave him an exact account of everything; but my feelings may be imagined, when it came to the mother's turn, and I heard her declare and maintain that she knew nothing at all about it! This was her statement, in which she never wavered. Not four days since, she had repeated all the details to me, and then, in my friend's presence, she flatly contradicted me. This attitude appeared to me decisive; and I then keenly felt my imprudence

[1] Diderot's visit (which was to be their last meeting) took place on 5 December 1757.

in having so long kept such a woman near me. I did not break out into invectives; I hardly condescended to say a few contemptuous words to her. I felt how much I owed to the daughter, whose unassailable uprightness contrasted strongly with her mother's contemptible cowardice. But, from that moment, my mind was made up in regard to the old woman, and I only waited for a suitable opportunity to carry out my determination.

This opportunity came sooner than I had expected. On the 10th of December I received an answer from Madame d'Epinay. Its contents were as follows (Packet B, No. 11):

"GENEVA, *December 1st*, 1757.

"After having given you, for several years, every possible proof of friendship and sympathy, I can now only pity you. You are very unhappy. I wish your conscience may be as clear as mine. That may be necessary for your future tranquillity.

"Since you wanted to leave the Hermitage, and ought to have done so, I am astonished that your friends have prevented you. As for myself, I do not consult my friends as to my duties, and I have nothing more to say to you concerning yours."

A dismissal so unexpected, but so clearly expressed, did not leave me a moment to hesitate. I was bound to leave the Hermitage at once, whatever the weather or the state of my health might be, even if I had to sleep in the woods or on the snow, with which the ground was covered, and in spite of anything Madame d'Houdetot might say or do; for, although I was ready to humour her in everything, I was not prepared to disgrace myself.

I found myself in the most terrible embarrassment of my life; but my mind was made up: I swore that, whatever might happen, I would not sleep in the Hermitage after a week. I set about removing my effects, having determined to leave them in the open field rather than keep the key longer than the week; for I was anxious, above all, that everything should be settled before anyone could write to Geneva and receive an answer. I was filled with a courage which I had never felt before: all my vigour had returned to me. Honour and indignation, upon which Madame d'Epinay had not reckoned, restored it to me.

Fortune assisted my boldness. M. Mathas, *procureur fiscal*[1] of M. le Prince de Condé, heard of my difficulties. He offered me a little house which stood in his garden at Mont-Louis,[2] in Montmorency. I accepted his offer with eagerness and gratitude. The bargain was soon concluded. I hastily bought some furniture, in addition to what I had already, that Thérèse and myself might have a bed to sleep on. With great trouble, and at great expense, I managed to get my goods removed in a cart. In spite of the ice and snow, my removal was effected in two days, and, on the 15th of December, I gave up the keys of the Hermitage, after having paid the gardener's wages, as I could not pay my rent.

I told Madame le Vasseur that we must separate; her daughter tried to shake my resolution, but I was inflexible. I saw her off to Paris in the messenger's cart, with all the furniture and effects belonging to her and her daughter in common. I gave her some money, and undertook to pay for her lodging with her children or elsewhere, to provide for her as long as it was in my power, and never to let her want for bread as long as I had any myself.

Lastly, the day after my arrival at Mont-Louis, I wrote the following letter to Madame d'Epinay:

"MONTMORENCY, *December 17th*, 1757.
"Madam,   Nothing is so simple or so necessary as to leave your house, since you do not approve of my remaining there. As you refused to allow me to spend the rest of the winter at the Hermitage, I left it on the 15th of December. I was fated to enter and to leave it in spite of myself. I thank you for the stay which you invited me to make there, and I would thank you still more if I had paid less dearly for it. You are right in thinking that I am unhappy: no one in the world knows better than yourself the extent of that unhappiness. If it is a misfortune to be deceived in the choice of one's friends, it is equally cruel to be disabused of so pleasant a mistake."

Such is the true story of my stay at the Hermitage, and of the reasons which caused me to leave it. I have been unable to

[1] The attorney who prosecutes in all cases in which the lord paramount or the public are concerned.
[2] He had rented a cottage at Montlouis, in the Montmorency district, belonging to a M. Mathas. It is now a Rousseau museum.

interrupt this narrative, and it was important to give the most exact details, since this period of my life has exercised an influence upon the future, the effects of which will last to my dying day.

BOOK X

[1758]

THE extraordinary energy with which a temporary irritation had enabled me to leave the Hermitage, left me as soon as I was out of it. I was no sooner settled in my new abode than severe and frequent attacks of retention of urine were complicated by the fresh inconvenience of a rupture, which had for some time tortured me, without my knowing that it was one. I soon became subject to the most painful attacks. My old friend Thierry came to see me, and enlightened me as to my condition. Probes, bougies, bandages, all the preparations for the infirmities of age which were collected around me, made me feel rudely, that one can no longer have a young heart without suffering for it, when the body has ceased to be young. The fine weather did not restore my strength, and I passed the whole of 1758 in a state of weakness which made me believe that I was near the end of my career. I saw it approaching almost with eagerness. Cured of idle dreams of friendship, separated from everything which had made me fond of life, I no longer saw anything in it which could make it agreeable; I saw nothing but misery and suffering, which prevented me from all self-enjoyment. I yearned for the moment when I should be free and beyond the reach of my enemies. But let us take up the thread of events again.

It appears that my retirement to Montmorency disconcerted Madame d'Epinay; probably she had not expected it. My melancholy condition, the severity of the weather, and my general loneliness, made her and Grimm believe that, by driving me to the last extremity, they would compel me to cry for mercy, and to degrade myself to the depths of meanness, in order to be left in the refuge which honour ordered me to leave. I changed my quarters so abruptly that they had not time to anticipate the step; no alternative was left to them except to go double or quits and ruin me completely, or to endeavour to get me back. Grimm was in favour of the former; but I believe that Madame d'Epinay would have preferred the latter. I am inclined to believe this from her answer to my last letter, in which she adopted a much milder tone, and seemed to open the door to reconciliation. The time she made me wait for an answer – a whole month – is a sufficient indication of the difficulty which she found in giving it a suitable turn, and of the anxious thought which she devoted to it. She could not go further without committing herself; but, after her previous letters, and my abrupt departure from her house, one cannot but be struck by the pains she has taken in this letter not to allow a single uncivil word to creep in. In order that the reader may judge for himself, I will give it in full (Packet B, No. 23):

"GENEVA, *January 17th*, 1758.

"Sir, – I did not receive your letter of the 17th of December until yesterday. It was sent to me in a box filled with different things, which has been all this time on its way. I will only answer the postscript; as for the letter itself, I do not clearly understand it; and, if it were possible for us to come to an explanation, I would gladly set down all that has passed to a misunderstanding. To return to the postscript. You may remember that we agreed that the gardener's wages should be paid through you, to make him feel that he was dependent upon you, and to spare you the laughable and unseemly scenes which his predecessor had caused. A proof of this is, that his first quarter's wages was handed to you, and, a few days before I left I arranged with you to repay what you advanced. I know that at first you made a difficulty about it; but I had asked you to make these advances; I had merely to discharge my obligations, and this we agreed upon. Cahouet has told me that you refused to accept this money. There must be some mistake about the matter. I have ordered it to be offered to you again; I do not see why you should want to pay my gardener, in spite of our agreement, even beyond the time of your stay at the Hermitage. Therefore, sir, I feel sure that, remembering all that I have the honour to tell you, you will not refuse to take back the money which you have been kind enough to advance."

After all that passed, being no longer able to trust Madame d'Epinay, I did not desire to renew my connection with her. I did not answer the letter at all, and our correspondence ended with it. Seeing that I had made up my mind, she did the same; and entering into all the plans of Grimm and the Holbachian clique, she united her efforts with theirs in order to ruin me. While they were working at Paris, she was working at Geneva. Grimm, who afterwards went to join her, finished what she had begun. Tronchin, whom they easily gained over, vigorously assisted them, and became my most violent persecutor, without having the least cause of complaint against me, any more than Grimm. All three, acting together, secretly sowed in Geneva the seed which, four years later, was seen to spring up.

They found more difficulty in Paris, where I was better known, and where people's hearts, less disposed to hatred, did not receive its impressions so easily. In order to deal their blows more adroitly, they began by spreading the report that it was I who had left them. (See Deleyre's letter, Packet B, No. 30.) Starting with that, and pretending to be still my friends, they cleverly sowed the seeds of their malicious accusations, in the form of complaints against the injustice of their friend. The result of this was that their hearers, thrown off their guard, were more inclined to listen to them and to blame me. The secret accusations of treachery and ingratitude were spread with greater precaution, and for that very reason with greater effect. I knew that they accused me of the most heinous crimes, without ever being able to learn in what, according to them, they consisted. All that I could infer from public report was, that they were reduced to these four capital offences: my retirement to the country, my love for Madame d'Houdetot, my refusal to accompany Madame d'Epinay to Geneva, my departure from the Hermitage. If they added other grievances, they took their measures so admirably, that it has been absolutely impossible for me ever to learn what was the nature of them.

From this time, therefore, I think that I can date the establishment of a system, subsequently adopted by those who have the disposal of my destiny, which has met with such rapid success, that it would seem almost marvellous to anyone who does not know how easy it is for everything which assists men's malice to secure approval. I must now endeavour to explain, as briefly as possible, what is visible to my eyes in this secret and deeply-laid system.

With a name already famous and known throughout Europe, I had preserved the simplicity of my early tastes. My deadly aversion to all that was called party, faction, or cabal, had kept me free and independent, without any other fetters than the attachments of my heart. Alone, a stranger, isolated, without support, without family, attached to nothing but my principles and duties, I followed without flinching the paths of uprightness, never flattering, never favouring anyone at the expense of justice and truth. Besides, during two years spent in solitude and retirement, without hearing any news, without any connection with the affairs of the world, without being informed or curious about anything, I lived, four leagues from Paris, separated from it by my carelessness as far as I should have been by the sea from the island of Tinian.[1]

On the other hand, Grimm, Diderot, and d'Holbach, in the midst of the vortex, lived in the society of the great world, and divided between them nearly all its circles. Great men, wits, men of letters, lawyers, women, all listened to them when they acted in concert. It is easy to see the advantage which such a position gives to three men united against a fourth in a position like my own. It is true that Diderot and d'Holbach were not – at least, I cannot believe it – the men to form very black designs; the one was not wicked enough,[*] the other was not sufficiently clever; but for that very reason they played their game better together. Grimm alone formed his plan in his head, and only disclosed so much of it to the other two as was necessary to enable them to assist in carrying it out. His ascendancy over them made this co-operation easy, and the effect of the whole corresponded to his superior abilities.

With these superior abilities, sensible of the advantage he could derive from our respective positions, he formed the design of utterly destroying my reputation, and changing it into one totally different, without compromising himself, by beginning to erect around me an edifice of obscurity which it was impossible for me to penetrate, so as to throw light upon his stratagems, and to unmask him.

This undertaking was difficult, seeing that it was necessary for him to palliate its injustice in the eyes of those who were to assist

[1]   In the Mariana islands.
[*]   I confess, since I wrote this work, that the glimpses which I have had of the mysteries which surround me, make me afraid that I did not know Diderot. (R)

in it. It was necessary to deceive those who were honourable; it was necessary to keep everyone away from me, and not to leave me a single friend, either great or small. What do I say? it was necessary for him not to allow a single word of truth to penetrate to me. If a single generous man had come and said to me, "You are playing the virtuous man; and yet, look how you are treated, and how you are judged – what have you to say?" Truth would have triumphed, and Grimm would have been lost. He knew it; but he had sounded his own heart, and estimated men at their true value. I regret, for the honour of humanity, that he calculated so accurately.

In these underground paths, his steps, to be sure, were obliged to be slow. He has for twelve years pursued his plans, and the most difficult thing still remains for him to do – to deceive the entire public. There are eyes which have watched him more closely than he thinks. He is afraid of this, and does not yet venture to expose his plot to the light of day.* But he has found the least difficult way of accompanying it with power, and this power disposes of me. With this to support him, he proceeds with less risk. As the satellites of power as a rule think but little of uprightness, and still less of frankness, he need not fear the indiscretion of any honourable man. Above all, it is necessary for him that I should be surrounded by impenetrable darkness, and that his plot should always be concealed from me, since he well knows that, however skilfully he may have laid his plans, they would never be able to resist a look from me. His great cleverness consists in appearing to treat me indulgently, while in reality defaming me, and in giving his perfidy the appearance of generosity.

I felt the first effects of this system through the secret accusations of the Holbachian clique, without it being possible for me to know, or even to conjecture, what formed the subject of these accusations. Deleyre, in his letters, told me that I was accused of most disgraceful offences. Diderot, more mysteriously, told me the same thing; and when I entered upon an explanation with

* Since these words were written, he has taken the plunge with the most complete and inconceivable success. I believe that it is Tronchin who has supplied him with the courage and the means. (R)

both, the whole was reduced to the four heads already mentioned. I became conscious of a growing coolness in Madame d'Houdetot's letters. I could not attribute this coolness to Saint-Lambert, who continued to correspond with me with the same friendliness, and even came to see me after his return. Nor could I blame myself either, since we had parted very amicably, and, on my side, I had done nothing since then, except leave the Hermitage, a step which she herself had felt to be necessary. Consequently, not knowing what to consider responsible for this coolness – which she did not admit, although my heart could not be deceived – I felt generally uneasy. I knew that she was extremely cautious in her behaviour to her sister-in-law and Grimm, on account of their relation to Saint-Lambert; I was afraid of their schemes. This agitation reopened my wounds, and made our correspondence so stormy, that she became quite disgusted. I caught a glimpse of a thousand cruel circumstances, without seeing anything distinctly. My position was most unbearable for a man whose fancy is so easily inflamed. If I had been altogether isolated, if I had known nothing at all, I should have been calmer; but my heart still clung to the attachments which gave my enemies a thousand handles against me; and the feeble rays which penetrated my refuge only served to show me the blackness of the mysteries which were concealed from me.

I have no doubt that I should have succumbed to this cruel torture, which was too much for my frank and open disposition, which, while it makes it utterly impossible for me to conceal my own feelings, makes me fear everything from those which are concealed from me; but, fortunately, other things presented themselves, sufficiently interesting to my heart to create a healthy diversion from those which, in spite of myself, engaged my attention. During the last visit which Diderot had paid to the Hermitage, he had spoken to me about the article on "Geneva" which D'Alembert had inserted in the "Encyclopaedia"; he had told me that this article, which had been agreed upon together with some Genevese of high standing, had in view the establishment of a theatre at Geneva; that the necessary steps had been taken, and that it would soon be carried out. As Diderot seemed to look favourably upon the scheme, and had no doubt of its success, and as I had too many other things to discuss with him to have time to argue further upon the point, I said nothing; but, feeling indignant at all these intrigues to corrupt my country, I awaited with impatience the volume of the "Encyclopaedia" which contained the article, that I might see whether I could not find some means of answering it in such a manner as to ward off the blow. I received the volume soon after I was settled at Mont-Louis, and I found that the article was written with considerable skill and cleverness, and was worthy of the pen from which it had proceeded. However, this did not deter me from my intention of replying to it; and, in spite of my low spirits, in spite of my grief and suffering, the severity of the weather, and the uncomfortableness of my new abode, in which I had not yet had time to settle down, I set to work with an eagerness which overcame all.

During a somewhat severe winter, in the month of February, and in the condition I have already described, I spent two hours, morning and afternoon, in an open turret at the bottom of the garden in which my house stood. This turret, which stood at the end of a terraced walk, looked upon the valley and fishpond of Montmorency, and showed me in the distance, as far as I could see, the simple but stately château of Saint Gratien, the retreat of the virtuous Catinat.[1] In this place, which at that time was bitterly cold, unsheltered from the wind and snow, and with no other fire except that in my heart, I composed, in three weeks, my letter to D'Alembert upon Theatres. This was the first of my writings — for "Julie" was not half finished — in which I have found delight in work. Hitherto, virtuous indignation had been my Apollo; on this occasion, tenderness and gentleness of soul supplied his place. The injustices of which I had only been a spectator had irritated me: those by which I had myself been attacked saddened me; and this sadness, free from all gall and bitterness, was nothing but the sadness of a too loving and tender heart, which, deceived by those whom it believed to be of its own stamp, had been forced to retire into itself. Full of all that had just happened to me, still shaken by so many violent

[1] Nicholas de Catinat (1637–1712), marshal of France.

emotions, my heart mingled the feelings of its sufferings with the ideas with which meditation upon my subject had inspired me: my work showed evident traces of this mingling. Without perceiving it, I described my situation at that time: I portrayed Grimm, Madame d'Epinay, Madame d'Houdetot, Saint-Lambert and myself. While writing, what delightful tears I shed! Alas! in what I wrote it is only too evident that love, the fatal love of which I was doing my utmost to cure myself, was not yet banished from my heart. With all this was mingled a certain feeling of tenderness in regard to myself, as I felt that I was dying, and believed that I was saying farewell to the public for the last time. Far from being alarmed at death, I beheld its approach with joy, but I felt regret at leaving my fellows before they had learned to appreciate me properly, before they knew how much I should have deserved their affection if they had known me better. These are the secret reasons of the singular tone which prevails in this work, and which offers so striking a contrast to that which preceded it.[1]

I revised and made a fair copy of this letter, and was about to get it printed, when, after a long silence, I received a letter from Madame d'Houdetot, which overwhelmed me with a fresh affliction, the most painful that I had as yet suffered. She told me in this letter (Packet B, No. 34), that my passion for her was known throughout Paris; that I had spoken of it to persons who had made it public; that these rumours had reached the ears of her lover, and had nearly cost him his life; that at last he did her justice, and that they had become reconciled; but that she owed it to him, as well as to herself and her reputation, to break off all intercourse with me; that, in the meanwhile, she assured me that they would never cease to take an interest in me, that they would defend me before the public, and that she would send from time to time to inquire after me.

"And you too, Diderot!" I exclaimed. Unworthy friend! Nevertheless, I could not make up my mind to condemn him yet. My weakness was known by other persons who might have caused it to be talked about. I wanted to doubt; but soon I was unable to do so any longer. Soon afterwards, Saint-Lambert

[1] The "Discours sur l'Inégalité des Conditions."

behaved in a manner worthy of his generosity. Knowing my heart tolerably well, he guessed the state of mind in which I must be, betrayed by one section of my friends, and abandoned by the rest. He came to see me. When he came first, he had very little time to spare. He came again. Unfortunately, as I did not expect him, I was not at home. Thérèse, who was, had a conversation with him, which lasted more than two hours, in the course of which they told each other of several things which it was of great importance for both of us to know. The surprise with which I learned that no one doubted that I had lived with Madame d'Epinay, as Grimm was living with her at that time, was only equalled by his own, when he learned that the report was utterly false. Saint-Lambert, to the lady's great displeasure, was in the same case as myself; and all the explanations, which were the result of this conversation, utterly stifled any regrets I may have felt at having irrevocably broken with her. As for Madame d'Houdetot, he gave Thérèse a detailed account of many circumstances with which neither she nor even Madame d'Houdetot were acquainted – things which I alone knew, which I had mentioned to Diderot alone under the seal of friendship; and it was Saint-Lambert himself to whom he had chosen to confide them. This finally decided me. Resolved to break with Diderot once and for all, I had nothing further to think about, except the manner of doing it; for I had perceived that secret ruptures always proved prejudicial to me, since they left the mask of friendship to my most cruel enemies.

The rules of good breeding established in the world upon this point seem to be dictated by the spirit of falsehood and treachery. To appear to be the friend of a man, when one has ceased to be so, is to reserve to oneself the means of injuring him by deceiving honourable men. I recalled to mind that when the illustrious Montesquieu broke with Father de Tournemine, he hastened to announce it openly, and said to everybody, "Do not listen either to Father de Tournemine or myself, when one speaks of the other, for we are no longer friends." His conduct was highly applauded, and its frankness and generosity were universally praised. I determined to follow his example in dealing with Diderot; but how was I to announce the rupture authentically from my retreat, and, in addition, without causing a scandal? I decided to insert in my work, in the form of a note, a passage from Ecclesiasticus, which announced it and even the attendant circumstances, in terms sufficiently clear to anyone who was well informed, while it had no meaning for others.[1] I further took care only to allude to the friend whom I was renouncing in the respectful terms which are always due to friendship even when it no longer exists. All this may be seen in the work itself.

There is nothing in this world but good and bad fortune;[2] and it appears that in adversity every act of courage is a crime. The very same thing which had been admired in Montesquieu only brought upon me blame and reproach. As soon as my work was printed and I had received copies of it, I sent one to Saint-Lambert, who, the very day before, had written to me, in Madame d'Houdetot's name and his own, a letter full of the tenderest expressions of friendship (Packet B, No. 37). He returned my copy, accompanied by the following letter (Packet B, No. 38):

"EAUBONNE, *October 10th*, 1758.

"Really, sir, I am unable to accept the present which you have just sent me. At the passage in your Preface, where, mentioning Diderot, you quote a passage from Ecclesiastes" (he is wrong, it is Ecclesiasticus), "the book fell from my hands. After our conversations during this summer, you appeared to me to be convinced that Diderot was innocent of the pretended indiscretions which you laid to his charge. He may have treated you wrongly; I do not know; but I do know that this does not give you the right to insult him publicly. You are not ignorant of the persecutions to which he has to submit, and now you unite the voice of an old friend to the cries of the envious! I cannot conceal from you, sir, how greatly this outrageous conduct shocks me. I do not live with Diderot, but I honour him, and I feel keenly the pain which you cause to a man whom you have never reproached, at least in my presence, with anything more than a little weakness. Sir, we differ

---

[1]   The passage ran: "I had a severe and judicious Aristarchus. I have him no longer, I no longer want him, but I shall never cease to regret him, and he is a greater loss to my heart even than to my writings." A footnote added a quotation from *Ecclesiasticus*, condemning those who disclosed their friends' secrets.

[2]   *Il n'y a qu'heur et malheur dans ce monde*: a proverbial expression, meaning, "In this world everything depends upon luck."

too much in our principles ever to be able to agree. Forget my existence; this ought not to be difficult for you. I have never done men either good or harm which they remember for long. I promise you, sir, to forget your person, and to remember your talents alone."

I felt no less afflicted than indignant, when I read this letter, and, in the excess of my wretchedness, finding my pride again, I replied to him as follows:

"MONTMORENCY, *October 11th*, 1758.

"Sir, – When I read your letter, I did you the honour of being surprised at it, and I was foolish enough to be affected by it; but now I find that it is unworthy of an answer.

"I have no wish to continue the copies for Madame d'Houdetot. If it is not agreeable to her to keep what she has, she can send it back to me; I will return her money. If she keeps it, she must still send for the rest of her paper and money. I beg, at the same time, that she will return me the prospectus which she has in her keeping. Farewell, sir."

Courage in misfortune irritates cowardly hearts, but pleases those that are generous. It appears that this letter caused Saint-Lambert to reflect, and that he was sorry for what he had done; but, being too proud on his side to admit it openly, he seized, perhaps prepared, the means of deadening the force of the blow which he had dealt me. A fortnight later, I received the following letter from M. d'Epinay (Packet B, No. 10):

"*Thursday, 26th.*

"Sir, – I have received the book which you have been kind enough to send me; I read it with great pleasure. This is always the feeling with which I have read all the works which have proceeded from your pen. Accept my best thanks for it. I would have offered them to you in person, if my affairs had allowed me to stay any time in your neighbourhood; but I have lived very little this year at La Chevrette. M. and Madame Dupin are coming to dine with me next Sunday. I expect that MM. de Francueil and Saint-Lambert, and Madame d'Houdetot will be of the party. You would do me a real favour by consenting to join us. All those who will be my guests are anxious for your company, and will be delighted to share with me the pleasure of spending a portion of the day with you. I have the honour to be, with the most perfect esteem, etc."

This letter made my heart beat terribly. After having been for a year the talk of Paris, the idea of going to exhibit myself before Madame d'Houdetot made me tremble, and I could scarcely muster up sufficient courage to sustain this ordeal. However, since she and Saint-Lambert desired it, since D'Epinay spoke in the name of all those who had been invited, and mentioned no one whom I should not be glad to see, I came to the conclusion that, after all, I was not compromising myself by accepting an invitation to dinner which was sent me, as it were, by all the guests. I accordingly promised to go. On Sunday, the weather was bad: M. d'Epinay sent his carriage for me, and I went.

My arrival created a sensation. I have never met with a more cordial reception. One would have said that the whole company felt how greatly I needed cheering. Only French hearts know how to show tenderness of this kind. However, I found more people there than I had expected; amongst others, the Comte d'Houdetot, whom I did not know at all, and his sister, Madame de Blainville, whose company I could very well have dispensed with. She had visited Eaubonne several times during the preceding year; and her sister-in-law, during our solitary walks, had often made her dance attendance until she was tired out. She cherished a resentment against me which she gratified during this dinner to her heart's content; for it may be guessed that the presence of the Comte d'Houdetot and Saint-Lambert did not give me the laugh on my side, and that a man who found himself at a loss during the most ordinary conversations did not shine very much on that occasion. I have never suffered so much, never cut such a bad figure, or been subjected to more unexpected attacks. When at length we left the table, I escaped from this vixen; I had the pleasure of seeing Saint-Lambert and Madame d'Houdetot come up to me, and we talked together during part of the afternoon, concerning matters which it is true were of no importance, but with the same familiarity as before my fit of madness. This friendliness did not escape my heart; and if Saint-Lambert had been able to read therein, he would certainly have been satisfied. I can swear that, although, on my arrival, the sight of Madame d'Houdetot caused my heart to beat so violently that I almost fainted, when I took my leave I scarcely thought of her at all, my mind being entirely occupied with Saint-Lambert.

Notwithstanding Madame de Blainville's spiteful sarcasms, this dinner did me a great deal of good, and I heartily congratulated myself upon not having refused the invitation. It showed me not only that the intrigues of Grimm and the Holbachians had not separated my old friends from me,* but, what was still more flattering to me, that the feelings of Madame d'Houdetot and Saint-Lambert were less changed than I had expected; and I at last understood that jealousy had more to do with his keeping her away from me than disesteem. This consoled and calmed me. Sure of not being an object of contempt to those whom I esteemed, I worked upon my own heart with greater courage and success. If I did not succeed in completely extinguishing in it a guilty and unfortunate passion, I at least kept its remains so well in order, that since that time they have not caused me to commit a single error. Madame d'Houdetot's copying, which she persuaded me to resume; my works, which I continued to send her when they appeared, still brought me, from time to time, messages and notes from her, of no great importance, but couched in polite terms. She even did more, as will be subsequently seen; and the reciprocal conduct of all the three, after our intercourse had ceased, may serve as an example of the way in which honourable persons separate, when it is no longer agreeable to them to associate.

Another advantage resulting from this dinner was, that it was spoken of in Paris, and served to refute unanswerably the report which was everywhere circulated by my enemies, that I was at daggers-drawn with all those who had been present, especially with M. d'Epinay. On leaving the Hermitage, I had written to him a very polite letter of thanks, to which he replied with equal politeness; and this mutual interchange of civilities continued between ourselves and his brother, M. de Lalive, who even came to see me at Montmorency, and sent me his engravings. With the exception of Madame d'Houdetot's two sisters-in-law, I have never been on bad terms with any member of his family.

My letter to D'Alembert met with great success. All my works had done the same, but this was even more profitable to me. It

---

* This was what, in the simplicity of my heart, I still believed when I wrote my "Confessions." (R)

taught the public to mistrust the Holbachian clique. When I went to the Hermitage, they predicted, with their usual self-assurance, that I should not stop there for three months. When they saw that I stopped twenty, and that, when obliged to leave it, I still remained in the country, they declared that it was pure obstinacy: that I was wearying myself to death in my retirement; but that, eaten up with pride, I preferred to die there, the victim of my own obstinacy, rather than to give in and return to Paris. The letter to D'Alembert breathed a gentleness of soul which it was easy to see was not pretended. If I had been devoured by ill-humour in my retreat, it would have made itself felt in the style of the letter. It showed itself in all the writings which I had written at Paris: it ceased to show itself in the first work which I had written in the country. For those who are capable of observing, this indication was decisive. They saw that I had returned to my proper element.

Nevertheless, this same work, full of gentleness though it was, owing to my awkwardness and my usual ill-luck, made me another enemy in the literary world. At M. de la Poplinière's I had made the acquaintance of Marmontel, and this acquaintance had been kept up at the Baron's. At that time Marmontel was editor of the *Mercure de France*. As I was too proud to send my works to those who wrote for the newspapers, and yet wanted to send him this, without letting him think that it was meant for him in his editorial capacity, or that I desired a notice of it in the *Mercure*, I wrote upon the copy, which I sent him, that it was not intended for the writer of the *Mercure*, but for M. Marmontel. I thought that I was paying him a very graceful compliment; but he appeared to see in it a deadly insult, and became my irreconcilable enemy. He wrote a polite article against my letter, but with evident bitterness; and from that time, he missed no opportunity of injuring me in society and of indirectly attacking me in his works. So difficult is it to manage the irritable *amour-propre* of literary men, and such great care is necessary, in paying them compliments, to leave nothing which can even be suspected of a double meaning.

[1759.] – Thus freed from all anxiety, I employed my leisure and independence in resuming my literary occupations with greater regularity. I finished "Julie" in the winter, and sent it to Rey, who had it printed in the following year. However, my work was again interrupted by a trifling, but rather unpleasant incident. I heard that arrangements were being made at the Opera for a reproduction of the *Devin du Village*. Highly indignant at the idea of these people so arrogantly claiming the right to dispose of my property, I again took up the memorial which I had sent to M. d'Argenson, to which I had received no reply; and having revised it, I sent it by M. Sellon, together with a letter which he was kind enough to take charge of, to M. le Comte de Saint-Florentin, who had succeeded M. d'Argenson in the management of the Opera. Duclos, whom I informed of what I had done, spoke of it to the "little violins," who offered to give me back, not my Opera, but my free pass, which was no longer of any use to me. Seeing that I could not hope for justice from any quarter, I gave up the affair; and the directors of the Opera, without either replying or listening to my arguments, continued to make what use they pleased of the *Devin*, which incontestably belongs to me alone,* as if it had been their own property, and to draw profits from it.

Since I had shaken off the yoke of my tyrants, I led a tolerably even and peaceful life; deprived of the charm of two strong attachments, I was also free from the weight of their chains. Disgusted with patronising friends, who wanted to have the absolute disposal of my destiny and to make me the slave of their pretended benefits in spite of myself, I was resolved for the future to keep to connections formed by simple goodwill, which, without putting any restraint upon perfect freedom, constitute the enjoyment of life, and are founded upon a footing of complete equality. I had sufficient connections of this kind to be able to taste the pleasures of society, without being obliged to submit to dependence upon it; and, as soon as I had tried this manner of life, I felt that it was most suitable to my age, to end my days in peace, far beyond the reach of the storms, quarrels, and annoyances by which I had recently been almost swamped.

* It now belongs to them by virtue of a fresh agreement made between us quite recently. (R)

During my stay at the Hermitage, and since my settlement at
Montmorency, I have made some agreeable acquaintances in the
neighbourhood, to whom I felt under no obligations. At the
head of these was young Loyseau de Mauléon, who was just
beginning his career at the Bar, but did not know what position
he would take. I had no such doubts as he had. I soon marked
out for him a brilliant career, which has culminated in his present
position. I predicted to him that, if he was rigidly careful in his
choice of cases, and always defended the cause of justice and
virtue, his talents, elevated by these lofty sentiments, would
make him the equal of the greatest orators. He has followed
my advice, and has felt the benefit of it. His defence of M. de
Portes is worthy of Demosthenes. He was in the habit of coming
every year to spend his vacations at Saint-Brice, a quarter of a
league from the Hermitage, in the fief of Mauléon, which
belonged to his mother, and where the great Bossuet had formerly lived. It is a fief, in which a succession of such proprietors
would render it difficult to keep up the old nobility.

Another of my friends, in the same village, was Guérin the
bookseller, a man of wit, learning, and amiable character, and in
the first rank of his business. Through him I made the acquaintance of Jean Néaulme, an Amsterdam bookseller, his friend and
correspondent, who afterwards printed "Émile." Nearer than
Saint-Brice, I had M. Maltor, *curé* of Grosley, more fitted to be a
minister and statesman than a village *curé*, who should at least
have had the administration of a diocese, if places were
bestowed according to ability. He had been secretary to the
Comte du Luc, and had known Jean Baptiste Rousseau intimately. As full of esteem for the memory of that illustrious exile
as of loathing for that of the rascal Saurin who had ruined him,
he knew a number of curious anecdotes about both, which
Seguy had not inserted in the as yet unprinted life of the former;
and he assured me that the Comte du Luc, far from ever having
had reason to complain of him, had preserved the warmest
friendship for him to the end of his life. M. Maltor, upon
whom M. de Vintimille had bestowed this comfortable retreat
after the death of his patron, had been formerly employed in
several affairs, of which, in spite of his years, he still had a vivid

recollection, and which he discussed very sensibly. His conversation, as instructive as it was amusing, in no way reminded one of a village *curé*: he combined the air of a man of the world with the learning of a student. Of all my permanent neighbours, he was the one whose society was the most agreeable to me, and whom I left with the greatest regret.

At Montmorency I had the members of the Oratory; amongst others Father Berthier, professor of physics, to whom I became attached, owing to a certain air of geniality which I discovered in him, in spite of a slight dash of pedantry. I found it difficult, however, to reconcile this excessive simplicity with his eagerness and adroitness in thrusting himself everywhere; amongst the great, the ladies, the devotees, and the philosophers. He knew how to be all things to all men. I found great pleasure in his society. I spoke of him to everybody; and what I said apparently went back to him. One day he thanked me, with a grin, for having found him a good fellow. There appeared to me something sardonic in his smile, which totally altered his features in my eyes, and which I have often thought of since then. This smile may be most fitly compared to that of Panurge, when buying Dindenaut's sheep. Our acquaintance had commenced soon after my arrival at the Hermitage, where he frequently came to see me. I was already settled at Montmorency, when he left to return to Paris. He often saw Madame le Vasseur there. One day, when nothing was further from my thoughts, he wrote me a letter on her behalf, to inform me that Grimm had offered to support her, and to ask my permission to accept the offer. I heard that he offered her an allowance of 300 *livres*, on condition that she went to live at Deuil, between La Chevrette and Montmorency. I will not describe the impression which this information produced upon me: it would have been less surprising if Grimm had had an income of 10,000 *livres*, or any more intelligible connection with this woman, and if it had not been considered such a crime on my part to have taken her into the country, to which he was now inclined to take her back, as if she had grown younger since then. I understood that the good old lady only asked this permission, which she could easily have dispensed with if I had refused it, in order not to run the risk of losing what she received from me. Although this exhibition of charity on the part of Grimm appeared to me very extraordinary, it did not strike me so much at the time as it did afterwards. But, even if I had known all that I have since found out, I should have given my consent just the same as I did, and was obliged to do, unless I had been prepared to outbid Grimm. From that time, Father Berthier somewhat cured me of the belief in his geniality, which had seemed to him so amusing, and of which I had so thoughtlessly accused him.

This same Father Berthier enjoyed the acquaintance of two persons, who, for some unknown reason, also sought mine: for there was certainly very little sympathy between their tastes and my own. They were children of Melchisedec,[1] whose country and family no one knew – probably, not even their real names. They were Jansenists, and passed for priests in disguise – perhaps in consequence of their absurd fashion of wearing long swords, by which they set great store. The prodigious secrecy which marked all their proceedings gave them the appearance of party-chiefs, and I have always felt convinced that they managed the *Gazette Ecclésiastique*. One of them, tall, benevolent, and wheedling, was named M. Ferrand; the other, short, dumpy, sneering, and punctilious, was named M. Minard. They called each other cousin. They lived at Paris with D'Alembert in his nurse's house; and had taken a small house at Montmorency, where they spent their summers. They managed for themselves, without servant or messenger. They took it in turns each week to go to market, do the cooking, and sweep the house. They were pretty comfortable, and we sometimes had our meals together. I do not know what made them care about me: the only thing I cared about in them was, that they played chess; and, for the sake of a poor little game, I endured four hours of weariness. As they wanted to poke their noses in everywhere, Thérèse called them "the gossips," and this name stuck to them at Montmorency.

Such, together with my landlord, M. Mathas, who was a worthy fellow, were my chief country acquaintances. I still had a sufficient number at Paris to make it pleasant for me to live there, whenever I might wish, outside the circle of literary men,

[1] *i.e.*, persons of whom nothing is known.

amongst whom I could reckon no friend except Duclos. Deleyre was too young: and although, upon a closer acquaintance with the intrigues of the philosophical clique against me, he had detached himself from it altogether – or, at least, I thought so – I was not yet able to forget the readiness he had shown in making himself the speaking-trumpet of the whole tribe.

In the first place, I had my old and worthy friend, M. Roguin. He was a friend of the good old times, whose friendship I did not owe to my writings, but to my own merits; and for this reason I have always preserved that friendship. I had the worthy Lenieps, my fellow-countryman, and his daughter, Madame Lambert, who was alive at the time. I had a young Genevese named Coindet, who seemed to me a good fellow, careful, obliging, and zealous, but ignorant, credulous, gluttonous, and presuming; he came to see me immediately after I had gone to live at the Hermitage, and, acting as his own introducer, soon established himself on a firm footing, in spite of me. He had some taste for drawing, and was acquainted with several artists. I found him useful for the illustrations of "Julie"; he undertook to see after the drawings and plates, and executed his commission very successfully.

M. Dupin's house was open to me; and although the society to be met there was less brilliant than in Madame Dupin's best days, it was still one of the best houses in Paris, owing to the distinguished qualities of its heads, and the select company which assembled there. As I had always preferred them to all others, and had only left them in order to be independent, they had never ceased to regard me with friendship, and I was always sure of a welcome from Madame Dupin. I could even reckon her as one of my country neighbours, since they had set up an establishment at Clichy, where I sometimes spent a day or two; and I should have gone there oftener, if Madame Dupin and Madame Chenonceaux had been on more friendly terms. But the difficulty of dividing my attentions in the same house between two women who had no sympathy with each other, made my position at Clichy too constrained. Being on more equal and familiar terms with Madame Chenonceaux, I had the pleasure of enjoying her society with less restraint at Deuil, close to my doors, where she had taken a little house, and even at my own place, where she came to see me pretty frequently.

Another of my friends was Madame de Créqui, who had devoted herself to a religious life, and had given up the society of D'Alembert, Marmontel, and most literary men, with the exception, I believe, of the Abbé Trublet, who at that time was a sort of canting hypocrite, of whom she herself was tolerably weary. I, whose society she had sought, did not lose her good-will, and always kept up a correspondence with her. She sent me some fat pullets from Le Mans as a new year's present; and she had made up her mind to come and see me in the following year, when a journey undertaken by Madame de Luxembourg at the same time interfered with her plans. I owe her a place by herself; she will always hold a prominent place in my recollections.

I also had a friend who deserves the next place after Roguin; my old colleague De Carrio, formerly nominal secretary to the Spanish embassy at Venice, afterwards in Sweden, where his Court appointed him *chargé d'affaires*, who had since become the actual secretary to the embassy in Paris. He surprised me at Montmorency when I least expected it. He was decorated with some Spanish order, the name of which I forget, and wore a splendid cross of precious stones. He had been obliged, in his proofs of ancestry, to add another letter to his name, and now called himself the Chevalier de Carrion. I found him just the same – the same excellent heart, and a mind that developed greater amiability day by day. I should have resumed my former intimacy with him, had not Coindet, thrusting himself between us in his usual fashion, taken advantage of my distance from Paris to worm himself into my place, and, in my name, into his confidence, and to supplant me, from his excessive eagerness to serve me.

The recollection of Carrion reminds me of one of my country neighbours, whom it would be the more unpardonable on my part to omit to mention, as I have to confess myself guilty of an inexcusable wrong towards him. This was the worthy M. le Blond, who had rendered me considerable services at Venice; and who, after making a journey in France with his family, had taken a country house at La Briche, not far from

Montmorency.* As soon as I heard that he was my neighbour, in the joy of my heart I went to call upon him, more as a pleasure than a duty. I set out the very next day. I met some people who were coming to see me, and I was obliged to turn back with them. Two days afterwards I set out again; he had gone to dine in Paris with all his family. The third time I called, he was at home: I heard women's voices, and saw at the door a carriage which alarmed me. I wished to see him, at any rate for the first time, without interruption, and to talk over our old acquaintance. In short, I put off my visit from one day to another, until at last my shame at deferring so long the fulfilment of such a duty prevented me from fulfilling it at all: having dared to wait so long, I no longer dared to show myself. This neglect, at which M. le Blond was justly indignant, made my idleness appear ingratitude; and yet, in my heart, I felt myself so little to blame, that, if I had been able to afford him any real pleasure, even unknown to him, I am sure that he would not have found me slow in doing so. But indolence, carelessness, and delay in the performance of trifling duties, have always been more prejudicial to me than great vices. My worst faults have been those of omission; I have seldom done what I ought not to have done, but, unfortunately, I have still less often done what I ought to have done.

Since I have returned to the acquaintances I made at Venice, I ought not to forget one which is connected with them, and which has lasted much longer than the rest. I refer to M. de Jonville, who, since his return from Genoa, had continued to show his friendship for me in many ways. He was very fond of my society, and liked to talk about Italian affairs and the mad folly of M. de Montaigu, concerning whom he had heard several characteristic anecdotes through his connection with the Foreign Office. I was also glad to meet at his house my old comrade Dupont, who had bought a commission in his province, and was sometimes obliged to visit Paris on business. M. de Jonville gradually showed such fondness for my society, that it became somewhat irksome; and, although we lived at a great distance from each other, it created a disturbance, if I let a

* When writing this, full of my usual blind confidence, I was far from suspecting the real reason and result of this journey to Paris. (R)

week pass without going to dine with him. When he went to Jonville, he always wanted to take me with him; but after I had once spent a week there, which seemed interminably long, I had no desire to go there again. He was certainly an honourable man and an agreeable companion, even amiable in certain respects, but he had little intellectual capacity; he was handsome, somewhat proud of his personal appearance, and tolerably wearisome. He had a singular collection, perhaps unique of its kind, to which he devoted a great deal of his attention, and in which he also endeavoured to interest his friends, who sometimes found less amusement in it than he did. This was a very complete collection of all the Court and Parisian vaudevilles of the last fifty years, in which many anecdotes were to be found, which it would have been useless to look for elsewhere. There is a collection of Memoirs for the History of France, which would scarcely be thought of in any other nation.

One day, while we were on the best of terms, he gave me so cold and freezing a reception, so little after his usual manner, that, after I had given him an opportunity of explanation, and even begged him to give me one, I left his house, resolved never to set foot in it again, and I kept my resolution; for I am rarely seen again where I have once been ill received, and here there was no Diderot to plead for M. de Jonville. In vain I puzzled my brains to discover how I had offended him; I could think of nothing. I felt certain that I had never spoken of him or his except in terms of the greatest respect, for I was sincerely attached to him; and, besides that I had nothing but good to say of him, it has always been my inviolable principle, never to speak of the houses at which I visited in other than respectful terms.

At length, after long pondering, I arrived at the following conjecture. The last time that we had seen each other, he had invited me to supper at the rooms of some girls with whom he was acquainted, together with two or three Foreign Office clerks, very worthy fellows, who had neither the manner nor the appearance of libertines; and I can swear that, for my part, I spent the evening in melancholy reflections upon the unhappy lot of these poor creatures. I did not contribute towards the expenses, because M. de Jonville gave the supper; and I gave the girls nothing, because I did not give them the chance of earning the present which I might have been able to offer them. We left together, in high spirits and on the best of terms. Without having paid another visit to the girls, three or four days afterwards, I went to dine with M. de Jonville, whom I had not seen since. It was on this occasion that he received me in the manner I have mentioned. As I could not attribute it to anything else but some misunderstanding in reference to the supper, and as I saw that he was not disposed to offer an explanation, I made up my mind and gave up visiting him. I continued, however, to send him my works, and he often sent me his compliments. One evening, when I met him in the *foyer* of the Comedy, he politely reproached me for not going to see him; but this did not make me return to him. Thus the whole affair had the appearance of a fit of sulkiness rather than a regular rupture. However, as I never saw him again, and never heard anything more of him since that time, it would have been too late, after our intercourse had been broken off for several years, to renew the acquaintance. This is the reason why I do not here mention M. de Jonville in my list, although I had for a long time been a visitor at his house.

I will not swell this same list with the names of other less intimate acquaintances, or of those with whom, in consequence of my absence, I had gradually become less intimate, although I still sometimes saw them in the country, either at my own or my neighbours' houses, such, for instance, as the Abbés de Condillac and de Mably, MM. de Mairan, de Lalive, de Boisgelou, Watelet, Ancelet, and others whom it would be tedious to mention. I will just mention, in passing, M. de Margency, the King's chamberlain, a former member of the Holbachian clique, which, like myself, he had left, and an old friend of Madame d'Epinay, whom, in this also like myself, he had given up; lastly, his friend Desmahis, the famous but soon-forgotten author of the comedy called *L'Impertinent*. The former was my country neighbour, his estate at Margency being close to Montmorency. We were old acquaintances; but our nearness to each other and a certain similarity in our experiences brought us still closer together. The latter died shortly afterwards. He was a man of wit and ability; but he in some respects resembled the original of his comedy, being a bit of a coxcomb with the ladies, by whom his loss was not particularly regretted.

I cannot, however, leave unnoticed a fresh correspondence, which began at that time, and which has had too much influence upon the remainder of my life for me to omit to indicate its origin. I am speaking of M. de Lamoignon de Malesherbes, first President of the Excise Office, who at this time was censor of published books, an office which he filled with equal intelligence and mildness, to the complete satisfaction of literary men. I had not even visited him in Paris; but I had always met with the most courteous civility from him, in matters connected with the censorship; and I knew that, on more than one occasion, he had severely rebuked those who were in the habit of writing against me. In reference to the printing of "Julie," he gave me fresh proofs of his kindness: the cost of postage from Amsterdam of the proof sheets of a work of such size was considerable; and, as all communications were sent to him post free, he allowed them to be addressed to him, and he forwarded them on to me, franked by his father the Chancellor. When the work was printed, he did not allow it to be sold in the kingdom until an edition had been sold, the profits of which he insisted that I should take, notwithstanding my opposition. As acceptance on my part would have been a fraud upon Rey, to whom I had sold my manuscript, I not only refused to accept the present, which was intended for me, without his consent, which he very generously gave, but I wanted to share with him the 100 *pistoles* to which it amounted; but he refused to accept anything. These 100 *pistoles* caused me the annoyance, for which M. de Malesherbes had not prepared me, of seeing my work fearfully mutilated, and prevented the sale of the good edition until the bad was exhausted.

I have always considered M. de Malesherbes as a man of unassailable uprightness. Nothing that has ever occurred has made me doubt his honesty for a moment; but since his weakness is as great as his honour, he sometimes injures those, in whom he takes an interest, by his efforts to protect them. He not only ordered more than a hundred pages of the Paris edition to be cut out, but he mutilated the copy of the good edition which he sent to Madame de Pompadour, in a manner which deserved to be called a breach of faith. I have said somewhere in this work, that a coal-heaver's wife is more worthy of respect than the mistress of a Prince. This phrase had occurred to me in the fervour of composition, and I swear that no personal allusion was intended. On reading the work over again, I saw that others would certainly see one. However, I would not strike out the phrase, in accordance with my very injudicious principle of leaving nothing out, because it might be considered to contain some personal allusion, provided my conscience assured me that nothing of the kind had been intended when I wrote it; and I contented myself with substituting the word "Prince" for "King," which I had at first written. This alteration did not satisfy M. de Malesherbes; he suppressed the whole sentence in a fresh sheet, which he had printed on purpose and glued in as neatly as possible in Madame de Pompadour's copy. She did not remain in ignorance of this piece of jugglery: some worthy souls were kind enough to inform her of it. I myself did not hear of it until some time afterwards, when I began to feel the consequences.

Is not this also the origin of the secret but implacable hatred of another lady whose case was similar, without my knowing anything of it, and with whom I was not even acquainted when I wrote the passage? When the book was published, the acquaintance was made, and I felt very uneasy. I told the Chevalier de Lorenzi, who laughed at me, and said that the lady in question felt so little offended, that she had not even taken any notice of it. I believed it, perhaps rather too readily, and regained my calmness at a very inopportune moment.

At the beginning of winter, I received a further mark of M. de Malesherbes' kindness, which I greatly appreciated, although I did not consider it advisable to take advantage of it. There was a place vacant on the *Journal des Savants*; Margency wrote to offer it to me, as if on his own initiative. But it was easy for me to see, from the style of his letter (Packet C, No. 33), that he was acting under instructions and authority; and he himself in a subsequent letter (Packet C, No. 47) gave me to understand that he had been commissioned to make the offer. The work was trifling; it consisted of two extracts a month, to be made from books which were to be brought to me, so that there would never be any need for me to go to Paris, not even to pay a visit of thanks to the magistrate. This gave me admission into the society of literary men of the first rank, MM. de Mairan, Clairaut, de Guignes, and the Abbé Barthélemy. I was already acquainted with the first two, and I looked forward with pleasure to making the acquaintance of the last two. Lastly, for this by no means laborious work, which I could easily perform, I was to receive a honorarium of 800 *francs*. I deliberated a few hours before deciding, and I can swear that the only reason for my hesitation was the fear of annoying Margency and displeasing M. de Malesherbes. But, at length, the insupportable restraint of not being able to work when I pleased, and of being tied to time, and, still more, the certainty of inefficiently performing the duties which I should have been obliged to undertake, prevailed over all, and made me decide to refuse a post for which I was not adapted. I knew that my talent consisted entirely in a certain lively interest in the subjects which I had to treat, and that nothing but the love of the great, the true, and the beautiful, could enliven my genius. What would the contents of the different books, from which I should have had to make extracts, or even the books themselves, have mattered to me? My indifference to the whole thing would have frozen my pen and deadened my mind. It was thought that I could write according to the rules of a trade, like all other literary men, whereas I have never been able to write except from inspiration. That was certainly not the kind of thing that was wanted for the *Journal des Savants*. I accordingly wrote a letter of thanks to Margency, couched in the politest terms possible, in which I explained my reasons so fully, that neither he nor M. de Malesherbes can possibly have believed that ill temper or pride had anything to do with my refusal. They both approved of it; it made no alteration in their friendship for me, and the secret was so well kept, that the public never got the least scent of it.

The proposal was not made at a favourable moment for me to accept it; for I had for some time intended to abandon literature altogether, especially the profession of an author. All that had just occurred had completely disgusted me with literary men, and I had cause to feel that it was impossible for me to pursue the same career, without coming into contact with them. I was equally disgusted with men of the world, and, in general, with the mixed life which I had recently led, half by myself, and half in society for which I was utterly unfitted. I felt more than ever, from constant experience, that all association on unequal terms is always prejudicial to the weaker party. Living with wealthy people, who belonged to a different state of life from that which I had chosen, without keeping house as they did, I was nevertheless obliged to imitate them in many respects; and certain petty expenses, which were nothing to them, were for me as ruinous as they were indispensable. If another man goes to visit at a country-house, he is waited upon by his lackey, at table as well as in his room; he sends him to fetch whatever he wants; without coming directly into contact with the servants of the house, perhaps not even seeing them, he only gives them a gratuity whenever and as it pleases him; whereas I, alone, without a servant of my own, was at the mercy of the people of the house, whose good graces it was absolutely necessary to gain, if I did not want to suffer many annoyances; and, being treated as their master's equal, I was obliged to treat his servants accordingly, and even to do more for them than anyone else, because, in fact, I had much greater need of their services. Where there are only few servants, this is not a matter of such importance; but, in the houses at which I visited, they were very numerous, all very uppish, great rascals, and keenly alive – to their own interests; and the rascals knew how to manage so that I needed the services of each of them in turn. The women of Paris, with all their wit and intelligence, are entirely wrong in their ideas upon this point; and, in their anxiety to save my purse, they ruined me. If I went out to supper a little distance from home, instead of letting me send for a coach, the lady of the house ordered her horses to be put to to drive me back; she was delighted to spare me the expense of the carriage, twenty-four *sous*; but she never thought of the crown which I gave the footman and coachman. If a lady wrote to me from Paris to the Hermitage or Montmorency, in order to spare me the four *sous* for postage, she sent the letter by one of her servants, who made the journey on foot and arrived bathed in perspiration, and I had to give him a crown and a dinner, which he had certainly well earned. If she invited me to stay a week or a fortnight at her country-house, she said to herself: Anyhow, it will be a saving for the poor fellow; he will not have to pay for his food while he is here. She forgot that, during that time, I did no work; that my rent, household expenses, washing, and clothes, still had to be paid for; that it cost me twice as much for my barber, and that it was more expensive for me to live in her house than at home. Although I limited my trifling gratuities to the houses in which I was in the habit of staying, they were none the less ruinous to me. I am convinced that it cost me more than twenty-five crowns at Madame d'Houdetot's house at Eaubonne, where I only slept four or five times, and more than a hundred *pistoles* at Épinay and La Chevrette, during the five or six years in which I was a constant visitor there. These expenses are unavoidable for a man of my disposition, who does not know how to do anything for himself or to set his wits to work upon anything, who cannot endure the sight of a lackey who grumbles and performs his duties sulkily. Even at Madame Dupin's, where I was one of the family, and where I rendered many services to the servants, I never received any from them unless I paid for them on the nail.[1] Subsequently I was obliged altogether to discontinue these trifling gratuities, which my position no longer allowed me to give; and then it was that I felt even more keenly the disadvantage of associating with persons in a different station of life to one's own.

Again, if this life had been to my taste, I should have felt consoled for the heavy expenditure on my pleasures; but I could not endure to ruin myself, simply for the sake of becoming utterly wearied; and I had felt so strongly the burden of this manner of life, that, taking advantage of the interval of freedom which I then enjoyed, I determined to make it lasting, to renounce fashionable and literary society altogether, to give up

[1] *À la pointe de mon argent*: lit., I never received any from them except at the point of – my money.

writing books, and to confine myself for the remainder of my days to the limited and peaceful sphere for which I felt that I was born.

The profits of the "Letter to D'Alembert" and the "New Héloïse" had somewhat improved the state of my finances, which had been almost exhausted at the Hermitage. I saw about 1,000 crowns in prospect. "Émile," to which I seriously began to devote my attention after I had finished "Héloïse," was well advanced, and I expected that its profits would at least double that sum. I formed the resolution of investing this fund in such a manner as to bring me in a small annuity, which, together with my copying, would be sufficient to keep me without writing any more. I still had two works in hand. The first was my "Institutions politiques." I examined the state of this work, and found that it would still require several years of labour. I had not the courage to continue it and to wait until it was finished, before carrying out my resolution. I accordingly abandoned it, and decided to extract what was possible, and to burn the rest; and, pushing on this work vigorously, without discontinuing "Émile," in less than two years I put the finishing touch to the "Contrat Social."

There still remained the "Dictionnaire de Musique." This was a purely mechanical work which could be taken up at any time, and which I had undertaken merely for the sake of the money. I reserved to myself the right of abandoning it, or finishing it at my leisure, according as my other combined resources might render it necessary or superfluous. In regard to the "Morale sensitive," of which I had only made an outline, I abandoned it altogether.

As my last intention, if I could dispense with copying altogether, was to remove to a distance from Paris, where the constant stream of visitors made it expensive for me to live, and deprived me of the time to make provision for myself, I kept in reserve, in order to prevent in my retirement the feeling of weariness which is said to come upon an author when he has laid down his pen, an occupation which might fill up the void in my solitude, without leading me into the temptation of publishing anything more during my lifetime. I do not know what whim had prompted Rey, for a long time past, to urge me to write the Memoirs of my life. Although, as far as incidents were concerned, they were not at that time particularly interesting, I felt that they might be made so by the candour with which I was capable of treating the subject; and I was determined to make it a work unique of its kind, by an unexampled veracity, which, for once at least, would enable the outside world to behold a man as he really was in his inmost self. I had always ridiculed the false ingenuousness of Montaigne, who, while pretending to confess his defects, is most careful to attribute to himself only such as are amiable; whereas I, who have always believed, and still believe, myself to be, all things considered, the best of men, felt that there is no human heart, however pure it may be, which does not conceal some odious vice. I knew that I was represented in the world under features so utterly different from my own, and sometimes so distorted, that, in spite of my defects, none of which I had the least desire to conceal, I could not help being the gainer by showing myself in my true character. Besides, this was impossible without also showing others as they were, and consequently this work could not be published until after my own death and that of several others. This further emboldened me to write my Confessions, for which I shall never have to blush before anybody. I accordingly determined to devote my leisure to carrying out this undertaking, and I commenced to collect the letters and papers which might guide or assist my memory, greatly regretting all that I had torn up, burned, or lost, up to this time.

This project of complete retirement, one of the most sensible that I had ever formed, made a very strong impression on my mind, and I had already commenced to carry it out, when Heaven, which was preparing a different destiny for me, flung me into a fresh whirl of excitement.

Montmorency, the ancient and splendid patrimony of the family of that name, has been confiscated, and no longer belongs to it. Through the sister of Duc Henri, it has passed to the house of Condé, which has changed the name of Montmorency to Enghien; and the Duchy has no other château except an old tower, in which the archives are kept, and where the vassals come to render homage. But at Montmorency, or Enghien, may be seen a private house, built by Croiset (called *le pauvre*) which, equal in magnificence to the most superb château, deserves and bears the name of one. The imposing aspect of this fine building, the terrace upon which it stands, the view from it, which is perhaps unequalled in the world, its spacious *salon*, painted by a master-hand, its garden, laid out by the celebrated Le Nostre – all this forms a whole, the striking majesty of which nevertheless presents a certain simplicity, which arouses a lasting admiration. M. le Maréchal, Duc de Luxembourg, who at that time occupied the house, came twice every year into the district where his forefathers had formerly been masters, to spend five or six weeks as an ordinary inhabitant, but in great style, which in no way fell short of the old magnificence of his house. The first time he visited it, after I had settled at Montmorency, M. and Madame la Maréchale sent their compliments to me by a footman, and an invitation to sup with them whenever I pleased. Each time that they came again, they never failed to repeat their compliments and invitation. This reminded me of Madame de Beuzenval[1] sending me to dine in the servants' hall. Times were changed, but I was still the same. I had no desire to be sent to dine in the servants' hall, and I cared but little for the tables of the great. I should have preferred that they had left me for what I was, without making much of or humiliating me. I replied to M. and Madame de Luxembourg's civilities politely and respectfully, but I did not accept their invitations. My ill-health, as much as a natural shyness and awkwardness in conversation, made me shudder at the mere idea of presenting myself before an assembly of Court grandees; and I did not even go to the château to pay a complimentary visit of thanks, although I understood well enough that this was what they wanted, and that all their eagerness was due to curiosity more than goodwill.

Nevertheless, they continued to make advances, and even with greater persistency. Madame la Comtesse de Boufflers,[2] who was very intimate with Madame la Maréchale, had come to Montmorency. She sent to inquire after me, and asked whether

[1] [Mme de Beuzenval] See Book VII, p. 305.
[2] [Boufflers] See *Biographies*, p. 707.

she might pay me a visit. I replied politely, but did not stir. During the Easter visit of the following year (1759), the Chevalier de Lorenzi, who belonged to the suite of M. le Prince de Conti, and to Madame de Luxembourg's circle, came to visit me several times. We became acquainted; he pressed me to go to the château. I refused. At last, one afternoon, when I least expected it, I saw M. le Maréchal de Luxembourg[1] approaching, attended by five or six persons. There no longer remained any means of escape; and I could not, without being considered arrogant and ill-bred, avoid returning his visit, and paying my respects to Madame la Maréchale, on the part of whom he overwhelmed me with polite messages. Thus commenced, under fatal auspices, a connection which I could no longer escape, but which a presentiment, only too well founded, made me dread, until I found myself committed to it.

I was terribly afraid of Madame de Luxembourg. I knew that she was amiable. I had seen her several times at the theatre, and at Madame Dupin's ten or twelve years ago, when she was Duchesse de Boufflers, and was still in the first brilliancy of her beauty. But she had the reputation of being spiteful; and this, in so great a lady, made me tremble. No sooner did I see her than I was vanquished. I found her charming, with that charm which is proof against time, and is most calculated to act upon my heart. I expected to find her conversation sarcastic and full of epigrams. This was not the case; it was something far better. Her conversation does not sparkle with wit; it exhibits no flights of fancy, or even, properly speaking, *finesse*; but it is marked by an exquisite refinement, which is never striking, but is always pleasing. Her flatteries are the more intoxicating in proportion to their simplicity; it seems as if they fall from her lips without thinking, and are the overflowings of a heart which is too full. I fancied that I perceived, at my first visit, that, in spite of my awkward manner and clumsy phrases, she found my society agreeable. All Court ladies know how to produce this impression whenever they please, whether it be true or not; but all do not know, as Madame de Luxembourg did, how to produce it in so

[1] [Luxembourg] See *Biographies*, p. 712.

charming a manner, that one no longer thinks of doubting it. From the first day, my confidence in her would have been as complete as it soon afterwards became had not Madame la Duchesse de Montmorency, her daughter-in-law, a somewhat spiteful, and, as I believe, quarrelsome young fool, taken it into her head to attack me, and, in the midst of all her mamma's civilities and her own coquetries, made me suspect that they were only laughing at me.

I should, perhaps, have found it difficult to make myself easy in regard to this apprehension in the case of the two ladies, had not the very great kindness of M. le Maréchal convinced me that theirs also was genuine. Considering my timid disposition, nothing is more surprising than the readiness with which I took him at his word as to the footing of equality on which he wanted to put himself with me, except perhaps the equal readiness with which he himself took my word as to the complete independence in which I wanted to live. Convinced that I was right to be satisfied with my position and not to desire any change in it, neither he nor Madame de Luxembourg appeared for a moment to trouble themselves about my purse or my means. Although I could not doubt the warm interest which they both took in me, they never offered to find me a place or to assist me with their influence, except once, when Madame de Luxembourg seemed desirous that I should enter the Académie Française. I raised the objection of my religious faith; she said that that was no obstacle, or that, if it was one, she would undertake to remove it. I replied that, in spite of the great honour I should consider it, to be a member of so illustrious a body, as I had refused the invitation of M. de Tressan, and, in a manner, of the King of Poland, to enter the Académie of Nancy, I could not with propriety become a member of any other. Madame de Luxembourg did not press the matter further, and nothing more was said about it. The simplicity of intercourse with such great people, who could have done anything for me, since M. de Luxembourg was, and deserved to be, the special friend of the King, is in singular contrast with the continual fussiness, as troublesome as it was officious, of the patronising friends I had just left, and whose object was rather to humiliate than to serve me.

When M. le Maréchal had visited me at Mont-Louis, I had received him and his suite in my one room with a feeling of embarrassment; not because I was obliged to ask him to sit down in the middle of my dirty plates and broken jugs, but because my floor was rotten and falling to pieces, and I was afraid that the weight of his suite might make it give way altogether. Thinking less of my own danger than of that to which this worthy gentleman's affability exposed him, I hastened to get him out of it, by taking him, in spite of the weather, which was still very cold, to my tower, which was completely exposed and had no fireplace. When we were there, I told him the reason why I had brought him; he repeated it to Madame la Maréchale, and both pressed me to stay at the château until the floor had been repaired; or, if I preferred, at a detached building in the middle of the park, which was called the "little château." This enchanted abode deserves special mention.

The park or garden of Montmorency is not on a level, like that of La Chevrette. It is uneven, hilly, with alternate elevations and depressions, which the clever artist has taken advantage of to give variety to the groves, waters, decorations, and different views, and to multiply, so to speak, with the aid of genius and art, a space which in itself is somewhat confined. This park is crowned at the top by the terrace and the château; at the bottom, it forms a ravine, which opens and widens in the direction of the valley, the angle of which is filled by a large sheet of water. Between the orangery, which occupies this enlarged space, and this sheet of water surrounded by elevations adorned with groves and trees, is the little château of which I have spoken. This building and the ground which surrounds it formerly belonged to the celebrated Le Brun,[1] who amused himself with building and ornamenting it with the exquisite taste in architecture and decoration which this great painter had made his own. Since then, this château has been rebuilt, but after its first owner's designs. It is small, simple, but elegant. As it lies between the basin of the orangery and the large sheet of water, and is consequently exposed to the damp, it has been pierced in the middle by an open peristyle between two rows of columns,

[1] A celebrated French painter (1619–1690).

so that the air, blowing through the whole building, keeps it dry, notwithstanding its situation. On looking at this building from the opposite height in perspective, it appears completely surrounded by water, like an enchanted island, or the most beautiful of the three Borromean Islands, Isola Bella, in Lago Maggiore.

In this solitary building, I was offered the choice of one of the four complete apartments which it contains, in addition to the ground floor, which consists of a ball-room, a billiard-room, and a kitchen. I chose the smallest and simplest, above the kitchen, which I had as well. It was delightfully neat, with furniture in blue and white. In this profound and delightful solitude, in the midst of woods and waters, to the accompaniment of the songs of birds of every kind, surrounded by the perfumes of orange blossoms, I composed, in a continued state of ecstasy, the fifth book of "Émile," the fresh colouring of which is in great part due to the lively impression of the locality in which I wrote.

How eagerly I ran every morning at sunrise to breathe the perfumed air of the peristyle! What delicious *café au lait* I took there with my Thérèse! My cat and dog kept us company. This retinue alone would have been enough for my whole life; I should never have experienced a moment's weariness. I was in an earthly paradise; I lived there in the same state of innocence, and enjoyed the same happiness.

During their July visit, M. and Madame de Luxembourg showed me so many attentions, and treated me with such kindness, that, living in their house and overwhelmed by their civilities, I could not do less than repay it by visiting them frequently. I hardly left them at all: in the morning, I went to pay my respects to Madame la Maréchale; after dining there, I took a walk in the afternoon with M. le Maréchal; but I did not stay to supper, at which a number of great persons were always present; besides, they supped too late for me. Up to this time, all went on without a hitch, and no harm would have resulted, if I had known how to leave things alone. But I have never been able to preserve a mean in my friendships, and simply to fulfil the duties of society. I have always been everything or nothing. Soon I was everything: and finding myself made much of and spoiled by people of such importance, I overstepped the proper limits,

and conceived for them a friendship, which it is only allowable
to feel towards one's equals. I showed it by the familiarity which
I assumed in my manners, while they, on their part, never
abandoned the politeness to which they had accustomed me.
Yet I never felt quite at my ease with Madame la Maréchale.
Although not completely reassured as to her character, I feared
it less than her wit, of which I particularly stood in awe. I knew
that she was difficult to satisfy in conversation, and that she had
the right to be so. I knew that women, especially great ladies,
must be amused, and that it is better to offend them than to bore
them; and I judged, from her remarks upon the conversation of
the people who had just taken leave of her, what she must have
thought of *my* silly nonsense. I thought of an expedient to save
myself from the embarrassment of talking to her: this was, to
read to her. She had heard "Julie" spoken of; she knew that it
was being printed; she showed an eagerness to see the work; I
offered to read it to her, and she consented. I went to her every
morning at ten o'clock: M. de Luxembourg came, and the door
was shut. I read by the side of her bed, and portioned out my
readings so well, that they would have lasted throughout her
stay, even if it had not been interrupted.* The success of this
expedient surpassed my expectations. Madame de Luxembourg
took a violent fancy to "Julie" and its author; she spoke of
nothing but me, thought of nothing but me, flattered me the
whole of the day, and embraced me ten times a day. She insisted
that I should always sit by her at table, and when any great
noblemen wanted to take this place, she told them that it
belonged to me, and made them sit somewhere else. It is easy
to imagine the impression which these charming manners
produced upon me, who am subjugated by the slightest
marks of affection. I became sincerely attached to her, in
proportion to the attachment which she showed for me. My
only fear, when I perceived this infatuation, was that, as I felt I
was not sufficiently agreeable to keep it alive, it might change to
disgust, and, unfortunately for me, this fear was only too well
founded.

* The loss of a great battle, which greatly afflicted the King, obliged M. de
Luxembourg to return suddenly to Court. (R)

There must have been a natural opposition between her turn of mind and my own, since, independently of the many stupid and injudicious remarks which every moment escaped me in the course of conversation, and even in my letters, and when I was on the best of terms with her, there were certain things which displeased her, without my being able to imagine the reason. I will only mention one instance out of twenty. She knew that I was making a copy of "Héloïse" for Madame d'Houdetot, at so much a page; she wanted me to make one for her on the same terms. I promised to do so; and, consequently, entering her name as one of my customers, I wrote her a few lines of polite thanks, or, at least, I had intended them as such. I received the following answer, which utterly astonished me (Packet C, No. 43):

"VERSAILLES, *Tuesday*.

"I am delighted, I am satisfied; your letter has given me infinite pleasure; I hasten to inform you and to thank you for it.

"Here are the exact words of your letter: 'Although you are certainly a very good customer, I feel some difficulty about taking your money; properly speaking, I ought to pay for the pleasure of being permitted to work for you.' I will not mention the subject again. I regret that you do not tell me more about the state of your health. Nothing interests me more. I love you with all my heart; and, I assure you, it is with great sorrow that I write this to you for it would be a great pleasure to me to tell it to you by word of mouth. M. de Luxembourg loves you and embraces you in all sincerity."

On receiving this letter, I hastened to reply to it before examining it more fully, in order to protest against any impolite interpretation; and, after having devoted several days to this examination with a feeling of uneasiness which may be imagined, without being able to understand what was the matter, I wrote the following note as a final answer on the subject:

"MONTMORENCY, *December 8th*, 1759.

"Since writing my letter, I have examined the passage in question hundreds and hundreds of times. I have considered it in its own natural meaning, I have considered it in every meaning that could be put upon it, and I confess, Madame la Maréchale, that I am at a loss to know whether it is I who owe you excuses or whether it is not rather yourself who owe them to me."

It is now ten years since these letters were written. I have often thought of them since then: and, even to this day, I am so stupid on this point, that I have not been able to understand what she could find in the passage in question that was, I will not say offensive, but even calculated to cause her displeasure.

In reference to this manuscript of "Héloïse," which Madame de Luxembourg wanted to have, I ought to mention here what I had intended to do, in order to give it some special distinction above all the rest. I had written the adventures of Lord Edward separately, and I had long been undecided whether I should insert them, either wholly or in extracts, in this work, in which they seemed to me to be out of place. I finally decided to cut them out altogether, because, not being in keeping with the tone of the remainder, they would have spoiled its touching simplicity. I had a weightier reason, when I made the acquaintance of Madame de Luxembourg. In these adventures there was a Roman Marchioness of very odious character, some features of which, without being applicable to her, might perhaps have been applied to her by those who only knew her by reputation. I therefore congratulated myself upon the resolution I had taken, and determined to keep to it. But, being extremely desirous of enriching her copy with something which was not contained in any others, I was misguided enough to think of these unfortunate adventures, and I formed the plan of making a selection of them and adding it to the work – a mad project, the extravagance of which can only be explained by the blind fatality which was dragging me to my destruction. *Quos vult perdere Jupiter dementat.*[1]

I was foolish enough to make this extract with great care and labour, and to send it to her as if it had been the most beautiful thing in the world, at the same time informing her, as was true, that I had burnt the original, that the extract was intended for her alone, and would never be seen by anybody, unless she herself showed it; and this action on my part, far from proving to her my prudence and discretion, as I expected, only gave her an idea of the opinion which I myself held as to the application of the features of the work, by which she might have felt

[1] "Those whom Jupiter wishes to destroy, he [first] makes mad". This famous tag is thought to belong to a lost Greek tragedy.

offended. My imbecility was so great, that I entertained no doubt that she would be enchanted by what I had done. She did not compliment me upon it as heartily as I expected, and, to my very great surprise, never spoke to me of the manuscript which I had sent her. I myself, delighted with my conduct in the matter, did not suspect till long afterwards, in consequence of other indications, the effect which it had produced.

In regard to her manuscript, I had another idea, which was more sensible, but which, in its remoter effects, was almost equally prejudicial to me. So greatly does everything assist the work of destiny, when it summons a man to misfortune. I thought of ornamenting this manuscript with the drawings of the engravings of "Julie," which were of the same size as the manuscript. I asked Coindet for the drawings, to which I had every possible claim, the more so as I had allowed him the profits of the plates, which had a large sale. Coindet is as cunning as I am the reverse. My repeated requests for them at last made him understand for what purpose I wanted them. Then, under pretence of improving them, he induced me to leave them with him, and finally presented them himself. *Ego versiculos feci: tulit alter honores.*[1]

This introduced him to the Hôtel de Luxembourg and gave him a certain footing in it. After my removal to the little château, he frequently came to see me, and always in the morning, especially when M. and Madame de Luxembourg were at Montmorency. The consequence was that, in order to spend the day with him, I did not go to the château at all. I was reproached for these absences; I explained the reason. I was pressed to take M. Coindet with me; I did so. This was just what the rascal had been scheming for. Thus, thanks to the extraordinary kindness with which I was treated, M. Thélusson's clerk, who was sometimes invited to dine with his master when there were no other guests, suddenly found himself admitted to the table of a Marshal of France, and the company of Princes, Duchesses, and the highest personages of the Court. I shall never forget that, one day, when he was obliged to return to

[1] "I wrote the verses; another enjoyed the glory of them": a line attributed to Virgil.

Paris early, M. le Maréchal said to the company after dinner, "Let us walk along the road to Saint-Denis, then we can give M. Coindet our company." The poor fellow could not stand it: he lost his head completely. As for me, I felt so affected that I could not utter a word. I followed behind, weeping like a child, and longing to kiss the footprints of this good Maréchal. But the continuation of the history of this manuscript has made me anticipate events. Let me now take them up in their proper order, as far as my memory will allow me.

As soon as the little house at Mont-Louis was ready, I furnished it neatly and simply, and returned there to live, being unable to renounce the determination to which I had come when I left the Hermitage, namely, always to live in a place of my own: but neither could I make up my mind to give up my apartment in the little château. I kept the key of it, and in my fondness for the nice little breakfasts in the peristyle, I often slept there, and sometimes spent two or three days, as if it had been my country-house. I perhaps had more comfortable and agreeable apartments at that time than any private individual in Europe. My landlord, M. Mathas, who was the best fellow in the world, had left me the complete control of the repairs at Mont-Louis, and insisted that I should make use of his workmen as I pleased, without any interference on his part. I found means to make a complete suite of apartments out of a single room on the first floor, consisting of a bedroom, an antechamber, and a wardrobe. On the ground floor were the kitchen and Thérèse's room. The turret served as a study, after a glazed partition and a fire-place had been added. When I was there, I amused myself with decorating the terrace, which was already shaded by two rows of young lime-trees; I planted two more rows, in order to make a regular arbour; I had a table and some stone benches put there; I surrounded it with lilac, seringa and honeysuckle; I had a pretty border of flowers laid out, parallel to the two rows of trees; and this terrace, which was higher than that of the château, from which the view was at least as fine, and which was inhabited by a number of birds which I had tamed, served me as a kind of reception room, when I had company, such as M. and Madame de Luxembourg, M. le Duc de Villeroy, M. le Prince de Tingry, M. le Marquis de Armentières, Madame la Duchesse de Montmorency, Madame la Duchesse de Boufflers, Madame la Comtesse de Valentinois, Madame la Comtesse de Boufflers, and other persons of similar rank, who condescended to undertake, by a very fatiguing climb, the pilgrimage from the château to Mont-Louis. I owed the compliment of all these visits to M. and Madame de Luxembourg: I was sensible of this, and my heart rendered them the homage of gratitude. It was in one of my transports of emotion that I said to M. de Luxembourg, "Ah! M. le Maréchal, I used to hate the great before I knew you; and I hate them still more, since you have made me feel how easy it would be for them to make themselves adored." More than this, I put the question to all those who knew me during this period, whether they have ever observed that this brilliancy has dazzled me for a single moment, that the fumes of this incense have mounted to my head; whether they have seen me less uniform in my conduct, less simple in my manners, less affable towards the people, less familiar with my neighbours, less ready to assist everyone when I have had the power, without ever being offended by the numberless and frequently unreasonable importunities, with which I was incessantly overwhelmed. If my heart drew me towards the château of Montmorency, owing to my sincere attachment for its owners, it brought me back in the same manner to my own neighbourhood, to taste the sweets of that even and simple life, outside which there is no happiness for me. Thérèse had formed a friendship with the daughter of one of my neighbours, a bricklayer, named Pilleu: I did the same with the father, and, after having lunched at the château in the morning, not without some unwillingness, in order to please Madame la Maréchale, I eagerly returned in the evening to sup with the worthy Pilleu and his family, sometimes at his house, sometimes at mine.

Besides these two lodgings, I soon had a third at the Hôtel de Luxembourg, the owners of which pressed me so earnestly to go and see them sometimes, that I agreed, in spite of my aversion to Paris, where I had only been on the two occasions I have mentioned, after my retirement to the Hermitage; even then I only went on days that had been agreed upon beforehand, simply to supper, and returned the following morning. I entered and left by the garden adjoining the boulevard; so that I was enabled to say, with strict truth, that I had never set foot upon the pavement of Paris.

In the midst of this temporary prosperity, the catastrophe which was to mark the end of it was preparing in the distance. Shortly after my return to Mont-Louis, I made, in spite of myself as usual, a new acquaintance, which also marks an epoch in my history: whether for good or evil, will be afterwards seen. I refer to my neighbour, the Marquise de Verdelin, whose husband had just bought a country-house at Soisy, near Montmorency. Mademoiselle d'Ars, daughter of the Comte d'Ars, a man of position but poor, had married M. de Verdelin, old, ugly, deaf, harsh, brutal, jealous, covered with scars, and one-eyed; in other respects a good sort of fellow, when one knew how to take him, and possessed of an income of 15,000 to 20,000 *livres*, to which his wife's parents married her. This paragon of amiability, who swore, shouted, grumbled, stormed, and made his wife cry all day long, always ended by doing what she wanted, with the idea of putting her in a rage, seeing that she knew how to make him believe that it was he, and not she, who wanted it done. M. de Margency, of whom I have spoken, was Madame's friend, and became her husband's. Some years ago he had let to them his château of Margency, near Eaubonne and Ardilly, where they were living just at the time of my amour with Madame d'Houdetot. Madame de Verdelin and the latter had made each other's acquaintance through their mutual friend, Madame d'Aubeterre; and as the garden of Margency was on the road which Madame d'Houdetot had to take to get to Mont-Olympe, her favourite walk, Madame de Verdelin gave her a key, that she might go through the garden. Thanks to this key, I often went with her; but I was not fond of unexpected meetings; and when Madame de Verdelin happened to meet us, I left them together without saying a word, and walked on. This ungallant behaviour on my part could not have given her a very favourable impression of me. However, when she was at Soisy, she nevertheless sought my society. She came to see me several times at Mont-Louis, without finding me at home; and as I did not return her visit, she bethought herself of sending me some pots of flowers for my terrace, in order to force me to do so. I was obliged to go and thank her; that was enough; the acquaintance was made.

This connection was stormy at first, like all those which I made in spite of myself. It was never even really peaceful; Madame de Verdelin's turn of mind was too antipathetic to my own. She utters spiteful and epigrammatic remarks with such an air of simplicity, that it requires the closest attention, which is very fatiguing to me, to know when she is laughing at anybody. One instance of her silliness which I remember will be enough to give an idea of her manner. Her brother had just been appointed to the command of a frigate which was starting on a cruise against the English. I was speaking of the manner in which this frigate had been armed, without any injury to its speed. "Yes," said she, without changing her tone, "only as many cannon are taken as are wanted for fighting." I have rarely heard her say anything good of any of her absent friends without slipping in something against them. What she did not put a bad construction upon she turned into ridicule; her friend Margency was not excepted. Another thing which I found unendurable was the continual nuisance of her little messages, presents, and notes, which I was obliged to rack my brains to know how to answer, and which were always a source of fresh embarrassment, whether I had to write a letter of thanks or a refusal. However, from continually seeing her, I at last became attached to her. She, like myself, had her sorrows; our mutual confidences made our *tête-à-têtes* interesting. Nothing unites hearts so much as the pleasure of shedding tears together. We sought each other's society in order to console ourselves, and the need for this made me overlook much. I had shown such roughness in my outspokenness to her, and had sometimes shown so little respect for her character, that I really must have felt a great deal, to believe that she could sincerely pardon me. The following is a sample of the letters which I sometimes wrote to her, in regard to which it is worthy of notice that she never, in any of her answers, showed the least sign of annoyance:

"MONTMORENCY, *November 5th*, 1760.

"You inform me, madame, that you have not expressed yourself very well, in order to give me to understand that I have expressed myself very badly. You speak of your pretended stupidity, in order to make me sensible of my own. You boast of being nothing more than a 'good woman,' as if you were afraid of being taken at your word, and you make excuses to me in order to make me feel that I owe you some in return. Yes, madame, I know it well; it is I who am a fool, a 'good man,' and worse still, if it is possible. It is I who do not choose my terms sufficiently well to please a fine French lady, who pays as much attention to phrases and speaks as well as you do. But you must consider that I take them in the ordinary meaning of the language, without being familiar with the polite acceptations which are sometimes attached to them in the virtuous society of Paris. If my expressions are sometimes ambiguous, I endeavour, by my conduct, to give them a definite meaning," etc.

The remainder of the letter is after the same style. Her answer (Packet D, No. 41) will give an idea of the incredible self-restraint of a woman's heart, who can feel no greater resentment against such a letter than is shown in her reply, and than she herself has exhibited towards me. Coindet, bold and daring to the verge of effrontery, who was ever lying in wait for my friends, was not slow to introduce himself at Madame de Verdelin's in my name, and soon became, unknown to me, more intimate there than myself. This Coindet was a queer fellow. He introduced himself from me to all my acquaintances, made himself at home, and took his meals with them without ceremony. In his devoted zeal for me, he never spoke of me except with tears in his eyes; but, when he came to see me, he preserved the most profound silence about all these connections, and everything in which he knew I must feel interested. Instead of telling me what he had heard, said, or seen, which was of interest to me, he listened to me, and even asked me questions. He never knew anything about Paris except what I told him; in short, although everyone spoke to me of him, he never spoke to me of anybody. He was only close and mysterious with his friend. But let us leave Coindet and Madame de Verdelin for the present; we will return to them later.

Some time after my return to Mont-Louis, Latour, the painter, came to see me, and brought me my portrait in pastil, which he had exhibited some years before at the Salon. He had wanted to make me a present of it, but I had refused it. Madame d'Epinay, who had given me hers and wanted mine, had made me promise to ask him for it back. He had taken some time to touch it up. In the meantime, my rupture with Madame d'Epinay occurred. I gave her back her portrait, and, as I could no longer think of giving her mine, I hung it up in my room in the little château. M. de Luxembourg saw it there, and took a fancy to it. I offered it to him; he accepted it, and I sent it to him. He and Madame la Maréchale understood that I should be very pleased to have theirs. They had them taken in miniature by a very clever artist, and set in a sweetmeat-box of rock-crystal, mounted in gold, which they presented to me in a most handsome manner, with which I was delighted. Madame de Luxembourg would never consent that her portrait should be on the upper part of the box. She had several times reproached me with being fonder of the Marshal than of herself; and I had not denied it, because it was true. She proved to me very politely, but at the same time very cleverly, by this manner of placing her portrait, that she did not forget my preference.

About the same time, I was guilty of an act of folly which did not help to keep me in her good graces. Although I had no acquaintance with M. de Silhouette,[1] and was little inclined to like him, I had a great opinion of his administrative powers. When he began to lay a heavy hand upon the financiers, I saw that he was not commencing the operation at a favourable moment. Nevertheless, I wished him all success; and, when I heard that he had been removed from office, I was so thoughtless as to write the following letter to him, which assuredly I do not attempt to justify:

"MONTMORENCY, *December 2nd*, 1759.

"Condescend, sir, to accept the homage of a recluse who is unknown to you, but who esteems you for your talents, who respects you for your administration, and who has done you the honour of

---

[1] The attempted national economies, and attack on the privileges of the farmers-general, by Etienne de Silhouette, during his brief career as Controller-general of Finance (March–November 1759), ended in failure and ridicule. (Hence the satirical application of this name to shadow-portraits or "silhouettes".)

believing that it would not long remain in your hands. Unable to save the State, except at the expense of the capital which has destroyed it, you have dared to brave the outcries of the money-grubbers. When I saw how you crushed these wretches, I envied you your office. Now that I see how you have abandoned it without belying yourself, I admire you. Be satisfied with yourself, sir; you take with you from it an honour which you will long enjoy without a rival. The execrations of rascals are the glory of an upright man."

[1760.] — Madame de Luxembourg, who knew that I had written this letter, spoke to me about it when she came out at Easter; I showed it to her; she wished for a copy, and I gave her one; but I did not know, when I did so, that she herself was one of those money-grubbers who had an interest in sub-leases and had caused the removal of Silhouette. To judge from my numerous follies, it seemed as if I purposely wanted to arouse the hatred of an amiable and influential woman, to whom I was becoming more sincerely attached every day, and whose displeasure I was far from wishing to bring upon myself, although by my repeated acts of stupidity, I was doing everything that was wanted to produce such a result. I think it is hardly necessary to mention that it is to her that the story of M. Tronchin's opiate,[1] of which I have spoken in the first part of my Confessions, refers; the other lady was Madame de Mirepoix. Neither of them has ever mentioned it to me again, or appeared to have the slightest recollection of it; but I find it difficult, even if one did not know anything of subsequent events, to assume that Madame de Luxembourg can have really forgotten it. For my own part, I tried to reassure myself as to the effect of my follies by the evidence which I produced to myself, that none of them had been committed with the intention of offending her; as if a woman could ever pardon such follies, even though she is perfectly certain that they were not the result of deliberate intention.

However, although she seemed to see and feel nothing, although I found no abatement in her warmth, and no alteration in her manner towards me, a continually growing presentiment, which was only too well founded, made me tremble incessantly, for fear her infatuation for me might be succeeded by disgust.

[1] [opiate] See Book III, p. 122.

Could I expect, on the part of so great a lady, a constancy which would be proof against my lack of address to support it? I did not even know how to conceal from her this dim presentiment, which disquieted me and only made me more sullen and awkward. This may be seen from the following letter, which contains a very singular prediction.

N.B. – This letter, which is undated in my rough copy, was written in October, 1760, at the latest.

"How cruel your kindness is! Why disturb the tranquillity of a recluse, who renounced the pleasures of life, in order to feel the weariness of them no longer? I have spent my life in the vain endeavour to find lasting attachments: I have been unable to form any in the ranks which were accessible to me. Am I to look for them in yours? Neither interest nor ambition has any temptations for me; I have little vanity: I am rather timid; I can resist everything except affection. Why do you both attack me in a weakness which I must overcome, since, considering the distance which separates us, the overflowings of tender hearts cannot bring mine near to you. Will gratitude be sufficient for a heart which knows not two ways of bestowing itself and only feels capable of friendship? Friendship, Madame la Maréchale! Ah! therein lies my misfortune. It is very handsome of you and Monsieur le Maréchal to use this term; but I am a fool to take you at your word. You are amusing yourselves: I am forming an attachment to you, and the end of the game has fresh sorrows in store for me! How I hate all your titles, and how I pity you for having them! You seem to me so worthy to taste the charms of private life. Why do you not live at Clarens? I would go there in search of the happiness of my life; but – the château of Montmorency, the Hôtel de Luxembourg! Is that where one ought to see Jean Jacques? Is that where a friend of equality, who, in thus paying for the esteem which is shown for him, believes that he is returning as much as he receives, ought to carry the affections of a tender heart? You are good, and also feeling: I know it: I have seen it. I regret that I have not been able to believe it sooner; but, considering the position which you hold, and the manner in which you live, nothing can make a lasting impression upon you: and so many new interests efface each other, that not one is permanent. You will forget me, madame, after you have made it impossible for me to imitate you. You will have done much to make me unhappy and unable to justify myself."

I coupled M. de Luxembourg's name with hers, in order to make the compliment less harsh for her; besides, I was so sure of him, that I had never for a moment felt any anxiety as to the duration of his friendship. None of my apprehensions in regard to his wife ever extended to him. I have never felt the least mistrust of his character, which I knew was weak, but trustworthy. I had no more fear of a coldness on his part than expectation of a heroic attachment. The simplicity and familiarity of our intercourse showed how each of us depended upon the other. We were both right: as long as I live I shall honour and cherish the memory of this worthy gentleman; and, whatever attempts may have been made to part him from me, I am as certain that he died my friend, as if I had received his last sigh.

During their second stay at Montmorency, in 1760, having come to the end of "Julie," I had recourse to "Émile," in order to keep in with Madame de Luxembourg; but this did not prove so successful, either because the subject was less to her taste, or because she was at last tired of so much reading. However, as she reproached me with allowing myself to be cheated by my publishers, she wanted me to leave the printing and publication of it to her, that she might make a better bargain. I accepted her proposal, expressly stipulating that the work should not be printed in France. We had a long dispute upon this point: I maintained that it was impossible to obtain, and even imprudent to ask for tacit permission, and I would not hear of its being printed in the kingdom on any other terms; while she insisted that there would not be the least difficulty about the censorship, under the system which had been adopted by the Government. She found the means of bringing M. de Malesherbes over to her views; he wrote me a long letter himself, in order to prove that the *Profession de foi du vicaire savoyard* was just the kind of thing to meet with the approval of the human race everywhere, and, under the circumstances, even of the Court. I was surprised to find this official, who was as a rule so timid, so easy-going in this matter. As his mere approval was enough to legalise the printing of a book, I could make no further objection. However, in consequence of a singular scruple, I still insisted that the work should be printed in Holland, and by Néaulme, whom, not satisfied with mentioning him, I apprised of my intention. I agreed that the profits of the edition should go to a French publisher, and that, when it was ready, it should be sold in Paris or anywhere else, since the sale did not concern me. These were the exact terms of the agreement made by Madame de Luxembourg and myself, after which I handed over the manuscript to her.

She had brought with her on this occasion her grand-daughter, Mademoiselle de Boufflers, now Madame la Duchesse de Lauzun. Her name was Amélie. She was a charming person. Her face, gentleness, and timidity were truly maidenly. Nothing could have been more amiable or more interesting than her features, nothing tenderer or more chaste than the feelings which they inspired. Besides, she was a mere child, not yet eleven years of age. Madame la Maréchale, finding her too shy, did her best to rouse her. She several times allowed me to kiss her, which I did with my usual awkwardness. Instead of the pretty things which anyone else in my place would have said, I stood mute and utterly confused. I do not know which of us was the more bashful, the poor little one or myself. One day I met her alone on the staircase of the little château; she was coming to see Thérèse, with whom her governess still was. Not knowing what to say to her, I asked her to give me a kiss, which, in the innocence of her heart, she did not refuse, as she had already given me one that very morning, by her grandmamma's orders, and in her presence. The next day, while reading "Émile" at Madame la Maréchale's bedside, I came upon a passage, in which I have justly censured the very thing that I had myself done the day before. She found the observation very just, and made some sensible remark upon it, which caused me to blush. How I curse my incredible stupidity, which has often caused me to appear vile and guilty, when I have only been foolish and embarrassed — a foolishness which is regarded as only a false excuse in the case of a man who is known to be not wanting in intelligence! I can swear that in this kiss, which was so blameable, as in all the rest, Mademoiselle Amélie's heart and feelings were no purer than my own. I can even swear that, if at that moment I could have avoided meeting her, I would have done so; for, although I was very pleased to see her, I was greatly at a loss to find something agreeable to say to her in passing. How is it that a child can intimidate a man whom the power of kings fails to alarm? What is a man to do? How is he to behave, if he is utterly destitute of presence of mind? If I force myself to speak to people whom I meet, I infallibly utter some foolish remark; if I say nothing, then I am a misanthrope, a wild animal, a bear. Complete imbecility would have been far more favourable to me; but the talents which I lacked in society have made those which I possessed the instruments of my ruin.

At the end of her stay on this occasion, Madame de Luxembourg carried out a good work, in which I had some share. Diderot had very rashly offended Madame la Princesse de Robeck, a daughter of M. de Luxembourg. Her *protégé* Palissot avenged her by the comedy of the *Philosophes*,[1] in which I was held up to ridicule, and Diderot was very severely handled. The author was more merciful to me, not so much, I believe, on account of the obligations under which he was to me, as for fear of displeasing his patroness's father, who he knew entertained an affection for me. Duchesne, the bookseller, with whom I was not acquainted at the time, sent me the piece when it was printed, I suspect by Palissot's instructions, who perhaps thought that I should be glad to see a man pulled to pieces, with whom I had broken off relations. He was greatly mistaken. When I broke with Diderot, whom I believed to be weak and indiscreet rather than absolutely wicked, I still preserved in my heart a feeling of attachment, even of esteem, for him, and of respect for our old friendship, which I am convinced was for a long time as sincere on his part as on my own. The case is quite different with Grimm, a man whose character is false, who never loved me, who is not even capable of loving, and who, with a light heart, without any reason for complaint, simply in order to satisfy his spiteful jealousy, has secretly become my bitterest calumniator. He is no longer anything to me. Diderot will always be my old friend. My tenderest feelings were moved at the sight of this hateful piece; I could not bear to read it, and, without finishing it, I sent it back to Duchesne, together with the following letter:

[1] Palissot's play, first performed on 2 May 1769, contains a *coup de théâtre* in which Crispin, who was once a valet to a prickly and unsociable sage, enters upon all fours, with a bunch of lettuce protruding from his pocket – as it were, epitomising Rousseau's *Second Discourse*.

"MONTMORENCY, *May 21st*, 1760.

"Sir, – On looking through the piece which you have sent me, I have shuddered at finding myself praised. I refuse to accept this horrible present. I am convinced that, in sending it to me, you did not intend to insult me; but you either do not know, or you have forgotten, that I have had the honour of being the friend of a man deserving of respect, who is unworthily traduced and calumniated in this libellous production."

Duchesne handed this letter round. Diderot, who ought to have been touched by it, was annoyed. His *amour-propre* could not pardon me the superiority of a generous action, and I heard that his wife attacked me on every possible occasion, with a rage which affected me but little, since I knew that everybody looked upon her as a regular "fish-hag."

Diderot, in his turn, found an avenger in the Abbé Morellet, who wrote a little *brochure* against Palissot, after the manner of the "Petit Prophète," called "La Vision." In this pamphlet he very imprudently insulted Madame de Robeck, whose friends caused him to be imprisoned in the Bastille; she herself was not of a sufficiently revengeful disposition – not to mention that at that time she was a dying woman – to have had anything to do with it.

D'Alembert, who was very intimate with the Abbé Morellet, wrote and asked me to beg Madame de Luxembourg to procure his release, promising, in token of his gratitude, to praise her in the "Encyclopédie."* The following was my reply:

"Sir, – I have not waited for your letter, before expressing to Madame la Maréchale de Luxembourg the pain which the imprisonment of the Abbé Morellet caused me. She knows the interest which I take in the matter, she shall also know the interest that you take in it; it will be sufficient for her, in order that she herself may take an interest in it, to know that he is a person of merit. Further, although she and M. le Maréchal honour me with a kindness which is the consolation of my life, and although your friend's name is, in their opinion, a recommendation in favour of the Abbé Morellet, I do not know how far they may consider it fitting, on this occasion, to make use of the influence attached to their position and the personal esteem in which they are held. I do not even feel convinced, that the act of

* This letter, together with several others, disappeared at the Hôtel de Luxembourg, while my papers were deposited there. (R)

vengeance in question concerns Madame la Princesse de Robeck so much as you appear to think; and, even should you be correct, one must not suppose that the pleasure of avenging oneself is the exclusive property of philosophers, and that, when they choose to be women, women will be philosophers.

"I will inform you of what Madame de Luxembourg says to me when I have shown her your letter. Meanwhile, I think that I am sufficiently well acquainted with her, to be able to assure you before-hand that, even if she should have the pleasure of contributing to the release of the Abbé Morellet, she would certainly refuse to accept the tribute of gratitude which you promise to render her in the columns of the 'Encyclopédie,' although she might feel herself honoured by it, because she does not do good for the sake of praise, but only in order to satisfy her goodness of heart."

I spared no pains to arouse the zeal and compassion of Madame de Luxembourg on behalf of the poor prisoner, and I succeeded. She took a journey to Versailles on purpose to see M. le Comte de Saint-Florentin; and this journey shortened her stay at Montmorency, which the Maréchal was obliged to leave at the same time, his presence being required at Rouen, whither the King was sending him as the Governor of Normandy, in connection with certain proceedings in the Parliament, which it was desired to suppress. The following is the letter which Madame de Luxembourg wrote to me the second day after her departure (Packet D, No. 23):

"VERSAILLES, *Wednesday.*

"M. de Luxembourg left yesterday at six o'clock in the morning. I do not yet know whether I shall join him. I am waiting to hear from him, because he does not know himself how long he will be there. I have seen M. de Saint-Florentin, who is most favourably disposed towards the Abbé Morellet; but he finds that there are difficulties, which, however, he hopes to surmount the first time he has to see the King, which will be next week. I have also asked as a favour, that he shall not be banished, which was talked of: it was intended to send him to Nancy. This, sir, is as much as I have been able to do; but I promise you that I will not leave M. de Saint-Florentin alone, until the matter is arranged as you desire. And now let me tell you how sorry I was to be obliged to leave you so soon, but I flatter myself that you have no doubt of it. I love you with all my heart, and shall do so as long as I live."

A few days later I received the following letter from D'Alembert, which caused me real joy (Packet D, No. 26):

"August 1st.

"Thanks to your efforts, my dear philosopher, the Abbé has left the Bastille, and his imprisonment will have no further consequences. He is setting out for the country, and, together with myself, sends you a thousand thanks and compliments. *Vale et me ama.*"

The Abbé also, a few days afterwards, wrote me a letter of thanks (Packet D, No. 29), which did not appear to me to come straight from the heart, and in which he appeared to some extent to depreciate the service which I had rendered him; and, some time afterwards, I found that he and D'Alembert had in a manner, I will not say supplanted, but succeeded me in Madame de Luxembourg's favour, and that I had lost in her esteem as much as they had gained. However, I am far from suspecting the Abbé Morellet of having contributed to my loss of favour; I esteem him too highly to think that. As for M. d'Alembert, I say nothing about him here; I will return to him later.

At the same time I had another affair on hand, which was the occasion of the last letter I ever wrote to Voltaire—a letter which he exclaimed loudly against as an abominable insult, but which he never showed to anyone. I will here supply the omission.

The Abbé Trublet, with whom I was slightly acquainted, but of whom I had seen very little, wrote to me on the 13th of June, 1760 (Packet D, No. 11), to inform me that M. Formey, his friend and correspondent, had printed in his journal my letter to M. de Voltaire about the disaster at Lisbon. The Abbé Trublet wanted to know how this publication had been rendered possible; and, with his Jesuitical slyness, asked me my opinion of the reprinting of the letter, without wanting to tell me his own. As I thoroughly detest cunning persons of this sort, I thanked him, as he deserved, but somewhat stiffly: he noticed this, but nevertheless it did not prevent him from trying to get over me in one or two more letters, until he had found out everything he wanted to know.

I well understood, whatever Trublet might say, that Formey had not found the letter printed, and that it had been printed by him for the first time. I knew that he was an unblushing pilferer, who, without ceremony, earned an income from the works of others, although he had not yet ventured upon the astounding impudence of removing the author's name from a book already published, putting his own to it, and selling it for his own profit.*

But how had this manuscript come into his hands? That was the question. It was not a difficult one to answer, but I was simple enough to be puzzled by it. Although Voltaire was honoured beyond all measure in this letter, he would have had reason to complain, in spite of his uncivil behaviour, if I had had it printed without his consent, and I accordingly decided to write to him on the matter. Here is this second letter, to which he made no reply, and at which, in order to give freer vent to his brutality, he pretended to be irritated even to madness:

"MONTMORENCY, *June 17th*, 1760.

"Sir, – I never thought to find myself writing to you again. But, having learnt that the letter which I wrote to you in 1756 has been printed at Berlin, I feel it my duty to give you an account of my conduct in regard to it, and I will fulfil this duty in all truthfulness and sincerity.

"This letter, having been really addressed to yourself, was never meant to be printed. I communicated its contents, conditionally, to three persons to whom the rights of friendship did not permit me to refuse anything of the kind, and whom these same rights of friendship still less permitted to abuse their trust by violating their promise. These three persons are: Madame de Chenonceaux, Madame Dupin's stepdaughter; Madame la Comtesse d'Houdetot; and a German named Grimm. Madame de Chenonceaux was anxious for the letter to be printed, and asked my consent. I told her that it depended upon you. Your consent was asked; you refused it, and nothing more was said about the matter.

"Nevertheless, M. l'Abbé Trublet, with whom I have no sort of connection, has just written, with a most friendly mark of attention, to inform me, that he has received the sheets of a journal belonging to M. Formey, in which he has read this identical letter, accompanied by a note, in which the editor, under date of the 23rd October, 1759, says that he found it some weeks ago in the Berlin booksellers' shops, and that, since it is one of those pamphlets which soon disappear beyond hope of return, he thought it his duty to allot it a place in his journal.

"This, sir, is all that I know about the matter. It is quite certain that hitherto this letter has never even been heard of in Paris. It is quite certain that the copy, whether in manuscript or print, which has fallen into M. Formey's hands, can only have come to him either through you, which is not likely, or through one of the three persons whom I have

* In this fashion he afterwards appropriated "Émile." (R)

just mentioned. Lastly, it is quite certain that the two ladies are incapable of such a breach of confidence. From my retreat, I cannot gain any further information about the matter. You have correspondents, by whose assistance it would be easy for you, if it were worth the trouble, to trace it back to its source, and learn the truth about the facts.

"In the same letter, M. l'Abbé Trublet informs me that he is keeping back the number of the journal, and will not lend it without my consent, which I certainly will never give. But this copy may not be the only one in Paris. My wish is that the letter may not be printed there, and I will do my best to prevent it; but, in case I am unable to succeed, and, being informed in time, may be able to secure the prior right, then I will not hesitate to have it printed myself. This appears to me to be only fair and natural.

"As for your reply to the same letter, it has not been communicated to anyone, and you may feel assured that it will never be printed without your consent,* which I shall never be so indiscreet as to ask for, for I know well, that what one man writes to another, is not meant for the public. But if you like to write an answer for publication, addressed to me, I promise you that I will faithfully add it to my letter, without a single word of reply on my part.

"I do not love you, sir: you have done me injuries, which I could not but feel most deeply – me, your disciple and most enthusiastic admirer. You have ruined Geneva in return for the shelter you have found there: you have alienated my fellow-citizens from me, in return for the eulogies which I have lavished upon you in their midst: it is you who have made life in my native country unendurable for me: it is you who will cause me to die in a foreign land, deprived of all the consolations of a dying man, and to be thrown into a gutter, as the last token of respect: while you will be followed to the grave with all the honours that a man can expect. In fact, I hate you, since you have so willed it; but I hate you as a man who is more worthy loving you, if you had so chosen. Of all the sentiments towards you, with which my heart was filled, the only one that survives is the admiration which one cannot refuse to your splendid genius, and admiration for your writings. If I can honour nothing but your talents, the fault is not mine. I shall never fail in the respect that is due to them, or in the behaviour which such respect demands. Farewell, sir!"†

* That is to say, during his life-time and mine: and surely, the most scrupulous behaviour, especially in dealing with a man who tramples it ruthlessly under foot, cannot require more. (R)

† It will be observed that, although this letter has been written nearly seven years, I have neither mentioned it nor shown it to a living soul. This has also been the case with the two letters which M. Hume forced me to write to him last summer, until he made the noise about them, which everybody knows of. The evil that I have to say about my enemies, I say to themselves privately; as for the good, when there is any, I say it openly and with a good heart. (R)

In the midst of all these petty literary squabbles, which only confirmed me more and more in my resolution, I was the recipient of the greatest honour which the profession of letters has ever conferred upon me, and of which I felt most proud: M. le Prince de Conti[1] condescended to visit me twice, once at the little château, and once at Mont-Louis. On both occasions, he selected the time when Madame de Luxembourg was not at Montmorency, in order to make it clearer that he only came to see me. I have never had any doubt that I owed his kindness originally to Madame de Luxembourg and Madame de Boufflers; but neither have I any doubt that I owe the kindness with which he has never ceased to honour me since then, to his own feelings and myself.*

As my apartment at Mont-Louis was very small, and the situation of the turret was delightful, I took the Prince there; and he, to crown his favours, desired that I would have the honour of playing a game of chess with him. I knew that he could beat the Chevalier de Lorenzi, who was a much better player than myself. However, in spite of the signs and grimaces of the Chevalier and those who were present, which I pretended not to see, I won the two games which we played. When they were finished, I said to him in a respectful, but serious tone, "My Lord, I have too much respect for your most serene Highness, not to beat you always at chess." This great Prince, so witty and learned, who deserved to be spared from flattery, felt – at least, I think so – that I was the only person present who treated him as a man, and I have every reason to believe that he felt really grateful to me for it.

Even if he had been displeased, I could not reproach myself with wishing to deceive him in anything, and I certainly have not to reproach myself with having ill-requited his goodness in my heart, although I certainly sometimes requited it with a bad grace, whereas he himself displayed infinite delicacy in the manner in which he showed it. A few days afterwards, he sent

---

[1] [Conti] See *Biographies*, p. 708.

* Notice the persistency of this blind and stupid confidence, in the midst of all the ill-treatment, which ought to have disabused me of it. It never disappeared until after my return to Paris in 1770. (R)

me a hamper of game, which I accepted in a proper manner. Some time after that, he sent me a second hamper, accompanied by a note from one of his officers of the hunt, written by his instructions, informing me that the contents had been shot by His Highness himself. I accepted it; but I wrote to Madame de Boufflers that I would accept no more. This letter was generally blamed, and deservedly. To refuse presents of game from a Prince of the blood, who, besides, displays such delicacy in sending them, shows rather the boorishness of an ill-bred person who forgets himself, than the delicate feeling of a proud man, who desires to preserve his independence. I have never read over this letter without blushing for it, or without reproaching myself for having written it. However, I have not undertaken to write my Confessions in order to be silent upon my follies, and the present instance disgusts me with myself too much for me to allow myself to conceal it.

If I did not commit the additional folly of becoming his rival, I very nearly did so; for, at the time, Madame de Boufflers was still his mistress, and I knew nothing about it. She came to see me pretty often with the Chevalier de Lorenzi. She was handsome and still young. She affected the old Roman spirit, while I was always romantic; this was a sufficient similarity. I was nearly caught; I believe she saw it. The Chevalier saw it also; at least, he spoke to me about it, and in a manner not calculated to discourage me. But this time I was prudent – and it was time to be so, at fifty years of age. Full of the good advice which I had just given to the grey-beards in my letter to D'Alembert, I was ashamed to profit so little by it myself. Besides, after learning what I did not know before, I must have lost my head entirely, if I had dared to carry my rivalry so high! Lastly, being perhaps not yet thoroughly cured of my passion for Madame d'Houdetot, I felt that nothing could henceforth take her place in my heart, and I bade adieu to love for the remainder of my life. At the moment of writing these lines, a young woman, who had her designs upon me, has just made dangerous advances to me, and that with very significant glances; but, if she had pretended to forget my fifty years, I have remembered them. After having extricated myself from this snare, I have no longer any fear of falling, and I feel that I can answer for myself for the rest of my days.

Madame de Boufflers had observed the emotion which her presence caused me, and could also see that I had triumphed over it. I am neither foolish nor vain enough to believe that, at my age, I can have inspired her with any fancy for me; but, from certain expressions which she made use of to Thérèse, I believe that I aroused a certain feeling of curiosity in her mind. If this is the case, and if she has not forgiven me for not having satisfied this curiosity, it must be admitted that I was born to be the victim of my weaknesses, since victorious love was so fatal to me, and vanquished love even more fatal still.

Here ends the collection of letters which has served me as a guide in these two books. Henceforth, I can only follow in the footsteps of my recollections; which, however, in reference to this cruel period of my life, are so vivid, and have left so strong an impression upon me that, lost in the vast ocean of my misfortunes, I am unable to forget the details of my first ship-wreck, although its results only afford me confused recollections. Accordingly, in the following book, I can still proceed with tolerable certainty. If I go further, I shall have to grope in the dark.

BOOK XI

[1761]

ALTHOUGH "Julie," which had been in the press for a long time, was not yet published at the end of 1760, it was beginning to make a great stir. Madame de Luxembourg had spoken of it at Court, Madame d'Houdetot in Paris. The latter had even obtained permission from me for Saint-Lambert to have it read in manuscript to the King of Poland, who was delighted with it. Duclos, to whom I had also had it read, had spoken of it to the Academy. All Paris was impatient to see this romance; the booksellers' shops in the Rue Saint-Jacques and the Palais-Royal were besieged by persons making inquiries about it. At last it appeared, and its success, contrary to what is usually the case, corresponded to the eagerness with which it had been expected. Madame la Dauphine, who was one of the first who read it, spoke of it to M. de Luxembourg as a delightful work. Opinions were divided amongst men of letters; but amongst the general public the verdict was unanimous; the ladies, especially, became infatuated with the book and the author to such an extent, that there were few, even amongst the highest circles, whose conquest I could not have made, if I had been so disposed. I possess proofs of this, which I do not wish to commit to writing, but which, without any need of putting them to the test, confirm my opinion. It is singular that this work has met with greater success in France than in the rest of Europe, although the French, both men and women, are not very well treated in it. Quite contrary to my expectation, it was least successful in Switzerland, most successful in Paris. Do then friendship, love, and virtue, prevail more in Paris than elsewhere? Most certainly, no; but there still prevails there that exquisite feeling, by which the heart is transported, when these qualities are portrayed, and which makes us cherish in others the pure, tender, and virtuous feelings, which we ourselves no longer possess. The corruption of manners is at the present day everywhere the same; virtue and morality no longer exist in Europe; but, if there be a place where affection for them still exists, it is in Paris that we must look for it.*

Amidst so many prejudices and factitious passions, one must know how to analyse properly the human heart, in order to disentangle the true feelings of nature. A delicacy of tact is necessary, which can only be acquired by intercourse with the great world, in order to feel, if I may so venture to say, the delicacies of heart of which this work is full. I unhesitatingly place the fourth part of it by the side of the "Princesse de Clèves," and I assert that, if these two works had been read only in the provinces, their true value would never have been recognised. It is, therefore, not surprising that the book met with the greatest success at Court. It abounds in piquant, but veiled allusions, which were bound to please, because those at Court are more practised in seeing through them. However, a further distinction must here be made. The reading of such works is certainly not suited to those witty people, whose cunning and *finesse* is only of avail to see through what is bad, and who see nothing at all where there is only good to be seen. If, for instance, "Julie" had been published in a certain country which I have in my mind, I am sure no one would have read it to the end, and that it would have died at its birth.

I have collected most of the letters, which were written to me on the subject of this work, in a packet which is in the hands of Madame de Nadaillac. If this collection ever sees the light, it will disclose several curious things, amongst others, a diversity of opinion, which shows what it is to have anything to do with the public. The feature which has been least observed, and which will always make it a work unique of its kind, is the simplicity of the subject and the sustained interest which, confined to three persons, is kept up through six volumes, without the aid of incidents, romantic adventures, or improprieties of any kind, either in the characters or in their actions. Diderot has paid great compliments to Richardson upon the enormous variety of his situations and the number of characters introduced by him. Richardson certainly has the merit of having given them all distinctive characteristics; but, in regard to their number, he

* I wrote these words in 1769. (R)

has the fault common to most insipid writers of romance, who make up for the barrenness of their ideas by the aid of characters and incidents. It is easy to excite interest by incessantly presenting unheard-of incidents and new faces, who pass like the figures in a magic-lantern; but it is far more difficult to sustain this interest continually by means of the same objects, without the aid of wonderful adventures. And if, other things being equal, the simplicity of the subject adds to the beauty of the work, the romances of Richardson, though superior in so many other things, cannot, in this respect, be compared to mine. However, it is dead – I know it, and I know the reason; but it will come to life again.

My only fear was that, owing to its extreme simplicity, the development of the story might prove wearisome, and that I had not been able to keep up a sufficiently lively interest to the end. I was reassured by an incident which, of itself alone, flattered me more than all the compliments which this work has procured me.

It appeared at the beginning of the Carnival. A book-hawker took it to Madame la Princesse de Talmont* one day when there was a ball at the Opera. After supper she dressed herself to go, and, while waiting, began to read the new romance. At midnight she ordered her horses to be put in, and went on reading. She was informed that her carriage was waiting; she made no reply. Her servants, seeing that she had forgotten herself, went to tell her that it was two o'clock. "There is no hurry yet," she answered, and still went on reading. Some time afterwards, her watch having stopped, she rang the bell to know what time it was. When she heard that it was four o'clock, she said, "Then it is too late to go to the ball; take out the horses," undressed herself, and spent the rest of the night in reading.

Since hearing of this incident, I have always wanted to see Madame de Talmont, not only to learn from her own lips if it is strictly true, but also because I have never thought it possible that anyone could feel so lively an interest in "Julie" without possessing the sixth sense, that moral sense, with which so few

* It was not she, but another lady whose name I do not know; but I have been assured of the fact. (R)

hearts are endowed, and without which it is impossible for anyone to understand my own.

What made the women so favourably disposed towards me was their conviction that I had written my own history, and that I myself was the hero of this romance. This belief was so firmly established, that Madame de Polignac wrote to Madame de Verdelin, begging her to persuade me to let her see the portrait of Julie. Everyone was convinced that it was impossible to express sentiments so vividly without having felt them, or to describe the transports of love so glowingly, unless they came straight from the heart. In this they were right. It is quite true that I wrote this romance in a state of most feverish ecstasy, but they were wrong in thinking that it had needed real objects to produce this condition; they were far from understanding to what an extent I am capable of being inflamed by beings of the imagination. Had it not been for a few reminiscences of my youth and Madame d'Houdetot, the love which I felt and described would have had only the nymphs of the air for its object. I did not desire either to confirm or refute an error which was to my advantage. It may be seen in the preface, in the form of a dialogue, which I had printed separately, how I left the public in suspense on that point. Rigid moralists may say that I ought to have declared the truth without reserve. For my own part, I do not see what obligation there was for me to do so; and I think that I should have shown far more stupidity than frankness in making such a declaration, when there was no necessity for it.

Nearly about the same time appeared the "Paix Perpetuelle," the manuscript of which I had given up in the preceding year to a certain M. de Bastide, editor of a journal called *Le Monde*, into which, whether I liked it or not, he would have been glad to cram all my manuscripts. He was acquainted with M. Duclos, and came in his name to try and induce me to help him to fill his journal. He had heard "Julie" spoken of, and wanted me to let it appear in it, as well as "Émile"; he would also have liked to have the "Contrat Social," if he had had any suspicion of its existence. At length, wearied by his importunities, I decided to let him have my extracts from the "Paix Perpetuelle" for twelve *louis*. The agreement was, that it should be printed in his journal; but, as soon as he became the owner of the manuscript, he thought fit to have it printed by itself, after certain passages had been cut out, in accordance with the requirements of the censorship. What would have been the result, if I had added my own criticisms of the work, which, fortunately, I did not mention to M. de Bastide, and which were not included in our agreement! These criticisms are still unprinted, and I have them amongst my papers. If they ever appear, it will be seen how Voltaire's witticisms and self-complacency on this subject must have made me laugh – me, who understood so well the extent of this poor man's intelligence in regard to the political matters in which he ventured to interfere.

In the midst of the successful reception of my work by the public and the favour of the ladies, I felt that I was losing ground at the Hôtel de Luxembourg, not with M. de Luxembourg, whose kindness and friendship seemed to increase daily, but with Madame de Luxembourg. Since I had found nothing more to read to her, her room had not been so freely open to me; and, during her visits to Montmorency, although I presented myself with great regularity, I hardly ever saw her except at table. My place at her side, even, was no longer reserved for me as before. As she no longer offered it to me, spoke to me but little, and I had not much to say to her either, I was glad to find another place, where I was more at my ease, especially in the evening; for I unconsciously made a practice of sitting closer to M. le Maréchal.

In regard to "the evening," I remember that I have said that I did not sup at the château, and this was true at the commencement of our acquaintance; but, as M. de Luxembourg did not dine at all, and did not even appear at table, the result was that, at the end of several months, although I was on a very familiar footing in the house, I had never been at a meal with him. He was kind enough to make a remark to that effect. This decided me to go to supper there sometimes, when there were not many guests; and I greatly enjoyed myself, seeing that we took our dinner almost in the open, and, as is said, *sur le bout du banc*;[1]

[1] Without ceremony.

whereas supper was a very lengthy meal, because the guests made themselves comfortable, in order to rest themselves after a long walk; it was a very good meal, because M. de Luxembourg was somewhat of a gourmand; and a very agreeable one, because Madame de Luxembourg did the honours with charming grace. Without this explanation, it would be difficult to understand the concluding portion of one of M. de Luxembourg's letters (Packet C, No. 36), in which he tells me that he recalls our walks with great pleasure, especially, he adds, when, on our return to the courtyard in the evening, we found no marks of carriage wheels; for, as the ruts in the sand were raked over every morning, I guessed, from the number of wheel-tracks, how many guests had arrived during the afternoon.

This year (1761) filled to the brim the cup of the afflictions, which this worthy gentleman had suffered, since I had had the honour of knowing him; as if the evils which destiny was preparing for myself were fated to commence with the man to whom I felt the most sincere attachment, and who was most worthy of it. In the first year, he lost his sister, Madame la Duchesse de Villeroy; in the second, his daughter, Madame la Princesse de Robeck; in the third, his only son, the Duc de Montmorency, and his grandson, the Comte de Luxembourg, the last and only inheritors of his name and family. Outwardly, he endured all these losses with apparent courage; but his heart did not cease to bleed inwardly for the rest of his life, and his health gradually declined. He must have felt the unexpected and tragic end of his son the more keenly, as it happened at the very moment when the King had just granted him for his son, and promised him for his grandson, the reversion of his commission as Captain of the Gardes du Corps. He had the sorrow of seeing, before his own eyes, the life of this child, in whom such hopes were centred, gradually wasting away, in consequence of the mother's blind confidence in the physician who caused the poor child's death from sheer want of nourishment, owing to his being fed upon nothing but drugs. Alas! if they had only trusted in me, the grandfather and the grandson would both be still alive. I said everything I could; I wrote to M. le Maréchal; I remonstrated with Madame de Montmorency upon the more than strict diet, which, in her faith in her physician, she prescribed for her son. Madame de Luxembourg, whose opinions coincided with my own, did not wish to usurp the mother's authority. M. de Luxembourg, who was weak and gentle, never cared to oppose anyone. Madame de Montmorency felt a confidence in Bordeu, of which her son finally became the victim. How delighted the poor child was, when he was able to get permission to come to Mont-Louis with Madame de Boufflers, to ask Thérèse for something to eat, and to put a little nourishment into his famished stomach! How I deplored, in my own heart, the miseries of greatness, when I saw the only heir of so large an estate, of so great a name, of so many titles and dignities, devour with the greediness of a beggar a sorry morsel of bread. But it was no use for me to say or do anything; the physician triumphed, and the child starved.

The same confidence in quacks, which caused the death of the grandson, dug the grave of the grandfather, and, in addition to this, he was weak-minded enough to attempt to conceal from himself the infirmities of old age. M. de Luxembourg suffered at times from pains in his great toe; he had an attack while at Montmorency, which prevented him from sleeping, and made him somewhat feverish. I ventured to pronounce the word "gout"; Madame de Luxembourg scolded me. The Maréchal's *valet de chambre* and surgeon declared that it was not the gout, and proceeded to dress the part afflicted with some healing ointment. Unfortunately, the pain abated, and, when it returned, recourse was invariably had to the same remedy which had previously given relief; his constitution broke up, his sufferings increased, and the remedies in proportion. Madame de Luxembourg, who at last saw that it was the gout, opposed this senseless treatment. They afterwards concealed his condition from her, and he died at the end of a few years, through his own fault and his persistent efforts to cure himself. But let me not so far anticipate misfortunes; how many others have I to relate before I come to that!

It is strange by what fatality all that I could say or do seemed doomed to displease Madame de Luxembourg, even when I was exceedingly anxious to preserve her goodwill. The blows which

M. de Luxembourg sustained one after another only made me more attached to him, and consequently to Madame de Luxembourg; for they always seemed to me so sincerely united, that the feelings which I entertained for the one naturally extended to the other. M. le Maréchal was getting old. His constant attendance at Court, the duties entailed by it, the continual hunting-expeditions, above all, the fatigues of his office during the three months he was on duty, would have required the vigour of a young man, and I no longer saw anything which could keep up his strength in the position which he occupied. Since his dignities would be distributed amongst others, and his name would become extinct after his death, there was little need for him to continue a laborious life, the chief object of which had been to secure the Prince's favour for his children. One day, when we three were alone, and he was complaining of the fatigue of his Court duties like a man disheartened by his losses, I ventured to speak to him of retiring, and to give him the advice which Cineas[1] gave to Pyrrhus. He sighed, but made no decided answer. But, the very first time she saw me alone, Madame de Luxembourg scolded me severely for this advice, which seemed to me to have alarmed her. She added a remark, the justice of which I felt, and which made me abandon the idea of ever referring to the same topic again; that the habit of living so long at the Court had become a real necessity; that, even at that moment, it was a diversion for M. de Luxembourg; and that the retirement which I recommended to him would not be so much a rest for him as an exile, in which idleness, weariness, and grief would soon put an end to his life. Although she must have seen that she had convinced me, although she could depend upon the promise which I made and kept, she never seemed to me quite easy in regard to the matter, and I remember that, since that time, my *tête-à-têtes* with M. le Maréchal were less frequent and were nearly always interrupted.

While my awkwardness and ill-luck thus united to injure me in her opinion, the people of whom she saw most, and for whom she entertained the greatest affection, did not promote my

[1] [Cineas] See Book V, p. 202.

interests in that quarter. The Abbé de Boufflers, especially, who was as brilliant as a young man could possibly be, never seemed particularly well-disposed towards me; not only is he the only person, in Madame la Maréchale's circle, who has never shown me the slightest marks of attention, but I fancied that I observed that, after each of his visits to Montmorency, I lost ground with her. Certainly, however, it is true that, without any attention on his part, the mere fact of his presence was sufficient to account for it, so dull and heavy did my clumsy *spropositi*[1] appear by the side of his graceful and refined wit. During the first two years, his visits to Montmorency had been very rare; and, thanks to the indulgence of Madame la Marquise, I had held my ground tolerably well; but, as soon as he made his appearance with tolerable regularity, I was crushed beyond hope of recovery.

I should have liked to take refuge under his wing, and to make him my friend; but the same awkwardness which made his favour a necessity to me prevented me from gaining it; and my maladroit efforts in that direction ended by completely ruining me with Madame la Maréchale, without being of any service to me in regard to him. With his intellect, he might have succeeded in everything; but his total incapacity for steady application, and his taste for amusement only permitted him to acquire imperfect accomplishments of every description. By way of compensation, these attainments were extensive; and that is all that is necessary in the great world in which he is anxious to shine. He can compose pretty little poems, write pretty little notes, can play a little on the cithern, and daub a little in pastil. He undertook to paint Madame de Luxembourg's portrait; the result was horrible. She declared that it was not in the least like her, which was quite true. The traitorous Abbé consulted me; and I, like a fool and a liar, said that it was like her. I wanted to flatter the Abbé; but I did not flatter Madame la Maréchale, who scored it down against me; and the Abbé, after his trick had succeeded, laughed at me. I learned, through the result of my tardy first attempt, never again to attempt to play the sycophant and flatterer, *invita Minerva.*[2]

---

[1] Absurdities, blunders.
[2] *Malgré Minerve*: specially applied to a poet, who persists in writing verses, in spite of his having no talent for it.

My ability lay in telling useful but hard truths to mankind with a certain amount of energy and courage; and I ought to have stopped at that. I was not born, I will not say to flatter, but to praise. The awkwardness of the praises which I attempted to bestow has done me more harm than all the severity of my reproaches. I will here quote a terrible example of this, the consequences of which have not only decided my destiny for the rest of my life, but will perhaps decide my reputation among posterity.

When the family stayed at Montmorency, M. de Choiseul[1] sometimes came to supper at the château. He came one day as I was leaving it. They spoke about me: M. de Luxembourg told him the history of my relations with M. de Montaigu at Venice. M. de Choiseul said that it was a pity that I had abandoned the diplomatic career, and that, if I was inclined to enter it again, it would give him great pleasure to find me employment. M. de Luxembourg repeated this to me: as I was not accustomed to be spoiled by ministers, I felt it all the more; and I am not at all sure that, if my health had permitted me to entertain the idea, I should not have made a fool of myself again, in spite of my resolutions. Ambition only took possession of me during the brief intervals when all other passions left me alone; but one of these intervals would have been sufficient to enlist my sympathies again. This kindly intention on M. de Choiseul's part gained my affection and strengthened the esteem which some of the proceedings of his ministry had caused me to entertain for his talents: the *pacte de famille*,[2] in particular, appeared to me to indicate a statesman of the first rank. He gained my esteem still more from the poor opinion I had of his predecessors, not even excepting Madame de Pompadour, whom I looked upon as a sort of Prime Minister; and when it was currently reported that one of those two would drive out the other, I believed that I was offering prayers for the glory of France when I prayed for the triumph of M. de Choiseul. I had always had a feeling of antipathy against Madame de Pompadour even when I saw her, before she had risen to

---

[1] [Choiseul] See *Biographies*, p. 707.
[2] A treaty of defensive alliance, concluded in 1761, between the two branches of the house of Bourbon in France and Spain.

power, at Madame de Poplinière's, while she was still Madame d'Etioles. Since then, I had been annoyed by her silence in the matter of Diderot, and the manner in which she had behaved towards me, both in regard to the *Fêtes de Ramire*, the *Muses Galantes*, and the *Devin du Village*, which had by no means brought me advantages proportionate to its success: in all these cases I had found very little inclination on her part to oblige me: this, however, did not prevent the Chevalier de Lorenzi from proposing to me to write something in praise of this lady, at the same time giving me to understand that it might be useful to me. This proposal made me the more indignant, as I saw clearly that it did not come from him: I knew well that this man, who was totally insignificant in himself, never thought or acted except as he was prompted by others. I am not sufficiently capable of putting restraint upon myself to have been able to conceal from him my contempt for his proposition, or, from anyone else, my dislike for the favourite, which I am convinced she knew; all these considerations united my self-interest to my natural inclination, in the prayers which I offered for the success of M. de Choiseul. Already prepossessed in favour of his abilities, which was the extent of my acquaintance with him: full of gratitude for his good intentions; in addition, totally ignorant, in my retirement, of his tastes and manner of life, I regarded him by anticipation as the avenger of the public and myself; and, as I was at the time engaged in putting the finishing touches to the "Contrat Social," I set down, in a single passage, my opinion of preceding ministries, and of that which was beginning to eclipse them all. On this occasion, I offended against my most firmly established principle; and, further, I did not reflect that, when one desires to praise or blame strongly in the same article, without mentioning names, it is necessary to apportion the praise to those for whom it is intended in such a manner that the most sensitive *amour-propre* cannot possibly misunderstand it. In regard to this, I felt so foolishly secure, that it never even occurred that it could be possible for anyone to be mistaken. It will soon be seen whether I was right.

It had been one of my misfortunes to be always connected with authoresses. I thought that, amongst the great, I should at least be free from this. Not at all; my misfortune still pursued me. As far as I know, Madame de Luxembourg was never attacked by this complaint; but Madame de Boufflers was. She wrote a tragedy in prose, which was at first read, sent round, and praised up in M. le Prince de Conti's circle; and, not satisfied with all these eulogies, she wanted to ask my opinion also, in order to secure my approbation. I gave it, and praised the work in the moderate terms which it deserved. I also informed her, as I thought was only right, that her piece, entitled *L'Esclave Généreux*, had a great resemblance to a little known English play, which, however, had been translated into French, called *Oroonoko*.[1] Madame de Boufflers thanked me for my opinion, but assured me that her piece had not the least resemblance to the English. I have never mentioned this plagiarism to a single person except herself, and then only to fulfil a duty which she herself had imposed upon me; but this has not prevented me from often thinking since then of the manner in which Gil Blas[2] fulfilled his duty to the preaching archbishop, and its results.

Without mentioning the Abbé de Boufflers, who was not fond of me, and Madame de Boufflers, whom I had offended in a manner which women and authors never forgive, none of Madame le Maréchale's other friends seemed particularly inclined to become mine. I may mention M. le Président Hénault, who, as a member of the society of authors, was not free from their faults; Madame du Deffand and Mademoiselle de Lespinasse, both of them on intimate terms with Voltaire and D'Alembert, with the latter of whom Mademoiselle de Lespinasse finally lived – of course, in a most respectable manner: let no one imagine that I mean anything else. I had begun by feeling a lively interest in Madame du Deffand, whom I pitied on account of the loss of her eyesight; but her manner of living, so entirely contrary to mine, that she got up about the time that I went to bed; her extravagant passion for trifling displays of wit; the importance which she attached to the most contemptible

[1] Thomas Southerne's play (1696), based on Aphra Behn's *Orinooko; or the Royal Slave*.

[2] Begged by the Archbishop of Granada to give his opinion of the latter's sermons, the valet Gil Blas is rewarded for his frankness by being thrown into prison. (See Le Sage, *Gil Blas*, Book VII.)

rags which appeared, whether complimentary or abusive; the despotic violence of her oracular utterances; her exaggerated prepossessions in favour of or against everything, which prevented her from speaking of any subject except hysterically; her incredible prejudices, her unconquerable obstinacy, her unreasoning enthusiasm to which she was carried away by the stubbornness of her impassioned judgments – all this soon discouraged me from the attentions which I was ready to pay her. I neglected her; she noticed it. This was sufficient to put her in a rage; and, although I felt how greatly a woman of this character was to be feared, I preferred to expose myself to the scourge of her hatred than to that of her friendship.

As if it was not enough for me to have so few friends in Madame de Luxembourg's circle, I had enemies in her family – only one, certainly, but one who, in the situation in which I now find myself, is equal to a hundred. It was certainly not her brother, M. le Duc de Villeroy, who not only came to see me, but invited me several times to Villeroy; and, as I had answered this invitation with all possible politeness and respect, he had taken this vague answer as an acceptance, and arranged that M. and Madame de Luxembourg should pay him a fortnight's visit, on which it was proposed that I should accompany them. As the care which my health required rendered it dangerous for me at that time to change my quarters, I begged M. de Luxembourg to be good enough to make my excuses. It may be seen from his answer (Packet D, No. 3) that he did so with the best grace in the world; and M. le Duc de Villeroy's kindness towards me showed no alteration. His nephew and heir, the young Marquis de Villeroy, did not share the kindly feelings with which his uncle honoured me, nor, I must confess, did I entertain the same respect for him. His frivolous behaviour made him unendurable to me, and my coldness brought upon me his dislike. One evening, at table, he wantonly insulted me; I came out very badly, because I am a fool and utterly without presence of mind, and anger, instead of sharpening the little ready wit I may possess, entirely deprives me of it. I had a dog which had been given to me when it was quite a puppy, almost immediately after my arrival at the Hermitage, and which I had named

"Duke." This dog, which, although no beauty, was of an uncommon breed, I had made my friend and companion; and it certainly deserved the name better than the majority of those who have assumed it. It had become a favourite at the château of Montmorency, owing to its sensible and affectionate disposition, and the attachment which we felt for each other; but, in a moment of foolish weakness, I had changed its name to "Turk," as if there had not been hundreds of dogs called "Marquis," without any Marquis being offended at it. The Marquis de Villeroy, who knew of this change of name, pressed me so hard upon the point that I was obliged to relate, in the presence of the company, what I had done. What gave offence in the story was, not so much that I had given the dog the name of "Duke," as that I had afterwards altered it. The worst thing was, that there were several dukes present, amongst others, M. de Luxembourg and his son. The Marquis de Villeroy, who was a duke presumptive, and bears that title at the present day, cruelly enjoyed the embarrassing position in which he had placed me, and the effect produced by it. I was assured, the next day, that his aunt had severely scolded him; and it may be imagined how far this reprimand, if he really received it, must have improved my relations with him.

My only protector against all these enemies, both at the Hôtel de Luxembourg and at the Temple, was the Chevalier de Lorenzi, who professed to be my friend; but he was still more the friend of D'Alembert, under whose wings he passed amongst the ladies for a great geometrician. He was, besides, the gallant, or rather the tame cat, of Madame la Comtesse de Boufflers, who was herself a great friend of D'Alembert; the Chevalier de Lorenzi's very existence and thoughts depended upon her. Thus, far from my possessing any outside counterpoise to my folly which could keep me in Madame de Luxembourg's good graces, all who approached her seemed to work together to injure me in her esteem. However, besides her kindness in undertaking to see after "Émile," she showed me an additional mark of favour and sympathy, which caused me to believe that, even if she was getting tired of me, she still preserved, and would always preserve, the friendship which she had so often promised to entertain for me to the end of my life.

As soon as I thought that I could reckon upon this feeling on her part, I began to relieve my heart by making a confession of all my faults to her; since it is an inviolable principle with me, to show myself to my friends exactly as I am, neither better nor worse. I informed her of my relations with Thérèse, and all their consequences, not omitting the manner in which I had disposed of my children. She received my confessions kindly, even too kindly, and spared me the censure which I deserved; and what especially touched me was the kindness which she lavished upon Thérèse: she gave her little presents, sent for her, encouraged her to go and see her, received her most tenderly, and frequently kissed her before everybody. The poor girl was transported with joy and gratitude, which I certainly shared; the kindness with which M. and Madame de Luxembourg overwhelmed me through her touched me more than that which they showed to me directly.

For a considerable time matters remained on this footing; but at last Madame la Maréchale pushed her kindness so far as to express a wish to remove and adopt one of my children. She knew that I had put a monogram upon the eldest one's linen; she asked me for the duplicate of it, and I gave it to her. In the search she employed La Roche, her *valet de chambre* and confidential servant, whose inquiries proved useless; he found out nothing, although only twelve or fourteen years had elapsed; if the registers of the Foundling Hospital had been regularly kept, or if the inquiry had been properly conducted, the mark ought not to have been so difficult to discover. However that may be, I was less annoyed at his failure than I should have been, if I had followed the child's career from its birth. If, with the assistance of the information afforded, any child had been presented to me as mine, the doubt, whether it really was so, or whether another had been substituted for it, would have tormented my heart with uncertainty, and I should not have enjoyed in all its charm the true feeling of nature, which, in order to be kept alive, must be kept up by constant familiarity at least during infancy. The continued absence of a child whom one does not yet know, weakens and at last utterly destroys the feelings of a parent; it is impossible to love a child which has been put out to nurse as much as one which is brought up at home. This reflection may extenuate the effects of my faults, but only aggravates their origin.

It may be useful to observe that, through the medium of Thérèse, this same La Roche made the acquaintance of Madame le Vasseur, whom Grimm still kept at Deuil, close to La Chevrette, and only a little distance from Montmorency. After I left, it was through M. la Roche that I continued to send this woman the money which I never ceased to supply her with, and I believe that he very often took presents to her from Madame la Maréchale; thus, although she was always complaining, she was certainly not to be pitied. In regard to Grimm, as I am not fond of speaking of people whom I feel bound to hate, I never mentioned him to Madame de Luxembourg unless I was obliged to; but she several times introduced his name without telling me what she thought of him, and without ever letting me discover whether she was acquainted with the man or not. As reserve with those whom I love, and who are perfectly frank with me, is by no means to my taste, especially in what concerns them, I have sometimes reflected since then upon the reserve which she showed towards me, but only when such reflection has been rendered natural by other events.

After having waited a considerable time since I had handed "Emile" to Madame de Luxembourg, without hearing anything about it, I at length was informed that an arrangement had been made at Paris with the bookseller Duchesne, and by him with Néaulme of Amsterdam. Madame de Luxembourg sent me the two copies of the agreement with Duchesne to sign. I recognised the writing as that of M. de Malesherbes's letters, which he did not write himself. The certainty that my agreement had been concluded with the consent and under the eyes of the magistrate made me sign it with confidence. Duchesne gave me 6,000 *francs* for the manuscript, half down, and, I think, 100 to 200 copies. Having signed the two documents, I sent them both to Madame de Luxembourg, in accordance with her desire; she gave one to Duchesne and kept the other herself, instead of sending it back to me, and I have never seen it again.

Although my acquaintance with M. and Madame de Luxembourg had interrupted my plans of retirement, they had not caused me to renounce them altogether. Even at the time when I was most in favour with Madame la Maréchale, I always felt that nothing but my sincere attachment to her and her husband could render their surroundings endurable; my whole difficulty was to unite this attachment with a manner of life more agreeable to my taste and less injurious to my health, which the perpetual restraint and the late suppers continually undermined, in spite of all the care which they took to avoid exposing me to any risk; for, in this respect, as in everything else, they showed the greatest possible attention. For instance, every evening, after supper, M. de Maréchal, who went to bed early, never failed to take me away with him, whether I liked it or not, in order that I might do the same. It was not until just before my catastrophe that he ceased, for some reason unknown to me, to show me this attention.

Even before I perceived any coldness on the part of Madame la Maréchale, I was anxious, in order to avoid exposing myself to it, to carry out my old plan; but, as I was without the means, I was obliged to wait until the agreement of "Emile" was concluded, and in the meantime I put the final touches to the "Contrat Social," and sent it to Rey, fixing the price of the manuscript at 1,000 *francs*, which he gave me. I ought not perhaps to omit a little incident which has reference to that manuscript. I handed it, carefully sealed, to Duvoisin, a minister from the Pays de Vaud, and chaplain at the hôtel de Hollande, who sometimes came to see me, and undertook to forward it to Rey, with whom he was acquainted. This manuscript, written in a very fine hand, was very small, and did not fill his pocket. However, as he was passing the *barrière*,[1] it somehow or other fell into the hands of the clerks, who, after having opened and examined it, afterwards returned it to him, when he claimed it in the name of the Ambassador. This gave him the opportunity of reading it himself, which, as he ingenuously informed me, he

[1] The gate where the offices of the *octroi*, or town dues, were.

did, at the same time praising the work highly, without a word of blame or criticism, no doubt reserving to himself the right of playing the part of the avenger of Christianity when the work should have appeared. He resealed the manuscript, and sent it to Rey. Such was essentially the story which he told me in the letter in which he gave me an account of the matter, and that is all that I have heard about it.

Besides these two works and my "Dictionnaire de Musique," at which I worked from time to time, I had some other writings of less importance, all ready for publication, which I intended to bring out, either separately or in a general collection of my works, if I ever undertook to produce one. The most important of these, most of which are still in manuscript in the hands of Du Peyrou, was an "Essai sur l'Origine des Langues," which I had read to M. de Malesherbes and the Chevalier de Lorenzi, who expressed his approval of it. I calculated that all these works together, after all expenses, would be worth to me at least 8,000 or 10,000 *francs*, which I intended to sink in a life-annuity for myself and Thérèse. After this, we would go and live together in the corner of some province, where I would no longer trouble the public with myself, or trouble myself about anything further, except how to end my days peacefully, while continuing to do as much good around me as was possible, and to write at my leisure the Memoirs which I meditated.

Such was my scheme, the execution of which was rendered still easier to me by the generosity of Rey, which I must not pass by in silence. This publisher, of whom I heard so much that was bad at Paris, is nevertheless the only one, of all those with whom I have had anything to do, that I have always had reason to be satisfied with.* We certainly often quarrelled about the publication of my books; he was careless, and I was hasty. But, in financial matters and others connected with them, although I never had a regular agreement with him, I always found him strictly honourable. He is also the only one who has openly admitted that he made a good thing out of me; and he has often

---

* When I wrote these lines, I was far from imagining, or conceiving, much less believing, the frauds which I subsequently discovered in the printing of my works, which he was obliged to admit. (R)

told me that he owed his fortune to me, and offered to share it with me. Being unable to show his gratitude to myself directly, he desired to prove it at least in the person of my better-half, upon whom he settled an annuity of 300 *francs*, stating in the deed that it was an acknowledgement of the advantages he owed to me. We settled the matter between us, without any show or pretentiousness; and if I had not been the first to let everybody know of it, no one would ever have heard of it. I was so affected by his behaviour, that from that I became sincerely attached to him. Some time afterwards, he asked me to stand godfather to one of his children; I consented; and one of my regrets, in the condition to which I have been reduced, is that I have been deprived of all opportunity of ever making my attachment of any service to my goddaughter and her parents. How is it that I, who am so grateful for the modest generosity of this publisher, feel so little gratitude for the noisy attentions of so many distinguished personages, who boastfully fill the world with an account of the benefits which they claim to have bestowed upon me, the results of which I have never felt? Is it their fault, or is it mine? Is it merely vanity on their part, or ungratefulness on mine? I ask the intelligent reader to consider and decide the matter; for myself, I am dumb.

This pension was a great assistance to Thérèse, and a great relief for me. But I was far from desiring any direct profit for myself from it, any more than from any other presents which she received. She has always had the absolute disposal of it. If I kept her money, I rendered her a faithful account of it, without ever deducting a farthing for our common expenses, even when she was better off than I was. "That which is mine is ours," I said to her, "and that which is yours is yours." I always behaved, in money matters, in accordance with this principle, which I often repeated to her. Those who are base enough to accuse me of accepting through her hands what I refused to accept with my own, no doubt judged my heart by their own, and had but little knowledge of me. I would gladly eat with her the bread she may earn, but never that which may be given to her. I appeal to her own testimony on this point, both now and hereafter, when, in the course of nature, she shall have survived me. Unfortunately, she knows little about economy in anything, and she is careless and extravagant, not from vanity or fondness of delicacies, but from sheer thoughtlessness. No one is perfect in this world; and, since her excellent qualities must be counterbalanced, I prefer that she should have faults rather than vices, although these faults are sometimes more prejudicial to us both. The efforts which I have made for her sake, as formerly for mamma's, to put by a little hoard which might some day be useful to her, are inconceivable; but it has always been labour lost. Neither of them ever reckoned with herself; and, in spite of all my endeavours, all that I earned was immediately gone. Notwithstanding the simplicity with which she dresses, Rey's pension has never been sufficient, and I have always been obliged to assist her every year. Neither she nor I was born to be rich, and I certainly do not reckon that as one of our misfortunes.

The "Contrat Social" was printed with little delay. It was different with "Émile," for the publication of which I was obliged to wait, before I could carry out my project of retirement. From time to time, Duchesne sent me specimens of type to choose from; and after I had made a choice, instead of putting the work in hand, he sent me fresh ones. When we had at last settled upon the size and type, and several sheets had already been struck off, in consequence of a slight alteration which I made in a proof he began all over again, and, at the end of six months, we were not so far advanced as on the first day. While these experiments were going on, I discovered that the book was being printed in France as well as in Holland, and in two separate editions. What could I do? The manuscript was no longer under my control. Far from having had anything to do with the French edition, I had always opposed it; but, at length, since it was being brought out, whether I liked it or not, and served as a model for the other, I was obliged to glance over it and look at the proofs, to prevent my work being mutilated and disfigured. Besides, the work was being printed with such definite approval on the part of the magistrate, that the undertaking was in some sort under his direction; he frequently wrote to me, and even came to see me on the subject, on a certain occasion of which I will speak presently.

While Duchesne proceeded at a tortoise-pace, Néaulme, whom he kept back, proceeded even more slowly. The sheets were not sent to him regularly as they were printed. He thought that Duchesne, that is to say De Guy, who acted for him, was not behaving in good faith; and, seeing that the agreement was not being carried out, he wrote to me letter after letter full of complaints and grievances, which I could no more remedy than my own. His friend Guérin, who at that time saw me pretty frequently, was always talking to me about the book, but with the greatest reserve. He did and he did not know that it was being printed in France; he did and he did not know that the magistrate was interesting himself in it; he sympathised with me upon the embarrassment the book would cause me, while at the same time he seemed to accuse me of imprudence, without ever telling me in what it consisted; he equivocated and shuffled incessantly; he seemed to talk only to make me talk. At that time, I fancied myself so secure, that I laughed at the cautious and mysterious tone which he adopted in the matter, as a habit contracted by constant intercourse with ministerial and magisterial offices. Feeling sure that everything connected with the work was in order, firmly convinced that it enjoyed not only the approval and protection of the magistrate, but even deserved and had obtained the favour of the ministry, I congratulated myself upon my courage in acting rightly, and laughed at the faintheartedness of my friends, who seemed anxious about me. Duclos was amongst the number, and I confess that my confidence in his uprightness and shrewdness might have alarmed me if I had felt less confidence in the usefulness of the work and the honour of its patrons. He came to see me on the part of M. Baille, while "Émile" was in the press, and spoke to me about it. I read to him the "Savoyard Vicar's Profession of Faith"; he listened to it quietly, and, as it seemed to me, with great pleasure. When I had finished, he said to me: "What, citizen! is this part of a book which is being printed in Paris?" "Yes," I answered; "and it was to be printed at the Louvre, by order of the King." "I admit it," said he; "but be kind enough not to tell anyone that you have read me this extract." This singular way of expressing himself surprised, but did not alarm me. I knew that Duclos saw a good deal of M. de Malesherbes; and I found it difficult to understand how he could hold so different an opinion in regard to the same thing.

I had lived at Montmorency for more than four years, without having enjoyed one single day of good health. Although the air is excellent, the water is bad; and this may very well have been one of the causes which aggravated my usual complaints. About the end of the autumn of 1761 I fell seriously ill, and spent the whole winter in almost constant suffering. My physical ailments, increased by numerous uneasinesses, made them still more painful to me. For some time secret and gloomy forebodings had been disturbing me, although I did not know to what they referred. I received several curious anonymous letters, and even signed ones which were equally curious; one from a councillor of the Parliament of Paris, who, dissatisfied with the present constitution of affairs, and prognosticating no good from its results, wished to consult me as to the choice of an asylum in Geneva or Switzerland, to which he and his family might retire; another from M. de — *président à mortier* in the Parliament of — [1] who proposed to me to draw up a memorandum and remonstrances for this Parliament, which at that time was out of favour with the Court, at the same time offering to supply me with all the materials and documents which I might require.

When I am suffering, I am easily irritated. This was what happened when I received these letters, and I showed it by my answers, in which I flatly refused to do what I was asked. I certainly do not reproach myself for refusing, since these letters might have been snares set for me by my enemies,* and what I was asked to do was opposed to the principles from which I was still less than ever inclined to depart; but, when I might have refused politely, I refused rudely; and therefore in that I was wrong.

The two letters of which I have just spoken will be found amongst my papers. The letter from the councillor did not altogether surprise me, because, in common with him and

---

[1] Charles de Brosses (1709–77), *président à mortier* of the *Parlement* of Dijon.

* For instance, I knew that the President of — was intimately connected with the Encyclopaedists and the Holbachians. (R)

many others, I thought that the break up of the constitution threatened France with speedy destruction. The disasters of an unfortunate war,[1] which were all the fault of the Government; the incredible financial disorders; the continued disagreements in the administration, which had hitherto been conducted by two or three ministers openly opposed, and who, in order to injure each other, were ruining the kingdom; the general discontent of the people and of all classes in the State; the stubbornness of an obstinate woman, who, ever sacrificing her intellectual powers, if she possessed any, to her inclinations, almost invariably kept the most capable men out of offices, in order to fill them with those who were her favourites; all these things contributed to justify the forebodings of the councillor, the public, and myself. These forebodings several times made me consider whether I should not act wisely in seeking a refuge for myself outside the kingdom, before the troubles, which seemed to threaten it, broke out; but, reassured by my insignificance and peaceful disposition, I believed that, in the retirement in which I intended to live, no storm could reach me. My only regret was that, when things were in this condition, M. de Luxembourg undertook commissions which could not fail to make him disliked in his government. I could have wished him to prepare a retreat for himself there, ready for all emergencies, in case the great machine should fall to pieces, which there seemed reason to fear under existing circumstances; and it still seems to me at the present time that there can be no doubt that, if the reins of government had not fallen completely into the hands of one man, the French monarchy would now be in its last agonies.

While my condition grew worse, the printing of "Émile" proceeded more slowly, and was at last entirely suspended. I was unable to learn the reason. Guy did not condescend either to write to me again or to answer my letters. I could not procure information from anyone, and knew nothing of what was going on, M. de Malesherbes being in the country at the time. No misfortune, whatever it may be, ever troubles or overwhelms me, provided that I know in what it consists; but I am naturally

[1] The Seven Years' War.

afraid of darkness; I dread and hate its gloomy appearance; mystery always makes me uneasy; it is too much opposed to my disposition, which is frank to the verge of imprudence. During the daytime, the sight of the most hideous monster would, I believe, alarm me but little; but if I were to see by night a figure in a white sheet, I should be afraid. Thus my fancy, kindled by this prolonged silence, busied itself in conjuring up for me a number of phantoms. The more I had at heart the publication of my last and best work, the more I tormented myself to find out what could be delaying it; and, as I always went to extremes in everything, I saw in the suspension of the printing the suppression of the book. Meanwhile, as I was unable to imagine the reason or the manner of this interruption, I remained a prey to the most cruel uncertainty. I wrote letter after letter to Guy, M. de Malesherbes, and Madame de Luxembourg; and as no answers came at all, or did not come when I expected them, I was utterly confused and almost beside myself. Unfortunately I heard, at the same time, that Father Griffet, a Jesuit, had spoken of "Émile," and had even quoted passages from it. In a moment my imagination, like a flash of lightning, disclosed the whole iniquitous mystery; I saw its progress as clearly and as surely as if it had been revealed to me. I imagined that the Jesuits, furious at the tone of contempt in which I had spoken of their colleges, had got possession of my work; that it was they who were delaying its publication; that, having been informed by their friend Guérin of my present condition, and foreseeing my speedy death, of which I myself entertained no doubt, their object was to delay the printing until that event occurred, with the intention of mutilating and altering the work, and, in order to serve their own ends, of attributing to me opinions totally different from my own. It is astonishing what a crowd of facts and circumstances entered my head to accommodate themselves to this mad idea, and to give it an air of probability – nay, to prove and demonstrate its truth. I knew that Guérin was completely devoted to the Jesuits. I attributed to them all the friendly advances which he had made to me. I persuaded myself that it was at their instigation that he had urged me to enter into negotiations with Néaulme; that it was through the latter that they had got hold of the first sheets of my work; and that they had subsequently found means to make Duchesne stop printing, and perhaps to get possession of my manuscript, in order to work upon it at their leisure, until my death should leave them free to publish their travesty of it. I had always felt, in spite of Father Berthier's show of affection, that the Jesuits had no love for me, not only as being an Encyclopaedist, but also because my views were even more hostile to their principles and influence than the unbelief of my colleagues, since atheistic and religious fanaticism, which approach closely in their common intolerance, are even capable of uniting, as they have done towards China,[1] and as they do now against myself; whereas rational and moral religion, which takes away all human control over the conscience, deprives of further resource those who claim that power. I knew that the Chancellor also was a great friend of the Jesuits; I was afraid that the son, intimidated by the father, might find himself compelled to abandon to them the manuscript which he had taken under his protection. I even imagined that I could see the effect of this abandonment in the chicanery which was stirred up against me in regard to the two first volumes, in which fresh sheets were required for mere trifles; while the two remaining volumes, as was well known, were full of such outspoken sentiments, that it would have been necessary to recast them entirely, if they had been criticised by the censor like the two first. I knew besides – and M. de Malesherbes himself told me – that the Abbé de Grave, who had been charged with the inspection of this edition, was another partisan of the Jesuits. I saw nothing but Jesuits everywhere, without reflecting that they, on the eve of their annihilation, and fully occupied with their own defence, had something else to do than to intrigue against the printing of a book in which they were not concerned. I am wrong, however, in saying, "without reflection"; I certainly did think of it. M. de Malesherbes himself even took care to make the objection, as

---

[1] *i.e.*, the Jesuits agreed with the Encyclopaedists, though for opposite motives, in extolling the Chinese. In the spring of the following year *Parlement* succeeded in forcing the closure of Jesuit schools, and this was followed in 1764 by the expulsion of Jesuits from France.

soon as he heard of my fantastic idea; but, owing to another of these caprices, to which a man is subject who attempts, in the bosom of obscurity, to judge of secret and important affairs of which he knows nothing, I refused to believe that the Jesuits were in danger, and I regarded such rumours as a ruse on their part to lull their adversaries to sleep. Their past and ever consistent successes gave me so terrible an idea of their power, that I already lamented the degradation of the Parliament. I knew that M. de Choiseul had studied amongst the Jesuits, that Madame de Pompadour was not on bad terms with them, and that their league with the favourites and ministers had always been considered of great service to both parties against their common enemies. The Court appeared to be neutral; and feeling convinced that, if the society one day met with a severe check, the Parliament would never be strong enough to give it, I drew from this inaction on the part of the Court the justification of their confidence and the augury of their triumph. In short, seeing in all the rumours of the day nothing but a feint and snares on their part, and believing that, in their position of security, they had time to attend to everything, I had no doubt that they would soon crush Jansenism, the Parliament, the Encyclopaedists, and all who had not submitted to their yoke; and that, if they permitted my book to appear, it would not be until they had transformed it into a weapon for themselves, by making use of my name in order to deceive my readers.

I felt that I was dying. I can scarcely understand how it was that my extravagant notions did not prove my death-blow, so terribly was I alarmed at the idea that my memory would be dishonoured in a work which was my best and most worthy of me. I never felt such dread of death; and I believe that, if I had died then, I should have died in a state of utter despair. Even at the present day, when I see the blackest and most hideous conspiracy which has ever been entered into against a man's memory advancing without hindrance to its accomplishment, I shall die much more peacefully, feeling sure of leaving behind me in my writings a witness in my favour which, sooner or later, will triumph over the conspiracies of men.

[1762.] – M. de Malesherbes, the witness and confidant of my agitation, did his utmost to calm it, in a manner which proved his inexhaustible goodness of heart. M. de Luxembourg assisted in this good work, and went to see Duchesne several times, in order to find out how the edition was progressing. At last the printing was resumed and proceeded more rapidly; and I have never known why it had been suspended. M. de Malesherbes took the trouble to come to Montmorency to calm my agitation, and he succeeded. My perfect confidence in his uprightness, having overcome the derangement of my poor head, rendered effectual every effort on his part to restore its equilibrium. After what he had seen of my distress and frenzy, it was natural that he should consider that I greatly deserved to be pitied. The talk of the philosophical cabal, by which he was surrounded, repeated over and over again, came back to his mind. When I went to live at the Hermitage, they publicly declared, as I have already said, that I should not be able to stand it long. When they saw that I persevered, they said that it was due to obstinacy, pride, and shame at the idea of giving in, but that I was really wearied to death, and was very unhappy. M. de Malesherbes believed it and wrote to me. Feeling deeply this mistake on the part of a man whom I so highly esteemed, I wrote to him four letters one after the other, in which I explained the true reasons for my conduct, and at the same time faithfully described my tastes, my character, and all the feelings of my inmost heart. These four letters, written offhand, hurriedly, with a single stroke of the pen, and which I never even read over, are perhaps the only compositions which I have ever written with perfect ease during the whole of my life, and, what is even more astonishing, at a time when I was suffering deeply and was in a state of the utmost depression. Feeling my strength giving way, I sighed at the thought that I was leaving behind, in the minds of honourable men, so unjust an opinion of myself; and, by means of the sketch hastily thrown off in these four letters, I attempted, in some degree, to supply the place of the Memoirs which I had proposed to write. These letters, which pleased M. de Malesherbes, and which he showed to people in Paris, are to a certain extent the summary of that which I here set forth in detail, and, on this ground, are worthy of being preserved. The copy of them, which he had made at my request, and which he sent me some years afterwards, will be found amongst my papers.

From that time the only thing which troubled me, when I thought of my approaching death, was the want of a literary friend whom I could trust, in whose hands I could deposit my papers, so that, after my death, he might pick and choose from them. After my journey to Geneva, I had become friendly with Moultou;[1] I was fond of this young man, and should have liked him to close my eyes. I told him of my desire, and I believe that he would have performed this act of humanity with pleasure, if his affairs and his family had permitted him. Deprived of this consolation, I wished at least to give him a proof of my confidence, by sending him the "Savoyard Vicar's Profession of Faith" before it was published. He was very pleased with it; but, from the tone of his reply, he did not appear to me to share the feeling of confidence, with which at that time I awaited its effect. He expressed a wish to have something of mine which no one else possessed. I sent him a "Funeral Oration upon the late Duke of Orleans," which I had written for the Abbé d'Arty, but which had not been delivered because, contrary to his expectation, that duty had not been intrusted to him.

The printing, when it had once been resumed, was quietly continued and finished; and I noticed as a singular fact, that, after the fresh sheets, which had been stringently exacted for the first two volumes, the last two were passed without a word, and no objection of any kind was taken to their contents. However, I still felt an uneasiness, which I must not omit to mention. After having been alarmed at the Jesuits, I became alarmed at the Jansenists and philosophers. An enemy to everything that comes under the denomination of party, faction, and cabal, I have never expected any good from those who belong to them. The "Gossips" had left their former abode some time ago, and had established themselves so close to me, that, from their room, it was possible to hear everything that was said either in mine or on my terrace, and it was perfectly easy to climb, from their garden, the low wall which separated it from my turret. I had made this

[1] [Moultou] See *Biographies*, p. 713.

turret my study, and in it there was a table covered with proofs and sheets of "Émile" and the "Contrat Social"; these sheets I stitched together as they were sent to me, and thus had complete copies of all the volumes long before they were published. My thoughtlessness, carelessness, and confidence in M. Mathas, in the garden by which I was enclosed, often made me forget to shut my turret at night, and in the morning I found it wide open. This would not have caused me the least uneasiness, had I not fancied that I noticed that my papers had been disturbed. Having noticed this several times, I became more careful about shutting the turret. The lock was bad, and the key would only turn half-way in it. A more careful examination showed me that my papers were disturbed even more than when I left the door wide open. At last, one of my volumes disappeared for a day and two nights, and I was utterly unable to find what had become of it until the morning of the third day, when I found it on my table again. I neither felt then, nor ever have felt, any suspicion of M. Mathas, or his nephew M. Dumoulin, as I know that both had a sincere regard for me, and I felt every confidence in them. I began to feel less sure about the "Gossips." I knew that, although they were Jansenists, they had some connection with D'Alembert and lived in the same house. This caused me some uneasiness, and made me more careful. I removed my papers to my room, and entirely gave up visiting these people, as I had also heard that they had exhibited in several houses the first volume of "Émile," which I had been imprudent enough to lend them. Although they continued to be my neighbours until I left, I held no further communication with them from that time forth.

The "Contrat Social" appeared a month or two before "Émile."[1] Rey, whom I had made promise never to introduce any of my books secretly into France, applied to the magistrate for permission to introduce this by way of Rouen, to which place he sent his consignments by sea. He received no reply; his packages

[1] The *Contrat social* came off the presses at the beginning of April 1762 and was soon on sale in Switzerland and Britain. It was forbidden entry into France, though clandestine copies circulated there. *Émile* went on sale in Paris at the end of May.

remained at Rouen for several months, when they were sent back to him, after an attempt had been made to confiscate them; but he created such a disturbance that they were returned to him. Certain persons, out of curiosity, procured some copies from Amsterdam, which circulated without making much stir. Mauléon, who had heard and even seen something of this, spoke to me about it with an air of mystery which surprised me, and would even have made me uneasy, unless, feeling sure that I had acted in order in everything, and had done nothing with which I could reproach myself, I had reassured myself by my grand principle. I entertained no doubt that M. de Choiseul, who had already shown himself favourably disposed towards me, and appreciated the eulogy which my esteem had caused me to pronounce upon him in this work, would support me on this occasion against the ill-will of Madame de Pompadour.

At that time, I certainly had as much reason as ever to reckon upon the kindness of M. de Luxembourg, and his support in case of necessity; for he never gave me more frequent or more touching proofs of his friendship. During his Easter visit, my melancholy state of health did not allow me to go to the château; but he never let a day pass without paying me a visit, and, seeing that my sufferings were incessant, he at last persuaded me to let him send for Brother Côme.[1] He brought him to me himself, and had the courage, certainly rare and meritorious in a great nobleman, to remain with me during the operation, which was a long and painful one. However, it was only a question of being probed; but I had never been able to submit to it, even at the hands of Morand, who made the attempt several times, but always unsuccessfully. Brother Côme, whose skill and lightness of hand was unequalled, at last succeeded in introducing a very small probe, after having caused me great suffering for more than two hours, during which I did my utmost to restrain my cries, to avoid distressing the tender-hearted Marquis. On the first examination, Brother Côme thought he had discovered a

---

[1] Jean Baseilhac (1703–1781), a great authority on stone and diseases of the bladder. He was a member of the religious order, founded by Robert de Molesme, in the village of Cîteaux, in 1098.

large stone, and told me so; on the second, he could not find it. After having made a second and third examination, with a care and exactitude which made the time seem very long, he declared that there was no stone at all, but that the prostate gland was scirrhous and abnormally swollen. He found the bladder large and in good condition, and he ended by expressing his opinion that I should suffer greatly, and that I should live for a long time. If the second prediction is fulfilled as completely as the first, my sufferings are not nearly at an end.

Thus, after having been successively treated for so many years for complaints which I never had, I ended by learning that my malady, incurable without being fatal, would last as long as myself. My imagination, checked by this knowledge, no longer presented to me the prospect of a cruel death in the agonies of stone. I ceased to fear that the end of a bougie, which had long ago been broken off in the urethra, had laid the foundation for the formation of a stone. Freed from imaginary evils, more cruel than those which were real, I endured the latter more patiently. There is no doubt that, since that time, I have suffered much less from my malady than I had ever done before, and I never remember that I owe this relief to M. de Luxembourg, without being stirred to fresh emotion when I think of him.

Thus restored, so to speak, to life, and more than ever occupied with my plans for passing what still remained of it, I only waited for the publication of "Émile" in order to put them into execution. I thought of Touraine, which I had already visited, and which pleased me greatly, owing to the mildness of its climate and the gentleness of its inhabitants.

> "La terra molle e lieta e dilettosa
> Simile a se gli abitator produce."[1]

I had already mentioned my plan to M. de Luxembourg, who endeavoured to dissuade me from it. I spoke to him of it again, as a step upon which I had decided. He then proposed to me the Château of Merlou, fifteen leagues from Paris, as a refuge which might possibly suit me, where he and his wife would be delighted

[1] "The country, agreeable, fertile and delightful, produces inhabitants like itself." (Tasso, *Gerusalemme Liberata*, I, 62.)

to see me settled. The proposal touched me, and made a favourable impression upon my mind. First of all, it was necessary to see the place, and we agreed that he should send his *valet de chambre* with a carriage, on a day which was fixed upon, to drive me there. On that day I was very unwell, the journey had to be put off, and various disappointments prevented the plan from being carried out. As I subsequently heard that Merlou belonged, not to M. de Luxembourg, but to his wife, I had less difficulty in consoling myself for not having gone there.

"Émile" at last appeared, without my having heard any more about fresh proofs or other difficulties. Before its publication, M. de Luxembourg asked me to return all the letters from M. de Malesherbes, which had reference to the work. My great confidence in both, my feeling of perfect security, prevented me from considering the extraordinary, and even alarming, aspect of this request. I gave up the letters, with the exception of one or two which had inadvertently been left in some books. Some time previously, M. de Malesherbes had observed to me that he would withdraw the letters which I had written to Duchesne at the time when I was alarmed about the Jesuits; and I must confess that these letters were not very creditable to my intelligence. But I told him that I was not desirous of appearing better in any respect than I really was, and that he might leave the letters with Duchesne. I do not know whether he did so.

The publication of this book did not take place with the outburst of approval which had followed that of all my other writings. Never did a work meet with such praise from private individuals, and so little approbation from the public. What those who were most capable of judging said and wrote to me about it, confirmed me in the opinion that it was the best, as well as the most important, of my writings. But all this was told me with the most curious circumspection, as if it had been a matter of importance to keep all favourable opinion of it secret. Madame de Boufflers, who declared to me that the author of such a work deserved statues and the homage of all mankind, without any ceremony begged me, at the end of her note, to send it back to her. D'Alembert, who wrote to me to the effect that the work decided my superiority, and was bound to place me at the head of all men of letters, did not sign his note, although he had signed all those which he had previously written to me. Duclos, a friend on whom I could depend, an upright but cautious man, and who thought highly of the work, avoided expressing any opinion of it in writing. La Condamine fell upon the "Profession of Faith," and beat about the bush. Clairaut, in his letter, confined himself to the same part of the book, but was not afraid to declare how greatly he had been touched by reading it: he told me, in so many words, that the perusal of it had warmed his old soul. Of all those to whom I sent my book, he was the only one who told the world, openly and unreservedly, how highly he thought of it.

Mathas, to whom I had also given a copy before it was on sale, lent it to M. Blaire, Parliamentary Councillor, and father of the Intendant of Strasburg. M. de Blaire had a country house at Saint-Gratien, and Mathas, who was an old acquaintance, sometimes went to see him when he was able. He made him read "Émile" before it came out. M. de Blaire, on giving it back to him, made the following remark, which was repeated to me on the same day: "M. Mathas, this is a very fine book; but it will soon be spoken of more than is desirable for the author." When he repeated this to me, I merely laughed, and saw nothing more in it than the self-importance of a magistrate, who makes a mystery of everything. All the disturbing expressions, which were repeated to me, made equally little impression upon me; and, far from foreseeing in the least the catastrophe which was close at hand, convinced of the beauty and usefulness of my work, certain that I was in order in all respects, sure, as I believed I had a right to be, of all the influence of Madame de Luxembourg, and even of the favour of Ministers, I congratulated myself upon the resolution which I had taken – to retire in the midst of my triumphs, and when I had just crushed all those who were jealous of me.

One thing alone alarmed me in regard to the publication of the work, not so much out of consideration of my own safety as from a desire to quiet my conscience. At the Hermitage and at

Montmorency, close to my doors, I had seen with indignation the vexatious annoyances inflicted, owing to the jealous care with which the pleasures of princes are guarded, upon the unfortunate peasants, who are obliged to put up with the damage caused to their fields by the game, not venturing to protect themselves further than by making a noise, and compelled to spend the nights amidst their beans and peas, beating kettles, drums, and bells, to keep off the wild boars. A witness of the barbarous severity with which M. le Comte de Charolois caused these poor people to be treated, I had made an attack upon this cruel behaviour, towards the end of "Émile." This was another violation of my principles, which has not remained unpunished. I heard that the officers of M. le Prince de Conti treated the peasants upon his estates with hardly less cruelty. I trembled for fear that this Prince, towards whom I entertained the deepest feelings of respect and gratitude, might apply to himself the attack which a feeling of revolted humanity had caused me to make upon his uncle, and be offended at it. However, as my conscience completely justified me on this point, I quieted myself by its testimony, and I was right. At least, I have never heard that this great Prince paid the slightest attention to this passage, which was written long before I had the honour of his acquaintance.

A few days before or after the publication of my book – I do not exactly remember the time – another work on the same subject appeared, taken word for word from my first volume, with the exception of a few platitudes, scattered over the extract. This book bore the name of a Genevese, named Balexsert; and, according to the title, it had gained the prize at the Haarlem Academy. I easily understood that this Academy and this prize had been quite recently founded, in order to disguise the plagiarism in the eyes of the public; but I also saw that there must have been some previous intriguing, which I was at a loss to understand, either through the communication of my manuscript, without which the theft would have been impossible, or for the purpose of establishing the story of this pretended prize, for which it had been necessary to find some foundation. It was not until several years afterwards that I penetrated the mystery, in consequence of a word which D'Ivernois[1] let fall, and saw, as it were between the lines, who it was that had drawn M. Balexsert into the affair.

The dull murmur which precedes the storm began to make itself heard. All keen-witted persons saw clearly that, in regard to my book and myself, some plot was brewing, which would soon explode. As for me, my feeling of security and stupidity were so great, that, far from having any idea of my misfortune, I did not even suspect the cause, after I had felt the effects of it. My opponents began by cleverly spreading the idea that, while the Jesuits were severely treated, no favouritism could be shown towards books and authors who attacked religion. I was reproached for having put my name to "Émile," as if I had not put it to all my other writings, against which nothing had been said. It seemed as if people were afraid of being forced to take certain steps which they would regret, but which circumstances rendered necessary, and to which my imprudence had given occasion. These rumours reached my ears, but caused me scarcely any uneasiness. It never even occurred to me that in the whole affair there could be anything which personally affected me — me, who felt myself so completely beyond reproach, so strongly supported, and so entirely in order in all respects, and who had no fear that Madame de Luxembourg would leave me in difficulties on account of an error, which, if it had been committed, was entirely due to her. But, as I knew the usual course of things in similar cases, that it is the custom to rage against the booksellers while the authors are spared, I was not without some uneasiness in regard to poor Duchesne, if M. de Malesherbes should abandon him.

I remained calm. The rumours increased and soon assumed a different character. The public, and, above all, the Parliament, appeared irritated by my calmness. At the end of a few days the excitement became terrible; the threats changed their object, and were addressed directly to myself. Members of Parliament might be heard saying quite openly, that it was no good to burn the books; that the authors ought to be burnt as well. As for the

[1] François-Henri d'Ivernois (1722–78), a Genevan businessman and self-appointed friend of Rousseau's.

booksellers, not a word was said about them. The first time that these expressions of opinion, more worthy of an inquisitor of Goa than of a senator, were repeated to me, I had no doubt that they were an invention of the Holbachians intended to frighten me and drive me out of the country. I laughed at this childish trick, and said to myself that if they had known the real state of things, they would have sought some other means of frightening me; but at length the rumour became so pronounced, that it was clear that it was serious. M. and Madame de Luxembourg had made their second visit to Montmorency somewhat earlier than usual this year, and were there at the beginning of June. I heard very little said about my new books, in spite of the stir which they created in Paris; and neither M. nor Madame de Luxembourg said a word to me on the matter.

One morning, however, when I was alone with M. de Luxembourg, he asked me, "Have you said anything against M. de Choiseul in the 'Contrat Social'?" Starting back with surprise, I replied, "I? No, certainly not; that I swear to you; on the contrary, I have pronounced upon him, with a pen which is not given to flattery, the most splendid eulogy that a minister has ever received." With that, I quoted the whole passage to him. "And in 'Émile'?" he went on to ask. "Not a word," I answered; "there is not even a single word in it which refers to him." "Ah!" said he, with more vivacity than usual, "you ought to have done the same thing in the other book, or to have made yourself clearer." "I thought that I had done so," I answered; "I esteemed him highly enough for that." He was on the point of speaking again; I saw that he was ready to unbosom himself; but he checked himself and remained silent. Oh! the misery of a courtier's diplomacy, which, even in the best of hearts, overpowers friendship itself!

This conversation, although brief, enlightened me upon my situation, at least, in regard to certain things, and made me understand that it was certainly I who was attacked. I deplored this unheard-of fatality, which turned to my disadvantage all the good that I said and did. However, believing that I had Madame de Luxembourg and M. de Malesherbes to protect me in this matter, I did not see how it would be possible for my enemies to thrust them aside and reach me; for, in addition, I felt from that moment that it would no longer be a question of equity and justice, and that no one would trouble himself to examine whether I was really right or wrong. However, the storm roared louder and louder. Even Néaulme himself, in his wearisome chatter, showed me how greatly he regretted having had anything to do with this work, and the certainty which he seemed to entertain of the fate which threatened both the book and its author. One thing, however, still comforted me. I found Madame de Luxembourg so calm, so contented, so cheerful even, that she must have known what she was about, since she did not show the least anxiety on my account, did not utter a word of sympathy or apology, and regarded the turn the affair was taking with as much coolness as if she had nothing to do with it, and had never taken the least interest in myself. The only thing that surprised me was, that she said nothing at all to me. It appeared to me that she ought to have said something. Madame de Boufflers seemed more uneasy. She came to and fro in an agitated manner, showed great activity, assured me that M. le Prince de Conti was also exerting himself to ward off the blow which was being prepared for me, and which she attributed simply to the present state of affairs, in which it was of importance to the Parliament not to give the Jesuits an opportunity of accusing it of indifference in religious matters. She seemed, however, to have little confidence in the success of the Prince's efforts or her own. The drift of all her conversations, which were more alarming than reassuring, was the same: to induce me to leave the country and retire to England, where she offered to find me several friends, amongst others the celebrated Hume, with whom she had long been acquainted. Seeing that I persisted in remaining calm, she adopted a line which was more calculated to shake my resolution. She gave me to understand that, if I was arrested and examined, I should be obliged to mention Madame de Luxembourg, and that her friendship for me certainly deserved that I should not expose myself to the danger of being forced to compromise her. I replied that she might make herself easy, and that in such a case I would certainly not compromise her. She answered, that such a resolution was easier to take than to keep, and in this she was right, especially in my case, since I was quite determined never to perjure myself, or speak falsely before the judges, whatever risk there might be in telling the truth.

Seeing that, although this observation had made a certain impression upon me, I could not yet bring myself to decide upon flight, she spoke to me of the Bastille for a few weeks, as a means of escaping from the jurisdiction of the Parliament, which does not interfere with State prisoners. I made no objection to this singular favour, provided that it was not solicited in my name. As she said no more about it, I afterwards assumed that she had only proposed the idea in order to try me, and that an expedient, which would have put an end to everything, was not desired.

A few days afterwards, M. le Maréchal received from the *curé* of Deuil, a friend of Grimm and Madame d'Epinay, a letter, containing the information, which he declared came from a trustworthy source, that the Parliament intended to proceed against me with extreme severity, and that, on a certain day, which he mentioned, a warrant would be issued for my apprehension. I regarded this as an invention on the part of the Holbachians: I knew that the Parliament paid great attention to forms, and that it would be an infringement of them all, to commence on this occasion with a warrant of arrest, before it had been judicially established whether I acknowledged the book and was really its author. I said to Madame de Boufflers: "It is only in the case of those crimes which disturb the public safety, that a warrant is issued, upon a simple information, for the arrest of the accused, for fear they may escape punishment. But, when it is desired to punish an offence like mine, which deserves honours and rewards, the custom is, to proceed against the book, and to avoid attacking the author as much as possible." Upon this, she pointed out to me a very subtle distinction, which I had forgotten, in order to prove to me that it was a favour to me to issue a warrant, instead of summoning me to be heard. On the following day, I received a letter from Guy, in which he informed me that, having been with M. le Procureur-général the same day, he had seen upon his desk the rough draft of a "Requisition" against "Émile" and its author. Observe that the said Guy was a partner of Duchesne, who had printed the work, and also, having no anxiety on his own account, gave this information to the author out of charity. One may imagine how likely it all appeared to me! It was so simple, so natural, that a bookseller, when admitted to an audience of the *procureur-général*, should quietly read the manuscripts and rough drafts scattered over his desk! Madame de Boufflers and others assured me that it was true. In consequence of the absurdities which were being continually dinned into my ears, I was inclined to believe that everybody had gone mad.

Feeling sure that, under all this, there was some secret which was being withheld from me, I quietly awaited the issue of events, having full confidence in my upright behaviour and innocence throughout the affair, and being only too happy, whatever persecution might await me, to be summoned to the honour of suffering for the truth's sake. Far from being afraid, and keeping myself concealed, I went every day to the château, and took my usual walk in the afternoon. On the 8th of June, the day before the issue of the decree, I took it in company with two professors belonging to the Oratory, Father Alamanni and Father Mandard. We took some provisions with us to Champeaux, where we enjoyed a hearty meal. We had forgotten to take glasses, and supplied their place with stalks of rye, through which we sucked the wine from the bottles, eagerly picking out the thickest stalks, in order to see which could suck the hardest. I have never been so gay in my life.

I have mentioned how I suffered from sleeplessness in my youth. Since then, I had accustomed myself to read in bed every night, until I found my eyes getting heavy. Then I put out my candle, and tried to doze for a few minutes, which did not last long. My usual evening reading was the Bible, and in this manner I have read the whole of it through at least five or six times. On this particular evening, finding myself more wakeful than usual, I continued my reading for a longer time, and read the whole book, which ends with the history of the Levite of Ephraim – the Book of Judges, if I am not mistaken, for I have never looked at it since then. This history greatly affected me, and I was pondering over it in a half-dreamy state, from which I was suddenly roused by a noise and a light. The latter was carried by Thérèse, who was showing the way to M. le Roche, who, seeing me start up abruptly, said to me, "Do not be alarmed: I come from Madame la Maréchale, who has written to you herself, and also sends you a letter from M. le Prince de Conti." Inside Madame de Luxembourg's letter I found another, which had been brought to her by a special messenger from the Prince, containing the information that, in spite of all his efforts, it had been decided to proceed against me with the utmost rigour of the law. "The excitement," so he wrote, "is very great: nothing can avert the blow: the Court demands it, the Parliament wills it: at seven o'clock to-morrow morning the warrant of arrest will be issued, and executed immediately. I have obtained an assurance that, if he makes his escape, he will not be pursued; but, if he persists in his wish to allow himself to be taken, then he will be arrested." La Roche besought me, in Madame de Luxembourg's name, to get up and go and consult with her. It was two o'clock: she had just gone to bed. "She is waiting for you," he added, "and will not go to sleep until she has seen you." I hurriedly dressed myself, and hastened to her.

For the first time in her life she appeared to me agitated. Her anxiety touched me. In this moment of surprise, in the middle of the night, I myself was not free from excitement, but when I saw her I forgot myself, and thought only of her and the melancholy part which she would play if I allowed myself to be taken; for, while I felt that I had courage enough never to speak anything but the truth, even though it was bound to injure and ruin me, I did not feel that I had sufficient presence of mind or cleverness, or even, perhaps, sufficient firmness, to avoid compromising her, if I was hard pressed. This decided me to sacrifice my reputation for the sake of her peace of mind, and, on this occasion, to do for her, that which nothing would have induced me to do for myself. The moment my mind was made up, I told her, as I did not wish to depreciate the value of my sacrifice, by allowing it to be purchased from me. I am convinced that she could not have been mistaken as to my motives, but she did not say a single word to me which showed that she appreciated them. I was so shocked at this indifference that I even hesitated whether I should not draw back, but M. de Luxembourg appeared upon the scene, and Madame de Boufflers arrived from Paris a few moments afterwards. They did what Madame de Luxembourg ought to have done. I allowed myself to be flattered, I was ashamed to go back from my word, and the only question remaining was, where I should go, and when I should start. M. de Luxembourg proposed that I should stay a few days at his house, *incognito*, which would give me more time to consider and decide upon my course of action. I would not agree to this, any more than to the suggestion that I should go secretly to the Temple. I persisted in my intention of setting out the same day, rather than remain in concealment anywhere.

Feeling that I had secret and powerful enemies in the kingdom, I thought that, in spite of my attachment for France, I ought to leave it to make sure of not being disturbed. My first impulse was to retire to Geneva, but a moment's reflection was sufficient to dissuade me from committing so great an act of folly. I knew that the French Ministry, which had even greater power in Geneva than in Paris, would not leave me in peace in one of these two cities any more than in the other, if it was determined to persecute me. I knew that the "Discours sur l'Inégalité" had aroused against me, in the Council, a feeling of hatred, which was the more dangerous, as that body did not venture to show it openly. Lastly, I knew that when the "Nouvelle Héloïse" appeared it had been eager to prohibit it, at the urgent request of Doctor Tronchin; but, finding that no one imitated its example, not even in Paris, it was ashamed of its blunder and withdrew the prohibition. I had no doubt that, finding the present opportunity more favourable, it would do its best to profit by it. I knew that, in spite of all appearances, a secret jealousy prevailed against me in the hearts of all the Genevese, which only waited for an opportunity to satisfy itself. Nevertheless, patriotism called me back to my country, and if I could have ventured to hope that I could live there in peace, I should not have hesitated for a moment; but, since neither honour nor reason allowed me to take refuge there as a fugitive, I resolved only to retire to its neighbourhood, and to wait in

Switzerland until I saw what course would be taken in regard to me at Geneva. It will presently be seen that this state of uncertainty did not last long.

Madame de Boufflers strongly disapproved of this resolution, and made fresh efforts to persuade me to cross over to England. She did not shake my determination. I have never liked England or the English, and all the eloquence of Madame de Boufflers, far from overcoming my dislike, only seemed to increase it, without my knowing why.

Being determined to set out the same day, as soon as morning came, I had already started, as far as everybody else was concerned; La Roche, whom I sent to fetch my papers, would not tell even Thérèse whether I had left or not. Ever since I had decided some day to write the Memoirs of my life, I had accumulated a number of letters and papers, so that he was obliged to make several journeys. Those papers which had already been sorted were laid aside, and I spent the rest of the morning in sorting the others, intending only to take away with me such as might be useful and to burn the rest. M. de Luxembourg was kind enough to help me in this task, which took up so much time, that we were unable to finish it in the morning, and I had not time to burn anything. He offered to sort the papers which remained, and to burn the rubbish himself, without leaving anyone else to do it, and to send me all that he put aside. I accepted his offer, very glad to be freed from this anxiety, so that I might be able to spend the few hours which still remained to me together with those who were so dear, whom I was on the point of leaving for ever. He took the key of the room where I left the papers, and, at my earnest entreaty, sent for my poor "aunt," who was consumed by most cruel anxiety to know what had become of me and what was going to become of me, and was expecting the officers of justice to arrive at any moment, without knowing what she was to do or what she was to say to them. La Roche brought her to the château, without telling her anything; she believed that I was already far away; when she saw me, she uttered a piercing cry, and flung herself into my arms. Oh, friendship, union of hearts, intercourse, and intimacy! During this sweet and cruel moment all the happy, tender, and peaceful days which we had spent in company, crowding together, made me feel the more keenly the anguish of our first separation, after we had rarely lost sight of each other for a single day, during a period of nearly seventeen years. M. de Luxembourg, who witnessed our embrace, was unable to restrain his tears, and left us alone. Thérèse did not want to leave me. I represented to her the difficulties in the way of her following me at this moment, and the necessity for her remaining to dispose of my effects and to collect my money. When a warrant of arrest is issued against a man, it is the custom to seize his papers, to set a seal upon his belongings, or to make an inventory of them and appoint some one to take charge of them. It was very necessary that she should remain, to observe what took place, and do the best she could. I promised her that she should soon rejoin me; M. le Maréchal confirmed my promise; but I refused to tell her where I was going, so that, if questioned by those who came to arrest me, she might be able to declare with truth her ignorance on this point. When I embraced her at the moment of separation, I was conscious of a most singular emotion, and I said to her, with a fervour, which was, alas! only too prophetic: "My child, you must arm yourself with courage. You have shared the prosperity of my happy days; it now remains for you, since you desire it, to share my misery. You must expect nothing but insults and affliction if you follow me. The lot, which begins for me on this melancholy day, will attend me until my last hour."

Nothing further remained for me to do, except to think about my departure. The officers of justice were to have arrived at ten o'clock. It was four o'clock in the afternoon when I started, and they had not yet arrived.[1] It had been settled that I should travel by the post; I had no conveyance. M. le Maréchal made me a present of a cabriolet,[2] and lent me horses and a postillion as far as the first post, where, thanks to the arrangements he had made, no difficulty was made about providing me with horses.

---

[1] *Parlement* condemned *Émile* to be burnt and Rousseau to be arrested at its morning session, on 9 June 1762.
[2] A light two-wheeled carriage.

As I had not dined at table, and had not shown myself in the château, the ladies came to say good-bye to me in the *entresol*, where I had spent the day. Madame la Maréchale embraced me several times, with every appearance of melancholy; but I no longer perceived in her embraces the heartiness of those which she had lavished upon me two or three years before. Madame de Boufflers also embraced me and spoke very kindly to me. Madame de Mirepoix, who was present, also embraced me, which considerably surprised me. This lady is extremely cold, formal, and reserved, and, as it seems to me, not altogether free from the haughtiness which is natural to the house of Lorraine. She had never paid much attention to me. Whether it was that, flattered by the unexpected honour, I was inclined to attach greater value to it, or that she really mingled with her embrace a little of that pity which is natural to generous hearts, I found in her movements and looks a certain earnestness, which deeply affected me. On thinking of it afterwards, I have often suspected that she, knowing the lot to which I was condemned, had been unable to resist a momentary feeling of sympathy for my destiny.

M. le Maréchal did not open his mouth; he was as pale as death. He persisted in accompanying me as far as the conveyance, which was waiting for me at the watering-place. We crossed the garden without uttering a word. I had a key of the park, with which I opened the gate; after which, instead of putting it back into my pocket, I gave it to him without a word. He took it with surprising eagerness, of which I have been unable to avoid thinking frequently since then. I have rarely in my life experienced a more bitter moment than that of this separation. Our embrace was long and silent; we both felt that it was a last farewell.

Between La Barre and Montmorency I met, in a hired coach, four men dressed in black, who saluted me with a smile. From what Thérèse afterwards told me concerning the appearance of the officers, the hour of their arrival, and the manner in which they behaved, I have always been convinced that it was they whom I met; especially as I subsequently heard that, instead of the warrant having been issued against me at seven o'clock, as I had been informed, it had not been put in force until midday.

I had to pass right through Paris. There is not much facility for concealment in an open carriage. In the streets, I saw several persons who saluted me as if they knew me, but I did not recognise one of them. The same evening I turned aside to pass Villeroy. At Lyons, travellers[1] had to go before the town-major. This might have been embarrassing for a man who desired neither to lie nor to change his name. I went with a letter from Madame de Luxembourg, to ask M. de Villeroy that I might be excused from this duty. M. de Villeroy gave me a letter, which I did not make use of, since I did not pass through Lyons. This letter may still be found, sealed up, amongst my papers. M. le Duc pressed me to sleep at Villeroy, but I preferred to take the high road again, and I accomplished two more stages the same day.

My conveyance was uncomfortable, and I was too unwell to make long-day journeys. Besides, my appearance was not sufficiently imposing to ensure my being well served; and everybody knows that, in France, post-horses only feel the whip upon the postillions' shoulders. By feeing the guides handsomely, I thought I could supply the place of threatening words and gestures; but this only made matters much worse. They took me for a poor wretch travelling on commission, who was journeying by post for the first time in his life. From that time I was supplied with nothing but the most sorry nags, and became the laughing-stock of the postillions. I ended, as I ought to have begun, by being patient and saying nothing, and let them go on as they pleased.

In abandoning myself to the reflections upon all that had recently happened to me, which presented themselves to my mind, I had ample resources against weariness during my journey; but this suited neither the bent of my mind nor the inclinations of my heart. It is astonishing how easily I forget misfortunes, when once they are past, however recent they may be. The recollection of them grows weaker and finally disappears without difficulty as soon as they have happened, to the same extent as the thought of them, as long as they are in the future, alarms and troubles me. My cruel imagination, which

[1] *Courriers*: those who make use of post-horses.

tortures itself incessantly in anticipating misfortunes which do not yet exist, distracts my memory, and prevents me from recalling to mind those which are past. No further precautions are possible against what has happened, and it is useless to trouble oneself about it. In a manner I exhaust my misfortunes in advance. The greater my suffering in foreseeing them, the more easily I forget them; while, on the contrary, incessantly occupied with the thought of my past happiness, I recall it and, so to speak, chew the cud of it to such an extent that, when I desire it, I am able to enjoy it over again. It is due to this happy frame of mind, I am convinced, that I have never known that spiteful disposition which ferments in a revengeful heart, which never forgets affronts received, and worries itself with all the evil it would like to inflict upon its enemy by way of requital. Naturally hot-tempered, I have felt angry, even enraged, in the impulse of the moment; but a desire for vengeance has never taken root in my heart. I think too little about the offence to think much about the offender. I only think of the injury which I have received from him on account of that which I may still receive from him; and, if I were sure that he would inflict no further injury upon me, that which he has already inflicted would be immediately forgotten. Forgiveness of offences is constantly preached to us. This is, no doubt, a most beautiful virtue, but it is not meant for me. I do not know whether my heart can conquer its hatred, for it has never felt any; and I think too little about my enemies to have the merit of forgiving them. I will not say to what extent they torment themselves, in order to torment me. I am at their mercy, they have absolute power, they make use of it. There is only one thing beyond their power, which I defy them to do. Although they torment themselves about me, they cannot compel me to torment myself about them.

The day after my departure, I had so completely forgotten all that had recently happened – the Parliament, Madame de Pompadour, M. de Choiseul, Grimm, D'Alembert, their plots, and their accomplices – that I should never have thought of it again, had it not been for the precautions which I was obliged to take. In place of all this, I recalled to mind the subject of my last reading on the eve of my departure. I also recalled the Idylls of Gessner,[1] which his translator, Hubert, had sent me some time ago. These two remembrances took so strong a hold upon me, and became so blended in my thoughts, that I determined to try and combine them, by treating, after the manner of Gessner, the theme of the Levite of Ephraim. This idyllic and simple style appeared little suited for so fearful a subject, and it was hardly to be imagined that my present situation would furnish me with many cheerful ideas to relieve its sombreness. However, I made the attempt, simply to amuse myself in my chaise, and without any hope of succeeding. No sooner had I begun, than I was astonished at the agreeable turn of my ideas, and the ease with which I expressed them. In three days, I wrote the three first cantos of this little poem, which I subsequently finished at Motiers; and I am convinced that I have never written anything in my life which is pervaded by a more touching gentleness of character, a fresher colouring, a more simple delineation, a more faithful characterisation, a more old-fashioned simplicity in every respect – and that in spite of the horrible nature of the subject, which is essentially abominable; so that, in addition to everything else, I had the credit of overcoming a further difficulty. The "Levite d'Ephraim," if it is not the best of my works, will always be my favourite. I have never read it again, I never shall read it again, without being sensible of the approval of a heart free from bitterness, which, far from being soured by misfortune, finds consolation for it with itself, and, in itself, the means of compensation for it. If all those great philosophers who, in their works, profess themselves so superior to that adversity which they have never experienced, were gathered together and placed in a position similar to mine – if, in the first outbursts of the indignation of insulted honour, a similar task were set them to accomplish, it would soon be seen how they would acquit themselves.

When leaving Montmorency for Switzerland, I had made up my mind to go and stay at Yverdun with my good old friend Roguin, who had been living there in retirement for some years, and had invited me to go and see him. On the road, I heard that

[1] A celebrated Swiss poet and landscape-painter (1730–1788).

Lyons would be out of my way, and this prevented me from passing through it. But, on the other hand, I was obliged to pass Besançon, a fortified town, which, consequently, exposed me to the same inconvenience. I accordingly decided to turn to the left, and travel by way of Salins, under pretence of visiting M. de Mairan, M. Dupin's nephew, who held a post at the salt-works, and from whom I had frequently received pressing invitations to go and see him. The expedient was successful; I did not find M. de Mairan, and, highly pleased at having avoided delay, I continued my journey, without a word being said to me by anyone.

On entering the territory of Berne I ordered a halt. I got out of the carriage, flung myself upon the ground, kissed and embraced it, and, in my delight, cried out: "O Heaven, protector of virtue, I offer my praise to thee! I set foot in a land of liberty." Thus it is that, in the blind confidence of my hopes, I have always been seized with passionate fondness for that which was destined to bring misfortune upon me. The surprised postillion thought I was mad. I got into the carriage again, and, a few hours afterwards, I had the pure and lively satisfaction of being pressed in the arms of the worthy Roguin. Ah! let us take breath for a few moments with this worthy host! I must recover my courage and strength; I shall soon have need of both.

It is not without reason that, in this narrative, I have described in detail all the circumstances which I have been able to recollect. Although they may not seem very clear in themselves, they may throw light upon the course of events, when the reader once holds the thread of the plot; for instance, although they do not give the first idea of the problem which I have to propose, they afford considerable assistance in solving it.

If we assume that, in order to carry out the plot which was directed against me, my removal was absolutely necessary, then, in order to bring it about, everything was bound to happen almost exactly as it did. But if, instead of allowing myself to be terrified by Madame de Luxembourg's nocturnal embassy and disturbed by her anxiety, I had continued to hold out as I had begun; and if, instead of remaining at the château, I had returned from it to my bed and slept quietly until morning, would the warrant have been put into execution just the same? This is an important question, upon the answer to which depends the answer to many others; and, in order to investigate it, it is important to observe the hour of the decree of arrest that was threatened and the hour of its actual issue. This is a homely but expressive example of the importance of the most trifling details in the exposition of facts, the secret causes of which are investigated, in order to discover them by a process of induction.

BOOK XII

HERE commences the work of darkness, in which, for eight years past, I have been entombed, without ever having been able, in spite of all my efforts, to penetrate its frightful obscurity. In the abyss of misfortune in which I am submerged, I feel the strokes of the blows which are directed against me. I perceive their immediate instrument, but I cannot see either the hand which guides them or the means which it employs. Shame and misfortune fall upon me as if of themselves, and unawares. When my heart, torn with grief, gives vent to lamentation, I seem like a man who complains without reason, and the authors of my ruin have discovered the incomprehensible art of making the public the accomplice of their plot, without their suspecting it or perceiving its effect. Therefore, while narrating the events which concern me, the treatment which I have suffered, and all that has happened to me, I am not in a position to trace them back to the moving spirit, or to assign the causes, while stating the facts. These first causes are all indicated in the three preceding books. All the interests that concern me and all the secret motives are there set forth. But it is impossible for me to explain, even conjecturally, how these various causes are combined in order to bring about the strange events of my life. If, amongst my readers, there are any sufficiently generous to desire to fathom these mysteries and discover the truth, let them carefully read again the three preceding books, let them make use of the information within their reach in dealing with each fact they read of in what follows, let them go back from intrigue to intrigue, from agent to agent, until they come to the prime movers of all. I know well what will be the result of their inquiries, but I myself am lost in the dark and tortuous windings of the subterranean paths which will lead them to it.

During my stay at Yverdun I made the acquaintance of M. Roguin's whole family; amongst others his niece, Madame Boy de la Tour, and her daughters, whose father, as I think I have already mentioned, I had known at Lyons. She had come to Yverdun on a visit to her uncle and sisters. Her eldest daughter, who was about fifteen years of age, delighted me by her intelligence and her excellent character. I became most tenderly attached to the mother and daughter. M. Roguin intended the latter to marry his nephew, the colonel, a man already somewhat advanced in years, who also displayed great affection for myself; but, although the uncle was mad for this marriage, although the nephew also strongly desired it, and I took a lively interest in satisfying the wishes of both, the great disparity of age and the extreme repugnance of the young girl caused me to support the mother in preventing the marriage, which did not take place. The colonel subsequently married Mademoiselle Dillan, one of his relatives, a lady whose beauty and character were after my own heart, and who has made him the happiest of husbands and fathers. In spite of this, M. Roguin has never been able to forget that on this occasion I opposed his wishes. I am consoled for this by the certainty that I fulfilled the holiest duty of friendship, both towards himself and his family, which does not consist in always making oneself agreeable, but in always advising for the best.

I did not long remain in doubt as to the reception which awaited me at Geneva, in case I felt inclined to return there. My book was burned there, and a warrant was issued against me on the 18th of June, that is to say, nine days after it had been issued in Paris. In this second decree, so many incredible absurdities were heaped together, and the ecclesiastical edict was so distinctly violated,[1] that at first I refused to believe the news when it reached me, and, when it was actually confirmed, I trembled lest so manifest and crying an infringement of every law, commencing with that of common sense, should turn Geneva upside down. But I need not have disturbed myself; everything remained quiet. If there was any disturbance amongst the people, it was only directed against me, and I was publicly treated by all the town-gossips and *cuistres* like a pupil threatened with a flogging for having said his catechism badly.

---

[1] The "Ecclesiastical edict" of 1568 specified that the author of heretical opinions should be summoned to defend himself before the Consistory.

These two decrees gave the signal for the cry of execration which went up against me throughout Europe with unexampled fury. All the newspapers, journals, and pamphlets sounded a most terrible note of alarm. The French especially – that gentle, polite, and generous people, who so pride themselves on their good-breeding and respect for the unfortunate – suddenly forgetting their favourite virtues, distinguished themselves by the number and violence of the insults with which they vied with one another in overwhelming me. I was called an infidel, an atheist, a lunatic, a madman, a wild beast, a wolf. The continuer of the *Journal de Trévoux*[1] made a side attack upon my pretended wolfishness, which was a fairly convincing proof of his own. In short, it almost seemed as if people in Paris were afraid of coming into collision with the police, if, when publishing a book upon any subject whatever, they omitted to interlard it with insults against myself. Seeking in vain for the cause of this universal animosity, I was ready to believe that all the world had gone mad. What! the compiler of the "Paix Perpetuelle" the promoter of discord! the editor of the "Vicaire Savoyard" an infidel! the author of the "Nouvelle Héloïse" a wolf! the author of "Émile" a madman! Good heavens! what then should I have been if I had published the work upon "L'Esprit,"[2] or something of the same kind? And yet, in the storm which burst upon the head of the author of that book, the public, instead of uniting its voice to that of his persecutors, avenged him by its eulogies. Compare his book and mine, the different reception which they have met with, the manner in which the two authors have been treated in the different countries of Europe, and then find, if possible, reasons for these differences which can satisfy a sensible man. That is all I ask, then I will say no more.

I was so comfortable at Yverdun that I decided to stay there, at the earnest entreaty of M. de Roguin and all his family. The kindness of M. de Moiry de Gingins, *bailli* of this town, also encouraged me to remain within his jurisdiction. The colonel

---

[1] 'Continuer', because the Jesuit *Journal* (or *Mémoires*) *de Trévoux* continued after the dispersal of the Jesuits in 1764, surviving until 1775.
[2] Helvétius's materialistic *De l'Esprit* (1758) caused great scandal, and the author had to publish a retraction.

pressed me so strongly to accept a lodging in a little detached building, between the court and garden of his house, that I consented; and he immediately set about furnishing and providing it with everything necessary for my humble wants. Roguin, the banneret,[1] was so assiduous in my behalf, that he never left me for a moment during the day. I highly appreciated all his kindness, but I was sometimes considerably bored by it. The day of my installation in my new abode was already settled, and I had written to Thérèse to rejoin me, when suddenly I heard that a storm was brewing against me in Berne, which was attributed to the extreme religionists, and of which I have never been able to discover the origin. The Senate, aroused by no one knows whom, seemed determined not to leave me in peace in my retreat. Directly the *bailli* heard of this excitement, he wrote on my behalf to several members of the Government, reproaching them for their unreasoning intolerance, and calling it a shame on their part to wish to refuse a persecuted and worthy man the refuge which so many bandits found in their States. Shrewd persons have conjectured that the warmth of his reproaches rather exasperated than soothed their minds. However that may be, neither his reputation nor his eloquence could ward off the blow. Having received an intimation of the order which he had to make known to me, he gave me a hint of it beforehand, and I decided to leave on the following day, before the same arrived. My difficulty was, to know where to go. Geneva and France were closed to me, and I clearly foresaw that, in this matter, everyone would be eager to imitate his neighbour's example.

Madame Boy de la Tour proposed to me to take up my quarters in an empty furnished house, belonging to her son, in the village of Motiers, in Val-de-Travers, in the county of Neufchâtel. I only had to cross a mountain to get there. The offer was the more opportune, since, in the territory of the King of Prussia, I should naturally be sheltered from persecution; at least, religion could not be alleged as an excuse for it. But a secret objection, which it did not become me to express, was calculated to make me hesitate. The innate love of justice, by which my

---

[1] A "banneret" (the title is military in origin) was holder of a civic office in the *pays de Vaud*.

heart was always consumed, united to my secret liking for France, had inspired me with aversion for the King of Prussia, who, in his principles and conduct, appeared to me to trample underfoot all respect for natural law and human obligations. Amongst the framed engravings, with which I had decorated the walls of my turret at Montmorency, was a portrait of this Prince, underneath which I had written a distich, which concluded as follows:

"Il pense en philosophe, et se conduit en roi."[1]

This line, which, proceeding from any other pen, would have been high praise, contained, coming from mine, a meaning which was by no means ambiguous, and which, besides, was only too clearly explained by the line which preceded it.[2] My numerous visitors had all seen this distich. The Chevalier de Lorenzi had even copied it for D'Alembert, and I had no doubt that the latter had taken care to make use of it to present me in a favourable light to the King.[3] I had further aggravated my first offence by a passage in "Émile," in which, under the name of Adrastus,[4] King of the Daunians, I had sufficiently indicated whom I had in view. I knew that the remark had not escaped the critics, since Madame de Boufflers had on several occasions mentioned the subject. I therefore felt sure of being inscribed in red ink on the registers of the King of Prussia; and supposing, besides, that his principles were such as I had ventured to attribute to him, my writings and their author could not fail to meet with his disapproval; for it is well known that the wicked and tyrants have always conceived a deadly hatred towards me, even without knowing me, on a simple perusal of my works.

However, I ventured to throw myself upon his mercy, and I believed that I was running but little risk. I knew that the baser

[1] He thinks as a philosopher, and acts as a king.
[2] "La gloire, l'intérêt, voilà son Dieu, sa loi." From a note in the Firmin-Didot edition we learn that this line did not really precede the one quoted above. The latter was underneath the portrait, the other verse was written at the back.
[3] This must be meant ironically, if the text be correct.
[4] Imaginary king of the Daunians in Fénelon's *Télémaque*, a cruel and perfidious but intrepid and resourceful character. He is mentioned near the end of Book V of *Émile*.

passions only overmaster the weak, and have but little hold upon minds of a strong stamp, such as I had always recognised in his. I argued that it was part of his plan of government to show himself magnanimous on such an occasion, and that it was not beyond the reach of his character to be so in reality. I argued that the desire of a mean and easy vengeance would never for a moment counterbalance in him the love of glory; and, putting myself in his place, I thought it not impossible that he might take advantage of circumstances to overwhelm with the weight of his generosity the man who had ventured to think ill of him. I accordingly went to settle at Motiers, with a confidence, the value of which I considered him capable of appreciating. I said to myself, When Jean Jacques raises himself to the level of Coriolanus, will Frederic show himself lower than the Volscian general?

Colonel Roguin insisted on crossing the mountain with me, to see me installed at Motiers. A sister-in-law of Madame Boy de la Tour, by name Madame Girardier, who found the house which I was to occupy a great convenience to herself, was not particularly pleased at my arrival. However, she let me take possession politely enough, and I took my meals with her, until Thérèse arrived, and my little establishment was set in order.

Since my departure from Montmorency, feeling certain that I should henceforth be a wanderer upon the face of the earth, I hesitated about allowing her to join me and share the wandering life to which I saw myself condemned. I felt that, owing to this catastrophe, the relations between us would be altered, and that what had hitherto been a favour and a kindness on my part would henceforth be the same on hers. If her attachment remained proof against my misfortunes, she would be greatly distressed by them, and her grief would only add to my woes. If, on the other hand, my misfortune cooled her affection for me, she would look upon it as a sacrifice if she remained constant to me; and, instead of feeling the pleasure which I felt in sharing my last crust of bread with her, she would only be sensible of her own merit in consenting to follow me whithersoever destiny might force me to go.

I must speak without reserve. I have never concealed either my poor mamma's faults or my own. I must not show greater favour to Thérèse either; and, pleased as I am to render honour to one who is so dear to me, neither do I wish to conceal her faults, if so be that an involuntary change in the heart's affections is really a fault. I had long since observed that her affection for me had cooled. I felt that she no longer was towards me what she had been in our best days; and I felt it the more, as I was always the same towards her. I was conscious again of an unpleasantness, the effects of which I had formerly felt when with mamma; and the effect was the same with Thérèse. Let us not look for perfections which are not to be found in nature; it would be the same with any other woman whatsoever. The course of action I had taken in regard to my children, however rational it had appeared to me, had not always left my heart in peace. While thinking over my "Traité de l'Education," I felt that I had neglected duties from which nothing could excuse me. My remorse at length became so keen, that it almost extorted from me a public confession of my error at the beginning of "Émile"; and the allusion itself is so obvious in a certain passage, that it is surprising to me how anyone, after having read it, can have had the courage to reproach me.[1] My situation, however, was at that time the same, and even aggravated by the animosity of my enemies, who only sought to find me at fault. I was afraid of a repetition; and, not desiring to run the risk of it, I preferred to condemn myself to strict continence, than to expose Thérèse to the risk of finding herself in the same condition again. Besides, I had observed that intercourse with women distinctly aggravated my ill-health; the corresponding vice, of which I have never been able to cure myself completely, appeared to me to produce less injurious results. These two reasons combined caused me to form resolutions which I had sometimes been very inconsistent

---

[1] In Book I of *Émile* Rousseau wrote: "He who cannot fulfil the duties of a father has not the right to become one. Neither poverty not labour nor other human claims dispense him from the duty of feeding his children and bringing them up himself. Readers, you may take my word for this. I foretell that any man of feeling who neglects such sacred duties will for long shed bitter tears over his fault and will never find consolation."

in keeping, but in which I had persevered with greater firmness for the last three or four years. Since then I had observed a coldness on the part of Thérèse; she had the same attachment for me from a feeling of duty, no longer from love. This naturally made our intercourse less pleasant, and I thought that, feeling sure that I should continue to look after her wherever she might be, she would perhaps prefer to remain in Paris than to wander through the world with me. However, she had exhibited such grief at our separation, she had exacted from me such positive promises that we should come together again, she had so strongly expressed a desire to that effect since my departure, both to the Prince de Conti and M. de Luxembourg, that, far from having the courage to speak to her of separation, I could scarcely bear to think of it myself; and, when I once felt how utterly impossible it was for me to do without her, my only thought was to call her back to me immediately. I accordingly wrote to her to set out; she came. It was hardly two months since I had left her; but it was our first separation, after the many years we had been together. We had both felt it cruelly. What a shock, when we embraced each other! How sweet are tears of tenderness and joy! How my heart revels in them! Why have I been permitted to shed so few!

On my arrival at Motiers, I had written to Lord Keith,[1] Marshal of Scotland, Governor of Neufchâtel, to inform him that I had taken refuge in His Majesty's territory, and to ask him for his protection. He replied with the well-known generosity which I expected from him. He invited me to go and see him. I went with M. Martinet, lord of the manor of Val-de-Travers, who stood high in his Excellency's esteem. The venerable appearance of this illustrious and virtuous Scotchman made a powerful impression upon my heart, and that very moment was the commencement of that strong attachment between us, which on my part has always remained the same, and would still be the same on his, had not the traitors, who have robbed me of all the consolations of life, profited by my absence to deceive him, weakened as he is by old age, and to misrepresent me in his eyes.

[1] [Keith] See *Biographies*, p. 712.

George Keith, hereditary Marshal of Scotland, and brother of
the celebrated General Keith, who, after a glorious life, died an
honourable death, had left his native land when a young man,
having been outlawed for his attachment to the house of Stuart,
with which the unjust and tyrannical spirit which he found in it,
and which was always its ruling characteristic, soon disgusted
him. He lived for some time in Spain, the climate of which suited
him, and at last, like his brother, attached himself to the King of
Prussia, who was a judge of men and received them as they
deserved. He was amply repaid for this reception of them by the
great services rendered him by Marshal Keith, and by what was
even more valuable, his sincere friendship. The great soul of this
worthy man, thoroughly proud and republican, could only bow
to the yoke of friendship; but to this it bowed so completely that,
although his principles were very different, he no longer saw
anyone but Frederic from the moment he became attached to
him. The King intrusted him with important commissions, and
sent him to Paris and Spain; and, finally, seeing that, already
advanced in years, he needed repose, he bestowed upon him the
government of Neufchâtel, where he spent the rest of his life in
retirement, occupied with the delightful task of rendering this
little country happy.

The inhabitants of Neufchâtel, who are fond of nothing but
trifles[1] and tinsel, who are no judge of genuine goods, and think
that talent consists in long phrases, when they saw a man who
was unemotional and unaffected, took his simplicity for pride,
his frankness for rudeness, and his conciseness for stupidity, and
revolted against his beneficent measures, because, desiring to be
useful without cajolery, he did not know how to flatter those
whom he did not esteem. In the ridiculous affair of Petitpierre,
who was driven out by his brother clergymen, because he had
refused to believe that they were eternally damned, the Marshal,
who had opposed their encroachments, found the whole
country, whose part he took, up in arms against him; and, at
the time of my arrival, this foolish excitement was not yet
allayed. He was, at least, still regarded as a man who allowed
himself to be prejudiced; and, of all the imputations brought

---

[1] *Prétintaille*: literally, some kind of dress trimming.

against him, this was perhaps the least unjust. My first feeling, on seeing this venerable old man, was one of emotion at the leanness of his body, already emaciated by old age; but when I lifted my eyes towards his animated, frank, and noble features, this was succeeded by a feeling of respect mingled with confidence, which overcame every other sentiment. To the brief compliment which I paid him when I presented myself, he replied by speaking of something else, as if I had been there a week. He did not even bid us sit down. The starchy lord of the manor remained standing, but I saw in my lord's keen and penetrating eye something so genial and friendly, that, feeling at my ease at once, without further ceremony I went and sat down on the sofa by his side. From the familiar tone, which he immediately assumed, I felt that this freedom on my part was agreeable to him, and that he said to himself, "This is no Neufchâtelois."

Singular effect of strong similarity of character! At an age when the heart has already lost its natural warmth, that of this good old man warmed towards me in a manner which surprised everyone. He came to see me at Motiers, under pretence of shooting quails, and spent two days without touching a gun. We became so friendly – that is the correct word – that we could not do without each other. The château of Colombier, where he lived in the summer, was six leagues distant from Motiers: I went at least every fortnight to spend twenty-four hours there, and then returned like a pilgrim, with my heart always full of him. The emotions of which I was formerly sensible during my journeys from the Hermitage to Eaubonne were certainly very different, but they were not sweeter than those with which I approached Colombier. What tears of tenderness I have often shed on my way, while thinking of the paternal kindness, the amiable virtues, and the gentle philosophy of this worthy old man! I called him my father, and he called me his child. These sweet names give a partial idea of the attachment which united us, but they do not give an idea of the need of each other which we felt, and of our continued desire to be together. He insisted upon putting me up at the château of Colombier, and for a long time pressed me to take up my quarters permanently in the apartment which I occupied. At last, I told him that I was freer at my own house, and that I preferred to spend my time in going to see him. He approved of my frankness, and said no more about the matter. O my good lord! O my worthy father! how my heart is still stirred by emotion when I think of you! Oh! the barbarians! What a blow have they dealt me in separating you from me! But, no, no, great man: you are, and always will be, the same for me, who am ever the same! They have deceived you, but they have not altered you.

My Lord Marshal is not entirely free from faults: he is a wise man, but still a man. Although gifted with the most penetrating intellect, the most delicate tact that a man can possibly possess, and the most profound knowledge of men, he sometimes allows himself to be deceived, and cannot be undeceived. His temper is curious; there is something whimsical and strange in his turn of mind. He appears to forget people whom he sees every day, and remembers them at the moment when they least expect it, and his attentions seem out of place. His presents are given capriciously, without regard to their suitability. On the spur of the moment he sends or gives whatever occurs to him, without discrimination, whether it be very valuable or absolutely worthless. A young Genevese, who desired to enter the service of the King of Prussia, presented himself before him; my lord gave him, instead of a letter, a little bag full of peas which he commissioned him to deliver to the King, who, on receipt of this singular letter of recommendation, immediately gave a place to the bearer. These lofty geniuses have a language of their own, which vulgar minds will never understand. These little oddities, resembling the caprices of a pretty woman, only served to render my Lord Marshal more interesting. I was quite sure, and I have since found it to be the case, that they had exercised no influence either upon his feelings or upon the attention which friendship imposes upon him in serious matters. But it is true that, in conferring an obligation, he exhibits the same singularity as in his manners. I will quote a single instance of this in regard to a matter of trifling importance. As the journey from Motiers to Colombier was too much for me to make in a day, I generally broke it by starting after dinner, and sleeping at an inn at Brot, about half-way. The landlord, named Sandoz, who wanted to solicit at Berlin a favour which was of the greatest importance to him, begged me to induce his Excellency to ask it on his behalf. I gladly consented. I took him with me, left him in the antechamber, and mentioned his business to my lord, who made no reply. The morning passed, and on walking through the hall on my way to dinner, I saw poor Sandoz, who was utterly tired of waiting. Thinking that my lord had forgotten him, I spoke about him again before we sat down to table. Not a word, as before. I found this manner of hinting to me that I was troublesome somewhat severe, and I held my tongue, pitying poor Sandoz in my own mind. On returning home the next day, I was greatly surprised by his profuse thanks for the kindly reception and the good dinner which his Excellency had given him, besides taking charge of his papers. Three weeks later, my lord sent him the rescript for which he had asked, made out by the minister and signed by the King, and this without having said a single word or made an answer to either myself or Sandoz in regard to the matter, with which I believed he did not wish to have anything to do.

I should like to speak incessantly of George Keith. It is with him that my last happy recollections are connected; the rest of my life has been nothing but sorrow and affliction. The remembrance of it has been so melancholy, and comes back to me so confusedly, that it is no longer possible for me to introduce any order into my narrative. I shall be obliged, from this time forth, to arrange the facts haphazard, as they present themselves to me.

I was soon relieved of my uneasiness in regard to my asylum, by the answer of the King to the Marshal, in whom, as may be imagined, I had found a powerful advocate. His Majesty not only approved of what I had done, but also – for I must conceal nothing – commissioned him to give me twelve *louis*. The worthy Marshal, embarrassed by such a commission, and not knowing how to acquit himself of it delicately, endeavoured to soften the affront by changing the money into provisions, and informing me that he had been ordered to supply me with wood and coal to start my housekeeping; he even added, perhaps on his own initiative, that the King would be pleased to have a small

house built for me, according to my own taste, if I would choose
a site for it. This last offer touched me greatly, and made me
forget the stinginess of the other. Without accepting either,
I looked upon Frederic as my benefactor and protector, and
conceived so sincere an attachment to him, that from that time
forth I took as much interest in his reputation as I had hitherto
found injustice in his success. When peace was concluded
shortly afterwards, I testified my joy by an illumination, which
showed very good taste. This was a row of garlands, with which I
decorated the house in which I was living, and upon which, it is
true, I spent, in a spirit of revengeful pride, almost as much
money as he had wanted to give me. Peace being concluded, I
imagined that, since his military and political reputation was at
its height, he intended to secure for himself one of a different
kind, by reviving the prosperity of his States, through the
restoration of commerce and husbandry; by creating a new soil
and peopling it anew; by continuing at peace with all his neighbours, and making himself the umpire of Europe, after having
been its terror. He could lay down the sword without risk, in the
full confidence that he would not be obliged to take it up again.
Seeing that he did not disarm, I was afraid that he would not
know how to use his advantages aright, and that he was only half
a great man. I ventured to write to him on this subject, and
adopted the tone of familiarity best adapted to please men of his
stamp, in order that the holy voice of truth, which so few kings
are born to hear, might reach him. It was only in confidence,
between our two selves, that I took this liberty. I did not even
communicate my secret to the Marshal, and I sent him my letter
to the King, carefully sealed. My lord sent the letter without
inquiring about its contents. The King made no reply; and, some
time afterwards, when the Marshal went to Berlin, he merely
told him that I had severely scolded him. I understood from this
that my letter had been ill received, and that my outspoken zeal
had been looked upon as pedantic awkwardness. At bottom, this
may have been really the case. Perhaps I did not say what I ought
to have said, and had not adopted the tone which I ought to have
adopted. I can only answer for the feeling which made me take
the pen into my hand.

Shortly after my establishment at Motiers-Travers, having received every possible assurance that I should be left in peace, I assumed the Armenian costume. This was not a new idea of mine; it had often occurred to me in the course of my life, and it often occurred to me again at Montmorency, where the constant use of bougies, which frequently compelled me to keep my room, made me sensible of the advantages of a long garment. The chance afforded by an Armenian tailor, who frequently came on a visit to a relation at Montmorency, tempted me to take advantage of it, in order to assume this new costume, in spite of what people might say, to which I paid but little heed. However, before adopting this new outfit, I desired to have the advice of Madame de Luxembourg, who strongly advised me to do so. I accordingly procured a little Armenian wardrobe; but the storm, which was roused against me, made me put off wearing it until the times were calmer, and it was not until several months later that, being obliged by fresh attacks of my complaint to have recourse to bougies, I thought that I might, without risk, assume this dress at Motiers, especially after having consulted the pastor of the place, who told me that I could wear it even in church without giving offence. I accordingly put on the jacket, caftan, fur cap, and girdle; and, after having been present at divine service in it, I saw no impropriety in wearing it in the presence of my Lord Marshal. His Excellency, when he saw me thus attired, said, by way of compliment, "*Salaam alek*";[1] this ended the matter, and I never afterwards wore any other dress.

Having entirely abandoned literature, I only thought of leading a quiet and peaceful life, as far as it depended upon myself. When alone, I have never known what it is to feel weary, even when I am entirely unemployed; my imagination fills up every void, and is alone sufficient to occupy me. It is only the idle gossip of a room, when people sit opposite each other, moving nothing but their tongues, that I have never been able to endure. When walking or moving, I can put up with it; the feet and eyes are at least employed; but, to remain with folded arms, talking about the weather and the flies buzzing round, or, what is worse,

---

[1] "Peace be with you" – a form of salutation only interchanged between Mussulmans.

exchanging compliments, that is to me unendurable torture. That I might not live quite like a savage, I took it into my head to learn to make laces. I took my cushion with me on my visits, or, like the women, I worked at my door, and talked with the passers-by. This made the empty chatter endurable, and enabled me to spend my time without weariness amongst my neighbours, several of whom were agreeable enough and not destitute of intelligence. One of them, named Isabelle d'Ivernois, the daughter of the *procureur-général* of Neufchâtel, appeared to me deserving of my particular friendship, of which she has had no reason to complain, for I gave her some very useful advice, and rendered her considerable services on important occasions; so that now, a respected and virtuous mother of a family, she perhaps owes her insight, her husband, her life, and her happiness to me. On my part, I am indebted to her for much gentle consolation, especially during a very dull winter, when, whilst my maladies and sufferings were at their height, she came to spend, with Thérèse and myself, long evenings which she knew how to make seem short by her cheerful disposition and our mutual confidences. She called me "papa," I called her "daughter"; and these names, which we still give each other, will, I hope, never cease to be as dear to her as to me. To make some use of my laces, I presented them to my young friends on their marriage, on condition that they brought up their children. Her eldest sister received one by virtue of this, and deserved it; Isabelle also had one, and, as far as good intentions went, equally deserved it; but she has not had the happiness of being able to carry them out. When sending them these laces, I wrote a letter to each, the first of which has travelled about the world; the second did not obtain such celebrity; the progress of friendship is not accompanied by so much noise.

Amongst the connections which I formed in my neighbourhood, into the details of which I do not propose to enter, I must not omit to mention Colonel Pury, who had a house on the mountains, where he was in the habit of coming to spend the summer. I was not very anxious to make his acquaintance, because I knew that he was in bad odour at the Court, and on bad terms with my Lord Marshal, whom he never visited.

However, as he called upon me and showed me great civility, I was obliged to return his call. We continued to visit, and sometimes dined with each other. At his house I made the acquaintance of M. du Peyrou, with whom I became so intimate that I cannot avoid saying something about him.

M. du Peyrou was an American, son of a commandant of Surinam, whose widow married his successor, M. de Chambrier of Neufchâtel. Being left a widow for the second time, she came to settle with her son in her husband's native country. Du Peyrou, an only son, very rich, and the darling of his mother, had been brought up with great care, and had made good use of his education. He had acquired a great deal of partial knowledge, a certain taste for the arts, and he specially prided himself on having cultivated his reasoning powers. His manner, cold and philosophical, resembling that of a Dutchman, his tawny complexion, his silent and reserved disposition, strongly favoured this opinion. He was deaf and gouty, although still young. This rendered all his movements very deliberate and solemn; and, although he was fond of arguing, sometimes even at length, as a rule he spoke little, because he could not hear. His whole appearance inspired me with respect. I said to myself: Here is a thinker, a wise man, such as one might be happy to have for a friend. To complete his conquest of me, he often addressed me, without ever paying me a compliment. He rarely spoke to me about himself, me, or my books. He was not without ideas, and everything that he said was fairly accurate. This accuracy and precision attracted me. His mind possessed neither the loftiness nor delicacy of that of my Lord Marshal, but it was just as simple; and thus, in one respect, he always represented him. I did not become infatuated with him, but was attracted to him by a feeling of esteem; and this esteem gradually led to friendship. In his case, I entirely forgot the objection which I had made to Baron d'Holbach – that he was too wealthy; and I believe that I was wrong. I have learned to doubt whether a man, who is the possessor of a large fortune, whoever he may be, can be sincerely fond of my principles and their originator.

For a considerable time I saw little of Du Peyrou, because I never went to Neufchâtel, and he only came once a year to see

Colonel Pury on his mountain. Why did I never go to Neufchâtel? For a childish reason, which I must not conceal.

Although, under the protection of the King of Prussia and my Lord Marshal, I at first escaped persecution in my retreat, I did not escape the hostility of the public, the municipal magistrates, and the clergy. After France had given the signal, it was no longer good taste not to offer me some kind of insult at least: these persons would have been afraid of seeming to disapprove of the conduct of my persecutors, if they did not imitate them. The chief class of Neufchâtel, that is to say, the society of the clergy of the town, gave the first impulse, by attempting to stir up the State Council against me. This attempt having proved unsuccessful, the clergy turned to the municipal authorities, who immediately prohibited my book, and, treating me on every occasion with scant politeness, gave me to understand, even in so many words, that, if I had desired to take up my abode in the town, it would not have been allowed. They filled the columns of their *Mercure* with absurdities and the most insipid cant, which, although it only excited the ridicule of sensible persons, none the less provoked the people and stirred them up against me. All this, however, to listen to them, ought not have prevented me from being extremely grateful to them for allowing me to live at Motiers, where they had no authority; they would willingly have measured out the air to me by the pint, on condition that I paid a heavy price for it. They desired that I should feel under a great obligation to them for the protection which the King granted me in spite of them, and of which they were persistently working to deprive me. At last, finding that they could not succeed, and having done me all the harm they could, and abused me with all their might, they made a virtue of their impotence, by exalting their kindness in suffering me to remain in their country. My only answer ought to have been – to laugh in their face; instead of this, I was silly enough to feel annoyed, and foolish enough to make up my mind never to go to Neufchâtel: a resolution which I kept for nearly two years, as if I were not showing such creatures too much honour by taking any notice of their conduct, for which, whether good or bad, they cannot be considered responsible, since they never act except under compulsion! Besides, uncultivated and narrow minds, which know no other object of esteem but reputation, power, and money, are far from even suspecting that any respect is due to talent, and that there is any dishonour in insulting it.

A certain village *maire*, who had been deprived of his office for his malpractices, once said to the lieutenant of Val-de-Travers, who was my Isabelle's husband, "This Rousseau is said to be a man of great talent: bring him to me, that I may see whether it is true." Assuredly, the displeasure of a man who adopts such a tone ought not to trouble those who are the objects of it.

Judging from the manner in which I was treated at Paris, Geneva, Berne, and Neufchâtel, I expected no greater consideration from the pastor of the place. However, I had been recommended to him by Madame Boy de la Tour, and he had received me very kindly; but, in this country, where flattery is universal, courtesies go for nothing. But, after my solemn reunion with the Reformed Church, and living in a Protestant country, I could not, without breaking my vows and failing in my duties as a citizen, neglect the public profession of the religion which I had again adopted: I therefore attended divine service. On the other hand, I was afraid that, by presenting myself at the Lord's table, I might expose myself to the insult of a refusal; and it was highly improbable that, after the stir that had been created at Geneva by the Council and at Neufchâtel by the clergy, he would quietly administer the Holy Communion to me in his church. As the time for Communion was near, I decided to write to M. de Montmollin – this was the minister's name – in order to prove my good intentions, and to inform him that, at heart, I had always been a member of the Reformed Church. I told him at the same time that, in order to avoid all disputes about the articles of faith, I declined to listen to any special explanation upon points of dogma. Having thus set myself right in this quarter, I remained quiet, not feeling the least doubt that M. de Montmollin would refuse to admit me without the preliminary discussion, with which I absolutely declined to have anything to do, and that the matter would thus be settled, without any blame being attached to me. But nothing of the kind happened. At the moment when I least expected it, M. de Montmollin came to tell me, not only that

he was willing to admit me to the Communion, under the condition for which I had stipulated, but, more than this, that he and
his elders considered it a great honour to have me as one of the
members of their flock. I was never so surprised in my life, and
nothing has ever afforded me greater consolation. It appeared to
me a most gloomy fate, to live always isolated in the world,
especially in time of adversity. In the midst of so many proscrip-
tions and persecutions, I found the greatest consolation in being
able to say to myself, At least I am amongst my brethren; and I
went to Communion with a heart greatly moved and affected to
tears, which was perhaps the preparation most acceptable to God
that one could take to His table.

Some time afterwards, my lord sent me a letter from Madame
de Boufflers, which – so at least I imagine – came through
D'Alembert, who was acquainted with him. In this letter, the
first that this lady had written to me since my departure from
Montmorency, she severely scolded me for having written to
M. de Montmollin, and, above all, for having taken Communion.
I was the less able to understand what was the object of her
reprimand, since, from the time of my journey to Geneva, I had
always openly proclaimed myself a Protestant, and had publicly
attended the Hôtel de Hollande,[1] and no one in the world had
made any objection. It seemed highly amusing that Madame la
Comtesse de Boufflers should desire to interfere with the direction of my conscience in matters of religion. However, as I did
not doubt that her intentions – although I utterly failed to
understand them – were the best possible, I took no offence at
this remarkable attack, and I replied to her without irritation, at
the same time quietly explaining my reasons.

Meanwhile, the printed abuse against me continued as before,
and its kindly authors reproached the authorities with treating
me too leniently. This chorus of yelping, the leaders of which
continued to act under cover, was somewhat ill-omened and
alarming. For my part, I let them yelp, without troubling myself.
I was assured that a decree of censure had been obtained from
the Sorbonne;[2] I refused to believe it. How could the Sorbonne

---

[1] The chapel of the Dutch embassy in Paris.
[2] A famous school of theology at the time.

interfere in the matter? Did the members desire to settle that I was not a Catholic? Everybody knew this already. Did they desire to prove that I was not a good Calvinist? What did it matter to them? That would be to take a singular responsibility upon themselves, and to pose as the substitutes of our ministers. Before I had seen the document, I believed that it was being circulated in the name of the Sorbonne, in order to insult its members; I felt even more convinced of this after I had read it. At last, when I was unable to doubt its genuineness any longer, nothing was left for me to believe except that the proper place for the Sorbonne was a lunatic asylum.

[1763.] – Another document affected me more, because it proceeded from a man whom I had always esteemed, and whose firmness I admired, while pitying his blindness. I am speaking of the "charge" written by the Archbishop of Paris against me.[1]

I thought it incumbent upon me to reply to it. I could do so without lowering myself; it was a case almost similar to that of the King of Poland.[2] I have never been fond of brutal quarrels, *à la Voltaire*. I can only fight in a dignified manner, and, before I condescend to defend myself, I must be assured that he who attacks me will not dishonour my blows. I had no doubt that this mandatory letter was the work of the Jesuits; and, although they were themselves in very great distress at the time, I recognised in it their ancient maxim – that of crushing the unfortunate. I was thus enabled to follow my own established principle – that of honouring the author whose name the work bore, and of pulverising the work itself; and this I think I did with great success.

I found my stay at Motiers very agreeable; nothing but an assured means of livelihood was wanting to make me decide to end my days there; but living was rather expensive, and all my former schemes had been upset by the break-up of my old household and the establishment of a new one, by the sale or dispersal of my effects, and by the expenses which I had been

---

[1] The pastoral "charge" denouncing *Émile* by the Archbishop of Paris, Christophe de Beaumont, bore the date 20 August 1762; Rousseau's *Letter* in reply is dated 18 November 1762.
[2] [King of Poland] See Book VIII, p. 389.

obliged to incur since my departure from Montmorency. I saw my little capital dwindling daily; two or three years would be sufficient to consume what was left, while I saw no means of replacing it, unless I began to write books again – a fatal profession, which I had already abandoned.

Convinced that my situation would soon alter, and that the public, recovering from its madness, would put the authorities to the blush, my only desire was to make my means last until this happy alteration took place, which would make it easier for me to take my choice of such means of subsistence as might present themselves. With this object, I again took up my "Dictionnaire de Musique," which, after ten years' labour, was already far advanced, and only needed a final revision, and to be copied out fairly. My book, which had recently been sent on to me, furnished me with the means of finishing this work: my papers, which were sent at the same time, enabled me to start upon my Memoirs, to which I intended henceforth to devote my sole attention. I began by copying some letters in a collection, to serve as a guide to my memory in the order of events and dates. I had already picked out those which I intended to keep for this purpose, and they were arranged in an almost unbroken series for the last ten years. However, while arranging them for copying, I found a gap which surprised me. This embraced a period of nearly six months, from October, 1756, to the following March. I perfectly remembered having included in my collection a number of letters from Diderot, Deleyre, Madame d'Epinay, Madame Chenonceaux, and others, which bridged over this gap and could no longer be found. What had become of them? Had anyone touched my papers during the few months they had remained at the Hôtel de Luxembourg? This was inconceivable: for I had seen M. de Luxembourg himself take the key of the room in which I had deposited them. As several letters from ladies, and all those from Diderot, were undated, and as I had been obliged to fill in these dates from memory and, as it were, groping in the dark, in order to arrange these letters in order, I at first thought that I had made some mistakes in dates, and I went over all the letters which were undated, or in which I had myself inserted the dates, to see if I could not find those which were needed to fill up the gap. This attempt was unsuccessful: I found that the gap was a real one, and that the letters had certainly been abstracted. By whom and for what reason? This was beyond my powers of comprehension. These letters, prior to my great quarrels, and belonging to the time of my first infatuation for "Julie," were of no interest to anybody. They contained, at most, some bickerings of Diderot, some bantering from Deleyre, some assurances of friendship from Madame de Chenonceaux, and even from Madame d'Epinay, with whom I was then on the best possible terms. To whom could these letters be of any importance? What was intended to be done with them? It was not until seven years later that I suspected the frightful purpose of this theft.

Having settled the fact of this deficiency, I proceeded to examine my rough copies, to see whether I could discover any further loss. I found several missing, and this, as I had a very bad memory, made me imagine I should find it the same with my multitudinous papers. Those which I missed were the rough copy of "La Morale Sensitive," and the extract of the "Aventures de Mylord Édouard." The absence of the latter, I confess, caused me to suspect Madame de Luxembourg. It was her *valet de chambre*, La Roche, who had forwarded my papers, and I could not think of anyone else who could feel any interest in this fragment; but how could the other have interested her; or the letters which had been abstracted, of which no use could be made, even with the worst intentions to injure me, unless they were fraudulently altered? As for M. de Luxembourg, of whose invariable uprightness and genuine friendship I felt assured, I could not for a moment suspect him. I could not even fix the suspicion upon Madame la Maréchale. The most reasonable supposition that I could think of, after long racking my brains to discover the thief, was to fix the guilt upon D'Alembert, who, having already made his way into Madame de Luxembourg's good graces, might have found means to rummage amongst these papers, and to abstract whatever he pleased, whether manuscripts or letters, either with the intention of stirring up some annoyance against me, or of appropriating to himself what might be useful to him. I imagined that, misled by the title of

"La Morale Sensitive," he expected to find in it the sketch of a real treatise upon Materialism, which he might have been able to use against me in a manner which may easily be imagined. Feeling sure that he would soon be undeceived on examining the rough copy, and having made up my mind to abandon literature altogether, I troubled myself little about these petty larcenies, which were, perhaps, not the first committed by the same hand which I have endured without complaining.* I soon thought no more of this disloyalty, as if no similar act had ever been committed against me, and I began to arrange the materials which had been left to me, in order to work at my Confessions.

I had long believed that the society of the clergy at Geneva, or, at least, the citizens and burgesses, would protest against the infringement of the edict involved in the decree against myself. All remained quiet, at least in outward appearance, for a general feeling of discontent prevailed, which only waited for an opportunity of manifesting itself. My friends, or those who called themselves such, wrote letter after letter, urging me to go and put myself at their head, and assuring me of a public apology on the part of the Council. The fear of the disorder and disturbance, which my presence might cause, prevented me from yielding to their entreaties; and, faithful to the vow I had formerly made – never to mix myself up in any civil quarrel in my own country – I preferred to let the offence against justice remain as it was and to exile myself from my native land for ever, than to enter it again by violent and dangerous means. I had certainly expected, on the part of the burgesses, legal and peaceful remonstrances against an infringement which greatly concerned them. But nothing of the kind took place. Those at their head were less anxious for the real redress of wrongs than for an opportunity of making themselves necessary. They intrigued, but kept silence, and allowed the gossips and hypocrites to prate, who were put forward by the Council to render me odious in the eyes of the

* I had found, in his "Eléments de Musique," several things which had been taken from my article in the "Encyclopédie," which had been sent to him several years before the publication of his "Eléments." I do not know what share he may have had in a work entitled "Dictionnaire des Beaux-arts," but I have found in it articles copied word for word from mine, long before these same articles were printed in the "Encyclopédie." (R)

people, and to cause its insolence to be attributed to religious zeal.

After having waited in vain, for more than a year, for some-one to protest against an illegal procedure, I at last made up my mind; and, finding myself abandoned by my fellow-citizens, I determined to renounce my ungrateful country, in which I had never lived, from which I had received no kindness or assistance, and by which, as the reward of the honour which I had endeavoured to bestow upon it, I found myself, by unanimous consent, so unworthily treated, seeing that those who ought to have spoken had never uttered a word. I accordingly wrote to the chief syndic for that year, who was, I believe, M. Favre, a letter in which I solemnly renounced my burgess rights, at the same time being careful to observe in it the becoming and moderate language, which I have always employed, when acting in accordance with the dictates of my pride, as I have frequently been compelled to do by the cruelty of my enemies, in time of misfortune.

This step at last opened the eyes of the citizens; feeling that they had acted against their own interests in abandoning my defence, they took it up when it was too late. They had other grievances, which they added to mine, and made them the subject of several very well-reasoned remonstrances, which they extended and strengthened, in proportion as the rude and discouraging refusals of the Council, which felt itself supported by the French ministry, made them feel more strongly the design which had been formed for keeping them in a state of subjection. These disputes called forth various pamphlets, which decided nothing, until there suddenly appeared the "Lettres écrites de la Campagne," a work written in support of the Council with infinite skill, and which for a time reduced to silence and crushed the party of remonstrance. This work, a lasting memorial of the rare talents of its author, was the production of the *Procureur-général* Tronchin, an enlightened and talented man, who had a profound knowledge of the laws and constitution of the Republic *Siluit terra.*[1]

[1] See *Maccabees* I, I, 3.

[1764.] – The party of remonstrance,[1] recovering from their first defeat, undertook to reply, and in time acquitted themselves tolerably well. But all turned their eyes towards me, as the only person capable of entering the lists against such an adversary, with any hope of overthrowing him. I confess that I thought the same; and, urged on by my old fellow-citizens, who represented it to me as my duty to assist them with my pen in a difficulty of which I had been the cause, I undertook the refutation of the "Lettres écrites de la Campagne," and parodied its title by that of "Lettres écrites de la Montagne,"[2] which I gave to mine. I conceived and carried out this undertaking so secretly, that, at a meeting which took place at Thonon between myself and the party of remonstrance, in order to discuss their affairs, and at which they showed me the outline of their reply, I did not say a word about my own, which was already written; for I was afraid that some obstacle might be thrown in the way of its being printed, if either the magistrates or my private enemies got the least wind of it. I could not, however, prevent the work becoming known in France before it was published; but it was thought better to let it appear than to let me understand too clearly how my secret had been discovered. I will afterwards state what I have been able to learn positively about the matter, which is not much; I will say nothing about my own conjectures.

At Motiers I had almost as many visitors as at the Hermitage and Montmorency, but, for the most part, of a very different kind. Those who had hitherto come to see me had been people who, being connected with me by common talents, tastes, and principles, made them the excuse for their visits, and immediately introduced subjects on which I was able to converse with them. At Motiers this was no longer the case, especially as far as the French were concerned. My visitors were officers or others who had no taste for literature, the majority of whom had never even read my works, and who, nevertheless, according to their own account, had travelled thirty, forty, sixty, a hundred leagues to see me and admire the illustrious, famous, very famous man,

---

[1] *i.e.*, the "popular" party, the opponent of the oligarchic "Little Council".
[2] Rousseau's *Letters Written from the Mountain* were published in October–November 1764 in Amsterdam.

the very great man, and so forth. From that time people never ceased to fling in my face the coarsest and most shameless flatteries, from which the esteem of those who came to see me had hitherto protected me. As the majority of these visitors did not condescend to mention their names or position, as their knowledge and mine had no common object, as they had neither read nor even glanced over my works, I did not know what to talk to them about. I waited for them to speak, since it was their place to know and to inform me what was the object of their visit. It may be imagined that this did not lead to conversations particularly interesting to me, although they may have been so to them, according to what they wanted to know; for, as I was never mistrustful, I expressed myself without reserve upon all the questions which they thought fit to put to me; and they left me, as a rule, quite as well informed as myself in regard to all the details connected with my situation.

Such a visitor, for instance, was M. de Feins, equerry to the Queen, and a captain of cavalry in the Queen's regiment, who was so persevering as to spend several days at Motiers, and even to accompany me on foot as far as La Ferrière, leading his horse by the bridle, without having anything else in common with me, except that we both knew Mademoiselle Fel, and both played at cup-and-ball. Before and after M. de Feins, I received another much more extraordinary visit. Two men arrived on foot, each leading a mule carrying his scanty baggage. They put up at the inn, and, after rubbing down their mules themselves, asked to see me. From the general appearance of these muleteers, the villagers took them for smugglers; and the report immediately spread that some smugglers had come to pay me a visit. But the manner in which they accosted me at once informed me that they were persons of quite a different sort; but, although they were certainly not smugglers, they might well have been adventurers, and this uncertainty kept me on my guard for some time. However, they very soon allayed my suspicions. One of them was M. de Montauban, called the Comte de la Tour du Pin, a gentleman from Dauphiné; the other was M. Dastier, from Carpentras, an old soldier, who had put his cross of Saint-Louis in his pocket, to avoid displaying it. These gentlemen, who were both very amiable, were also very good company; their conversation was interesting and agreeable. Their manner of travelling, so greatly to my taste, and so little in keeping with that of French gentlemen, made me feel a kind of attachment for them which intercourse with them could not fail to strengthen. The acquaintance did not even end there. It still continues, and they have paid me several visits since then, but not on foot, although that was well enough for the first introduction. But the more I have seen of these gentlemen, the less sympathy I have found between their tastes and mine, the less I have felt that their principles were mine, that they were familiar with my writings, or that there was any real sympathy between us. What, then, did they want of me? Why did they visit me with such an equipage? Why did they remain several days? Why did they return several times? Why were they so anxious to have me for their guest? At that time it never occurred to me to ask myself all these questions. I have often put them to myself since.

Touched by their friendly advances, my heart surrendered without reflection, especially to M. Dastier, whose manner, being more frank and open, pleased me most. I even continued to correspond with him; and, when I wanted to get the "Lettres de la Montagne" printed, I thought of applying to him, in order to put those, who were waiting for my parcel on the route to Holland, on the wrong scent. He had often spoken to me, and perhaps designedly, of the liberty enjoyed by the press at Avignon, and had offered his services, if I ever wanted to get anything printed there. I availed myself of this offer, and sent him my first sheets, one after the other, by post. After he had kept them for a considerable time he sent them back, at the same time informing me that no printer would venture to undertake the work; and I was obliged to go back to Rey, taking the precaution of sending my sheets one after the other, and not letting the succeeding ones go until I had been advised of the receipt of those which preceded them. Before the publication of the work, I learned that it had been seen in the ministerial offices; and D'Escherny, of Neufchâtel, spoke to me of a book called "De l'Homme de la Montagne," which he had been told by Holbach was written by me. I assured him, as was quite true, that

I had never written a book called by this name. When the letters appeared he was furious, and accused me of falsehood, although I had told him the simple truth. This is how I was convinced that my manuscript was known. Feeling sure of Rey's trustworthiness, I was obliged to transfer my suspicions elsewhere; and the most rational conjecture, and the one to which I was most inclined to adhere, was that my packets had been opened in the post.

Another person, whose acquaintance I made almost at the same time, at first merely through the medium of correspondence, was M. Laliaud, of Nîmes, who wrote to me from Paris, asking me to send him my profile in silhouette, which he said he required for a bust of myself in marble, which he was having made by Le Moine, with the intention of placing it in his library. If this was a piece of flattery, simply intended to disarm me, it was completely successful. I imagined that a man who desired to have my bust in marble in his library must be full of my works, and consequently of my principles, and that he must love me, because his soul was in unison with mine. This idea was bound to attract me. I have seen M. Laliaud subsequently. I have found him eager to render me several trifling services, and to meddle with my humble affairs. But, beyond that, I doubt whether any single work of mine has been included in the very limited number of books which he has read in the course of his life. I am ignorant whether he has a library, and whether it is a piece of furniture which he is likely to use; and as for the bust, it is limited to a poor figure in clay, executed by Le Moine, from which he has had a hideous portrait engraved, which nevertheless passes current under my name, as if it had some resemblance to me.

The only Frenchman whose visits seemed to be due to a partiality for my sentiments and writing, was a young officer of the Limousin regiment, by name Séguier de Saint-Brisson, who cut a brilliant figure in Paris and in the world, and perhaps still does, through the amiability of his talents and his pretentions to wit. He had come to see me at Montmorency during the winter preceding my catastrophe. I found in him a liveliness which pleased me. He afterwards wrote to me at Motiers; and, whether it was that he wanted to flatter me, or that his head was really turned by "Émile," he told me that he intended to leave the service, in order to live independently, and that he was learning the trade of a carpenter. He had an elder brother, a captain in the same regiment, the favourite of the mother, who, being a violent devotee, and under the thumb of some hypocritical *abbé*, treated her younger son very badly, accusing him of irreligion, and even of the unpardonable offence of being intimate with myself. These were the grievances which induced him to break with his mother, and adopt the resolution of which I have just spoken – all, to play the little "Émile."

Alarmed at this impetuous eagerness, I hastened to write to him, to try and dissuade him from carrying out his resolution, and I made my exhortations as forcible as I could. He listened to them; he returned to his duty as a son, and withdrew from his colonel's hands the resignation which he had handed in, and which the former had prudently not accepted, in order to allow him time to think better of it. Saint-Brisson, cured of these follies, committed another, which was not quite so outrageous, but which was hardly more to my taste; he became an author. He produced two or three pamphlets one after the other, which showed a certain amount of talent, but in regard to which I shall never have to reproach myself with having praised them in sufficiently encouraging terms to induce him to follow such a career.

Some time afterwards, he came to see me, and we made an excursion together to the island of Saint-Pierre.[1] I found him, during this journey, somewhat different from what he had been at Montmorency. There was something affected about him, which at first did not particularly offend me, but which I have often thought of since then. He came to see me once again at the Hôtel de Saint-Simon, when I was passing through Paris on my way to England. There I heard – which he had not told me before – that he went into fashionable society, and that he frequently saw Madame de Luxembourg. He gave no sign of life when I was at Trye, and did not send me any message through Mademoiselle Séguier, who was my neighbour, and who never seemed particularly well disposed towards me. In a

[1] In the Lake of Bienne; see p. 683.

word, M. de Saint-Brisson's infatuation suddenly came to an end, like my connection with M. de Feins, but, whereas the latter owed me nothing, the former owed me something, unless the follies which I had prevented him from committing were only a joke on his part, which really may very well have been the case.

I also had as many and even more visitors from Geneva. The Delucs, father and son, successively chose me for their nurse. The father fell ill on the road; the son was already ill when he started from Geneva; both came to recruit themselves at my house. Clergymen, relatives, bigots, persons of all sorts, came from Geneva and Switzerland, not for the purpose of admiring or making fun of me, like those who came from France, but to scold and catechise me. The only one whom I was glad to see was Moultou, who came to spend three or four days with me, and whom I should have been glad to keep longer. The most obstinately persistent of all, and the one who finally conquered me by his importunities, was one M. d'Ivernois, a Genevese merchant, a French refugee, and a relative of the *procureur-général* of Neufchâtel. This M. d'Ivernois came twice a year from Geneva to Motiers on purpose to see me, stayed with me from morning till evening several days in succession, accompanied me on my walks, brought me hundreds of little presents, wormed himself into my confidence in spite of myself, interfered in all my affairs, without our having any ideas, tastes, sentiments, or knowledge in common. I doubt whether, in the whole course of his life, he has ever read through a single book of any kind, or whether he even knows the subjects of which my works treat. When I began to collect plants, he accompanied me on my botanical excursions, although he had no taste for such amusement, and we had not a word to say to each other. He even had the courage to spend three whole days with me *tête-à-tête* in a public-house at Goumoins, from which I had hoped to drive him away by dint of boring him and making him feel how greatly he bored me; but I was never able to discourage his incredible persistency, or to discover the reason of it.

Amongst all these acquaintances, which I only made and kept up under compulsion, I must not omit the only one which has been agreeable to me, and which aroused a real interest in my heart; I refer to a young Hungarian, who came to reside at Neufchâtel, and afterwards at Motiers, some months after I was settled there myself. In the district he was called the Baron de Sauttern, under which name he had been accredited from Zurich. He was tall and well-built, his features were pleasant, his manners gentle and affable. He told everybody, and also gave me to understand, that he had come to Neufchâtel solely to see me, and to train his youth to virtue by intercourse with me. His expression, his tone, his manners, appeared to me in agreement with his words; and I should have considered myself failing in a most important duty, if I had refused to receive a young man in whom I saw nothing but amiability, and whose motive in seeking my acquaintance was so worthy of respect. My heart is incapable of surrendering itself by halves. He soon possessed my entire friendship and my entire confidence; we became inseparable. He accompanied me on all my walking excursions, and greatly enjoyed them. I took him to my Lord Marshal, who showed him the greatest kindness. As he was not yet able to express himself in French, he spoke and wrote to me in Latin; I answered him in French, but this mixture of the two languages did not make our conversations less fluent or lively in any respect. He spoke to me of his family, his affairs, his adventures, and the Court of Vienna, with the domestic details of which he appeared to be intimately acquainted. In short, for nearly two years, during which we lived on terms of the closest intimacy, I invariably found in him a gentleness of character which nothing could alter, manners not only polite but refined, great personal cleanliness, and extreme propriety of language; in short, all the characteristics of a well-bred man, which made me esteem him too highly not to regard him with affection.

At the time of my greatest intimacy with him, D'Ivernois wrote to me from Geneva, warning me against the young Hungarian who had come to settle in my neighbourhood; adding that he had been assured that he was a spy sent by the French ministry to watch me. This warning was calculated to cause me the more uneasiness, since, in the country where I was, everybody advised me to keep on my guard because I was being watched, and it was designed to entice me into French territory, and then to pounce upon me.

In order to shut, once for all, the mouths of these silly monitors, I proposed to Sauttern, without saying a word to him beforehand, a walk to Pontarlier. He agreed to go. When we reached Pontarlier, I gave him D'Ivernois's letter to read, and then, fervently embracing him, said, "Sauttern needs no proof of my confidence; but the public needs a proof that I know who is worthy of it." This embrace was very sweet. It was one of those enjoyments of the soul which persecutors can never know, and of which they cannot deprive the oppressed.

I will never believe that Sauttern was a spy, or that he betrayed me; but he deceived me. When I opened my heart to him without reserve, he was firm enough to keep his own shut, and to deceive me with his lies. He invented some story, which caused me to believe that his presence was required in his own country. I exhorted him to set out without delay. He did so, and, when I thought he was already in Hungary, I heard that he was at Strasburg. This was not the first time that he had been there. He had caused dissension in a family in the town, and the husband, knowing that I was in the habit of seeing him, wrote to me. I had spared no efforts to bring the wife back to the path of virtue, and Sauttern to his duty. When I thought that their separation was complete, they came together again, and the husband was obliging enough to take the young man into his house again. After that I had nothing more to say. I discovered that the pretended Baron had imposed upon me with a heap of lies. His name was not Sauttern at all, but Sauttersheim. As for the title of Baron, which had been bestowed upon him in Switzerland, I could not reproach him on that score, because he had never assumed it. But I have no doubt that he was really a gentleman, and my Lord Marshal, who was a judge of men, and who had been in his country, always looked upon and treated him as one.

As soon as he had left, the servant at the inn where he took his meals declared that she was in the family way by him. She was so dirty a slut, and Sauttern, who was generally esteemed and looked up to in the district as a well-conducted and respectable young man, was known to take such pride in cleanliness, that

this impudent assertion disgusted everybody. The most attractive women in the district, who had in vain lavished their
fascinations upon him, were furious. I was beside myself with
indignation. I did all I could to get the shameless hussy arrested,
offering to pay all expenses and go bail for Sauttersheim. I wrote
to him, firmly convinced not only that this pregnancy was not
his work, but that it was in reality only pretended, and that the
whole affair was a joke on the part of his enemies and my own. I
wanted him to return to the district, to confound the jade, and
those who had prompted her. I was surprised at the feebleness
of his reply. He wrote to the pastor of the girl's parish, and tried
to hush up the affair. I accordingly ceased to trouble myself
about the matter, feeling greatly astonished that a man whose
tastes were so low could have been sufficiently master of himself
to impose upon me by his reserve during our closest intimacy.

From Strasburg, Sauttersheim went to Paris to seek his fortune, but only found misery. He wrote to me, confessing his sins.
My heart was moved at the recollection of our old friendship.
I sent him some money. The following year, when passing
through Paris, I saw him again. He was in much the same
circumstances, but on very friendly terms with M. Laliaud. I
have never been able to learn how he made his acquaintance, or
whether it was recent or of long standing. Two years later,
Sauttersheim returned to Strasburg, from which place he
wrote to me, and where he died. Such is, in brief, the story of
my connection with him, and of his adventures; but, while
deploring the unhappy lot of this unfortunate young man, I
shall always believe that he was a gentleman by birth, and that
his irregular life was the result of the situations to which he was
reduced.

Such were my acquisitions, in the way of connections and
friendships, at Motiers. I should have needed many such to
compensate for the cruel losses which I suffered at the same
time!

First, I lost M. de Luxembourg,[1] who, having suffered great
torture at the hands of the physicians, at last fell a victim to them,

---

[1] The Maréchal de Luxembourg died 18 May 1764.

who treated his gout, which they persistently refused to acknowledge, as a malady which they were able to cure.

If we can believe the written account of La Roche, Madame la Maréchale's confidential servant, M. de Luxembourg's case is a cruel and memorable example, how deplorable are the miseries of greatness!

I felt the loss of this worthy gentleman the more keenly, as he was the only friend I had in France; and the gentleness of his character was so great, that it made me altogether forget his rank and associate with him as an equal. Our relations did not come to an end after my retirement, and he continued to write to me as before. I fancied, however, that absence or my misfortunes had somewhat cooled his affections. It is difficult for a courtier to preserve the same attachment for anyone whom he knows to be out of favour with the authorities. Besides, I came to the conclusion that the great influence which Madame de Luxembourg possessed over him had not been favourable to me, and that she had taken advantage of my absence to injure me in his esteem. She herself, in spite of affected demonstrations of friendship, which became less and less frequent, was at less pains every day to conceal the alteration in her feelings towards me. She wrote to me four or five times in Switzerland, at intervals, after which she left off writing altogether; and it needed all my preconceived opinions, all my confidence, all my blindness, which still clung to me, to prevent me from seeing that her feelings towards me were something more than simple coolness.

Guy, the bookseller, and partner of Duchesne, who, after me, was a frequent visitor at the Hôtel de Luxembourg, wrote to inform me that my name was down in M. le Maréchal's will. In this there was nothing singular or incredible; accordingly, I did not doubt what he said. This made me deliberate how I should behave in regard to the legacy. After careful consideration, I decided to accept it, whatever it might be, and to pay this respect to an honourable man, who entertained a true friendship for me, in spite of his rank, which is rarely accessible to such a feeling. I have been relieved of this duty, since I have never heard this legacy, whether the story was true or false, mentioned again; and, to tell the truth, I should have been grieved to violate one of my great moral principles, by profiting by the death of anyone who had been dear to me. During our friend Mussard's last illness, Lenieps proposed to me that we should take advantage of the gratefulness, which he showed for our attentions to him, to suggest to him gently that he should leave us something in his will. "Ah! my dear Lenieps," I said to him, "let us not degrade, by thoughts of self-interest, the melancholy but sacred duties which we are discharging towards our dying friend." I hope that I may never be mentioned in anyone's will, least of all, in that of a friend. It was about the same time that my Lord Marshal spoke to me about his will, and what he intended to do for me, on which occasion I made the answer which I have mentioned in the first part of these Confessions.

My second loss, more painful and irreparable, was that of the best of women and mothers,[1] who, already burdened with years, and overburdened with misery and infirmities, left this valley of tears for the abode of the blessed, where the pleasing recollection of the good we have done in this world below is its everlasting reward. Go, gentle and kindly soul, to join Fénélon, Bernex, Catinat, and those who, like them, have opened their hearts to genuine charity. Go, taste the fruit of your own, and prepare for your pupil the place which he one day hopes to occupy by your side! Happy, amidst all your misfortunes, since Heaven, by putting an end to them, has spared you the cruel spectacle of his! Afraid of saddening her heart by the narrative of my early disasters, I had not written to her at all after my arrival in Switzerland; but I wrote to M. de Conzié[2] for news of her, and it was from him that I learned that she had ceased to alleviate the sufferings of others, and that her own were over. I, also, shall soon cease to suffer; but, if I did not believe that I should see her again in the next world, my feeble imagination would refuse to entertain the idea of the perfect happiness to which I look forward.

My third and last loss – for I had then no more friends to lose – was that of my Lord Marshal. I did not lose him by death; but,

---

[1] Mme de Warens had died at Chambéry on 29 July 1762.
[2] For François-Joseph de Conzié, Comte des Charmettes, see Book V, p. 228.

tired of serving ungrateful masters, he left Neufchâtel, and I have never seen him again. He still lives, and will, I hope, survive me; he still lives, and, thanks to him, all my ties upon earth are not broken; there is still left a man worthy of my friendship, the real value of which consists even more in that friendship which one feels than in that which one inspires; but I have lost the delight with which his friendship filled me, and I can now do no more than reckon him amongst those whom I still love, but with whom I have no further connection. He went to England to receive the King's pardon, and to redeem his property which had been confiscated. We did not separate without arranging to meet again, the prospect of which appeared to afford him as much pleasure as myself. He intended to settle at Keith Hall, near Aberdeen, and it was agreed that I should visit him there; but the prospect was too delightful for me to hope that it would ever be realised. He did not stay in Scotland. The tender entreaties of the King of Prussia brought him back to Berlin, and it will presently be seen how I was prevented from going there to rejoin him.

Before his departure, foreseeing the storm which was about to be raised against me, he sent me, of his own accord, letters of naturalisation, which seemed to be a very safe precautionary measure, to make it impossible for me to be driven out of the country. The Corporation of Couvet in Val-de-Travers imitated the Governor's example, and granted me the rights of a native, free of charge, like the first. Thus, being a full citizen in every respect, I was protected against legal expulsion, even by the Prince; but my enemies have never been able to use legal means in persecuting a man who, more than any other, has always shown the greatest respect for the laws.

Amongst the losses which I suffered at this time, I do not think that I ought to reckon that of the Abbé de Mably.[1] Having lived at his brother's house, I had become slightly acquainted with him, but never intimate; and I have some reason to believe

[1] The *abbé* Gabriel Bonnot de Mably was brother to Jean Bonnet de Mably, whose children Rousseau tutored in 1740/41 (see Book VI, p. 285). Rousseau is incorrect in saying that Mably never replied; in fact he wrote reproaching Rousseau for (unlike Socrates in similar circumstances) attempting to revenge himself on his judges.

that his feelings towards me had changed since I had acquired greater celebrity than himself. But it was after the publication of the "Lettres de la Montagne" that I had the first indication of his ill-will. A letter to Madame Saladin, which was attributed to him, was circulated in Geneva, in which he spoke of the work as the seditious vapourings of a violent demagogue. My esteem for the Abbé, and the high opinion which I entertained of his abilities, did not allow me to believe for an instant that this extravagant letter was written by him. I decided to act as my frankness prompted me. I sent him a copy of the letter, informing him that it was attributed to him. He made no reply. This silence on his part surprised me; but my astonishment may be imagined, when Madame de Chenonceaux informed me that he had really written the letter, and that my own had greatly embarrassed him. For, even if he had been right, that was no excuse for a step which was bound to create a stir, and was taken publicly and with a light heart, without obligation or necessity, with the sole object of still further overwhelming, at the height of his misfortunes, a man towards whom he had always shown goodwill, and who had never done him any injury. Some time afterwards appeared the "Dialogues de Phocion," which appeared to me a barefaced and shameless compilation from my works. When I read the book, I felt that the author had made up his mind in regard to me, and that, from that time forth, I should have no bitterer enemy. I believe that he was never able to forgive me for having written the "Contrat Social," which was far above his powers, or for the "Paix Perpetuelle," and that he only wanted me to make a selection from the Abbé de Saint-Pierre's writings, because he thought that I should not be so successful in it.

The further I advance in my narrative, the less I am able to preserve its proper order and sequence. The unsettled condition of the rest of my life has not left events time to arrange themselves in succession in my head. They have been too numerous, too mixed up, too disagreeable to be able to be related without confusion. The only strong impression which they have left upon my mind is that of the horrible mystery in which their causes are enveloped, and of the deplorable condition to which they have reduced me. My narrative can only proceed at haphazard, as the ideas come back to me. I remember that, during the time of which I am speaking, being absorbed in my Confessions, I was so imprudent as to talk about them to everybody, never once imagining that anyone had any interest or desire, and, still less, the power, to throw obstacles in the way of this undertaking; and, even had I thought so, I should not have shown any greater discretion, since my disposition renders it absolutely impossible for me to conceal any of my thoughts or feelings. As far as I can judge, the fact of this undertaking becoming known was the real cause of the storm which was raised with the object of driving me out of Switzerland, and delivering me into the hands of those who might prevent me from carrying it out.[1]

I had another work in view, which was regarded with little less disfavour by those who were afraid of the first: this was a general edition of my works. Such an edition appeared to me necessary, in order to establish the authenticity of the books bearing my name, which were really by me, and to put the public in a position to be able to distinguish them from the pseudonymous writings, which my enemies attributed to me, in order to discredit and degrade me. In addition to that, this edition would be a simple and honourable way of insuring a means of subsistence; in fact, it was the only one, for I had abandoned book-making, my Memoirs could not be published during my lifetime, I did not earn a penny in any other manner, and was always spending money; so that I saw that I should be at the end of my resources as soon as the profits of my last writings were exhausted. These considerations had strongly inclined me to bring out my "Dictionnaire de Musique," which was as yet incomplete. It had brought me in 100 *louis* in ready money and an annuity of 100 crowns; but it was easy to see that 100 *louis* would not long last a man, who spent more than sixty every year; and an income of 100 crowns was nothing for one, upon whom beggars and others swooped down incessantly like a flock of starlings.

A company of Neufchâtel business-men offered to undertake the collected edition, and a printer or bookseller of Lyons, named Reguillat, somehow or other managed to thrust himself

---

[1] He means those of David Hume, whose invitation to England he had come to regard as having been a trap.

among them in the capacity of manager. An agreement was concluded on reasonable and satisfactory terms, considering the object I had in view. My printed works and others still in manuscript were enough to fill six volumes quarto. I further agreed to exercise a general supervision over the edition, in return for which I was to receive an annuity of 1,600 French *livres*, and 1,000 crowns down.

[1765.] – The agreement was concluded, but not signed, when the "Lettres écrites de la Montagne" appeared. The terrible outburst against this infernal work and its abominable author alarmed the company, and the enterprise fell through. I should compare the effect of this last work to that of the "Lettre sur la Musique Française," only that this letter, while bringing hatred upon me and exposing me to danger, at least left me in possession of esteem and respect. But, after this last work, the inhabitants of Geneva and Versailles seemed to be astonished that a monster like myself was permitted to live. The Little Council, egged on by the French Resident, and instructed by the *Procureur-général*, issued a declaration concerning my work, in which, after stigmatising it in most outrageous terms, that body declared that it was not even worthy of being burned by the hands of the executioner, and added, with a cleverness bordering on burlesque, that it would be impossible for anyone to answer it without disgracing himself, or even to mention it. I wish I could give a copy of this curious document, but, unfortunately, I have not got it, and I do not remember a single word of it. I sincerely wish that some one of my readers, animated by a desire for truth and justice, would read the whole of the "Lettres écrites de la Montagne" over again. I venture to assert that he will recognise the stoical moderation which characterises this work, after the violent and cruel insults which people had just vied with one another in heaping upon the author. But, being unable to reply to the abuse, because it contained none, or to the arguments, because they were unanswerable, my enemies had recourse to the expedient of pretending to be too indignant to answer; and it is certainly true that, if they took irrefutable arguments for insults, they must have felt themselves greatly insulted!

The party of remonstrance, far from complaining of this hateful declaration, followed the path which it marked out for them, and, instead of glorying in the "Lettres de la Montagne" as a trophy of victory, they covered them up to serve as a shield, and were too cowardly to render either honour or justice to this work, which was written in their defence and at their solicitation, or even to quote or mention it, although they secretly drew all their arguments from it, and the careful manner in which they have followed the advice given at the end of the work has been the sole cause of their salvation and their victory. They had imposed this duty upon me: I had fulfilled it. I had served the country and their cause to the end. I begged them to abandon mine, and only think of themselves in their quarrels. They took me at my word, and I interfered no further in their affairs, except to exhort them without ceasing to make peace, as I had no doubt that, if they persisted, they would be crushed by France. This has not happened. I understand the reason, but this is not the place to mention it.

The effect of the "Lettres de la Montagne" at Neufchâtel was at first insignificant. I sent a copy of it to M. de Montmollin. He was glad to have it, and read it without finding any fault with it. He was ill like myself; he paid me a friendly visit when his health was re-established, and said nothing about the book. However, the excitement was beginning. The book was publicly burnt – I do not know where.[1] From Geneva, from Berne, and, perhaps, from Versailles, the focus of disturbance soon shifted to Neufchâtel, especially Val-de-Travers, where, even before the "Class"[2] had given any signs of movement, they had begun to hound on the people by underhand means. I venture to say that I ought to have been loved by the people of that country, as I have been by all those amongst whom I have lived. I bestowed alms freely, left none of the needy in my neighbourhood without assistance, never refused to render any service within my power which was consistent with justice, perhaps even making myself

[1] At Paris, together with Voltaire's *Dictionnaire Philosophique*.
[2] The "Class" of pastors which met at Neuchâtel on 12/13 March declared that after his *Letters Written from the Mountain* it could not regard Rousseau any longer as a Christian and a member of the church.

too familiar with everybody, and, as far as I was able, I refused every distinction which might have aroused jealousy. All this, however, did not prevent the people, secretly stirred up by someone unknown to me, from gradually becoming infuriated against me, and publicly insulting me in broad daylight, not only in the country and on the roads, but in the open street. Those to whom I had rendered the greatest services were the most virulent; and even people to whom I continued to render them, although they did not venture to show themselves, urged on the rest, and seemed anxious to avenge themselves in this manner for the humiliation of being under an obligation to me. Montmollin seemed to see nothing and did not as yet show himself; but, as a celebration of the Communion was close at hand, he paid me a visit to advise me not to present myself, at the same time assuring me that he was not at all angry with me, and that he would leave me undisturbed. I thought this a curious kind of compliment. It reminded me of Madame de Boufflers's letter, and I could not imagine to whom it could be a matter of such importance whether I communicated or not. As I considered it would be an act of cowardice to give way to him, and, besides, did not desire to give the people a fresh excuse to raise the cry of "infidel" against me, I bluntly refused to do what he asked, and he went home highly displeased, at the same time giving me to understand that I should be sorry for it.

He could not refuse to admit me to Communion on his authority alone; that of the Consistory, which had admitted me, was also necessary: and, as long as the Consistory had said nothing, I could present myself boldly, without fear of being refused. Montmollin procured from the clergy the commission of summoning me before the Consistory to give an account of my belief, and of excommunicating me, in case I refused to appear. This excommunication, again, could only be pronounced by a majority of the votes of the Consistory. But the peasants who, under the name of Elders, composed this assembly, being under the presidency and, as may be supposed, the rule of their minister, would naturally have no other opinion but his, especially upon theological questions, which they understood still less than he did. I was accordingly summoned, and decided to appear.

What a lucky circumstance, and what a triumph would it have been for me, if I had been able to speak, and, so to say, had carried my pen in my mouth! With what overwhelming superiority, with what ease should I have overthrown the poor minister in the midst of his six peasants! Greed of authority had caused the Protestant clergy to forget all the principles of the Reformation: all that I needed, in order to remind him of this, and to reduce him to silence, was to explain my first "Lettres de la Montagne," for which they had been foolish enough to censure me. My text was ready, I had only to expand it, and my enemy was reduced to silence. I should not have been so silly as to confine myself to the defensive: it was easy enough for me to take the offensive without his even perceiving it, or being able to protect himself against it. The wretched members of the "Class," as thoughtless as they were ignorant, had themselves placed me in the most favourable position I could have desired, for crushing them as I pleased. But – I should have been obliged to speak, and to speak on the spot, to find ideas, turns of expression, and suitable words on the spur of the moment, never to lose my presence of mind or coolness, never to be flustered for a moment. What could I hope from myself – I who felt so strongly my inability to express myself impromptu? I had been most humiliatingly reduced to silence at Geneva,[1] in the presence of an assembly which was entirely favourable to me, and had made up its mind beforehand to approve of everything that I said. Here, it was quite the contrary: I had to do with a person who was prepared to cavil, who substituted cunning for knowledge, who would lay a hundred traps for me before I perceived one, and was fully determined to put me in the wrong, at whatever cost. The more I considered my position, the more perilous it seemed to me; and, convinced that it would be impossible for me to extricate myself with success, I bethought myself of another expedient. I pondered over a speech which I proposed to deliver before the Consistory, in order to challenge its authority and to relieve myself from the

[1] [Geneva] See p. 647.

necessity of replying. The matter was very simple: I wrote the speech, and proceeded to learn it by heart with unequalled enthusiasm. Thérèse, hearing me muttering and incessantly repeating the same phrases, in the endeavour to cram them into my head, laughed at me. I hoped in the end to know my speech by heart. I knew that the lord of the manor, as the Prince's official, would be present at the meeting of the Consistory, and that, in spite of the bottles of wine distributed by Montmollin, and his intrigues, most of the Elders were well disposed towards me. I had on my side reason, truth, justice, the King's protection, the authority of the Council of State, and the wishes of all good patriots who were affected by the establishment of this inquisition; in fact, everything contributed to my encouragement.

The day before the time appointed, I knew my speech by heart; I recited it without a mistake. I went over it again all night in my head: in the morning I had forgotten it: I hesitated at each word, I fancied myself already in the presence of the illustrious assembly; I was confused, I stammered, I lost my head; at last, almost at the moment of starting, my courage failed me entirely. I remained at home, I determined to write to the Consistory, hastily giving my reasons for not appearing, and alleging as an excuse my ill-health, which, considering the state I was in, would really have made it almost impossible for me to go through the whole sitting.

The minister, embarrassed by my letter, put off the matter to another sitting. In the meantime, he and his creatures made every effort to seduce those of the Elders who, following the dictates of their own conscience rather than his, were not of the same opinion as he and the clergy were. However powerful his arguments drawn from his cellar must have been for people of this kind, he could not win over any others except the two or three who were already devoted to him, and who were called his *âmes damnées*. The Prince's officer and Colonel de Pury, who was very energetic in the matter, kept the others to their duty; and, when Montmollin wanted to proceed to the excommunication, the Consistory, by a majority of votes, flatly vetoed it. Reduced to the last resource of stirring up the people, he proceeded, with the aid of his colleagues and others, to work openly and with such success, that, in spite of the frequent and strongly-worded rescripts of the King, in spite of all the orders of the Council of State, I was at last obliged to leave the country, to avoid exposing the Prince's officer to the risk of being assassinated, in consequence of his efforts to defend me.

My only recollections of the whole affair are so confused, that it is impossible for me to introduce any order or connection into the ideas which come back to me; I can only produce them, scattered and isolated, as they present themselves to my mind. I remember that some sort of negotiations had taken place with the clergy, in which Montmollin had been the mediator. He had pretended that it was feared that, by my writings, I should disturb the tranquillity of the country, which would be held responsible for allowing me to write. He had given me to understand that, if I undertook to lay aside my pen, the past would be winked at. I had already made this engagement with myself, and I had no hesitation in making it with the clerical party, but conditionally, and only as far as matters of religion were concerned. He managed to get two copies of the agreement made, in consequence of some alteration which he required. The condition was rejected, and I demanded the return of what I had written; he gave me back one of the duplicates, and kept the other, pretending that he had lost it. After this, the people, openly egged on by the clergy, laughed the King's rescripts and the orders of the Council of State to scorn, and became utterly uncontrollable. I was preached at from the pulpit, called the Antichrist, and chased in the country like a were-wolf. My Armenian costume was sufficient description for the people: I felt the disadvantage of it cruelly, but to abandon it under the circumstances appeared to me an act of cowardice. I could not make up my mind to do this, and I calmly walked about the country in my caftan and fur cap, pursued by the hue and cry of the rabble, and sometimes by their stones. Several times, when passing in front of the houses, I heard those inside say, "Bring me my gun: let me fire at him." I did not walk any faster, and this only increased their fury; but they always confined themselves to threats, at least as far as firearms were concerned.

During the whole time of this excitement, I nevertheless, on two occasions, had great cause for satisfaction, which afforded me genuine pleasure. The first was, that, through my Lord Marshal, I was enabled to perform an act of gratitude. All the respectable inhabitants of Neufchâtel, indignant at the treatment which I received and the intrigues of which I was the victim, were greatly incensed against the clerical party, being well aware that it was under foreign influence, and that it was merely the tool of others, who kept themselves in the background while urging it on to act; and they began to fear that the precedent established in my case might result in the establishment of a veritable inquisition. The magistrates, and particularly M. Meuron, who had succeeded M. d'Ivernois in the office of *procureur-général*, did all they could to protect me. Colonel de Pury, although merely a private individual, did even more and succeeded better. It was he who found the means of making Montmollin knock under in his Consistory, by keeping the Elders to their duty. As he had considerable reputation, he made the most use of it to check the outbreak; but he only had the authority of the laws, justice, and reason, to oppose to that of money and wine. The odds were against him, and in this respect Montmollin triumphed. However, appreciating his zeal and efforts on my behalf, I was anxious, if possible, to do him a service in return, and in some degree to discharge my obligations to him. I knew that he was very anxious to become a councillor of State; but, having offended the Court in the matter of the minister Petitpierre, he was out of favour with the Prince and the Governor. However, I ventured to write on his behalf to my Lord Marshal; I even mentioned the position which he was anxious to obtain, and my efforts were so successful that, contrary to general expectation, it was almost immediately bestowed upon him by the King. Thus destiny, which has always placed me too high and too low at the same time, continued to toss me from one extreme to the other; and, while the people covered me with mud, I appointed a councillor of State.

Another thing that caused me great pleasure was a visit from Madame de Verdelin and her daughter, whom she had brought to the baths of Bourbonne, whence she came on to Motiers, and spent two or three days with me. By her constant attentions and trouble on my behalf, she had finally overcome the feelings of dislike which I had so long entertained towards her; and my heart, vanquished by her tenderness, returned to the full the friendship which she had so long exhibited towards me. I felt touched by this visit, especially considering my circumstances at the time, when I greatly needed the consolations of friendship, to support my courage. I was afraid that she would feel deeply the insults which I suffered from the people, and I should have liked to spare her the sight of them, to avoid distressing her; but this was impossible; and, although her presence put some check upon their insolence during our walks, she saw enough to be able to judge what took place on other occasions. It was during her stay, in fact, that I began to be subjected to nightly attacks in my own house. One morning, her lady's-maid found a number of stones in front of my window which had been thrown at it during the night. A large, heavy bench, which stood in the street by the side of my door and was securely fixed, was torn up, removed, and set up on end against the door; so that, unless someone had seen it, the first person who had opened the door to go out would have been knocked down. Madame de Verdelin knew all that was going on; for, in addition to what she could see for herself, her confidential servant made himself very well known in the village, talked to everybody, and was even seen in conversation with Montmollin. However, she did not appear to take any notice of anything that happened, never mentioned Montmollin or anyone else, and only replied briefly to remarks which I sometimes made about him. She only seemed to be convinced that England would be the best place for me to stay in. She spoke much of Hume, who was in Paris at the time, of his friendship for me, and of his desire to be of service to me in his country. It is time to say something about M. Hume.

He had acquired a great reputation in France, especially amongst the Encyclopaedists, through his commercial and political treatises, and, lastly, by his "History of the House of Stuart," the only one of his writings of which I had read something in the Abbé Prévost's translation. Not having read his other works, I felt convinced, from what I had heard of him, that he united a genuine republican spirit with the paradoxical English prejudices in favour of luxury. In accordance with this opinion, I looked upon the whole of his apology for Charles I as a marvel of impartiality, and I entertained as high an opinion of his virtue as of his genius. The desire of making the acquaintance of this singular man and gaining his friendship, had greatly increased the temptation to cross over to England, which the earnest entreaties of Madame de Boufflers, his intimate friend, had aroused in me. On my arrival in Switzerland, I received from him, through her, an extremely flattering letter, in which after praising my talents most highly, he gave me a pressing invitation to cross over to England, and offered to use all his influence and that of his friends to make my stay agreeable. I went on the spot to my Lord Marshal, Hume's friend and fellow-countryman, who confirmed my good opinion of him, and told me a literary anecdote about him, which struck me as much as it had struck him. Wallace, who had written against Hume on the subject of the population of the ancient world, was absent while his book was being printed. Hume undertook to revise the proofs and superintend the publication of the work. Such conduct was after my own heart. In the same manner, I had sold copies of a song which had been written against me, at six *sous* each. I accordingly had every reason to be prejudiced in favour of Hume, when Madame de Verdelin came and spoke strongly of the friendship which he professed to entertain for me, and of his eagerness to do me the honours of England, to use her own expression. She strongly urged me to take advantage of Hume's enthusiasm and to write to him. As I had no liking for England, and did not wish to adopt this course until I was actually obliged, I refused either to write or to make any promise; but I left it to her discretion to do whatever she thought fit, to keep Hume favourably disposed towards me. When she left Motiers, she left me fully persuaded, from all that she had said to me concerning this famous man, that he was one of my friends, and that she was a still greater friend of his.

After her departure, Montmollin pushed on his intrigues, and the people became uncontrollable. However, I continued to take my walks quietly, undisturbed by their hue and cry; the taste for botany, which I had begun to acquire through Doctor d'Ivernois, gave a new interest to my walks, and made me roam the country collecting plants, undisturbed by the shouts of the rabble, whose fury was only increased by my indifference. One of the things which most affected me was, to see the families of my friends,* or people who called themselves such, openly join the ranks of my persecutors; such as the D'Ivernois, even the father and brother of my Isabelle not excepted; Boy de la Tour, a relation of the lady friend with whom I lodged, and Madame Girardier, her sister-in-law. This Pierre Boy was such a booby, so stupid, and behaved so brutally that, to avoid getting in a rage, I took it upon myself to treat him with ridicule. I wrote, in the style of the "Petit Prophète,"[1] a little pamphlet of a few pages, entitled "The Vision of Peter of the Mountain, named the Seer," in which I found opportunities of humorously attacking the miracles which at that time formed the chief excuse for my persecution. Du Peyrou had this fragment, which only met with moderate success in the district, printed at Geneva; since the inhabitants of Neufchâtel, with all their wit, are little able to appreciate Attic salt or humour, as soon as it becomes at all refined.

I took more pains about another composition, which belongs to the same period, the manuscript of which will be found amongst my papers. I must here give some account of the subject of it.

When the fury of decrees and persecutions was at its height, the Genevese had particularly distinguished themselves by

* This fatality had commenced from the time of my stay at Yverdun; for when Roguin, the *banneret*, died, a year or two after I left that town, old Papa Roguin was honest enough to inform me, with regret, that it had been proved, from his relation's papers, that he had entered into the plot to expel me from Yverdun and the State of Berne. This clearly proved that the plot was not, as people wished it to be believed, a matter of hypocrisy, since Roguin the *banneret*, far from being a devotee, pushed his materialism and unbelief even to intolerance and fanaticism. Besides, no one at Yverdun had so completely taken possession of me, or lavished upon me, in such an abundance, affection, praise, and flattery, as this same Roguin. He loyally followed the favourite system of my persecutors. (R)

[1] [Petit Prophète] See Book VIII, p. 410. In his skit, Rousseau plays on the double sense of "Pierre", which also means "stone", and of "Boy", the imperative of *Boire* ("Drink").

joining in the hue and cry with all their might. My friend Vernes, amongst others, with a truly theological generosity, chose just this moment to publish some letters against me, in which he claimed to prove that I was not a Christian. These letters, written in a conceited style, were none the better for it, although it was stated positively that Bonnet, the naturalist, had assisted in their composition, for the said Bonnet, although a materialist, is notwithstanding most intolerantly orthodox, the moment it is a question of myself. I certainly did not feel tempted to answer this production; but, as the opportunity presented itself of saying a few words about it in the "Lettres de la Montagne," I inserted a somewhat contemptuous note, which made Vernes furious. He filled Geneva with his cries of rage, and D'Ivernois informed me that he was out of his mind. Some time afterwards an anonymous pamphlet appeared, which seemed to be written with the water of Phlegethon[1] instead of ink. In this letter I was accused of having exposed my children in the streets, of taking about with me a soldiers' trollop, of being worn out by debauchery, rotten with the pox, and similar politenesses. It was easy for me to recognise my man. On reading this libellous production, my first thought was to estimate at its true value everything that is called renown and reputation amongst men; when I saw a man treated as a whoremonger who had never been in a brothel in his life, and whose greatest fault was a constant timidity and shyness, like that of a virgin; when I saw that I was supposed to be eaten up by the pox – I, who had not only never had the slightest attack of any venereal disease, but who, according to the physicians, was so formed that it would have been impossible for me to contract it. After careful consideration, I came to the conclusion that I could not better refute this libel than by having it printed in the town in which I had lived longest. I sent it to Duchesne to be printed just as it was, with a prefatory notice, in which I mentioned M. Vernes,[2] and a few brief notes, in order to explain the facts. Not content with having had this pamphlet

---

[1] One of the rivers of the infernal regions.
[2] Rousseau jumped to the conclusion that the pamphlet, in reality by Voltaire, was by his erstwhile friend the Genevan pastor Jacob Vernes (1728–91).

printed, I sent it to several persons, amongst others to Prince Louis of Wurtemburg, who had shown great civility to me, and with whom I was in correspondence at the time. The Prince, Du Peyrou, and others, seemed to doubt whether Vernes was the author of the libel, and blamed me for having mentioned his name without due investigation. In consequence of their remonstrances, I regretted what I had done, and wrote to Duchesne to suppress the pamphlet. Guy wrote to me that this had been done. I do not know whether this was true. I have found him out in so many lies on so many occasions, that one more would be nothing surprising; and at that time I was surrounded by that profound darkness, which it is impossible for me to penetrate, so as to arrive at any kind of truth.

M. Vernes bore the imputation with an equanimity which was more than surprising in a man, if he had not deserved it, after his previous outburst of rage. He wrote to me two or three cautiously worded letters, the object of which seemed to me to be, to endeavour to find out, from my answers, how much I knew, and whether I had any proof against him. I wrote two short answers, dry, and severe in the meaning they conveyed, but couched in most polite terms, at which he was not at all annoyed. I did not answer his third letter at all, since I saw that he wanted to draw me into correspondence; and he sent D'Ivernois to speak to me. Madame Cramer wrote to Du Peyrou that she was certain that the libel was not the work of Vernes. All this failed to shake my own conviction; but, since it was possible that I was mistaken, and in this case owed Vernes an apology, I sent him a message by D'Ivernois that I would make him a most handsome one, if he could inform me of the real author of the libel, or, at least, prove to me that it was not himself. I did more, feeling that, after all, if he was not guilty, I had no right to demand that he should prove anything to me; I resolved to explain, in a tolerably lengthy memoir, the reasons for my conviction, and to submit them to the decision of an umpire, whom Vernes could not refuse. No one would guess who was the umpire that I chose: it was the Council of Geneva. I declared, at the end of the memoir, that if the Council, after having examined it and made such inquiries as it might consider necessary, and which it was easy for it to carry out successfully, was of opinion that M. Vernes was not the author of the libel, I would from that moment sincerely abandon my belief that he was, and would go and throw myself at his feet, and ask his pardon until I had obtained it. I venture to say, that never did the ardour of my zeal for justice, never did the uprightness and generosity of my soul, never did my confidence in this love of justice, which is natural to the hearts of all, display themselves more fully or more clearly than in this memoir, at the same time prudent and affecting, in which I unhesitatingly accepted my most implacable enemies as umpires between the slanderer and myself. I read the pamphlet to Du Peyrou; he advised me to suppress it, and I suppressed it. He recommended me to wait for the proofs which Vernes promised. I waited, and am still waiting for them; he advised me to remain silent while I was waiting; I remained silent, and shall remain silent for the rest of my life, blamed for having brought against Vernes a serious imputation, that was false and not proved, although, in my own mind, I am as firmly convinced and persuaded that he is the author of the libel as of my own existence. My memoir is in Du Peyrou's hands. If it ever sees the light, my reasons for thinking so will be found there, and the soul of Jean Jacques, which my contemporaries refused to understand, will then, I hope, be understood.

It is time to proceed to the final catastrophe at Motiers, and my departure from Val-de-Travers, after a residence of two years and a half, and eight months of unshaken firmness in enduring most unworthy treatment. It is impossible for me to recall clearly the details of this unpleasant period of my life; but they will be found in the account of it published by Du Peyrou,[1] of which I shall have to speak later.

After Madame de Verdelin's departure, the excitement became more violent; and, in spite of the repeated rescripts of the King, in spite of the frequent orders of the Council of State, in spite of the efforts of the lord of the manor and the magistrates of the place, the people seriously regarded me as the

---

[1] Du Peyrou related the stoning incident in the third of his *Letters from Goa*, written in defence of Rousseau against the pastors in the summer and autumn of 1765.

Antichrist; and, finding all their clamours useless, seemed at last inclined to proceed to acts of violence. In the streets, stones already began to roll after me, which had been thrown from too great a distance to be able to reach me. At last, on the night after the fair at Motiers, at the beginning of September, I was attacked in the house where I lived in a manner which imperilled the lives of the inmates.

At midnight, I heard a loud noise in the gallery which ran along the back part of the house. A shower of stones, thrown against the window and the door which led to this gallery, fell into it with such a noise that my dog, who slept in the gallery, and at first commenced to bark, was terrified into silence, and ran into a corner, where he scratched and gnawed the boards in his endeavours to escape. Hearing the noise, I got up. I was on the point of leaving my room to go into the kitchen, when a stone thrown by a powerful hand, smashed the window of the kitchen, flew across it, burst open the door of my room, and fell at the foot of my bed; and, if I had been a second sooner, I should have had it in my stomach. I concluded that the noise had been made in order to attract my attention, and the stone thrown to receive me when I left my room. I dashed into the kitchen. There I found Thérèse, who had also got up and ran trembling towards me. We stood close against a wall, out of the line of the window, to avoid being hit by the stones, and to think of what we should do; for to go out to call for help would have been certain death. Fortunately, the servant of a worthy old man, who lodged below me, got up at the noise, and ran to call the lord of the manor, who lived next door. He jumped out of bed, threw on his dressing-gown, and immediately came with the watch, who, on account of the fair, were making the round, and were close at hand. When he saw the havoc, he grew pale with affright; and, at the sight of the stones, of which the gallery was full, he exclaimed, "Good God! it is a regular quarry!" On going below, we found that the door of a small yard had been broken open, and that an attempt had been made to get into the house through the gallery. When inquiry was made, why the watchmen had neither perceived nor prevented the disturbance, it was found that, although those of another village ought properly to have done duty, those from Motiers had persisted in taking this watch out of their turn. On the following day, the lord of the manor sent in his report to the Council of State, who, two days afterwards, commissioned him to institute an inquiry into the matter, and to offer a reward, under promise of secrecy, to those who informed against the guilty parties. In the meantime, he was to set a guard, at the Government expense, to protect my house and his own, which adjoined it. The next day, Colonel de Pury; Meuron, the *procureur-général*; Martinet, the lord of the manor; Guyenet, the receiver of taxes; D'Ivernois, the treasurer, and his father – in a word, all the persons of importance in the district, came to see me, and united their entreaties to induce me to bow to the storm, and to leave, at least for a time, a parish in which I could no longer live with safety or honour. I even noticed that the lord of the manor, terrified by the fury of the frenzied populace, and alarmed lest it might extend to him, would have been very glad to see me leave at once, that he might be relieved from the responsibility of protecting me, and might be able to leave the place himself, as in fact he did, after my own departure. I accordingly yielded, and even with little reluctance; for the sight of the hatred of the people caused me such heart-breaking anguish, that I could no longer endure it.[1]

More than one place of refuge was open to me. Madame de Verdelin, after her return to Paris, had mentioned, in several of her letters, a certain M. Walpole, whom she called My Lord, who took a great interest in me, and offered me a refuge on one of his estates, of which she gave me a most delightful description, and entered into details, in regard to board and lodging, which showed me how far my Lord Walpole had interested himself together with her in this plan. My Lord Marshal had always recommended to me England or Scotland, where he also offered me a refuge on his estates, but he offered me another, which tempted me far more, at Potsdam, in his neighbourhood. He had recently informed me of a conversation which the King had held with him concerning me, and which amounted to an

---

[1] It is said that Thérèse was really responsible for this disturbance; and that, being tired of the place, it was got up by her to bring about Rousseau's removal from it.

invitation; and Madame la Duchesse de Saxe-Gotha felt so sure of my accepting it, that she wrote to me, pressing me to pay her a visit on the way, and to stay a few days with her; but I felt so strongly attached to Switzerland, that I could not make up my mind to leave it as long as it was possible for me to live there, and I took advantage of this opportunity to carry out a plan which had occupied my attention for several months, and which I have hitherto been unable to mention, for fear of interrupting the thread of my narrative.

This plan was, to go and settle in the island of Saint-Pierre, a domain belonging to the hospital of Berne, in the middle of the Lake of Bienne. During a walking tour, which I had taken the year before with Du Peyrou, we had visited this island, and I had been so delighted with it, that, since then, I had never ceased to think how I might contrive to fix my abode there. The chief obstacle was, that the island belonged to the Bernese, who, three years before, had disgracefully driven me from their territory; and, not to mention that my pride would have been hurt by going back to live amongst people who had received me so ill, I had reason to fear that they would not leave me undisturbed on this island any more than at Yverdun. I had consulted my Lord Marshal on the matter; he thought, like myself, that the Bernese would be only too pleased to see me banished to this island, and to keep me there as a hostage for any further works I might be tempted to write, and had sounded them through a certain M. Sturler, his former neighbour at Colombier. This gentleman made inquiries of several of the chief men of the State, and, in consequence of the answer he received, assured my Lord Marshal that the Bernese, ashamed of their former behaviour, would be delighted to see me domiciled in the island of Saint-Pierre, and to leave me in peace there. By way of further precaution, before venturing to go and reside there, I procured further information through Colonel Chaillet, who gave me the same assurances; and, as the receiver of taxes of the island had obtained permission from his superiors to receive me in his own house, I thought I ran no risk in going there, with the tacit consent both of the supreme authority and the owners; for I did not venture to hope that the gentlemen of Berne would openly acknowledge the injustice they had done me, and offend against the most inviolable principle of all supreme authorities.

The island of Saint-Pierre, called the Ile de la Motte at Neufchâtel, in the middle of the Lake of Bienne, is only about half a league in circumference; but within this small space it produces all the chief necessaries of existence. It contains fields, meadows, orchards, woods, and vineyards; the whole, thanks to the diversified and mountainous nature of the ground, exhibits a variety that is the more agreeable, since its different aspects, not disclosing themselves all at the same time, mutually set each other off, and cause the island to seem larger than it really is. The western portion of it, which faces Gleresse and Bonneville, is formed by a very lofty terrace. This terrace has been planted with a long row of trees, intersected in the middle by a large *salon*,[1] where, during the vintage, the inhabitants assemble on Sundays from the neighbouring shores, to dance and enjoy themselves. There is only one house in the island, where the receiver of taxes lives; but it is large and commodious, and situated in a recess, which shelters it from the wind.

Five or six hundred yards from Saint-Pierre, in a southerly direction, is another island, much smaller, uncultivated, and uninhabited, which appears to have been at some time separated from the larger one by the violence of the storms; its gravelly soil produces nothing but willows and persicaria, but it contains some rising ground, covered with turf and very pleasant. The shape of the lake is almost a perfect oval. Its shores, not so fertile as those of the Lakes of Geneva and Neufchâtel, nevertheless form a most ornamental scene, especially on the west side, which is very populous, and, at the foot of a chain of hills, has a border of vines which are like those of Côte-Rôtie,[2] but do not produce such good wine. On the way from south to north, is the bailiwick of Saint-Jean, Bonneville, Bienne, and Nidau, at the end of the lake, the whole being dotted with a number of pleasant villages.

[1] Grassy enclosure.
[2] A noted vineyard in the *département* of the Rhône.

Such was the refuge which I had secured for myself, where I made up my mind to settle on leaving Val-de-Travers.* This choice was so entirely suited to my quiet tastes and to my solitary and indolent disposition, that I reckon it as one of the delightful dreams for which I have conceived a most passionate affection. It seemed to me that, in this island, I should be more removed from the society of men, more sheltered from their insults, more completely forgotten by them, and, in a word, more at liberty to abandon myself to the delights of idleness and a life of contemplation. I should have liked to be shut up in this island so completely as to have no further intercourse with any living man; and I undoubtedly took all possible steps to relieve myself of the necessity of keeping it up any longer.

It was necessary to live, and, in consequence of the high price of provisions and the difficulty of transport, living was very expensive in this island; in addition to this, one is at the mercy of the receiver. This difficulty was removed by an arrangement which Du Peyrou was good enough to make with me, by which he took the place of the company which had undertaken and abandoned the production of a complete edition of my works. I put into his hands all the necessary materials. I undertook the arrangement and distribution of it. I also bound myself to hand over to him the Memoirs of my life, and I made him the general trustee of all my papers, expressly stipulating that he should make no use of them until after my death, as I had set my heart upon ending my career peacefully, without reminding the public of my existence. The annuity which he undertook to pay me in return was sufficient for my wants. My Lord Marshal, who had recovered all his property, had also offered me an annuity of 1,200 *francs*, of which I only accepted half. He wanted to send me the capital, which I refused, since I should not have known how to invest it. He accordingly sent it to Du Peyrou, in whose hands

---

* It is perhaps not irrelevant to observe that I left behind me a personal enemy in a certain M. de Terraux, *maire* of Verrières, who was not held in particular esteem in the country, but who has a brother, who is said to be an honourable man, in M. de Saint-Florentin's offices. The *maire* had paid him a visit some time before my adventure. Little remarks of this kind, which in themselves are quite insignificant, may subsequently assist in the discovery of many underhand proceedings. (R)

it has remained, and he hands me over the interest accruing from it in accordance with the terms agreed upon between him and my patron.[1] Including my agreement with Du Peyrou, my Lord Marshal's pension, two-thirds of which was to revert to Thérèse after my death, and the yearly sum of 300 *francs* which I received from Duchesne, I was able to count upon a respectable income, both for myself and, after my death, for Thérèse, to whom I left an income of 700 *francs*, from Rey's pension as well as my Lord Marshal's; so that I had no longer any fear that she would ever want for bread, any more than myself. But it was written, that honour should compel me to reject all the resources which fortune or my own labours placed within my reach, and that I should die as poor as I have lived. The reader will be able to judge whether, without degrading myself to the lowest depths of infamy, I could have adhered to arrangements which others have always been careful to make disgraceful for me, by at the same time depriving me of all other resources, in order to compel me to consent to my dishonour. How could they have felt any doubt as to my course of action in such an alternative? They have always judged my heart by their own.

My mind being easy in regard to my means of livelihood, I had no other anxiety. Although, in the world, I left the field free for my enemies, I was leaving behind me, in the noble enthusiasm which had prompted all my writings, and in the consistent uniformity of my principles, a testimony on behalf of my soul which corresponded to that which my whole course of behaviour rendered to my character. I needed no other defence against my calumniators. They might, under my name, represent a totally different man; but they could only deceive those who wanted to be deceived. I could leave them my life to criticise, from one end to the other; I felt certain that, amidst all my faults and weaknesses, and my unfitness for submitting to any yoke, they would always find a man who was just, good, free from bitterness, hatred and jealousy, ever ready to acknowledge his own injustice, and still more ready to forget that of others, who sought all his happiness in loving and gentle emotions, and

[1] *Constituant*: a term specially applied to one who settles an annuity on another.

displayed in everything sincerity even to the extent of imprudence and the most incredible disinterestedness.

Accordingly, I in a measure took leave of my generation and my contemporaries, and said farewell to the world, by confining myself within this island for the remainder of my days; for such was my resolution, and it was there that I hoped at last to be able to carry out the grand scheme of a life of idleness, to which I had hitherto devoted in vain all the little energy which Heaven had bestowed upon me. This island should be my Papimania,[1] that happy country where one sleeps:

"Where one does even more, one does nothing at all."

This "something more" was everything for me; for I have never much regretted the loss of sleep; idleness is enough for me. Provided that I have nothing to do, I much prefer to dream awake than asleep. As the age for romantic schemes was over, and the incense of vainglory had rather made me giddy than flattered me, there remained nothing for me, as a last hope, but a life free from restraint, spent in perpetual leisure. This is the life of the blessed in the next world, and, from this time forth, I fixed upon it my supreme happiness in this.

Those who reproach me with so many inconsistencies, will not fail here to reproach me with another. I have said that the idleness of society made it unendurable to me; and yet, here was I seeking solitude with the sole object of abandoning myself to idleness. And yet such is my disposition; if there is any inconsistency in this, the fault is in nature and not in me; but it is so trifling, that it is just that which makes me always consistent. The idleness of society is tedious, because it is obligatory; that of solitude is delightful, because it is free and voluntary. In company it is a cruel task for me to do nothing, because I am under compulsion. I am obliged to remain there, nailed to my chair, or standing bolt upright like a sentinel, without moving hand or

---

[1] A quotation from La Fontaine's fable *Le Diable de Papefiguière*:
"Master François [Rabelais] says that Papimanie
Is a country where people are happy.
True sleep exists only for them...
One does even more, one does nothing at all."
[1] *i.e.*, "Flora of the Isle of Saint-Pierre".

foot, afraid to run, to jump, to sing, to cry out, or gesticulate when I have a mind to, afraid even to dream. I feel at once all the weariness of idleness and all the torture of constraint. I am obliged to listen attentively to all the silly things that are said and the compliments that are interchanged, and to rack my brains incessantly, that I may not fail in my turn to bring in my pun or my lie. And that is called idleness! It is the work of a galley-slave!

The idleness that I love is not that of an idler who remains with folded arms in a state of total inactivity, no more thinking than acting. That which I love is the combined idleness of a child who is incessantly in motion without ever doing anything, and that of a dotard, who wanders from one thing to another while his arms are still. I love to busy myself about trifles, to begin a hundred things and finish none, to come and go as the fancy takes me, to change my plans every moment, to follow a fly in all its movements, to try and pull up a rock to see what is underneath, to undertake with eagerness a work that would last ten years, and to abandon it without regret at the end of ten minutes – in a word, to spend the day in trifling without order or sequence, and, in everything, to follow nothing but the caprice of the moment.

Botany, such as I have already regarded it, and such as it began to be a passion for me, was exactly the kind of idle study which was calculated to fill up the void of my leisure time, without leaving room for the extravagances of imagination or the weariness of absolute idleness. To wander carelessly in the woods and in the country, to pluck mechanically, here and there, sometimes a flower, sometimes a branch, to munch my food almost haphazard, to observe the same things thousands and thousands of times, and always with the same interest, because I always forgot them – that was the way to spend eternity without a moment's weariness. However delicate, however admirable, however different the structure of plants may be, it never strikes an ignorant eye sufficiently to interest it. The consistent analogy and, at the same time, the enormous variety which characterises their organism, only delights those who already have some idea of the system of the vegetable world. Others, when they behold all these treasures of nature, only feel a stupid and monotonous admiration. They see nothing in detail, because they do not even know what they are to look at: they see the whole as little, because they have no idea of the chain of relations and combinations which overwhelms with its marvels the mind of the observer. I myself was, and my bad memory was always destined to keep me, in the happy condition of knowing little enough for everything to appear new to me, and yet enough to make everything intelligible to me. The different kinds of soil distributed over the island, in spite of its small size, afforded me a sufficient variety of plants for study and amusement during the rest of my life. I did not intend to leave a blade of grass unexamined, and I already began to make arrangements to write an account of the "Flora Petrinsularis,"[1] with a huge collection of curious observations.

I sent for Thérèse with my books and belongings. We boarded with the receiver of the island. His wife's sisters, who lived at Nidau, came to see her in turns, and this was company for Thérèse. Here I first experienced the pleasures of a life which I could have wished might last out my own; but the taste which I acquired for it only served to make me feel more keenly the bitterness of that life which was so soon to succeed it.

I have always been passionately fond of the water, and the sight of it throws me into a delightful state of dreaminess, although often without any definite object. When it was fine weather, I always hastened to the terrace as soon as I was up, to inhale the fresh and healthy morning air, and let my eyes roam over the horizon of this beautiful lake, the shores of which, surrounded by mountains, formed an enchanting prospect. I can think of no worthier homage to the Divinity than the mute admiration which is aroused by the contemplation of His works, and does not find expression in outward acts. I can understand how it is that the inhabitants of cities, who see nothing but walls, streets and crimes, have so little religious belief; but I cannot understand how those who live in the country, especially in solitude, can have none. How is it that

---

[1] *i.e.*, "Flora of the Isle of Saint-Pierre".

their soul is not lifted up in ecstasy a hundred times a day to the Author of the wonders which strike them? As far as I am concerned, it is especially after rising, weakened by a night of sleeplessness, that I am led by long-standing habit to those upliftings of the heart, which do not impose upon me the trouble of thinking. But, for this to take place, my eyes must be smitten by the enchanting spectacle of nature. In my room, my prayers are not so frequent or so fervent; but, at the sight of a beautiful landscape, I feel myself moved without knowing why. I remember reading of a wise bishop, who, during a visit to his diocese, came upon an old woman who, by way of prayer, could say nothing but "Oh!". "Good mother," said the bishop, "continue to pray in this manner; your prayer is better than ours." This better prayer is also mine.

After breakfast I hastily wrote a few miserable letters, with a sulky air, longing eagerly for the happy moment when I need write no more. I bustled about my books and papers for a few moments, more for the sake of unpacking and arranging than of reading them; and this, which became for me the task of Penelope, afforded me the pleasure of idling away my time for a few moments, after which I became tired of the task, and spent the three or four remaining hours of the morning in the study of botany, especially the system of Linnaeus, of which I became so passionately fond that I have never been able to give it up entirely, even after discovering its deficiencies. This great observer is, in my opinion, with the exception of Ludwig, the only man who has as yet considered botany from the point of view of a naturalist and a philosopher; but he has studied too much from gardens and collections of dried plants, and too little from nature herself. I, whose garden was the whole island, as soon as I required to make or verify some observation, ran into the woods or meadows with a book under my arm: there, I threw myself on the ground by the side of the plant in question, to examine it, where it stood, at my leisure. This method has greatly assisted me in acquiring a knowledge of plants in their natural state, before they have been cultivated and disfigured by the hand of man. It is said that Fagon, chief physician to Louis XIV, who was thoroughly familiar with, and able to name all the plants in the Jardin Royal, was so ignorant in the country, that he was no longer able to recognise them. It is exactly the opposite with me: I know something of the work of nature, nothing of that of the gardener.

In the afternoon I abandoned myself entirely to my idle and careless disposition, and followed, without any system, the impulse of the moment. Frequently, when the weather was calm, immediately after dinner, I jumped by myself into a little boat, which the receiver had taught me how to manage with a single oar, and rowed out into the middle of the lake. The moment at which I left the bank, I felt ready to leap for joy. It is impossible for me to explain or understand the reason of this feeling, unless it was a secret self-congratulation on being thus out of the reach of the wicked. I rowed by myself all over the lake, sometimes near the bank, but never landing. Frequently, leaving my boat at the mercy of the wind and water, I abandoned myself to aimless reveries, which, although foolish, were none the less delightful. I sometimes exclaimed with emotion, "O Nature! O my mother! behold me under thy protection alone! Here there is no cunning or knavish mortal to thrust himself between me and thee." In this manner I got out half a league from land. I could have wished that this lake had been the ocean. However, in order to please my poor dog, who was not so fond of long excursions on the water as I was, as a rule I followed a definite plan. I landed on the small island, walked about for an hour or two, or stretched myself on the grass at the top of the rising ground, to sate myself with the pleasure of admiring this lake and its surroundings, to examine and anatomise all the plants within my reach, and to build for myself, like a second Robinson, an imaginary dwelling on this little island. I became passionately attached to this hillock. When I was able to take Thérèse, the receiver's wife and her sisters, for a walk there, how proud I felt to be their pilot and their guide! We solemnly took some rabbits to it, to stock it. Another gala for Jean Jacques! This colony made the little island still more interesting to me. I visited it more frequently and with greater pleasure from that time, to look for signs of the progress of the new inhabitants.

To these amusements I united another, which reminded me of the delightful life at Les Charmettes, and for which the season was particularly suitable. This was the occupations of a country life; and we gathered in the fruit and vegetables, which Thérèse and myself were delighted to share with the receiver and his family. I remember that a Bernese, named M. Kirchberger, when he came to see me, found me perched on the branches of a tall tree, with a bag tied round my waist, so full of apples that I could not move. I was not at all sorry that he and others should find me thus. I hoped that the Bernese, seeing how I employed my leisure time, would no longer think about disturbing its tranquillity, and would leave me in peace in my solitude. I should have preferred to be shut up there by their will than by my own; for, in that case, I should have felt more certain of not seeing my rest disturbed.

I am now again coming to one of those confessions, in regard to which I feel sure beforehand that those readers will be incredulous, who are always determined to judge me by their own standard, although they have been compelled to see, throughout the whole course of my life, a thousand inner emotions which have not the least resemblance to their own. The most extraordinary thing is that, while denying to me all the good or indifferent feelings which they do not themselves possess, they are always ready to attribute to me others so utterly bad that they could not even enter into the heart of a man. They find it perfectly simple to put me into contradiction with nature, and to make me out a monster such as cannot possibly exist. No absurdity appears incredible to them, if only it is calculated to blacken me; nothing that is at all out of the common seems to them possible, if only it is calculated to bring honour upon me.

But, whatever they may believe or say, I will none the less continue faithfully to set forth what Jean Jacques Rousseau was, did, and thought, without either explaining or justifying the singularity of his sentiments and ideas, or inquiring whether others have thought as he. I took such a fancy to the island of Saint-Pierre, and was so comfortable there, that, from continually concentrating all my desires upon this island, I formed the design of never leaving it. The visits which I had to pay in the neighbourhood, the excursions which I should have been obliged to make to Neufchâtel, Bienne, Yverdun, and Nidau, already wearied me in imagination. A day to be spent out of the island seemed to me a curtailment of my happiness; and to go beyond the circumference of the lake was, for me, to leave my element. Besides, my experience of the past had made me timid. It only needed something to make me happy and soothe my heart, to make me expect to lose it; and my ardent desire of ending my days in this island was inseparably united with the fear of being compelled to leave it. I was in the habit of going every evening to sit upon the shore, especially when the lake was rough. I felt a singular pleasure in seeing the waves break at my feet. They represented to me the tumult of the world and the peacefulness of my own abode; and I was sometimes so touched by this delightful idea, that I felt the tears trickling down from my eyes. This repose, which I passionately enjoyed, was only troubled by the apprehension of losing it; but this feeling of uneasiness spoilt its charm. I felt my position to be so precarious that I could not reckon upon its continuance. Ah! said I to myself, how gladly would I exchange the permission to leave the island, for which I do not care at all, for the assurance of being able to remain there always! Instead of being allowed here by sufferance, why am I not kept here by force? Those who only leave me here on sufferance, can drive me away at any moment; can I venture to hope that my persecutors, seeing me happy here, will allow me to continue to be so? It is little enough that I am permitted to live here; I could wished to be condemned, to be forced to remain in this island, so as not to be forced to leave it. I regarded with envy the happy Micheli Ducret, who, quietly resting in the fortress at Arberg, in order to be happy, had only needed to wish to be so. At last, from constantly abandoning myself to these reflections, and to the disquieting forebodings of fresh storms always ready to burst upon my head, I at last came to wish, with incredible eagerness, that, instead of merely tolerating my stay in the island, my persecutors would assign it to me as a prison for life; and I can swear that, if it had only rested with myself to secure my condemnation to that effect, I would have done so with the greatest delight, since I preferred a thousand times the necessity of spending the rest of my life there to the danger of being driven out of it.

My apprehensions did not long remain unfulfilled. At the moment when I least expected it, I received a letter from the *Bailli* of Nidau, within whose jurisdiction the island of Saint-Pierre was included; in this letter he conveyed to me, on the part of their Excellencies, the order to leave the island and their States. I thought I was dreaming when I read it. Nothing could have been less natural, less reasonable, less expected than such an order; for I had rather looked upon my forebodings as the uneasiness of a man alarmed by his misfortunes, than as a presentiment which rested upon the slightest foundation. The steps which I had taken to assure myself of the tacit consent of the Sovereign, the peaceful manner in which I had been permitted to establish myself on the island, the visits of several Bernese and the *Bailli* himself, who had overwhelmed me with demonstrations of friendship and attention, the severity of the weather, which made it absolutely barbarous to drive out a man in ill-health – all these considerations caused me and many others to believe that there was some misunderstanding about the order, and that those who were ill-disposed towards me had purposely chosen the time when the grapes were being gathered and when several members of the Senate were absent, to deal me this blow unexpectedly.

If I had listened to the first impulse of my indignation, I should have set out at once. But where was I to go? what was to become of me, at the beginning of winter, when I had made no plans or preparations, and was without a guide or conveyance. Unless I was prepared to leave everything in confusion, my papers, belongings, and affairs generally, I required time to see to them, and it was not mentioned in the order whether this was to be allowed me or not. My continued misfortunes began to weaken my courage. For the first time in my life, I felt my natural pride bend beneath the yoke of necessity; and, in spite of the murmurings of my heart, I was obliged to humiliate myself by asking for delay. It was to M. de Graffenried, who had sent me the order, that I addressed myself for an explanation of it. In his letter, he expressed strong disapproval of this order, which he had only communicated to me with the greatest regret; and the evidences of sorrow and esteem, of which it was full, seemed to me a kindly invitation to speak to him with perfect frankness, which I did. I had no doubt that my letter would open the eyes of these unjust men to their barbarous conduct, and that, even if they did not revoke so cruel an order, they would at least grant me a reasonable delay, perhaps the whole winter, to make preparations for retreat, and to select another place of refuge.

While awaiting their reply, I began to consider my situation, and to reflect upon the course of action which I had to adopt. I saw so many difficulties on all sides, my sorrow had so greatly affected me, and my health, at this moment, was so bad, that I allowed myself to give way altogether, and the effect of my despair was, to deprive me of the few expedients, which might possibly remain in my head, for getting out of my melancholy situation as successfully as was possible. In whatever asylum I might take refuge, it was clear that I could not avoid being exposed to the two methods which had been employed in order to drive me out; the one, to stir up the people against me by underhand intrigues; the other, to expel me by open force, without assigning any reason for it. Thus, I could not reckon upon any refuge where I should be safe from attack, without going further to look for it than my own strength and the weather seemed to permit me. All these considerations led me back to the ideas with which I had just been busying myself; I ventured to desire and to propose that I should rather be imprisoned for life than driven incessantly as a wanderer over the face of the earth, expelled in succession from all the places of refuge which I might choose. Two days after my first letter, I wrote a second to M. de Graffenried, asking him to lay my proposal before their Excellencies. The reply from Berne to both these letters was an order, couched in most harsh and formal terms, to leave the island and all the territory belonging directly or indirectly[1] to the Republic within the space of twenty-four hours, and never to enter it again, under pain of the severest penalties.

[1] *Médiats et immédiats*: terms used of fiefs held, or persons holding fiefs directly or indirectly from the King or Emperor.

It was a terrible moment. Since then I have often been in greater distress, never in greater embarrassment. But what afflicted me most was, to be obliged to give up the scheme which had made me wish to spend the winter in the island. It is now time to relate the fatal circumstance which has crowned my disasters, and which has involved in my ruin an unfortunate people, whose growing virtues already gave promise of some day equalling those of Sparta and Rome. In the "Contrat Social" I had spoken of the Corsicans as a new people, the only one in Europe which had not yet been ruined by legislation[1]; and I had pointed out the great hopes which might be entertained of such a people, if it should be fortunate to find a wise instructor. My work was read by some Corsicans, who appreciated the terms of respect in which I had spoken of them; and, finding themselves obliged to devote their energies to the establishment of their republic, some of their chiefs bethought themselves of asking my opinion upon this important work. A certain M. Buttafuoco, who belonged to one of the chief families of the country and was a captain in the French Royal Italian regiment, wrote to me on the subject and furnished me with a number of documents, which I had asked him for, to make myself acquainted with the history of the nation and the state of the country. M. Paoli also wrote to me several times; and, although I felt that such an undertaking was beyond my strength, I thought that I could not refuse my assistance in so great and noble a task, after I had procured all the information which I required. It was to this effect that I replied to both; and this correspondence continued until my departure from Saint-Pierre.

Exactly at the same time, I heard that France was sending troops to Corsica, and had concluded a treaty with the Genoese.[2] This treaty and this despatch of troops made me uneasy, and, without imagining that I was in any way connected with it, I considered that it would be impossible, and even

[1] *Le Contrat social*, Book II, chapter 10.
[2] At the end of the Seven Years' War France had made an agreement with Genoa, the titular possessor of Corsica, to be allowed to install garrisons at various spots on the Corsican coast. (In 1768 these would be ceded to France, and in 1769, after a struggle with Paoli, Corsica as a whole would be annexed by France.)

absurd, to devote my attention to a work, which requires such profound tranquillity – the organisation of a people, at the moment when it was perhaps on the point of being brought under the yoke. I did not conceal my uneasiness from M. Buttafuoco, who calmed me by the assurance that, if this treaty had contained anything detrimental to the liberty of his country, a good citizen like himself would not remain, as he did, in the service of France. In fact, his zeal for the legislative arrangements of Corsica, and his intimate connection with M. Paoli, prevented me from entertaining any suspicions in regard to him; and, when I heard that he made frequent journeys to Versailles and Fontainebleau, and had interviews with M. de Choiseul, I could only conclude that he had assurances in regard to the real intentions of the French Court, which he left me to understand, but about which he did not desire to express himself openly in a letter.

All this to some extent reassured me. However, as I could not understand the meaning of the despatch of French troops, and could not, with any show of reason, think that they were there in order to protect the liberty of the Corsicans, which they were very well able by themselves to defend against the Genoese, I was unable to feel perfectly easy or to devote my attention seriously to the proposed work of legislation, until I had convincing proof that it was not all a mere joke at my expense. I should have greatly liked an interview with M. Buttafuoco, which was the only means of getting from him the explanations which I wanted. He held out hopes of one, and I awaited it with the utmost impatience. I do not know whether he really intended to grant me one; but even if this had been the case, my misfortunes would have prevented me from taking advantage of it.

The longer I thought over the proposed undertaking, and the more I studied the documents I had in my hands, the more I felt the necessity of studying on the spot both the people who were to be legislated for, and the country which they inhabited, and of examining, in all their relations, the circumstances, the aid of which was necessary for them, in order to adopt such legislation. I understood more clearly every day, that it was impossible for me to acquire from a distance all the information necessary for my guidance. I wrote to this effect to Buttafuoco: he agreed with me, and, if I did not exactly make up my mind to go over to Corsica, I thought a good deal about the means of undertaking the journey. I spoke of it to M. Dastier, who, having formerly served in the island under M. de Maillebois, was, of course, well acquainted with it. He spared no effort to dissuade me from my intention; and I confess that the frightful picture, which he drew of the Corsicans and their country, greatly cooled my ardent desire to go and live amongst them.

But, when the persecutions to which I was subjected at Motiers made me think of leaving Switzerland, this desire was revived by the hope of at last finding amongst those islanders the tranquillity which was denied me everywhere else. One thing only alarmed me in regard to the journey – my unfitness for, and the aversion which I had always felt to, the active life to which I should be condemned. Fitted by nature to meditate at leisure by myself, I was utterly unfitted to speak, act, and conduct affairs amongst men. Nature, who had endowed me with a capacity for the former, had refused it for the latter. However, I felt that, without directly taking part in public affairs, I should be obliged, as soon as I arrived in Corsica, to throw myself into the eagerness of the people, and to hold frequent conferences with the chief personages of the island. The object of my journey itself required that, instead of seeking retirement, I should seek, in the midst of the nation, the information which I needed. It was clear that I should no longer be my own master; that, hurried along, in spite of myself, into a whirl of activity, for which I was not adapted by nature, I should lead a life utterly opposed to my tastes, and should only be seen at a disadvantage. I foresaw that, ill-sustaining by my presence the opinion of my capabilities which they might have formed from my books, I should lose credit with the Corsicans, and, in addition, as much to their detriment as my own, the confidence which they had bestowed upon me, and without which I could not successfully carry out the work which they expected from me. I felt sure that in thus going beyond my own sphere I should only become useless to them and make myself unhappy.

Tormented, buffeted by storms of every kind, worn out by journeys and persecutions for many years past, I strongly felt the need of the repose of which my barbarous enemies, by way of amusing themselves, deprived me. I sighed more than ever for the delightful idleness, for the sweet repose of body and soul, which I had so longed for, to which the supreme happiness of my heart, now cured of its idle dreams of love and friendship, was limited. I only regarded with alarm the task which I was on the point of undertaking, the stormy life to which I proposed to abandon myself; and if the greatness, the beauty, and the usefulness of the object in view inspired my courage, the impossibility of exposing myself to risk with any chance of success completely deprived me of it. Twenty years of profound and solitary meditation would have been less painful to me than six months of an active life in the midst of men and public affairs with the certainty of failure.

I thought of an expedient, which seemed to me well adapted to settle everything. Pursued, wherever I took shelter, by the underhand intrigues of my secret persecutors, and seeing no other place but Corsica where I could look forward, in my old age, to the repose which they refused to allow me anywhere, I decided to go there, in accordance with the instructions of Buttafuoco, as soon as it should be possible for me to do so; but, in order to live quietly there, I made up my mind to abandon, at least to all appearance, the work of legislation, and in order to repay my hosts in some measure for their hospitality, to confine myself to writing their history on the spot, with the reservation of quietly acquiring the information necessary to make me of greater use to them, if I saw any prospect of success. By thus binding myself to nothing at first, I hoped to be able to think, by myself and at greater leisure, of a suitable plan, without either abandoning my cherished hopes of solitude, or adopting the kind of life which was unendurable to me, and for which I had no qualifications.

But in my position, this journey was not easy of accomplishment. To judge from what M. Dastier had told me about Corsica, I did not expect to find there the simplest comforts of life, unless I took them with me: linen, clothes, plates and dishes, kitchen utensils, paper, books – all these would have to be taken with me. In order to remove thither with Thérèse, it would be necessary to cross the Alps, and to drag after me, for two hundred leagues, a houseful of baggage; it would be necessary to pass through the territories of several different princes; and, considering the attitude adopted towards me by the whole of Europe, I should naturally have to be prepared, after my misfortunes, to meet with obstacles everywhere, and to find everyone proud to overwhelm me with some fresh misfortune, and to violate, in my person, all the rights of nations and humanity. The enormous expense, the fatigues, the risks of such a journey compelled me to consider in advance and carefully weigh all its difficulties. The idea of at last finding myself alone, without resources, at my time of life, far from all my acquaintances, at the mercy of a barbarous and ferocious people, such as M. Dastier represented the Corsicans to be, was well calculated to make me ponder such a resolution carefully before I carried it out. I was passionately eager for the interview which Buttafuoco had led me to hope for, and I awaited the result of it, before finally making up my mind.

While I was thus hesitating, the persecutions at Motiers occurred, which forced me to withdraw. I was not prepared for a long journey, especially to Corsica. I was waiting to hear from Buttafuoco: I took refuge in the island of Saint-Pierre, whence I was driven at the commencement of winter, as I have already said. The snow, with which the Alps were covered, made it impossible for me to leave the country by that route, especially at such short notice. It is true that the extravagance of such an order made it an impossibility to obey it; for, in the midst of this lonely retreat surrounded by water, with only twenty-four hours allowed me, from the time of the notification of the order, to make preparations for my departure and to procure boats and conveyances in which to leave the island and the district – even if I had had wings, I should hardly have been able to obey. I told the *Bailli* of Nidau this in my answer to his letter, and then made all haste to leave this land of unrighteousness. Thus I was compelled to abandon my cherished scheme, and having been unable, in my discouragement, to prevail upon my enemies to dispose of me as they thought fit, I decided, at the invitation of my Lord Marshal, to go to Berlin, leaving Thérèse behind to spend the winter in the island with my books and belongings, and depositing my papers in the hands of Du Peyrou. I made such haste that, on the next morning, I left the island and reached Bienne before noon. My journey was nearly terminated by an incident which I must not omit to describe.

As soon as the report spread that I had been ordered to leave my refuge, I had a crowd of visitors from the neighbourhood, especially Bernese, who, with the most detestable falseness, came to flatter and soothe me, and to assure me that advantage had been taken of the holidays and the absence of several members of the Senate, to draw up and send me notice of this order, at which, so they declared, all the "Two Hundred" were indignant. Amongst this crowd of consolers were certain persons from the town of Bienne, a little free State, included in that of Berne; amongst others, a young man named Wildremet, whose family held the first rank and enjoyed the highest reputation in that little town. Wildremet earnestly entreated me, in the name of his fellow-citizens, to take shelter amongst them, assuring me that they were eager and anxious to receive me; that they would consider it an honour and a duty to help me to forget the persecutions which I had suffered; that amongst them I had nothing to fear from the influence of the Bernese; that Bienne was a free city, which was under no one's jurisdiction; and that all its citizens were unanimously resolved to listen to no request which was prejudicial to myself.

When Wildremet saw that he could not shake my resolution, he appealed for support to several other persons from Bienne and the neighbourhood, and even from Berne itself, amongst others, the same Kirchberger of whom I have spoken, who had sought me out after my retirement to Switzerland and interested me by his abilities and principles. More unexpected and more weighty were the entreaties of M. Barthès, secretary to the French Embassy, who called upon me with Wildremet, strongly advised me to accept his invitation, and surprised me by the lively and tender interest which he seemed to take in me. I did not know M. Barthès at all; nevertheless, I recognised in his

words the warmth and fervour of friendship, and I saw that he
was really anxious to persuade me to settle at Bienne. He praised,
in most high-flown language, the town and its inhabitants, with
whom he appeared on such intimate terms that, on several
occasions, he called them, in my presence, his patrons and
fathers.

This behaviour on the part of Barthès upset all my conjectures. I had always suspected M. de Choiseul of being the secret
author of all the persecutions to which I had been subjected in
Switzerland. The behaviour of the French Resident at Geneva
and of the ambassador at Soleure confirmed these suspicions
only too strongly. I saw the secret influence of France in all that
had happened to me at Berne, Geneva and Neufchâtel, and
I thought that the only powerful enemy I had in France was
the Duc de Choiseul. What, then, was I to think of the visit of
Barthès and of the tender interest which he seemed to take in my
destiny? My misfortunes had not yet destroyed my natural
trustfulness, and experience had not yet taught me to see a
snare in every demonstration of affection. Greatly surprised,
I tried to discover the cause of this kindness on the part of
Barthès. I was not foolish enough to believe that he was acting
on his own initiative. I saw in his behaviour an ostentation and
even an air of affectation, which was evidence of some hidden
purpose, and I was far from ever having found in these inferior
agents that high-spirited intrepidity, which, when I held a similar
position, had often made my blood boil.

I had formerly had some slight acquaintance with the
Chevalier de Beauteville at M. de Luxembourg's house, where
he had shown me some kindness. Since his appointment to the
embassy, he had shown that he had not forgotten me, and had
even invited me to go and see him at Soleure; although I did not
accept the invitation, I had felt touched by it, as I was not
accustomed to be treated so politely by those in high places. I
accordingly assumed that M. de Beauteville, although he had
been obliged to obey instructions in what concerned the affairs
of Geneva, nevertheless pitied me in my misfortune, and had
procured me, by his private exertions, this refuge at Bienne, that
I might be able to live there at peace under his auspices. I was

grateful for this mark of attention, although I did not intend to take advantage of it; and, having quite made up my mind to go to Berlin, I eagerly awaited the moment when I should rejoin my Lord Marshal, convinced that only with him should I be able to find true repose and lasting happiness.

When I left the island, Kirchberger accompanied me as far as Bienne, where I found Wildremet and some other Biennese waiting for me. We all dined together at the inn; and the first thing I did, on arriving, was to order a conveyance, as I intended to set out on the following morning. During dinner, these gentlemen renewed their entreaties to me, to remain amongst them, with such warmth and such touching assurances, that, in spite of all my resolutions, my heart, which has never been able to resist affection, felt moved by theirs. As soon as they saw that I began to hesitate, they redoubled their efforts, and with such success that I finally allowed myself to be overcome, and consented to remain at Bienne, at any rate until the following spring.

Wildremet immediately made haste to find me a lodging, and highly recommended to me, as a great find, a wretched little room, on the third floor back, looking upon a yard, where I could feast my eyes upon the stinking skins of a leather-dresser's establishment which were displayed there. My landlord was a little, low looking man, a tolerable rascal, of whom I heard the next day, that he was a rake and a gambler, and in very bad repute in the district. He had neither wife nor children nor servants; and I, shut up in melancholy confinement in my solitary room, and in the most pleasant country in the world, was lodged in a manner calculated to make a man die of melancholy in a few days. What affected me most, in spite of all that I had been told as to the eagerness of the inhabitants to have me amongst them, was, that I did not observe, when walking through the streets, any politeness in their behaviour, or friendliness in their looks. However, I had quite made up my mind to remain there, when, even on the next day, I learned, saw, and perceived myself, that the town was in a terrible state of excitement on my account. Several persons were obliging enough to hasten to inform me that, on the next day, I should be told, as harshly as possible, to leave the State, that is to say, the town, immediately. I had no one in whom I could trust; all those who had urged me to stay had dispersed. Wildremet had disappeared; I heard nothing more of Barthès, and it did not seem as if his recommendation had done much to ingratiate me with the "patrons" and "fathers" of whom he had boasted to me. A certain M. de Vau-Travers, however, a Bernese, who had a nice house near the town, offered me a refuge in the meantime, in the hope, as he said, that I might escape being stoned. This recommendation did not seem to me sufficiently enticing to tempt me to prolong my stay amongst this hospitable people.

Having lost three days by this delay, I had already considerably exceeded the twenty-four hours which the Bernese had allowed me to leave their States, and, as I knew their harshness, I was not free from some anxiety as to the manner in which they would allow me to pass through them, when the *Bailli* of Nidau most opportunely relieved me of embarrassment. As he had openly expressed his disapproval of the violent measures adopted by their Excellencies, he believed, in his generosity, that it was his duty to testify publicly, that he had had nothing to do with them, and he had the courage to leave his bailiwick and pay me a visit at Bienne. He came the day before I left, by no means *incognito*, but even with a certain amount of ceremony; he came in state[1] in his carriage, accompanied by his secretary, and brought me a passport in his name which would enable me to cross the State of Berne without fear of being molested. The visit touched me more than the passport. I should have been equally sensible of it, if it had been paid to anyone else. I know nothing which exercises a more powerful influence upon my heart than an act of courage, performed at an opportune moment, on behalf of the weak who are unjustly oppressed.

At last, having with difficulty procured a conveyance, I set out on the following morning from this murderous land, before the arrival of the deputation, with which it was proposed to honour me, even before I was able to see Thérèse again, to whom, when I thought that I was going to stay in Berne, I had written to join me, and whom I had hardly time enough to put off by a few lines, in which I informed her of my fresh misfortune. It will be seen,

[1] *Fiocchi*: lit., the tufts or tassels on a cardinal's hat.

in the third part of my Confessions, if I ever have strength to write it, how, when I thought that I was setting out for Berlin, I was really setting out for England, and how the two ladies who were anxious to control my movements, after having driven me by their continued intrigues from Switzerland, where I was not sufficiently in their power, at last succeeded in delivering me into the hands of their friend.

I added what follows on the occasion of my reading these Confessions to M. and Madame la Comtesse d'Egmont, M. le Prince Pignatelli, Madame la Marquise de Mesmes, and M. le Marquis de Juigné.

"I have told the truth; if anyone knows things that contradict what I have just related, even though they be proved a thousand times over, he knows what is false and an imposture; and, if he declines to investigate and inquire into them together with me while I am still in the land of the living, he loves neither justice nor truth. As for myself, I declare openly and fearlessly: whosoever, even without having read my writings, after examining with his own eyes my disposition, my character, my manners, my inclinations, my pleasures, and my habits, can believe me to be a dishonourable man, is himself a man who deserves to be choked."

Thus I concluded the reading of my Confessions, and everyone was silent.[1] Madame d'Egmont was the only person who appeared to be affected; she trembled visibly, but she quickly recovered herself and remained silent, like the rest of the company. Such were the results of this reading and my declaration.

THE END

---

[1] This reading, of the Second Part of the *Confessions*, took place at the home of the Comtesse d'Egmont between 4 and 8 May 1771.

BIOGRAPHIES

ALEMBERT, Jean le Rond d' (1717–83). D'Alembert won fame early as a mathematician. He was introduced to Rousseau by Diderot in 1746, at which time he and Diderot were planning the *Encyclopédie*, for which they commissioned Rousseau to write articles on music and political economy. It was d'Alembert's article "Geneva" in the *Encyclopédie*, which praised the Genevan pastors for possessing "enlightened" and Socinian views and criticised the Genevan ban on the theatre, which prompted Rousseau's *Letter to d'Alembert on Stage Spectacles* of 1758. D'Alembert, who made efforts to help Rousseau during his troubles, took a detached attitude towards him, writing to Voltaire that he was "a sick man of much genius, who only possesses genius when he has fever and should neither be cured nor outraged".

ANET, Claude (1706–34). He was born in Montreux, the nephew of one of Madame de Warens's gardeners, and abjured Protestantism and quitted Switzerland at the same time as her. He lived with her from 1729 onwards and became her lover and man of affairs. At his death he was on the brink of a successful career as a botanist. It has been suggested that his attempted suicide arose from jealousy of Rousseau.

BOUFFLERS, Marie-Charlotte-Hippolyte de Campet de Saujon, Comtesse de (1724–1800). She married the Comte de Boufflers in 1746 and in about 1750 became the mistress of the Prince de Conti, for whom she conducted an influential *salon*. She befriended Rousseau and, being a close friend of David Hume, strongly encouraged Rousseau to accept Hume's invitation to England, a fact which in later years Rousseau came to regard as a sign of her covert but "implacable" enmity.

CHOISEUL, Etienne-François, Duc de (1719–85), a native of Lorraine. He won the favour of Madame de Pompadour and in 1758 was appointed Minister of Foreign Affairs, controlling French policy through the Seven Years' War and engineering the alliance with Spain and other Bourbon monarchies known as the Family Compact. An energetic and subtle politician, his antagonism towards the King's new mistress, du Barry, led to his dismissal in 1770. In 1761 he invited Rousseau to rejoin the diplomatic service. Rousseau, however, having once been invited to draft a constitution for an independent Corsica, was resentful at Choiseul's part in the French annexation of that country in 1768. He also persuaded himself that Choiseul, offended by a sentence in the *Contrat social*, nursed malevolent feelings towards him personally; and eventually he came to picture him as the very heart of the "conspiracy" against himself.

CONDILLAC, Etienne Bonnot de (1715–80), philosopher. He was the brother of François-Paul de Mably, whose children Rousseau tutored in Lyons in 1740/41, and of the abbé Gabriel de Mably. Rousseau got to know him in Lyons, and he, Diderot and Rousseau used to meet for a weekly lunch in Paris at the time of his important Lockean *Essay on the Origins of Human Knowledge* (1746). He influenced Rousseau by his sensationalist philosophical doctrines and also by his theories about language. Rousseau refers to him eulogistically in his *Second Discourse* and in *Émile*, and it was to Condillac that he entrusted the manuscript of his *Rousseau Judge of Jean-Jacques* after his abortive attempt to deposit it on the high altar of Notre-Dame.

CONTI, Louis-François de Bourbon, Prince de (1717–76). He was first cousin to Louis XV; named Grand Prior of France in 1749, he settled in the Temple in Paris, surrounding himself with a miniature court. As a protector of French Protestants he was suspected of disloyalty to the King and even of possible involvement in Damiens's assassination attempt. Having made Rousseau's acquaintance through Rousseau's friends the Maréchal de Luxembourg and his wife he became one of his most active protectors. It was he who warned Rousseau of his impending arrest in June 1762; he gave him sanctuary at the Temple during his sojourn in Paris in December 1765; and he provided him with a refuge at the Château de Trye on his return from England in 1767.

DIDEROT, Denis (1713–84). He was the son of a master-cutler in Langres and was originally intended for the Church, but in due course became famous as editor of the *Encyclopédie*, and as an atheist philosopher, dramatist, art critic and (posthumously) as novelist; he played a leading role in the *philosophic* salon of the Baron d'Holbach (*see* HOLBACH). Rousseau and he met in Paris in 1742, and he was Rousseau's great encourager in the earlier stages of his writing career. (According to Rousseau his influence was particularly strong on the *Second Discourse*.) A quarrel between them developed after Rousseau quitted Paris for the Hermitage, Rousseau persuading himself that a line in Diderot's play *The Natural Son* ("Only the wicked man is alone") was aimed at himself; and their friendship ended in 1757, being one of the many casualties of the imbroglio over Rousseau's love affair with Sophie d'Houdetot. For some years after this they thought of each other with a certain kindliness, but eventually Rousseau came to suspect Diderot of having been one of the worst and most devious of all his enemies, and Diderot himself grew almost as unbalanced about Rousseau, suspecting him of deliberately planning to blacken his reputation in the *Confessions*.

DU PEYROU, Pierre-Alexandre (1729–94). He was born in Dutch Guiana of a wealthy French colonial family and, after studies in Amsterdam, joined his mother and step-father in Neuchâtel, acquiring rights of citizenship there. He met Rousseau in 1762 and gave him much hospitality during Rousseau's stay in Môtiers in 1764, writing some *Letters from Goa* in Rousseau's defence during his quarrel with the Genevan pastors. When Rousseau left for England in 1766, he left his papers in the charge of du Peyrou, for him to forward; and on his return to France he once more gave the papers into du Peyrou's keeping as executor, in exchange for an annuity. In November 1767, however, while du Peyrou was visiting Rousseau in the Château de Trye, Rousseau got into his head the fantastic notion that du Peyrou believed that he (Rousseau) intended to poison him. As a result their arrangement was broken off. Du Peyrou nevertheless retained some of Rousseau's papers, and he played a large and responsible part in the posthumous publication of the *Confessions*.

DUPIN, Louise-Marie-Madeleine, *née* de Fontaine (1704?–99). She was the illegitimate daughter of the financier Samuel Bernard and in 1722 married the widowed Claude Dupin, whom her father aided to become a farmer-general. The Dupins, who first made their married home in the Rue Platrière in Paris, acquired and restored the great château of Chenonceaux. Rousseau, as a young man, helped Madame Dupin and her stepson Charles-Louis Dupin de Francueil (*see* FRANCUEIL) as secretary and was a frequent visitor to Chenonceaux. Madame Dupin took a kindly interest in Thérèse and her mother and was one of the few friends to whom Rousseau revealed the secret of his children. Many of his first friendships among the rich and aristocratic were formed in the Dupin circle.

EPINAY, Louise-Florence-Pétronille d', *née* d'Esclavelles (1726–83). She was the daughter of the Governor of the Citadel of Valenciennes and was related through her mother to the farmer-general Lalive de Bellegarde, marrying her cousin Denis-Joseph Lalive d'Epinay, who became a farmer-general likewise and inherited the grand mansion of La Chevrette, near Montmorency. The marriage was unhappy, leading to a formal separation, and she became the lover of Dupin de Francueil (*see* FRANCUEIL) and subsequently, for the remainder of her life, of Melchior Grimm (*see* GRIMM). She was admired by Voltaire and was a frequent contributor to Grimm's manuscript journal *La Correspondance littéraire*, and in later years she published a well-known educational dialogue, *Conversations d'Emilie*. Diderot, who initially refused to meet her, eventually became one of her closest friends. Her husband, who was a spendthrift and a *roué*, was dismissed as farmer-general in 1762, whereupon she was forced to give up La Chevrette for a smaller house. Her loan of the Hermitage to Rousseau in 1756 led ultimately to the disastrous quarrel described in detail in Book IX of the *Confessions*. Madame d'Epinay wrote a voluminous semi-autobiographical novel, *Histoire de Madame de Montbrillant*, which was published in garbled form in 1818 and in which Rousseau figures in a bad light.

FRANCUEIL, Charles-Louis Dupin de (1716–80?). He was the son of Claude Dupin (*see* DUPIN) by his father's first marriage. He married twice, becoming by his second marriage the grandfather of the novelist George Sand. Rousseau and he became friendly in 1743, and he employed Rousseau, as did his step-mother, as a secretary and, briefly, as an accountant. The two attended Rouelle's lecture courses in chemistry and collaborated on their own projected treatise or compilation on chemistry.

GAIME, Jean-Claude (1692–1761). He was born in Geneva and when Rousseau got to know him in Turin he was tutor in the household of the Savoyard Minister of the Interior. Later he became professor at the Turin Military Academy. According to Rousseau he was the model for the "Savoyard Vicar" in *Émile*.

GRIMM, Friedrich-Melchior (1723–1807). He was born in Ratisbon, the son of a Lutheran pastor, and came to Paris in 1748, becoming secretary and companion to a nephew of the Maréchal de Saxe and tutor to the young hereditary Prince of Saxe-Gotha. Rousseau met him on a visit to the Prince's country home and for a time was very intimate with him; he introduced him to the rest of his circle, including Diderot, who came to regard Grimm as his closest friend. In 1753 Grimm acquired control of a manuscript journal or newsletter, the *Correspondance littéraire*, intended for the eyes of foreign royalty, in which he would give special prominence to the doings and writings of Diderot. As Madame d'Epinay's companion and lover, he figured actively in the "Hermitage affair", by which time his relations with Rousseau had become exceedingly hostile. Eventually he abandoned literature for diplomacy, acting as representative in Paris for several small German courts and becoming the close friend and unofficial agent of Catherine the Great. He quitted France during the Revolution, his possessions and savings being confiscated, and he ended his days, a nearly blind and embittered man, in Gotha. His *Correspondance littéraire* is an important source for contemporary reactions to Rousseau.

HOLBACH, Paul-Henri Thiry, Baron d' (1723–89). He was born in the Palatinate and brought up in Paris by an uncle, from whom he inherited great wealth. After university studies in Leyden and England, he devoted himself to the spread of "enlightened" and atheistic views, setting up a sort of private "factory" for translating German scientific treatises and anti Christian works and entertaining his fellow-*philosophes* at twice-weekly dinners at his home in the Rue Royale. He contributed extensively on scientific topics to the *Encyclopédie*, and in 1770 published his long-meditated *System of Nature*, a complete system of atheism, materialism and determinism. At the insistence of Diderot, Rousseau accepted a certain amount of hospitality from d'Holbach but always claimed to have disliked his attitudes and his sardonic manner and once told him he was "too rich". D'Holbach, for his part, came to regard Rousseau as an ill-intentioned troublemaker, and he gave Hume an earnest warning against him on the eve of their departure for England. According to Rousseau, the (not unfavourable) portrait of the sceptical Baron Wolmar in *La Nouvelle Héloïse* is based in part on d'Holbach.

HOUDETOT, Elisabeth-Sophie-Françoise d', *née* Lalive de Bellegarde (1730–1813). She was sister-in-law to Madame d'Epinay (*see* EPINAY), married the Comte Claude d'Houdetot, an army officer, in 1748, and in 1751 began a life-long love affair with the Marquis de Saint-Lambert (*see* SAINT-LAMBERT). She wrote verse and was reputed to be the author of a mildly scandalous "Hymn to Breasts". A visit that she paid to Rousseau at the Hermitage in 1756 led to his falling desperately in love with her and to a disastrous quarrel with various of his friends. In her old age she was frequently sought out by people curious to meet the model for Julie in *La Nouvelle Héloïse*.

KEITH, George (1686–1778), Rousseau's "Milord Marshal". He was a Jacobite, inheriting the title "Lord Marshal of Scotland" and refusing to abandon it when officially stripped of it because of his part in the 1715 rising. Keith – like his younger brother the famous general James Keith – entered the service of Frederick the Great, and when Rousseau arrived in Neuchâtel in 1762 he was Governor of the principality and treated Rousseau with great kindness. He was one of those who encouraged him to accept Hume's invitation to England, and he later settled a small annuity on him.

LUXEMBOURG, Charles-François-Frédéric de Montmorency, Duc de (1702–64). He was a "Peer of France" and served with distinction in the War of the Austrian Succession and the Seven Years' War, becoming Marshal of France in 1757. He would spend a month or two each summer at a small château in the

Montmorency district (he was himself a Montmorency), and when in 1758 Rousseau moved to Montlouis in the same neighbourhood, the Duc and his wife went out of their way to secure his friendship, overcoming his social timidity and giving him the use of a lodge in their park, known as the *petit château*. The Duc had in 1750 married Madeleine-Angélique, *née* de Neufville-Villeroy (1707–87), the widow of the Duc de Boufflers, and she, like her husband, busied herself on Rousseau's behalf, making efforts to have him elected to the Académie, attempting to trace his children and helping in the publishing of *Émile*. He claimed always to have been nervous of her and eventually to have lost her goodwill, but never that of the Duc, for whom he had great affection.

MOULTOU, Paul (1725–87). Originally from Montpellier, he became a pastor and a citizen of Geneva, getting to know Rousseau on his stay there in 1754. Later he resigned from the ministry on conscientious grounds. He came to visit Rousseau at Môtiers in 1763, and Rousseau at one point thought of appointing him as his literary executor. Rousseau, in his last months, entrusted the "Geneva" manuscript of the *Confessions* to Moultou, on the understanding that it might not be possible to publish it for many years. In the event, Moultou and du Peyrou joined in publishing the First Part in 1782.

REY, Marc-Michel (1720–80). A native of Geneva, Rey ran an extensive bookselling and printing business in Amsterdam, specialising in "dangerous" and freethinking works which it was not possible to publish in France. He got to know Rousseau in Geneva in 1754 and published his *Second Discourse*, *La Nouvelle Héloïse*, *Le Contrat social* and *Lettres écrites de la montagne*. Diderot and others accused him of financial meanness, but he treated Rousseau with generosity, settling an annuity on Thérèse in recognition of his gains from Rousseau as a writer. Rousseau was sufficiently friendly with him to stand as godfather to one of his children, and his repeated encouragements played a large part in prompting Rousseau to write the *Confessions*.

ROUSSEAU, Isaac (16??–1747). Rousseau's father Isaac came from a French Huguenot family which had settled in Geneva some time in the sixteenth century. He was an independent-minded and pleasure-loving man who, though a skilled watchmaker, deserted his trade for a year or two to become a dancing-master and after his marriage to Rousseau's mother in 1704 went off for six years to Constantinople, to work as a watchmaker in the Sultan's seraglio. After his self-exiling from Geneva in 1722 he went to live in Nyon in the *pays de Vaud*, marrying for a second time in 1726.

SAINT-LAMBERT, Jean-François, Marquis de (1716–1803). His military career, in which he served as *aide-major de l'infanterie* at Minorca and in the Army of the Lower Rhine during the Seven Years' War, was cut short by an attack of paralysis, and on retirement from the army he took up a literary career, becoming a leading member of the d'Holbach (*see* HOLBACH) circle and an Academician. His poem *Les Saisons*, written in imitation of Thomson's *Seasons*, was highly thought of. He had an affair with Voltaire's mistress Madame du Châtelet, who died bearing a child by him, and later he became the devoted lover of the Comtesse d'Houdetot (*see* HOUDETOT).

SARDINIA, kings of:

Victor Amadeus II (1666–1732). He became Duke of Savoy in 1675 and in 1684 married Anne d'Orléans, a niece of Louis XIV. For his support of Austria in the War of the Spanish Succession he received the kingdom of Sicily, but he was persuaded in 1720 to exchange it for Sardinia, adopting the title of King of Sardinia. In 1730 he abdicated in favour of his son Charles Emmanuel. On attempting subsequently to regain the throne, he was arrested by his son and imprisoned in the château of Rivoli, where he died. Piedmont belonged to the house of Savoy, and Victor Amadeus did much to beautify its capital, Turin.

Charles Emmanuel III (1701–73). Son of Victor Amadeus II. For his support of France during the War of the Polish Succession (1733–6) he was promised Milan but eventually he had to content himself with Novara and Tortona.

STANISLAS LECZINSKI, King of Poland and Duke of Lorraine (1677–1766). His father was Grand Treasurer of Poland, and in 1704, after the toppling of Augustus II, the Saxon occupant of the Polish throne, by Charles XII of Sweden, Stanislas was elected king; as a result of Charles's defeat at Pultawa in 1709, Augustus was, however, restored to the throne. In 1725 Louis XV of France married Stanislas's daughter Marie Leczinska; and upon the death of Augustus II in 1733 Stanislas, with France's support, was once again elected King of Poland, in the teeth of opposition from Austria and Russia, who were supporting a rival candidate. He was able to sustain his position for no more than twelve days, being then compelled to quit Warsaw by the approach of a Russian army. A war ensued – between on the one hand France, Spain and Sardinia, and on the other Austria and Russia – and the treaty which concluded it laid down a complicated arrangement, by which Francis, Duke of Lorraine, who was due to marry Maria Theresa of Austria, should succeed to the reversion of Tuscany and, in exchange, should resign Lorraine to Stanislas (and after Stanislas's death to France). Stanislas and his court at Lunéville figure frequently in Rousseau's career. The ex-king wrote a counterblast to Rousseau's *Second Discourse*, to which Rousseau composed a firm though respectful reply, and he was one of the first admirers of *La Nouvelle Héloïse*, which Rousseau allowed him to read in manuscript. Palissot, the satirist of Rousseau and his associates, was a member of the Academy of Nancy, founded by Stanislas, and, by an ironic reversal, Rousseau once generously intervened to prevent his expulsion.

TRONCHIN. The various branches of the Tronchin family were very influential in Geneva and a mainstay of the oligarchic or "negative" (anti-popular) party in the Council of Two Hundred. We may distinguish the following members:

Théodore Tronchin (1709–81). He was a pioneer of inoculation (on which he wrote the article in the *Encyclopédie*) and the most fashionable physician of his day, coming to Paris in 1765 as personal physician to the Duc d'Orléans. He acted as an intermediary between Rousseau and Voltaire in their polemic about the Lisbon earthquake, but he helped induce the Council of Geneva to ban *La Nouvelle Héloïse*, and it may have been he who told Voltaire about Rousseau's abandonment of his children.

François Tronchin (1704–98), cousin-german to Théodore. He was Voltaire's landlord at Les Délices and a wealthy connoisseur, possessing one of the largest collections of antiques and paintings in Geneva (where in fact such collections were illegal).

Jean-Robert Tronchin (1710–93), brother of François. He was Procureur-General and in 1762 persuaded the Petit Conseil to order the burning of the *Contrat social* and *Émile*; he was the author of the *Lettres de la campagne* to which Rousseau's *Lettres de la montagne* were a reply.

WARENS, Françoise-Louise, *née* de La Tour. She was born at Vevey and received her education there from a Pietist. At the age of thirteen she married Sebastien-Isaac de Loys de Villardin, later seigneur de Warens, but in 1726 she left her husband and went to live in Savoy, where she renounced the Protestant faith, earning by so doing the protection of King Victor Amadeus II (*see* SARDINIA), who granted her a pension. Her divorce was confirmed by the Berne Consistory in 1727. After a brief spell in a convent in Annecy she set up house there, receiving financial help from the Church to offer hospitality to new Catholic converts. When Rousseau first encountered her she had been in residence there for two years. With her passion for "projects" she was a natural prey to crooks and charlatans; nevertheless it would seem that, at least on one occasion, she was commissioned to perform a delicate political mission in Paris, on behalf of the King of Sardinia. The complicated motive of her removal to Chambéry is explained by Rousseau in his *Confessions*. His account of their idyll at Les Charmettes is, on the other hand, not altogether faithful to the facts. He gives a touching account of the desperate straits to which she was reduced in later years.

This book is set in GARAMOND, the first typeface in
the ambitious programme of matrix production
undertaken by the Monotype Corporation
under the guidance of Stanley Morrison
in 1922. Although named after the
great French royal typographer,
Claude Garamond (1499–
1561), it owes much to
Jean Jannon of Sedan
(1580–1658).